Thomas & Renee Glaudz
5/25/94

International Scientific Committee for the Drafting of a General History of Africa (UNESCO)

General History of Africa · II

Ancient Civilizations of Africa

EDITOR G. MOKHTAR

Abridged Edition

JAMES CURREY · CALIFORNIA · UNESCO

First published 1990 by the
United Nations Educational, Scientific
and Cultural Organization
7 Place de Fontenoy, 75700, Paris

James Currey Ltd
54b Thornhill Square, Islington
London N1 1BE

and

University of California Press
2120 Berkeley Way, Berkeley
California 94720, United States of America

ISBN (Unesco): 92 – 3 – 102585 – 6

British Library Cataloguing in Publication Data
General history of Africa. – Abridged ed.
2, Ancient civilization of Africa.
1. Africa, to 1980
1. Mokhtar, G. II. Unesco *International Scientific Committee for the drafting of a General History of Africa*
960

ISBN 0–85255–092–8 (James Currey)

Library of Congress Cataloging-in-Publication Data
Ancient civilizations of Africa / editor, G. Mokhtar. — Abridged ed.
p. cm. — (General history of Africa / International Scientific Committee for the Drafting of a General History of Africa (UNESCO) : 2)
ISBN 0–520–06697–9 (University of California Press)
1. Africa—History—To 1498. I. Mokhtār, Gamal el Din 1918 II. Series: General history of Africa (Abridged version) : 2.
DT20.G452 vol. 2
[DT25]
960 s—dc20
[960′.2] 89–20358
CIP

2 3 4 5 6 7 8 9 10

Typeset in Bembo by Colset Pte Ltd, Singapore
Printed in the United States

General History of Africa · II

Ancient Civilizations of Africa

Abridged Edition

Volume I	*Methodology and African Prehistory* Editor **J. Ki-Zerbo**
Volume II	*Ancient Civilizations of Africa* Editor **G. Mokhtar**
Volume III	*Africa from the Seventh to Eleventh Century** Editor **M. El Fasi** Assistant editor **I. Hrbek**
Volume IV	*Africa from the Twelfth to Sixteenth Century** Editor **D. T. Niane**
Volume V	*Africa from the Sixteenth to Eighteenth Century** Editor **B. A. Ogot**
Volume VI	*Africa in the Nineteenth Century until the 1880s** Editor **J. F. A. Ajayi**
Volume VII	*Africa under Foreign Domination* 1880–1935 Editor **A. Adu Boahen**
Volume VIII	*Africa since* 1935* Editor **A. A. Mazrui** Assistant editor **C. Wondji**

*forthcoming

The abridged edition of
THE UNESCO GENERAL HISTORY OF AFRICA
is published by the following publishers

In Ghana, Sierra Leone,
the Gambia and Cameroon by
Ott–Attafua
P.O. Box 2692
Accra, Ghana

In Kenya by
Heinemann Kenya
P.O. Box 45314
Nairobi, Kenya

In Nigeria by
Heinemann Nigeria
P.O. Box 6205
Ibadan, Nigeria

In Tanzania by
Tanzania Publishing House
P.O. Box 2138
Dar es Salaam, Tanzania

In Uganda by
Uganda Bookshop Publishing
P.O. Box 7145
Kampala, Uganda

In Zambia by
Multimedia Zambia
Box 320199
Lusaka, Zambia

In Zimbabwe,
Botswana, Swaziland and Malawi by
Baobab Books
P.O. Box 1559
Harare, Zimbabwe

In the United States of America
and Canada by
The University of California Press
2120 Berkeley Way
Berkeley, California 94720

And in the United Kingdom, Europe
and the rest of the world by
James Currey *Publishers*
54B Thornhill Square
Islington, London N1 1 BE

and

UNESCO
7 Place de Fontenoy, 75700, Paris

Contents

Preface by Amadou-Mahtar M'Bow, former Director-General of Unesco *vii*
Description of the project by B. A. Ogot, former President, International Scientific Committee for the Drafting of a General History of Africa *xii*
Note on chronology *xiv*
List of the Members of the International Scientific Committee for the Drafting of a General History of Africa *xvii*
Biographies of authors *xix*

Introduction 1

1 *Origin of the Ancient Egyptians* 15
Annex to Chapter 1: Report of the symposium on 'The Peopling of Ancient Egypt and the Deciphering of the Meroitic Script' 33
2 *Pharaonic Egypt* 62
3 *Pharaonic Egypt: society, economy and culture* 79
4 *Egypt's relations with the rest of Africa* 90
5 *The legacy of Pharaonic Egypt* 103
6 *Egypt in the Hellenistic era* 119
7 *Egypt under Roman domination* 131
8 *The importance of Nubia: a link between Central Africa and the Mediterranean* 141

9	*Nubia before Napata (−3100 to −750)*	*148*
10	*The Empire of Kush: Napata and Meroe*	*161*
11	*The civilization of Napata and Meroe*	*172*
12	*The spreading of Christianity in Nubia*	*185*
13	*Pre-Axumite culture*	*192*
14	*The civilization of Axum from the first to the seventh century*	*203*
15	*Axum: political system, economics and culture, first to fourth century*	*214*
16	*Christian Axum*	*224*
17	*The proto-Berbers*	*236*
18	*The Carthaginian period*	*246*
19	*The Roman and post-Roman period in North Africa*	*261*
20	*The Sahara in classical antiquity*	*286*
21	*Introduction to the later prehistory of sub-Saharan Africa*	*296*
22	*The East African coast and its role in maritime trade*	*306*
23	*East Africa before the seventh century*	*313*
24	*West Africa before the seventh century*	*325*
25	*Central Africa*	*339*
26	*Southern Africa: hunters and food-gatherers*	*351*
27	*The beginnings of the Iron Age in southern Africa*	*362*
28	*Madagascar*	*373*
29	*The societies of Africa south of the Sahara in the Early Iron Age*	*383*
	Conclusion	*390*
	Bibliography	*394*
	Index	*412*

Preface

AMADOU-MAHTAR M'BOW
Former Director-General of Unesco (1974–1987)

For a long time, all kinds of myths and prejudices concealed the true history of Africa from the world at large. African societies were looked upon as societies that could have no history. In spite of important work done by such pioneers as Leo Frobenius, Maurice Delafosse and Arturo Labriola, as early as the first decades of this century, a great many non-African experts could not rid themselves of certain preconceptions and argued that the lack of written sources and documents made it impossible to engage in any scientific study of such societies.

Although the *Iliad* and *Odyssey* were rightly regarded as essential sources for the history of ancient Greece, African oral tradition, the collective memory of peoples which holds the thread of many events marking their lives, was rejected as worthless. In writing the history of a large part of Africa, the only sources used were from outside the continent, and the final product gave a picture not so much of the paths actually taken by the African peoples as of those that the authors thought they must have taken. Since the European Middle Ages were often used as a yardstick, modes of production, social relations and political institutions were visualized only by reference to the European past.

In fact, there was a refusal to see Africans as the creators of original cultures which flowered and survived over the centuries in patterns of their own making and which historians are unable to grasp unless they forgo their prejudices and rethink their approach.

Furthermore, the continent of Africa was hardly ever looked upon as a historical entity. On the contrary, emphasis was laid on everything likely to lend credence to the idea that a split had existed, from time immemorial, between a 'white Africa' and a 'black Africa', each unaware of the other's existence. The Sahara was often presented as an impenetrable space preventing any intermingling of ethnic groups and peoples or any exchange of goods, beliefs, customs and ideas between the societies that had grown up on either side of the desert. Hermetic frontiers were drawn between the civilizations of Ancient Egypt and Nubia and those of the peoples south of the Sahara.

It is true that the history of Africa north of the Sahara has been more closely linked with that of the Mediterranean basin than has the history of sub-Saharan Africa, but it is now widely recognized that the various civilizations of the African continent, for all their differing languages and cultures, represent, to a greater or lesser degree, the historical offshoots of a set of peoples and societies united by bonds centuries old.

Another phenomenon which did great disservice to the objective study of the African past was the appearance, with the slave trade and colonization, of racial stereotypes which bred contempt and lack of understanding and became so deep-rooted that they distorted even the basic concepts of historiography. From the time when the notions of 'white' and 'black' were used as generic labels by the colonialists, who were regarded as superior, the colonized Africans had to struggle against both economic and psychological enslavement. Africans were identifiable by the colour of their skin, they had become a kind of merchandise, they were earmarked for hard labour and eventually, in the minds of those dominating them, they came to symbolize an imaginary and allegedly inferior *Negro* race. This pattern of spurious identification relegated the history of the African peoples in many minds to the rank of ethno-history, in which appreciation of the historical and cultural facts was bound to be warped.

The situation has changed significantly since the end of the Second World War and in particular since the African countries became independent and began to take an active part in the life of the international community and in the mutual exchanges that are its *raison d'être*. An increasing number of historians has endeavoured to tackle the study of Africa with a more rigorous, objective and open-minded outlook by using – with all due precautions – actual African sources. In exercising their right to take the historical initiative, Africans themselves have felt a deep-seated need to re-establish the historical authenticity of their societies on solid foundations.

In this context, the importance of the eight-volume *General History of Africa*, which Unesco is publishing, speaks for itself.

The experts from many countries working on this project began by laying down the theoretical and methodological basis for the *History*. They have been at pains to call in question the over-simplifications arising from a linear and restrictive conception of world history and to re-establish the true facts wherever necessary and possible. They have endeavoured to highlight the historical data that give a clearer picture of the evolution of the different peoples of Africa in their specific socio-cultural setting.

To tackle this huge task, made all the more complex and difficult by the vast range of sources and the fact that documents were widely scattered, Unesco has had to proceed by stages. The first stage, from 1965 to 1969, was devoted to gathering documentation and planning the work. Operational assignments were conducted in the field and included campaigns to collect oral traditions, the creation of regional documentation centres for oral traditions, the collection of unpublished manuscripts in Arabic and Ajami (African languages written in Arabic script), the compilation of archival inventories and the preparation of a *Guide of the Sources of the History of Africa*, culled from the archives and libraries of the countries of Europe and later published in eleven volumes. In addition, meetings were organized to enable experts from Africa and other continents to discuss questions of methodology and lay down the broad lines for the project after careful examination of the available sources.

The second stage, which lasted from 1969 to 1971, was devoted to shaping the *History* and linking its different parts. The purpose of the international meetings of experts held in Paris in 1969 and Addis Ababa in 1970 was to study and define the problems involved in drafting and publishing the *History*; presentation in eight volumes, the principal edition in English, French and Arabic, translation into African languages such as Kiswahili, Hausa, Fulfulde, Yoruba or Lingala, prospective versions in German, Russian, Portuguese, Spanish and Chinese, as well as abridged editions designed for a wide African and international public.[1]

The third stage has involved actual drafting and publication. This began with the appointment of the 39-member International Scientific Committee, two-thirds African and one-third non-African, which assumes intellectual responsibility for the *History*.

The method used is interdisciplinary and is based on a multi-faceted approach and a wide variety of sources. The first among these is archaeology, which holds many of the keys to the history of African cultures and civilizations. Thanks to archaeology, it is now acknowledged that Africa was very probably the cradle of mankind and the scene – in the Neolithic period – of one of the first technological revolutions in history. Archaeology has also shown that Egypt was the setting for one of the most brilliant ancient civilizations of the world. But another very important source is oral tradition, which, after being long despised, has now emerged as an invaluable instrument for discovering the history of Africa, making it possible to follow the movements of its different peoples in both space and time, to understand the African vision of the world from the inside and to grasp the original features of the values on which the cultures and institutions of the continent are based.

We are indebted to the International Scientific Committee in charge of this *General History of Africa*, and to its Rapporteur and the editors and authors of the various volumes and chapters, for having shed a new light on the African past in its authentic and all-encompassing form and for having avoided any dogmatism in the study of essential issues. Among these issues we might cite: the slave trade, that 'endlessly bleeding wound', which was responsible for one of the cruellest mass deportations in the history of mankind, which sapped the African continent of its life-blood while contributing significantly to the economic and commercial expansion of Europe; colonization, with all the effects it had on population, economics, psychology and culture; relations between Africa south of the Sahara and the Arab world; and, finally, the process of decolonization and nation-building which mobilized the intelligence and passion of people still alive and sometimes still active today. All these issues have been broached with a concern for honesty and rigour which is not the least of the *History*'s merits. By taking stock of our knowledge of Africa, putting forward a variety of viewpoints on African cultures and offering a new reading of history, the *History* has the signal advantage of showing up the light and shade and of openly portraying the differences of opinion that may exist between scholars.

By demonstrating the inadequacy of the methodological approaches which have long been used in research on Africa, this *History* calls for a new and careful study of the twofold problem areas of historiography and cultural identity, which are united by links of reciprocity. Like any historical work of value, the *History* paves the way for a great deal of further research on a variety of topics.

It is for this reason that the International Scientific Committee, in close collaboration

1. At the time of going to press, Volumes I and II have been published in Arabic, Chinese, Italian, Korean, Portuguese and Spanish; Volume IV in Arabic, Spanish and Portuguese and Volume VII in Spanish.

with Unesco, decided to embark on additional studies in an attempt to go deeper into a number of issues that will permit a clearer understanding of certain aspects of the African past. The findings being published in the series 'Unesco Studies and Documents – General History of Africa'[2] will prove a useful supplement to the *History*, as will the works planned on aspects of national or subregional history.

The *General History* sheds light both on the historical unity of Africa and also its relations with the other continents, particularly the Americas and the Caribbean. For a long time, the creative manifestations of the descendants of Africans in the Americas were lumped together by some historians as a heterogeneous collection of *Africanisms*. Needless to say, this is not the attitude of the authors of the *History*, in which the resistance of the slaves shipped to America, the constant and massive participation of the descendants of Africans in the struggles for the initial independence of America and in national liberation movements, are rightly perceived for what they were: vigorous assertions of identity, which helped forge the universal concept of mankind. Although the phenomenon may vary in different places, it is now quite clear that ways of feeling, thinking, dreaming and acting in certain nations of the western hemisphere have been marked by their African heritage. The cultural inheritance of Africa is visible everywhere, from the southern United States to northern Brazil, across the Caribbean and on the Pacific seaboard. In certain places it even underpins the cultural identity of some of the most important elements of the population.

The *History* also clearly brings out Africa's relations with southern Asia across the Indian Ocean and the African contributions to other civilizations through mutual exchanges.

I am convinced that the efforts of the peoples of Africa to conquer or strengthen their independence, secure their development and assert their cultural characteristics must be rooted in historical awareness renewed, keenly felt and taken up by each succeeding generation.

My own background, the experience I gained as a teacher and as chairman, from the early days of independence, of the first commision set up to reform history and geography curricula in some of the countries of West and Central Africa, taught me how necessary it was for the education of young people and for the information of the public at large to have a history book produced by scholars with inside knowledge of the problems and hopes of Africa and with the ability to apprehend the continent in its entirety.

For all these reasons, Unesco's goal will be to ensure that this *General History of Africa* is widely disseminated in a large number of languages and is used as a basis for producing children's books, school textbooks and radio and television programmes. Young people, whether schoolchildren or students, and adults in Africa and elsewhere will thus be able to form a truer picture of the African continent's past and the factors

2. The following eleven volumes have already been published in this series: *The peopling of Ancient Egypt and the deciphering of Meroitic script; The African slave trade from the fifteenth to the nineteenth century; Historical relations across the Indian Ocean; The historiography of Southern Africa; The decolonization of Africa: Southern Africa and the Horn of Africa; African ethnonyms and toponyms; Historical and socio-cultural relations between black Africa and the Arab world from 1935 to the present; The methodology of contemporary African history; Africa and the Second World War; The educational process and historiography in Africa; Libya Antiqua.*

that explain it, as well as a fairer understanding of its cultural heritage and its contribution to the general progress of mankind. The *History* should thus contribute to improved international co-operation and stronger solidarity among peoples in their aspirations to justice, progress and peace. This is, at least, my most cherished hope.

It remains for me to express my deep gratitude to the members of the International Scientific Committee, the Rapporteur, the different volume editors, the authors and all those who have collaborated in this tremendous undertaking. The work they have accomplished and the contribution they have made plainly go to show how people from different backgrounds, but all imbued with the same spirit of goodwill and enthusiasm in the service of universal truth can, within the international framework provided by Unesco, bring to fruition a project of considerable scientific and cultural import. My thanks also go to the organizations and governments whose generosity has made it possible for Unesco to publish this *History* in different languages and thus ensure that it will have the worldwide impact it deserves and thereby serve the international community as a whole.

Description of the Project

B. A. OGOT[1]
President, International Scientific Committee for the Drafting of a General History of Africa

The General Conference of Unesco at its 16th Session instructed the Director-General to undertake the drafting of a *General History of Africa*. The enormous task of implementing the project was entrusted to an International Scientific Committee which was established by the Executive Board in 1970. This Committee, under the Statutes adopted by the Executive Board of Unesco in 1971, is composed of thirty-nine members (two-thirds of whom are African and one-third non-African) serving in their personal capacity and appointed by the Director-General of Unesco for the duration of the Committee's mandate.

The first task of the Committee was to define the principal characteristics of the work. These were defined at the first session of the Committee as follows:

(a) Although aiming at the highest possible scientific level, the history does not seek to be exhaustive and is a work of synthesis avoiding dogmatism. In many respects, it is a statement of problems showing the present state of knowledge and the main trends in research, and it does not hesitate to show divergencies of views where these exist. In this way, it prepares the ground for future work.

(b) Africa is considered in this work as a totality. The aim is to show the historical relationships between the various parts of the continent, too frequently subdivided in works published to date. Africa's historical connections with the other continents receive due attention, these connections being analysed in terms of mutual exchanges and multilateral influences, bringing out, in its appropriate light, Africa's contribution to the history of mankind.

(c) *The General History of Africa* is, in particular, a history of ideas and civilizations, societies and institutions. It is based on a wide variety of sources, including oral tradition and art forms.

(d) The *History* is viewed essentially from the inside. Although a scholarly work, it is also, in large measure, a faithful reflection of the way in which African authors view their own civilization. While prepared in an international framework and drawing to the full on the present stock of scientific knowledge, it should also be a

1. During the Sixth Plenary Session of the International Scientific Committee for the Drafting of a General History of Africa (Brazzaville, August 1983), an election of the new Bureau was held and Professor Ogot was replaced by Professor A. Adu Boahen.

> vitally important element in the recognition of the African heritage and should bring out the factors making for unity in the continent. This effort to view things from within is the novel feature of the project and should, in addition to its scientific quality, give it great topical significance. By showing the true face of Africa, the *History* could, in an era absorbed in economic and technical struggles, offer a particular conception of human values.

The Committee has decided to present the work covering over three million years of African history in eight volumes, each containing about eight hundred pages of text with illustrations, photographs, maps and line drawings.

A chief editor, assisted if necessary by one or two assistant editors, is responsible for the preparation of each volume. The editors are elected by the Committee either from among its members or from outside by a two-thirds majority. They are responsible for preparing the volumes in accordance with the decisions and plans adopted by the Committee. On scientific matters, they are accountable to the Committee or, between two sessions of the Committee, to its Bureau for the contents of the volumes, the final version of the texts, the illustrations and, in general, for all scientific and technical aspects of the *History*. The Bureau ultimately approves the final manuscript. When it considers the manuscript ready for publication, it transmits it to the Director-General of Unesco. Thus the Committee, or the Bureau between committee sessions, remains fully in charge of the project.

Each volume consists of some thirty chapters. Each chapter is the work of a principal author assisted, if necessary, by one or two collaborators. The authors are selected by the Committee on the basis of their *curricula vitae*. Preference is given to African authors, provided they have requisite qualifications. Special effort is also made to ensure, as far as possible, that all regions of the continent, as well as other regions having historical or cultural ties with Africa, are equitably represented among the authors.

When the editor of a volume has approved texts of chapters, they are then sent to all members of the Committee for criticism. In addition, the text of the volume editor is submitted for examination to a Reading Committee, set up within the International Scientific Committee on the basis of the members' fields of competence. The Reading Committee analyses the chapters from the standpoint of both substance and form. The Bureau then gives final approval to the manuscripts.

Such a seemingly long and involved procedure has proved necessary, since it provides the best possible guarantee of the scientific objectivity of the *General History of Africa*. There have, in fact, been instances when the Bureau has rejected manuscripts or insisted on major revisions or even reassigned the drafting of a chapter to another author. Occasionally, specialists in a particular period of history or in a particular question are consulted to put the finishing touches to a volume.

The work will be published first in a hard-cover edition in English, French and Arabic, and later in paperback editions in the same languages. An abridged version in English and French will serve as a basis for translation into African languages. The Committee has chosen Kiswahili and Hausa as the first African languages into which the work will be translated.

Also, every effort will be made to ensure publication of the *General History of Africa* in other languages of wide international currency such as Chinese, Portuguese, Russian, German, Italian, Spanish, Japanese, etc.

It is thus evident that this is a gigantic task which constitutes an immense challenge to African historians and to the scholarly community at large, as well as to Unesco under whose auspices the work is being done. For the writing of a continental history of Africa, covering the last three million years, using the highest canons of scholarship and involving, as it must do, scholars drawn from diverse countries, cultures, ideologies and historical traditions, is surely a complex undertaking. It constitutes a continental, international and interdisciplinary project of great proportions.

In conclusion, I would like to underline the significance of this work for Africa and for the world. At a time when the peoples of Africa are striving towards unity and greater co-operation in shaping their individual destinies, a proper understanding of Africa's past, with an awareness of common ties among Africans and between Africa and other continents, should not only be a major contribution towards mutual understanding among the people of the earth, but also a source of knowledge of a cultural heritage that belongs to all mankind.

Note on chronology

It has been agreed to adopt the following method for writing dates. With regard to prehistory, dates may be written in two different ways.

One way is by reference to the present era, that is, dates BP (before present), the reference year being + 1950; all dates are negative in relation to + 1950.

The other way is by reference to the beginning of the Christian era. Dates are represented in relation to the Christian era by a simple + or − sign before the date. When referring to centuries, the terms BC and AD are replaced by 'before the Christian era' and 'of the Christian era'.

Some examples are as follows:

(i) 2300 BP = − 350
(ii) 2900 BC = − 2900
AD 1800 = + 1800
(iii) Fifth century BC = Fifth century before the Christian era
Third century AD = Third century of the Christian era.

Members of the International Scientific Committee for the Drafting of a General History of Africa

The dates cited below refer to dates of membership.

Professor J. F. A. Ajayi
(Nigeria), from 1971
Editor Volume VI

Professor F. A. Albuquerque Mourao
(Brazil), from 1975

Professor A. A. Boahen
(Ghana), from 1971
Editor Volume VII

The late H. E. Boubou Hama
(Niger), 1971–8 (resigned in 1978); deceased 1982

Dr (Mrs) Mutumba M. Bull
(Zambia), from 1971

Professor D. Chanaiwa
(Zimbabwe), from 1975

Professor P. D. Curtin
(USA), from 1975

Professor J. Devisse
(France), from 1971

Professor M. Difuila
(Angola), from 1978

The late Professor Cheikh Anta Diop
(Senegal), 1971–86; deceased 1986

Professor H. Djait
(Tunisia), from 1975

Professor J. D. Fage
(UK), 1971–81 (resigned)

H. E. M. El Fasi
(Morocco), from 1971
Editor Volume III

The late Professor J. L. Franco
(Cuba), from 1971; deceased 1989

The late Mr M. H. I. Galaal
(Somalia), 1971–81; deceased 1981

Professor Dr V. L. Grottanelli
(Italy), from 1971

Professor E. Haberland
(Federal Republic of Germany), from 1971

Dr Aklilu Habte
(Ethiopia), from 1971

H. E. A. Hampâté Bâ
(Mali), 1971–8 (resigned)

Dr I. S. El-Hareir
(Libya), from 1978

Dr I. Hrbek
(Czechoslovakia), from 1971
Assistant Editor Volume III

Dr (Mrs) A. Jones
(Liberia), from 1971

The late Abbé Alexis Kagame
(Rwanda), 1971–81; deceased 1981

Professor I. M. Kimambo
(Tanzania), from 1971

Professor J. Ki-Zerbo
(Burkina Faso) from 1971
Editor Volume I

Mr D. Laya
(Niger), from 1979

Dr A. Letnev
(USSR), from 1971

Dr G. Mokhtar
(Egypt), from 1971
Editor Volume II

Professor P. Mutibwa
(Uganda), from 1975

Professor D. T. Niane
(Senegal), from 1971
Editor Volume IV

Professor L. D. Ngcongco
(Botswana), from 1971

Professor T. Obenga
(People's Republic of the Congo), from 1975

Professor B. A. Ogot
(Kenya), from 1971
Editor Volume V

Professor C. Ravoajanahary
(Madagascar), from 1971

The late Professor W. Rodney
(Guyana), 1979–80; deceased 1980

The late Professor M. Shibeika
(Sudan), 1971–80; deceased 1980

Professor Y. A. Talib
(Singapore), from 1975

The late Professor A. Teixeira da Mota
(Portugal), 1978–82; deceased 1982

Mgr T. Tshibangu
(Zaïre), from 1971

Professor J. Vansina
(Belgium), from 1971

The late Rt. Hon. Dr E. Williams
(Trinidad and Tobago), 1976–8; resigned 1978; deceased 1980

Professor A. A. Mazrui
(Kenya)
Editor Volume VIII,
not a member of the Committee

Professor C. Wondji
(Ivory Coast)
Assistant Editor Volume VIII,
not a member of the Committee

Secretariat of the International Scientific Committee
A. Gatera, Director,
Division of Cultural Studies
and Policies
I, rue Miollis, 75015 Paris

Biographies of the authors who contributed to the main edition

The abridged version was prepared from the texts of the main version written by the following authors:

INTRODUCTION G. Mokhtar (Egypt); specialist in archaeology; author of numerous publications on the history of Ancient Egypt; former Director of the Service of Antiquities.

CHAPTER 1 Cheikh Anta Diop (Senegal); specialist in human sciences; author of numerous works and articles on Africa and the origin of man; Director of the Radiocarbon Laboratory, University of Dakar.

CHAPTER 2 A. Abu Bakr (Egypt); specialist in the ancient history of Egypt and Nubia; author of numerous publications on Ancient Egypt; Professor at the University of Cairo; deceased.

CHAPTER 3 J. Yoyotte (France); specialist in Egyptology; author of numerous publications on Egyptology; Director of Studies at the *Ecole Pratique des Hautes Etudes*.

CHAPTER 4 A. H. Zayed (Egypt); specialist in Egyptology and ancient history; author of numerous works and articles on Ancient Egypt; Professor of Ancient History.

CHAPTER 5 R. El Nadoury (Egypt); specialist in ancient history; author of numerous works and articles on the history of the Maghrib and of Egypt; Professor of Ancient History and Vice-Chairman of the Faculty of Arts, University of Alexandria.

CHAPTER 6 H. Riad (Egypt); specialist in history and archaeology; author of numerous works on the Pharaonic and Graeco-Roman periods; Chief Curator of the Museum of Cairo.

CHAPTER 7 S. Donadoni (Italy); specialist in the history of Ancient Egypt; author of a number of works on cultural history; Professor at the University of Rome.

CHAPTER 8 S. Adam (Egypt); specialist in Egyptian history and archaeology; author of numerous publications on Ancient Egypt; Director of the Centre of Documentation and Studies on the Art and Civilization of Ancient Egypt.

CHAPTER 9 N. M. Sherif (Sudan); specialist in archaeology; author of numerous works on the archaeology of Sudan; Director of the National Museum at Khartoum.

CHAPTER 10 J. Leclant (France); specialist in Egyptology; author of numerous works and articles on Ancient Egypt; Professor at the Sorbonne; Member of the Académie des Inscriptions et Belles Lettres.

CHAPTER 11 A. A. Hakem (Sudan); specialist in ancient history; author of numerous works on ancient Sudan; Head of the Department of History at the University of Khartoum.

CHAPTER 12 K. Michalowski (Poland); specialist in Mediterranean archaeology; author of numerous publications on the art of Ancient Egypt; Professor of Archaeology; Deputy Director of the National Museum, Warsaw.

CHAPTER 13 H. de Contenson (France); specialist in African history; author of works on Ethiopian archaeology and Christian Nubia; engaged in research at the Centre National de la Recherche Scientifique (CNRS).

CHAPTER 14 F. Anfray (France); specialist in archaeology; author of a number of articles on archaeological research in Ethiopia; Head of the French Archaeological Mission to Ethiopia.

CHAPTER 15 Y. M. Kobishanov (USSR); historian, author of numerous articles on African anthropology; member of the USSR Academy of Sciences.

CHAPTER 16 Tekle Tsadik Mekouria (Ethiopia); historian; writer; specialist in the political, economic and social history of Ethiopia from its origins to the 20th century; retired.

CHAPTER 17 J. Desanges (France); specialist in the history of Ancient Africa, author of numerous works and articles on Ancient Africa; lecturer at the University of Nantes.

CHAPTER 18 B. H. Warmington (UK); specialist in the history of ancient Rome: author of many works on North Africa; lecturer in Ancient History.

CHAPTER 19 A. Mahjoubi (Tunisia); specialist in Ancient History of North Africa; author of numerous works and articles on Tunisian archaeology, assistant professor at the University of Tunis.
P. Salama (Algeria); archaeologist; specialist in the history of the ancient institutions of the Maghrib; professor at the University of Algiers.

CHAPTER 20 P. Salama.

CHAPTER 21 M. Posnansky (UK); historian and archaeologist; author of a number of important works on the archaeological history of East Africa.

CHAPTER 22 A. M. H. Sheriff (Tanzania); specialist in the history of the East African slave trade; lecturer at the University of Dar-es-Salaam.

CHAPTER 23 J. E. G. Sutton (UK); specialist in prehistory; author of numerous works and articles on African history; former President of the Department of Archaeology at the University of Oxford.

CHAPTER 24 B. Wai-Andah (Nigeria); specialist in archaeology; author of works on the archaeology of West Africa; lecturer at the University of Ibadan.

CHAPTER 25 F. Van Noten (Belgium); specialist in prehistory and archaeology; author of numerous works and publications on prehistory of Central Africa; Curator at the Royal Museum of Prehistory and Archaeology.

CHAPTER 26 J. E. Parkington (UK); archaeologist; author of works on the prehistory of Southern Africa; professor of archaeology.

CHAPTER 27 D. W. Phillipson (UK); archaeologist; author of works on the archaeology of East and Southern Africa.

CHAPTER 28 P. Verin (France); specialist in history and archaeology; author of numerous publications on Madagascar and the civilizations of the Indian Ocean; engaged in research on Madagascar.

CHAPTER 29 M. Posnansky.

CONCLUSION G. Mokhtar.

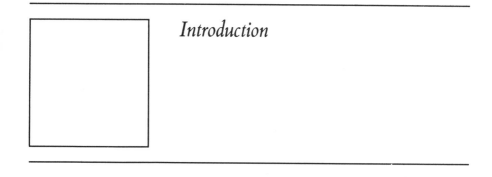

Introduction

The present volume of *A General History of Africa* deals with that long period of the continent's history extending from the end of the Neolithic era (Stone Age), that is, from around the eighth millennium before the Christian era to the beginning of the seventh century of the Christian era.

That period, which covers some nine thousand years of Africa's history, has been roughly sub-divided into four major geographical zones:

(1) the corridor of the Nile, Egypt and Nubia (Chapters 1 to 12);
(2) the Ethiopian highlands (Chapters 13 to 16);
(3) that part of Africa often later called the Maghrib, and its Saharan hinterland (Chapters 17 to 20);
(4) the rest of Africa, including the African islands in the Indian Ocean (Chapters 21 to 29).

This division is largely determined by the present regional compartmental nature of research into African history. It might have seemed more logical to arrange the volume according to the continent's chief ecological divisions, which offer the same living conditions to the human groups inhabiting them, without any true physical barriers.

Such a division, more satisfying than the one that has had to be used, was unfortunately impossible. The separation into sections which is reflected in the plan adopted here derives very largely from the colonization of the nineteenth and twentieth centuries. The archives of the history of Africa, which consist of reports of excavations or of texts and iconography, are for some regions assembled, classified and published according to an order which is irrelevant and arbitrary to the present situation in Africa, but which is very difficult to call in question.

This volume of *A General History of Africa*, perhaps even more than the one that preceded it, must depend on inconclusive and tentative assessments. This is because the period it covers is obscure, owing to the scarcity of sources in general, and of solidly-dated sources in particular – except in respect of certain relatively privileged regions such as the Nile Valley and the Maghrib. For the greater part of the continent, it must be repeated, hard verifiable facts in the period are exceptions rather than the rule.

Yet another point should be stressed: the archaeological sources available to the historian are extremely inadequate. Because of the prohibitive costliness in men and money, excavations are not uniformly spread over the continent as a whole. There is not everywhere the density of excavation that is found notably along the coast, in the hinterland of the northern fringe and, above all, in the Nile Valley from the sea to the Second Cataract.

This lack of archaeological information cannot, unfortunately, be supplemented by reports of foreign travellers, contemporaries of the events or facts that concern this volume. The forbidding nature of the continent deterred outsiders. The continent's rugged nature, and its very size, discouraged, in antiquity as later, deep penetration by those from outside. It will be noted that, in the present state of our knowledge, Africa is the only continent where voyages around the coastline have thrown an important light on history.

These considerations notwithstanding, the inconclusive assessments of Africa from −8000 to +700 are not mere guesses or suppositions; they are based on available data, although these are often rare and inadequate. As should be expected, the task of contributors to this work has been to collect, weigh and assess those sources very carefully. As specialists in the regions whose history – no matter how fragmentary – they trace, they present here the synthesis of what may legitimately be deduced from the data at their disposal. Their assessments, subject to re-examination when further sources are available, will, we are persuaded, provide encouragement and research guidelines to future historians.

Some evaluation of the density of Africa's population during the crucial period between −8000 and −5000 is very necessary, because this is in fact the birth period of the cultures that were later to become differentiated. Moreover the demographic pattern of the period would have a bearing on the evolution of the art of writing: a high or low population density would encourage or make unnecessary the development of writing. The originality of Ancient Egypt, in contrast with the rest of Africa at the same period, perhaps, resides mainly in the fact that the high population density found in ancient times along the banks of the Nile between the First Cataract and the southern portion of the Delta gradually compelled the use of writing, simply in order to co-ordinate the irrigation system vital to these peoples' survival. In contrast, the use of writing was not essential south of the Aswan Cataract, which was a region of low population density where the small somatic groups who occupied the country remained independent of each other. Thus it is regrettable that the population density pattern during that period is beyond scientific investigation and certification.

Lastly ecology, which altered considerably both in space and in time, played an important part. The environment of −7000 to −2400, a period of 4,600 years, which is much more than half the period studied in this volume, was very different from that which obtained after the second half of the third millennium. This latter environment, which seems to have been very similar to the present, strongly determined the pattern of human societies living in it. Community life is not and cannot be the same in the great subtropical desert zones, southern as well as northern, as in the great equatorial forest; or in the mountain ranges as in the great river basins; or in the swamps as in the great lakes. The influence of these major ecological zones is of capital importance for the growth of the routes which permitted movement from one sphere to another, for example, from the Maghrib or mountainous Ethiopia or the Nile Valley towards the central basins of the Congo, Niger and Senegal rivers; or again, from the Atlantic coast towards the Red Sea and the Indian Ocean. Yet those routes are still very little explored. They are guessed at or rather they are 'presumed', much more than actually known. A systematic archaeological study of them should teach us a great deal about the history of Africa. In fact, it is only when they have been discovered and fully investigated that we shall be able to undertake a fruitful study of the migrations between −8000 and −2500 which followed the last great climatic changes and which profoundly altered the distribution of human groups in Africa.

As may be seen, the chapters of Volume II of A *General History of Africa* constitute points of departures for future research much more than a rehearsal of well-established facts. Unfortunately, as has been stressed before, such facts are extremely rare except in the case of some regions that are very small in comparison with the immense size of the continent of Africa.

Egypt: geographical position

In large part parallel to the shores of the Red Sea and the Indian Ocean, to which depressions perpendicular to its course give it access, the Nile Valley, south of the eighth parallel north and as far as the Mediterranean, is also wide open to the west, thanks to valleys starting in the Chad region, the Tibesti and the Ennedi and ending in its course. Lastly, the broad span of the Delta, the Libyan oases and the Suez isthmus give it wide access to the Mediterranean. Thus open to east and west, to south and north, the Nile Corridor is a zone of privileged contacts, not only between the African regions bordering it, but also with the more distant centres of ancient civilization of the Arabian peninsula, the Indian Ocean and the Mediterranean world, western as well as eastern.

However, the importance of this geographical position varied with time. In Africa the end of the Neolithic Age was characterized by a final wet phase that lasted till around −2300 in the northern hemisphere. During that period, which extended from the seventh to the third millennium before the Christian era, the regions east and west of the Nile enjoyed climatic conditions favourable to human settlement and, consequently, contacts and relations between the east and west of the continent were as important as those established between the north and the south.

In contrast, after −2400, the very drying-up of that part of Africa lying between the thirtieth and fifteenth parallels north made the Nile Valley the major route of communication between the continent's Mediterranean coast and what is now called Africa south of the Sahara. It was via the Nile Valley that raw materials, manufactured objects and, no doubt, ideas moved from north to south and vice versa.

It is clear that, because of climatic variations, the geographical position of the middle Nile Valley, as of Egypt, did not have the same importance, or more exactly the same impact, during the period from −7000 to −2400 as it did after that date. Between those years, human groups and cultures could move freely in the northern hemisphere between east and west as well as between south and north. This was the primordial period for the formation and individualization of African cultures.

From −2400 to the seventh century of the Christian era, however, the Nile Valley became the privileged route between the continent's north and south. It was via that valley that exchanges of various kinds took place between black Africa and the Mediterranean basin.

Sources for the history of the Nile Valley in antiquity

The sources at our disposal are of an archaeological nature and thus silent – at least apparently – and literary. The former, especially for the earliest periods have only recently been sought out and collected together. The literary sources, on the other hand, have a long tradition.

Well before Jean-François Champollion (+1790 to +1832), who in the nineteenth century deciphered old Egyptian scripts, mysterious Egypt had aroused curiosity. As early as the sixth century before the Christian era the Greeks had already called attention to the differences between their customs and beliefs and those of the Nile Valley. Thanks to Herodotus, their observations have come down to us. To gain a better understanding of their new subjects, the Ptolemaic kings had a history of Pharaonic Egypt compiled on their own behalf in the third century before the Christian era. Manetho, an Egyptian, was put in charge of writing this general history of Egypt. He had access to the ancient archives and was able to read them. If his work had come down to us in its entirety, we would have been spared many uncertainties. Unfortunately it disappeared when the Library of Alexandria was burned. The excerpts preserved in various compilations, which were too often assembled for apologetic purposes, none the less provide us with a solid framework of Egyptian history. In fact, the thirty-one Manethonian dynasties remain today the firm foundation of the relative chronology of Egypt.

The closing of the last Egyptian temples under Justinian I in the sixth century of the Christian era led to the abandonment of Pharaonic forms of writing, whether hieroglyphic, hieratic or demotic. Only the spoken language survived, in Coptic; the written sources gradually fell into disuse. It was not until +1822, when Jean-François Champollion deciphered the script that we once again had access to ancient documents drawn up by the Egyptians themselves.

Of course these Ancient Egyptian literary sources have to be used with caution, for they are of a particular nature. Most often they were prepared with a specific purpose: to enumerate a Pharaoh's achievements or to ensure eternal worship. Into these two categories of documents fall the lengthy texts and historical images that adorn some parts of Egyptian temples, and also the venerable ancestor lists such as those carved in the Karnak temples during the Eighteenth Dynasty and at Abydos during the Nineteenth.

For compiling royal lists like those referred to above, the scribes used documents drawn up either by priests or by royal officals, which presupposes the existence of properly maintained official archives. Unfortunately only two of these documents have come down to us, but even they are incomplete. They are:

The Palermo Stone (so called because the largest fragment of the text is preserved in the museum of that Sicilian city) is a diorite slab carved on both faces, which preserves

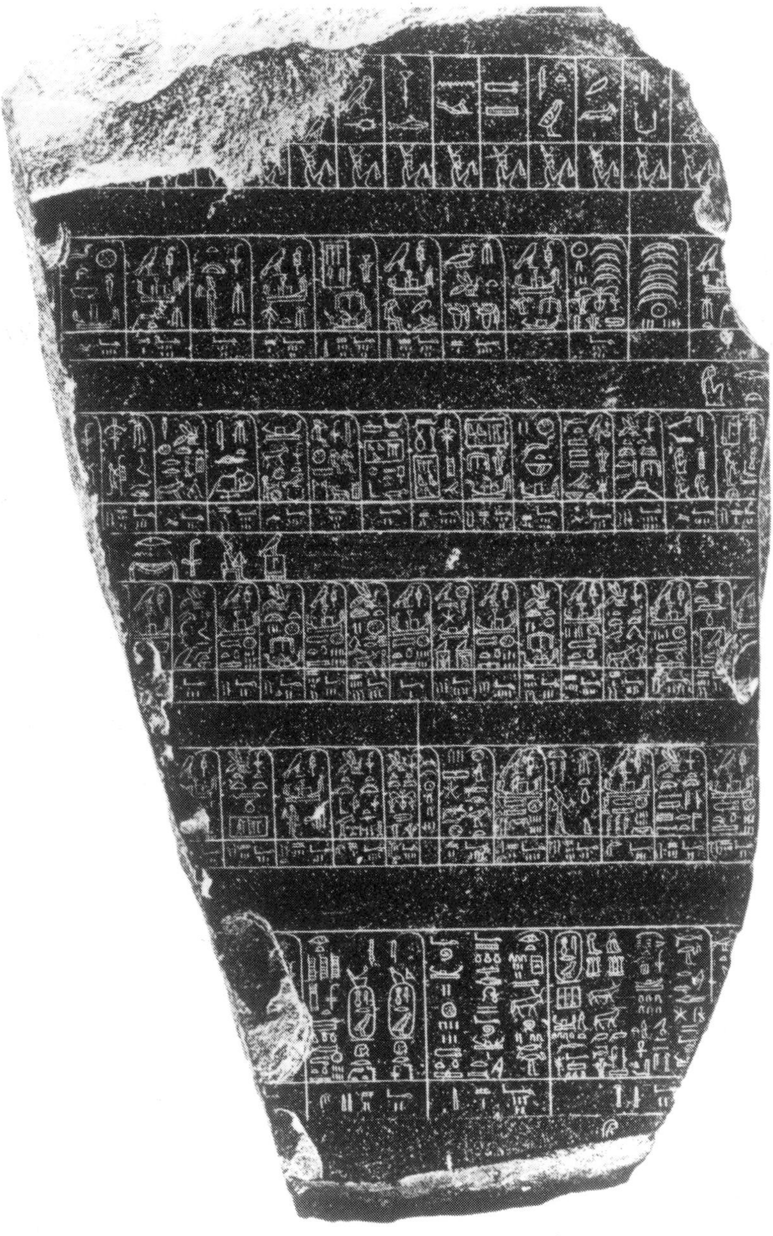

The Palermo Stone (A. H. Gardiner, The Egypt of the Pharoahs, *Oxford University Press, 1961)*

The Papyrus of Turin (A. H. Gardiner, The Royal Canon of Turin, *Oxford, 1954. Photo, Griffith Institute, Ashmolean Museum, Oxford)*

for us the names of all the Pharaohs who reigned in Egypt from the beginning to the Fifth Dynasty, around −2450. Starting with the Third Dynasty, the Palermo Stone lists not only the names of the sovereigns in the order of their succession but also, year by year, the most important events of each reign.

The Turin Papyrus, preserved in that city's museum, is no less important, although it consists only of a list of rulers, with their complete protocol and the number of years, months and days of their reigns, arranged in chronological order. It provides a complete list of all the Pharaohs from the earliest times to around −1200.

Egyptian chronology

The Palermo Stone, the Turin Papyrus and the royal lists on monuments are all the more important for the history of Egypt in that the Egyptians did not use any continuous or cyclical eras similar to our systems: such as, for example, before or after Christ, the years of the Hegira, or the Olympiads. Their computation was based on the person of the Pharaoh himself and each date was given by reference to the sovereign ruling at the time the document was drawn up. This practice explains the importance, for establishing chronology, of knowing both the names of all the Pharaohs who reigned and the duration of each one's reign. Not only does the order of succession itself remain controversial for certain periods, when the Turin Papyrus and Palermo Stone have no references, but even the exact length of reign of some sovereigns remains unknown. At best, we have only the earliest known date of a given Pharaoh, but his reign may have lasted long after the erection of the monument carrying that date.

Even with these gaps, all the dates provided by the sources at our disposal added together give a total of over 4,000 years. This is the long chronology accepted by the first Egyptologists until about +1900. It was then realized that such a time span was impossible, for further study of the texts and monuments showed, first, that at certain periods several Pharaohs reigned simultaneously and that there were thus parallel dynasties, and, secondly, that occasionally a Pharaoh took one of his sons as co-regent. Since each of the rulers dated his monuments according to his own reign, there was thus some overlapping, and by adding together the reigns of parallel dynasties and those of co-regents, with the reigns of the official sovereigns, one necessarily arrived at a total figure which was much too high.

It would probably have been impossible to solve this problem, if one peculiarity of the ancient Pharaonic calendar had not provided a sure chronological framework, by linking that calendar to a permanent astronomical phenomenon the tables for which were easy to establish. We are here referring to the rising of the star Sothis – our Sirius – co-ordinated with the rising of the sun, at a latitude of Heliopolis-Memphis. This is what is called the 'heliacal rising of Sothis', which was observed and noted in antiquity by the Egyptians. These observations supplied the 'Sothic' dates on which Egyptian chronology rests today.

At the outset the Egyptians, like most of the peoples of antiquity, seem to have used a lunar calendar, notably to set the dates of religious festivals. But alongside that astronomical calendar they used another, a natural calendar based on the periodic repetition of an event that was all-important for their existence – the flood of the Nile.

In that calendar the first season of the year, called 'Akhet' in Egyptian, saw the beginning of the flood. For about four months the fields would become saturated with water. In the next season the land gradually coming out from the flood waters became ready for sowing. This was the season of Peret, literally 'coming out'. In the third and final season the Egyptians harvested and then stored the harvest. This was the season of Shemou.

Whatever their reasons, the Egyptians, by linking the beginning of the flood, and consequently the first day of the new year, with an astronomical phenomenon, have provided us with a means of setting positive reference points for their long history.

At the latitude of Memphis the very gentle beginning of the flood took place about the middle of July. Observation over a few years appears to have sufficed to show the Egyptians that the beginning of the flood recurred on average every 365 days. They thereupon divided their year of three empirical seasons into a year of twelve months of thirty days each. They then assigned four months to each of the seasons. By adding five additional days (in Egyptian the '5 *heryou renepet*', the five over – in addition to – the year), the scribes obtained a year of 365 days which was by far the best of all those adopted in antiquity. However, although very good, that year was not perfect. In fact, the earth completes its revolution around the sun, not in 365 days, but 365¼ days. Every four years the Egyptians' official year lagged one day behind the astronomical year, and it was only after 1,460 years – what is called a Sothic Period – that the three phenomena, sunrise, rise of Sothis and beginning of the flood occurred simultaneously on the first day of the official year.

This gradual lag between the two years had an important consequence: it enabled modern astronomers to determine when the Egyptians adopted their calendar, that date necessarily having to coincide with the beginning of a Sothic period.

By combining the astronomical dates with the relative dates provided by the sources at our disposal – the Turin Papyrus, the Palermo Stone, the dated monuments of various epochs – we have been able to reach a basic chronology, the most certain of all those of the ancient Orient. It sets the beginning of the history of Egypt at –3000.

The conquest by Alexander of Macedon in –332 marks the end of the history of Pharaonic Egypt and the beginning of the Hellenistic period (cf. Chapter 6).

The Nilotic environment

It is perhaps useful to quote here a sentence written by Herodotus (II,35) at the end of his description of Egypt: 'Not only is the Egyptian climate peculiar to that country, and the Nile different in its behaviour from other rivers elsewhere, but the Egyptians themselves in their manners and customs seem to have reversed the ordinary practices of mankind.' Of course, when he wrote that sentence Herodotus was thinking only of the countries bordering on the Mediterranean. It is none the less true that, of all the countries of Africa, Egypt is the one with the most distinctive environment. It owes this to the regime of the Nile. Without the river, Egypt would not exist. This has been said over and over again since Herodotus: it is a basic truth.

From the end of the Neolithic Age, around −3300 to −2400, north-western Africa, the Sahara included, enjoyed a relatively moist climatic system. At that period Egypt was not dependent solely on the Nile for its subsistence. The steppe still extended both east and west of the valley, providing cover for abundant game and favouring considerable cattle-raising. Agriculture was then still only one of the components of daily life, and cattle-raising – even hunting – played at least as important a role. A census of this basic wealth was made every two years. The scenes decorating the mastabas of the Old Kingdom from the end of the Fourth Dynasty to the Sixth Dynasty (−2500 to −2200) clearly show that cattle-raising occupied an essential place in Egyptian life at that time.

We may thus suspect that man's search for control of the river – the fundamental achievement of Egyptian civilization, which enabled it to flourish – was probably stimulated in the beginning not by the desire to make better use of the flood for agriculture, but more especially to prevent damage by the rising waters. It is sometimes forgotten that the overflowing of the Nile is not solely beneficial: it can bring disaster, and it was no doubt for themselves that the valley's inhabitants learned to build dykes and dams to shield their villages and to dig canals to dry out their fields. So they slowly acquired experience that became vital for them when the climate of Africa between the thirtieth and fifteenth parallels north gradually became as dry as it is today, transforming into absolute desert the immediate neighbourhood of the Nile Valley, both in Egypt and in Nubia. Thereafter, all life in the valley was strictly conditioned by the river's rise.

Using the dyke-building and canal-digging techniques which they had perfected over the centuries, the Egyptians little by little developed the system of irrigation by basins (hods), thus securing not only their survival in a climate increasingly desert-like, but even the possibility of expansion (see Chapters 4 and 8 below).

It is no exaggeration to say that this unique system of irrigation is at the very root of the development of Egyptian civilization. It explains how human ingenuity slowly managed to overcome great difficulties and succeeded in changing the valley's natural ecology.

By profoundly changing the conditions imposed upon him by nature, man played an essential part in the emergence and expansion of civilization in the Nile Valley. Egypt is not only a gift of the Nile; it is, above all, a creation of man.

The settlement of the Nile Valley

As early as the Palaeolithic Era (Ice Age) man occupied, if not the actual valley, at least its immediate neighbourhood and notably the terraces overlooking it. Successions of wet and dry periods during the Palaeolithic and Neolithic Ages (see Volume I) inevitably changed the population density, first one way then the other, but the fact remains that, as far back in time as we can go, *homo sapiens* has always been living in Egypt.

To what race did he belong? Few anthropological problems have given rise to so much impassioned discussion. Yet this problem is not new. Already in +1874 there was argument about whether the Ancient Egyptians were 'white' or 'black'. A century later a Unesco-sponsored symposium in Cairo proved that the discussion was not, nor was likely soon to be, closed. Recently an anthropologist cast doubt upon the very possibility of finding positive means of determing the race to which a given skeleton belongs – at least as regards very ancient human remains, such as those from the Palaeolithic Era, for instance. The traditional criteria applied by physical anthropoligists – facial index, length of limbs, etc. – are no longer accepted by everyone today. Nevertheless, it is highly doubtful whether the inhabitants who introduced civilization into the Nile Valley ever belonged to one single, pure race. The very history of the peopling of the valley refutes such a possibility.

Man did not penetrate all at once into a valley that was empty or inhabited only by wild animals. He settled there gradually in the course of thousands of years, as the very density of the human groups or the variations in climate forced him to seek additional resources or greater security. Owing to its position at the north-eastern corner of the African continent, it was inevitable that the Nile Valley as a whole, and Egypt in particular, should become the terminal point for movements of people coming not only from Africa but also from the Middle East, not to mention more distant Europe. It is, therefore, not surprising that anthropologists should have believed they could discern, among the several very ancient Nilotic skeletons at their disposal, representatives of the Cro-Magnon race, Armenoids, negroids, leucoderms, etc., although these terms should only be accepted with caution. If an Egyptian race ever existed – and this is open to doubt – it was the result of mixtures whose basic elements varied in time as well as in space.

One fact remains, however, and that is the continued existence in Egypt, as in Nubia, of a certain physical type which it would be vain to call a race, since it varies slightly according to whether we are concerned with Lower or Upper Egypt. Darker in the south than in the north, it is in general darker than in the rest of the Mediterranean basin, including North Africa. The hair is black and curly and the face, rather round and hairless, is in the Old Kingdom sometimes adorned with a moustache. Relatively slim as a rule, it is the human type that frescoes, bas-reliefs and statues of the Pharaohs have made familiar to us.

This shows that in the Nile Valley we have to do with a human type, not a race, a type gradually brought into being as much by the habits and conditions of life peculiar to the valley as by the mixtures of which it is the product. It is more than probable that the African strain, black or light, is preponderant in the Ancient Egyptian, but in the present state of our knowledge it is impossible to say more.

Writing and environment

Egypt was the first African country to make use of writing, if we judge from the employment in the hieroglyphic system of pictograms representing objects that had long ago ceased to be used. It is possible to set its invention at the Amratian period, called also the Nagada I (see Volume I), that is, around −4000, if we follow the dates suggested by carbon 14 dating, at the beginning of the historic period. Thus it is one of the oldest known systems of writing. It developed very rapidly, since it appears already established on the Narmer palette, the first historic Egyptian monument, which can be dated at −3000. Moreover, the fauna and flora used in the signs are essentially African.

Egyptian writing is fundamentally pictographic, like many ancient types of writing, but, whereas in China and Mesopotamia, for example, the originally pictographic signs rapidly evolved towards abstract forms, Egypt remained faithful to its system till the end of its history.

But this system thus completed had several flaws. It necessarily utilized a greater number of signs – more than 400 ordinary ones are known – which could leave the reader perplexed as to how to read them. In addition, it was impossible at first sight to know whether a given sign was employed as a word-sign designating the object represented, or whether it was used as a phonetic sign. The Ancient Egyptians invented also what Egyptologists call phonetic complements. These consist of twenty-four word-signs each of which has only one consonant. The scribes gradually came to use them to indicate phonetic reading of the signs.

It is evident that these twenty-four simple signs in fact play the part of our letters, and that we have here in embryo the invention of the alphabet, since these signs express all the consonants of the Egyptian language and since Egyptian, like Arabic and Hebrew, does not write the vowels. Hence there was no word in the language that could not have been written simply by means of signs. However, the Egyptians never took the final step in this direction, and, far from employing only the simple, almost alphabetic signs alone they further complicated their writing system by bringing into it, in addition to the signs used phonetically and their phonetic complements, new purely ideographic signs. These signs were placed at the end of the words. They made it possible to classify those words into a given category at first sight. For example, verbs designating a physical action, such as 'to strike', 'to kill', were followed by the sign of a human arm holding a weapon.

With its intricate system of word-signs, plurisyllabic phonetic signs, phonetic complements and ideographic determinatives – a medley of signs, some to be pronounced and others not to be pronounced – hieroglyphic writing is complex, certainly, but it is also very evocative.

One of the forces presiding over the invention and development of hieroglyphic writing in the Nile Valley is undoubtedly to be found in the need for its inhabitants to act together in a concerted manner to combat the disasters periodically threatening them, among others the flooding of the Nile.

The political unification of Egypt by Menes around −3000 was bound to strengthen further the development of administration and, therefore, of writing. Moreover, because of the very fickleness of the flood, one of the central government's responsibilities was to stock as much food as possible in times of plenty, to palliate the shortages which might always occur at short notice. Consequently the leaders, in this case the Pharaoh, must know exactly what the country had available, so as to be able, in case of need, either to ration or to distribute the existing resources to the regions most seriously affected by the famine. This was the basis of Egypt's economic organization and, in fact, of its very existence. It required on the material level a complex accounting system for incomings and outgoings, as regards both commodities and personnel, which explains the essential role devolving on the scribe in the civilization of Ancient Egypt.

The contrast between Egypt and the Nubian Nile Valley gives us a better understanding of the role of writing and the reasons for its existence in the emergence and development of the Egyptian civilization. South of the First Cataract we are in the presence of a population having the same composition as that of Upper Egypt. However, Nubia was always unwilling to accept the use of writing, although the permanent contacts which it maintained with the Egyptian valley could not have left it in ignorance of that use. The reason for this stage of affairs seems to reside in the difference in the way of life. On the one hand, we have a dense population that the requirements of irrigation and control of the river on which its very existence depends have closely bound into a hierachical society in which each individual plays a specific role in the country's development.

On the other hand, in Nubia we have a population that at the dawn of history possessed a material culture equal, if not superior, to that of Upper Egypt, but the population of which was divided into smaller groups spaced farther apart. Those groups were more independent and more mobile, because stock-raising required frequent moves and played at least as important a part in the economy as did agriculture, the latter very limited in a valley narrower than in Egypt. The Nubian peoples did not feel the need for writing. They were always to remain in the domain of oral tradition, only very occasionally using writing and then solely, it seems, for religious purposes, or when they were subject to a central monarchical type of government (see below, Chapters 10 and 11).

African Egypt – receptacle of influence

Around −3700 a unification of the material culture in the two centres of civilization in the Nile Valley occurred. Or, to be more precise, the southern centre, while still maintaining its distinctive characteristics, partially adopted the culture of the northern centre. This penetration southward of the northern civilization is often associated, on the one hand, with the invention of writing and, on the other, with the appearance in Egypt of invaders more advanced than the autochthonous inhabitants.

As regards writing, we have seen earlier that a purely Nilotic, hence African origin not only is not excluded, but probably reflects the reality. However, the originality and the antiquity of the Egyptian civilization should not hide the fact that it was also a receptacle for many influences. Moreover, its geographical position predisposed it in this direction.

The relatively moist climate at the end of the Neolithic Era and throughout the pre-dynastic period, which saw the crystallization of civilization in Egypt, made the Arabian desert between the Red Sea and the Nile Valley permeable, so to speak. It was undoubtedly by that route that Mesopotamian influences, whose importance, incidentally, may have been exaggerated, penetrated into Egypt. It would seem also, in spite of the lack of sufficient investigation, that some contacts existed between the population of the Libyan desert and those of the Nile Valley.

To the north, it seems that in very early times the links, by way of the isthmus of Suez between Egypt and the Syro-Palestinian corridor, were not as close as they were to become after the establishment of the Old Kingdom. However, there again, very ancient traces of contacts with Palestine are to be noted, and the Osiris myth may have risen out of relationships between the Deltaic centre of civilization and the wooded coast of Lebanon – relationships which would thus date back to extremely ancient times.

At first glance the ties with the south seem much clearer, but their importance is difficult to assess. From the fourth century before the Christian era, people south of the First Cataract (see Chapter 10 below) were in close contact with the lower Nile Valley. In the pre- and proto-dynastic eras exchanges between the two groups of peoples were numerous in pottery techniques and the manufacture of enamelled clay (Egyptian faience), use of the same pigments, use of similar weapons, the same belief in a life after death, related funerary rites. During these contacts the Egyptians must have had relations, direct or through intermediaries, with the people of more distant Africa, as may be deduced from the number of ivory and ebony objects that have been collected from the oldest Egyptian tombs. Even if we accept that the ecological boundary line of ebony was farther north than it is today, it was still very far from Lower Nubia, and this provides us with a precious piece of evidence of contacts between Africa south of the Sahara and Egypt. Apart from ivory and ebony, incense – which appears very early – and obsidian, both items foreign to the Nile Valley, could have been imported by the Egyptians. Through this trade, techniques and ideas would have passed the more easily from one area to the other in that, as we have seen, there was in the Egyptians a considerable African strain.

Thus, whichever way we turn, whether west or east, north or south, we see that Egypt received outside influences. However, these never profoundly affected the originality of the civilization that was gradually taking shape on the banks of the Nile, before in its turn influencing adjoining regions. To allow of an estimation of the part that outside influences may have played at the beginning of civilization in the Nile Valley, a good knowledge would be needed of the archaeology of the whole country in ancient times.

A very comprehensive knowledge is required for a profitable comparison of the archaeological material collected in Egypt with that provided by the neighbouring cultures, designed to bring to light importations or imitations, the sole tangible proof of large-scale contacts.

But, while the archaeology of the fourth millennium before the Christian era is fairly well known, both in Upper Egypt and in Lower Nubia (between the First and Second Cataracts), the same does not apply to the other parts of the Nile Valley. The Delta, in particular, is virtually unknown to us in respect of the pre- and proto-dynastic periods, except for some very rare localities on its desert fringe. All references to possible influences coming from Asia during those periods, by way of the Suez isthmus or the Mediterranean coast, are yet to be authenticated by investigation.

We encounter the same difficulties in the case of the upper Nile Valley, between the Second and Sixth Cataracts. Our ignorance of the earliest archaeology of this vast region is all the more regrettable, in that it must have been there that contacts and trade between the Egyptian part of the Nile Valley and Africa south of the Sahara took place.

1

Origin of the Ancient Egyptians

The general acceptance, as a sequel to the work of Professor Leakey, of the hypothesis of mankind's monogenetic and African origin, makes it possible to pose the question of the peopling of Egypt and even of the world in completely new terms. More than 150,000 years ago, beings morphologically identical with the man of today were living in the region of the great lakes at the sources of the Nile and nowhere else. This notion means that the whole human race had its origin, just as the ancients had guessed, at the foot of the Mountains of the Moon. From this two facts of capital importance result:

(a) The earliest men were ethnically homogeneous and negroid. Gloger's Law, which would also appear to be applicable to human beings, lays it down that warm-blooded animals evolving in a warm, humid climate will secrete a black pigment (eumelanin). Hence if mankind originated in the tropics around the latitude of the great lakes, he was bound to have brown pigmentation from the start and it was by differentiation in other climates that the original stock later split into different races.

(b) There were only two routes available by which these early men could move out to people the other continents, namely, the Sahara and the Nile Valley. It is the latter region which will be discussed here.

From the Upper Palaeolithic to the dynastic epoch, the whole of the river's basin was taken over progressively by these negroid peoples.

Evidence of physical anthropology on the race of the Ancient Egyptians

It might have been thought that, working on physiological evidence, the findings of the anthropologists would dissipate all doubts by providing reliable and definitive truths. This is by no means so: the arbitrary nature of the criteria used, as well as abolishing any notion of a conclusion acceptable without qualification, introduces a considerate amount of scientific hair-splitting.

Nevertheless, although the conclusions of these anthropological studies stop short of the full truth, they still speak unanimously of the existence of a negro race from the most distant ages of prehistory down to the dynastic period. It is not possible in this paper to cite all these conclusions: they will be found summarized in Chapter X of

Dr Emile Massoulard's *Historie et protohistorie d'Egypte* (Institut d'Ethnologie, Paris, 1949). We shall quote selected items only.

> Miss Fawcett considers that the Negadah skulls form a sufficiently homogeneous collection to warrant the assumption of a Negadah race. In the total height of the skull, the auricular height, the length and breadth of the face, nasal length, cephalic index and facial index, this race would seem to approximate to the negro; in nasal breadth, height of orbit, length of the palate and nasal index, it would seem closer to the Germanic peoples; accordingly the Pre-Dynastic Negadians are likely to have resembled the negroes in certain of their characteristics and the white races in others. (pp. 402–3)

These measurements, which would leave an open choice between the two extremes represented by the negro and the Germanic races, give an idea of the elasticity of the criteria employed.

'Falkenburger reopened the anthropological study of the Egyptian population in a recent work in which he discusses 1,787 male skulls varying in date from the old Pre-Dynastic to our own day. He distinguished four main groups.' The sorting of the pre-dynastic skulls into these four groups gives the following results for the whole pre-dynastic period: '36% negroid, 33% Mediterranean, 11% Cro-Magnoid and 20% of individuals not falling in any of these groups but approximating either to the Cro-Magnoid or the the negroid.'

The point about these conclusions is that despite their discrepancies the degree to which they converge proves that the basis of the Egyptian population was negro in the pre-dynastic epoch. Thus they are all incompatible with the theory that the negro element only infiltrated into Egypt at a late stage. Far otherwise, the facts prove that it was preponderant from the beginning to the end of Egyptian history, particularly when we note once more that 'Mediterranean' is not a synonym for 'white', Elliot-Smith's 'brown or Mediterranean race' being nearer the mark. Elliot-Smith classes these proto-Egyptians as a branch of what he calls the brown race, which is the same as Sergi's 'Mediterranean or Eurafrican race'. The term 'brown' in this context refers to skin colour and is simply a euphemism for negro. It is thus clear that it was the whole of the Egyptian population which was negro, barring an infiltration of white nomads in the proto-dynastic epoch.

In Petrie's study of the Egyptian race we are introduced to a possible classification element in great abundance which cannot fail to surprise the reader.

> Petrie . . . published a study of the races of Egypt in the Pre-Dynastic and Proto-Dynastic periods working only on portrayals of them. Apart from the steatopygian race, he distinguishes six separate types: an aquiline type belonging to an invading race coming perhaps from the shores of the Red Sea; a 'sharp nosed' type almost certainly from the Arabian desert; a 'tilted nose' type from Middle Egypt; a 'jutting beard' type from Lower Egypt and a 'narrow-nosed' type from Upper Egypt. Going on the images, there would thus have been seven different racial types in Egypt during the epochs we are considering.

The above mode of classification gives an idea of the arbitary nature of the criteria used to define the Egyptian races. Be that as it may, it is clear that anthropology is far from having established the existence of a white Egyptian race and would indeed tend to suggest the opposite.

Nevertheless, in current textbooks the question is suppressed: in most cases it is simply and flatly asserted that the Egyptians were white and the honest layman is left with the impression that any such assertion must necessarily have a prior basis of solid research. But there is no such basis, as this chapter has shown. And so generation after generation has been misled.

Human images of the proto-historic period: their anthropological value

The study of human images made by Flinders Petrie on another plane shows that the ethnic type was black: according to Petrie these people were the Anu, whose name has been traced to the proto-historic epoch.

As we shall see later Min, who was worshipped by the Anu, was called by the tradition of Egypt itself 'the great negro'.

After a glance at the various foreign types of humanity who disputed the valley with the indigenous blacks, Petrie describes the Anu, who occupied southern Egypt and Nubia, according to a certain portrait of Tera Neter, as blacks.

Amélineau lists in geographical order the fortified towns built along the length of the Nile Valley by the Anu blacks: Esneh, 'the southern On' or Hermonthis, Denderah, a town called On in the nome of Tinis, and 'the northern On', or Heliopolis.

The mural in tomb SD63 (Sequence Date 63) of Hierakonpolis shows the native-born blacks subjugating the foreign intruders into the valley, if we accept Petrie's interpretation: 'Below is the black ship at Hierakonpolis belonging to the black men who are shown as conquering the red men.'

The images of men of the proto-historic and of the dynastic period in no way square with the idea of the Egyptian race popular with Western anthropologists. Wherever the autochthonous racial type is represented with any degree of clearness, it is evidently negroid. Nowhere are the Indo-European and Semitic elements shown even as ordinary freemen serving a local chief, but invariably as conquered foreigners. The rare portrayals found are always shown with the distinctive marks of captivity, hands tied behind the back or strained over the shoulders. A proto-dynastic figurine represents an Indo-European prisoner with a long plait on his knees, with his hands bound tight to his body. The characteristics of this object show that it was intended as the foot of a piece of furniture and represented a conquered race.

The typically negroid features of the Pharaohs (Narmer, First Dynasty, the actual founder of the Pharaonic line; Zoser, Third Dynasty,; Cheops, the builder of the Great Pyramid, a Cameroon type; Menthuhotep, founder of the Eleventh Dynasty, very black; Sesostris I; Queen Ahmosis Nefertari; and Amenhophis I) show that all classes of Egyptian society belong to the same black race.

There are two variants of the black race:

(a) straight-haired, represented in Asia by the Dravidians and in Africa by the Nubians and the Tubu or Teda, all three with jet-black skins:
(b) the kinky-haired blacks of the Equatorial regions.

Both types entered into the composition of the Egyptian population.

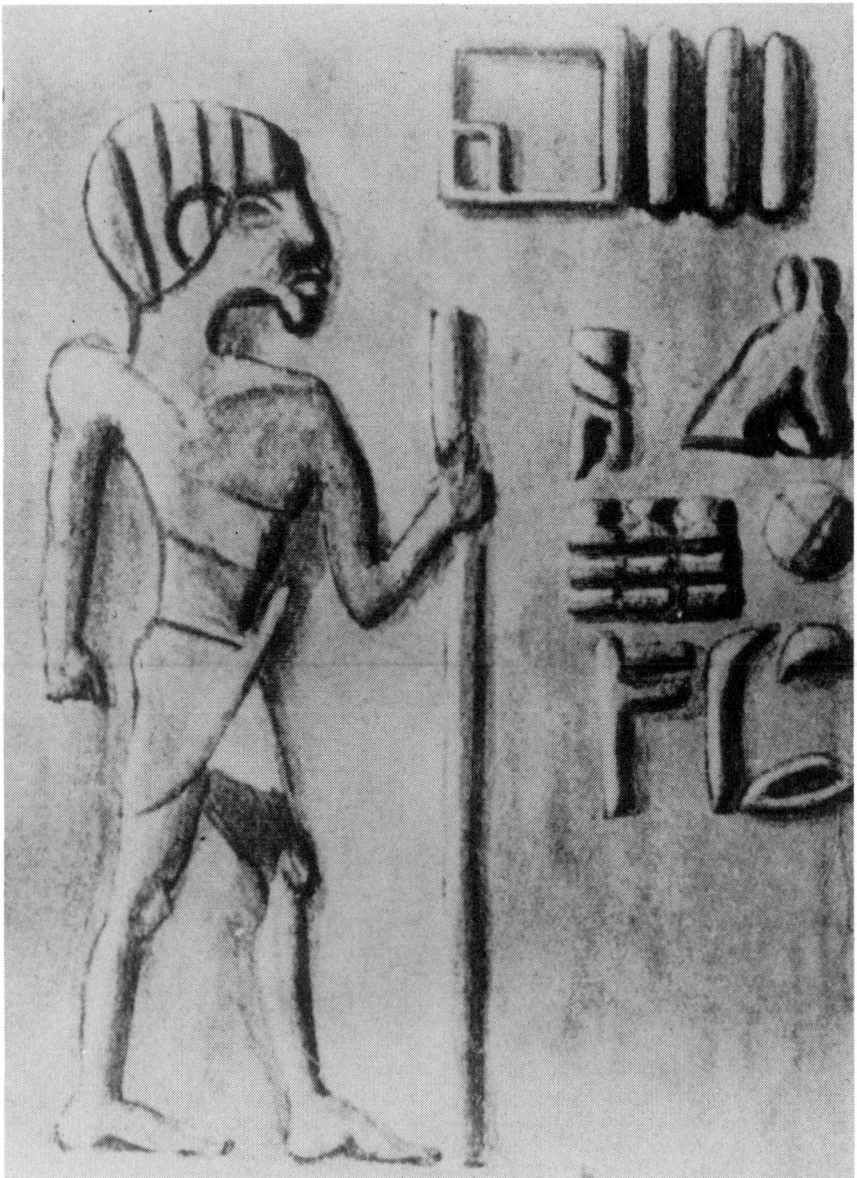

1.1 *Proto-historic figure of Tera-Neter, a negro nobleman of the Anous race who were the first inhabitants of Egypt (C. A. Diop,* Antériorité des civilisations nègres: mythe ou vérité historique? *Présence Africaine, 1967)*

1.2 *A pharaoh of the First Egyptian Dynasty, said to be Narmer (C. A. Diop,* Antériorité des civilisations nègres: mythe ou vérité historique? *Présence Africaine, 1967)*

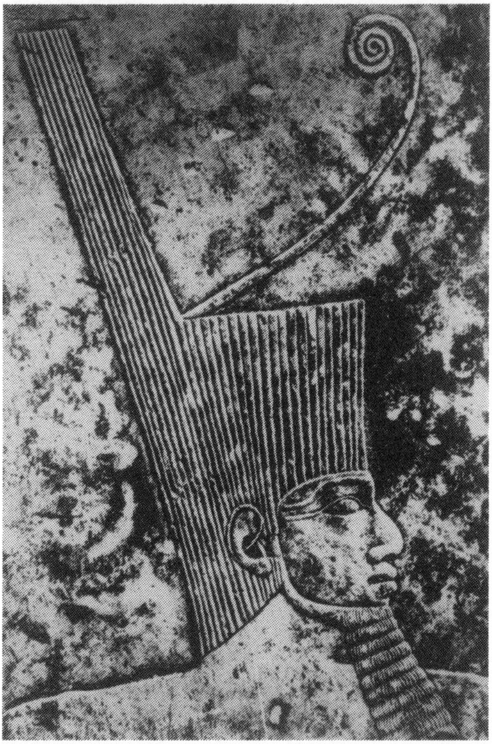

1.3 *Djeser – typical negro, pharoah of the Third Dynasty (C. A. Diop,* Antériorité des civilisations nègres: mythe ou vérité historique? *Présence Africaine, 1967)*

Melanin dosage test

In practice it is possible to determine directly the skin colour, and hence the ethnic affiliations of the Ancient Egyptians, by microscopic analysis in the laboratory; I doubt if the sagacity of the researchers who have studied the question has overlooked the possibility.

Melanin (eumelanin), the chemical substance responsible for skin pigmentation, is, broadly speaking, insoluble and is preserved for millions of years in the skin of fossil animals. There is thus all the more reason for it to be readily recoverable in the skins of Egyptian mummies. Although the epidermis is the main site of the melanin, the melanocytes penetrating the derm at the boundary between it and the epidermis – even where the latter has mostly been destroyed by the embalming materials – show a melanin level which is non-existent in the white-skinned races. The samples I myself analysed were taken in the physical anthropology laboratory of the Musée de L'Homme in Paris off the mummies from the Marietta excavations in Egypt. The same method is perfectly suitable for use on the royal mummies of Thutmoses III, Seti I and Ramses II in the Cairo Museum, which are in an excellent state of preservation. No more than a few square millimetres of skin would be required to mount a specimen, the preparations being a few μm in thickness and lightened with ethyl benzoate. They can be studied by natural light or with ultraviolet lighting which renders the melanin grains fluorescent.

Either way let us simply say that the evaluation of melanin level by microscopic examination is a laboratory method which enables us to classify the Ancient Egyptians unquestionably among the black races.

Osteological measurements

Among the criteria accepted in physical anthropology for classifying races, the osteological measurements are perhaps the least misleading (in contrast to craniometry) for distinguishing a black man from a white man. By this criterion, also, the Egyptians belong among the black races. This study was made by Lepsius at the end of the nineteenth century and his conclusions remain valid. Subsequent methodological progress in the domain of physical anthropology in no way undermines what is called the 'Lepsius Canon' which, in round figures, gives the bodily proportions of the ideal Egyptian, short-armed and of negroid or negrito physical type.

Blood groups

It is a notable fact that even today Egyptians, particularly in Upper Egypt, belong to the same Group B as the populations of western Africa on the Atlantic seaboard and not to the A2 Group characteristic of the white race prior to any cross-breeding. It would be interesting to study the extent of Group A2 distribution in Egyptian mummies, which present-day techniques make possible.

The Egyptian race according to the classical authors of antiquity

To the Greek and Latin writers contemporary with the Ancient Egyptians the latter's physical classification posed no problems: the Egyptians were negroes, thick-lipped, kinky-haired and thin-legged. Some of the following evidence drives home the point.

(a) Herodotus, 'the father of history', −480 (?) to −425.

With regard to the origins of the Colchians who lived on the shores of the Black Sea, he writes:

> It is in fact manifest that the Colchidians are Egyptians by race . . . several Egyptians told me that in their opinion the Colchidians were descended from soldiers of Sesostris. I had conjectured as much myself from two pointers, firstly because they have black skins and kinky hair and secondly and more reliably for the reason that alone among mankind the Egyptians and the Ethiopians have practised circumcision since time immemorial. The Phoenicians and Syrians of Palestine themselves admit that they learnt the practice from the Egyptians while the Syrians in the river Thermodon and Pathenios region and their neighbours the Macrons say they learnt it recently from the Colchidians. These are the only races which practise circumcision and it is observable that they do it in the same way as the Egyptians.

Herodotus reverts several times to the negroid character of the Egyptians and each time uses it as a fact of observation to argue more or less complex theses.

(b) Aristotle, −389 to −332, scientist, philosopher and tutor of Alexander the Great.

In one of his minor works Aristotle attempts to establish a correlation between the physical and moral natures of living beings and leaves us evidence on the Egyptian–Ethiopian race which confirms what Herodotus says.

(c) Lucian, Greek writer, +125 (?) to +190.

The evidence of Lucian is as explicit as that of the two previous writers. He introduces two Greeks, Lycinus and Timolaus, who start a conversation.

> *Lycinus* (describing a young Egyptian): This boy is not merely black; he has thick lips and his legs are too thin . . . his hair worn in a plait behind shows that he is not a freeman.
>
> *Timolaus*: But that is a sign of really distinguished birth in Egypt, Lycinus. All freeborn children plait their hair until they reach manhood. It is the exact opposite of the custom of our ancestors who thought it seemly for old men to secure their hair with a gold brooch to keep it in place.

(d) Apollodorus, first century before the Christian era, Greek philosopher.

> 'Aegyptos conquered the country of the black-footed ones and called it Egypt after himself.'

1.4 ▲ *Indo-European captives (C. A. Diop,* Antériorité des civilisations nègres: mythe ou vérité historique? *Présence Africaine, 1967)*

1.5 ◄ *Semitic captives at the time of the pharoahs; Sinai rock (C. A. Diop,* Antériorité des civilisations nègres: mythe ou vérité historique? *Présence Africaine, 1967)*

1.6 ▼ *Libyan prisoner (C. A. Diop,* Antériorité des civilisations nègres: mythe ou vérité historique? *Présence Africaine, 1967)*

1.7 *Cheops, Pharoah of the Fourth Egyptian Dynasty, builder of the Great Pyramid (C. A. Diop,* Antériorité des civilisations nègres: mythe ou vérité historique? *Présence Africaine, 1967)*

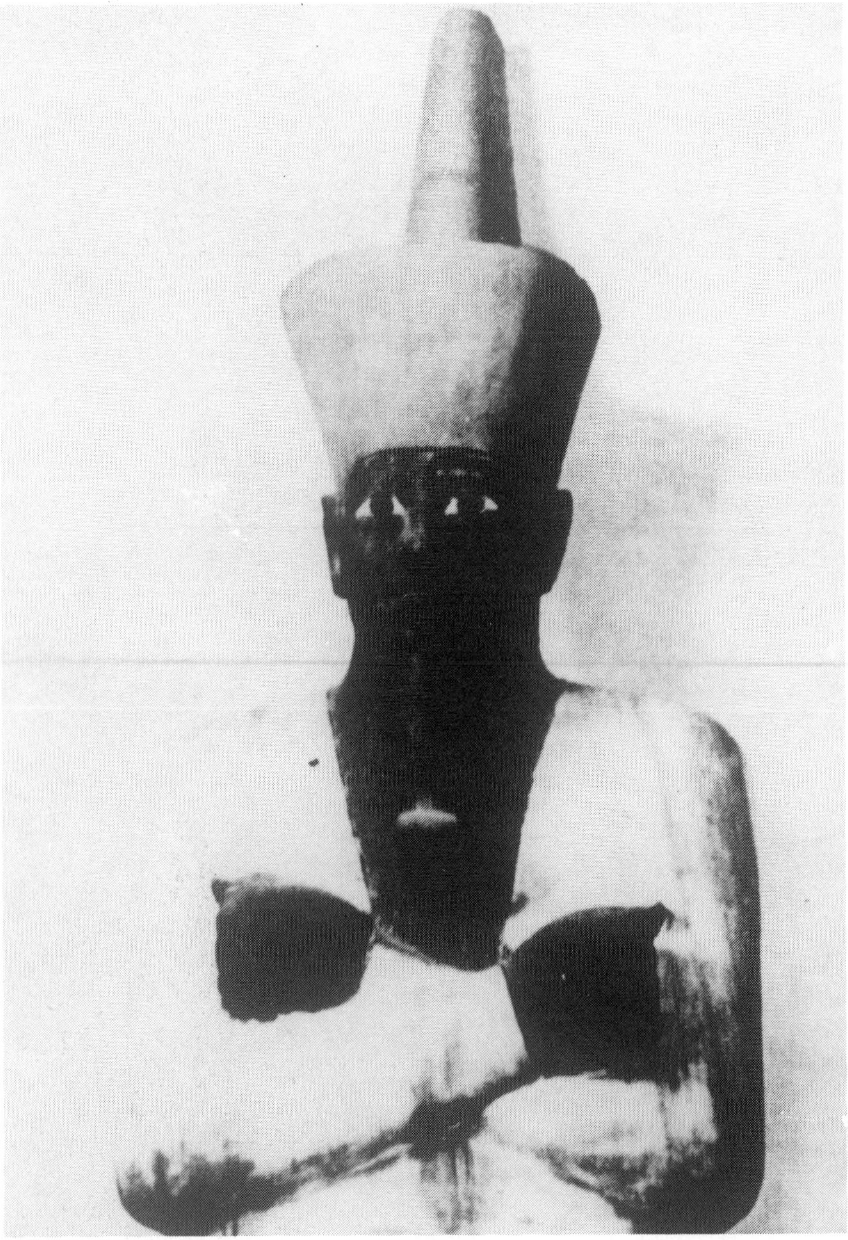

1.8 *Mentuhotep I (C.A. Diop,* Antériorité des civilisations nègres: mythe ou vérité historique? *Présence Africaine, 1967)*

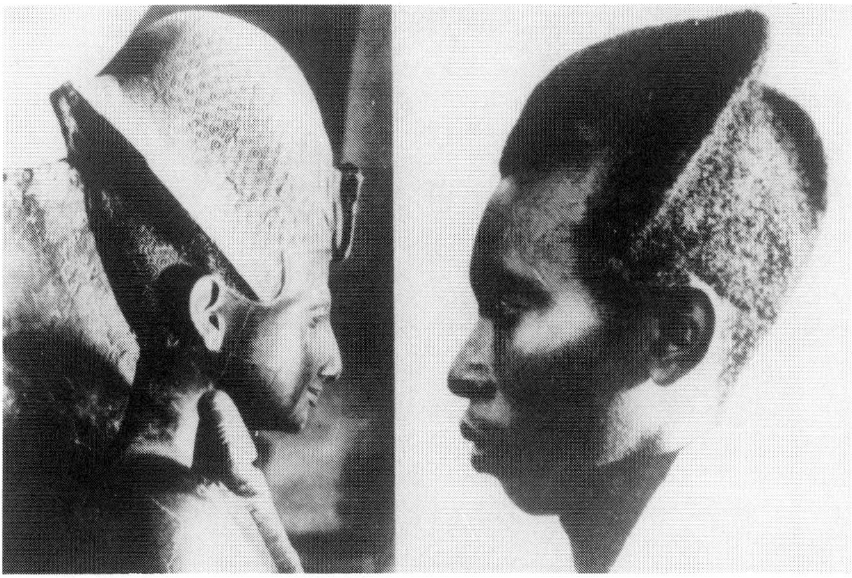

1.9 *Ramses II and a modern Batutsi (C. A. Diop,* Antériorité des civilisations nègres: mythe ou vérité historique? *Présence Africaine, 1967)*

1.10 *The Sphinx as found by the first French scientific mission in the nineteenth century. The typically Negro profile is thought to be that of the pharoah Khafre or Khefren (ca.–2600, IV Dynasty, the builder of the second pyramid of Giza (C. A. Diop,* Antériorité des civilisations nègres: mythe ou vérité historique? *Présence Africaine, 1967)*

(e) Aeschylus, −525 (?) to −456, tragic poet and creator of Greek tragedy.

In *The Suppliants*, Danaos, fleeing with his daughters, the Danaids, and pursued by his brother Aegyptos with his sons, the Aegyptiads, who seek to wed their cousins by force, climbs a hillock, looks out to sea and describes the Aegyptiads at the oars afar off in these terms: 'I can see the crew with their black limbs and white tunics.'

A similar description of the Egyptian type of man recurs a few lines later in verse 745.

(f) Achilles Tatius of Alexandria.

He compares the herdsmen of the Delta to the Ethiopians and explains that they are blackish, like half-castes.

(g) Strabo, −58 to about +25.

He concurs in the theory that the Egyptians and the Colchoi are of the same race but holds that the migrations to Ethiopia and Colchoi had been from Egypt only. 'Egyptians settled in Ethiopia and in Colchoi.'

(h) Diodorus of Sicily, about −63 to +14. Greek historian and contemporary of Caesar Augustus.

According to Diodorus it was probably Ethiopia which colonized Egypt, and was led into Egypt by Osiris.

Ammianus Marcellinus, about +330 to +400, Latin historian, writes: '. . . the men of Egypt are mostly brown or black with a skinny and desiccated look'.

This cursory review of the evidence of the ancient Graeco-Latin writers on the Egyptians' race shows that the extent of agreement between them is impressive and is an objective fact difficult to minimize or conceal.

We add here the evidence of Volney, who travelled in Egypt between +1783 and +1785, i.e. at the peak period of negro slavery, and who made the following observations on the true Egyptian race, the same which produced the Pharaohs, namely, the Copts:

> All of them are puffy-faced, heavy-eyed and thick-lipped, in a word, real mulatto faces. I was tempted to attribute this to the climate until, on visiting the Sphinx, the look of it gave me the clue to the enigma. Beholding that head characteristically Negro in all its features, I recalled the well-known passage of Herodotus which reads: 'For my part I consider the Colchoi are a colony of the Egyptians because, like them, they are black-skinned and kinky-haired.' In other words the ancient Egyptians were true negroes of the same stock as all the autochthonous peoples of Africa and from that datum one sees how their race, after some centuries of mixing with the blood of Romans and Greeks, must have lost the full blackness of its original colour but retained the impress of its original mould.

To this testimony of Volney, Champollion-Figeac, brother of Champollion the Younger, was to reply in the following terms: 'The two physical traits of black skin and kinky hair are not enough to stamp a race as negro and Volney's conclusion as to the negro origin of the ancient population of Egypt is glaringly forced and inadmissible.'

The Egyptians as they saw themselves

It is no waste of time to get the views of those principally concerned. How did the Ancient Egyptians see themselves? Into which ethnic category did they put themselves? What did they call themselves? The language and literature left to us by Egyptians of the Pharaonic epoch supply explicit answers to these questions which the scholars cannot refrain from minimizing, twisting or 'interpreting'.

The Egyptians had only one term to designate themselves: = kmt = the negroes (literally). This is the strongest term existing in the Pharaonic tongue to indicate blackness. This word is the etymological origin of the well-known root *kamit* which has proliferated in modern anthropological literature. The biblical root *kam* is probably derived from it and it has, therefore, been necessary to distort the facts to enable this root today to mean 'white' in Egyptological terms whereas, in the Pharaonic mother tongue which gave it birth, it meant 'black'.

It is a remarkable circumstance that the Ancient Egyptians should never have had the idea of applying these qualificatives to the Nubians and other populations of Africa to distinguish them from themselves. The Egyptians used the expression = nahas to designate the Nubians; and 'nahas' is the name of a people, with no colour connotation in Egyptian. It is a deliberate mistranslation to render it as 'negro' as is done in almost all present-day publications.

The divine epithets

Finally, 'black' or 'negro' is the divine epithet, invariably used for the chief beneficent gods of Egypt, whereas all the malevolent spirits are qualified as desrêt = red; we also know that to Africans this form applied to the white nations; it is practically certain that this held good for Egypt too, but I want in this chapter to keep to the least debatable facts.

The surnames of the gods are these:

= Kmwr = the 'Great Negro' for Osiris.
= km = the black + the name of the god.
= kmt = the black + the name of the goddess.

The km (black) qualificative is applied to Hathor, Apis, Min, Thoth, etc. set kmt = the black woman = Isis. On the other hand 'seth', the sterile desert, is qualified by the term desrêt = red. The wild animals which Horus fought to create civilization are qualified as desrêt = red, especially the hippopotamus.

The witness of the Bible

The Bible tells us: '. . . the sons of Ham (were) Kush, and Mizraim (i.e. Egypt), and Phut, and Canaan. And the sons of Kush; Seba, and Havilah, and Sabtah, and Raamah, and Sabtechah'.

Generally speaking, all Semitic tradition (Jewish and Arab) classes Ancient Egypt with the countries of the blacks.

The importance of these depositions cannot be ignored, for these are peoples (the Jews) who lived side by side with the Ancient Egyptians and had nothing to gain by presenting a false ethnic picture of them. Nor is the notion of an erroneous interpretation of the facts any more tenable.

Culture data

Among the innumerable identical cultural traits recorded in Egypt and in present-day black Africa, it is proposed to refer only to circumcision and totemism.

According to the extract from Herodotus quoted earlier, circumcision is of African origin. Archaeology has confirmed the judgement of the 'father of history', for Elliot-Smith was able to determine from the examination of well-preserved mummies that circumcision was the rule among the Egyptians as long ago as the proto-historic era, i.e. earlier than –4000.

Egyptian totemism retained its vitality down to the Roman period and Plutarch also mentions it. The researches of Amélineau, Loret, Moret and Adolphe Reinach have clearly demonstrated the existence of an Egyptian totemic system.

Linguistic Affinity

Wolof, a Senegalese language spoken in the extreme west of Africa on the Atlantic Ocean, is perhaps as close to Ancient Egyptian as Coptic. An exhaustive study of this question has recently been carried out. In this chapter enough is presented to show that the kinship between Ancient Egyptian and the languages of Africa is not hypothetical but a demonstrable fact which it is impossible for modern scholarship to thrust aside.

As we shall see, the kinship is genealogical in nature:

	EGYPTIAN	COPTIC	WOLOF
	= kef = to grasp, to take a strip (of something)	(Saïdique dialect) keh = to tame	kef = to seize a prey

	EGYPTIAN	WOLOF
	= feh = go away	feh = rush off

We have the following correspondence between the verb forms, with identity or similarity of meaning: all the Egyptian verb forms, except for two, are also recorded in Wolof.

EGYPTIAN	WOLOF
feh-ef	feh-ef
feh-es	feh-es
feh-n-ef	feh-ôn-ef

feh-n-es	feh-ôn-es
feh-w	feh-w
feh-wef	feh-w-ef
feh-w-es	feh-w-es
feh-w-n-ef	feh-w-ôn-ef
feh-w-n-es	feh-w-ôn-es
feh-in-ef	feh-il-ef
feh-in-es	feh-il-es
feh-t-ef	feh-t-ef
feh-t-es	feh-t-es
feh-tyfy	feh-ati-fy
feh-tysy	feh-at-ef
feh-tw-ef	mar-tw-ef
feh-tw-es	mar-tw-es
feh-kw(i)	fahi-kw
feh-n-tw-ef	feh-an-tw-ef
feh-n-tw-es	feh-an-tw-es
feh-y-ef	feh-y-ef
feh-y-es	feh-y-es

		EGYPTIAN	WOLOF
=		mer = love	mar = lick

Egyptian and Wolof demonstratives

There are the following phonetic correspondences between Egyptian and Wolof demonstratives.

EGYPTIAN		WOLOF		
	= pw (ipw) →	bw		ep → w p → b w → w
	= pwy (ipw) →	bwy		p → b̄ w → w y → y
	- pn (ipn) →		bané balé	p → b̄ n → n p→b̄ n→ l
	= pf (ipf) →	bafe		p → b f → f
	= pf3 →	bafa		p → b̄

f → f
3 → a

 = pfy (ipfy)/ → bafy — p → b̄, f → f, y → y

 = p3 → ba — p → b, 3 → â

 = iptw → ba<u>t</u>w — p → b, <u>t</u> → t, w → w

 = iptn → { batné / Batalé } — { p → b, <u>t</u> → t, { n → n / n → l } }

 = iptf
= iptf batafé — p → b̄, t → t, f → t

The comparison could be carried further to show that the majority of the phonemes remain unchanged between the two languages. The few changes which are of great interest are the following.

(*a*) The correspondence n (E) → 1 (W)

EGYPTIAN			WOLOF
n			l
		= na<u>d</u> = ask	la<u>d</u> = ask
		= nah = protect	lah = protect
		= ben ben = well up	bel bel = well up
	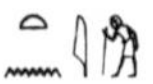	= teni = grow old	talé = important
		= tefnwt = the goddess born of Ra's spittle	tefnit = 'spit out' a human being teflit = spittle tefli = spitter
		= nebt = plait	let = plait nâb = to plait hair temporarily

(*b*) The correspondence h (E) → g (W)

EGYPTIAN		WOLOF
h		g
	= hen = phallus	gen = phallus
	= hwn = adolescent	gwne / gone } = adolescent
	= hor = Horus	gor = vir (? male ?)
	= hor gwn = the youth Horus	gor gwné = young man (m.ǎ.m)

It is still early to talk with precision of the vocalic accompaniment of the Egyptian phonemes. But the way is open for the rediscovery of the vocalics of Ancient Egyptian from comparative studies with the languages of Africa.

Conclusion

The structure of African royalty, with the king put to death, either really or symbolically, after a reign which varied but was in the region of eight years, recalls the ceremony of the Pharaoh's regeneration through the Sed feast. Also reminiscent of Egypt are the circumcision rites mentioned earlier and the totemism, cosmogonies, architecture, musical instruments, etc., of black Africa. Egyptian antiquity is to African culture what Graeco-Roman antiquity is to Western culture. The building up of a corpus of African humanities should be based on this fact.

It will be understood how difficult it is to write such a chapter in a work of this kind, where euphemism and compromise are the rule. In an attempt to avoid sacrificing scientific truth, therefore, we made a point of suggesting three preliminaries to the preparation of this volume, all of which were agreed to at the plenary session held in 1971. The first two led to the holding of the Cairo Symposium from 28 January to 3 February 1974. In this connection I should like to refer to certain passages in the report of that symposium. Professor Vercoutter, who had been commissioned by Unesco to write the introductory report, acknowledged after a thorough discussion that the conventional idea that the Egyptian population was equally divided between blacks, whites and half-castes could not be upheld. On the subject of Egyptian culture: 'Professor Vercoutter remarked that, in his view, Egypt was African in its way of writing, in its culture and in its way of thinking.'

Professor Leclant, for his part, 'recognized the same African character in the Egyptian temperament and way of thinking'.

In regard to linguistics, it is stated in the report that 'this item, in contrast to those previously discussed, revealed a large measure of agreement among the participants. The outline report by Professor Diop and the report by Professor Obenga were regarded as being very constructive.'

Similarly, the symposium rejected the idea that Pharaonic Egyptian was a Semitic language. 'Turning to wider issues, Professor Sauneron drew attention to the interest of the method suggested by Professor Obenga following Professor Diop. Egyptian remained a stable language for a period of at least 4,500 years. Egypt was situated at the point of convergence of outside influence and it was to be expected that borrowing had been made from foreign languages, but the Semitic roots numbered only a few hundred as compared with a total of several thousand words. The Egyptian language could not be isolated from its African context and its origin could not be fully explained in terms of Semitic; it was thus quite normal to expect to find related languages in Africa.'

The genetic, that is, non-accidental relationship between Egyptian and the African languages was recognized: 'Professor Sauneron noted that the method which had been used was of considerable interest, since it could not be purely fortuitous that there was a similarity between the third person singular suffixed pronouns in Ancient Egyptian and in Wolof; he hoped that an attempt would be made to reconstitute a paleo-African language using present-day languages as a starting point.'

A new page of African historiography was accordingly written in Cairo. The symposium recommended that further studies be made on the concept of race. Such studies have since been carried out, but they have not contributed anything new to the historical discussion.

The rediscovery of the true past of the African peoples should not be a divisive factor, but should contribute to uniting them, each and all, binding them together from the north to the south of the continent so as to enable them to carry out together a new historical mission for the greater good of mankind; and that is in keeping with the ideal of Unesco.[1]

1. NOTE BY THE EDITOR OF THE VOLUME
The opinions expressed by Professor Cheikh Anta Diop in this chapter are those which he presented and developed at the Unesco symposium on 'The peopling of Ancient Egypt' which was held in Cairo in 1974. The arguments put forward in this chapter have not been accepted by all the experts interested in the problem (cf. Introduction, above).
Gamal MOKHTAR

Annex to Chapter 1: Report of the symposium on 'The Peopling of Ancient Egypt and the Deciphering of the Meroitic Script'[1]

Cairo, 28 January–3 February 1974

Summary report[2]

The symposium was held in two stages: the first took place from 28 to 31 January 1974 and concerned 'The peopling of Ancient Egypt', the second dealt with 'The deciphering of the Meroitic script' and took place from 1 to 3 February 1974.

The participants were as follows:

Professor Abdelgadir M. Abdalla (Sudan)
Professor Abu Bakr (Arab Republic of Egypt)
Mrs N. Blanc (France)
Professor F. Debono (Malta)
Professor J. Devisse (France)
Professor Cheikh Anta Diop (Senegal)
Professor Ghallab (Arab Republic of Egypt)
Mrs J. Gordon-Jaquet (United States of America)
Professor L. Habachi (Arab Republic of Egypt)
Professor R. Holthoer (Finland)
Professor S. Husein (Arab Republic of Egypt)
Professor Kaiser (Federal Republic of Germany)
Professor J. Leclant (France)
Professor G. Mokhtar (Arab Republic of Egypt)
Professor R. El Nadury (Arab Republic of Egypt)
Professor Th. Obenga (People's Republic of the Congo)
Professor S. Sauneron (France)
Professor T. Säve-Söderbergh (Sweden)
Professor P. L. Shinnie (Canada)
Professor J. Vercoutter (France)

Professor Hintze (German Democratic Republic), Professor Knorossov, Professor

1. This annex should have been inserted as an Annex to the whole volume and placed after the Conclusion.

2. The present report is an abridged version of the final report of the symposium. It was prepared by the International Scientific Committee's Rapporteur at the request of the Committee, for insertion in this volume. The Proceedings of the Symposium have been published in the series *The General History of Africa – Studies and Documents* No. 1, Unesco, Paris, 1978.

Piotrovski (Union of Soviet Socialist Republics) and Professor Ki-Zerbo (Burkina Faso) were invited to the symposium but were unable to attend and sent their apologies.

In accordance with the decisions of the International Scientific Committee, Professor J. Devisse, the Committee's Rapporteur, was present and prepared the final report of the symposium.

Unesco was represented by Mr Maurice Glélé, programme specialist, Division of Cultural Studies, representing the Director-General, and Mrs Monique Melcer, Division of Cultural Studies.

1 Symposium on the peopling of Ancient Egypt

Two papers previously commissioned by Unesco from Professor J. Vercoutter and Mrs N. Blanc[3] provided a basis for discussion.

Three important stages may be distinguished in the discussion.

A Summary of the introductory papers.

B Preliminary statements made by most of the participants.

C General discussion.

A Summary of the introductory papers

(1) Professor Vercoutter drew attention to a number of points dealt with in greater detail in his written report, and made a number of further observations.

(a) In spite of recent progress, physical anthropology had so far provided relatively little reliable data except in Nubia. The information available was insufficient to enable provisional conclusions to be drawn with regard to the peopling of Ancient Egypt and the successive phases through which it may have passed. Furthermore, this information was not homogeneous as regarded either time or space and historians often disagreed as to how it should be interpreted. The methods themselves were being called in question; but it was now generally agreed that craniometry did not meet the requirements of such research.

A number of regions had still not been studied in any depth. This applied to the entire Delta during the pre-dynastic and proto-dynastic periods, and to Upper Egypt prior to Neolithic times. Little was known of the area between the Second and Sixth Cataracts in Neolithic and proto-dynastic times. Similarly, the links existing in ancient times between the Sahara, Dārfūr and the Nile had as yet been very little studied.

In that respect, the work that had been done lagged behind what had been achieved in North Africa and in the Syria–Palestine zone.

Evidence at present available did not warrant the assertion that the populations of northern Egypt had been different from those in the south. Similarly, the gap between Palaeolithic and Neolithic was probably due to the fact that insufficient research had yet been done in that field.

3. These documents are attached to the Final Report, 1974.

(b) Insufficient and unsatisfactory use had been made of iconography; the studies which had been carried out were based mainly on cultural criteria. The iconographic material available, however, has extremely significant characteristics from the the Eighteenth Dynasty onwards.

(c) Outline of the two opposing theories in their most extreme form:

(i) The people who lived in Ancient Egypt were 'white', even though their pigmentation was dark, or even black, as early as the pre-dynastic period. Negroes made their appearance only from the Eighteenth Dynasty onwards.

From the proto-dynastic period onwards, according to some, the population remained the same; others believed that foreign penetration into Africa profoundly altered the conditions of cultural life.

(ii) Ancient Egypt was peopled, 'from its Neolithic infancy to the end of the native dynasties', by black Africans.

(2) Mrs Blanc reported on her research findings.

(a) Mindful of the fact that, for reasons which were themselves historical, the historiography of the valleys of the Nile had been based on the assumption that there was a civilized Egyptian valley providing a wealth of historical evidence, and another valley farther south, which was black and primitive, and of interest only to anthropologists, Mrs Blanc hoped that historical research in the valley as a whole would in future be more balanced. This would mean abandoning traditional historical methods and broadening the field of inquiry to embrace a new methodology. Mrs Blanc saw the work which had been going on in Nubia for the last twenty years or so as a first step towards the re-examination of the question which faced the symposium.

(b) In order to escape from the traditional view of the Nile Valley which traced its historical development in a north–south direction, from the 'more civilized' to the 'less civilized', Mrs Blanc drew attention to the Nile regions situated between the twenty-third parallel and the sources of the river in Uganda. Her analysis took into account the dividing line, which she regarded as being of fundamental ecological importance, along the tenth parallel, where the advance of Islam stopped.

Between the twenty-third and the tenth parallels, the Nile, being a navigable waterway, could apparently have played a role comparable to that which it played farther north, in Egypt. This did not occur, and the ecological conditions in this reach of the river no doubt provided the principal explanation.

Mrs Blanc went on to make an overall examination, in the light of this fact, of the respective contributions of settled and nomadic populations throughout the area considered.

But, after tracing the history of the population changes since the coming of the Muslim Arabs, she concentrated particularly on reviewing hypotheses concerning the peopling of this zone prior to their arrival. She emphasized that the Nile Valley facilitated communication with West Africa and sub-Saharan Africa and that it was reasonable to put forward the hypothesis that the civilizations which emerged there might be authentically African rather than civilizations intermediate between the Mediterranean world and black Africa.

Dārfūr, to the west, about the social and political organization of which, prior to the seventeenth century, little is known, nevertheless played an important part as a regional centre of economic development.

To the east, the region of Sennār, inhabited by the Fundj, was the centre of a 'black sultanate' which was originally neither Arab nor Muslīm.

The zone between the Nile and the Red Sea occupied by the Bedja was barely able to support settled populations, on account of the harsh ecological conditions.

South of the tenth parallel, the ecological conditions were totally different. In this area, there were isolated populations about which little was known either from archaeological research or from oral tradition. Hypotheses on the peopling and history of this zone today have little evidence to support them, and it is only in more southerly regions, in the interlacustrine zone in East Africa, that fairly thorough historical studies have been carried out.

B Preliminary statements by participants

(1) Professor Säve-Söderbergh gave information about the Scandinavian excavations in the Sudan between 1960 and 1964. These excavations established that there were contacts between the Nile Valley and North Africa and the Sahara. The subjects covered by the publications[4] included 7,000 rock drawings and the analysis of the remains of 1,546 human individuals. Van Nielson (Vol. 9) had defined relations between the A Group, C Group, New Kingdom Group, etc. Comparative studies yielded different results, depending on whether craniometry only was used or anthropological and technological factors as a whole. Iconographical and physical anthropology studies lent support to the idea that there had been a migration of Saharan peoples and of groups coming from the south, and that they also had had considerable contacts with the Ancient Egyptians. For the Mesolithic period, comparisons had to be made on the basis of fewer than 100 skeletons. Valid conclusions were impossible in the case of Nubia, but more accurate data could be obtained on the Neolithic period.

In any event, Professor Säve-Söderbergh thought that it was impossible to base a study of the peopling of Egypt in ancient times, or any other similar study, on racial distinctions. In future, other lines of inquiry should be followed. Different cultures, contemporary with one another but isolated, might nevertheless belong to the same techno-complex. This new method confirmed that Egypt was African. But, if one looked beyond this finding, it was apparent that there were many other problems. Nagada I and II did not belong to the same techno-complex as Nubia or the contemporary Sudan. In the Sudan, the zone extending from Kassala to Chad and from Wādī Halfa to Khartoum was a single, large techno-complex unit. The A

4. See Scandinavian Joint Expedition to Sudanese Nubia, publications (especially Vol. 1, *Rock Pictures*, Vol. 2, *Pre-Ceramic Sites*, Vol. 3, *Neolithic and A-Group Sites*, and Vol. 9, *Human Remains*).

Group constituted another and more recent techno-complex between the First and Third Cataracts and possibly beyond.

(2) Professor Cheikh Anta Diop gave an extensive account of his ideas. He summarized a written paper, picking out the main points.

(a) From the anthropological point of view, research carried out since the discoveries of Professor Leakey led to the conclusion that the human race first came into existence in Africa in the region of the sources of the Nile. Gloger's Law, which presumably applied just as much to the human race as the other species, stated that warm-blooded animals which evolved in a warm, humid climate had a dark (eumelanin) pigmentation. The earliest human beings on earth were therefore ethnically homogeneous and negroid. The population spread out from this original area, reaching other regions of the earth by only two routes: the Nile Valley and the Sahara.

In the Nile Valley, this spread took place from the south in a northerly direction, in a progressive movement, between the Upper Palaeolithic and the proto-historic periods.

Even Professor Massoulard had reached the conclusion that the population of Ancient Egypt perhaps comprised at least three different racial elements: negroids, amounting to over one-third of the total, 'Mediterranean' people and people of the Cro-Magnon type. Professor Diop inferred from this that the population of Egypt was basically negro during the pre-dynastic period, a conclusion contradicting the theory that the negro element spread to Egypt in later times.

Skeletons with fragments of skin attached, dating from very ancient times, before the practice of mummification was introduced, had been discovered by Elliot-Smith. These fragments, stated Professor Diop, contain melanin in sufficient quantity to establish them as negro skin.

In the quest for positive proof, Professor Diop had studied a number of preparations being subjected to laboratory examination in Dakar. These consisted of samples of skin taken from mummies found in the Mariette excavations. They all revealed – and Professor Diop invited the specialists present to examine the samples – the presence of a considerable quantity of melanin between the epidermis and the dermis. Melanin, which was not present in white skin, persisted for millions of years (notwithstanding frequent affirmations to the contrary) as could be seen from an examination of the skins of fossil animals. Professor Diop hoped to be given the opportunity of carrying out similar research on the skins of the Pharaohs whose mummies were in the Cairo Museum collection.

He went on to state that a conclusive anthropological study would also include osteological measurements and the study of blood groups. It was remarkable, for example, that present-day Egyptians, particularly in Upper Egypt, belonged to the same blood group, B, as the population of West Africa, and not to Group A2, which was characteristic of the white race.

(b) *Iconography:* On the basis of an important iconographical drawing and the definitions given in this work, Professor Diop contended that it was unnecessary to dwell on details which, for example, distinguished negroes from other personages – the latter being aristocratic – in the same tomb: this difference of representation was of social origin. The common people were iconographically distinguished from members of the ruling class.

(c) Professor Diop went on to speak of the evidence provided by *ancient written sources*, pointing out that Greek and Latin authors described the Egyptians as negroes. He referred to the testimony of Herodotus, Aristotle, Lucian, Apollodorus, Aeschylus, Achilles Tatius, Strabo, Diodorus Siculus, Diogenes Laertius and Ammianus Marcellinus. Modern scholars, he said, refused to take account of those texts. By contrast, an eighteenth-century author, Volney, did speak of the inhabitants of Ancient Egypt as negroes. Furthermore, the biblical tradition also considered Egypt as belonging to the descendants of Ham. Professor Diop considered that the science of Egyptology, a product of imperialism, had much to answer for in denying all the facts to which he had just referred.

(d) Professor Diop then turned his attention to the way in which the Egyptians described themselves. They used only one word for this purpose: KMT,[5] 'the strongest term existing in the language of the Pharaohs to indicate blackness', which was translated by Professor Diop as 'the negroes'. Consequently, this hieroglyph was not written with crocodile scales but with a piece of charcoal.

(3) Professor Debono contributed an extensive review of the information given in Volume 1.

(4) Professor Leclant began by stressing the African character of Egyptian civilization. But it was necessary to distinguish clearly, as Professor Vercoutter had done, between 'race' and culture.

Physical anthropology in Egypt was in its infancy. Nevertheless, there was no justification for relying on the totally outmoded studies of Chantre, Elliot Smith, Sergi, or Dr Derry. Furthermore, there had already been important restatements of current knowledge such as that by Wierczinski.[6] Groups working in Nubia had also shown considerable interest in physical anthropology, with the result that Nubia, reputedly 'poor' in archaeological remains, paradoxically seemed likely to become far better known than Egypt in this respect.[7] Archaeological expeditions now gave great prominence to osteological studies, an innovation which was greatly to be welcomed.[8]

In cultural studies, rock engravings, which showed an enormous degree of uniformity from the Red Sea to the Atlantic, were worthy of careful study. These traces had been left by successive cultural groups, hunters, herdsmen, or others.

5. This word gave rise to the term 'Hamite' which has been much used subsequently. It is also found in the Bible in the form 'Ham'.

6. *Bulletin of the Egyptian Geographical Society*, 31, 1958, pp. 73–83.

7. Professor Leclant referred to the work of Nielsen, Strouhal, Armelagos, Rogalsky, Prominska, Chemla and Billy.

8. See an important recent article, D. P. Van Gerven, D. S. Carlson and G. J. Armelagos, 'Racial history and bio-cultural adaptation of Nubian archaeological populations', *JAH*, vol. XIV, no. 4, 1973, pp. 555–64.

The peopling of Ancient Egypt was a considerable problem and it would be very premature, at this stage, to adopt a synoptic approach as a means of solving it. The problem should be approached through separate, precise studies. For this purpose, the collaboration of specialists in disciplines not represented at this symposium was indispensable. All the participants were 'general historians', qualified to compile and synthesize data supplied by specialists; such data were, for the moment, very inadequate.

In any case, it was retrograde to have recourse to authorities who were today completely outdated, such as Lepsius or Petrie. They might be recognized as having 'historical' importance but Egyptology had made great progress since their day.

As for iconographical evidence, the only problem was to know how the Egyptians considered themselves in relation to other men. They called themselves RMT (Rame), that is to say 'men'; other people they regarded as an amophous mass extending in all directions, designated by the cardinal points. For example, the statues of prisoners at Sakkara (Sixth Dynasty, 2300 before the Christian era) were partly northerners (Asians, Libyans) and partly southerners (Nubians, negroes). Stereotypes of northerners (whites) and southerners (negroes) under the sandals of Pharaoh confirmed that representation.

(5) Professor Ghallab spoke of the successive elements which could be identified in the peopling of Africa between the Palaeolithic period and the third millennium before the Christian era.

In north-east Africa, a large quantity of stone objects dating from the second pluvial period had been found in the Nile Valley and the oases. Professor Ghallab distinguished at least six ethnic groups in the Egyptian population during the Mesolithic period, which, however, were united by a homogeneous culture. He considered that the human race during the Palaeolithic period was more or less homogeneous and 'Caucasian'; the first negro types in Africa were Asselar man and Omdurman man. In the late Palaeolithic period, the black race appeared from the Atlantic to the Red Sea. Among the earliest Egyptians, however, traces had been found of 'Bushmen', some of whose characteristics were modified as a result of their becoming acclimatized to Mediterranean ecological conditions. Even today, there were vestiges of this 'Bushman' type in the population of Egypt. A negro culture did not really appear prior to the Neolithic period.

(6) Professor Abdelgadir M. Abdalla did not think it important to establish whether the Ancient Egyptians were black or negroid: what was most remarkable was the degree of civilization they had achieved.

Iconographic evidence made it clear that the creators of the Napata culture had nothing in common with the Egyptians: their anatomical characteristics were completely different. If the Egyptians were black, what colour were the men of the Napata culture?

Turning to the subject of linguistics, Professor Abdalla stated that KM (Kem) did not mean 'black' and its derivatives did not refer to the colour of individuals. He gave a linguistic demonstration in his turn to illustrate his theory, which differed from that of Professor Diop. He concluded that the Egyptian language was not a purely African language; it belonged to a proto-Semitic group, as could be abundantly demonstrated by supporting examples. Professor Abdalla considered that the linguistic examples given by Professor Diop were neither convincing nor conclusive and that it was hazardous to make too uncompromising a correlation between a language and an ethnic structure or an individual. A comparison drawn between a dead language and living languages was bound to be inconclusive; the similarities which had been pointed out were fortuitous and nothing was so far known of the evolution of ancient African languages. The evidence which had been given to support the theory of kinship was in fact far more consistent with the theory of the spread of Ancient Egyptian throughout Africa than of its kinship with present-day African languages. Why should it be assumed that Ancient Egyptian and Wolof were related, but not ancient Egyptian and Meroitic, for example? The language of Napata and Meroitic were at opposite poles from one another.

Professor Abdalla hoped that the inquiry would be pursued in the strictest fashion.

(a) He considered it impossible to establish any automatic correlation between an ethnic group, a socio-economic system and a language.
(b) It was impossible to reach scientifically valid conclusions by working 'on a large scale'. There were almost no unambiguous examples in history of major migrations accompanying major cultural transformations.
(c) 'Negro' was not a clearly defined concept today as far as physical anthropologists were concerned. A skeleton did not provide evidence of skin colour. Only the tissues and the skin itself were important in that respect.
(d) It was imperative to broach the study of palaeo-pathology and of funerary practices without delay.

(7) Professor Sauneron intervened in the course of a lively exchange of views on linguistic matters between Professors Abdalla and Diop. Professor Sauneron stated that in Egyptian *KM* (feminine *KMT*) meant 'black', the masculine plural was *KMU* (Kemou), and the feminine plural *KMNT*.

The form *KMTYW* could mean only two things: 'those of Kmt', 'the inhabitants of Kmt' ('the black country'). It was a derived adjective (*nisba*) formed from a geographical term which had become a proper name; it was not necessarily 'felt' with its original meaning (cf. Frank, France, French).

To designate 'black people', the Egyptians would have said *Kmt* or *Kmu*, not *Kmtyw*. In any case, they never used this adjective to indicate the black people of the African hinterland whom they knew about from the time of the New Kingdom onwards, nor, in general, did they use names of colours to distinguish different peoples.

(8) Professor Obenga in his turn reverted to the linguistic demonstration which had been begun by Professor Diop.[9]

(a) After criticizing Professor Greenberg's method, on the basis of the recent work by Professor Istvan Fodor[10] and remarking that, since the work of Ferdinand de

9. The full text, as transmitted to the Rapporteur by Professor Obenga, is attached as Annex II in the Final Report of the symposium.

10. I.Fodor, *The Problems in the Classification of the African Languages* (Centre for Afro-Asian Research of the Hungarian Academy of Sciences, Budapest, 1966), p. 158.

Saussure, it was an accepted fact that linguistic evidence was the most obvious means of establishing whether two or more than two peoples were culturally related, Professor Obenga endeavoured to prove that there was a genetic linguistic relationship between Egyptian (Ancient Egyptian and Coptic) and modern negro-African languages.

Before making any comparison, one must be on one's guard against confusing typological linguistic relationship, which gave no clue as to the pre-dialectal ancestor common to the languages being compared, and genetic relationship. For example, modern English, considered from the typological point of view, had affinities with Chinese; but, from the genetic point of view, the two languages belonged to distinct language families. Similarly, Professor Obenga rejected the notion of a mixed language as linguistic nonsense.

Genetic relationship depended on establishing phonetic laws discovered by comparison between morphemes and phonemes of similar languages. On the basis of such morphological, lexicological and phonetic correspondences, one could arrive at common earlier forms. In this way, a theoretical 'Indo-European' language had been reconstructed in the abstract and had been used as an operational model. It was indicative of a common cultural macrostructure shared by languages which subsequently evolved along separate lines.

(b) Professor Obenga drew attention to important typological similarities in grammar: the feminine gender formed by the use of the suffix *–t,* the plural of nouns by the suffix *-w(ou, u)*. He next analysed complete word-forms and noted similarities between those of Ancient Egyptian and a considerable number of African languages; between Egyptian and Wolof the correspondence was total. This series of demonstrations led Professor Obenga to the conclusion that morphological, lexicological and syntactic similarities amounted to convincing proof of the close relationship between Ancient Egyptian and negro-African languages of today. This kind of parallelism was impossible between Semitic, Berber and Egyptian.

He then dealt with comparisons of ways of expressing 'to be' in verb–noun combinations: the common archaic form in the Bantu language was the same in this respect as that of the most archaic form of Ancient Egyptian. The analysis of negative morphemes, of the emphatic future and of linking particles led to the same conclusions as the previous examples. Professor Obenga considered, therefore, that it would prove possible to discover a common genetic structure.

(c) Lastly, Professor Obenga spoke of what he considered to be the most interesting aspect of the comparison.

He drew parallels between the forms taken in different languages by certain words: palm, spirit, tree, place; and also between certain small phonemes: for example, *KM* (*Kem*), black in Ancient Egyptian, becomes *Kame, kemi, kem* in Coptic; *ikama* in Bantu (with the meaning of charred by exposure to excessive heat), *kame* in Azer (cinder). *Romé,* 'man' in ancient Egyptian, becomes *lomi* in Bantu. The same phonemes have the same functions in the different languages compared.

Professor Obenga inferred from these comparisons that it would be possible in the future to identify a 'negro-Egyptian' language, analogous to 'Indo-European'. In this context, and in view of the undeniable common cultural background of all these languages, there was a sound basis for the development of future studies.

(9) Professor Gordon-Jaquet stated that the study of Egyptian toponomy could perhaps be brought to bear in support of the assertion that no massive immigrations or invasions of foreign populations had arrived in Egypt at least since Neolithic times. It was a well-known phenomenon that topographical names were extremely long-lived and that each successive language group inhabiting the same area would leave its mark on that area in the form of place names, more or less numerous, depending on the size of the population and the length of time of its predominance in that area. Any important permanent addition to the Egyptian population from the exterior would certainly have left its mark on the toponomy of the country. This was not the case. The toponomy of Egypt was very homogeneous, displaying names whose etymology could almost without exception be explained by the Egyption language itself. It was only at the Ptolemaic period and still later, after the Arab conquest, that names of respectively Greek and Arabic origin were added to the basic fund of Egyptian names. It was only in the peripheral regions, Nubia, the Western Oases and the Eastern Delta – regions in immediate contact with neighbouring peoples speaking other languages – where names whose etymology could be traced to these foreign languages were to be found.

(10) Professor Devisse briefly abandoned his role as Rapporteur to inform the symposium of the unexpected results of an iconographic study.[11]

Three manuscripts[12] included representations of black Egyptians which merited consideration. After eliminating what could be attributed to biblical tradition (the descendants of Ham), and allegorical representations in a consciously archaic manner (Hades, Night), there remained a variable proportion of Egyptians represented with negro features and colouring. Admittedly, some of these were servants, but – and on this point the scenes selected were extremely interesting – others were free Egyptians. Some of them – about a third of the participants – were around the table of Joseph, who was giving a banquet for his Israelite brothers seated at another table; others were taking part in the sale of Joseph to Potiphar, who was himself represented as white. Probably the most remarkable aspect of these representations, which were consistently realistic in their details, lay in the characteristic costume worn by these black Egyptians (particularly in the eleventh-century octateuch). The negroes, who were clearly differentiated from Egyptians wearing beards and turbans, were in many cases carrying spears and wore a 'panther skin' leaving the right shoulder bare. Professor Devisse considered these observations all the more interesting because there were considerable contacts between Byzantium and Egypt during the Fatimid period,

11. This very wide-ranging international study will be the subject of a publication in three volumes two of which have already been published. The study has been carried out by the Menil Foundation (Houston, United States of America), a unit of which in Paris has co-ordinated the collection of a vast quantity of iconographic material.

12. Paris, Bibliothèque Nationale, New Acquisitions: latin 2334 (VI–VIIe?), Vatican grec 747 (XIe), Vatican grec 746 (XIIe).

and because the representations which dated from this period were far more realistic than in the older manuscript.

It was very difficult to interpret these documents: they pointed both to the Byzantine cultural background and to the biblical tradition. Nevertheless, they reflected a 'northerner's view' of the Egyptians which was not consistent with the standard 'white-skinned' theory.

C General discussion

The general discussion made it clear that a number of participants, in varying degrees, thought it desirable, in the present state of knowledge, to undertake macro-analyses embracing the history of Ancient Egypt as a whole, or, in some cases, the entire continent of Africa; certain other participants, on the other hand, thought that it would be wiser to take geographical micro-analyses very much further on a disciplinary or interdisciplinary basis.

(I) Chronological analysis of the results achieved
The discussion on this point was opened by Professor Cheikh Anta Diop. Since the Upper Palaeolithic period, the initial homogeneity of the human race had gradually declined; the population of Egypt was neither more nor less homogeneous than the population of other parts of the world. The first appearance of the human race was currently believed to have occurred in Africa 5,300,000 years ago BP. The origins were African.

Homo sapiens appeared about –150,000 and progressively spread to all the then habitable parts of the Nile basin. Men living in Egypt at that time were black.

Rejecting the opposing theory, referred to by Professor Vercoutter in his report concerning the peopling of Egypt during the pre-dynastic period, Professor Diop stated that the 33 per cent of 'white' Egyptians with a fairly dark, or even black, pigmentation were in fact black, as were the 33 per cent of half-castes; adding the last 33 per cent of the population mentioned by Dr Massoulard and admitted to be black, Professor Diop expressed the opinion that the population of Egypt as a whole was black throughout the proto-dynastic period.

He went on to reassert the general theory which he had previously outlined concerning the black population of Egypt which gradually became hybridized.

At another point in the discussion, Professor Diop explicitly stated that the black population of Upper Egypt began to retreat only at the time of the Persian occupation.

He ended by making two general observations: one concerned the use of the word *negroid*, a term which he considered unnecessary and pejorative; the other concerned the arguments which were being put forward to contest his ideas, and which he considered to be negative, lacking in critical rigour and not based on the facts.

Professor Diop's theory was rejected in its entirety by one participant.

None of the participants explicitly voiced support for the earlier theory concerning a population which was 'white' with a dark, even black, pigmentation. There was no more than tacit agreement to abandon this old theory.

Numerous objections were made to the ideas propounded by Professor Diop. These objections revealed the extent of a disagreement which remained profound even though it was not voiced explicitly. In respect of certain sequences, the criticisms arose out of the line of argument put forward.

In so far as very ancient times were concerned – those earlier than what the French still called the 'Neolithic' period – participants agreed that it was very difficult to find satisfactory answers.

Professor Debono noted the considerable similarity between pebble cultures in the different regions where they had been discovered (Kenya, Ethiopia, Uganda, Egypt). The same was true of the Acheulean period, during which biface core tools were similar in a number of regions of Africa.

On the other hand, the homogeneity of the Sangoan industry, found in East Africa, progressively diminished as one moved farther north. At Khor Abu Anga (Sai Island in the Sudan), there was a more or less complete range of tools. From Wādī Halfa onwards, a number of elements were apparently lost. In Egypt, only one of the industry's typological characteristics was retained, between Thebes and Dahshur near Cairo.

In the Middle Palaeolithic period, the striking of Levallois flakes with Mousterian variants differed greatly between Egypt and areas situated farther south or west.

In the Palaeolithic period, for reasons which remain obscure but which were probably due to changed climatic and ecological conditions, Egypt became isolated from the rest of Africa with regard to the stone tool-making industry, and original industries were created (Sebilian, Epi-Levalloisian or Hawarian, Khargian).

Furthermore, at the same period there was an attempt at foreign penetration by the Aterians from north-east Africa. Traces of them were found as far as the southern Sahara. Having reached the Siwa Oasis and also, in large numbers, the Khargah Oasis, they spread out in the Nile Valley and their traces had been found at Thebes. Other evidence dating from the same period had been noted at Wādī Hamamat (Eastern Desert), at Esna (mingled with Khargian remains), at Dara, at Djabal Ahmar near Cairo, and as far as Wādī Tumilat in the Eastern Delta (mingled with Epi-Levalloisian remains). It was probable that at the same time there was a small-scale admixture of other races, rapidly absorbed by the native population.

An equally interesting intrusion of foreign peoples into Egypt was that of the Natoufians of Palestine, whose presence at Halwan near Cairo had long been an established fact. Recent excavations had shown that these people inhabited a larger area. Stone implements, attributable to these Natoufians, had been found at Fayyūm and in the Eastern Desert along a belt extending in an east–west direction across the Nile Valley at this point.

Professor Sauneron considered that, in view of the existence of chipped pebbles in the old Pleistocene strata of the Theban hills, it could be inferred that human beings had inhabited the Nile Valley since very ancient times.

Professor Ghallab stated that the inhabitants of Egypt in Palaeolithic times were Caucasoids. He went on to say the recent excavations had provided evidence of the existence of men of the 'San' type in the population during the pre-dynastic period.

Professor Shinnie was in agreement regarding the settlement of *Homo sapiens*, but without mentioning the colour of his skin, and dated the first settled population of the Nile Valley at about 20,000 years ago. Subsequently, various human groups came from different regions, increasing this population and altering its composition.

The discussion was no less lively concerning the Neolithic and pre-dynastic periods. Professor Abu Bakr emphasized that the Egyptians had never been isolated from other peoples. They had never constituted a pure race and it was impossible to accept the idea that in the Neolithic period the population of Egypt was entirely black. The population of Egypt in Neolithic times was a mingling of men from the west and east, who had been incorrectly called Hamitic.

This was also the theory of Professor El Nadury. In Neolithic times migrants from all parts of the Sahara had infiltrated the sedentary population settled in the north-western part of the Delta, resulting in an intermingling of many ethnic groups. From that period onwards there was no break in continuity as regards the population until dynastic times. The site of Merimdé with its wealth of clearly stratified archaeological material showed that the peopling of this area had been a gradual process.

Professor Vercoutter firmly stated his conviction, with regard to the peopling of Egypt in ancient times, that the inhabitants of the Nile Valley had always been mixed; outside elements coming from west and east had been numerous, particularly in pre-dynastic times.

During the pre-dynastic period and the beginning of the dynastic period, a further element, coming from the north-east and described as Semitic, was added to the population. Like Professor Abu Bakr, Professor El Nadury thought it a striking fact that, during the First Dynasty, fortifications had been built at Abydos, in all probability for the purpose of preventing immigration from the south towards the north.

Professor Abu Bakr referred to the case of the yellow-haired, blue-eyed wife of Cheops as an example of the existence of 'non-black' people in Egypt. Professor Diop regarded this isolated instance as an exception which proved the rule.

In the course of the discussion, Professor Obenga added some important points and emphasized the interest of ancient written sources concerning the population of Egypt. Herodotus, in a passage concerning the Colchians which was neither disputed by modern scholarship nor invalidated by the comparative critical study of manuscripts, endeavoured to show, through a series of critical arguments, that the Colchians were similar to the Egyptians: 'They speak in the same way as they do, they and the Egyptians are the only peoples to practise circumcision, they weave linen like the Egyptians'; these similarities were in addition to two other features which they had in common, their black pigmentation and their crinkly hair.

Professor Leclant maintained that ancient writers used the expression 'burnt face' (Ethiopians) to refer to Nubians and negroes but not to Egyptians. Professor Obenga replied that the Greeks applied the word 'black' (*melas*) to the Egyptians. Professor Vercoutter, in particular, asked in what precise context Herodotus had defined the Egyptians as negroes. Professor Diop replied that Herodotus referred to them on three occasions: in speaking of the origin of the Colchians, in speaking of the origin of the Nile floods, and in discussing the oracle of Zeus-Amon.

In Professor Leclant's opinion, the unity of the Egyptian people was not racial but cultural. Egyptian civilization had remained stable for three millennia; the Egyptians described themselves as REMET (*Rome* in Coptic) and, particularly in their iconographic representations, drew a distinction between themselves and the peoples of the north and those of the south who differed from them. Professor Obenga denied that Egyptians, in using the word REMET, drew a racial distinction between themselves and their neighbours; he considered the distinction made to be similar to that which led to Greeks to differentiate between themselves and other peoples, whom they termed Barbarians.

Professor Leclant noted that important palaeo-African features in the cultural life of Egypt were worthy of study. As an example, he mentioned the baboon, which was an attribute of the God Thoth, and the frequent appearance in iconography of 'panther' skins as a ritual garment during the worship of Osiris by Horus. In his opinion, however, the Egyptians, whose civilization was culturally stable for three millennia, were neither white nor negro.

Professor Sauneron then questioned the very idea of a homogeneous population, particularly if it was alleged to have existed from the earliest appearance of man in Egypt up to the pre-dynastic period. He considered that none of the evidence currently available gave grounds for doubting that the population of Egypt was mixed.

The conclusion of the experts who did not accept the theory, put forward by Professors Cheikh Anta Diop and Obenga, that the Nile Valley population had been homogeneous from the earliest times until the Persian invasion, was that the basic population of Egypt settled there in Neolithic times, that it originated largely in the Sahara and that it comprised people from the north and from the south of the Sahara who were differentiated by their colour. In opposition to this theory, Professors Diop and Obenga submitted their own theory to the effect that the valley was peopled uniformly by black people and that the movement had been from south to north.

(2) Existence or non-existence of migrations of consequence towards the Nile Valley

As regards this item, the proceedings of the symposium remained very confused. More than one discussion was inconclusive.

Generally speaking, participants considered that the 'large-scale migrations' theory was no longer tenable as an explanation of the peopling of the Nile Valley, at least up to the Hyksos period, when linguistic exchanges with the Near East began to take place (Holthoer). On the other hand, several experts thought that population exchanges had evidently occurred with immediately adjacent regions in the valley, although very divergent opinions were expressed concerning the role played by geographical or ecological factors in creating natural or artificial obstacles to such population movements.

At all events, it was generally agreed that Egypt had absorbed these migrants of various ethnic origins. It followed that the participants in the symposium implicitly recognized that the substratum of the Nile Valley population remained generally stable and was affected only to a limited extent by migrations during three millennia.

When the later periods came to be examined, however, it proved impossible to reach this very broad measure of theoretical agreement.

As regards the Palaeolithic period, Professor Cheikh Anta Diop put forward the hypothesis that *Homo sapiens* settled progressively in the valley as far as the latitude of Memphis. Professor Abu Bakr said that too little information was available concerning this period and that the northern part of the Nile Valley might not have been inhabited at all. Professor Obenga, on the other hand, considered that between the Upper Palaeolithic and the Neolithic periods there had been continuous settlement by a uniform population; the Egyptians themselves had laid emphasis on this in their oral traditions, mentioning the Great Lakes as their original homeland and Nubia as a country identical with theirs.

Where the Mesolithic merged with the Neolithic (Professor Vercoutter) or during the Neolithic period (Professors Habachi and Ghallab), it seemed likely that fairly large movements of population took place from the Sahara towards the Nile Valley. Professor Vercoutter hoped that these movements, about which very little was at present known, would be dated accurately and that the relevant archaeological material would be collected and studied.

Professor Cheikh Anta Diop submitted certain details by way of reply. Radiocarbon dating for the Western Sahara showed that a period of damp climate had extended from about 30,000 BP to 8,000 BP, with intermittent periods of drought, similarly, the dating of the ensuing dry period was becoming clearer. Similar datings should be obtained for the Eastern Sahara; by combining the results obtained with palaeo-climatic research and with studies of tombs and carvings, the information which Professor Vercoutter wanted would be obtained.

Professor Habachi unreservedly supported the theory of migrations from the Sahara on the basis of known studies. Professor Säve-Söderbergh considered that the majority of Neolithic cultures in the Nile Valley belonged to a techno-complex of Saharan and Sudanese cultures; nevertheless, migratory movements were probably intense, especially prior to and at the end of the Neolithic subpluvial period.

As an alternative to the hypothesis postulating a migration from the Sahara largely during Neolithic times, Professor Diop put forward the hypothesis that the population had spread northwards from the south. He restated the idea, to which reference had been made several times during the discussion, that, during the Capsian period, this culture covered a vast area extending from Kenya to Palestine.

On the subject of the proto-dynastic and pre-dynastic periods, Professors Diop and Vercoutter agreed that the population of the Egyptian reaches of the Nile Valley was homogeneous as far as the southern extremity of the Delta. These two experts were in partial agreement on the hypothesis of migration southwards from the north, Professor Vercoutter finding this theory difficult to accept and Professor Diop rejecting it. Disagreement emerged on the subject of defining the nature of these people more precisely. Professor Diop regarded them as being the Anu and identified them in the picture noted by Petrie in the temple of Abydos.

During the dynastic period, the stability of the population of the Egyptian reaches of the Nile Valley was attested by the stability of its culture; Professor Diop showed that the Egyptian calendar had been in use as early as −4236, and from the beginning, had a cyclic pattern of 1,461 years. He considered that, until the Persian invasion, that stability had been threatened only by a very powerful earthquake which occurred in about −1450. This had given rise to a series of migrations which affected the equilibrium of all countries bordering the eastern Mediterranean basin. Seafaring peoples then attacked the Egyptian Delta at a period contemporaneous with the disappearance of the Hittites and the appearance of the proto-Berbers in North Africa. Apart from this major upheaval, the only important episode in the life of the Egyptian people, even if it were not associated with a migration, was the conquest of Egypt in a south–north direction by the unifying Pharaoh Narmer in about −3300.

There was no discussion of this analysis, but other analyses were put forward: Professor Säve-Söderbergh sought to establish, on the basis of the Nubian excavations, at what periods and in what conditions the Egypt of the Pharaohs had become cut off from the south. In Nubia, the most ancient culture gradually disappeared at the end of the First Dynasty or perhaps at the beginning of the Second. The C Group which succeeded it did not appear before the Sixth Dynasty. This meant that there was a 'chronological gap' of about 500 years, between −2800 and −2300, on which no infomation was available today. It was clear that, as a result of this situation, active contacts between Pharaonic Egypt and the south were destroyed or discontinued.

There was another instance of the same situation: no archaeological remains dating from the period between −1000 and the beginning of the Christian era were to be found in Lower Nubia. The earliest Meroitic remains which had been discovered there dated from the first century of the Christian era; exchanges between Egypt and the south had therefore varied considerably between −2800 and the Meroitic period.

Professors Vercoutter and Leclant noted the appearance, from the Eighteenth Dynasty onwards, of a type of negro representation which was totally different from anything that had existed earlier (the tomb of *Houy* or the tomb of *Rekhmire*, for example). How did these new populations make their appearance in Egyptian iconography? Was it the result of contacts between Egyptians and the south or because of migrations northwards into Nubia of populations living farther south? Professor Shinnie objected that this information gave no grounds for inferring that there had been a northward migration from the south which had affected the population of Egypt.

Professor Leclant considered that, with the exception of the Eighteenth-Dynasty example already mentioned, no important change had occurred prior to the Twenty-fifth Dynasty, when the Kushites from the Dongola region appeared in Egypt. He was inclined, incidentally, to regard this as attributable rather to the transitory increase of a particular influence in the life of the Egyptian population than to migrations of peoples.

Two main facts became very plain during the discussion and were not seriously contested:

(a) There is a twofold problem in connection with the Nile Delta[13] in prehistoric times.

Firstly, as Professor Debono pointed out, this region, unlike Upper Egypt, is

13. Professor Holthoer drew attention to the following work: D. G. Réder, 'The economic development of Lower Egypt (Delta) during the archaic period (V–IV [centuries] before our era)', a collection of articles which appeared in the *Journal of Ancient Egypt*, 1960 (translation of the Russian title).

very little known, as the excavations being carried out at Merimde, El Omari and Meadi-Heliopolis have not yet been completed.

The human remains so far discovered dating from prehistoric times and from the archaic period are different from those found in Upper Egypt.

Secondly, it appears certain that human factors which affected life in Lower Egypt or the Delta, in so far as they can be discerned prior to the dynastic period, differ from those which were operative in the valley south of this region.

(b) The study of the ancient substratum of the population has been made possible in northern Nubia by the intensive archaeological research organized under Unesco's auspices. For a great variety of reasons, this has not been the case in the remainder of the Egyptian part of the Nile Valley, where research concerning pre-dynastic times and ancient material cultures had produced far fewer results than in northern Nubia. The reservations and the unwillingness of some of the experts to draw final conclusions are probably due in part to this fact.

There is no doubt that one other factor at least added to the complexity of a discussion which often took the form of successive and mutually contradictory monologues. This factor emerged clearly from a phrase uttered by Professor Obenga, although it was not commented upon. Professor Obenga considers it self-evident that a homogeneous cultural substratum necessarily implies a homogeneous ethnic substratum.

Whether or not these two ideas lend themselves to simultaneous consideration, it seems likely that they were not kept sufficiently apart during the discussions and that, as a result, the conclusions reached were less clear-cut than they might otherwise have been. The possibility of finding points of agreement was probably affected by this fact.

Nevertheless, if they are considered without reference to racial issues, two major themes did ultimately meet with almost unanimous agreement, at least as working hypotheses.

It was probably in Neolithic times that the population of the Egyptian Nile Valley was most affected by large-scale migrations. Two theories are current in this connection: according to one, the migrants came, in the main, in a north–south direction from the entire area of the Eastern Sahara; according to the other, these movements of population came along the Nile from the south; from proto-dynastic times onwards, the population of Egypt was very stable. The nature of the peopling was not radically altered by the various population movements which affected the political life and the military situation of Egypt, by the consequences of Egypt's commercial relations, by the internal efforts towards agricultural settlement of by infiltrations from nearby regions. This ethnic stability was accompanied by a high degree of cultural stability.

However, during the discussion of the hypothesis of a homogeneous population, which was favoured by Professor Diop, and the hypothesis of a mixed population, which was supported by several other experts, it became clear that there was total disagreement.

(3) Results of the physical anthropology inquiry

At various points in the discussion, it became apparent that the terms used hitherto for the purposes of racial description required to be more clearly defined.

Mr Glélé, the representative of the Director-General of Unesco, intervened to reassure those experts who advocated outlawing the terms 'negro', 'black' and 'negroid' on the grounds that the concept of race was outmoded and efforts should be made to bring men closer together by repudiating any reference to race. Mr Glélé reminded the participants that Unesco was committed to the cause of promoting international understanding and co-operation in the cultural sphere and that it had not been the intention of the Organization, when deciding to hold the symposium, to give rise to tensions between peoples or races but rather, as far as the present state of knowledge permitted, to elucidate and clarify one of several subjects which were matters of doubt, namely, the question of the peopling of Ancient Egypt from the point of view of its ethnic origin and of its anthropological relationships. What was needed, therefore, was to compare the alternative theories, to assess the scientific arguments on which they were based, and to take stock of the situation, drawing attention, where appropriate, to any gaps. He emphasized that the terms negro, negroid, black, had, in any case, been used hitherto; that they appeared in all scientific studies, as also did the word 'Hamitic' or 'Chamitic', even though doubts had been expressed on their validity in the course of the current symposium; he also stated that the authors of the *General History of Africa* would make use of those words, to which readers were already accustomed. Whatever general opinion one might have, it remained true that these words, as used in both scholarly and popular works, were not devoid of meaning and were inseparable from value judgements, whether implicit or otherwise. He corroborated a statement made by one expert with reference to Unesco's publications on racial problems. Unesco had not repudiated the idea of race; the Organization had drawn up a special programme to study race relations and had stepped up its efforts to combat racial discrimination. There had been several publications on this important problem. It was therefore out of the question for the symposium, in studying problems bearing on the peopling of Ancient Egypt, to reject out of hand, and without proposing any new system, the generally accepted classification of peoples as white, yellow and black – a typology which had traditionally been used by Egyptologists to classify the people of Egypt. Furthermore, if the traditional vocabulary currently used by historians needed revision, it should not be revised merely for the history of Africa but for the entire world; if the symposium considered the matter important, it could be submitted for consideration at the international level to the historians' association. Pending the introduction of new terms, the terms black, negro, negroid and Hamitic, which were currently used, should be more clearly defined.

The debate on this point was opened by Professor Vercoutter. He recalled that the problem had been raised by the work of Junker, when he used the word 'negro' to denote the type of representations which appeared under the Eighteenth Dynasty, and was subsequently caricatured by the Egyptians. Junker used the word negro primarily in reference to West Africa, emphasizing both the pigmentation and certain facial characteristics.

Professor Vercoutter was inclined to think that, in place of this old point of view, more specific criteria were essential in order to provide a scientific definition of the black race; in particular, he mentioned a blood criterion, the question of the precise significance of the degree of skin pigmentation and whether, for example, the Nubians should be considered as negroes.

Various attitudes emerged with regard to these questions. Several participants hoped that the word 'race', which on a number of recent occasions had aroused strong feelings, would be used with circumspection. Professor Obenga replied that the notion of race was recognized as valid by scientific research and that the study of races did not necessarily involve racialism.

The discussion brought out the difficulty of giving a scientific content to the terms under review. Even more, perhaps, it brought out the fact that more than one expert was reluctant, for highly respectable reasons, to use those terms, which could rightly be regarded as having dangerous or pejorative implications. Some experts pointed out, moreover, that the basic answers on this issue could not be expected to come from historians and archaeologists, but only from specialists in physical anthropology.

Professor Säve-Söderbergh was supported by a considerable number of the participants when he expressed the hope that racial terminology would be studied by specialists on modern physical anthropology. A strict scientific definition would be of use with regard not only to Africa but also, and perhaps more so, to Asia; similarly, the concepts of mixed population, composite population and groups of populations needed sharper definition. Unesco already had before it a request to this effect in connection with research being carried out in Nubia.

Mr Glélé said that if the criteria for classifying a person as black, white or yellow were so debatable, and if the concepts which had been discussed were so ill-defined and perhaps so subjective or inseparable from habitual patterns of thought, this should be frankly stated and a revision should be made of the entire terminology of world history in the light of new scientific criteria, so that the vocabulary should be the same for everyone and that words should have the same connotations, thus avoiding misconceptions and being conducive to understanding and agreement.

Professors Diop and Obenga were ill-advised, however, to refer to the series of criteria established by anthropologists to characterize the negro: black skin, facial prognathism, crinkly hair, flat nose (the facial and nasal indicators being very arbitrarily selected by different anthropologists), negritic bone structure (ratio between upper and lower limbs). According to Montel, the negro had a flat and 'horizontal' face. Professor Abu Bakr observed that, if that were the case, the Egyptians could certainly not be considered as negroes.

Professor Diop went on to specify that cranial measurements had never provided any statistical basis for specifying that a particular brain size was characteristic of one race or another.

He considered that there were two black races, one with smooth hair and the other with crinkly hair and, if the skin colour was black, it was unlikely that the other fundamental characteristics which he had previously enumerated would not be found. Lastly, whereas the blood-group A2 was characteristic of white people, black people tended to have Group B, or, in a more limited number of cases, Group C.

Professor Shinnie replied that the American specialists whom he had consulted while preparing for the symposium had told him that skeletal studies had some importance but that they did not in themselves provide a basis for determining race, and that the criteria regarded as adequate by Professor Diop were, rightly or wrongly, no longer considered to be so by American specialists.

Professor Obenga considered that there were two groups within a single black race, one with smooth hair and the other crinkly hair. Professor Obenga reverted to the general question which was before the symposium: if the notion of race was accepted as valid and if the notion of a black race was not rejected, what was to be said of the relationship between this race and the Ancient Egyptians?

Professor Diop considered that the findings of the anthropological inquiry already provided an adequate basis on which to draw conclusions. Negroid Grimaldian man appeared about −32000. Cro-Magnon man, the prototype of the white race, about −20000, Chancelade man, the prototype of the yellow race, in the Magdalenian period, about −15000. The Semitic races were a social phenomenon characteristic of an urban environment and were a cross between black and white races.

He was, therefore, in no doubt: the first inhabitants of the Nile Valley belonged to the black race, as defined by the research findings currently accepted by specialists in anthropology and prehistory. Professor Diop considered that only psychological and educational factors prevented the truth of this from being accepted.

As the assumption behind the research being carried out in Nubia was favourable to a universalistic view, the research findings were of little use in the current discussion. Professor Diop was not in favour of setting up commissions to verify patent facts which, at the present time, simply needed formal recognition: in his view, all the information currently available, even that which derived from the superficial studies made in the nineteenth century, supported the theory that, in the most ancient times, the Egyptians were black-skinned and that they remained so until Egypt ultimately lost its independence. In response to the various questions put to him, Professor Diop stated that the samples already provided by archaeology were adequate to support his argument. He was unable to accept Professor Vercoutter's proposal that anthropological documentation antedating about 1939 should be regarded as of dubious reliability owing to its lack of scientific rigour.

Professor Diop's forceful affirmation was criticized by many participants.

The main criticism was voiced by Professor Sauneron, who observed that the total number of people who had occupied the Nile Valley between the beginning of historical times and the present day could reasonably be estimated at several hundred million individuals. A few hundred sites had been excavated and some 2,000 bodies studied; in view of the sparseness of the data thus obtained, it was totally unrealistic to infer from them such ambitious general conclusions. As the available samples gave nothing like a complete picture, it was advisable to wait until a rigorous and sufficiently comprehensive inquiry into general features had provided universally acceptable evidence.

(4) The validity of the iconographic inquiry

In this field also there were two opposing theories. Professor Diop considered that, as the Egyptians were black, their painted iconography, which, incidentally, he had not cited in support of his argument, could represent only black people. Professor Vercoutter, who was supported by Professors Ghallab and Leclant, considered that Egyptian iconography, from the Eighteenth Dynasty onwards, showed characteristic representations of black people who had not previously been depicted; these representations meant, therefore, that at least from that dynasty onwards the Egyptians had been in contact with peoples who were considered ethnically distinct from them.

Professor Diop remarked that, in the course of his introductory statement, he had submitted a series of representations drawn exclusively from sculpture. He regarded all these as representing black people or as showing features characteristic of black societies. He asked for specific criticisms of these records and invited participants to produce comparable representations of whites in dignified or commanding postures dating from early Pharaonic times. Various participants replied that there had never been any question of discovering in Egypt representations comparable to those of Greek statuary, for example. Professor Vercoutter said that numerous representations could be produced in which human beings were painted red rather than black, but that Professor Diop would refuse to recognize these as non-black. Professor El Nadury did not deny that there were black elements in the population of Egypt during the Old Kingdom but said that it seemed hardly likely that the entire population was black.

Professor Vercoutter stated that the photographic reproduction of Pharaoh Narmer was considerably enlarged, that the features were probably distorted, and that to regard the person represented as black involved a subjective assessment. This was also the opinion of Professor Säve-Söderbergh, who said that the photograph could just as well be interpreted as a picture of a Laplander.

Professor Vercoutter did not dispute that there might have been black elements in Egypt throughout history, and he himself adduced a number of further examples of their being represented graphically. He took issue with the facts as presented, however, on two counts: they had been drawn indiscriminately from the whole Pharaonic period, without clear references; and the selection had been made to support a theory. On this score, Professor Diop replied that he had made a point of submitting only carved objects or scenes in order to avoid the likelihood of discussion on the significance of colours, but that he had been obliged to use the material available to him at Dakar. The list was comprehensive; it extended from the Old Kingdom to the end of the Pharaonic period. The evidence did, indeed, support a theory and any contrary theory must of necessity be supported by iconographic representations of 'non-black' Egyptians.

During the lengthy discussion on colours, Professors Vercoutter, Sauneron and Säve-Söderbergh, on the one hand, and Professor Diop, on the other, were again in disagreement. During the discussion, nothing was conceded by either side. The only apparent point of agreement was that the matter warranted further study, in particular with the help of specialized laboratories.

Professor Vercoutter conceded that there were representations of black people in Egyptian sculpture during the Old Kingdom, and he gave supporting examples. But he did not consider that they were representative of the Egyptian population as a whole, which was, in any case, also represented by contemporay sculptures showing quite different features.

Professor Vercoutter wondered why the Egyptians, if they did regard themselves as black, rarely, if ever, used carbon black in their representations of themselves but used a red colour instead. Professor Diop considered that this red colour was indicative of the black Egyptian race and that the yellow colouring of the womenfolk illustrated the fact, to which attention had been drawn by American anthropologists, that women, in a number of racial groups studied, were, as a rule, of a paler hue than the men.

(5) Linguistic analyses

This item, in contrast to those previously discussed, revealed a large measure of agreement among the participants. The outline report by Professor Diop and the report by Professor Obenga were regarded as being very constructive.

Discussion took place on two levels.

In response to Professor Diop's statement that Egyptian was not a Semitic language, Professor Abdalla observed that the opposite opinion had often been expressed.

A grammatical and semantic debate took place between Professor Diop on the radical which he reads *KMT*, derives from *KM* 'black' and considers to be a collective noun meaning 'blacks, i.e. negroes' and Professor Abdelgadir M. Abdalla who adopts the accepted reading of it as *KMTYW* and translation as 'Egyptians', the plural of *KMTY* 'Egyptian', the *nisba*-form from *KMT* 'black land, i.e. Egypt'. The latter reading and translation were affirmed by Professor Sauneron.

Turning to wider issues, Professor Sauneron drew attention to the interest of the method suggested by Professor Obenga following Professor Diop. Egyptian remained a stable language for a period of at least 4,500 years. Egypt was situated at the point of convergence of outside influence and it was to be expected that borrowings had been made from foreign languages, but the Semitic roots numbered only a few hundred as compared with a total of several thousand words. The Egyptian language could not be isolated from its African context and its origin could not be fully explained in terms of Semitic, it was thus quite normal to expect to find related languages in Africa.

However, a rigorous methodical approach required the difficult problem of the 5,000-year gap to be faced: this was the period separating Ancient Egyptian from present-day African languages.

Professor Obenga drew attention to the fact that a language which was not fixed by a written form and which developed normally might retain certain ancient forms; he had cited examples of this in the communication he had given on the first day of the symposium.

Professor Sauneron noted that the method which had been used was of considerable interest, since it could not be purely fortuitous that there was a similarity between the third person singular suffixed pronouns in Ancient Egyptian and in Wolof; he hoped that an attempt would be made to reconstitute a palaeo-African language, using present-day languages as a starting-point. This would facilitate comparison with Ancient Egyptian. Professor Obenga considered this method to be acceptable. Professor Diop thought it essential to derive a research method from linguistic comparisons, and he provided a specific example of what he had in mind. He regarded the Dinka, Nuer and Shilluk groups and their respective languages, on the one hand, and Wolof, on the other, as being ethnically and, to a lesser extent, linguistically related. Senegalese proper names occurred in the groups in question at clan level. More specifically, Professor Diop believed that he had found among the Kaw-Kaw, in the Nubian hills, the clearest link between Ancient Egyptian and Wolof.

Professor Vercoutter pointed out, as a matter of interest, that in the tomb of Sebek-Hotep there were representations of three Nilotes who were indubitably ancestors of the Dinka or the Nuer.

(6) Development of an interdisciplinary and pluridisciplinary methodology

There was complete agreement on this point as to the necessity of studying in as much detail as possible all the zones bordering on the Nile Valley which were likely to provide fresh information on the question submitted to the symposium.

Professor Vercoutter considered it necessary to give due weight to the palaeo-ecology of the Delta and to the vast region which Professor Balout had termed the African Fertile Crescent.

Professor Cheikh Anta Diop advocated tracing the paths taken by peoples who migrated westwards from Dārfūr, reaching the Atlantic seaboard by separate routes, to the south along the Zaïre Valley and to the north towards Senegal, on either side of the Yoruba. He also pointed out how worth while it might be to study Egypt's relations with the rest of Africa in greater detail than hitherto, and he mentioned the discovery, in the province of Shaba, of a statuette of Osiris dating from the seventh century before the Christian era.

Similarly, a general study might be made of the working hypothesis that the major events which affected the Nile Valley, such as the sacking of Thebes by the Syrians, or the Persian invasion of –525, had far-reaching repercussions on the African continent as a whole.

D General conclusion

It is to be expected that the overall results of the symposium will be very differently assessed by the various participants.

Although the preparatory working paper sent out by Unesco gave particulars of what was desired, not all participants had prepared communications comparable with the painstakingly researched contributions of Professors Cheikh Anta Diop and Obenga. There was consequently a real lack of balance in the discussions.

Nevertheless, for a number of reasons, the discussions were very constructive.

1 In many cases, they clearly showed the importance of exchanging new scientific information.
2 They brought home to almost all the participants the shortcomings of the methodological criteria which had hitherto been used in research.
3 They drew attention to examples of new methodological approaches on the basis

of which the question before the symposium could be studied in a more scientific manner.

4 This first meeting should, in any case, be regarded as providing a basis for further international and interdisciplinary discussions, and as a starting-point for further researches which were clearly shown to be necessary. The large number of recommendations is a reflection of the desire of the symposium to suggest a future programme of research.

5 Lastly, the symposium enabled specialists who had never previously had the opportunity of comparing and contrasting their points of view to discover other approaches to problems, other sources of information and other lines of research than those to which they were accustomed. From this point of view also, the symposium undeniably proved constructive.

E Recommendations

The symposium draws the attention of Unesco and other competent bodies to the following recommendations.

(1) Physical anthropology

It is desirable:

(i) that an international inquiry be organized by Unesco, either by consulting universities in a sufficient number of countries, or by consulting individual experts of international repute, or alternatively by convening a symposium, with a view to establishing very precise standards on the strictest possible scientific principles for defining races and for identifying the racial type of exhumed skeletons;

(ii) that the collaboration of the medical services of several Unesco member states be sought for the purpose of carrying out statistical observations during post-mortem examinations on the osteological characteristics of skeletons;

(iii) that a re-examination be made of human remains which are already in the possession of museums throughout the world, and that a rapid study be made of remains discovered during recent excavations in Egypt, in particular in the Delta, with a view to adding to the available information;

(iv) that the Egyptian authorities do everything in their power to facilitate the necessary study of examinable vestiges of skin, and that these authorities agree to set up a department specializing in physical anthropology.

(2) Study of migrations

It is desirable that the following studies be undertaken:

(i) a systematic archaeological study of the earliest periods during which the Delta was inhabited. This operation might be preceded by the analysis of a core sample taken from the soil of the Delta. The study and the dating of this geological core sample could be carried out simultaneously in Cairo and in Dakar;

(ii) a comparable inquiry in the regions of the Sahara near to Egypt and in the oases. This inquiry should comprise the simultaneous study of rock drawings and paintings and of all available archaeological material. Here again, geological samples might be analysed and dated at the same time;

(iii) a survey in the valley itself, comparable to that which has been carried out in northern Nubia, which would be concerned with non-Pharaonic tombs, with the study of ancient material cultures and, in general, with the prehistory of the valley as a whole;

(iv) an inquiry on palaeo-African vestiges in Egyptian iconography and their historical significance. The cases of the baboon and of the leopard ('panther') skin have already been cited by the symposium. It would undoubtedly be possible to discover others.

(3) Linguistics

The symposium recommends that a linguisitc study be made without delay on the African languages which are in imminent danger of disappearing: Kaw-Kaw has been suggested as a very significant case in point.

At the same time, the co-operation of specialists in comparative linguistics should be enlisted at international level in order to establish all possible correlations between African languages and Ancient Egyptian.

(4) Interdisciplinary and pluridisciplinary methodology

The symposium earnestly hopes that:

(i) interdisciplinary regional studies may be undertaken in several regions, with the following priorities:
Dārfūr
the region between the Nile and the Red Sea
the eastern fringe of the Sahara
the Nile region south of the tenth parallel
the Nile Valley between the Second and Sixth Cataracts.

(ii) an interdisciplinary inquiry be made as a matter of urgency on the Kaw-Kaw, who are in imminent danger of extinction.

II Deciphering of the Meroitic script

(1) A preliminary report had been prepared by Professor J. Leclant at the request of Unesco.[14]

(a) The Meroitic language, which was used by the cultures of Napata and Meroe, was still not understood, although the script had already been deciphered.

The historical account of the studies made on Meroitic showed how systematic research on the inscriptions, which had gradually been collected in a haphazard way in the course of excavations, had been started only in recent years. Archaeological

14. See this preliminary report in Annex IV of the Final Report of the symposium (1974).

research was likely to bring to light more inscriptions in the future; none had so far been discoverd in the region between the Second and Fourth Cataracts: the same was true of the travel routes in the direction of the Red Sea, the great valleys of the west, Kordofān and Dārfūr.

It was particularly important to persevere with archaeological work as it could reasonably be hoped that a bilingual inscription might one day be discovered.

(b) The results were published in full in the *Meroitic Newsletters*, thirteen issues of which had so far appeared, which made it possible rapidly to publicize findings when they were sometimes still only tentative. Regular meetings of specialists had taken place – at Khartoum in December 1970, in East Berlin in September 1971, and in Paris in June 1972 and again in July 1973; the results of the last-mentioned meeting were set out in Information Note No. 34 issued by the International Scientific Committe for the Drafting of a General History of Africa, Unesco.

Computer processes had also been used for analysing the Meroitic language for a number of years. As a result, there had been considerable and rapid progress in this field.

By compiling lists of *stichs*, it had been possible to make a start on analysing the structure of the language. The index of words recorded now comprised 13,405 units and a means had been found of putting questions to the machine.

On this basis, an effort had been made, by using words of which the meaning was known or could be inferred, to compare the language with Egyptian or Nubian.

(c) Professor Leclant ended his presentation with an account of the lines of research now being followed:

Professor Hintze was working on structures;
Professor Schaenkel was working on improving the data to be recorded by the computer;
Professor Abdelgadir M. Abdalla was going forward with an inquiry about which he was to speak briefly; it had achieved results which corroborated the findings of the international team.

Future efforts would include making a comparison between Meroitic and other African languages and discovering its place among a group of African languages, in particular in relation to Nubian; other comparisons would be made with the languages spoken in areas bordering on the Ethiopian region. Lastly, it would be desirable to compare Meroitic with African languages as a whole.

Discussion

(2) Professor Abdalla confirmed that he endorsed the system adopted for transcribing Meroitic and the method which had been devised for recording the texts. He drew attention to the gaps in our knowledge: almost complete ignorance of the system of pronouns, of the use of demonstrative pronouns, of the nature of prefixes and suffixes. It was essential to know with what other languages Meroitic was linked.

Professor Abdalla was in favour of carrying out a kind of dissection of the language, so as to study its components. He drew attention to the mobility of the elements forming personal names in which these elements had social implications:

the same mobile elements recurred in the names of several members of a given family; the names of certain children comprised elements taken from the names of their mother and father; certain names were titles; others contained place-names.

(3) Professor Shinnie said that there were three possible methods of approach: the discovery of a bilingual text; the internal analysis of the structure of the language; and comparison with other African languages.

Direct comparison between the two principal non-Arabic languages of northern Sudan and of the M Group had proved fruitless: Meroitic might prove to be a help in making this comparison.

(4) Professor Kakosy, who was present as an observer, laid stress on the necessity of studying documentary sources. He stated that there were in Budapest fragments of offering tables which came from a site close to Abu Simbel; he proposed to include these fragments forthwith in the Repertory of Meroitic Epigraphy.

(5) Professor Cheikh Anta Diop was very pleased with the progress achieved. Pending the possible future discovery of a bilingual text, he suggested that use should be made of the computer-based methods which had made possible the partial deciphering of the Maya hieroglyphs by the Leningrad team headed by Professor Knorossov. Most scripts had been deciphered with the help of bilingual or multilingual texts. The correct procedure in the case of Meroitic would be to combine multilingualism and the potentialities of the computer in the following manner:

(a) Purely as a methodological procedure, a relationship should be postulated between Meroitic and negro-African languages, thus creating a multilingual situation.
(b) As, at the present time, 22,000 Meroitic words could be read with some degree of certainty, a 500-word basic vocabulary should be drawn up on punched cards for each of 100 African languages carefully selected by a suitable group of linguists. The words selected might be those indicating, for example, the parts of the body, terms of kingship, religious terminology, terms relating to material culture, and so on.
(c) The computer should be programmed to recognize, for example, three identical consonants, two identical consonants, etc.
(d) On the basis of the results obtained, a comparison should be made of the structures of the languages thus juxtaposed.

This method was more rational than the haphazard comparison of linguistic structures, because too little was as yet known about the grammar of Meroitic. The method was more efficient than awaiting the result of a non-comparative study of the internal structure of Meroitic.

Professor Leclant endorsed this investigatory and operational procedure as being likely to provide very valuable information. He thought that it would be useful not only to make a concordance of features actually present but also of features not present (the absence of certain structures or certain sequences).

Mr Glélé asked to what extent the methods used for deciphering other languages could also serve to clear up the mystery surrounding the Meroitic language. He stated that Professor Knorossov and Professor Piotrovski had been invited to the meeting on the same basis as Professor Holthoer and Professor Hintze in order to provide the required information.

Professor Leclant said that a very wide-ranging study of this matter had been made at meetings held in Paris and London during the summer of 1973. The work both on the Mohenjodaro script and on Maya had not yet got beyond the stage of working hypotheses.

Professor Diop hoped, however, that the idea of using comparative methods side by side with the study of structures would not be abandoned. His proposal was approved by Professor Sauneron, who took the opportunity of emphasizing the importance of the work which had already been done by the Meroitic Studies Group.

Subsequent discussion bore more especially on the languages of the Sudan; Professor Säve-Söderbergh emphasized that, in any case, it was important that they be studied, since quite apart from the comparison with Meroitic, a knowledge of these languages would assist in advancing African linguistics. Professor Säve-Söderbergh at this stage submitted the outline of a recommendation to this effect. He also emphasized that it was possible, even with quite small funds, to set up an efficient secretariat and to accelerate the collection of material, its processing by computer and the redistribution of information.

Lastly, there was discussion of the content of the recommendation. Professor Diop hoped that the excellent work done by the Meroitic Studies Group would be continued with full international collaboration, that a systematic compilation of the vocabulary would be made in the Sudan and that an identical compilation would be carried out in other regions of Africa with the collaboration of Professor Obenga. Professor Sauneron accepted these proposals in their entirety. As it was uncertain what bearing this work would ultimately prove to have on the deciphering of Meroitic, he hoped that the study of African languages would be developed independently, for its own sake, even if it were partly incorporated in the overall project. It was likely to be very protracted and it was essential that a thoroughly sound method should be established from the outset, after strict critical appraisal. Professor Obenga endorsed this idea and suggested that an inventory should be made of the grammatical features of Meroitic which were currently known. Professor Leclant considered that this proposal could be put into effect immediately. Professor Habachi hoped that the need for an archaeological inquiry would not be neglected.

In response to a methodological proposal made by Professor Obenga, Mr Glélé stated that the methods to be adopted would be decided when the membership of the international team responsible was finalized. He explained that Unesco was supporting the studies being carried out in Khartoum with regard to Sudanese languages and was in a position to provide study grants in accordance with its normal procedures. Unesco was financing and directing a programme on African linguistics and had just adopted a ten-year plan for this purpose.

Recommendations

(1)(a) The meeting expresses its satisfaction for the work accomplished by the Meroitic Study Group in Paris in collaboration with scholars of many other countries, and wishes to express its opinion that the work is well grounded and promises good results.

(b) The meeting has unanimously decided to suggest the following measures to further the project:

(i) the speeding up of the computer processes by making available additional funds, and circulating the information, in revised and improved form, to the main centres of Meroitic studies;

(ii) to produce lists and where possible, of Meroitic personal names, place names and titles, and to classify linguistic structures, and to pursue collaboration with specialists in African linguistics;

(iii) to establish and publish a complete corpus of all Meroitic texts with bibliography, photographs, facsimiles and transcriptions on the basis of the existing files (Répertoire d'Epigraphie Méroitique);

(iv) to produce a complete Meroitic vocabulary.

(c) Since the results of the project so far obtained are scientifically sound and promise a successful development, and since the greater expense of the project as a whole has already been met with funds from various sources, this meeting now considers it to be imperative to assure the continuation and completion of the project by providing funds for the following purposes:

(i) costs of secretariat and personnel for the documentation and scientific publication of the material;

(ii) costs of inquiries in collections and museums;

(iii) travel expenses of specialists;

(iv) costs of card punching and computer time.

(2) The next step of research would be comparative structural and lexicographical studies of African languages, in the first place the languages of the Sudan and the border regions of Ethiopia, some of which are now dying out. This would best be done by giving Sudanese students at the University of Khartoum a linguistic training, preferably such students who have these languages as their mother tongue.

Such training would also be of value for many other purposes. Such a project, which would complement the valuable work already under way in the Sudan, would require to be negotiated with the University of Khartoum, and funds would be required for the necessary scholarships.

(3) In addition a wider linguistic survey of all African languages with the purpose of collecting key words was desirable. Such a survey should be made in collaboration with the Meroitic Study Group and be directed by specialists chosen by Unesco in collaboration with the International Scientific Committee for the General History of Africa. The choice should be limited to about 500 words of selected categories from some 100 languages.

This collection, when computerized, would be a valuable tool not only for the deciphering of the Meroitic language but for many other linguistic problems of modern Africa.

2

Pharaonic Egypt

The end of the glacial period in Europe brought major climatic changes to the lands south of the Mediterranean. The decrease in rain caused the nomadic peoples of Saharan Africa to immigrate to the Nile Valley in search of a permanent water supply. The first actual settlement of the Nile Valley may thus have begun in early Neolithic times (about −7000). The Egyptians then entered on a pastoral and agricultural life.

Shortly before the dawn of history, the Egyptians learned the use of metals in what is called the Chalcolithic (or Cuprolithic) period, in which metal gradually supplanted flint. Gold and copper also made their first appearence, though bronze was not used until the Middle Kingdom and the use of iron apparently did not become widespread until the closing period of Pharaonic history.

Prehistory

The first settlers in Egypt did not find life easy and there must have been fierce competition among the different human groups to secure the land along the edge of the Nile and in the relatively restricted area of the Delta. These people, coming from the west and east as well as from the south, were doubtless of different somatic groups. It is not surprising that the different natural obstacles, together with the diversity of origin, should at first have separated from one another the groups which settled in different areas along the valley. In these groups, we can see the origin of the nomes, or territorial divisions, which formed the basis of the political structure of Egypt in historical times.

The great achievement of the prehistoric period was control of the land (see Introduction). The early Egyptians managed to clear the ground in their immediate neighbourhood for cultivation, drain the swamps and build dykes against the incursions of flood water. Gradually the benefits of using canals for irrigation were learned. Such work required organized effort on a large scale and this led to the growth of a local political structure within each district.

Some memory of the growth of political unity in Egypt may perhaps be deduced from some of the fragments of early literary evidence. This suggests that in the dim and distant past, the nomes of the Delta had apparently formed themselves into coalitions. The western nomes of this region were traditionally united under the god Horus, while those of the eastern part of the Delta were joined under the god Andjty,

Lord of Djedu, who was later assimilated by Osiris. The western nomes, it has been suggested, conquered those of the east and formed a united kingom in northern Egypt, so that the worship of Horus as the chief god prevailed throughout the Delta, spreading gradually to Upper Egypt to overwhelm Seth, the chief god of an Upper Egyptian coalition.

Archaic period (– 3200 to – 2900)

The first event of historical importance known to us is the union of these two prehistoric kingdoms, or rather the subjugation of Lower Egypt by the Upper Egyptian ruler whom tradition designated as Menes, while archaeological sources seem to call him Narmer. He begins the first of the thirty dynasties, or ruling families, into which the Egyptian historian Manetho (– 280) divided the long line of rulers down to the time of Alexander the Great. The family of Menes resided at Thinis in Upper Egypt, the foremost city of the district, which embraced the sacred town of Abydos. It was near Abydos, with its sanctuary of the god Osiris, that Petrie excavated the huge tombs of the kings of the first two dynasties. Certainly it was the southern kingdom which gained dominance over the whole country and, soon after its first victory, set up a capital at Memphis, near the junction of the two lands.

The kings of the first two dynasties of the archaic period still remain rather nebulous figures to us. Yet without doubt this period was one of hard work for consolidation. During the 300 years of the First and the Second Dynasties the culture of the later years of the pre-dynastic period continued, but during the Third and Fourth Dynasties political unity was achieved and the new state was stable enough to express itself in a distinctively Egyptian way.

The Old Kingdom (– 2900 to – 2280)

Third Dynasty

It has already been noted that the kings of the first two dynasties (archaic period) appear to have been primarily concerned with conquest and consolidation. We believe that the new dogma of divine kingship actually began with the Third Dynasty and that it was not until then that Egypt became a single, united nation. This Third Dynasty was founded by King Zoser, who was evidently a strong and able ruler. Yet his fame has been overshadowed, to a great extent, by that of his subject I-em-htp, a man renowned from his own day until now as an architect, physician, priest, magician, writer and maker of proverbs. Two thousand three hundred years after his death he became a god of medicine in whom the Greeks (who called him Imeuthes) recognized their own Askelepios. His outstanding accomplishment as an architect was the step pyramid, an extensive funerary complex built for his Pharaoh at Sakkara (Saqqara), on an area of 15 hectares in a rectangle 544 by 277 metres. He endowed the construction with a fortress-like enclosure wall, but introduced a striking innovation in substituting stone for brick.

The other kings of the Third Dynasty are as shadowy as those of the first two dynasties, although the huge unfinished step pyramid of King Sekhem-Khet (who was perhaps Zoser's son and successor) at Sakkara, is sufficient indication that Zoser's pyramid complex was not unique. King Huny, who closes the Third Dynasty, is the immediate predecessor of Snefru, the founder of the Fourth Dynasty. A pyramid at Meidum, some 70 kilometres to the south of Cairo, was built for him. This structure, originally constructed in steps, underwent several enlargements and changes of design before it was finished (perhaps by Snefru) as a true pyramid.

Fourth Dynasty

The Fourth Dynasty, one of the high points in Egyptian history, opens with the long and active reign of Snefru, whose annals, as preserved in part on the Palermo Stone, tell us of successful military campaigns against the Nubians to the south and the Libyan peoples to the west, the maintenance of traffic (particularly in timber) with the Syrian coast, and extensive building operations carried out year after year and involving the erection of temples, fortresses and palaces throughout Egypt. Snefru reigned for twenty-four years, and probably belonged to a minor branch of the royal family. To legitimize his position he married Hetep-Heres, the eldest daughter of Huny, thus carrying the royal blood over to the new dynasty. He had two pyramids constructed at Dahshur, the southern being rhomboidal in shape, the northern of true pyramid form and of a size which begins to approach that of the Great Pyramid of Khufu at Giza.

Snefru's successsors Khufu (Cheops), Khafre (Chephren) and Mankaure (Mycerinus) are remembered chiefly by the three pyramids which they erected on the high promontory at Giza, 10 kilometres south-west of modern Cairo. The pyramid of Khufu has the distinction of being the largest single building ever constructed by man, and for the excellence of its workmanship, accuracy of its planning and beauty of its proportions remains the chief of the Seven Wonders of the World. The pyramids of Khufu's son and grandson, though smaller, are similar in construction and in the arrangement of their subsidiary buildings.

Fifth Dynasty

This dynasty stemmed from the growing of the priesthood of Heliopolis. A legend in the Westcar Papyrus relates that the first three kings of the Fifth Dynasty were the offspring of the god Re and a lady named Radjeded, wife of a priest at Heliopolis. These three brothers were Weserkaf, Sahure and Neferirkare. Sahure is known chiefly for the splendid bas-reliefs which decorated his funerary temple at Abusir, north of Sakkara (Saqqara). It is well known that, though the royal pyramids of the Fifth Dynasty were far smaller than the great tombs of the Fourth Dynasty and of inferior construction, the funerary temples adjoining the pyramids were elaborate structures extensively decorated with painted bas-reliefs.

Near the pyramid complex most of the kings of this dynasty built great temples to the Sun-god, each dominated by a towering solar obelisk.

In addition to the erection and endowments of many temples listed in the Palermo Stone, the Pharaohs of the Fifth Dynasty were active in safeguarding the frontiers of

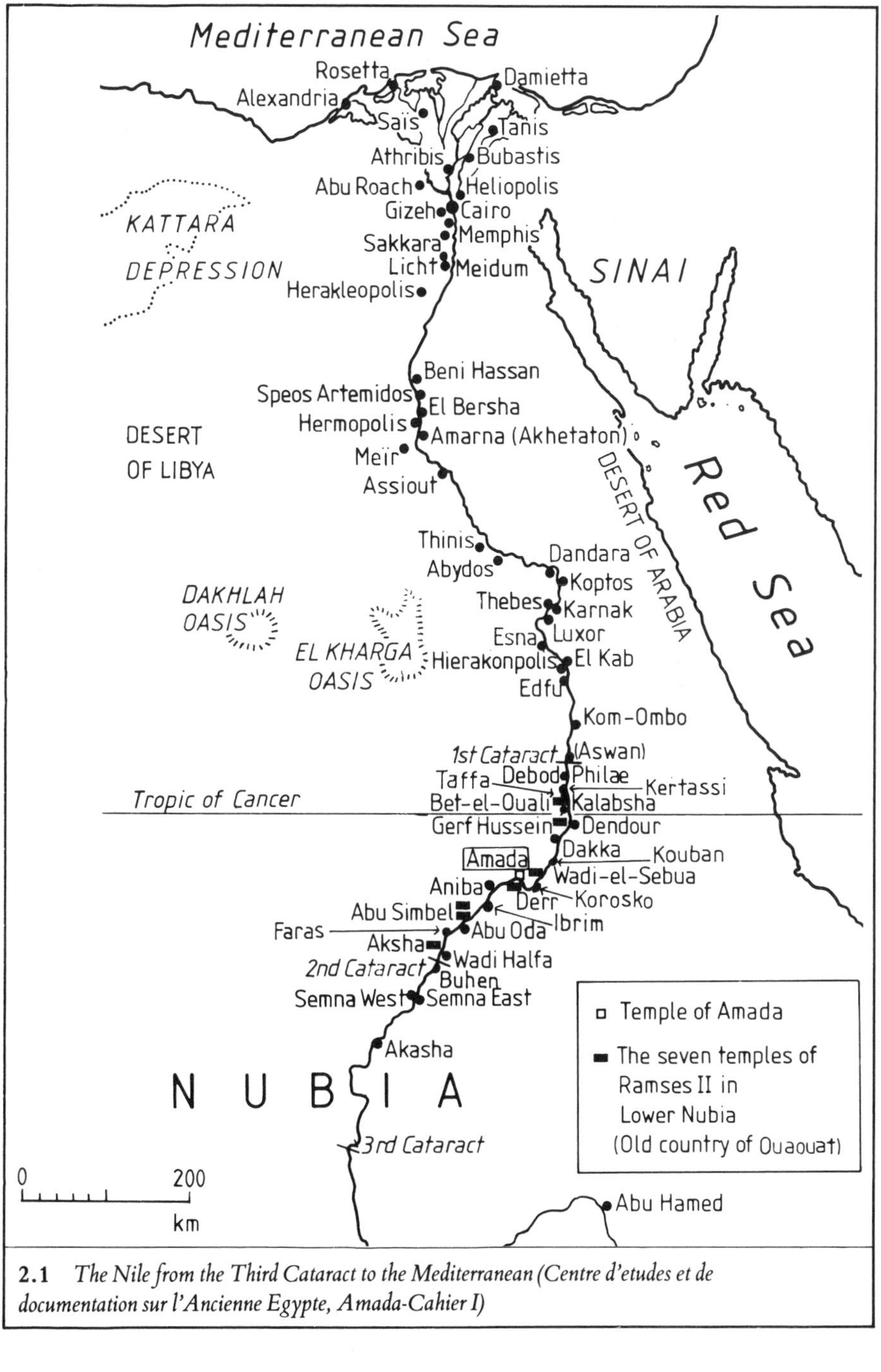

2.1 *The Nile from the Third Cataract to the Mediterranean (Centre d'etudes et de documentation sur l'Ancienne Egypte, Amada-Cahier I)*

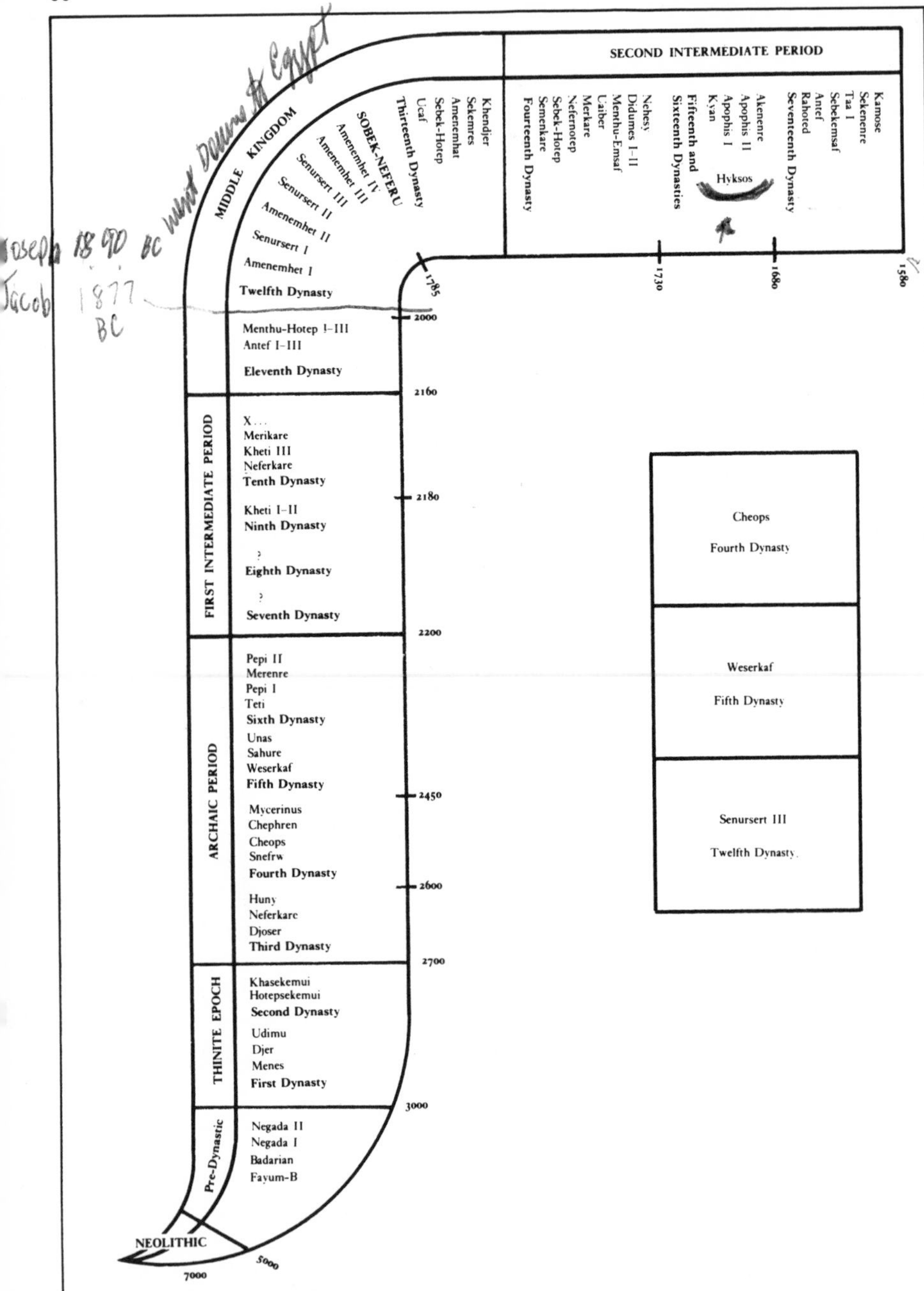

2.2 *Chronology of Egyptian history (Diagram by J. Vercoutter)*

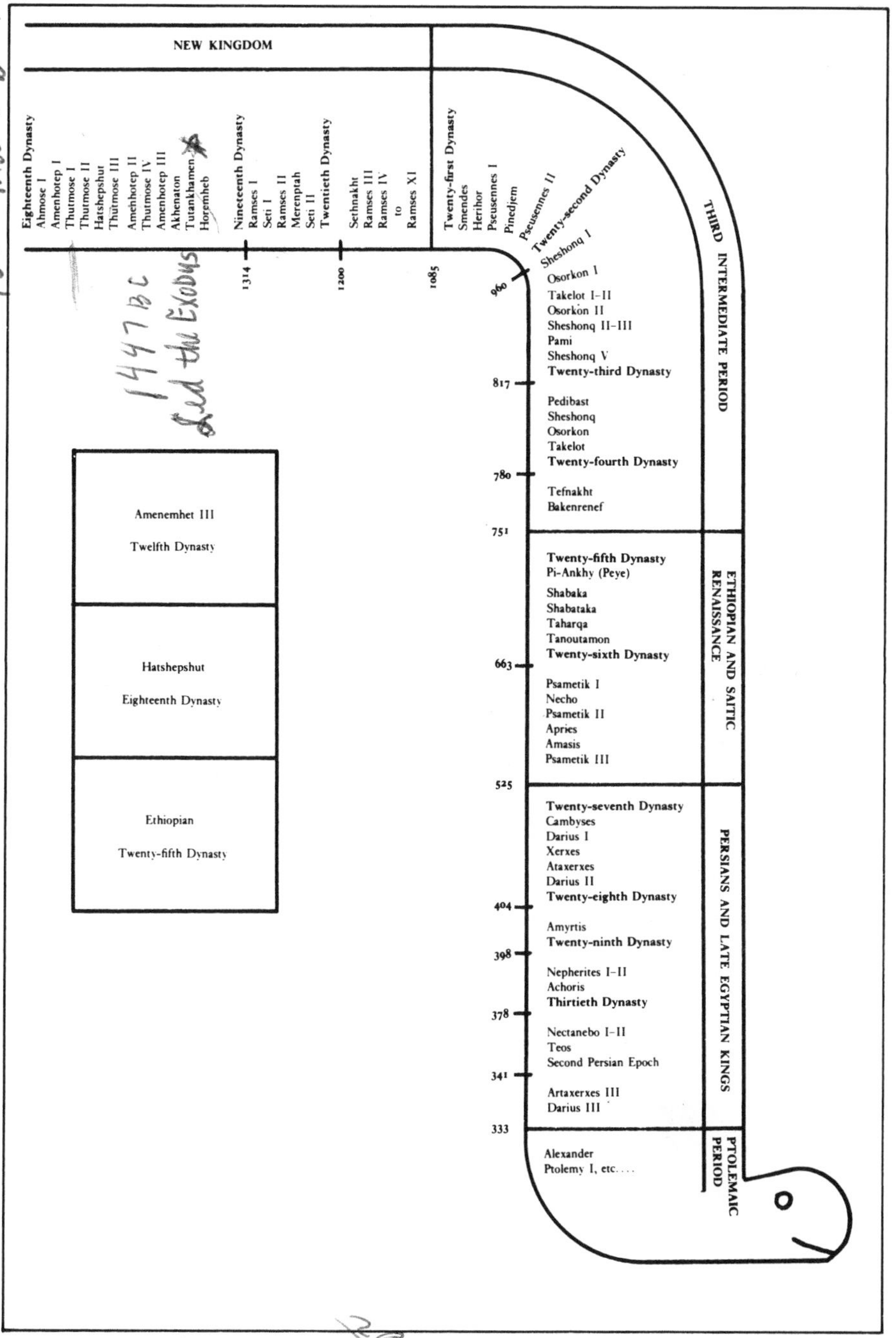
NEW KINGDOM
Eighteenth Dynasty
Ahmose I
Amenhotep I
Thutmose I
Thutmose II
Hatshepsut
Thutmose III
Amenhotep II
Thutmose IV
Amenhotep III
Akhenaton
Tutankhamen
Horemheb
Nineteenth Dynasty
Ramses I
Seti I
Ramses II
Merenptah
Seti II
Twentieth Dynasty
Sethnakht
Ramses III
Ramses IV
to
Ramses XI
1314
1200
1085
Twenty-first Dynasty
Smendes
Herihor
Pseusennes I
Pinedjem
Pseusennes II
Twenty-second Dynasty
Sheshonq I
960
Osorkon I
Takelot I–II
Osorkon II
Sheshonq II–III
Pami
Sheshonq V
Twenty-third Dynasty
817
Pedibast
Sheshonq
Osorkon
Takelot
Twenty-fourth Dynasty
780
Tefnakht
Bakenrenef
751
THIRD INTERMEDIATE PERIOD
Twenty-fifth Dynasty
Pi-Ankhy (Peye)
Shabaka
Shabataka
Taharqa
Tanoutamon
Twenty-sixth Dynasty
663
Psametik I
Necho
Psametik II
Apries
Amasis
Psametik III
525
ETHIOPIAN AND SAITIC RENAISSANCE
Twenty-seventh Dynasty
Cambyses
Darius I
Xerxes
Ataxerxes
Darius II
Twenty-eighth Dynasty
404
Amyrtis
Twenty-ninth Dynasty
398
Nepherites I–II
Achoris
Thirtieth Dynasty
378
Nectanebo I–II
Teos
Second Persian Epoch
341
Artaxerxes III
Darius III
333
PERSIANS AND LATE EGYPTIAN KINGS
Alexander
Ptolemy I, etc. . . .
PTOLEMAIC PERIOD
Amenemhet III
Twelfth Dynasty
Hatshepshut
Eighteenth Dynasty
Ethiopian
Twenty-fifth Dynasty

Egypt and in expanding the existing trade relations with neighbouring countries. Punitive expeditions against the Libyans of the western desert, the Bedouins of Sinai and the Semitic peoples of southern Palestine were recorded on the walls of their funerary temples. Great seagoing ships visited the coast of Palestine during the reigns of Sahure and Issessi. Egyptian ships also reached the shores of the land of Punt on the Somali coast to procure highly valued cargoes of myrrh, ebony and animals, among other goods. The traffic with Syria in cedar wood continued to thrive, and the ancient port of Byblos on the coast below the wooded slopes of Lebanon saw more and more of the Egyptian timber fleet.

Sixth Dynasty

There is no evidence that political disturbances in the country accompanied the transition from the Fifth to the Sixth Dynasty. With the long and vigorous reign of Pepi I (the second king) the dynasty showed its strength. For the first time an Egyptian king abandoned purely defensive military tactics and carried the might of his army into the heart of the enemy country. With the large army under Uni, the Egyptian general, the enemies were driven back to their homelands as far north as Mount Carmel and trapped, in the last five campaigns, by landing troops from an Egyptian fleet far up the Palestine coast. During this time, Pepi I did much to expand and consolidate Egyptian power in Nubia.

On the death of Pepi I's son Merenre, another of his sons, Pepi II, a child of six, ascended the throne and ruled the country for ninety-four years, dying in his hundredth year after one of the longest reigns in history.

The second year of Pepi II's reign was marked by the return of Herkhuf, the nomarch of Elephantine, who had been travelling in Nubia and had reached the province of Yam, whence he had brought back a rich cargo of treasures and a dancing pygmy as a gift for the king. With great enthusiasm, the eight-year-old king sent a letter of thanks to Herkhuf, requesting him to take every precaution that the pygmy should arrive at Memphis in good condition.

The very long reign of Pepi II came to an end in political confusion which can be traced back to the beginning of the Sixth Dynasty, when the growing power of the nomarchs of Upper Egypt enabled them to build their tombs in their own districts and not near the king's pyramid on the necropolis. A rapidly increasing process of decentralization took place. The impoverishment of the royal house is plain from the absence of monuments after those built by Pepi II. It is not clear whether the forces of disintegration were already too strong for any Pharaoh to combat, or whether the very long and feebly defensive reign of Pepi II hastened the collapse. What is clear is that the Old Kingdom ended almost immediately after his death and then began a period of anarchy which we call the First Intermediate Period.

The First Intermediate Period (– 2280 to – 2060)

On the death of Pepi II, Egypt disintegrated in an explosion of feudal disorder. A period of anarchy, social chaos and civil war began. Along the length of the Nile Valley local princelings battled with each other amid such confusion that Manetho mentioned in his history of Egypt that the Seventh Dynasty included seventy kings who reigned for seventy days.

Little is known of the Seventh Dynasty and, even when we have a record of the names of the kings, the order of their reigns is disputed. Soon, however, a new royal house emerged at Heracleopolis (in Middle Egypt) and some attempt was made to continue the Memphis culture. These kings of the Ninth and Tenth Dynasties evidently controlled the Delta, which had become a prey to marauding desert nomads. Upper Egypt, however, had split up into its old units, each nome under the control of a local ruler. The subsequent history of Egypt is characterized by the growth of a Theban power which, in the Eleventh Dynasty, was destined to gain control, first of Upper Egypt and, not very long afterwards, of the whole country.

The condition of Egypt following the collapse of the Old Kingdom, which had realized the highest material and intellectual achievements of the country, is best described by the sage Ipu-wer. His writings, which seemingly go back to the First Intermediate Period, have been preserved in a papyrus of the New Kingdom which is now in the Leiden Museum. In one of the passages he described the social revolution which took place in the early part of the First Intermediate Period and the absence of any sort of centralized authority.

Yet out of the turmoil certain positive values were born: an inspiring new emphasis on individualism, for example, social equality and the dignity of the common man. Thus, amidst the chaos, the Egyptians evolved a set of moral standards upholding the individual. This is apparent from the well-known papyrus known as the Protests of the Eloquent Peasant dating from the Tenth Dynasty. It is the story of a poor peasant who, having been robbed of his belongings by a wealthy landowner, insists upon his rights.

The Middle Kingdom (−2060 to −1785)

Although the Egyptians glimpsed democratic values, the vision did not endure. It seemed clear in times of trouble, yet dimmed with the return of prosperity and discipline in the Middle Kingdom, which was the second great period of national development. Egypt was once more reunited by force of arms. Thebes, previously an unknown and unimportant name, put an end to the rule of Heracleopolis and laid claim to the entire state of Egypt and in winning the war reunited the Two Lands under a single rule.

King Menthuhotep stands out as the dominant personality of the Eleventh Dynasty. His great task was the reorganization of the country's administration. All resistance to the royal house had been crushed, but there may have been occasional minor uprisings. Menthuhotep II, who had a long reign, built the funerary temple at Deir el Bahari which is the greatest monument of the period at Thebes.

Following Menthuhotep II's rule, the family began to decline. Under the last king of the Eleventh Dynasty, a certain Amenemhet, vizier to the king who also bore other titles, is probably identical with the founder of the Twelfth Dynasty, King Amenemhet, and the first of a succession of powerful rulers.

Amenemhet I adopted three important measures which were strictly adhered to by his successors. He established a new capital called Ithet-Tawi (Holder-of-the-Two-

2.3 *Kephren (J. Pirenne,* Histoire de la civilisation de l'Egypte Ancienne, *vol. 1, Neuchâtel, Paris, 1961)*

Lands) not far south of Memphis, from which he could better control Lower Egypt; he initiated the custom of placing his son beside him on the throne as co-regent; and he planned the subjugation of Nubia and established a trading station further south then had ever been attempted before.

Senusret I followed in the steps of his father and through his own energy, ability and breadth of vision was able to implement plans for the enrichment and expansion of Egypt. A series of expeditions led by the king himself, or by his able officers, tightened Egyptian control over Lower Nubia. The king's activities to the west seem to have been confined to punitive expeditions against the Temenw Libyans and to the maintenance of communications with the oases. His policy with the countries of the north-west was to defend his boundaries and to continue trading with the countries of western Asia.

The two subsequent kings, Amenemhet II and Senusret II, were apparently not interested in the consolidation and expansion of Egypt's foreign conquests. Senusret III, however, is remembered for the reconquest and subjugation of Lower Nubia, which he reduced to the status of a province of Egypt. The long and prosperous reign of his successor, Amenemhet III, was characterized by an ambitious programme of irrigation, leading to vast agricultural and economic expansion in the Fayyūm.

With Amenemhet IV the royal family was evidently beginning to lose its vigour. His brief and undistinguished reign, followed by the even briefer reign of Queen Sobek Neferu, marks the end of the dynasty.

The Second Intermediate Period (−1785 to −1580)

The names borne by some of the Pharaohs of the Thirteenth Dynasty reflect the existence in Lower Egypt of a large Asiatic population. This element was no doubt increased by the immigration of large groups from the lands north-east of Egypt, forced southward as a result of widespread population movements in western Asia. The leaders of these groups were called Hka-Hasut by the Egyptians, meaning Rulers of Foreign Countries, from which was derived the Manethonian term Hyksos which is now generally applied to the people as a whole.

The Hyksos only began seriously to challenge the political authority of the Thirteenth Dynasty about the year −1729. By −1700, however, they had emerged as a well-organized, well-equipped and warlike people, and they conquered the eastern part of the Delta, including the town of Hat-Wcrt (Avaris), which they refortified and used as their capital.

There is no doubt that the Hyksos occupation had a profound effect on the nation. They introduced the horse, the chariot and body-armour into Egypt. The Egyptians, who had never before had need of such equipment, eventually turned them successfully against the Hyksos and expelled them from the land. They began a war of liberation, conducted by the rulers of the Theban nome. The few surviving records of this period mostly concern the war fought by the kings of the late Seventeenth Dynasty against the Asiatic oppressors after nearly 150 years of occupation. Ahmose finally succeeded in driving the invaders out of the Delta, capturing their capital, Avaris, and following them into Palestine where he laid siege to the stronghold of Sharuhen. After that he proceeded northwards and raided the land of Zahi (the Phoenician coast). Thus Hyksos power was finally broken.

2.4 *Queen Hatshepsut seated (C. Alfred,* New Kingdom Art of Ancient Egypt. *Photo, The Metropolitan Museum of Art, New York)*

The New Kingdom (−1580 to −1085)

Eighteenth Dynasty

King Ahmose I was hailed by posterity as the father of the New Kingdom and the founder of the Eighteenth Dynasty.

Ahmose I's son, Amenhotep I, was followed by Thutmose I and II and then by Queen Hatshepsut, who married each of her half-brothers, Thutmose II and III, in turn. In the fifth year of her reign, however, Hatshepsut was powerful enough to declare herself supreme ruler of the country. The two peaceful decades of her reign were prosperous for Egypt. She concentrated her attention upon the country's internal affairs and upon great building enterprises (mainly her magnificent temple at Western Thebes). The two achievements of which she was most proud were the expedition to Punt and the raising of two great obelisks at the temple of Karnak.

Following the death of Hatshepsut, Thutmose III at last came into his own. His first act as king was to overthrow the statues of Hatshepsut and erase her name and image wherever they appeared. His revenge appeased, he swiftly formed an army and marched against a coalition of the city states of the Palestine–Syria–Lebanon region, which had joined forces at the city of Megiddo and which were preparing to revolt against Egypt's domination. Marching with astonishing speed, Thutmose III surprised the enemy and drove them to cover within the city walls. With the surrender of Megiddo the whole country as far as the southern Lebanon came under Egyptian control. In all, Thutmose III undertook seventeen campaigns abroad and Egyptian arms commanded respect in Syria for many years thereafter. Egypt was firmly established as a world power with a far-reaching empire.

Thutmose III was followed by two able and energetic Pharaohs, Amenhotep II and Thutmose IV, the latter being closely connected with the kingdom of Mittani, for he married the daughter of the royal house. It is this lady who appears on the monuments as the Pharaoh's chief queen and the mother of Amenhotep III.

When Amenhotep III succeeded his father he was probably already married to his principal queen, Teye. The young king's accession to the throne came at a time when the country was at the peak of its political power, and was economically prosperous and culturally developed. Moreover, the world was at peace and both the Pharaoh and his people could enjoy the many pleasures and luxuries which life now had to offer them. Towards the end of his reign, as is evident from the Tell-al-Amarna letters, the absence of a show of military force encouraged energetic men to scheme for independent power and to revolt against Egyptian authority. Amenhotep III, however, seems not to have been unduly concerned. It was as a builder and patron of the arts that he earned his reputation for magnificence. To him we owe the Luxor temple, the other large buildings at Karnak, and many others both in Egypt and elsewhere such as at Soleb in Nubia.

Though the cult of Aton began under Amenhotep III, its growth seems to have had little effect on the worship of the other gods until later in his reign, possibly not until the thirtieth year of the reign, the probable date when his son Amenhotep IV (later known as Akhenaton) became co-regent. Physically weak, with a frail, effeminate

2.5 *Akhenaton before the sun (G. Mokhtar)*

body, the new king had in him the makings of neither soldier nor statesman. He was mostly concerned with matters of the mind and spirit.

In his youthful fanaticism, Amenhotep IV instituted a radical change of policy which led to a direct attack on the priesthood of Amon. Amenhotep IV at first continued to live at Thebes, where he had a great temple to Aton erected east of Amon's temple at Karnak. Then, obviously embittered by the reaction to his reforms in Thebes, he decided to withdraw from the city. He founded a new residence at Tell-al-Amarna in Middle Egypt, which he called Akhot Aton (the horizon of Aton) where he lived until his death some fourteen years later. He changed his name to Akh-en-Aton (He-who-is-serviceable-to-Aton).

Not content with proclaiming Aton as the sole true god, Akhenaton assailed the older deities. While tumult raged about him, Akhenaton lived in his capital worshipping his sole god. This worship of the creative power of the sun in the name of Aton required no images of the god and was carried out in the open air of the temple court.

The Atonist revolution did not survive the death of Akhenaton. His co-regent and successor, Semenekh-Ka-Re, almost immediately initiated a reconciliation with the priesthood of Amon. Semenekh-Ka-Re did not reign for more than three years and was followed by Tut-Ankh-Aton, who eventually changed his name to Tutankhamun. Since we know that this young Pharaoh died at about 18 years of age and that he reigned for at least nine years, he was probably about eight years old at his accession. During the reign of Tut-Ankh-Amon, and even after his death, there was some hesitation in repudiating Aton who, in spite of the restoration of Amon, maintained a place among the gods which continued during the short reign of King Ay who followed Tut-Ankh-Amon. It was only with Horemheb, as the last king of the Eighteenth Dynasty, that the persecution of Aton began with the same persistence that had formerly applied to Amon.

Horemheb came from a line of provincial noblemen in a small town of Middle Egypt. His long career as commander of the Egyptian army and as an administrator gave him an opportunity of assessing the political corruption which had increased dangerously since the beginning of Akhenaton's reign. On accession he promptly initiated a widespread series of reforms which were beneficial to the country. He also issued a decree to expedite the collection of national revenue and abolished corruption among military and civil officials.

Ninteenth Dynasty

Horemheb showed great favour to an army officer called Pa-Ramesses whom he made vizier and chose to succeed him on the throne, establishing the Nineteenth Dynasty. However, Pa-Ramesses was already an old man and reigned for only two years, to be followed by his son and co-regent Seti I, the first of a line of warriors who turned all their efforts towards recovering Egypt's prestige abroad. As soon as Seti I came to the throne, he faced serious danger from a coalition of Syrian city-states encouraged, and even sustained, by the Hittites. He was able to defeat the coalition and enable Egypt to regain control over Palestine. After repulsing a Libyan attack, we find Seti once again in northern Syria where Egyptian troops came into contact with the Hittites for the first time. He captured Kadesh but though the Hittites were forced to retire temporarily they retained their influence in northern Syria. The war was continued by his successor Ramses II.

Under Ramses II the royal residence and administrative centre was moved to a city in the north-east part of the Delta, called Per-Ramesse, where a military base was established, suitable for marshalling large bodies of infantry and chariotry. In the fifth year of his reign Ramses II set out at the head of four armies against a powerful coalition of Asiatic people assembled by the Hittite king Mutawallis, and continued his father's attempts to regain Egypt's holdings in northern Syria. Though, in the famous battle near Kadesh, Ramses led the vanguard of his forces into an enemy trap, he nevertheless managed to gather his forces and convert what might have been defeat into questionable victory. Detailed representations and accounts of this battle, and some of the more successful campaigns in Palestine and Syria which preceded and followed it, were carved on the walls of Ramses II's rock-cut temples at Abu-Simbel and at El-Derr in Lower Nubia, in his temples at Abydos and Karnak, on the pylon which he added to the temple at Luxor as well as in his funerary temple called the Ramesseum. Hostilities between the two countries continued for a number of years. It was not, in fact, until the twenty-first year of his reign that Ramses II finally signed a remarkable peace treaty with the Hittite king Hattusilis. Thereafter cordial relations were maintained between the two powers and Ramses married the eldest daughter of Hattusilis in a ceremony widely announced as a symbol of peace and brotherhood. With the death of Hattusilis a new danger began with the movement of the Sea Peoples from the Balkans and the Black Sea regions, who soon overwhelmed the Hittite kingdom.

The ageing Ramses, who reigned for sixty-seven years after signing the treaty, neglected the ominous signs from abroad and his vigorous successor, Merneptah, found himself faced with a serious situation when he came to the throne.

In the meantime a great number of warlike Sea Peoples had moved into the coastal region to the west of the Delta and, entering into an alliance with the Libyans, threatened Egypt. Merneptah met them and, in a great battle in the western Delta in the fifth year of his reign, he inflicted an overwhelming defeat upon the invaders. On the Merneptah stelae he also recorded his military activities in the Syro-Palestine region and listed a number of conquered cities and states including Canaan, Askalon, Gezer, Yenoam and Israel – the last mentioned for the first time in Egyptian records.

Twentieth Dynasty

Merneptah's death was followed by a dynasty struggle and the throne was successively occupied by five rulers whose order and relationship one to another has not yet been clearly established. Order was restored by Sethnakhr, who reigned for two years as the first king of the Twentieth Dynasty. He was succeeded by his son Ramses III who, in a reign of thirty-one years, did as much as could be done to revive the glories of the New Kingdom. In his fifth and eleventh years of rule he decisively defeated invading hordes of western Libyans and in the eighth year beat back a systematic invasion by land and sea of the Sea Peoples.

In dealing with the internal ills which also beset the country, Ramses III was less successful than in defending it against foreign armies. The country was harassed by labour troubles, turbulence among government workers, an inflationary rise in wheat prices and a fall in the value of bronze and copper. Decadence grew in the reigns of subsequent kings from Ramses IV to Ramses XI. The feeble hold of the royal house became still more precarious as the power of the priests of Amon increased, till finally they chose a high priest, Heri-Hor, to ascend the throne and begin a new dynasty.

Period of decline

Twenty-first to Twenty-fourth Dynasties (−1085 to −720)

In the Twenty-first Dynasty, rule was divided by common consent between the princes of Tanis in the Delta and the Heri-Hor Dynasty at Thebes. On the death of the latter, Smendes (ruler of the Delta) seems to have taken control of the whole country. This period saw the flowering of a new power, a family of Libyan descent from the Fayyūm. One of the members of this family, named Sheshonq, seized the throne of Egypt and started a dynasty which lasted for about 200 years.

Towards the end of the Twenty-second Dynasty, Egypt was divided into squabbling petty kingdoms and was menaced both by Assyria and by a powerful independent Sudan. Then a man named Pedibast set up a rival dynasty, whose kings continued to bear the names of the Twenty-second Dynasty. At that time Egypt maintained peaceful relations with Solomon in Jerusalem, who even took an Egyptian princess to wife. In the fifth year of the reign of Solomon's successor, however, Sheshonq attacked Palestine. Though Egypt did not endeavour to hold Palestine, she regained something of her former influence and profited by a greatly increased foreign trade.

The Twenty-fourth Dynasty had one king only, namely Bakenrenef, whom the Greeks called Bocchoris, son of Tefnakht. Bocchoris endeavoured to give support to the king of Israel against the Assyrian king, Sargon II, but his army was beaten at Raphia in −720. His reign ended when the Sudanese king Shabaka invaded Egypt.

The Sudanese and Assyrian Twenty-fifth Dynasty (−720 to −658)

There was another invasion of Egypt in about −720, but this time from the south. From a capital at the Fourth Cataract, Piankhi, a Sudanese who ruled the Sudan between the First and Sixth Cataracts, found himself powerful enough to challenge the throne of the Pharaohs. His dynasty lasted for sixty years before the Assyrians, after many campaigns, succeeded in putting an end to it.

Saitic Kingdom (−658 to −530)

Egypt was freed from Assyrian domination by an Egyptian named Psammetik. In −658 he managed, with the help of Gyges of Lydia and Greek mercenaries, to throw off all vestiges of Assyrian overlordship and start a new dynasty, the Twenty-sixth. The kings of this dynasty tried valiantly to restore Egypt's position by promoting commercial expansion. Upper Egypt became a rich agricultural region, growing produce which Lower Egypt sold.

Persian period (– 530 to – 322)

In the reign of Psammetik III, Egypt had to endure conquest by the Persians under Cambyses, and with his occupation the history of the country as an independent power was in effect ended. The Twenty-seventh Dynasty was headed by Persian kings. The Twenty-eighth was a local dynasty established by Amyrtaios, who organized a revolt during the trouble-ridden reign of Darius II. By means of alliances with Athens and Sparta, the kings of the Twenty-ninth and Thirtieth Dynasties contrived to maintain the independence thus gained for about sixty years.

The second Persian domination of Egypt began under Artaxerxes III in – 341. This was soon brought to an end by Alexander the Great, who invaded Egypt in – 332, after defeating Persia at the battle of Issus.

3

Pharaonic Egypt: society, economy and culture

Economy and society

Fields and marshes

The establishment of the Pharaonic state around the year −3000 and the little-known period that followed undoubtedly corresponded with great economic development. There is no means of knowing whether the need to co-ordinate irrigation was the principal cause of the formation of a unified state, or whether the unification of the country under the Thinite kings, together with the development of writing, made it possible to co-ordinate the regional economies by rationalizing basic construction work and ensuring the organized distribution of food resources. What is clear is that, until the nineteenth century of the Christian era, Egypt's prosperity and vitality were to be tied to the cultivation of cereals (wheat, barley). A system of flood basins, which controlled and distributed the flood water and silt inside earth embankments, endured until the modern triumph of year-round irrigation: there is evidence that it existed as early as the Middle Kingdom, and in all probability it had taken shape even earlier. Obviously, this system only permitted one crop a year. On the other hand, the shortness of the agricultural cycle made plenty of manpower available for major operations on the construction of religious and royal buildings. The Ancient Egyptians also practised year-round irrigation by raising water from the canals or from pits dug down to the water-table, but for a long time human legs and human shoulders bearing yokes were the only 'machines' for raising water known, and watering by means of ditches was used only for vegetables, fruit trees and vineyards.

Bread and beer made from grain were the staple diet, but the Ancient Egyptians' food was astonishingly varied. One is struck by the types of cakes and bread listed in the texts. As today, gardens provided broad beans, chick peas and other pulses, onions, leeks, lettuces and cucumbers. Orchards furnished dates, figs, sycamore nuts and grapes. Skilful cultivation of the vine, practised mainly in the Delta and in the oases, produced a great variety of wines. Bee-keeping provided honey. Oil was extracted from sesame and nabk, the olive tree introduced during the New Kingdom remaining rare and not very successful.

Pharaonic Egypt did not transform the whole of the Nile Valley into productive land and gardens. The vast marshes and lakes along the northern edges of the Delta and the shores of Lake Moeris, and the low-lying land on the edge of the desert and in the meanders of the Nile were exploited differently. In these *pehu* abundant and varied wildfowl were hunted or trapped. There was fishing with seine-net, eel-pot, line or basket, for the Nile offered a wide variety of fish which had a definite place in the people's diet. Finally, the marshland gave pasturage for cows and oxen.

The tables of the gods and the great had to be well furnished with beef. The cutting-up of the carcass was a fine art, the animal fats being widely used to make perfumed unguents. We know that the Old Kingdom Egyptians tried to raise a number of species – oryx, antelope, etc., and even cranes and hyenas – but this proved labour-consuming and the results were disappointing. In contrast, they were very successful in raising poultry, notably the Nile goose. The meat of goats, so harmful to the valley's few trees, and sheep raised on fallow land and the fringes of the desert, as well as pigs (in spite of some prohibitions), acquired a considerable place in the people's diet. Two African species domesticated by the Egyptians were particularly successful and are closely linked in our minds with the Pharaonic past: the ass, used as early as the archaic period, not for riding but as a beast of burden, and the domestic cat, which did not appear until the end of the Old and the beginning of the Middle Kingdom.

Mining and industry

The nobility hunted hare and big game in the desert for sport and as a means of varying the ordinary fare, but this could not have had much economic importance. What the desert did offer was a wide range of mineral resources: the green and black dyes of the Arabian desert used to treat and embellish the eyes even in prehistoric times; the beautiful hard stone used by the builders and sculptors (limestone, granite, alabaster, quartzite and semi-precious stones like the Sinai turquoise or Nubian cornelians and amethysts. The manufacture of glazes developed very early, prompting the manufacture of objects with the look of turquoise or lapis lazuli. New Kingdom Egypt improved its glass-making techniques, and became a past master in these processes.

One of the riches derived by the country from the arid wastes surrounding it was gold, which came from the Arabian desert and Nubia, and which was more highly prized than silver, although the latter, an improved metal, was always rarer and, in the Old Kingdom, more precious than gold. The deserts contained a number of copper deposits, but these were of a rather low grade, except in Sinai, and Egypt soon became dependent on copper from Asia.

If Ancient Egypt had to import metals and timber from its Asian neighbours, its industrial capacity was unsurpassed in two domains. The Pharaohs exported textiles, Egyptian linen being then of an unequalled fineness, and paper. Papyrus, useful in so many ways – for sails, ropes, clothing, footwear – above all made possible the manufacture of a very flexible writing surface, which was the source of the scribe's power and which was in heavy demand abroad from the moment alphabetic writing spread around the eastern Mediterranean. Intensive cultivation of papyrus probably contributed greatly to the disappearance of the marshes, the haunt of the birds,

3.1 *Rendering the accounts (J. Pirenne,* Histoire de la civilisation de l'Egypte Ancienne, *vol. 1, Neuchâtel, Paris, 1961.* Photo, Fondation egyptologique Reine Elisabeth)

3.2 *Fishing (J. Pirenne,* Histoire de la civilisation de l'Egypte Ancienne, *vol. 1, Neuchâtel, Paris, 1961.* Photo, Archives photographiques, Paris)

crocodiles and hippopotamuses that, as the Ancient Egyptians themselves felt, brightened the landscape.

The development of transport was one determining factor in the progress of the Pharaonic regime. Oxen were hardly ever harnessed to anything but the plough or the funeral sledge; the ass, hardier and less demanding, was the ideal beast of burden in the fields as on the desert trails (we know that the horse, introduced during the second millennium, remained a luxury for warriors, and that the rich economic potential of the wheel, the principle of which was known as early as the Old Kingdom, was not exploited). Less efficient, certainly, although the technique of using them in teams was known, the ass preceded and supplemented the camel, which only came very slowly into use in the countryside after the Persian era. For bulk transport over long distances Egypt used its river and its canals: small craft and large boats were rapid and reliable. In addition, even at a very early date, sailing boats plied the Red Sea and the Mediterranean. For moving the heavy stone blocks needed for sacred buildings in particular, Pharaonic engineering had invented ingenious methods of an astonishing simplicity, using, for instance, the lubricating properties of wet mud to move simple sledges (without wheels or rollers), profiting from the rise of the Nile to float barges loaded with enormous blocks, or using reed matting for drogues.

The economic and social system

A survey of the available material on the economic and social system of Ancient Egypt gives the impression that everything stemmed from the king. He had a religious duty to ensure the cosmic order, the security of Egypt and the happiness of its people in this world and the next, not only by exercising his authority as king, but by maintaining the worship of the gods, with the result that he shared his economic prerogative with the temples. On the other hand, both in officiating in those temples and in managing the nation's affairs, Pharaoh, theoretically the sole priest, sole warrior, sole judge and sole producer, delegated his power to a whole hierarchy: one way of paying these officials was to assign them land, the revenue of which became theirs.

Certainly, the expeditions to Punt, Byblos, Nubia and the deserts to seek out exotic commodities and stones were normally sent out by the king and led by government officials. The building of the temples was likewise a government function, whilst, during the imperial era, the annexed territory of Kush and the Palestinian and Syrian protectorates were, for instance, directly exploited by the crown. In contrast, the development of the land in Egypt itself did not depend exclusively on the crown. Alongside the royal domain were the lands owned by the gods, who possessed fields, flocks, workshops, etc. Moreover, at least from the Eighteenth Dynasty on, warriors were given hereditary tenure of land. High officials received gifts of land that they managed themselves. We do not know how inheritable private fortunes were made, but it is obvious that there were some and that, apart from the official position that one could only hope to be able to hand on to one's children, there were 'household effects' that could be bequeathed freely. Smallholdings are known to have existed, notably in the New Kingdom, when the term 'fields of poor men' in fact designated the lands of small independent farmers who were quite distinct from tenants working the fields of the king or the gods. Relatively few in number, the foreigners deported to Egypt in the era of the great conquests were specialists (Palestinian viticulturists, Libyan drovers) or military settlers; the slaves acquired by private individuals were often only household servants and, although there is evidence that it existed, slave labour is believed to have provided only a limited amount of manpower for agriculture.

In the market towns, royal domains and temples, specialization was carried to a high degree. Guilds, sometimes with an elaborate hierarchy, of bakers, potters, flower-arrangers, founders, sculptors, draughtsmen, goldsmiths, water-carriers, watchmen of all kinds, dog-keepers, shepherds, goat-herds, goose-herds, etc. worked for the king or the temples, skills being handed down from father to son.

The civil service

The organization and distribution of production, the management of public order and the supervision of all activities were the responsibility of civil servants under the authority of either the prince – the Pharaoh or, in periods of schism, the local chiefs – or the temples. These officials were recruited from the scribes, the knowledge of writing being the gateway to all learning and all higher technical skills. Those scribes, trustees of both the religious and lay cultures, reigned over all professional activities. They might be engineers, agronomists, accountants, ritualists or even army officers and many combined several capacities. The greatest of them lived in fine style in this world and expected to do the same in the one to come, and their wealth, not to speak of their influence, gave them powers of patronage.

Pharaonic history seems to have been acted out to the rhythm of the struggle between high officialdom, which tended to set itself up as a hereditary and autonomous power, and the monarchy, clinging to the right to control appointments. Thus the Old Kingdom disappeared when, in the southern provinces, the dynasties of hereditary 'great chiefs' or prefects became strong. In the Second Intermediate Period, high office became a personal property that could be bought and sold. The end of the New Kingdom came when the Theban priesthood and the southern military command were joined and became the apanage of a dynasty of high priests of Amon.

Political organization

The avowed ideal of Egyptian society was thus a strong monarchy, regarded as the sole means of giving the country the driving force necessary for its well-being. The sovereign was the embodiment of the public service: the term 'Pharaoh' comes from *per-ao*, which the Old Kingdom designate the 'Great House' of the prince, including his residence and his ministers, and which in the New Kingdom finally came to designate the person of the king. He was of a different nature from the rest of mankind: the legends about his predestination, the four canonic names and the epithets that he added to his personal name, the protocol surrounding him, the pomp and circumstance accompanying his appearances and decisions, his endlessly repeated likenesses, cartouches and title lists in the sacred buildings, his jubilee celebrations, the style of his tomb (Memphis pyramid, Theban rock-cut tomb) all stress this difference.

There is some mystery about royal succession. It was certainly customary for son to succeed father on the throne, in conformity with the mythical model of Osiris and Horus, and in the New Kingdom designation or recognition of the new king by the oracle of Amon was the guarantee of the new monarch's legitimacy. Thus direct 'divine right' outweighed dynastic legitimacy.

Four women became Pharaohs. Strangely enough, the first two (Nitokris and Sebeknefru) mark the end of a dynasty and the other two (Hatshepsut and Tauosre) were treated as usurpers by posterity. Honours were showered on the mothers, wives and daughters of the king. Some princesses of the Middle Kingdom, and more especially later, Teye, first wife of Amenhotep III, and Nefertari, first wife of Ramses II, received exceptional honours. Ahhotep, under Amasis, or Ahmosis–Nefertari, under Amenhotep I, seem to have wielded a determining influence in political and religious matters. The attribution of the ritual function of 'divine wife of Amon' to princesses or queens shows the key role of femininity and the female in the worship of the cosmic god.

A study of the title lists of high and low officials and the few legislative and administrative texts that have come down to us gives a more or less accurate notion of government organization: the government of the nomes, the hierarchy of the priesthood and distribution of the religious obligations on the priests, royal or priestly administration of the arable land, flocks, mines, granaries, river transport, justice, and so on.

At the top of the system sat the *tjaty* or 'vizier', to use a traditional Egyptological term. This prime minister, responsible for public order, was before all else the supreme legal authority in the land after Pharaoh and the Minister of Justice. None the less, the *tjaty* (of whom there were two in the New Kingdom) was not the king's sole counsellor, or even necessarily the principal one. Many dignitaries boasted of having been consulted by their sovereign behind closed doors or having been selected for special missions and, in the imperial era, the governor of Nubia, an honorary 'royal son', was answerable directly to Pharaoh and was almost sovereign in his own territory. Some personalities, Amenhotep, the scribe of recruits and the son of Hapi, an architect gradually elevated to the rank of the gods for his wisdom, or Khamois, the high priest of Ptah and one of Ramses II's many sons, were no doubt as influential as the viziers of their time.

Military organization

The king was responsible for national security. In theory, all credit for victories and conquests was his. Ramses II made great propaganda capital, in words and images, from having stood alone with his bodyguard at Kadesh, reaffirming the primacy of the king, sole saviour by divine grace, over an army from which his dynasty had in fact emerged. As early as the time of the pyramids, the country had had a specialized high command, simultaneously military and naval, commanding troops already accustomed to manoeuvring and parading in disciplined ranks. In the third millennium, however, the peoples of the neighbouring countries posed no very great threat. Raiding parties easily thinned out the population of Nubia to Egypt's

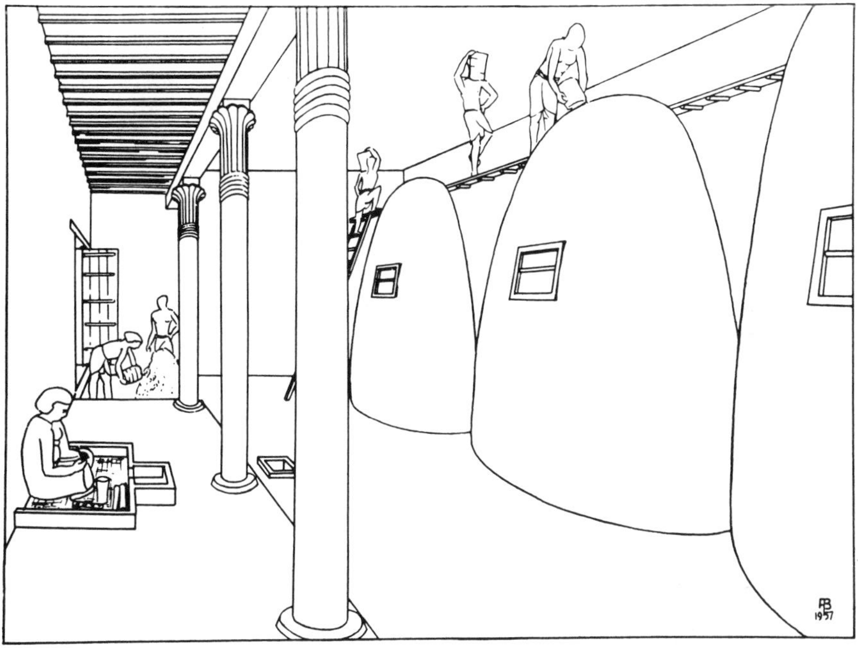

3.3 *Filling the granaries (A. Badawy,* A History of Egyptian architecture, *Los Angeles, 1966)*

advantage; triumphal campaigns for which the rural population was levied *en masse* were enough to intimidate and plunder the sedentary peoples on the Libyan and Asian borders, while 'desert scouts' supervised the movements of the hungry Bedouins. What we know best about the Memphis troops relates to their participation in operations of economic interest and in the great building operations. The 'teams of elite young recruits' serving as the king's bodyguard supervised the transport of stone for pyramids and some major expeditions to the Sinai mines or the eastern quarries. A specialized paramilitary corps, the *sementi*, prospected and exploited the gold mines of Nubia and the desert. With the First Intermediate Period, the division of the kingdom into rival principalities modified military organization: the prince's personal retinue and the contingents from the nomes were joined by auxiliary troops.

The New Kingdom, a time of great international conflicts, was to see an unprecedented expansion of the professional army, divided into two arms of service, chariots and infantry, and subdivided into large army corps. The soldiers received small grants of land, and under the Ramses many captives – Nubians, Syrians, Libyans, the pirate Sea Peoples – were enlisted and also given such grants. In spite of their relatively rapid assimilation the Libyans set themselves up as an autonomous force and ended by making their chieftain Pharaoh. In the new class of empires the Saite kings were to rely on new military settlers recruited from the Ionians, Carians, Phoenicians and Judaeans, whilst in the final wars against the Persian empire the last native Pharaohs, like their opponents, hired Greek mercenaries recruited by cosmopolitan adventures.

Religious and moral conceptions

Myths

Certainly one of the great achievements of Pharaonic civilization, and perhaps one of its weaknesses, was its splendid image of the world and the forces ruling it, a coherent image manifesting itself in its myths, rituals, art, language and works of wisdom. To apprehend the forces of nature and natural phenomena, mythology accepted all the images and legends handed down by tradition. There may be several 'sole' deities; the sky is a liquid ceiling, the belly of a cow, the body of woman, a sow, etc. Thus there existed several conceptions of the origins of the universe, which were combined in various ways into the great syntheses elaborated on a local basis through the ages, each of which could be re-enacted in all its purity through performance of a given ritual act, on which it conferred a cosmic dimension.

A divine dynasty ruled this world. In those days Seth killed Osiris; revived by the attentions of Isis and Anubis, the embalmer, Osiris became the paragon of all dead kings and, by extension, of all the dead. He is also the image of the sun that dies every evening, and the lymph that flowed from his body is taken to be the water that rises each year.

Corresponding to the divine order there are not only the structure and rhythms of the physical world, but a moral order – Ma'at – the norm of truth and justice which declares itself when Ra triumphs over his enemy and which, for the happiness of mankind, should reign in the functioning of institutions and in individual behaviour. 'Ra lives by Ma'at.' Thoth, the god of scholars, Ra's accountant, the judge of the gods, is 'happy by Ma'at'.

The gods

The doctrines and images we have just mentioned are accepted in all temples. The hymns singing the cosmic attributes and the wondrous providence of the god-creator take up the same themes, whether it be a primordial goddess like Neith, or an earth-god like Ptah. The great myths such as the passion of Osiris – as well as the basic ritual practices – are common to all centres of population; but different gods, each with his own name, traditional image, animal manifestation and associated gods, are the 'masters' of the various towns: Khnum at Elephantine, Isna and elsewhere, Min at Coptos and Akhmim, Mont at Hermonthis, Amon at Thebes, Sebek at Fayyūm and elsewhere, Ptah-Sẹker at Memphis, Ra-Harakhte-Atum at Heliopolis, Neith at Sais, Bast at Bubastis, Uadjit at Buto, Nekhbet at El Kah; and there were many local gods called by the name of Horus, many goddesses who are fearsome Sekhmets or kindly Hathors. It seems that this religion tended, through the identification of certain gods with others, to reduce that plurality to a few types: a supreme deity, generally a sun-god and often explicitly identified with Ra (Amon-Ra, Haroeris-Ra, etc.); a consort goddess (Mut = Bast = Sekhmet = Hathor, etc.); the warrior god-son of the Horus-Anhur type; a dead god of the Osiris type (Seker, Seph, etc.). The maze of theoretical problems presented by a multiform pantheon gave rise to much theological and even philosophical speculation. The attitude of the celebrated Akhenaton, who would recognize only the visible disc of the sun as the sole true god, still lay in the main stream of Egyptian thought, but was heretical in the manner in which it upset tradition, which, allowing for the mysterious, accepted and reconciled all forms of piety and thought.

The temple

Each god created his town, each looked after his own domain and, beyond that domain, all Egypt. The king concerned himself with all the gods simultaneously. To achieve this, sacred science employed the magic of word and gesture, of writing and images and of architectural forms, all processes also used to ensure the after-life of the dead. The ceremonies conducted by the initiate priests accompanied the ritual acts with verbal formulas reinforcing their power of compulsion by means of spells recalling mythical precedents. The depiction of these rites and the writing of these texts on the walls of the temples perpetuated their action. The architect made the temple a scale model of the universe, thus giving it permanence: the pylon is the mountain of the rising sun, the dark sanctuary is the place where the sun sleeps, the columns represent the primordial swamp out of which creation arose and the base of its walls are the soil of Egypt. A high brick perimeter wall isolates it and its gardens and service buildings from the impurities that might pollute the divine; the officiating priests and those privileged persons admitted to the temenos are required to perform ritual purifications and observe prohibitions relating to food, clothing and sexual activity. In order to show that it is actually Pharaoh performing the ritual, scenes carved into the walls depict him carrying out the various rites and presenting in long processions the nomes of Egypt, the phases of the flood and the minor gods that preside over the various economic activities of life. Throughout the day the idol, in other words the shape through which one may communicate with the god, is purified, censed, clothed, fed and invoked at length in hymns which exhort the god to awake, reaffirm his divine power and entreat his benevolent activity. During the great festivals, the god emerges in procession to recharge himself with divine energy from the rays of the sun, to visit the tombs of dead kings and past gods, and to re-enact the mythical events through which the world took shape.

Law

Religion and ethics in Ancient Egypt stress the maintenance of strict discipline, which benefits the whole community of subjects and the exclusive activity of the royal person in government ritual. It is thus all the more striking that Pharaonic law remained resolutely individualistic. In relation to royal decisions and to legal procedure and penalties, men and women of all classes seem to have been equals before the law. The family was limited to father, mother and their young children, and women enjoyed equal rights of property ownership and judicial relief. In general, responsibility was strictly personal. The extended family had no legal substance and the status of a man was not defined in relation to his lineage. In the domain of law, Pharaonic Egypt was distinctly different from traditional Africa and curiously anticipates the modern societies of Europe.

Funerary beliefs and practices

The same individualism reigned in regard to beliefs and practices concerning life after death. Each, according to his means, provided for his own after-life, that of his spouse and that of his children, in the event of their premature death. The son should participate in his father's funeral rites and, if the need should arise, ensure his burial. The human (or divine) being includes, in addition to the mortal flesh, several ingredients – the *Ka*, the *Ba*, and other lesser-known entities – whose nature remains difficult to define and whose interrelationships are obscure. Funerary practices are intended to ensure the survival of these 'souls', but a well-known feature of Egyptian religion is the linking of that survival to the preservation of the body itself by means of mummification, and the making of elaborate arrangements to enable the dead to enjoy an after-life at least as active and happy as life in this world. An Ancient Egyptian tomb was composed of a superstructure open to the surviving relatives and a vault where the deceased lay, accompanied by magical or domestic objects. Persons of wealth paid a regular stipend under contract to processional priests, who from father to son would be responsible for bringing offerings of food; and, as a final precaution, the compelling power of the spoken and written word and the magic of carved and painted images were employed. In the chapel – mastaba or hypogeum – the effective rituals of internment and offering are made eternal; other scenes recreate the work and pleasures of an ideal world; statues and statuettes create a multitude of substitute bodies. On the planks of the coffin, on the stones of the vault, on a 'Book of the Dead' given into the mummy's keeping, are copied the formulae recited at the time of burial and spells enabling the deceased to enjoy all his faculties, escape the dangers of the Other World and fulfil his divine destiny.

4 Egypt's relations with the rest of Africa

It is now commonly acknowledged that archaeological research has revealed no decisive evidence of contact between Egypt and Africa south of Meroe. A few years ago there was talk of the discovery of Egyptian objects far away in the heart of the continent. A statuette of Osiris, dating from the seventh century before the Christian era, was found in Zaïre on the banks of the River Lualaba, near the confluence of the Kalmengongo; a statue inscribed with the cartouche of Thutmose III (−1490 to −1468) was found south of the Zambezi. However, a critical study of the circumstances in which these objects were discovered makes it impossible at the present time to conclude that they indicate the existence of relations in the seventh or fifteenth centuries before the Christian era between Egypt and the regions mentioned above. A. Arkell reached the conclusion, on the strength of not very convincing evidence, that there were contacts between Byzantine Egypt and modern Ghana.

However, this by no means signifies that we should conclude on the basis of *a silentio* reasoning that no links existed in ancient times between Egypt and the rest of the African continent.

For instance, the influence, in certain respects, of Egyptian civilization on other African civilizations may be regarded by some as established. Eva Meyerowitz takes the fact that the Akan have adopted the vulture as the symbol of self-creation to be a proof of Egyptian influence. She also stresses the links between the god Ptah and the Akan god Odomankoma, both bisexual, who, after creating themselves, created the world with their own hands. Although an interesting association, this is not conclusive evidence that contacts existed between Ancient Egypt on the one hand and the ancient Akan or the region of the Bight of Benin on the other.

In the same way the serpent cult, arising from studies in all African civilizations by many distinguished scholars, was considered from early times likely to be derived from an Egyptian origin. But this view discounts the fact that ancient cultures observed their environment very closely and were perfectly capable of drawing their cults from their own observation.

Western neighbours: Saharans and Libyans

It is generally agreed that in the pre-dynastic period frequent human exchanges with the Sahara declined. Very little is known about these exchanges and it is sometimes claimed they did not exist. In the dynastic period it is certain that Egypt exerted an influence on the Sahara, although again very little is known about it.

In fact, for the Egyptians, according to the latest research, the Saharans during the dynastic period were mainly the Libyans who gradually concentrated in the north of one of the most vast and inhospitable deserts in the world. The situation was different in the Neolithic period when the rapid spread of the desert, which increased during the dynastic period, forced the Libyans, shepherds and hunters, back to the periphery of their former habitat, or led them, starving, to knock at the door of the Nilotic paradise which had to be defended against them. Their pressure continued unremittingly, but was seldom crowned with success, except perhaps in the western part of the Delta where the Saharan population is undoubtedly ancient and homogeneous. In the great oases encircled by their desert – Kh̲ariya, Dak̲h̲ila, Farafira and Sīwa – the Egyptian nobility took to hunting.

These oases had to be crossed in order to go southwards towards Chad or northwards towards the Fezzān and the Niger. However, we have today no proof that these routes were used regularly during the dynastic period.

Research on these routes, apart from their inherent interest, should certainly be undertaken. Archaeology and toponymy should make it possible to find out whether or not the Egyptians used these major African traffic routes to go to Tibesti, Dārfūr, Baḥr al G̲h̲azāl and Chad, or to the Fezzān and G̲h̲adamēs.

At all events, at least from the Nineteenth Dynasty onwards, the Libyans formed a reserve of manpower and soldiers for Egypt. Libyan captives, recognizable by the feathers they wore as a head-dress, had a good reputation as soldiers, particularly as charioteers. They were enrolled in the army where their proportion grew with the passing of centuries. As cattle breeders they supplied livestock for Egyptian consumption, either as tribute or seized from them as booty during raids. Thus they played an economic role comparable to that of the Nubians.

In the thirteenth and twelfth centuries before the Christian era, the Libyans were driven by necessity to try to penetrate into Egypt. Seti I and Ramses II erected a network of fortifications against them and captured the boldest invaders. After two vain attempts to return to the western part of the Delta whence they had been chased, the Libyans obtained from Ramses III, in the twelfth century before the Christian era, permission to settle there. In exchange, they played a greater part in the military defence of Egypt. In the tenth century, and for nearly two centuries thereafter, Libyans ruled Egypt under the Twenty-second and Twenty-third Dynasties. This new state of affairs aroused strong reactions in Upper Egypt where attempts were made to oust them with the support of the Kingdom of Napata.

When considering the relations between Egypt and other nations, whether African or not, the still almost unknown part played by the Delta should never be forgotten.

Southern neighbours

As an African nation, the Egyptians may have been tempted to penetrate a long way

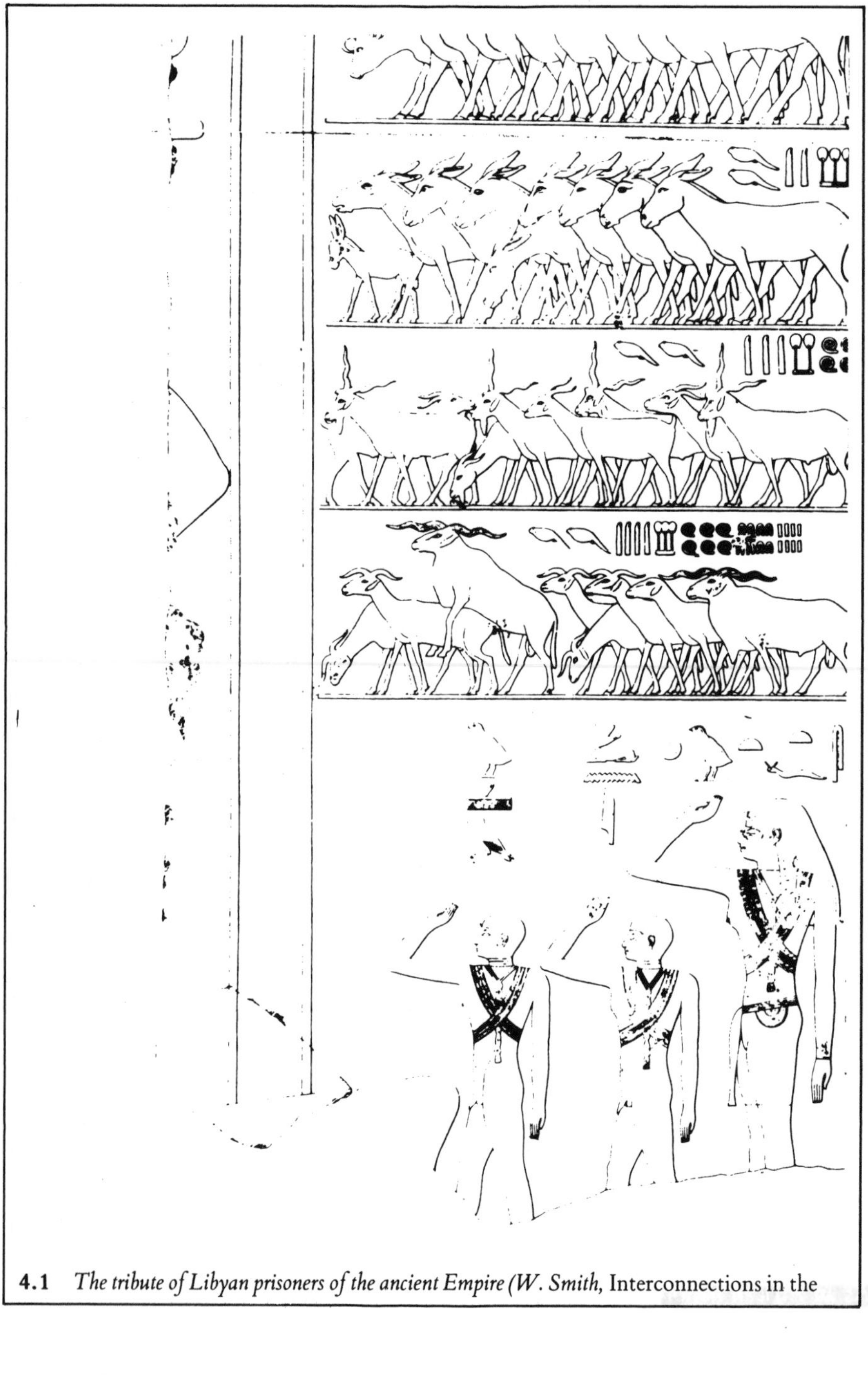

4.1 *The tribute of Libyan prisoners of the ancient Empire (W. Smith,* Interconnections in the

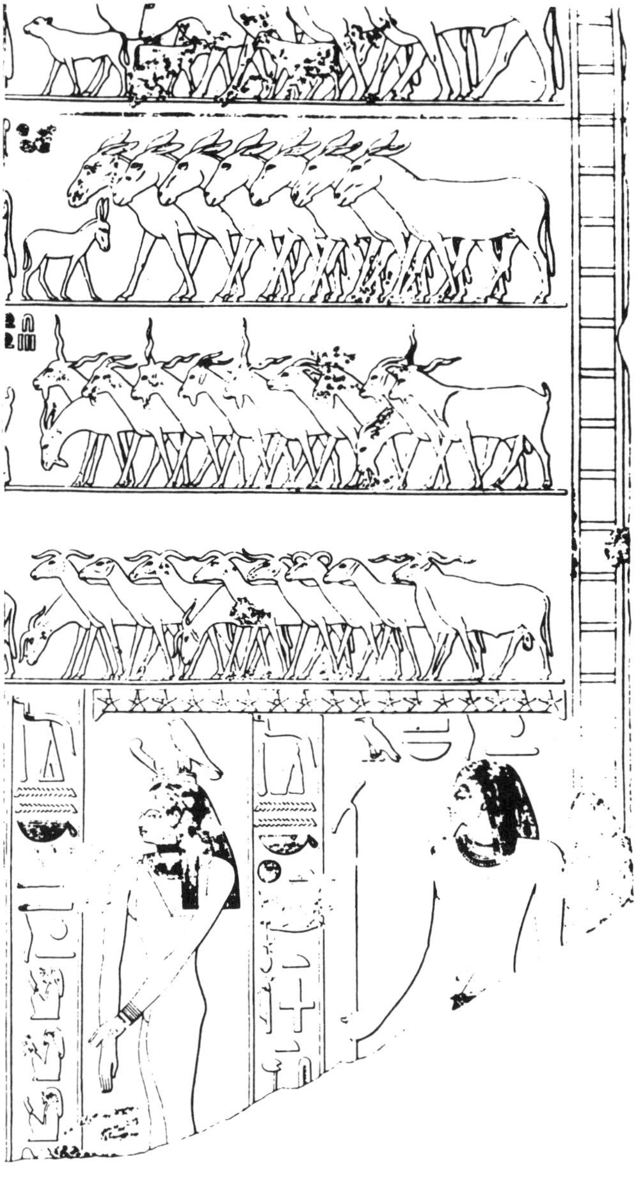

Ancient Near East, *1965. Photo, Yale University Press)*

inland along the Nile, at least as far as the Fourth Cataract. They may also have been attracted to Chad, passing through the ancient valleys which lead to the left bank of the Nile, and to Ethiopia with its wealth of ivory. Southwards a major obstacle would probably have been extensive marshlands which the Egyptians would have found difficult to reach or cross, which throughout antiquity protected the secrets of the high Nile valleys. Although we can today follow the history of Egypt's northern relations and of the portages between the Red Sea and the Nile fairly easily, archaeological data concerning the Ancient Egyptians' landward relations with the distant south are sadly lacking.

Already in the First Dynasty forts protected the south of Egypt against its southern neighbours. More and more, throughout their long common history, political and cultural differences and conflicting interests separated the territories north of the First Cataract from those that lie south of the Fourth Cataract. Nevertheless, relations, which were complex and diverse, were never completely broken off between the Egyptians and their southern neighbours, whom they called the Nehesi.

At all events, Lower Nubia interested the Egyptians on account of the gold it produced, and the more southerly Nilotic regions because of the routes leading to the African interior by the White Nile, the Saharan valleys or Dārfūr. Throughout the history of Egypt, access to the south was a predominant concern. This probably also explains the importance attributed to the control of the western oases, another access route parallel to the Nile.

From the beginning of the Old Kingdom, the Sudan, like Libya, represented for the Egyptians a source of manpower, livestock and minerals. The Nubians, famous for their archery, held a prominent place in the Egyptian army.

The Egyptians began to organize their links with the Sudan at the end of the Fifth Dynasty. During the same period, a new political and economic post, known as the Governorship of the South, was established. The holder was responsible for guarding the southern gate of Egypt, for organizing commercial exchanges and facilitating the circulation of trading expeditions. Unas, a Governor of the South under the Sixth Dynasty, was in command of recruits from different parts of Nubia: Nehesi (Nubians) from the land of Irhtet, Madja, Yam, Wawat and Kau.

At the end of the Old Kingdom trade relations between Egypt and the Sudan were interrupted. However, the Prince of Edfu relates on the wall of his tomb at Mealla that grain was sent to Wawat to prevent famine. This is evidence that relations between Egypt and Nubia continued at that time. Furthermore, Nubian soldiers played an important part in the battles in Middle Egypt during the First Intermediate Period. There exist painted wooden models of a company of Nubian archers, forty strong, which show the importance accorded by the Egyptians to the Sudanese soldier.

At the beginning of the Middle Kingdom the kings of Egypt, threatened by Asiatic Bedouins, appear to have asked the inhabitants of the Sudan for help. This tends to prove that relations between Egypt and the Sudan, interrupted during the First Intermediate Period, had been resumed. In all likelihood, some Egyptians crossed into the Sudan. From the stelae found at Buhen, we know that several Egyptian families lived in Nubia for a long time during the Middle Kingdom. They had Egyptian names and worshipped the local gods. The kings of that period built fourteen forts in Nubia to safeguard their frontiers and trading expeditions.

When the Hyksos seized the northern and middle parts of Egypt, Kush increased its independence and power. The Kingdom of Kush was a potential danger to the Pharaohs.

An Egyptian text reveals that during the war to overthrow the Hyksos, Kamose, the last Pharaoh of the Seventeenth Dynasty, was informed of the capture of a messenger from the Hyksos king inviting the King of Kush to be his ally against the Egyptians. With the Eighteenth Dynasty, pressure on the Sudan once again became very strong and relations were expanded on an unprecedented scale. Simultaneously the Egyptianization of the regions between the Second and the Fourth Cataracts gathered momentum. In the reign of Thutmose III, the shape of the tombs in this region changed. Egyptian-shaped tombs were built, and small pyramids like those found at Deir al-Medina were constructed. Hence the similarity of the cities of Buhen and Aniba to Egyptian cities. Likewise ushabtis and scarabs were found in tombs in the Sudan. The names and drawings on the princes' tombs were inscribed in a typically Egyptian way. The tomb of Heka-Nefer, prince of Aniba during the reign of Tutankhamun, is like the rock tombs in Egypt.

Nubia and Egypt had never been so close before. In −1400 the temple of Soleb was built. The military, and sometimes the administrative, part played by Sudanese was greater than ever before and reached its culmination when the Ethiopian dynasty dominated Egypt. Nevertheless, although Egyptianized, the inhabitants of the high valleys did not become Egyptian. A distinct culture continued to express itself, albeit in Egyptian form, even at the time of the Twenty-fifth Dynasty.

The latter restored to Egypt an African aspect recorded in the Bible, first when the Lord protects the Hebrews from the assault of the Assyrians, by inspiring their king in a dream with the fear of an attempt against him by Tir-hakah, the King of Ethiopia, and, second, when the Hebrew King Hezekiah sought an alliance with the Pharaoh and his people.

The conquest of Thebes by the Assyrians coincided with the rise in the south of the Meroitic empire. The defence of this region against the assault from the north became all the more necessary in that the Egyptian armies henceforth included large contingents of Hebrew, Phoenician and Greek mercenaries. In the absence of the necessary research, the relations, certainly difficult, between the new Nilotic empire and Egypt are little known.

Punt

As in the case of other problems of African history, a great deal of ink, not always of excellent quality, has flowed in order to locate the fabled land of Punt, with which the Egyptians had relations, at least during the New Empire, and which the images at Deir al-Bahri reveal. Attempts were made to place this country and, today, agreement has almost been reached on the location of Punt in the Horn of Africa, although much hesitation as to its exact boundaries still exists. One tempting theory is that it was

4.2 *Nubian tribute of Rekh-mi-Re (Metropolitan Museum of Art, New York)*

situated on that part of the African coast which stretches from the Poitialeh River in northern Somalia to Cape Guardafui. It is a mountain area with terraced plantations reminiscent of those depicted at Deir al-Bahri. Many trees, including the incense-producing balsam, grow on those terraces.

Agreement seems to have been virtually reached to the effect that Egyptian vessels sailed to Punt to seek precious incense and many other products. It seems also that Cape Guardafui was the southernmost point for ships for Punt and that the latter's southern boundaries were near this cape. As for its northern boundaries, they may be said to have changed from century to century.

In the light of other indications we can identify the two shores of the land of the god with the two banks of the strait of Bab al-Mandeb. Further proof is supplied by the fact that the incense-bearing tree grew equally well at Arabia Felix and in Africa.

We can trace successive stages in the relations between Egypt and Punt. The first preceded the reign of Queen Hatshepsut. At that time, the Egyptians had very little information about Punt. They obtained incense from middlemen who spread legends about the country in order to raise the price of incense. The few Egyptians known to have completed the voyage to Punt were bold men. The second period began with Queen Hatshepsut. A fleet of five ships, according to the artist who decorated the temple at Deir al-Bahri, was sent to bring back incense-bearing trees.

In a room of the same temple at Deir al-Bahri, there is a picture of Hatshepsut's divine birth in which her mother, Ahmose, is awakened by the scent of incense from the land of Punt. Here, the association of the name of Punt with her divine origin is evidence of the friendship between the Queen of Egypt and Punt, whose inhabitants worshipped Amon.

The pictures of this expedition have taught us about life in the land of Punt, its plants, animals and inhabitants, and its cone-shaped huts, built on piles amidst palm, ebony and balsam trees.

To judge by the pictures of Punt in the temples, there is nothing new to report after Queen Hatshepsut's reign. Then the texts mention the Puntite's arrival in Egypt. The Puntite chieftains were required to bring gifts to the Pharaoh, who ordered one of his subordinates to receive them and their gifts. There is some evidence of trading in Red Sea ports between Puntites and Egyptians and of the transporting of goods from Punt by land between the Red Sea and the Nile (Tomb of Amon-Mose at Thebes and Tomb No. 143).

Towards the end of the reign of Ramses IV, relations with Punt came to an end. But the memory of Punt remained in the minds of the Egyptians.

Perhaps we should include among the testimonies to these relations in ancient times the fact that a headrest in modern Somali is called a *barchi* or *barki*, which is similar to its name in Ancient Egyptian. Moreover, the Somalis call their New Year the Feast of Pharaoh.

The rest of Africa

Endeavours by a people or its leaders to establish relations with other countries arise from diverse motives which can, in the last resort, generally be reduced to simple terms. Needs are a powerful spur to exploration and efforts to establish relations.

Egypt's relations with Africa are too often thought of as a one-way flow, as the spreading of her culture abroad. This is to overlook the fact that she depended materially on the sale of certain African products. Consequently, influences may well have been reciprocal. In this field, everything has still to be done and investigation is very arduous.

A naval exploration of the African coasts at the time of Pharaoh Necho II, −610 to −595, has attracted the attention of research workers, but not all agree on the historical accuracy of the facts reported a century later by Herodotus. Necho II, who comes very late in the line of Pharaohs, undertook many other operations.

Should we also attribute to curiosity and a taste for the exotic the expedition which Harkuf undertook on behalf of Pepi II and which gave rise to conclusions both contradictory and difficult to accept? Harkuf, as mentioned below, brought back a dwarf dancer for Pepi II from the Land of Yam. The conclusion is sometimes drawn, on the assumption that the dwarf was a pygmy, that this example, unique of its kind, proves the existence of relations between Egypt, the Upper Nile and Chad. Harkuf's expedition belongs to history, whereas many others are more or less in the realm of legend or fiction. In the first place very little is known about the ancient habitat of the pygmies and it is dangerous to assume that they were found in large numbers in the upper regions of the Nile basins. Secondly, there is no proof that the dwarf concerned was a pygmy, and, lastly, it is still not known for certain where the Land of Yam was situated.

The observation often made, that African fauna is present in Egyptian iconography, is by no means conclusive evidence, in the present state of knowledge, of the existence of Egyptian relations with the heart of Africa. The ape, the sacred animal of Toth, and the panther skins, required for the priestly vestments for the rites of the cult of Osiris performed by Horus and also for the garb of the Pharaohs, may have come from bordering countries or from occasional chance exchanges between merchants. Before we can form a clear idea of the extent of the Egyptians' knowledge of Africa, a great deal of research must be done to investigate the chronology as well as the quantitative and qualitative significance of the many references to animals found in Egyptian texts and images.

Whether relations with Africa were impelled by need or by curiosity, the evidence assembled is very flimsy and its interpretation too difficult and too controversial for any conclusion to be reached in the present state of our knowledge. Yet there are many ways open for rewarding research.

The question has often arisen whether the column-based headrest invented by the Egyptians has spread with their civilization to other regions of Africa. Again, caution is advisable and the temptation to be diffuse must be avoided. Are this and other headrests exclusively African, originating from Egypt? Do they exist in other cultures far from Africa? Are they not rather of a functional nature and therefore likely to have been invented at different places far apart?

In another field, should it be concluded, as some research workers have perhaps been too quick to do, that any form of sacred royalty in Africa is of Egyptian origin, the result of a physical and historical relationship between Ancient Egypt and its

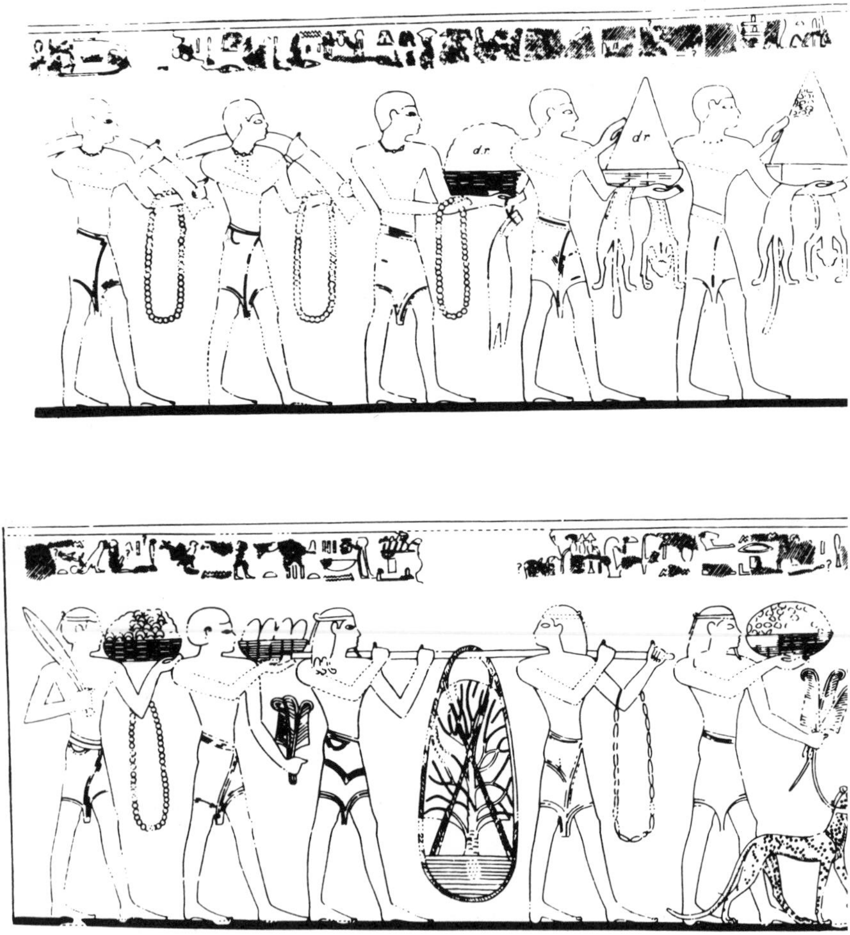

4.3 *The tribute of Punt (Metropolitan Museum of Art, New York)*

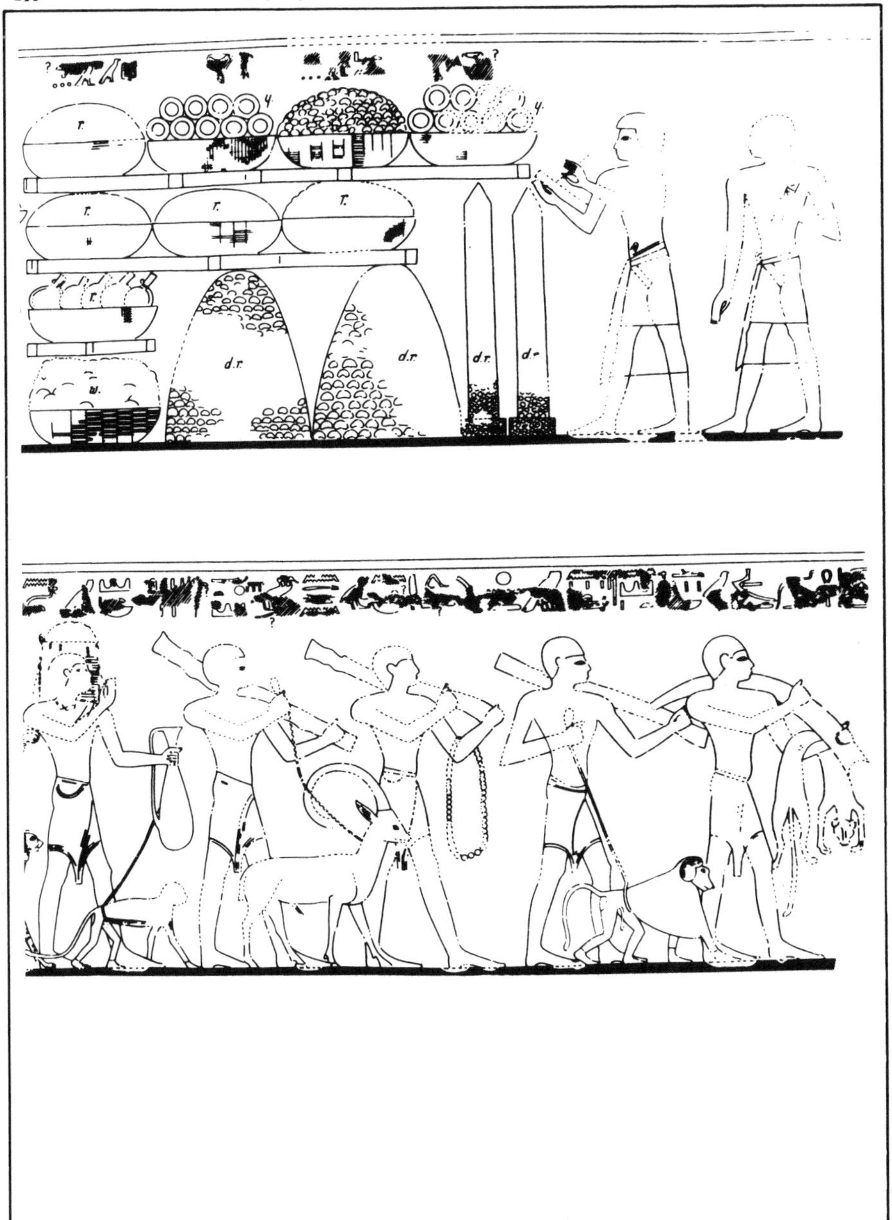
d.r.
d.r.
d.r.
d.r.

African creators? Should we not think of spontaneous developments more or less spaced out in time?

What were the routes taken by the cult of the ram, the sacred animal of Amon, which is honoured in Kush, in the Sahara, among the Yoruba and among the Fon? For the time being, all these resemblances and presences must be listed, without leaping to conclusions.

In many fields, it is possible to point to the similarity between Ancient Egyptian techniques, practices or beliefs and African ones of more or less recent origin. One of the most attractive examples at first sight is that of the doubles (known as *Kas* in Ancient Egypt) of the physical person to which the Egyptians and many present-day African societies attach importance. The after-life forms of these doubles among the Bantu, Ule or Akan, for instance, make it very tempting to associate them with Egyptian concepts in Pharaonic times.

A comparison has also been drawn between Egyptian inhumation rites and those described by al-Bakrī for the kings of Ghana in the eleventh century of the Christian era.

There would be no end to the list that could be made of practices of a similar nature accumulated for decades in studies of a more or less scientific nature. Linguistics also provides an enormous area for research, where probabilities at present outnumber certainties.

All this leads to the conclusion that Egyptian civilization very probably had an influence on more recent African civilizations, though to what extent is still little known. In trying to assess the latter, it would be wise also to consider how far influence was exercised in the opposite direction, that is to say, on Egypt. This is a fascinating inquiry which has only just been begun.

5

The legacy of Pharaonic Egypt

Pharaonic Egypt's valuable contributions to the world can be traced in many fields including history, economics, science, art and philosophy. Specialists in these, and many other fields, have long realized the importance of this legacy, even though it is often impossible to determine in what way it was passed on to neighbouring or subsequent cultures.

Indeed, that legacy, or at least the evidence we have of it, which is so important for the history of mankind, was transmitted in large part by classical antiquity (first by the Greeks, and later by the Romans) before passing to the Arabs. Now, the pre-Hellenes and Greeks did not come into contact with Egypt before −1600 or thereabouts and close ties were not established until the seventh century before the Christian era, with the spread of Greek adventurers, travellers and later settlers in the Mediterranean basin, particularly in Egypt. At the same time, the Greeks and their forerunners in the second and first millennia before the Christian era were in contact with the civilizations of Asia Minor and, through them, with the ancient Mesopotamian world of which they were the continuation. It is, accordingly, often very difficult to ascertain the exact cultural milieu, whether Asian or Egyptian, both so closely linked, in which this or that invention or technique first appeared.

In addition, the difficulty of establishing the chronology of the remote periods of antiquity makes attributions of the paternity of ideas very hazardous. Lastly, the possibility of convergences cannot be disregarded. To cite but one example: there is good reason to believe that writing was discovered at about the same time both in Egypt and Mesopotamia without there necessarily having been any influence of one civilization on the other.

For all that, the legacy bequeathed by Egypt to succeeding civilizations, and to the ancient civilizations of Africa in particular, is not to be underestimated.

Contribution of prehistoric Egypt

One of the earliest and most remarkable advances made by Egypt was in the field of economics. At the end of the Neolithic period, around −5000, the Ancient Egyptians gradually transformed the Nile Valley, enabling its inhabitants to progress from a food-gathering economy to a food-producing one, and this important transition in human development in the valley had great consequences, material as well as moral. For the growth of agriculture made it possible for the Ancient Egyptian to adopt a settled, integrated village life and this development affected his social and moral development not only in prehistoric times, but also during the dynastic periods.

One of the first results of this Neolithic revolution in the valley was that the Ancient Egyptian started to think of the natural forces around him. He saw these, especially the sun and the river, as gods, who were symbolized in many forms, especially in the animals and birds with which he was most familiar. In developing agriculture he also established the principle of co-operation within the community, for, without such co-operation among the people of the village, agricultural production would have been limited.

Pharaonic civilization was remarkable for the continuity of its development. Once a thing was acquired, it was passed on, with improvements, from the dawn of the history of Egypt to its close. This was how Neolithic techniques were transmitted and enriched in the pre-dynastic period (–3500 to –3000) and were subsequently preserved when the historical period was in full flower.

These changes in Neolithic times were characteristically reflected in the growth of town planning in Egypt. A striking example of this can be found in one of the oldest villages in the Nile valley: Merimda Beni Salama on the western edge of the Delta.

Historical times

In the Egyptian Pharaonic civilization of historical times two main currents can be discovered. The first is the material legacy. The second, also descended from the most distant past, is the more abstract cultural legacy. They are interrelated and together comprise the Egyptian cultural phenomenon. The material legacy includes crafts and science (geometry, astronomy, chemistry), applied mathematics, medicine, surgery and artistic productions. The cultural side covers religion, literature and philosophic theories.

Craft contribution

The Ancient Egyptians' contribution in the crafts can be traced in stone, metal, glass, ivory, bone and many other materials. They explored and exploited the various natural resources of the country and gradually refined the techniques required in making stone and copper tools such as axes, chisels, mallets and adzes designed with great skill for use in building as well as in industry for such purposes as drilling holes or fixing blocks. They also fashioned bows, arrows, daggers, shields and throwing-clubs.

For a long period, and even during historical times, the tools and arms inherited from the Neolithic period continued to be made of stone. The chalk cliffs bordering the Nile are rich in flints of large size and excellent quality which the Egyptians continued to use long after the discovery of the use of copper and bronze.

Very little use was made of iron for metal vases until the very end of the Pharaonic period, so Egyptian metal-working techniques are confined to the use of gold, silver, copper, and copper alloys such as bronze and brass. Traces of the mining and processing of copper ore by Egyptians have been found in Sinai as well as in Nubia.

As long ago as the early dynastic period (−3000), the Egyptians knew, and employed in making their copper tools, all the basic techniques of metal-working such as forging, hammering, casting, stamping, soldering and riveting techniques, which they mastered very rapidly. As well as tools, large Egyptian copper statues have been found which date from −2300. Texts of an earlier time, dating back to −2900, note the existence of statues of the same type, and scenes from mastabas of the very earliest period depict workshops where gold and electrum, which is a blend of gold and silver, are being fashioned into jewellery.

Egypt provides us with a wealth of information on the techniques used by craftsmen. In the workshops depicted in paintings or bas-reliefs on the tomb walls, both above and below ground, one sees, for example, carpenters and cabinet-makers at work making furniture and the tools they used, saws, drills, adzes, chisels and mallets, all faithfully represented and with infinite detail, as well as the manner in which they used them. As a result, we know that the Egyptian saw was a pull-saw and not a push-saw, like the modern saw.

As well as these pictorial representations, the Ancient Egyptians left in their tombs models of workshops with model craftsmen making various objects. These models are invaluable to the historian in interpreting the techniques and the manner in which they developed. Furthermore the large quantities of artisan objects which have been found attest to the variety of industries in Ancient Egypt. For example, in the making of jewellery they used gold, silver and precious and semi-precious stones such as felspar, lapis lazuli, turquoise, amethyst and cornelian, fashioning them with remarkable precision into crowns, necklaces and other items of adornment.

The cultivation of flax rapidly led to great ability in hand-spinning and linen-making. The latter was known from the start of the Neolithic period (*c.* −5000). The women spun the flax, doing so with great skill since they frequently handled two spindles simultaneously. Characteristic of Egyptian spinning was the length of the thread produced and this required a technique which placed the spindle some feet away from the raw fibre. To make the distance even greater, the women perched on high stools. Their looms were at first horizontal, and then, beginning in the Middle Empire, vertical, which enabled them to produce the very long fabrics required for the loose-fitting everyday clothing, as well as for the funerary ritual mummy wrapping and shrouds.

The wood, leather and metal industries were also perfected and the products of these industries have survived in good condition to the present day.

Other objects produced by Egyptian craftsmen included silver vases, wooden coffins, combs and decorated ivory handles. The Ancient Egyptians also had a special talent for weaving wild reeds into mats and the spun fibre of the palm-tree made possible the production of sturdy nets and ropes. Pottery manufacture, which started in prehistory in a rough form, developed into finer red, black-rimmed pottery, and then polished and incised pottery. These vessels were used for storing various materials, but some were for decorative purposes.

5.1 *Giza: Cheops' boat (the Solar boat). Source unknown*

Egypt contributed, if not the invention, at least the distribution of glass-making techniques to world civilization. While it is true that Mesopotamia and the civilizations of the Indus were likewise familiar at a very early time with glazing, the technique which is the basis of glass-making, there is no evidence to suggest that they spread it abroad. The most one can suppose, therefore, is that once again there was a phenomenon of convergence and that glass-making was discovered independently both in Asia and in the Nile Valley.

Glass was used for beads and also for vases of a great variety of shapes, from graceful stemmed chalices to vases in the form of fishes. They were usually polychromatic and always opaque. Transparent glass made its appearance under Tutankhamun (*c.* – 1300). Starting about – 700, Egyptian polychromatic glass vases, in the form called alabaster, spread throughout the Mediterranean area.

In the latter period, hieroglyphic signs, moulded in coloured glass, were set in wood or stone to make inscriptions. The techniques of the Pharaonic glass-makers were handed down to craftsmen of the Hellenistic period, who invented brown glass. Alexandria then became the main centre for the manufacture of glassware, exporting its products as far as China. The Meroitic empire later imported some glassware from Alexandria but, above all, adopted its manufacturing techniques and spread them to the upper Nile Valley.

One of the most important industries was that of the production of papyrus, which was invented by the Ancient Egyptians. No plant played a more significance role in Egypt than the papyrus reed. Its fibres were used for boat-making and for caulking, for the wicks of oil lamps, for mats, baskets, ropes and hawsers. The hawsers which served to moor the pontoon bridge that Xerxes tried to lay across the Hellespont were made in Egypt out of papyrus fibres. When tied together in bundles, papyrus stems served as pillars in early architecture until classical architects took them as a model for their simple or clustered columns, whose capitals were shaped like closed or open flowers. But, above all, papyrus fibre was used to make 'papyrus', from which the word 'paper' is derived.

Papyrus was made by placing crosswise successive layers of fine strips taken from the stem of the plant which, after pressing and drying, formed a large sheet.

Twenty sheets of papyrus joined together while they were still moist formed a scroll three to six metres in length. Several scrolls could be joined together and reach a length of 30 or 40 metres. It was this scroll that constituted the Egyptian book. Of all the writing materials employed in antiquity, papyrus was certainly the most practical. It was supple and light. Its sole drawback was its fragility.

The papyrus used in Egypt from the time of the First Dynasty (*c.* – 3000) until the end of the Pharaonic period was later adopted by the Greeks, the Romans, the Copts, the Byzantines, the Aramaeans and the Arabs. A large part of Greek and Latin literature has come down to us on papyrus. Papyrus scrolls were one of the principal exports of Egypt. Papyrus was, unquestionably, one of the major legacies bequeathed to civilization by Pharaonic Egypt.

All these industries depended on techniques and skills and led to the creation of a body of artisans, and to improved techniques. Museums and private collections throughout the world contain hundreds, even thousands, of archaeological examples of the various products of Ancient Egypt.

Not the least of their technical contributions to the world were their tradition and ability in stonemasonry. It was no easy task to transform huge blocks of granite, limestone, basalt and diorite from the raw material into the well-shaped, polished masonry required by various architectural designs.

Moreover, the search for stone to build their monuments, no less than prospecting for ores and efforts to discover fibres, semi-precious stones and coloured pigments, contributed to the spread of Egyptian techniques to Asia and Africa.

The Egyptians did not hesitate to fetch their stone from the open desert, sometimes going as far as 100 kilometres from the Nile. The quarry from which the diorite came for the famous statute of Chephren in the Cairo Museum lies in the Nubian desert some 65 kilometres to the north-west of Abu Simbel. Quarries were worked from the dawn of Egyptian history (*c.* –2800).

The only tools used by the Egyptian stoneworker were the wooden mallet and copper chisel for soft stones like limestone, and the pick, chisel and hard stone hammer for metamorphic rocks like granite, gneiss, diorite and basalt. When the quarry was located far from the Nile, an expedition was launched with sometimes as many as 1,400 men comprising officers and soldiers, porters and quarrymen, scribes and doctors. Such expeditions were equipped to remain for long periods out of Egypt and must have contributed to the spread of Egyptian civilization, especially in Africa.

The skills acquired by stoneworkers in the early dynastic period led the Egyptians, by the time of the Old Kingdom (*c.* –2400), to hew their final resting-places in solid rock. Much before this date, from –3000 to –2400, the building of tombs, planned as the dwelling-places of the dead, had already led them to build imposing superstructures which, in time, with the changes which occurred in architecture, led to the step pyramid and then to the pyramid proper.

The Egyptian expertise in woodworking is brilliantly manifested in their shipbuilding. The necessities of daily life in the Nile Valley, where the river is the only convenient thoroughfare, made expert boatmen of the Egyptians from the earliest times. Boats occupied a prominent position in their earliest works of art from prehistoric times on. Since in their belief an after-life was closely modelled on earthly life, it is not surprising that they placed models of boats in their tombs, or represented scenes of boat construction and river scenes on tomb walls. They would even sometimes bury actual boats near the tombs ready for use by the dead. This was the case at Heluan in a burial ground of the first two dynasties, and at Dahshur, near the pyramid of Sesostris III. But a more recent discovery is extraordinary. In 1952 two great pits, dug into the rock and covered with huge limestone slabs, were discovered along the southern side of the Great Pyramid. In the pits, partially disassembled, but complete with oars, cabins and rudders, were discovered the very boats used by Cheops. One of these boats has been removed from the pit and restored. The other one is still waiting to be taken out of its tomb.

Cheops' boat, now in a special museum, has been rebuilt. When found it consisted of 1,224 pieces of wood which had been partially disassembled and stacked in thirteen successive layers in the pit. The boat measures 43.4 metres long, 5.9 metres wide, and has a capacity of about 40 tons. The side planks are 13 and 14 centimetres thick. Its draught is difficult to calculate precisely, but was clearly very light in relation to the ship's mass. Although it does possess a rudimentary frame of timbers, Cheops' boat has no keel, and is flat-bottomed and narrow. The most remarkable fact is that it was built without any nails: the pieces of wood are held together solely by the use of tenon and mortise joints. The constituent elements, planks, timbers and cross-members, are tied to each other with ropes. The ship contains a large, spacious central cabin, as well as a covered shelter in the bow. There was no mast, and it was either propelled by oars or was towed, even though the sail had been in use in Egypt long before Cheops' reign. Amphibious military expeditions far from Egypt on the Red Sea and the Euphrates were made possible by this method of boat construction, assembling separate sections which were then tied to one another.

Scientific contributions

The Pharaonic contribution to science and applied mathematics has left a valuable legacy in the fields of physics, chemistry, zoology, geology, medicine, pharmacology, geometry and applied mathematics. In fact, the Ancient Egyptians gave to humanity a large store of experience in each of these fields, some of which were combined in order to execute a specific project.

Mummification

One outstanding example of the genius of the Ancient Egyptians is mummification. It shows their mastery of a number of sciences including physics, chemistry, medicine and surgery. Their ability in each branch was an accumulation of long experience. For example, they exploited their discovery of the chemical characteristic of natron, which was found in certain areas of Egypt, particularly in the Wādī el-Natrun, by using the chemical attributes of this substance in the practical fulfilment of the demands of their belief in the after-life. For the Ancient Egyptians believed in the continuity of life after death and emphasized this belief in a practical way by preserving the human body. The compounds of natron have been analysed in modern times as a mixture of sodium carbonate, sodium bicarbonate, salt and sodium sulphate. The Ancient Egyptian, therefore, was aware of the chemical functions of these substances. In the process of mummification he soaked the body in natron for seventy days. He drew the brain out through the nostrils and he also removed the intestines through an incision made in the side of the body. Such operations as these necessitated an accurate knowledge of anatomy, and the good state of preservation of the mummies illustrates this intimate knowledge.

Surgery

It was, undoubtedly, the knowledge they acquired from mummification that enabled the Egyptians to develop surgical techniques at a very early period in their history. We have quite a good knowledge of Egyptian surgery, in fact, thanks to the Smith Papyrus, a copy of an original which was composed under the Old Kingdom,

5.2 *Model of a weaver's workshop, twelfth dynasty, about –2000 (Metropolitan Museum of Art, New York)*

between −2600 and −2400. This papyrus is virtually a treatise on bone surgery and external pathology. Forty-eight cases are examined systematically. In each case, the author of the treatise begins his account under a general heading: 'Instructions concerning (such and such a case)', followed by a clinical description: 'If you observe (such symptoms)'. The descriptions are always precise and incisive. They are followed by the diagnosis. If the surgeon can treat the patient, the treatment to be administered is then described in detail.

Several of the treatments indicated in the Smith Papyrus are still used today. Examination of mummies has revealed traces of surgery, for example the jaw dating from the Old Kingdom which has two holes bored to drain an abscess, or the skull fractured by a blow from an axe or sword and successfully reset.

All this bears testimony to the skill of the surgeons of Ancient Egypt, a skill which it would be fair to assume was handed on in Africa as well as in Asia and to classical antiquity, by the doctors who were always attached to Egyptian expeditions to foreign lands. Moreover, it is known that foreign sovereigns like the Asian prince of Bakhtan, Bactria, or Cambyses himself brought in Egyptian doctors, that Hippocrates 'had access to the library of the Imhotep temple at Memphis' and that other Greek physicians later followed his example.

Medicine

Medical knowledge can be considered as one of the most important early scientific contributions of the Ancient Egyptians to the history of man. Documents show in detail the titles of Egyptian physicians and their different fields of specialization. In fact the civilization of the ancient Near East and the classical world recognized the ability and reputation of the Ancient Egyptians in medicine and pharmacology. One of the most significant personalities in the history of medicine is Imhotep, the vizier, architect and physician of King Zoser of the Third Dynasty. His fame survived throughout Egyptian ancient history to Greek times. Deified by the Egyptians under the name Imouthes, he was identified by the Greeks with Askelepios, the god of medicine. In fact, Egyptian influence on the Greek world in both medicine and pharmacology is easily recognizable in remedies and prescriptions. Some medical instruments used in surgical operations have been discovered during excavations.

Written evidence of Ancient Egyptian medicine comes in medical documents such as the Ebers Papyrus, the Berlin Papyrus, the Edwin Smith Surgical Papyrus and many others which illustrate the techniques of operations and detail the prescribed cures.

In contrast to the Edwin Smith Surgical Papyrus, which is highly scientific, the purely medical texts were based on magic. The Egyptians regarded sickness as the work of the gods or malevolent spirits, which provided justification for resorting to magic. This explains why some of the remedies prescribed on the Ebers Papyrus, for example, resemble a magical incantation rather than a medical prescription.

Despite this aspect, the Egyptian doctor examined his patient and determined the symptoms of his complaint. He than made his diagnosis and prescribed treatment. All the extant texts describe this sequence, from which it may be concluded that it was standard procedure. The examination was made in two stages, some days apart, if the case was unclear. Among the ailments identified and competently described and treated by Egyptian doctors were gastric disorders, stomach swelling, skin cancer, coryza, laryngitis, angina pectoris, diabetes, constipation, haemorrhoids, bronchitis, retention and incontinence of urine, bilharzia, opthalmia, etc.

The Egyptian doctor treated his patient by using suppositories, ointments, syrups, potions, oils, massages, enemas, poultices, and even inhalants, whose use the Egyptians taught to the Greeks. Their pharmacopoeia contained a large variety of medicinal herbs, the names of which, unfortunately, elude translation. Egyptian medical techniques and medicines enjoyed great prestige in antiquity, as we know from Herodotus. The names of nearly a hundred Ancient Egyptian physicians have been passed down to us through these texts. Among the specialists there were also veterinarians.

Mathematics (arithmetic, algebra and geometry)

Mathematics is an important field of science in which the Ancient Egyptians worked. The accurate measurements of their enormous architectural and sculptural monuments are worthy proof of their preoccupation with precision. They would never have been able to reach this pitch of perfection without a minimum of mathematical capacity.

Two important mathematical papyri have come down to us from the Middle Kingdom (– 2000 to – 1750), those of Moscow and Rhind. The Egyptian method of numeration, based on the decimal system, consisted of repeating the symbols for numbers (ones, tens, hundreds, thousands) as many times as necessary to obtain the desired figure. There was no zero. It is interesting to note that the Egyptian symbols for the fractions ½, ⅓, ¼, and so on originate in the myth of Horus and Seth, in which one of Horus' falcon eyes was torn out and cut into pieces by Seth. It is these pieces that symbolize certain fractions.

Egyptian mathematics may be considered under the three headings of arithmetic, algebra and geometry.

Egyptian administrative organization required a knowledge of arithmetic. It is not surprising that the scribes spent an enormous amount of time keeping records of the area of land under cultivation, the quantities of products available and their distribution, the size and quality of the staff, and so on.

All the problems posed and solved in Egyptian treatises on arithmetic have one trait in common: they are all material problems of the type that a scribe, isolated in some remote outpost, would have to solve daily, like the calculation of the number of bricks required to build an inclined plane. It was basically an empirical system, with little in it of an abstract nature.

It is not exactly clear whether one may properly speak of an Egyptian algebra, and specialists in the history of science hold different views on this matter. The question whether Egyptian algebra existed or not depends therefore on whether one accepts or rejects the possibility of doing algebra without abstract symbols.

The Greek writers Herodotus and Strabo concur in the view that geometry was invented by the Egyptians. The need to calculate the area of land eroded or added each year by the flooding of the Nile apparently led them to its discovery. As a matter of fact, Egyptian geometry, like mathematics, was empirical. In ancient treatises, the task was first and foremost to provide the scribe with a formula that would enable him to find rapidly the area of a field, the volume of grain in a silo or the number of bricks required for a building project. None the less, the Egyptians knew perfectly well how to calculate the area of a triangle or a circle, the volume of a cylinder, of a pyramid or a truncated pyramid, and probably that of a hemisphere. Their greatest success was the calculation of the area of a circle.

Knowledge of geometry proved of considerable practical use in land surveying, which played a significant role in Egypt. There are many tombs with paintings showing teams of surveyors busy checking that the boundary-stones of fields have not been shifted and then measuring with a knotted cord, the forerunner of our surveyor's chain, the area of the cultivated land. The surveyor's cord or *nouh* is mentioned in the earliest texts (*c.* –2800).

Astronomy

The documentation we possess on Egyptian astronomy is not at all comparable to the material available on mathematics, surgery and medicine. There is reason to believe, however, that treatises on astronomy did exist. Although the Carlsberg 9 Papyrus, which describes a method for determining the phases of the moon, was undoubtedly written during the Roman period, it derives from much earlier sources and is devoid of any Hellenistic influence; the same is true of the Carlsberg I Papyrus. Unfortunately the earlier sources are not extant and the Egyptian contribution to astronomy must therefore be deduced from practical applications made on the basis of observations. This contribution is, however, far from insignificant.

As we have seen in the Introduction, the Egyptian calendar year was divided into three seasons of four months, each having thirty days; to these 360 days, five were added at the end of the year. The 365-day calendar year, the most accurate known in antiquity, is at the origin of our own calendar year inasmuch as it served as the basis of the Julian reform (–47) and of the Gregorian reform of +1582. Side by side with this civil calendar, the Egyptians also used a religious, lunar calendar and were able to predict the moon's phases with adequate accuracy.

Ever since the Napoleonic expedition to Egypt, Europeans have been struck by the accuracy of the alignment of structures built at the time of the Pharaohs, particularly the Pyramids, the four façades of which face the four cardinal points. The Great Pyramids deviate from true north by less than one degree. Such accuracy could have been achieved only by astronomical observation. The Egyptians were perfectly capable of such accuracy because they possessed a corps of astronomers, working under the authority of the vizier, whose job it was to observe the night sky, to note the rising of the stars, especially of Sirius (Sothis), and, above all, to determine the passage of the hours of darkness. These, for the Egyptians, varied in length according to the seasons: night, which was supposed to contain twelve hours, always commenced at sunset and ended at sunrise. Tables have come down to us which indicate that each night hour was marked, month by month, at ten-day intervals, by the appearance of a constellation or a star of the first magnitude. The tables distinguished thirty-six such constellations or stars which constituted *decans*, each one of which inaugurated a ten-day period. Certain tombs have paintings representing the sky. The stars are represented in picture form, which has made it possible to identify some of the constellations recognized by the Egyptians. Ursa Major is called the Ox Leg; the stars surrounding Arcturus are represented by a crocodile and a hippopotamus coupled together; Cygnus is represented by a man with his arms extended; Orion by a person running with his head turned back; Cassiopeia by a figure with outstretched arms; and Draco, Pleiades, Scorpius and Aries by other figures.

To determine the daytime hours, which also varied according to the seasons, the Egyptians used a *gnomon*, a simple rod planted vertically on a graduated board with a plumb-line attached. This instrument served to measure the time spent on the irrigation of the fields, since the water had to be distributed impartially. As well as the *gnomon*, the Egyptians had water-clocks which were placed in their temples. These water-clocks were borrowed and perfected by the Greeks and are the clepsydras of antiquity.

Architecture

The Ancient Egyptians applied their mathematical knowledge to the extraction, transportation and positioning of the huge blocks of stone used in their architectural projects. They had a long tradition of using mud bricks and various kinds of stone from very early times. Their first use of heavy granite was during the beginning of the third millennium before the Christian era. It was used for the flooring of some tombs belonging to the First Dynasty at Abydos. In the Second Dynasty they used limestone in constructing the walls of tombs.

A new phase was started in the Third Dynasty. This was a vital development in the history of Egyptian architecture, for it was the construction of the first complete building in stone. This is the step pyramid at Sakkara (Saqqara), which forms a part of the huge funerary complex of King Zoser.

Egypt developed a wide variety of architectural forms, of which the pyramid is, undoubtedly, the most characteristic. The first pyramids were step pyramids and it was not until the Fourth Dynasty (*c.* – 2300) that they gradually became triangular in form. From that period, the architects gave up the use of the small stones of the Third Dynasty in favour of large blocks of limestone and granite.

Until the Roman conquest, civil architecture continued to use sun-dried brick, even in the building of royal palaces. The outbuildings of Ramses in Thebes and the great Nubian fortresses provide a very good idea of the versatility of this material. It could be used with the utmost refinement, as can be seen from the palace of Amenhotep IV at Tell-al-Amarna with its pavements and ceiling decorated with paintings. Another contribution in the field of architecture was the creation of the column. Columns were at first attached to the wall, but later became free-standing.

In developing this architectural skill the Ancient Egyptians were much influenced by the local environment. For example, in arriving at the idea of a column, they were inspired by their observation of wild plants such as reeds and papyrus. They cut the capitals of the columns into the shape of lotus flowers, papyrus and other plants, and this was another architectural innovation. The lotus, papyrus palm and fluted columns of Ancient Egypt were adopted in the architecture of other cultures.

It is likely that the Ancient Egyptians invented the vault during the Second Dynasty (*c.* –2900). To begin with it was built of bricks, but by the Sixth Dynasty the Egyptians were building stone vaults.

The great Giza Pyramid was one of the Seven Wonders of the Ancient World. A building of such great proportions stands proof of the architectural and administrative ability of the Ancient Egyptians. The construction of the ascending corridors, leading to the granite chamber of the king, and the existence of two openings or vents, on the northern and southern sides of the royal chamber, extending to the outside to provide ventilation, are good examples of their ingenuity.

The exact proportions, measurements and orientation of the chambers and corridors of the pyramids, to say nothing of the cutting and erection of giant obelisks in solid stone, indicate the possession of great technical skills from very early times.

The technical knowledge acquired by the Egyptians in construction and irrigation as the result of digging canals and building dykes or dams manifested itself in other fields allied to architecture. By –2550, they had sufficient skill to build a dam of hewn stone in a wadi near Cairo. Somewhat later, their engineers cut navigable channels in the rocks of the First Cataract at Aswan.

Garden design and town planning are other aspects of Egyptian architecture. The Egyptians had a great fondness for gardens. Even the poor managed to plant a tree or two in the narrow courtyards of their houses. When they were rich, their gardens rivalled their residences in size and luxury. The garden was arranged around the pool or pools, for there could be several of them. They served as fish ponds, as reservoirs for watering and as a source of cooling fresh air for the house near by. Frequently, the master of the house had a light wooden pavilion built near the pool where he could come for a breath of fresh air in the evening and receive friends for cold drinks.

These artificial pools were occasionally quite large. Snefru's palace lake was large enough for him to sail upon it, accompanied by young, lightly-clad girls plying the oars, and Amenhotep III had a vast pool built in his Theban palace. This very Egyptian taste for gardens and parks later passed to Rome.

There are earlier examples of town planning than those attributed to Greek genius. As early as –1895, under the reign of Sesostris II, the city of Lahun was built inside a rectangular wall. The city had both administrative and residential buildings. The workers' houses, nearly 250 of which have been excavated, were built in blocks along streets four metres wide which ran into a central thoroughfare eight metres wide. Each house occupied a ground area of 100 to 125 square metres and contained a dozen rooms on a single level. Located in another quarter of the city were the houses of the leading citizens – town houses which sometimes had as many as seventy rooms, or more modest homes which were, nevertheless, considerably larger than those of the workers. These houses were also built along rectilinear avenues running parallel to the city walls. The avenues had a drain running down the centre.

The large fortresses in Nubia were patterned on the same lines, and the same urban plan was adopted, under the New Kingdom, at Tell-al-Amarna, among other places, where the streets crossed at right angles, though the city itself did not have the geometrical severity of Lahun.

While Egypt unquestionably made a major contribution in the field of architecture, it is nevertheless more difficult to judge the impact it had on the world as a whole in this sphere. Architects in many cultures have used, and are still using, colonnades, pyramids and obelisks which are undeniably of Egyptian origin. It is difficult not to discern in the clustered columns of Sakkara (Saqqara) and the proto-Doric columns at Benī Ḥasan the remote ancestors of the columns of Greek, and later Roman, classical art. One fact, at least, seems established: the architectural traditions of the Pharaohs made their way into Africa first via Nubia, which transmitted forms such as pyramids and pylons, among others, as well as techniques such as building with small, well-shaped blocks of hewn stone.

Cultural contributions

This side of the Egyptian Pharaonic legacy is an abstract one. It includes the Egyptians' contributions in the fields of writing, literature, art and religion.

Literature

The Egyptians developed a hieroglyphic writing system in which many of the symbols came from their African environment. For this reason it can be assumed to be their original creation rather than borrowed (see Introduction).

The Ancient Egyptians at first expressed themselves in pictorial ideograms which were soon formalized into symbols reflecting phonetic sounds which, in their later abbreviated form, could be considered as a step towards an alphabetic script.

Cultural contacts with the Semitic script developed in Sinai, where there appeared distinctive forms of writing which borrowed forms possessing affinities with hieroglyphics, may have contributed to the invention of the true alphabet which was borrowed by the Greeks and had its influence on Europe. Apart from this, the Ancient Egyptians invented the tools of writing. Their discovery of papyrus, handed down to classical antiquity, thanks to its light weight, flexibility and the almost unlimited dimensions of papyrus 'scrolls', certainly played a role in the diffusion of thought and knowledge. There is an extensive literature dating from Pharaonic times covering every aspect of Egyptian life, from religious theories to literature, such as stories, plays, poetry, dialogues, etc. This literature can be considered as one of the most vital cultural legacies of Ancient Egypt.

Some of the most impressive examples of Egyptian literature are those written during the First Intermediate Period and during the early Middle Kingdom. One most eminent scholar of Egyptology, James Henry Breasted, considered this literature as an early sign of intellectual and social maturity. He described this period as a dawn of conscience when a man could debate with his own soul on metaphysical matters. Another example of the literature of this period was a work written by the 'Eloquent Peasant' which expresses dissatisfaction with the community and with the condition of the land. This could be considered as an early step towards social revolution and democracy.

Lastly, it is conceivable that certain specimens of Egyptian literature have survived to our day in the marvellous stories of Arabic literature. These stories seem at times to have their source in Egyptian oral tradition. It has, for example, been possible to establish a parallel between the story of 'Ali Baba and the Forty Thieves' from *The*

Arabian Nights and a Pharaonic story, 'The Taking of Joppe', and between 'Sindbad the Sailor' and 'The Shipwrecked Sailor,' a Pharaonic tale of the Middle Kingdom.

Art

In the field of art, the Ancient Egyptians expressed their ideas in a great many techniques including sculpture, painting, reliefs and architecture. They combined worldly affairs and activities with hopes for the after-life, and their art was particularly expressive because it gave representation to beliefs that were deeply held. For them there was only a semblance of death when all signs of life ceased, for the human being still continued to exist in every way. But to survive they required the support of the body, through mummification or, failing that, through an image. Statues and statuettes, bas-reliefs and tomb paintings are there to perpetuate the life of the individual in the after-world. To heighten the intensity of the gaze, the eyes of the statues were inlaid, and even the eyebrows were fashioned in copper or silver. The eyeballs were made of white quartz and the pupils were made of resin. This required great skill and experience in the shaping of metal, which can be seen in the large number of statues dating from every historical period which have been found at various archaeological sites.

In the field of minor arts, the Ancient Egyptians produced a very large number of amulets, scarabs and seals, and also ornamental objects and jewellery, which are no less beautiful because of their small size. It is undoubtedly these small objects which were most widespread and esteemed in Africa, the Near East and even in Europe. It is often the wide distribution of these objects that makes it possible to discover the bonds which linked Egypt to other nations long ago.

Religion

Religion can be considered as one of the philosophical contributions of Egypt. For the Ancient Egyptians developed a number of theories concerning the creation of life, the role of the natural powers, and the response of the human community towards them; also the world of the gods and their influence on human thought, the divine aspect of kingship, the role of the priesthood in the community and the belief in eternity and life in the after-world.

Their profound experience in such abstract thought influenced the Egyptian community to such an extent that it had a lasting effect on the outside world also. Particularly apparent to the historian is the Egyptian religious influence in certain Graeco-Roman religious objects, as can be seen by the popularity of the goddess Isis and her cult in classical antiquity.

Transmission of the Pharaonic legacy. Role of the Syro-Palestinian Corridor

Phoenicia played a special and important role in transmitting the Pharaonic legacy to the rest of the world.

Egypt's influence on Phoenicia can be traced through the economic and cultural contacts between the two areas. Such a relationship became apparent when trade and exploration started to expand during pre- and proto-dynastic times, in order to fulfil the vast needs of those periods. Even the invention of writing as an essential means of communication developed partly as a result of economic and religious factors. Contact with Phoenicia was indispensable for the importing of vital raw materials such as wood, which was necessary for the erection and construction of shrines and religious monuments.

The influence of Egyptian culture on biblical wisdom, among other things, is noteworthy. With regard to the Levant, commercial and cultural relations existed throughout the second and first millennia before the Christian era, which include the Middle and New Kingdom, as well as under the late dynasties. Relations naturally increased following Egyptian political and military expansion, and Egyptian artistic influence can be seen in various Syrian and Palestinian sites, in statues, sphinxes and decorative patterns. The exchange of gifts helped in expanding cultural and commercial relations. Phoenicians played an important cultural and commercial role in the Mediterranean world and carried elements of Egyptian culture to other areas.

Egyptian hieroglyphic writing has been traced in the Semitic script of the Levant. This can be observed by comparing some typical Egyptian hieroglyphs, the proto-Sinaitic signs, and the Phoenician alphabet. The proto-Sinaitic elements were influenced by the Egyptian hieroglyphic ideograms, and these ideograms were simplified in a way which may be considered as a step towards alphabetical signs. Proto-Sinaitic writing could be taken as a step towards the Phoenician alphabet and hence towards the European alphabet.

This vast Pharaonic legacy, disseminated through the ancient civilizations of the Near East, has in turn transmitted to modern Europe a civilization by way of the classical world.

6 *Egypt in the Hellenistic era*

At the death of Alexander the Great, his empire comprised Macedonia, a large part of Asia Minor, the eastern shores of the Mediterranean, and Egypt, extending into Asia to the east as far as the Punjab. After his death in −323, three dynasties founded by three of his generals were already well established to control the empire: the Antigonids in Macedonia, the Seleucids in Asia in what had been the Persian empire, and the Ptolemies in Egypt.

The Ptolemies reigned over Egypt for three centuries, initiating a period that was very different from preceding periods in the country's history.

A new type of state in Egypt

Under rather more than a dozen Ptolemies, Egypt was initially strongly marked by the stamp of the foreign rulers and the demands of the new policy, with subsequent slow assimilation, as before, of the new masters of the Delta.

The forward defence of the capital, which, probably from the time of Ptolemy II onwards, was situated on the sea coast for the first time in Egypt's history, in Alexandria, necessitated military and naval ascendancy in the eastern Mediterranean. To ensure an adequate supply of timber for shipbuilding it was necessary to limit construction work in Egypt, to develop royal plantations in the Nile Valley and to import timber from the Aegean and the islands. The most spectacular aspect of this maritime development was the establishment of bases for elephant-hunting all along the African coast as far as Somalia, and the construction, at enormous expense, of ships designed for transporting the beasts. Hippalus' discovery, in the reign of Ptolemy III, of the pattern of the monsoons shortened the journey to India and made it less dangerous and less expensive. Trade relations with Asia naturally increased. The Ptolemies spared no effort to improve relations between the Red Sea and the Delta. The canal dug by Darius I from the eastern arm of the Nile towards the Bitter Lakes was deepened in the reign of Ptolemy II and made more easily navigable by large vessels. He also established a route between Coptos in the Thebaid and Berenice on the Red Sea.

The foreign policy of the Ptolemies involved them in heavy expenditure, which had to be balanced by a very large income going into the royal coffers. A partial solution to the problem was provided by strict control over the economy and by the supervision of exports, some of which were systematically developed under royal monopoly. Increased production of exportable commodities led to a systematic policy of bringing virgin soil under cultivation at royal expense, but the ruler remained indifferent to the welfare of the Egyptian farmers.

Another way of meeting the vast cost of armaments and imports was the export to the Mediterranean of African products: ivory, gold, ostrich feathers and ostrich eggs were bought in places to the south of Egypt and in the Horn of Africa, for resale in the Mediterranean. Other merchandise was brought from the Indian Ocean; rare woods, dyes, silks and precious stones were re-exported to Greece and the whole of the eastern Mediterranean.

The processing industry was well developed in the Delta and the region of Alexandria. A special effort was made to obtain wool and to introduce Arab and Milesian sheep. Alexandria had the monopoly of the manufacture of papyrus. The art of glass-making reached a very high degree of refinement, new methods being perfected under the Ptolemies. For centuries Alexandria was renowned as a centre for the making of glassware. Alexandria also possessed great skill in the working of metals such as gold, silver and bronze, its inlaid vases being highly valued.

In order to deal with Egypt's financial problems, a strong currency was needed. To expand trade with the rest of the Hellenistic world, the currency had to be tied to that world's monetary standards, which were alien to Egypt. A complete, new financial system was therefore built up. A central state bank was set up in Alexandria, with branches in the capitals of the nomes and sub-branches in the major villages. There were also private banks, which had a secondary role in the country's economic life.

Foreigners were socially, politically and economically in a very different position from that of the native population and had far greater advantages. The high officials of the palace and the members of the government were foreigners, as were also the army officers and the soldiers. In agriculture, foreigners had a better chance than Egyptians of becoming landowners.

The Greeks, when they first came, had their own gods and their own religious beliefs, which were very different from those of the Egyptians. Very soon, however, there grew up a tendency to associate certain Greek gods with certain Egyptian gods, and a new trinity was created, consisting of Serapis as the father-god, Isis as the mother-goddess, and Harpocrates as the son-god. The focal point of this new religion was the Serapeion of Alexandria, which was erected to the west of the city. We have very little information about the appearance of this temple, but we know from Roman historians that it stood on a high platform reached by a stairway of a hundred steps. As early as the third century before the Christian era, the cult of Serapis was rapidly spreading on the islands of the Aegean Sea. By the first century, people everywhere were invoking Serapis and Isis as saviours. Worship of them spread far afield, the cult of Isis reaching Uruk in Babylonia and that of Serapis reaching India.

A renowned capital on the coast 'beside Egypt'

It was during the reign of the Ptolemies that Alexandria was founded, a city so prosperous that it became not only the capital of Egypt, but also the most important city of the Hellenistic world. It must be stressed that Egypt, which had suffered military defeat and been politically incorporated into the Macedonian empire, exerted a matchless fascination on Alexander, who wanted to make it the site of one of his most renowned urban schemes and perhaps thought of establishing the capital of his empire there. Furthermore, Egyptian learning was held in such esteem that the scholars of the empire soon began coming to live in Alexandria. Under the Ptolemies, Alexandria may be regarded as the intellectual capital of the Mediterranean world.

The site of the new city had been chosen by Alexander the Great while on his way from Memphis to the oasis of Ammonium (Siwa) to consult the famous oracle at the temple of Ammon in −331. He had been struck by the excellent position of the strip of land lying between the Mediterranean to the north and Lake Mareotis to the south, well away from the marshes of the Delta and yet close to the Canopic branch of the Nile. The site was occupied by a small village called Rhacotis, well protected from the waves and storms by the island of Pharos.

The architect Dinocrates devised a plan to connect the island of Pharos with the mainland by means of a wide mole called the Heptastadion because it was seven stadia (approximately 1,200 metres) long. This mole has now disappeared beneath the alluvial deposits that have built up from both sides.

The building of the Heptastadion resulted in the formation of two harbours: the one to the east – the 'Portus Magnus' – being larger than the one on the west side, which was called 'Portus Eunostos' or the port of safe return. There was also a third harbour on Lake Mareotis for inland trade.

Under Ptolemy I Soter, the major political role was still held by Memphis, but, after the body of Alexander had been transported (it is said) to the new capital, Ptolemy II established the seat of power of the dynasty permanently there.

The city was divided into five districts, called by the first five letters of the Greek alphabet. Unfortunately, we know very little about these districts. The royal quarter occupied nearly one-third of the city adjoining the eastern harbour. It was the most attractive part of the city, with the royal palaces surrounded by gardens with magnificent fountains and cages containing animals brought from all over the known world. This district also contained the famous museum, the library and the royal cemetery.

In the streets of the city many languages were spoken; Greek in its various dialects was, of course, the most widespread. Egyptian was the language of the inhabitants of the native quarters, while in the Jewish quarter Aramaic and Hebrew were the prevailing tongues and other Semitic languages might also be heard.

Alexandria was particularly famous for certain monuments whose location is now difficult to determine. Some of the most important parts of the Hellenistic city are today below sea-level, and the rest is buried deep below the modern city. When speaking of the monuments of the ancient city, therefore, we often rely as much on the description of ancient authors as on what archaeologists have uncovered.

In the southern part of the island of Pharos, at the entrance to the eastern harbour, stood the famous lighthouse (the *Pharos*), which ranked as one of the Seven Wonders of the World. The Alexandrian lighthouse gave its name and its basic form to all the lighthouses of antiquity.

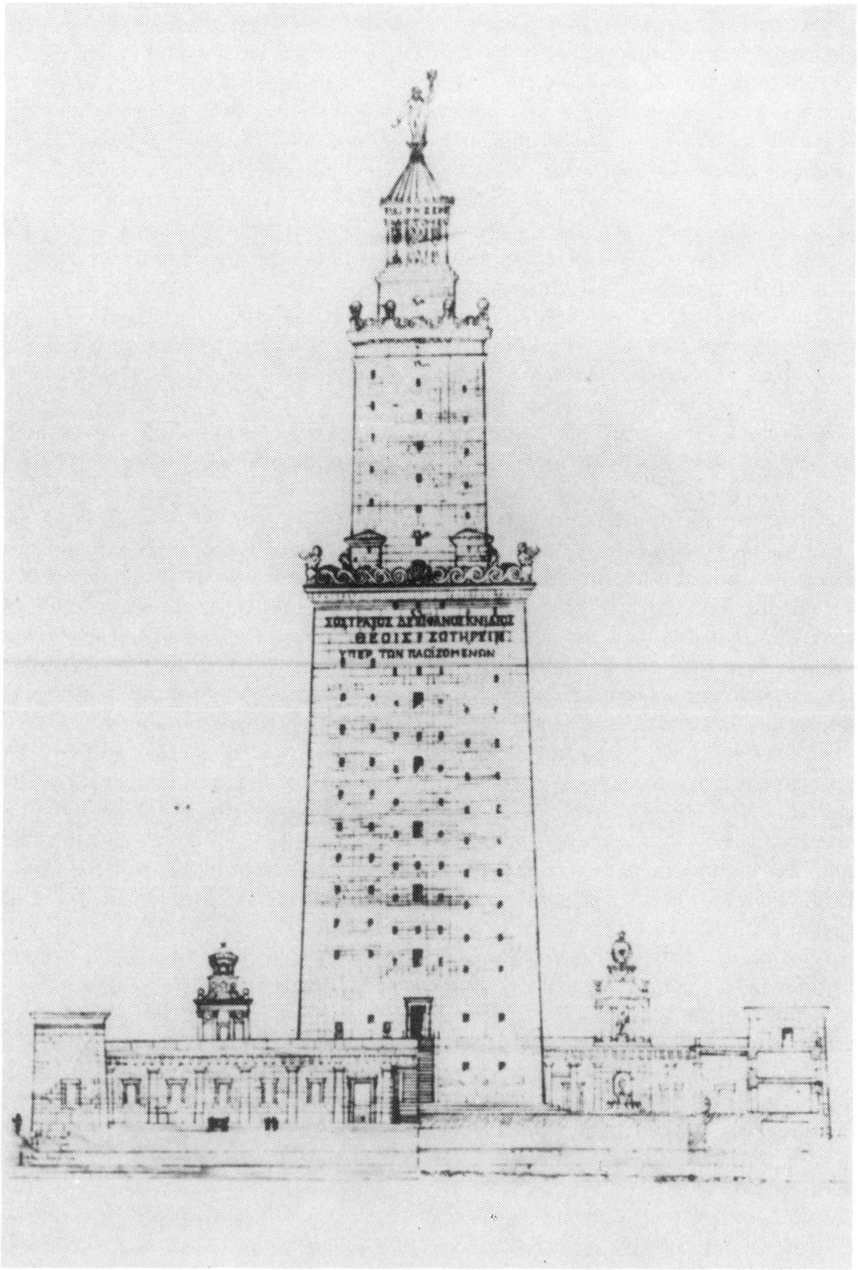

6.1 *Lighthouse at Alexandria (Thieresch,* Der Pharos Antike Islam und Occident)

This lighthouse was completely destroyed in the fourteenth century, so that our knowledge of its shape and arrangement is derived from a few classical references and some descriptions by Arab historians.

Ancient coins and representations on mosaics give us an idea of its shape. It was designed by Sostratus of Cnidus in about −280 in the reign of Ptolemy II. It was about 135 metres high and was constructed chiefly of limestone. The friezes and ornamental work were partly in marble and partly in bronze.

The museum, with its enormous library, was by far the most important achievement of the Ptolemies in Alexandria. It was started by Ptolemy I Soter on the advice of an Athenian refugee, Demetrius of Phaleron. The buildings have been described by Strabo as follows: 'The royal palaces also comprise the Museum, which contains a walk, an exedra and a vast hall in which the Museum's philologists take their meals together. There are also general funds for the maintenance of the college and a priest set over the Museum by kings, or, at the present time, by Caesar.' Scientists and men of letters lived in this institution. They were housed and fed and were able to give themselves up entirely to their research and studies, with no menial duties to perform.

Demetrius of Phaleron had advised Ptolemy Soter to create a library which would bring together the whole of contemporary culture by means of the purchase and systematic copying of manuscripts, and very soon more than 200,000 volumes had been collected. The management of this cultural repository was entrusted to illustrious specialists of the contemporary Greek world. There was also a smaller library in the Serapeion holding 45,000 volumes. No institution like the museum of Alexandria existed anywhere else in the Hellenistic world. The only library that could compete with that of Alexandria was the one at Pergamon. We are largely indebted to the library of Alexandria for the survival of the tragedies of Aeschylus, the comedies of Aristophanes, the odes of Pindar and Bacchylides and the histories of Herodotus and Thucydides.

Certain poets acted both as secretaries and as courtiers. Callimachus composed his famous elegy, *The Lock of Berenice*, there, as well as many other works. In the elegy Berenice, the wife of Ptolemy III Euergetes, vows to give the gods a lock of her hair if he returns safely from the war in Syria. On his return, the queen fulfils her vow. On the following day the royal lock was vanished from the temple. At that time, Conon, the astronomer, had just discovered a new constellation and so he christened it 'Berenice's Hair' and invented the myth that the gods themselves had carried off the lock from the temple and placed it in the heavens. The constellation still bears the name Coma Berenices to this day. Callimachus honoured the astronomer's courtly tribute in an elegy which we possess only in the Latin translation by Catullus (*c.* −84 to −54).

Geographers, cosmographers and astronomers played a large part in Alexandrian scientific development. We shall see, however, that they owed certain discoveries of theirs essentially to Egypt and not only to the library of Alexandria.

Eratosthenes, the father of scientific geography, was born at Cyrene in about −285. In about −245, Ptolemy offered him the post of librarian, which he had until his death. His most remarkable achievement was his attempt to measure the circumference of the earth, basing his calculations on the relationship between the shadow cast at the summer solstice on the sundial at Alexandria and the absence of shadow at Syene (Aswan). He concluded that the circumference of the entire earth was 252,000 stadia (i.e. 46,695 kilometres), which is greater by one-seventh than the actual circumference (40,008 kilometres). It was also Eratosthenes who catalogued 675 stars.

The geographer Strabo (*c.* –63 to +24), to whom we owe the oldest systematic account of the geography of Egypt, was born in Cappadocia, spent most of his life in Rome and Asia Minor, and finally settled in Alexandria. Although Strabo belongs to the Roman period, the core of his work was Hellenistic. His treatise on geography comprises seventeen volumes, with his description of Egypt taking up nearly two-thirds of the final volume.

Geography and astronomy presuppose a very advanced knowledge of mathematics. Among the museum's eminent men was the famous mathematician Euclid (–330 to –275), who was the first to be given charge of the mathematics department and wrote an important work on astronomy (the *Phaenomena*) as well as the famous treatise on geometry (the *Elements*), which remained the basic work on the subject and was translated into Latin and Arabic. Archimedes of Syracuse (–287 to –212), one of the greatest mathematicians of Euclid's school, discovered the relationship between diameter and circumference, the theory of the spiral and the law of gravity. His most important contribution to mathematics and mechanics, however, was his invention known as the Archimedean screw, a device still used in Egypt for raising water.

Apollonius of Perga, the great geometrician, came to Alexandria from Palmyra in about –240 to work in the mathematics school of Alexandria, and owes his renown to his work on conic section. He was the founder of trigonometry.

From the third century on, the mathematics school at Alexandria took on its own distinctive characteristics and became the principal focus of Greek mathematics.

Theophrastus, who lived at the time of Ptolemy I, is regarded, on account of his work on the history and physiology of plants, as the founder of scientific botany.

Diodorus Siculus, the historian, visited Egypt in –59. The first book of his historical work *Library of History*, written in Greek, is given over to an account of the myths, kings and customs of Egypt. According to Diodorus, the first appearance of man on earth took place in Egypt. He says (I, 10): 'At the beginning of the world, man first came into existence in Egypt, both because of the favourable climate of the country and because of the nature of the Nile.'

Physicians, too, came to work at the museum and at the library, the intellectual freedom which reigned there enabling them to make progress in the study of anatomy by dissecting corpses.

Herophilus of Asia Minor, who came to Egypt in the first half of the third century before the Christian era, was the first to discover the connection between the heartbeat and the pulse and to distinguish between arteries and veins. Some of the names he gave to the parts of the body are still in use today, e.g. the duodenum and the torcula herophili.

Erasistratus, another eminent surgeon who was also born in Asia Minor, threw new light on the anatomy of the heart while working in Alexandria.

Here again, the renown of the medical school of Alexandria was to be long-lived.

There is an obituary verse preserved in Milan which says of the physician to whom it relates: 'Egypt the all-sublime was his fatherland.'

In the course of time, the native Egyptian element made its presence felt more and more. Manetho, an Egyptian from Samanud in the Delta, was one of the most famous scholar-priests of the beginning of the third century before the Christian era. His chief work, the *Aegyptiaca*, would have been our best source of information on the history of ancient Egypt had it reached us in its entirety. The fragments which still exist contain lists of the names of kings arranged in dynasties and mentioning the duration of each king's reign, a method adopted by modern historians.

Egyptian influence on Hellenistic culture

We have seen that the Ptolemies strove to develop relations between Egypt and the Indian Ocean. Where land exploration is concerned there is still much discussion as to whether they had a systematic policy to trace the course of the Nile and make use of the river, far to the south, as a route for penetration and commerce. It is, however, certain that exploration to the south of Egypt took place. Timosthenes, navarch of Philadelphia, visited Nubia; Aristo reconnoitred the Arabian coasts; Satyrus followed the African coast to a point south of Cape Guardafui. The accounts of these explorations have been recorded and provide material for the work of scholars such as Agatharchides.

These explorers, furthermore, were following in illustrious footsteps. In about −500, Hecataeus of Miletus, the first Greek geographer to visit Egypt, wrote the first description of the world. Unfortunately only fragments of his geographical treatise have survived. In Egypt he travelled as far as Thebes and it seems very probable that he included a detailed description of Egypt in his treatise. Hecataeus considered the earth to be a flat disc with Greece at its centre. He divided the world into two continents, Europe and Asia, the latter consisting of Egypt and the whole of North Africa, known at that time under the name of Libya. He imagined that in the south the Nile connected with the River Oceanus, which encircled the whole world. Herodotus of Halicarnassus had visited Egypt in about −450. He went as far south as Elephantine, which he described as the frontier between Egypt and Ethiopia. Herodotus devoted the second of the nine books of his *History* to Egypt. He was the first geographer to mention Meroe by name, having actually met Meroites at Aswan.

Herodotus also thought that the earth was flat but, unlike Hecataeus, he did not think it was circular, nor did he believe that it was encircled by the River Oceanus. He divided the world into three continents: Europe, Asia and Libya (i.e. Africa), stating that the last was surrounded on all sides by the sea except at the point where it was joined to Asia.

Diodorus Siculus described the course of the Nile in the first book of his work. He was of the opinion that the Nile rose in Ethiopia and contained a large number of islands including the one called Meroe. Diodorus devoted the whole of his third book to Ethiopia, that is, to what is now called the Sudan. Strabo, like him, referred to the Meroe region as an island and also gave details of its inhabitants.

Even more surprising was the slow absorption of the Greek milieu by the

Egyptian. It would seem that the Egyptians did not give way to cultural pressure. They kept an independent attitude towards the Ptolemies, unlike the Greeks, who displayed a striking adulation of the sovereign. Yet the Greek language at that time enjoyed international status and was easier to write than Egyptian. Officially, everyone spoke Greek. It has been noticed by archaeologists, however, that almost as many papyri are found in demotic as in Greek. Greek law was very slow to be reflected in Egyptian legal instruments, while the Egyptian calendar gradually prevailed over the Greek. What is more, by means of the Greek language an entire Egyptian heritage became available to a world it would never have reached without the new linguistic medium which served to convey it.

Art can probably be said to be the sphere in which the Egyptian and even black African impregnation of Hellenistic culture was the most surprising and spectacular. The Greeks, lovers of the theatre as they had been in Athens, built monuments in Egypt which reflected their taste.

At first, naturally enough, artistic techniques and tastes among the Greek community in Egypt were similar to those in other Greek communities of the far-flung empire. It is also true that products from the Alexandrian workshops resembled those of Greece to some extent and showed the influence of fashions foreign to Africa. There are a great many examples of this important art in the Graeco–Roman Museum at Alexandria. One of the most remarkable is the head of Alexander which belongs to the tradition of the school of Lysippus. But innovation was also taking place in Alexandria, the most important new technique being that described by archaeologists by the Italian term *sfumato*, which is a blending of light and shade on the softened contours of the facial features, not much attention being paid to the representation of hair or cheeks. The latter were usually modelled in stucco, which lends itself to the soft modelling preferred by the Alexandrian artists. When these parts were added they were usually coloured.

In Pharaonic Egypt, the Nile had been depicted as a fat man with breasts, bearing lotus or papyrus, the plants growing in the Nile Valley. The Greeks represented him as a strong, bearded man either seated or reclining with hippopotamuses, crocodiles or a sphinx, the symbols of Egypt. Representations of royal personages followed the same pattern. Painting, which remained very faithful to the Greek models throughout the fourth and third centuries, began in the second to include scenes that were Egyptian in style side by side with others in Greek style, as, for example, in one of the tombs of Anfushi in Alexandria. The main burial chamber is decorated from the very entrance in a mixture of Egyptian and Greek styles, both in its architecture and in its painted decoration.

Mosaics appeared first in the eastern Mediterranean and possibly in Alexandria itself. Several mosaic pavements with pictorial motifs have been discovered in and around Alexandria. The most important is inscribed with the name 'Sophilos' and, inside the central rectangle, shows the head of a woman with a mast and yard-arm. This head is crowned with a head-dress in the form of a ship's prow and is thought to have been a personification of the city of Alexandria.

No doubt the most surprising aspect of Egypt's Hellenistic production, however, in the richness of its invention and tastes, was the proliferation of humorous, grotesque or realistic statuettes representing scenes from daily life and depicting Egyptians and black Africans. The small figurines in bronze, marble, terracotta or plaster were made for the common people, but the existence of more valuable pieces attest to the general popularity of these themes.

Egypt in the Hellenistic era: relations with Libya

Through Cyrenaica (the eastern part of Libya), certain aspects of Hellenistic civilization found their way from Egypt into North Africa. This was not the first time that Greek civilization had appeared in Cyrenaica, for we know that Greeks from the Dorian island of Thera emigrated to Cyrenaica, where they founded Cyrene, their first colony, in −631. This was followed by the founding of four more colonies, the port of Cyrene (later Apollonia), Tauchira, Barca (present-day Al-Merg) and Euhesperides. These colonies, especially Cyrene, were products of Greek civilization and underwent the normal political changes that took place in every Greek city. With the founding of Cyrene began the reign of the Battiad Dynasty, which came to an end as a result of internal strife in about −440. Then followed the usual conflict between aristocracy and democracy, and Cyrenaica became a land of confusion and strife.

The whole of the ancient world was at this time on the eve of a great upheaval with the coming of Alexander the Great, who invaded Egypt in the autumn of −332 and pressed westwards to Paraetonium (present-day Marsa-Matrûh) on his way to the Siwa oasis to consult the oracle of Ammon. Cyrene, and probably the other cities too (having in fact misunderstood Alexander's intentions and wishing to prevent his invasion of Cyrenaica), attempted to safeguard their independence by sending ambassadors to meet him at Paraetonium and profess their cities' loyalty. But they would not preserve their independence for ever, for in −323 after Alexander's death, Ptolemy, while still satrap of Egypt, seized the opportunity provided by the internal struggles at Cyrene and annexed Cyrenaica, thus initiating the Hellenistic period in that country. Except for a brief period of independence (*c.* −258 to −246), the domination of Cyrenaica by the Ptolemies lasted from −322 to −96, when Ptolemy Apion (son of Ptolemy Euergetes II), who was ruling over Cyrenaica, bequeathed it to the Roman people and it was combined with Crete into a Roman province.

Under the Ptolemies, the towns were given new names, some of which were Ptolemaic dynastic names. Cyrene kept its name, but Tauchira was rechristened Arsinoe (present-day Tokra), and Barka's port was given the name of Ptolemais (present-day Tolmeta) and superseded Barka as the official city centre. Euhesperides gave way to a new city which received the name of Berenice (present-day Benghazi) in honour of Berenice, the Cyrenaean princess and wife of Ptolemy III. Cyrene's port was raised to city rank and given the name of Apollonia (present-day Susa).

Cyrenaica was peopled by a mixture of races. In the cities, besides the Greeks there was a non-Greek population composed of Jews and many other foreigners. Outside the cities, the rural population (*georgoi*) consisted of native Libyans and mercenary soldiers who had settled there as cleruchs.

These *georgoi* tilled the arable lands of Cyrenaica, made up of the royal lands (*gêbasilikê*), the city lands (*gêpolitike*), and the land left to the native Libyans. This social structure resulted in a clash between the native Libyans and the Greek settlers.

Cyrenaica in the Hellenistic period was a country of great economic importance, being regarded as one of the granaries of the ancient world. It has been said that Cyrene sent a gift of 800,000 *medimni* of grain to the Greek cities in metropolitan Greece during the famine of –330 to –326. Much has been said about its wool, its horse-breeding, and the famous *silphium* of Cyrenaica, which was a monopoly of the Battiad kings and probably remained a monopoly of the Ptolemies.

This gift of grain is not the only evidence of the close relations existing between the Greeks of Cyrenaica and those in Greece itself. It is well known that Cyrene contributed greatly to the intellectual life of the Greeks, especially in the fourth century, through its renowned philosophers and mathematicians. As a result of its close intellectual contacts with Athens, Cyrene made it possible for philosophy and a great many branches of learning to flourish on the Cyrenaican plateau. It was here that the philosophical school known as the Cyrenaics developed. This was a minor Socratic school founded by Aristippus (*c.* –400 to –365), the grandson of the Aristippus who was friend and companion to Socrates. This intellectual activity and fertility were still evident in the Hellenistic era. We need only cite as evidence the names of Callimachus (–305 to –240) and Eratosthenes (–275 to –194) who were among those to leave Cyrene for Alexandria to enrich the latter's activity in the development of the sciences and literature. At the academy, the museum and the library, they added to the sum of creative intelligence in Alexandria and enabled the city to become the main pole of intellectual attraction in the Hellenistic era.

Many statues of philosophers, poets and the nine Muses have been discovered at Cyrene. The discovery of a bust of Demosthenes, albeit a Roman copy, is very significant since it shows the high esteem in which such a great Greek orator was held by the Greek population of Cyrene.

Some fine examples of Alexandrian sculpture have been found among the numerous marble statues at Cyrene. The few original portraits from Hellenistic times show very close affinities with what is known as the Hellenistic art of Alexandria. It is not surprising that the technique used in Alexandria was copied to a certain extent at Cyrene. Another similarity between the Greek sculpture of Cyrenaica and that of Alexandria can be seen in the Cyrenaean busts. A comparison of Cyrenaean funerary busts with Egyptian mummy portraits clearly reveals the close similarity between them. Even when the pieces in question are from the Roman era, there is no denying their Ptolemaic origin.

From Cyrene came painted Hellenistic pottery and terracotta figurines. These figurines were produced in local workshops which had started by reproducing and imitating Greek terracottas, but gradually evolved their own characteristic style. Study of these figurines is rewarding as they reflect the daily lives of the inhabitants of Cyrenaica, especially in the cities.

In the sphere of religion, the dynastic Ptolemaic cult found its way to Cyrenaica, as can be seen from the large number of dedicatory inscriptions to the Ptolemaic kings and queens. The cities of Cyrenaica also adopted the cult of Serapis, and temples to Isis and Osiris have been found at Cyrene and Ptolemais.

From Cyrenaica, this Graeco-Egyptian cult probably reached Tripolitania, which

6.2 *Cleopatra VII. Source unknown*

was never ruled by the Ptolemies in pre-Roman times. The sanctuary of Serapis and of Isis was discovered at Leptis Magna, and it is interesting to note that at Sabrata the cult of Isis was combined with Isiac rites. The cults of Isis and Serapis must have extended farther west as the cult of Isis became more general and as the Serapis cult started giving the ancient world a new hope of a better life.

Much of what has been said about Hellenistic Cyrenaica concerns only the Greeks, since information concerning the native Libyans and the extent to which they were influenced by Hellenistic civilization is scarce and hard to find. We know that the native Libyans, driven away from the fertile coastal lands and contained in the interior, did not welcome the presence of the Greeks. Hellenistic civilization, nevertheless, owed much to this region of North Africa which enabled it to develop and flourish for three centuries.

7

Egypt under Roman domination

Rome: from alliance to domination over Egypt

Egypt passed from the rule of the Ptolemies to that of Rome almost imperceptibly. Relations between Alexandria and Rome had for a long time, since Ptolemy Philadelphus, been very friendly. He was the first of the line to sign a treaty of friendship with Rome and send an embassy there, in –237. Half a century later Ptolemy Philopator had remained friendly to Rome during its war with Hannibal (–218 to –201) and Rome had reciprocated by saving Egypt's independence when Antiochus III invaded it in –168. Nevertheless, after establishing that position the republic had in practice become able and accustomed to controlling Egyptian affairs in a way that became all too obvious in the Ptolemies' last years. The aim of Cleopatra VII's intrigues with Roman generals between –51 and –30 had probably been to make them espouse her kingdom's interests, but her unconditional support of her friend Mark Antony lost her the throne for good as soon as Octavian conquered him in –31.

The attitude of its new master towards Egypt showed clearly the importance which Rome attached to this new province of its empire. It stationed three legions there, nearly 15,000 men. Their duty was to restore control over the country in which anarchy had raged during the Ptolemies' final reigns which led to the destruction of Thebes in –88.

The Roman emperor, therefore, succeeded the Ptolemies in Egypt, and tried to take their place in its structure. He took charge of its religion, and was soon known as the builder of numerous temples. He also took charge of its everyday well-being, and used the army not only to keep public order but also to repair the canal system, badly damaged during the disorders of the last Ptolemies.

Roman administration

The Roman emperor, however, copied the Ptolemies' administration of Egypt as a kind of vast personal estate, the whole income from which was managed by the crown. This exploitation by Augustus soon became the starting-point of the whole policy he devised for Egypt, which continued even though his successor reproached the prefect with excessive taxation, reminding him that sheep ought to be shorn but not flayed.

The emperor's direct authority was shown by his personal appointment of the prefect, who was always a knight (not a senator), to the highest office in the country, and of the other officers (the *procuratores*) who acted in his name. A small administrative detail clearly illustrates Egypt's special character: it was the only country in the whole empire where years were counted by the emperor's reign and not named after the consuls holding office. This perpetuated the ancient Ptolemaic and Pharaonic practice and invested the Roman head of state with an aura of royalty unrecognized anywhere else in the empire's organization.

The government's geographical unit was the nome which was subdivided into two *toparchiai* each containing a number of villages. The nomes of Upper Egypt formed together a higher unit, the *Thebaid*, which resembled the Heptanomis (the seven nomes of Middle Egypt) and the nomes of the Delta. A nome was governed by a *strategos* who had beside him as an administrative technician a royal scribe (also a Ptolemaic title). Junior officials administered lesser units, according to even older traditions.

The central government, however, was new. Its kernel was established in Alexandria, the old royal city. This general staff of the government was composed entirely of Roman citizens nominated by the emperor. First came the prefect, the head of all the departments, including the treasury, the army and the courts. His power was limited only by the power of appeal against his decisions to the emperor in person. The prefect, to enable him to perform his duties, had a council which also consisted of Roman knights. The *juridicus*, the *dikaiodotes* and the *archidikastes* helped him to administer justice; the *procurator usiacus* helped him to administer financially the funds which accrued to the emperor in person; and a knight had charge of the temples. The groups of nomes also came under the authority of the three *epistrategoni*, who were knights with the rank of procurator. The only judge was the prefect, who could obviously delegate his power to others, especially to the *strategos*, but who alone was responsible. He made a circuit of the country each year to settle the most difficult cases; it was called the *conventus*. He applied Roman law to Roman citizens and to others he applied the aliens' law, which took account of the manners and customs of the country, with a number of exceptions.

These examples alone show that the Roman presence had the capacity to change the structure of Ptolemy's Egypt. Since the beginning of the period of Augustus, however, other factors had still greater potentiality for change. The Ptolemaic administration was highly centralized and mostly consisted of paid officials, whose salaries came from their right to manage farms differing in size according to the importance of their duties. The army, likewise, was a hereditary organization which carried with it the right, also hereditary, to cultivate properties whose size was fixed according to certain criteria (whether the official was Greek or Egyptian, whether he had a horse to feed or not, and so on).

The Roman occupiers, in their need to set group against group, resorted to the ancient custom and restored to the Greeks their privileged position, this time not only in fact but also in law. The Egyptians paid a poll-tax (the *laographia* to which a man was liable merely by existing) from which the Greeks were exempt. The inhabitants of the provincial capitals, the *metropoles*, paid less than villagers; peasants might not leave the land they tilled, the *idia*. So the important thing was to belong to a Greek-educated family. A man could claim this only if he could show by documents that his two grandfathers had both attended a *gymnasion*, a Greek school. The right of the Egyptians as such disappeared in this new social setting, the chief purpose of which was to organize a solid middle class with a stake in the future of the empire.

It will be convenient here to mention the particular status of the autonomous cities (*poleis*) under the Ptolemies, such as Ptolemais in Upper Egypt and the ancient and glorious Naucratis in the Delta. The third *polis*, Alexandria, was still the greatest port in the Mediterranean, rivalling Rome in population and importance. Nevertheless, it lost its senate and became the base of the naval unit known as the Augusta Alexandrina fleet, while quite close to the city the Roman army was encamped at Nicopolis. The Alexandrians, whose scathing and forceful wit was famous, were never on good terms with their new masters and lost no opportunity of showing it.

Egypt under Roman domination

For quite a long time these bases of the Roman dominion were left alone. Provincial life went on in a *pax Romana* paid for by the taxes based on the wheat levy, the *annona*, which was a source of periodical rebellion and protest. Tiberius (+ 14 to + 37), who succeeded Augustus, was able to reduce to two the number of legions stationed in Egypt. It was under his successor that disorders between the Greeks of Alexandria and the many Jews who lived in the city broke out for the first time.

The relations between the government and the Jews of Egypt were embittered during the revolt in Judaea. Vespasian (+ 69 to + 79), who had become emperor in Syria and was acclaimed in Alexandria, recalled the legions from Nicopolis for the siege of Jerusalem. After its destruction in Trajan's reign (+ 98 to + 117) the Jews of Egypt rose in rebellion and besieged Alexandria, in troubles which were long remembered as the Jews' War. When the general Marcius Turbo defeated the rebels, the Jewish colony in Alexandria ceased to exist.

Apart, however, from these particular events, the empire's first century and the early years of its second were a period of relative calm and prosperity. The emperor Nero (+ 54 to + 68) sent explorers into the Kingdom of Meroe, with which Rome had peaceful trading relations; Vespasian became very popular in Alexandria, which attributed miraculous powers to him; Trajan reduced the legions stationed in Egypt to one only, which indicates that the situation was calm. He also drove a canal between the Nile and the Red Sea to increase trade with the East and compete with the caravan routes which led to Syria through countries outside Roman control. These measures benefited Alexandria, which was still the chief port in the whole Mediterranean. Moreover, when famine devastated the country, Trajan sent in much-needed wheat, reversing for once the principle that Egypt had to pay the *annona* to Rome.

Hadrian (+ 117 to + 138) showed still greater interest in the country, and in + 130 and + 131 made a fairly long journey there with his wife. Egypt owed to him the repair of the destruction caused in Alexandria by the Jews' War and the foundation in Middle Egypt of the town of Antinopolis to commemorate his favourite Antinous. There were, however, also practical reasons for founding that city, which was given the rank of a *polis*, or free city, and became a centre friendly to Rome in the interior of Egypt and the starting-point of a caravan route between the Red Sea and the Nile Valley.

The economic situation of the peasants and smallholders, which is documented in detail in papyri, nevertheless showed that the discrimination in favour of the middle class, which had been a principle of Roman policy, would bear bitter fruit. The humble folk became poor and unrest began to stir. One of its first signs was the murder of the prefect at Alexandria in the reign of Hadrian's successor, Antoninus Pius (+ 138 to + 161), who had to go to Egypt to restore order. His son Marcus Aurelius, the philosopher and philanthropist (+ 161 to + 180), faced a still more critical situation when the *boukoloi*, the cattlemen of the Delta, broke out in a ferocious revolt. It was headed by an Egyptian priest called Isidor and the rebels were united by a mystical enthusiasm due, some said, to the practice of ritual cannibalism; but they fought heroically for their right to a less miserable life and to racial recognition. The Alexandrians were this time on the Roman side because they had privileges which the Egyptians had not.

The tension between Rome and Egypt went on growing in spite of the reforms of Septimus Severus (+ 193 to + 211), who gave the Alexandrians back their senate, *boule*, which signified autonomy and which Augustus had dissolved. When Caracalla, his successor (+ 211 to + 217), visited Alexandria he was so enraged by the citizens' jeers that he proudly ordered a general massacre of youths after he had assembled them on the pretext of wishing to enrol them in the army. After the slaughter the troops left their quarters in Nicopolis and stayed in the city to force it into submission.

These episodes of blood and violence partly offset the importance of the emperor's best-known action, which was the grant of the Antoninian constitution in + 212. This supreme document made citizens of all the inhabitants of the empire and removed the barriers which until then had separated Roman citizens from provincials. Until then, except for officials from abroad, Roman citizens had very rarely been found in Egypt. They were mostly Egyptians who had served in the Roman army, had gained their citizenship on retirement after twenty or twenty-five years' service, and had gone back to their home towns as notables in the little group of metropolitans.

The constitution did away, in principle, with the dual status of the empire's inhabitants. The ordinary law became that of Rome and the general structure of the society accordingly completely changed. Nevertheless, if any country felt this social revolution less than the rest, it was Egypt. Together with the constitution the general administrative system was also changed. When Alexandria recovered its senate, a general reform altered the standing of the towns. The metropoles became cities (*poleis*) and took over the direct administration of their provinces.

Egypt was no longer the empire's granary. That function was performed by Africa (the present Maghrib), from the end of the second century onwards. This could only mean that Egypt was exhausted. A movement that started, spread and became

7.1 *Polish excavations at Kôm el-Dikka, Alexandria: Roman baths and hypocaust*

7.2 *Baouit painting (K. Wessel,* Koptische Kunst, *Recklinghausen, 1963. Photo, Cairo Museum)*

increasingly dangerous was the flight (*anachoresis*) of cultivators from their fields into the desert because they could no longer pay the taxes the state demanded of them.

Towards the middle of the third century a series of highly dramatic events happened. A prefect of Egypt, Marcus Julius Aemilianus, had himself proclaimed emperor in + 262 and was heavily defeated by Gallienus after reigning a few months. Foreign peoples appeared on the frontiers, raided the country and even occupied tracts of it for some time. It was not by chance that in the reign of Claudius II (+ 268 to + 270) an Egyptian named Thimagenes called the Palmyrians into the country. These people lived in a rich caravan town and were allied to the empire but independent of it. Their queen, Zenobia, without an open breach with Rome, sent in an army 70,000 strong which gave the legions a great deal of trouble because victories were useless when the people sided with the invaders. Even when Aurelian took the situation in hand and drove the Palmyrians out, some anti-Roman sections of the population led by one Firmus joined those of the invaders who still remained in Egypt. They also linked themselves to a race which began to be spoken of with terror, the Blemmyes. These were nomads who were spreading into Lower Nubia and often appeared in Upper Egypt out of the desert, which they dominated, and terrorized the cultivators.

The general who succeeded in dominating the Palmyrians, the Blemmyes and their allies, the Egyptian guerillas, was Probus (+ 276 to + 282), who succeeded Aurelian after commanding his forces. He made serious efforts to improve the situation of the country, which was well on the road to ruin and no longer reacted to a social life centred in a traditional administration. The welcome given even the Blemmyes, who behaved like nomad raiders, showed clearly that the community would have to be strengthened from inside by giving its members new confidence. This was doubtless Probus' aim when, having beaten the invading barbarians and become emperor, he set his army to dig canals and improve agriculture.

The new emperor saw the situation clearly and gave up Nubia which was open to invasion by the Blemmyes and to the Nobades, who were an African people akin to them, on condition that they should undertake to guard the empire's southern frontier. For this service they were paid sums which their petty kings (*reguli*, *basiliskoi*) enjoyed calling tribute.

Egypt itself was now divided into three provinces, each of which had formerly been an epistrategy. The two northern provinces, the Delta and Heptanomis (the seven nomes) were now named Aegyptus Jovia and Aegyptus Herculia and administered by a civil governor (*praeses*) who had no authority over the armed forces. The southern province, the Thebaid, which was more exposed to invasion, was placed under a *dux*, who held both the civil and the military power. Egypt lost its character as a separate province and struck the same coinage as the rest of the empire. The community tended, slowly at first and later more and more obviously, to fall into fixed patterns which provided a refuge for the taxpayer when taxation became too heavy. One consequence was that the state had to enforce immobility: no one was allowed to leave his post. Peasants had to remain peasants and stay on the same land, so that they became serfs of the soil, but also the *honestiores* (the respectable citizens) were bound fast to their duties as taxpayers and administrators. *Anachoresis* soon became a necessity for all social levels. Only persons with clear-cut political authority could defend their position. Naturally the less fortunate tended to join the groups surrounding these potentates, relying on their protection against the tax-gatherer and handing over their property to them to look after. The government used every legal means of opposing this slide towards a society dominated and organized by large landowners; but the law was powerless because it took no account of the causes underlying the trend it was trying to stop. When the large landowners had become entitled to regard themselves as the collectors of the taxes which they owed to the state (*autopragia*), the property system had become completely different. The smallholding which at the beginning of the empire had been the strength of the middle class disappeared before the baronial estate – and baronial authority – which broke up the old municipal administrative units into other economic units.

The impact of Christianity on Egyptian society

The religious experience of Egypt may have helped to spread another religion of salvation, which Christianity in some of its aspects could be considered to be, especially in a country where concern with the hereafter had always been a powerful factor in religious speculation. Egypt, moreover, had for long centuries had a Jewish colony whose presence had as early as Ptolemy Philadelphus been a motive for the Greek translation of the Bible called the Septuagint. A knowledge of the scriptural root of Christianity was, therefore, likely in Egypt from an early period and among different communities and may have helped to spread the new religion at its outset.

Very little is really known about all this. What seems important is that the spread of Christianity was similar to that of other religious experiences, such as those of the Gnostics or the Manichaeans, whose original texts Egypt has preserved on papyrus or parchment found in its soil. All this points to a crisis in the traditional world, whose traditional religion no longer satisfied the spiritual needs of the people. In Egypt religious precept demanded that the language of the country be adopted as the ritual tongue. Christianity as well as Gnosticism and Manichaeism adopted Coptic in one or other of its various provincial or regional dialects. Not only did this mean that preachers spoke to the humblest classes of the people, who had been shut out of the Greek culture of the ruling classes, but also that in religion the first place was given to the native population and to that national culture which had virtually been denied the benefits of the constitution of Antoninus and shut out of the new categories of citizens of the empire. Whereas in the official view the native Egyptian was a *dediticius* not worth the trouble of assimilating, for the Christians the word *Hellena* meant a 'pagan' and therefore an object of contempt.

The number and importance of Christians was reflected, by a strange but not uncommon paradox, in their frequent persecution by the emperors. That of Decius (+249 to +251) left a series of peculiar records in Egypt. Certificates were issued to persons who had made in the presence of the authorities a traditional sacrifice by burning a few grains of incense as a greeting to the emperor. Those who refused were presumed to be Christians and were liable to be punished as disloyal subjects. But the persecution which eclipsed all others in the popular memory and started the Coptic or the martyrs' era was that which Diocletian (+303) unleashed with all the energy and rigour of which that prince was capable. It was the final test, which showed the futility of opposing a movement which had already taken permanent hold. A few years later Constantine acknowledged at Milan (+313) the right to be a Christian, and began the long task of assimilating the Christian society to the needs of the empire. From that moment the history of Christianity in Egypt was bound up firmly with the relations between Alexandria and Constantinpole, the new imperial capital.

The distinctive role of Egypt within the Christian empire

From the time when the empire officially became Christian under Theodosius, the history of Egypt was directly affected by the official attitude of the emperors, who increasingly claimed the right to lay down, from Constantinople, the dogma to be taught and accepted throughout the empire. The desire for juridical unity was soon combined with an insistence on the religious uniformity known as orthodoxy.

As a religion, Christianity rests on certain articles of faith, and, from the earliest centuries of its existence, differing views and interpretations of these articles have brought Christians into fierce conflict with one another.

As long as the church was unable to come out into the open, quarrels among the faithful had no political significance, but as soon as the Christian community finally became representative of the majority of the subjects of the empire, their feuds became affairs of state. Even Constantine frequently had to intervene to settle discussions which were poisoning relations between groups of Christians and which, in the guise of theology, often threatened public order. To Constantine's practical and authoritarian mind, religious discussion – heresy – ought to disappear and give way to an order and definitively acknowledged conception of what was true and hence lawful. His successors followed his example, and his attitude was the root of the constant tension that existed between the court at Constantinople and the bishopric of Alexandria, each considering itself responsible for maintaining the true faith, or orthodoxy.

In Alexandria Christianity acquired, at a very early date and by the normal process of growth, a character that was rather different from that of Christianity in the rest of the country. The Greek culture with which the city was impregnated was visible even in the way the new religion had been received. The change to Christianity took the form not of a revolutionary act of faith but of an attempt to justify certain new concepts and integrate them into the broad framework of the philosophy and philology of antiquity. This attitude, however, had little appeal for the non-Greek population of the country, whose type of religious experience was more instinctive. As for the Bishop of Alexandria, his situation in relation to his priests (*presbyteroi*) was a very special one since they formed, as was usual in the early church, a very powerful college. To maintain his authority he therefore had to rely on the provincial bishops (the *chorepiskopoi* or bishops of the *chora*, i.e. Egypt outside Alexandria) who depended on him for their consecration.

In this conflict of interests and attitudes very serious disputes broke out. The first of these began when Bishop Melecius of Lycopolis (Asyut) supported the advocates of rigorism in refusing to admit into the bosom of the church those who had proved wanting during the persecutions.

Another dispute, which had much more serious consequences, arose from the differences of opinion between scholars and between philosophical schools concerning the dual human and divine nature of Christ. Did he have two indissociable natures, a single divine nature – his humanity being but an outward show – or two separate natures? The priest Arius, in Syria, opted for the second solution to the problem, stinging the church into an official rejoinder condemning him. The most ardent defender of orthodoxy was Saint Athanasius (+293 to +373), Patriarch of Alexandria, who in the midst of this storm successfully stood up even to those emperors who supported Arianism and who was recognized as the champion of the church both by the Greeks and by the Romans. Half a century later, another Patriarch of Alexandria, Cyril (+412 to +444), opposed the doctrine of Nestorius, the Patriarch of Constantinpole, and successfully stood up to the emperor, Theodosius II. On this occasion, Cyril corrected the previous affirmations of the theologians by stressing that there were in Christ one person and two natures. After his death, the monk Eutyches, backed by Cyril's successor, Disocurus, went a stage farther by maintaining that there was but one nature in Christ. The Council of Chalcedon condemned this doctrine in +451. It subsequently became a self-evident truth for the Alexandrians, with their pride in the learning and holiness of their patriarchs. This philosophico-theological movement was later to be known as Monophysitism.

The decision of the Council of Chalcedon (+451), which definitively settled the matter by declaring belief in the intimate union of two natures in Christ to be an article of faith, started a crisis in Alexandria which lasted until the Muslim conquest.

The bitter and sometimes bloody feuds between the faithful took place mainly in the city of Alexandria. Echoes of the often scandalous events which took place in that city reached the provinces, but the Christianity of the Nile Valley, in point of fact, succeeded in demonstrating its practical flavour. Hence the formation of religious communities which perhaps had precedents both in 'pagan' Egypt and among the Jews in Egypt (such as the *Therapeutes* whose virtuous practices Philo described) but which now became pillars of the new religion. Different phases can be distinguished in the history of this movement, known as monasticism. Its first outstanding figure was Paul of Thebes (+234 to +347), a hermit who, with his disciple Anthony (+251 to +336), fled the world and organized a group of anchorites. Last but not least there was Pachomius (+276 to +349), who with great practical sense devised groups who shared certain tasks and responsibilities, were subject to a code of discipline and lived together in a highly developed communal life (*Koinobia*). This brings us to Shenout of Atripa (+348 to +466) who, at the White Convent (Deir-al-Abyad), subjected men and women to the strictest discipline and perfected in Egypt the system which was further developed in medieval Europe.

In the end, however, the Alexandrian spirit of resistance, which was essentially theological, coincided in the sixth century with that of the anchorites. Constantinople was exerting increasingly heavy pressure to impose on a reluctant Egypt the doctrines of the Council of Chalcedon and many others subsequently laid down in Constantinople. Circumstances combined to discredit, in Egypt, the rich and authoritarian official church, which was responsible for keeping order, and to confer popularity on the persecuted Monophysites, who in the fifth century received tremendous doctrinal support from Syria and were joined in the sixth century by other persecuted Syrians. A general feeling of lassitude overcame Egyptians of all social classes. The firm belief that the Egyptian position was right and just was reinforced by many incidents in the growing number of apocryphal texts relating to episodes of Christ's life in Egypt. The Byzantines had become undesirable aliens, representing an unwelcome political occupation.

The papyri have preserved very precise information on the mood of the population at its various levels. The same feeling of fear, privation and weariness was everywhere. No wonder that the country, exhausted by a rapacious and ineffectual administration, divided internally by disputes and estranged from Constantinople by mutual distrust, was drained of its economic strength.

Not many years were to pass before the vulnerability of Byzantine rule was shown up by two military defeats.

The Sassanid king, Chosroes II, wanted to weaken the power of Byzantium. The Sassanids already dominated the southern part of Arabia and were hindering Byzantine trade in the Red Sea. They struck in three directions: towards Anatolia and Byzantium, towards Aleppo and Antioch, and towards Aqaba and Egypt, reaching the Nile Delta in +615. The Persian occupation was marked by the insurrection of the Jews, finally liberated from the long Roman oppression, and by the open reappearance of the Monophysite Church, which for some years became the only official church.

The reconquest of Egypt by Heraclius in +629 gave the Byzantines only a brief respite, compelled as they were to exercise surveillance over a colony which had by then become virtually ungovernable. Terror reigned in +632, under the Melchite Patriarch, when Byzantium decided to impose a new orthodoxy which was neither that of the Council of Chalcedon nor that of Rome nor yet Monophysitism. From +639 onwards the Muslims adopted a threatening posture, and in +642 the Egyptians gave themselves up to the new conquerors, who had promised to establish more equitable economic and fiscal conditions. The Arab conquest marked the beginning of a new era in Egyptian history.

8

The importance of Nubia: a link between Central Africa and the Mediterranean

A glance at a physical map of Africa is enough to bring out the importance of Nubia as a link between the Great Lakes and the Congo Basin of Central Africa on the one hand and the Mediterranean on the other. The Nile Valley, much of which runs parallel to the Red Sea down the Nubian 'Corridor', with the Sahara to the west and the Arabian or Nubian desert to the east, brought the ancient civilizations of the Mediterranean into direct contact with black Africa. The discovery of a fine bronze head of Augustus at Meroe, less than 200 kilometres from Khartoum, need cause no surprise. Nubia stands astride an African crossroads. It is a meeting-place for civilizations to the east and west, to the north and south of Africa, as well as those of the Near East, distant Asia and Mediterranean Europe.

Historically, as the most ancient Egyptian texts bear out, travellers coming from the north entered Nubia a little south of Al-Kab. The Egyptian province situated between Thebes and Aswan was long called Ta-Seti, the 'Land of the Bow', in Ancient Egyptian, and the hieroglyphic documents traditionally apply this term to what we call Nubia. Greater Nubia, in earliest times, thus began with the sandy areas of the Nile Valley, where the 'Nubian sands' take over from the limestone to the north. Originally it included the First Cataract. Its southern limit is more difficult to determine, but archaeological research has shown that from the fourth millennium before the Christian era the same or related cultures extended throughout the whole region from the edge of the Ethiopian highlands in the south to the Egyptian part of the Nile in the north.

The history and archaeology of Lower Nubia are fairly well known and, once all the historical, archaeological and anthropological studies under way have been published, we shall be able to form an accurate picture of the role this part of Nubia once played in linking north and south. However, the situation as regards Nubia south of Baṭn al-Ḥadjar is quite different and much less satisfactory. With the exception of a few very small regions, much of the country is still a *terra incognita* from the archaeological, and therefore historical, point of view.

Apart from archaeological research, ancient Pharaonic texts, as well as some in Latin and Greek, yield a little information about the early history of civilization in Nubia, and give us some idea of its role in the evolution of Africa. But these sources cannot make up for the lack of archaeological and literary information concerning the greater part of Nubia.

In short, Nubia is so situated that it ought to provide more well-dated information than any other African country concerning the historical links between Central and North Africa and between the east and west of the continent. But we have so little to go on, except for the northern part of the country, that our knowledge of the nature, importance and duration of these links is necessarily very inadequate.

From about −7000, and above all during the humid periods towards the end of Neolithic times, there seems to have been a common material culture throughout Nubia. It was only towards −3000 that a distinct difference developed between the civilization of the lower, Egyptian part of the Nile Valley and that of the upper, Nubian part. Until this time very similar, if not identical, funeral customs, pottery, stone and, later, metal instruments are found from Khartoum in the south to Matuar, near Asyut, in the north. They show how similar the various regions were as regards social organization, religious beliefs and funeral rites, as well as the general way of life, in which hunting, fishing and animal husbandry were associated with an as yet crude form of agriculture.

Towards −3200 the art of writing appeared in Egypt, whereas Nubia south of the First Cataract remained attached to its own social systems and its oral culture. By −2800 writing was in general use in Egypt. Yet there is a clear sign that exchanges between Egypt and the Nubian Corridor were frequent, and probably of greater historical importance than the occasional raids which from about −3000 onwards the Pharaohs were in the habit of launching against the Ta-Seti – the Land of the Bow – between the First and Second Cataracts.

These raids, however, which are referred to in the earliest Egyptian texts (see Chapter 9), provide the first indication of the dual aspect – military and economic – of north–south contacts along the Nile Valley. Despite their ambiguity, these contacts reveal the importance of the Nubian Corridor in providing a link between Africa and the Mediterranean.

By −3200, under the First Dynasty, the Egyptians already had sufficient knowledge of the country to risk sending a body of troops as far as the beginning of the Second Cataract. Thus we learn that under Snefru (about −2680) the Pharaoh's forces captured 110,000 prisoners and 200,000 head of cattle, figures which confirm both the size of the population, and the large scale of animal husbandry in their society.

An important archaeological find in +1961–2 has helped to cast a little more light on the background of the history of the Nubian Corridor. A settlement of the Egyptian Old Kingdom was discovered at Buhen, with Pharaonic seals, some dating from the end of the Fourth Dynasty, but most from the Fifth Dynasty. This settlement was linked to a group of furnaces used for smelting copper.

The discovery reveals, first, that the Egyptians did not depend solely on Asian copper – from Sinai in particular – and that they had already thoroughly prospected for metals in African Nubia. Secondly, it indicates something of great importance: that the Egyptians had been able – or had been obliged – to introduce smelting techniques to the upper Nile Valley. The Buhen find proves that African copper was produced at this time. The Egyptian documents of the Sixth Dynasty, the last dynasty of the Old Kingdom, include several accounts of expeditions into Upper Nubia (see Chapter 9). At the beginning of this dynasty these expeditions were clearly of a

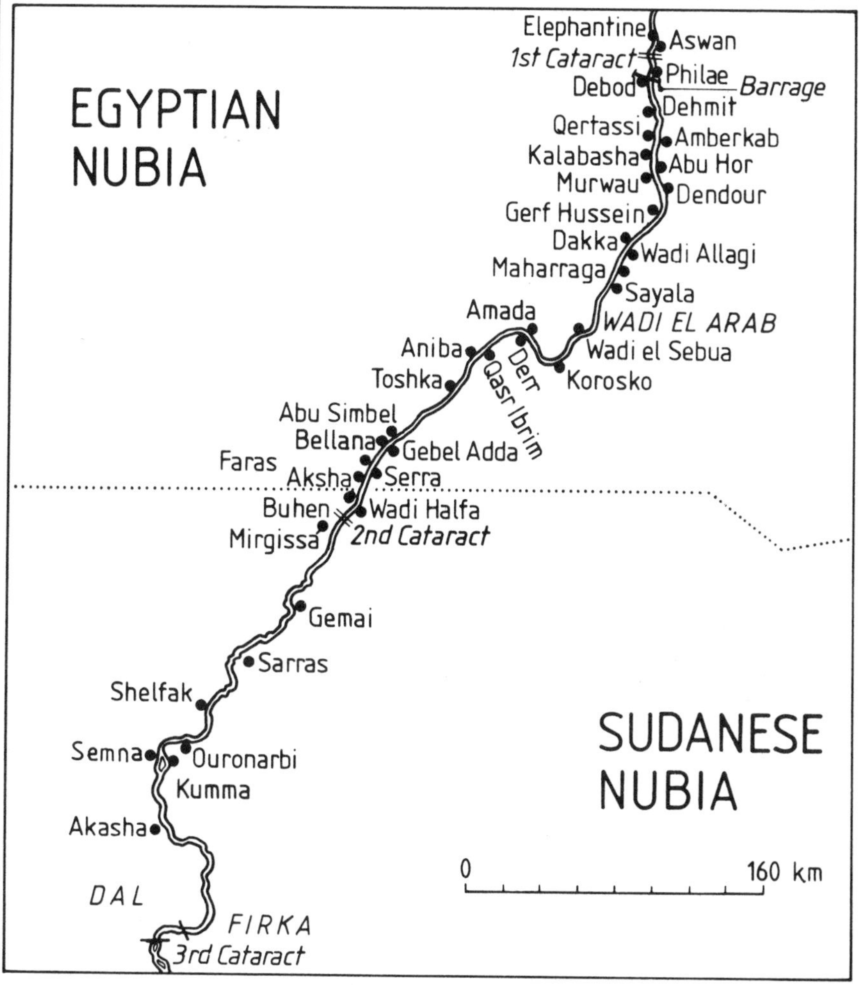

8.1 *Ancient Nubia (after K. Michalowski,* Faras: Die Kathedral aus dem Wistensand, *Benziger Verlag, 1967)*

commercial nature, and peaceful. Clearly this commerce also furthered the circulation of ideas and techniques in both directions. The Egyptian pantheon even acquired a new African deity, Dedun, provider of incense. To improve their communications with the south, the Egyptians dug out navigable channels in the rapids of the First Cataract at Aswan; this policy, initiated in the third millennium before the Christian era, was to be continued by the Pharaohs of the Middle Kingdom and later by those of the New Kingdom.

Egyptian expeditions took the overland routes as well as routes along the river valley. At that time the overland routes were certainly not desert tracks, because the Neolithic humid phase had barely ended; the journey south, if not in the shade, must have abounded with springs and water-holes, since pack-animals such as asses, which need regular supplies of water, were in normal use.

Whether they followed the valley or went overland, it seems very likely that, from these early times, the Egyptians were already in touch with Africa south of the Sahara, and that the Nubian Corridor played an important part in these contacts. Under Pepi II, towards −2200, an Egyptian expedition brought back from the distant south a 'dwarf for the sacred dance' (see Chapter 9). The word used to describe this person is *deneg*, whereas the usual term employed for a dwarf in the hieroglyphic texts is *nemu*. We might well wonder – and the answer is likely to be positive – whether *deneg* refers in fact to a pygmy. If this is so – and the translation *deneg* = pygmy is now broadly accepted – the Egyptians of the Old Kingdom must have been in direct or indirect contact with this race from the equatorial forest. We can therefore conclude that the Egyptians of the Old Kingdom had contacts with Central Africa, and that Nubia and its inhabitants did much to make such contacts possible.

In any case, contacts between Egypt and Central Africa probably go back a very long way, since the word *deneg* occurs in the Pyramid Texts. Admittedly, there is a great deal of disagreement as to when these texts were written, but even if we take the most conservative estimate they could not be later than the Fifth Dynasty, and it is very probable that they are much older.

From −2200 to −1580, the Nubians between Aswan and Baṭn al-Ḥadjar remained in close contact with Egypt, either because Egypt administered the region directly (*c.* −2000 to *c.* −1700), or because many Egyptians became permanent residents in the country (*c.* −1650 to *c.* −1580), very probably in the service of the new Kingdom of Kush. As they continued to keep in touch with their home region, Thebes, they helped to spread Egyptian ideas and techniques.

Farther south, from Baṭn al-Ḥadjar onwards, lay the Kingdom of Kerma, named after the most important centre so far discovered. Archaeological finds in the very few sites so far excavated reveal links not only with Egypt but also, from −1600 onwards, with the Asiatic Hyksos, who appear to have been in direct contact with them.

It is quite easy to determine the northern limit of the area administered by Kerma: it is Baṭn al-Ḥadjar. But the southern boundary is quite another matter. Finds of Kerma pottery between the White Nile and the Blue Nile south of Khartoum in +1973 appear to suggest that, even if the Kingdom of Kerma itself did not extend as far as the present-day Gezira, its influence did, and so brought it into close touch with the Nilotic world of the Sudds.

It is particularly unfortunate that we cannot be certain how far the Kingdom of Kerma extended towards equatorial Africa, since this kingdom, probably the first African 'empire' known to history, had achieved a high degree of civilization which enabled it to exert a profound influence on countries situated to its south, along the upper Nile and in Central Africa, as well as to the east and west.

We need only emphasize that this kingdom may have greatly influenced neighbouring cultures through its techniques, especially in metallurgy, and that its political strength, to which the size of its capital bears witness, may have enabled it to project its influence far afield. Unfortunately there has been little or no archaeological exploration in the outlying areas of the kingdom, so that we are not yet in a position to do more than speculate about the role of the Kingdom of Kerma in transmitting ideas, techniques or languages.

The improvements made by the Egyptians to the north–south route from −2000 to −1780 prove conclusively that the Nubian Corridor was still the principal artery between Africa, the lower Nile Valley and the Mediterranean world: the navigable channels through the First Cataract were kept clear, a *doilkos* – a track for hauling boats over land – was constructed parallel to the impassable rapids of the Second Cataract, and a dam was built at Semna to facilitate navigation of the minor rapids of Batn el-Ḥadjar. All this shows that the Pharaohs of the Twelfth Dynasty were bent on making the passage south as satisfactory as possible.

When Sesostris III fixed the Egyptian frontier at Semna, he further reinforced the military defences against the possibility of attacks by a powerful aggressor from the south, but a famous text records his command that these fortifications should not hinder the commercial traffic from which both Egyptians and Nubians had much to gain.

Not much is known about the troubled period from −1780 to −1580, which Egyptologists call the Second Intermediate Period, but it seems to have been a golden age for the Kingdom of Kush, the capital of which, Kerma, appears to have taken advantage of the weakening grip of Egyptian rulers to increase the amount of trade between the lower and upper Nile Valley, from which it profited.

Contact between the African Kingdom of Kush and Egypt seems to have been closest during the Hyksos period (−1650 to −1580). All along the Nubian Corridor scarabs and seal-marks bearing the names of the Asiatic kings then ruling Egypt have been found. The Africans of the middle Nile had such close links with the Asiatics of the Delta that when the Theban Pharaohs of the Seventeenth Dynasty embarked upon the reconquest of Middle and Lower Egypt the Hyksos king naturally turned for help to his African ally and proposed taking joint military action against their common enemy, the Pharaoh of Egypt (see Chapter 9).

In any case, the relations between Theban Upper Egypt and the Kushites of Kerma were both hostile and complementary. From −1650 to −1580 Thebans serving the King of Kush brought their technical expertise to Middle Nubia, and the presence of many Egyptians stationed in the fortresses of Lower Nubia ensured that Kush would maintain contact with the Hyksos rulers in the north. Moreover, the last Pharaohs of the Seventeenth Dynasty employed Madja mercenaries both in their internal struggles to unify Upper Egypt and in the war to drive out the Hyksos.

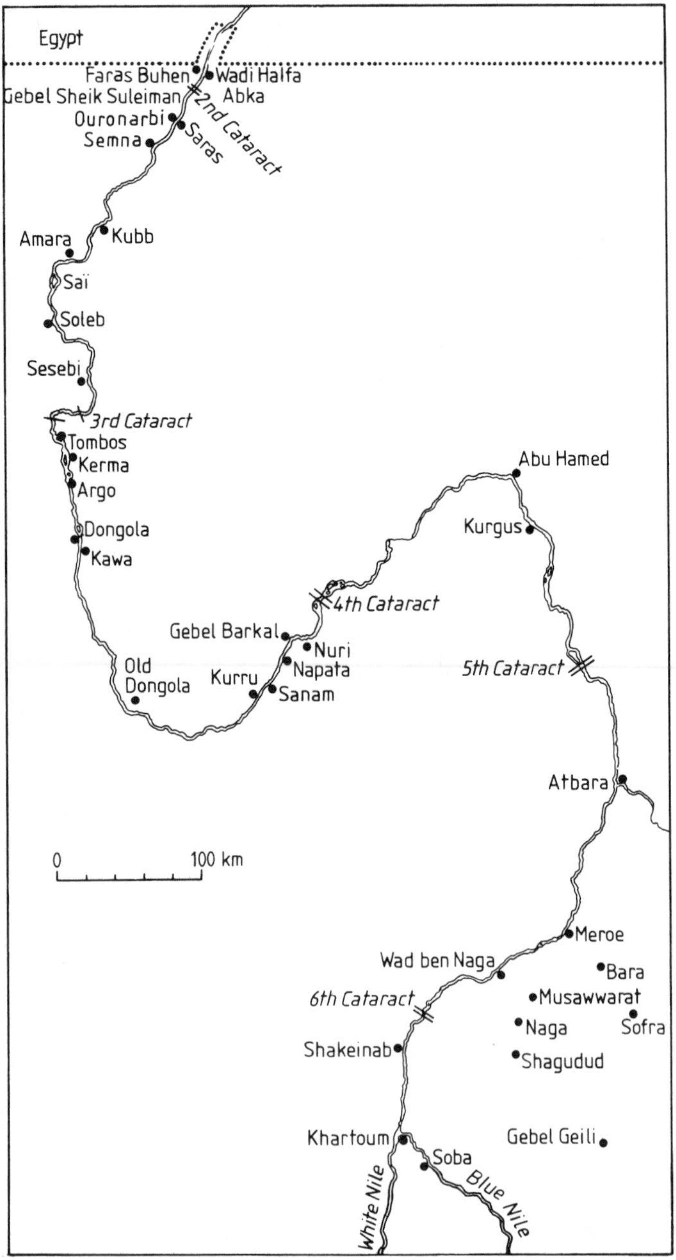

8.2 *Upper Sudanese Nubia (after F. and U. Hintze,* Alte Kulturen in Sudan, *Munich, 1966)*

The Pharaohs of the Eighteenth Dynasty, the Thutmosids, realized that a united African kingdom on the other side of its southern border could be dangerous for Egypt: a Hyksos–Kushite alliance had almost reduced Theban ambitions to nothing.

The Theban Pharaohs knew also that Africa south of Semna was richly endowed with the raw materials and manpower Egypt lacked, and they would not rest until they had complete control of the Nubian Corridor, the sole means of reaching that part of Africa whose resources were so essential to their Asian policy.

By the time of Thutmose I the entire region between the Second and Fourth Cataracts had been conquered. The Egyptians now had direct control of the desert roads to Dārfūr, Kordofān and Chad. But they could also advance towards the Great Lakes region of Africa, either by simply following the Nile from Abū Hāmād – stone inscriptions including cartouches of Thutmose I and Thutmose III have been found in this area – or by cutting across the Bayuda Desert from Korti to rejoin the main course of the Nile, via Wādī Muḳaddam and Wādī Abū Dom, at the Fifth Cataract. Besides being far shorter, this route avoided the difficulties of the south-west-north-east upstream journey between Korti and Abū Ḥamad, as well as those of navigating the Fourth and Sixth Cataracts.

The few thorough anthropological studies of the peoples that stayed in the Nile Valley between the Second and Fourth Cataracts, despite the Pharaonic occupation, throw up no evidence of important ethnic changes in Nubia at this time. On the contrary, they reveal that the physical type of the people living in the region has displayed a remarkable continuity. This means that, until we know more, we can accept that the negroes who appear in the iconography of the New Kingdom met the Egyptians in their own country; and we may conclude that direct contacts, even if only during brief military expeditions, existed between Egyptians and negroes in the heart of Africa between −1450 and −1200.

This short survey has shown that Nubia's special and sometimes involuntary role as an intermediary, which arose from its geographical position between Central Africa and the Mediterranean, was well established by −1800. It also brings out some constant features – the fact that it was important for Egypt to have access to African resources, together with Nubia's interest in the northern cultures – which brought about a continuing interchange that went on with varying degrees of intensity throughout the succeeding periods from −1200 to +700.

The kingdom of Napata (−800 to −300) and the empire of Meroe (−300 to +300), the civilizations of Ballana and Ḳustul (X-Group) (+300 to +600) and the Christian kingdoms after +600, all saw Nubia as the essential link between Central Africa and the Mediterranean civilizations. Like the Hyksos before them, the Persians, Greeks, Romans, Christians and Muslims all discovered the world of black Africa in Nubia.

9

Nubia before Napata (-3100 to -750)

The A-Group period

Around the end of the fourth millennium before the Christian era there flourished in Nubia a remarkable culture known to archaeologists as the A-Group. The copper tools and the pottery of Egyptian origin unearthed from A-Group graves show the flowering of the A-Group culture to have been contemporary with the First Dynasty in Egypt (– 3100). This culture is denoted, as are also some other Nubian cultures, by a letter of the alphabet because it was non-literate, no specific references to it exist on the part of literate peoples, nor can it be associated with any particular place of discovery or important centre. Yet it was a period of prosperity marked by a considerable increase in population.

Definite A-Group archaeological remains have so far been discovered in Nubia between the First Cataract in the north and Baṭn-al-Ḥadjar in the south. But pottery similar to that of the A-Group has been found on the surface in various sites farther south in the northern Sudan.

Ethnically the A-Group people were very similar in physical characteristics to the pre-dynastic Egyptians. They were semi-nomadic, probably herding sheep, goats and some cattle. They usually lived in small camps, moving whenever a pasturage became exhausted.

The A-Group belongs to the Chalcolithic culture. This means that essentially it was Neolithic, but with a limited usage of copper tools, all of which were imported from Egypt. One of the important characteristics of the A-Group culture is the pottery found in the graves of the people associated with it. Typical of the A-Group culture is a fine, thin pottery with a black-burnished inside, while its outside has red-painted decoration in imitation of basketwork. With this type of pottery are also found large bulbous jars with a pointed base, pots with 'wavy ledge' handles and deep-pink conical jars of Egyptian origin.

As for the burial customs of the A-Group people, two types of grave are known to us. The first type was a simple oval pit about 0.8 metres deep while the other was an oval pit 1.3 metres deep with a sunk chamber on one side. The body, which was enclosed in a leather shroud, was placed in a contracted position on the right with the head normally to the west.

The end of the A-Group

The A-Group, which is thought to have continued in Nubia to the end of the Second Dynasty in Egypt (– 2780), was followed by a period of marked cultural decline and poverty. This period lasted from the beginning of the Egyptian Third Dynasty (– 2780) to the Sixth Dynasty (– 2258). The culture found in Nubia during this era was termed the B-Group by the early archaeologists, who worked in the area. They claimed that Lower Nubia during the Egyptian Old Kingdom was inhabited by a distinct native group different from the preceding A-Group. Though some scholars still consider it valid, this hypothesis has been rejected by others.

The continuity of A-Group features in graves of the so-called B-Group culture makes it probable that they were simply graves of impoverished A-Group people when their culture was on the decline. The new features recognizable in the B-Group, which differentiate it in some aspects from its predecessor, were perhaps the outcome of the general decline and poverty.

Egypt in Nubia

From very early times the Ancient Egyptians were dazzled by Nubia because of its riches in gold and other luxury goods, and they continuously endeavoured to bring the trade and economic resources of that land under their own control. Thus we see that the history of Nubia is almost inseparable from that of Egypt. An ebony tablet from the time of Hor-aha, the first king of the Egyptian First Dynasty, seems to celebrate a victory over Nubia. The Egyptian artefacts discovered at Faras in the A-Group graves which belong to the reign of Djer and Ouadji, the third and fourth rulers of the First Dynasty, also indicate contact between the two countries even at that remote time.

However, the earliest record of Egyptian conquest in Nubia is the very important document now exhibited in the Antiquities Garden of the Sudan National Museum in Khartoum. This is a scene originally engraved on a sandstone slab on the top of a small knoll, known as Djabal Shaykh Sulaymān, about seven miles south of Wādī Halfa town on the west bank of the Nile. It belongs to the reign of King Djer, the third king of the First Dynasty already mentioned. The scene records a battle on the Nile waged by King Djer against the Nubians.

Another record of Egyptian hostile actions in Nubia is a fragment of an inscribed stone from Hierakonpolis which shows King Kasekhem of the Second Dynasty kneeling on a prisoner representing Nubia. The Palermo Stone tells us that King Snefru destroyed Ta-Nehasyu, the land of the Nubians, and captured 7,000 prisoners and 200,000 cattle and sheep.

It is evident that the Egyptians found no difficulty in exploiting the vast mineral resources of Nubia. Recent archaeological discoveries at Buhen, just below the Second Cataract, have shown the existence of a purely Egyptian colony at Buhen in the Fourth and Fifth Dynasties. One of the industries of this Egyptian settlement was working copper, as is shown by the furnaces and remains of copper ore found in it. The names of several kings of the Fourth and Fifth Dynasties were found there on papyrus and jar sealings.

Two records of King Merenre discovered at the First Cataract may be taken as an indication that Egypt's southern border was at Aswan during the Sixth Dynasty (– 2434 to – 2242); yet it seems that the Egyptians even at that period exerted some sort of political influence over the Nubian peoples, for these records show that King Merenre came to the district of the First Cataract to receive the homage of the chiefs of Medju, Irtet and Wawat. Peace reigned in Nubia during the Sixth Dynasty and the Egyptians recognized the great importance of the commercial potentialities of that land and its significance for the economic well-being of their own country. Harkhuf, the famous caravan leader who served in the reigns of Merenre and Pepi II, led four missions to the Land of Yam, a region not yet identified but certainly beyond the Second Cataract to the south.

The C-Group period

Towards the end of the Egyptian Old Empire or sometime during the period of Egyptian history called by Egyptologists the First Intermediate Period (– 2240 to – 2150) there appeared in Lower Nubia a new independent culture known to archaeologists as the C-Group. Similar to its forerunner, the A-Group, this culture was also a Chalcolithic culture. It lasted in this part of the Nile Valley up to the time when Nubia was completely Egyptianized in the sixteenth century before the Christian era.

One theory suggests that this culture might be a continuation of its predecessor the A-Group, for they were related to each other. Another claims that the culture grew out of influences introduced into Nubia by the arrival of a new people. The supporters of this theory differ among themselves on the question of the original home of these new people and on the direction from which they came. Cultural and anatomical data have been cited to support the various arguments. Some claim that the new people immigrated into Lower Nubia from the eastern desert or the region of the River Atbara. Others believe that they came from the west, specifically from Libya. A recent theory rejects the migration hypothesis and sees the C-Group culture as the outcome of cultural evolution.

It seems clear that the C-Group were essentially cattle-herding people who lived in small camps or occasionally settled in villages. The houses discovered in the region of Wādī Halfa were of two types: one had round rooms, the walls of which were built of stones plastered with mud, and the other type had square rooms built of mud-brick.

The earliest burials of the C-Group culture are characterized by small stone superstructures over round or oval pits. The semi-contracted body was laid on its right side with the head oriented east and often placed on a straw pillow. The body was frequently wrapped in a leather garment. This type of grave gave way to another of large stone superstructures over rectangular pits, often with rounded corners and sometimes lined with stone slabs. A third type, which is later in date, is also found among the C-Group. Now we find brick chapels often built against the north or east of the stone superstructures. Burials were commonly oriented north to south. The grave-goods consisted of different forms of pottery, stone, bone and ivory bracelets,

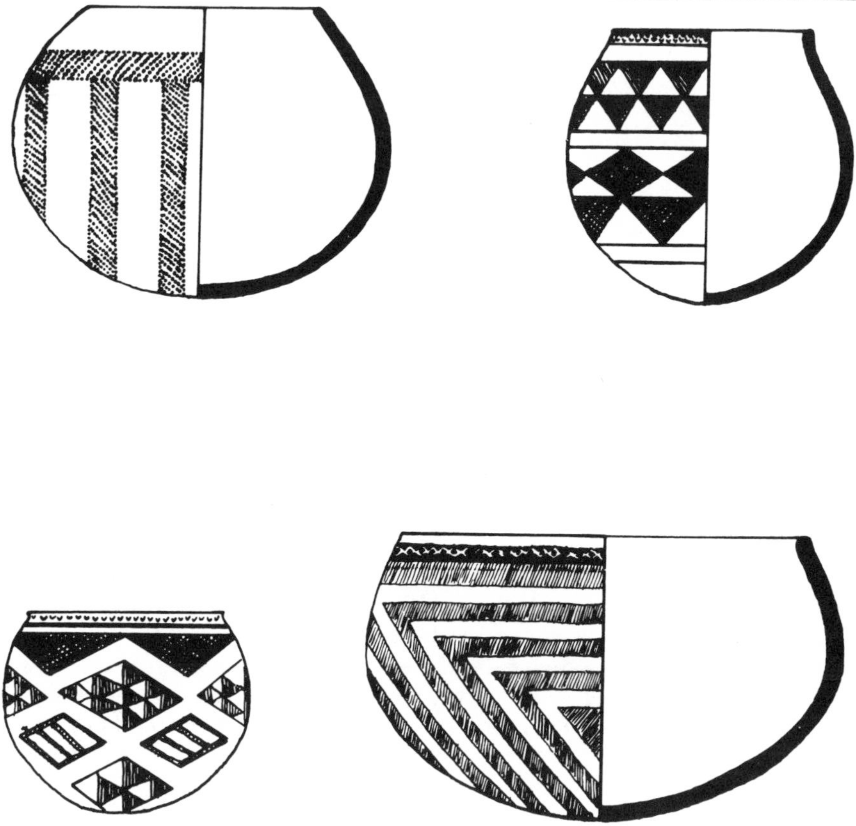

9.1 *C-Group pottery (Ministry of Culture and Information of the Democratic Republic of Sudan)*

shell ear-rings, bone and faience beads, leather sandals, mother-of-pearl discs for armlets and Egyptian scarabs.

The Middle Kingdom

The rulers of the Egyptian Middle Kingdom directed their attention to the land south of Egypt, namely, Nubia. This move began under the kings of the Theban Eleventh Dynasty. On a fragment from the temple of Gebelein in Upper Egypt, Menthuhotep II is depicted striking his enemies, among whom we find Nubians. A rock inscription of Menthuhotep III at the First Cataract refers to an expedition 'with ships to Wawat' which is the Shellal–Wādī Halfa reach of the Nile. Moreover, there are references which make it probable that the Egyptians of the Eleventh Dynasty had occupied Nubia as far south as Wādī Halfa. There are, for instance, several graffiti on two hills west and north of ʿAbd al-Gadir village on the west bank of the Nile just below the Second Cataract which mention Antef, Menthuhotep and Sebekhotep, and which relate to quarrying, hunting and clerical work.

Several pieces of evidence indicate that the permanent occupation of this part of Nubia was begun by Amenemhet I, the founder of the Twelfth Dynasty. He is thought to have been partly of Nubian origin. The occupation of Nubia commenced by Amenemhet I was completed by his son and successor Senusret I. On a large inscribed stone put up in the eighteenth year of Senusret I at Buhen by an officer named Mentuhotep, the Theban war-god Montu is shown presenting to the king a line of bound war-prisoners from ten Nubian localities.

Kush, though soon used by the Egyptians to describe a large southern land, was originally a restricted Nubian territory first heard of during the Middle Kingdom.

A second indication of the victory over Nubia won by Senusret I, which left the Pharaohs of the Twelfth Dynasty in full control of the country north of Semna, is provided by an inscription found in the tomb of Ameny, the monarch of Benī Ḥasan in Egypt. This tells us that Ameny sailed southward in the company of the king himself and 'passed beyond Kush and reached the end of the earth'.

The reasons which prompted the Egyptians to occupy part of Nubia were both economic and defensive. Economically they wanted, on the one hand, to secure skins, ivory and ebony and, on the other hand, to exploit the mineral wealth of Nubia. The security of their kingdom necessitated the defence of its southern frontier against the Nubians and the desert dwellers to their east. The strategy was to maintain a buffer between the border of Egypt proper in the region of the First Cataract and the land south of Semna, which constituted the source of real menace to them, in order to control traffic along the Nile and eradicate any threat to their country from Kush.

The defensive nature of the Egyptian occupation of Nubia during the Middle Kingdom period is clearly manifested by the number and the strength of the fortresses the kings of the Twelfth Dynasty were compelled to build in the occupied territory. A late Middle Kingdom papyrus discovered in a tomb near the Ramesseum at Luxor names seventeen Nubian forts between Semna in the south and Shellal in the north.

The strength of these forts and the effort made to render them impregnable can be seen from the fortress at Buhen, which was one of the best-preserved forts in Nubia

9.2 *The western fortifications of the Middle Kingdom fortress at Buhen (Ministry of Culture and Information of the Democratic Republic of Sudan)*

before it was flooded by the waters of the Aswan High Dam. This formidable Middle Kingdom fortress consisted of an elaborate series of fortifications within fortifications built on a rectangular plan measuring 172 by 160 metres.

Following the collapse of the Middle Kingdom and the Hyksos invasion, the Egyptians lost their control over Nubia. The forts were ransacked and burnt by the natives, who seem to have seized the opportunity of the collapse of the central government in Egypt to regain their independence.

Kerma (−1730 to −1580)

We have already noticed that the southern boundary of the Egyptian Middle Kingdom was unquestionably fixed at Semna by Senusret III. But the important excavations carried out by the American archaeologist G. A. Reisner, between 1913 and 1916 at Kerma, revealed what has come to be known as the Kerma culture. This culture has since been the subject of conflicting interpretations from scholars.

The ancient site of Kerma comprises two remarkable edifices locally known as the Western Dufufa and the Eastern Dufufa. The former is a solid mass of sun-dried brick and the latter is a funerary chapel, also in mud-brick, surrounded by a large cemetery of mound graves. Both buildings are typical of Middle Kingdom construction. In the light of these archaeological discoveries, Reisner concluded that: (a) the walls underneath the Western Dufufa are those of an Old Kingdom trading post; (b) the Western Dufufa was, in the Middle Kingdom, the southernmost stronghold in the chain of forts built by the Egyptians, between Aswan and Kerma, to safeguard their interests in Nubia; (c) Kerma was the headquarters of Egyptian Governors-General, the first of whom might have been Hapidjefa; (d) the Egyptian Governors-General were buried in the cemetery near the Eastern Dufufa in an Egyptian fashion; and (e) when the Hyksos invaded Egypt the fortified outpost at Kerma was destroyed by the Nubians.

Reisner's interpretation of the archaeological evidence discovered at Kerma was first questioned by Junker. The Western Dufufa was too small for a fort and was also dangerously isolated, being situated 400 kilometres away from the nearest Egyptian fort at Semna. Moreover, the raw materials, such as graphite, copper oxide, haematite, mica, resin, rock crystal, cornelian, ostrich egg-shell, discovered in the various rooms indicate that the Western Dufufa was a fortified trading post rather than an administrative centre.

As for the cemetery, Reisner's view that it was the burial place of Egyptian Governors was based solely on the discovery of the statues of Hapidjefa and his wife in one of the large burial mounds. The mode of burial in these large graves at Kerma was entirely Nubian. Here mummification was not practised and the dead man was buried on a bed with his wives, children and attendants in the same grave. Now, bearing in mind that these graves are Egyptian neither in their construction nor in their method of burial, and knowing that the Egyptians dreaded being buried abroad mainly because they might lose the appropriate burial rites, it becomes peculiarly difficult to believe that a person of Hapidjefa's social and political status would have been buried in a foreign land in a fashion utterly alien to Egyptian religious beliefs. Moreover, among the things found in the supposed tumulus of Hapidjefa were numerous grave-goods unquestionably dating from the Second Intermediate Period or the Hyksos period. From this, Säve-Söderbergh and Arkell concluded that the statues found in this mound grave had been exchanged by Egyptian traders for Nubian commodities with the local princes of Kerma during the Second Intermediate Period.

Thus Reisner's theory concerning the Western Dufufa and the cemetery around the Eastern Dufufa has been generally rejected. Instead most scholars advocate the view that the Western Dufufa was only an Egyptian trading post, while the cemetery was the burial ground of the native princes.

Hintze, re-examining the different theories put forward regarding the Kerma problem, sees that they 'contained inner contradictions making their correctness dubious'. In the first place he notes that the arguments raised by Junker, rejecting Reisner's interpretation, hold good also to refute Junker's own assumption that the Western Dufufa was a fortified trading post. Hintze also considers it unlikely that an Egyptian fortified trading post would have existed in this part of Nubia at this time, particularly if Kerma is taken as the political seat of Kush, which was the traditional enemy of Egypt during the Middle Kingdom. And as all the scholars whose views he has re-examined agree that the cemetery is a Nubian cemetery and that the Eastern Dufufa is a funerary chapel attached to it, Hintze points out the improbability of the Pharaoh sending an Egyptian official to 'vile Kush' in order to repair a chapel to a Nubian cemetery. Lastly, Hintze stresses what has already been shown by Säve-Söderbergh, namely, that the cemetery belongs to the Second Intermediate Period; that is to say, that it is later than the Western Dufufa and therefore the supposed Governors of the Western Dufufa in the Middle Kingdom could not have been buried there.

This is a simple theory which sounds nearer to the truth, especially as regards the evidence from the cemetery. The date of the objects found in the graves and the mode of their construction and burial rites clearly show that they were not built for the Middle Kingdom Egyptian Governors-General. But substantial evidence is still needed to prove that the Western Dufufa was the residence of the native ruler of Kush. The existence of an ordinary Egyptian trading post at Kerma during the Middle Kingdom cannot be ruled out as easily as Hintze contends. The site dug by Reisner is the only site so far excavated in the Dongola region, and even this single site is not yet fully excavated. The Dongola area is rich in Kerma sites, and, until systematic archaeological research is carried out there, a great deal will remain unknown regarding the Kerma culture.

Kerma culture

Typical sites of the Kerma culture have been discovered in Nubia only as far north as Mirgissa, indicating that the Second Cataract was the boundary between the Kerma and C-Group cultures. The characteristic features of the Kerma culture were a thin, highly-polished black-topped red ware that was made on a potter's wheel. It has been suggested that a great deal of the material in question was actually manufactured by

Egyptian craftsmen, but it could equally be said that it was produced to meet local taste by native craftsmen who had acquired Egyptian techniques.

The New Kingdom (−1580 to −1050)

When the Egyptians had re-established themselves after the liberation of their country from the Hyksos, they once again began to turn their attention to their southern frontier and this led to the largest conquest of Nubia ever achieved by Egypt throughout its ancient history.

The occupation of Nubia was accomplished by Amosis, successor of Kamose and founder of the Egyptian Eighteenth Dynasty. The main source of our information on his military activities in Nubia and also those of his immediate followers is the autobiography of the Admiral Ahmose, a simple shipmaster-captain, son of Ebana, inscribed on the walls of his tomb at El Kab in Egypt. Here we are told that 'His Majesty went up to Khent Hennefer (an unidentified region in Nubia) to overthrow the Nubians after he had destroyed the Asiatics.' Amosis was able to rebuild and enlarge the fortress of Buhen and erect a temple there. He may even have advanced to Sai Island, 190 kilometres upstream from Buhen, for a statue of him was found there together with inscriptions relating to himself and his wife.

However, it was Tuthmose I (−1530 to −1520) who accomplished the conquest of the northern Sudan, thus bringing the independence of the Kingdom of Kush to an end. On his arrival at Tumbus, the southern end of the Third Cataract, he set up his great inscription. From there he continued his push southwards, effectively occupying the whole reach between Kerma and Kurgus, 80 kilometres south of Abū Ḥāmād, where he left an inscription and perhaps built a fort. Thus Nubia came to be fully controlled by Egypt and a new and remarkable era in its history began, which left permanent marks on its cultural life throughout the following periods.

Nubia under the Eighteenth Dynasty

From a rock inscription between Aswan and Philae dating from the first year of Tuthmose II, we know that there was a revolt in Nubia after the death of Tuthmose I. It also informs us that an expedition had been sent and the rebels quelled. After this punitive mission, peace was restored and firmly established in Nubia for some years.

Peace prevailed throughout the reign of Queen Hatshepsut, who succeeded Tuthmose II. The most important monument of her time in Nubia is the magnificent temple she built inside the Middle Kingdom citadel walls at Buhen. It was dedicated to Horus, the falcon-headed god, Lord of Buhen. The importance of this temple lies in its great historical and artistic interest.

She also built a temple dedicated to the goddess Hathor at Faras, on the west bank of the Nile, just on the modern political border between Egypt and the Sudan.

The Annals of Tuthmose III inscribed on the walls of the great temple of Amon at Karnak show us the payment of the tribute of Wawat for eight years and of Kush for five years. This clearly indicates that the tribute of Nubia regularly flowed into the King's Chest, and that peaceful conditions continued in the reign of Tuthmose III. In his second year he rebuilt in stone the ruined mud-brick temple of Senusret III at

Semna West and dedicated it to the Nubian gods Dedwen and Khnum and to the deified Senusret III. This temple ranks among the best-preserved free-standing temples of pre-Ptolemaic date in the whole Nile Valley.

Tuthmose III was succeeded by Amenophis II, during whose reign Nubia was at peace. He finished building the temple of Amada started by his father Tuthmose III. On a stele dating from the third year of his reign and set up in that temple, Amenophis II records his victorious return from his campaign in Asia with the bodies of seven princes.

From the reign of Tuthmose IV, who followed Amenophis II, we have a record, at the island of Konosso near Philae, of one successful expedition to quell a revolt in Nubia. This record is dated the year eight of Tuthmose IV.

Tuthmose IV was succeeded by his son Amenophis III who led a campaign against Nubia as far as Karei in the fifth year of his reign. He erected at Soleb the most magnificent temple in the whole of Nubia. The temple was dedicated to his own living image. Amenophis III also built a temple for his queen, Teye, at Sedeinga, 21 kilometres north of Soleb on the same side of the Nile.

The political upheaval in Egypt caused by the religious revolution of Amenophis IV (– 1370 to – 1352) did not disrupt peace in Nubia and building activities continued as before. At Sesebi, south of Soleb opposite Delgo, Amenophis IV, before he changed his name to Akhenaton, built a group of three temples on a common substructure. They were inside a small walled town which included a shrine dedicated to Aton the new god. At Kawa a small temple was also built by his successor Tutankhamun. At Faras, Huy, viceroy of Nubia under Tutankhamun, built a temple and a walled settlement.

The end of the Eighteenth Dynasty brought trouble in Egypt, but seems to have had no effect on peace and stability in Nubia. On the whole Nubia developed peacefully during the whole of the Eighteenth Dynasty.

Nubia under the Nineteenth Dynasty

From the time of Akhenaton onwards, Egypt became continuously weaker internally and externally. Akhenaton was a man of dreams and his religious movement brought much harm to the empire. There was every reason to fear open civil war and general anarchy. At this critical moment Egypt was lucky enough to find a deliverer in the person of a general named Horemheb, an able and experienced leader.

Ramses I (– 1320 to – 1318), the real founder of the Nineteenth Dynasty, succeeded Horemheb. In the second year of his reign he put up a stele in the temple of Hatshepsut at Buhen on which he tells us that he increased the number of the priests of that temple and its slaves, and that he added new buildings.

After the death of Ramses I, his son Seti I (– 1318 to – 1298) ascended the throne. In Upper Nubia Seti I built a town at Amara West, some 180 kilometres south of Wādī Halfa. He probably also built the great temple of Amon at Djabal Barkal near Kereima. There is very little evidence of military activities in Nubia during the reign of Seti I. It seems that nothing necessitated serious military expeditions, but this does not mean that small punitive missions may not have been dispatched to Nubia.

Seti was succeeded by his son Ramses II (– 1298 to – 1232). We have numerous references to military activity in Nubia during the rule of this Pharaoh, who reigned for a long time, but as they give no dates or place names they are not very useful. In general, peace seems to have prevailed in Nubia during the time of Ramses II and this is supported by the enormous building activities undertaken by him throughout Nubia.

In the third year of his reign we find Ramses II at Memphis, consulting with his officials about the possibility of opening the Alaki country to develop the gold mines there, which his father had unsuccessfully attempted to exploit. The viceroy of Kush, who was present, explained the difficulty to the king and related the fruitless attempt of his father to supply the route with water. However, another attempt was ordered by the king and it proved successful, for water was reached only twelve cubits below the depth dug by Seti I. At Kuban, where the road leading to the Wādī al-ʿAllāḳī mines left the Nile Valley, a stele was erected commemorating this achievement.

Ramses II initiated enormous building activities in Nubia. The temple of Abu Simbel, one of the largest rock-cut structures in the whole world, is without doubt a unique piece of architectural work. It is hewn into a great head of sandstone rock on the left bank of the Nile. The site of this great temple was perhaps selected because the place was considered sacred long before the temple was cut there. It was dedicated to Re-Harakhte, the god of the rising sun, who is represented as a man with the head of a falcon wearing the solar disc.

Egyptianization of Nubia

The early stages of the Egyptian occupation of Nubia during the New Kingdom encountered resistance. But the Nubians soon settled down under the new Egyptian administration to a peaceful development of their country never before experienced. We have already seen that temples were built all over Nubia by the kings of the Eighteenth and Nineteenth Dynasties. Then towns important as religious, commercial and administrative centres grew around those temples. Nubia was entirely reorganized on purely Egyptian lines and a completely Egyptian system of administration was set up, entailing the presence of a considerable number of Egyptian scribes, priests, soldiers and artisans. This ultimately resulted in complete Egyptianization of Nubia. The natives adopted the Egyptian religion and worshipped Egyptian divinities. The old burial customs gave way to Egyptian rites.

The end of the New Kingdom

On account of its wealth and also because of the importance of its troops, Nubia towards the close of the New Kingdom started to play a significant role in the internal political affairs of Egypt itself. Disorder, weakness, corruption and struggles for power were the characteristic features of the time in Egypt. The competing parties in those struggles, fully appreciating the importance of Nubia in their dealings, endeavoured to win the support of the administration there. King Ramses-Siptah of the Nineteenth Dynasty went himself to Nubia in the first year of his reign in order to appoint Seti as the viceroy of Nubia. His delegate brought gifts and rewards from the king to the higher officials of Nubia. Merneptah-Siptah, the last king of the

9.3 *The temple of Amenophis III at Soleb (Ministry of Culture and Information of the Democratic Republic of Sudan)*

Nineteenth Dynasty, was even forced to send one of his officials to fetch the tribute of Nubia, although dispatching the tribute was the duty of the viceroy of Nubia when the Pharaoh exercised real power and actual control of his empire.

During the Twentieth Dynasty the situation in Egypt deteriorated enormously. There was a harem conspiracy in the time of Ramses III (– 1198 to – 1166) which aimed at deposing the reigning sovereign. One of the conspirators, the sister of the commander of the bowmen in Nubia, persuaded her brother to assist in the execution of the plot. But it is evident that the viceroy of Nubia remained loyal to the Pharaoh. Under Ramses XI, the last king of the Twentieth Dynasty, a rebellion-broke out in the region of Asyut. The king with the help of Pa-nehesi, the viceroy of Kush, and his troops succeeded in quelling the revolt and in restoring order in Upper Egypt. Following this rising, a certain Heri-Hor became the Chief Priest of Amar in Thebes. It seems that he was made the Chief Priest by Pa-nehesi and his Nubian soldiers and one supposes that he was one of his followers. In the nineteenth year of Ramses XI, after the death of Pa-nehesi, Heri-Hor was appointed viceroy of Nubia and vizier of Thebes. Thus he became the actual master of Upper Egypt and Nubia. Following the death of Ramses XI, he became king (– 1085) and with him started a new line of rulers in Egypt. Then chaos reigned in Egypt and with it a dark age commenced in Nubia, to continue until the eighth century before the Christian era, when Kush suddenly emerged as a great power.

10

The Empire of Kush: Napata and Meroe

Though today the region is extremely isolated, behind a barrier of deserts and the difficult hurdles of the Second, Third and Fourth Cataracts of the Nile, Dongola and the adjacent basin of the Middle Nile were formerly the centre of rich and powerful political structures. In the first half of the second millennium the so-called Kerma culture marked a rich and prosperous kingdom, the Kush of the Egyptian records. The extremely patchy archaeological prospection of this still little-known zone is quite inadequate for fixing the history of this sector after the brilliant but relatively short phase of Egyptian domination under the New Empire (– 1580 to – 1085); for nearly three centuries, the link between Africa and the Mediterranean world seems to be broken and almost total silence blankets Nubia. But from the end of the ninth century before the Christian era we get a reawakening: G. A. von Reisner's excavation of the El-Kurru necropolis near Napata below the Fourth Cataract revealed the tombs of a succession of princes: initially mounds, and later masonry structures of mastaba type.

Sudanese domination in Egypt: the Twenty-fifth or 'Ethiopian' Dynasty

These are the royal ancestors of the line which effected the union of Egypt and the Sudan, known in general history as the Twenty-fifth or 'Ethiopian' Dynasty of Egypt. It was long thought that this dynasty descended from Egyptian refugees from the Theban region, on the strength of the similarity of certain names and the position of the god Amon and his priesthood. Later some arrow-heads of Saharan type led to a belief in the dynasty's Libyan origin. In actual fact it sprang from the soil and may perhaps represent the succession of the ancient sovereigns of Kerma.

The Stele of Peye (Piankhi)

With the succeeding monarch, the illustrious Piankhi, whose name is nowadays normally written as 'Peye', we enter the main stream of history: one of the inscriptions which he caused to be carved at Napata, and which, rediscovered in the middle of the last century, is now preserved in the Cairo Museum and known as the Stele of Victory, is one of the longest and most detailed texts of Ancient Egypt. On front, back and sides are 159 lines of hieroglyphs describing the deliberations of the king in his palace and the phases of his campaign against the Libyan princes who were masters of Middle Egypt and the Delta. Another great stele of Peye's, discovered in 1920, defines the federative character of the Kushite empire conjointly with a proclamation of the supremacy of the god Amon.

King Shabaka

Towards −713, Shabaka, brother of Peye, ascended the throne. He brought the entire Nile Valley as far as the Delta under the empire of Kush and is reputed to have had Bocchoris, dynast of Sais, who resisted him, burnt to death; the compilers of the lists of the kings of Egypt regard him as the founder of the Twenty-fifth Dynasty. The *Weltpolitik* of the Middle East drew the Kushites towards Asia where Assyrian pressure was beginning to make itself felt; the appeals from princes and cities of Syria–Palestine and in particular from Jerusalem became urgent. But, to begin with, Shabaka seems to have preserved good relations with Assyria. In the Sudan and Egypt, he launched a policy of monument-building which was expanded under his successors, the two sons of Peye, first Shabataka (−698 to −690), and then the glorious Taharqa (−690 to −664).

King Taharqa: the struggle against the Assyrians

Taharqa's name is found on numerous monuments throughout the whole length of the Nile Valley. He built his sanctuaries at the foot of the holy mountain of Djabal Barkal, a kind of sandstone table formation which dominates the large fertile basin of Napata. His name is to be seen at several other places in Nubia such as Kawa. In the Theban region he erected colonnades on the four main faces of the Temple of Karnak and constructed in them large numbers of small chapels with which the cults of Amon and Osiris were associated. We have evidence of his presence at Memphis and in the Delta. Various texts, in particular a number of large stelae discovered by Griffith at Kawa, throw more light on the king's policy: shrine-building, sumptuous offerings of plate, sanctuary equipment, precious materials, endowments and personnel. The sixth year of the reign is particularly celebrated, when the lowering of a high flood of the Nile waters afforded an occasion for stressing the prosperity of the kingdom.

King Tanoutamon: the end of Sudanese domination in Egypt

By that time Taharqa had already been succeeded by his nephew Tanoutamon, son of Shabataka. The so-called Stele of the Dream shows successively the appearance of two serpents – an obvious allusion to the double Uraeus of the Ethiopian sovereigns – the crowning of Tanoutamon at Napata, his march to the north, the taking of Memphis, building works at Napata, a campaign in the desert and the ensuing submission of the local princes. But in actual fact, with the defeat inflicted by the Assyrians, the Kushites withdrew southward and their dynasty in Egypt ended.

A twin monarchy

We shall do well to pause over this fifty-year period during which Egypt and the Sudan combined as a great African power. The Kushite kingdom presents itself as a twin monarchy; its symbol is the double Uraeus. In their general style, their clothing and their attitudes the sovereigns of the Twenty-fifth Dynasty copy the Pharaohs of Egypt who preceded them and whose successors, if not descendants, they claim to be. The style of their monuments is typically Pharaonic. They also wear ornaments characteristic of the Sudan. A popular head-dress is a kind of close cap fitting tightly to the neck with a sidepiece protecting the temple; a thick knotted head-band holds it in place leaving two streamers hanging behind the shoulders. Ear-rings and the pendants of necklaces are adorned with rams' heads, the ram being the sacred animal of Amon. Amon is in fact the great god of the dynasty, worshipped in four major sanctuaries – Napata, Tore (probably Sanam), Kawa and Pnubs (Tabo in the Isle of Argo).

The glory of the Twenty-fifth Dynasty was great; a whole tradition about it developed among the classical authors. And in fact the art of this epoch shows great vigour. Taking over the best of the past tradition, the Kushites gave it new power and notable force.

Napata, the first capital of the Kushite Empire

After the retreat of the Kushites from Egypt under the assaults of Assyrians, their history is much more difficult to determine; even the chronology is extremely vague. For a millennium a state survived, becoming ever more African, the Kingdom of Kush, the name of its own choice from the ancient native name for the territory. In the eyes of conventional Egyptology this represents a long period of decadence during which the Pharaonic influences became progressively corrupted. In actual fact, it is a culture out of Africa which alternately entrenches itself in its specificity or seeks to align itself with the Egyptian civilization – itself, for that matter, African properly speaking; from time to time echoes reach it from the Mediterranean, in particular after the foundation of Alexandria.

To begin with, the capital remained at Napata at the foot of the sacred mountain, Djabal Barkal. Later, almost certainly in the sixth millenium before the Christian era, it was transferred much farther south to Meroe. There is little certainty as to the extent of the Kushite kingdom and so far the differences between its component regions are still unclarified. In the far north, Lower Nubia, a kind of no man's land, remained in dispute between the Meroites and whoever were masters of Egypt: Saites, Persians, Ptolemies and latterly Romans. Its revival then was probably due to the introduction of the *sāḳiya* (water-wheel) (see Chapter 11). In the heartland of the empire, Nubia proper, extending along the river (Napata, Dongola and Kerma basins), appears always to have been appreciably different from the steppe region of the 'Island of Meroe'. Eastward in Butana there are numerous unexcavated sites, while the caravan routes and the Red Sea littoral are still awaiting exploration.

At Napata the tombs of the Nuri cemetery are among the essential elements for determining the history, still very inadequately known, of the kings of the Napatan Dynasty. The first few rulers are still very much Egyptianized. As in the case of the Twenty-fifth Dynasty kings, their burial places are surmounted by Egyptian-style pyramids whose form is more reminiscent of those of the high dignitaries of the last days of the New Empire than of the royal pyramids of the Fourth Dynasty; the decoration of their burial chambers and their solid granite sarcophagi follow the Egyptian style in every particular.

Of the first two kings barely more than the names are known; they were Atlanarsa (−653 to −643), son of Taharqa, and the former's own son, Senkamanisken (−643 to −623). The two sons and successors of Senkamanisken, first Anlamani (−623 to −593), succeeded by Aspelta (−593 to −568), are better known. At Kawa a stele of Anlamani describes the king's progress through the provinces and his provision for their temples, a campaign against a people who could be the Blemmyes, the coming of the queen-mother, Nasalsa, and the consecration of the king's sisters as sistrum-players before the god Amon in each of his four great sanctuaries.

This king's brother and successor, Aspelta (−593 to −568), left two great inscriptions. The Enthronement or Coronation Text dates from the first year of the reign and shows the army mustered near Djabal Barkal, the decision of the leaders to consult Amon of Napata and the god's designation of Aspelta, whose descent through the 'Royal Sisters' is particularly distinguished, the king's assumption of the royal emblems and his thanks to and invocation of the god, his joyful reception by the army and his gifts to the temples. The Stele of the Appanaging of the Princesses, of the third year of the reign, is preserved in the Musée du Louvre: it is the description of the investiture of a princess as priestess. A further text discovered by G. A. Reisner at Djabal Barkal narrates the foundation by the sovereign of a chantry in honour, long after his death, of Khaliut, son of Peye. The attribution to Aspelta of the Stele of Excommunication is more doubtful, the names of the king having been defaced.

The expedition of Psammetik II and the fall of Napata

Aspelta was a contemporary of Psammetik II. This is one of the few really secure synchronisms, almost the only one in a thousand years of history. In −591, or the second year of the king's reign, the land of Kush was invaded by an Egyptian expedition, reinforced by Greek and Carian mercenaries, under two generals, Amasis and Potasimto, and Napata was captured.

Transfer of the capital to Meroe

Thenceforward the Kushites aimed at keeping a greater distance between themselves and their powerful northern neighbours; it is undoubtedly to this Egyptian raid, whose importance has long been underestimated, that we must attribute the transfer of the capital from Napata to Meroe, much farther south, at no great distance from the Sixth Cataract. Aspelta is in fact the first attested Meroe sovereign.

In −525 a Persian danger developed. We know the reply of the Nubian king to the ambassadors of Cambyses: 'When the Persians bend, as easily as I, bows as big as this, then let them march against the Ethiopians in superior numbers.' Cambyses did not take this advice: his army was unable to effect a crossing of the Baṭn al-Ḥadjar and had to retire with heavy losses. For all that, the Persians counted the inhabitants of Kush as their subjects. A shield is set aside for them on the pediment, inscribed with the peoples of the empire, of the magnificent statue of Darius recently brought to light at Susa. It is conceivable that a narrow belt of Nubian territory remained under their sway, and there were Kushite contingents in the armies of Darius and Xerxes.

A further possible explanation for the transfer of the Kushite capital may have been climatic and economic considerations. At Meroe the steppes were much more extensive than in the basins around Napata, hemmed in by deserts. To livestock was added agriculture, cultivation being perfectly possible in this zone of summer rainfall. Enormous irrigation basins (*hafirs*) were dug out adjacent to the principal sites. Commerce must have been brisk, as Meroe was an ideal entrepôt for the caravan routes between the Red Sea, the upper Nile and Chad.

For long centuries, which remain obscure, historians have little more to go on than royal tombs. Their excavator, G. A. Reisner, set about matching the list of attested royal names which the pyramids brought to light, with chancy results which have undergone many revisions since then and may be still liable to amendment. The last king buried at Nuri was Nastasen (a little before −300). Thereafter royal and princely interments took place in the Meroe cemeteries.

We have several inscriptions of King Amannoteyerike (a little before −400). The best describes the election of the king, a 'strong man of 41', and there are accounts of military expeditions, religious festivities, a torchlight tattoo, the visit of the queen-mother, restoration work on buildings and donations to sanctuaries.

Next we get Harsiotef, whose famous inscription is devoted partly to ceremonies and partly to campaigns against a multitude of different enemies. It is the same with the stele of Nastasen carried off by Lepsius to Berlin. This stele may, incidentally, give us a synchronism if one of the inscriptions is indeed the name of Khababash, fleetingly king of Egypt. In one of his campaigns Nastasen captured 202,120 head of cattle and 505,200 of small livestock. One would like to be able to 'place' all the peoples mentioned in the inscriptions; the spoils are often enormous and quite obviously we need to look in the Nilo-Chadian savannah for certain ethnic groups.

The philhellene Ergamenos

The renaissance which appears to mark the succeeding decades is confirmed in Greek historiography's account of 'Ergamenos'. After writing of the all-powerful position of the Kushite priests, who could even constrain the king to commit suicide if he had ceased to please the people, Diodorus of Sicily relates how a sovereign steeped in Greek culture, Ergamenos, dared to fight back and had a number of priests put to death. Doubts nevertheless subsist as to the identity of Ergamenos. At the same time, we also find reliefs in purely Meroitic style: head-dress, ornaments and royal regalia are of local inspiration and the faces do not conform to the Egyptian canon. Along with the Pharaonic divinities, worship is paid to purely Meroitic gods. Undoubtedly

10.1 *Ethiopian black granite statue of King Aspelta (Photo, Museum of Fine Arts, Boston)*

relations with Egypt subsisted, since we have sanctuaries of common Egyptian and Nubian dedication at Philae and at Dakka in Lower Nubia. However, the revolts in the south of Ptolemaic Egypt at the end of the third century before the Christian era may have been backed by the Nubian kings: Ptolemy V had to campaign in the country and Ptolemy VI established colonies in the Triacontaschone.

The Meroitic language and form of writing

With Queen Shanakdakhete (around −170 to −160) we appear to get the accession to full power of a typically local matriarchy. It is on an edifice in her name at Naga that we find inscriptions engraved in Meroitic hieroglyphs which are among the most ancient known.

These hieroglyphs are borrowed from Egyptian but differ in their values. They are written and read the other way round from Egyptian ones; this may attest a deliberate desire to be different. With these hieroglyphs there goes a cursive form of writing, often abbreviated; the signs seem to be derived in part from the demotic writing used in Egypt at that period for administrative and private documents. Whatever the case may be, the Meroitic language, whose nature is still not known, and the graphic system are completely different from the Egyptian: the twenty-three signs used represent the consonants, some vowels and syllabics; groups of 'colons' usually separate the individual words. In +1909 the English scholar F. L. Griffith found the key to transliteration. Since then the texts have been classified into different types, with comparable expressions set side by side in parallel, particularly those taken from funerary texts. In recent years computer techniques have made possible the systematic recording of texts which have been transliterated, together with their detailed analyses. For the time being, however, the translation as such of the 800-odd texts recovered remains as a whole impossible. The first long Meroitic texts appear on two stelae of King Taniydamani, who is dated about the end of the second century before the Christian era.

Rome and Meroe

Following the sack of Aswan by the Meroites (which was probably when the statue of Augustus was captured, the head of which has been discovered buried under the threshold of one of the palaces of Meroe), the prefect of Roman Egypt, Petronius, mounted a punitive expedition and captured Napata in −23. A permanent garrison was established by the Romans at Primis (Ḳasr Ibrīm), which held off the Meroites. In −21 or −20 a peace treaty was negotiated at Samos, where Augustus was staying at the time. The Roman garrison appears to have been withdrawn; the exaction of a tribute from the Meroites was renounced and the frontier between the Roman and Meroitic empires was fixed at Hiera Sycaminos (Muharraḳa).

The Meroitic empire at its height

This period around the start of the Christian era is one of the peaks of Meroitic civilization, as a number of buildings attest. The names of Akinidad and of Queen Amanishakheto are inscribed in Temple T at Kawa, and a palace discovered at Ouad ben Naga close by the river has been attributed to the queen. Her fine tomb is still to be seen in the Northern Cemetery of Meroe. The pyramid, with the traditional eastern approach of pylon chapel, is one of the most imposing in the old city and in 1834 yielded to the Italian adventurer Ferlini the elaborate jewels which are today the glory of the Munich and Berlin museums. Similar ornaments adorn the reliefs, where queens and princes display a rather flashy luxury which is to some degree reminiscent of that of another civilization – of rich merchants – on the frontiers of the Hellenized world, namely, Palmyra.

Natakamani, son-in-law and successor of Amanishakheto, and his wife, Queen Amanitere (− 12 to + 12), were also great builders, and their names are indisputably those recurring most frequently on the Kushite monuments. Throughout the major cities of the empire these monuments speak of the power of a dynasty at its apogee. In the north, at a site south of the Second Cataract, the king and queen built a temple at Amara in which the reliefs are Egyptian work, the only non-Egyptian element being the detail of the royal Meroitic head-dress. In the Isle of Argo just above the Third Cataract, the two colossi have long been accepted as Natekamani's. The royal couple also put in hand the restoration of Napata, devastated by Petronius' expedition, and in particular the temple of Amon. At Meroe itself, the names of Natekamani and his consort appear in the great Temple of Amon jointly with the name of the prince Arikankharor. At Ouad ben Naga, the South Temple is their work. They devoted particular attention to Naga, the great centre of the steppe-country south of Meroe: the frontal approach to the Temple of Amon became a pylon whose decoration combines Egyptian influences and purely Meroitic features, while the most famous building is the Naga Lion Temple whose reliefs are among the most representative examples of Meroitic art.

Meroe and the surrounding countries

It is in the next few years that we get the famous episode recorded in the Acts of the Apostles (8:28–39) of the deacon Philip's conversion, on the road from Jerusalem to Gaza, of 'an Ethiopian, an eunuch, a minister of Candace, the Queen of the Ethiopians, in charge of all her treasure'. Whatever the value and significance of this evidence, it does show that Meroe was known afar.

There is quite another direction in which researchers were long tempted to look for connections with the outer world: one representation of Apedemak, the Lion-god, shows him with a threefold lion's mask and four arms. This has suggested India, as have reliefs at Naga which show a lotus flower with a serpent rising from it. The neck of the serpent becomes a human body with one arm which is the mask of Apedemak wearing a triple crown. The most recent research, however, is inclined to abandon this hypothesis.

Meroe continued to intrigue the Romans. Towards + 60 Nero sent two centurions up the Nile; on their return they stated that the land was too poor to be worth conquering. An inscription in Latin is carved on one of the walls of Mussawwarat, while Roman coins, though in very small numbers, reached parts of Nubia and the Sudan; a coin of Claudius has been found in Meroe, one of Nero at Karanog, a coin of

10.2 *Queen Amanishakheto: relief from the Beg N6 pyramid at Meroe (J. Leclant)*

Diocletian far into Kordofān (El Obeid), and another of the middle of the fourth century of the Christian era at Sennār.

The most constant relations maintained by Meroe were with the Temple of Isis at Philae: embassies were sent regularly with rich gifts for the sanctuary of the goddess, where quantities of graffiti have been preserved in demotic, in Greek and in Meroitic. They enable us to establish the sole synchronism of one of the last Meroitic reigns, that of Teqorideamani (+246 to +266), who sent ambassadors to Philae in +253. We know very little of the last centuries of Meroe. The indigenous component in the culture becomes more and more important. The control of the caravan routes between the Nile Valley, the Red Sea and the Nilo-Chadian savannah was probably not easy to maintain.

Decline and fall of Meroe

The Meroites, who until then had beaten back the raids of the nomad peoples, thenceforward became a tempting prey for their neighbours, Axumites to the south, nomadic Blemmyes to the east and Nubas to the west. It is almost certainly this last group, mentioned for the first time by Eratosthenes in −200, to which should be ascribed the overthrow of the Meroitic empire.

On this we have no more than indirect evidence. Towards +330, the Kingdom of Axum, which had grown up on the high tablelands of present-day Ethiopia, had rapidly attained the summit of its power; Ezana, the first monarch to embrace Christianity, reached the confluence of the Atbara and boasts of having mounted an expedition yielding much booty 'against the Nubas'. From this we may conclude that the Meroitic kingdom had already collapsed at the time of Ezana's campaign. From then onwards inscriptions in Meroitic ceased and it may be that this was when the Meroitic language gave place to the tongue ancestral to present-day Nubian. Even the pottery, while remaining faithful to its millenary tradition, acquires new characteristics.

Whatever the importance of the penetration of Meroitic influences through the rest of Africa, the role of Kush should never be underestimated: for over a thousand years, first at Napata and then at Meroe, there flourished a strongly original civilization which, beneath an Egyptian-style veneer fairly constantly maintained, remained profoundly African.

Nubia after the fall of Meroe: 'Group X'

It can be taken that the Nubas from the west or south-west were the 'carriers' of the Nubian language, whose offshoots even today are living tongues both in certain mountainous regions of Dārfūr and in the various sectors of Upper and Lower Nubia.

The barbarian luxury of the Group X king was revealed in the period +1931–3, when the English archaeologists Emery and Kirwan, at Ballana and Ḳustul, a few miles south of Abū Simbel, excavated enormous tumuli which J. L. Burckhardt, the unwearying pioneer surveyor of Nubia, had already noted at the start of the previous century. Surrounded by their wives, their servants and their richly caparisoned horses, the dead reposed on litters as in the old days of Kerma. Their heavy diadems and silver bracelets set with coloured stones, have a wealth of reminders of Egypt or Meroe, such as the ram's head of Amon bearing a huge crown *atef*, the fringes of *uraei* or the busts of Isis. Alexandrian influences are clearly apparent in the treasures of silverware which strewed the floor; among the ewers, cups and patens, there was an incised plate showing Hermes seated on a globe with a griffin by his side; there are also huge bronze lamps and a wooden chest inlaid with panels of carved ivory. But the pottery is still of the traditional Meroitic type so that the qualities of a truly Nubian technique persist over the millennia.

Nobades or Blemmyes

Who were the people of Group X – Nobades or Blemmyes? The Blemmyes were warlike nomads customarily identified with the Bedja ethnic groups of the eastern desert. As regards the Nobades or Nobates, after mūch disputation they are accepted as Nubas.

In any event Blemmyes and Nobades are barely more than names for us, and it seems preferable to use the term 'Group X' or 'Ballana culture'.

Ancient literary evidences and epigraphic documents enable us to trace the main historical outlines. The historian Procopus claims that, towards the end of the third century, when the Roman emperor Diocletian pulled back the frontier to the First Cataract, he encouraged the Nobates to leave the oasis region and to establish themselves on the Nile, reckoning on their serving as a screen for Egypt against the incursions of the Blemmyes. In actual fact, under Theodosius towards +450, Philae was attacked by the Blemmyes and the Nobades; they were driven back eventually by forces commanded by Maximinus, and then by the prefect Florus.

After the advent of Christianity, the people of Nubia were permitted to continue to visit the sanctuary of Isis at Philae and for certain major feasts were allowed to borrow the statue of the goddess. Ḳasr Ibrīm may have been one of the staging posts for this pilgrimage, for what seems to have been a statuette of Isis in painted earthenware was found there. It was only under Justinian, between +535 and +537, that his general, Narses, closed the Temple of Philae and expelled the last priests.

11 The civilization of Napata and Meroe

Political organization

The nature of kingship

The most outstanding feature of political power in Nubia and central Sudan from the eighth century before the Christian era to the fourth century of the Christian era seems to have been its remarkable stability and continuity. Unlike many of the ancient kingdoms, the country escaped the upheavals associated with violent dynastic changes. Indeed one can say that basically the same royal lineage continued to rule uninterruptedly under the same traditions.

One of the peculiar features of the Meroitic political system was the choice of a new sovereign by election. Classical authors, from Herodotus, fifth century before the Christian era, to Diodorus of Sicily, first century before the Christian era, express their surprise about this usage, so different from that in other ancient kingdoms.

Fortunately we are able to reconstruct the succession procedures from Napatan inscriptions which describe the choice and coronation ceremonies in great detail. The Napatan coronation inscriptions are our best source for the understanding of the political institutions, in particular the features of kingship and the other related institutions. Although they are written in the contemporary style of Egyptian hieroglyphics, they show great differences from the usual run of similar New Kingdom inscriptions. Thus they have to be regarded as a product of their own culture.

Among these inscriptions the three latest, those of Amani-nete-yerike (−431 to −405), Harsiotef (−404 to −369) and Nastasen (−335 to −310) show that the kings were anxious to observe strict traditional practices and proclaim their insistence on the traditions and customs of their ancestors. At the same time, these texts give more details than the earlier ones, though their language is difficult to follow. They show a remarkable consistency in their subject matter and even sometimes in their phraseology. Thus, in all three cases, the king before his appointment was described as living among the other royal brethren at Meroe. He first succeeded to the throne at Meroe and then he journeyed northward to Napata for the ceremonies. Amani-nete-yerike says categorically that he was elected by the leaders of his armies to be king at the age of 41 and that he had fought a war before he could proceed to Napata for the coronation. Even when he reached Napata, he went into the royal palace where he received the crown of *Ta-Sti* as a further confirmation of his assumption of kingship. After this he entered the temple for the ceremony where he asked the god to grant him his kingship, which the god did as a matter of formality.

Earlier inscriptions confirm the conclusion that the succession to the throne was fixed before the king entered the temple. Thus the succession of Taharqa (– 689 to – 664) was decided by Shebitku (– 701 to – 689) who lived at Memphis in Egypt. Taharqa was summoned from among his royal brethren and journeyed northward, no doubt visiting Napata *en route*, and paid homage at Gematon (Kawa) before proceeding to Thebes.

Details of the ceremonies are given in Tanwetamani's (– 664 to – 653) stele: he lived somewhere outside Napata, perhaps among his other royal brothers with his mother Qalhata; there he was first proclaimed king and then started a festival procession, journeying northward to Napata and farther on to Elephantine and Karnak. It seems thus that the place where he had been before the start of the procession was south of Napata, i.e. Meroe. Consequently, the decision regarding the succession was made outside Napata, according to normal practice. Anlamani (– 623 to – 593) describes festivals at Gematon, where the stele was found, in similar terms and adds that he brought his mother to attend these ceremonies, as did Taharqa before him.

Important conclusions emerge from these inscriptions. One is that the journey northward to visit various temples was an important part of the coronation ceremony which every king would have to make on his accession to the throne; the second is that the Temple of Amun in Napata had a special role in this ceremony and that this remained unchallenged. All this has a direct bearing on G. A. Reisner's theory of the existence of two independent kingdoms of Napata recently restated by Hintze.

This theory was put forward by G. A. Reisner to explain the number of royal cemeteries. His basic assumption was that a royal burial was closely connected with the capital: a king would be buried not very far from his royal residence. Hence, the cemetery of El-Kurru, the earliest royal cemetery, and the cemetery of Nuri, which succeeded El-Kurru, were royal burial places up to the time of Nastasen, when the capital was Napata. Subsequently, the two cemeteries of Begrawiya South and North became royal cemeteries when the capital was moved to Meroe around – 300, after the reign of Nastasen. At Djabal Barkal, in Napata, however, there are two groups of pyramids. Archaeological and architectural considerations convinced Reisner that the first group fell immediately after Nastasen and the second group dated from the first century before the Christian era and ended when the Romans raided Napata in – 23 or soon after. Each group was assigned to a branch of the royal family ruling at Napata independently from the main ruling family at Meroe.

An analysis of all the relevant texts shows that the office of king was hereditary in the royal lineage. In Napata and Meroe the king was chosen among his royal brethren. The initiative in choosing a new sovereign came from the army leaders, high officials and clan chiefs. Any claimant of doubtful ability or unpopular with the electors might well be passed over. Further, it is plain that in theory the crown was to pass to the brothers of a king before descending to the next generation: from among twenty-seven kings ruling before Nastasen, fourteen were the brothers of preceding kings. There were, of course, exceptions when this or that king usurped the throne, but in such cases he tried to justify and legalize his action. There are also some signs that the right to the throne might depend even more on claims through the maternal line than on royal paternity. The role of the queen-mother in the choice of a new king is seen from many inscriptions. Some of these traits have close parallels among kingdoms and chiefdoms in various parts of Africa.

All the coronation ceremonies point to a sacral kingship in Napata and Meroe: the king was considered to be an adopted son of various deities. How far he himself was regarded as a god, or as the incarnation of a god, is not clear, but since he was chosen by the gods his actions were directed by them through the precepts of customary law. Strabo and Diodorus Siculus relate cases where priests, acting avowedly under divine instructions, ordered the king to commit suicide. They state that this custom persisted until the time of Ergamenos (about −250 to −125), who had had a Greek education which freed him from superstition and who executed the leading priests for their presumption. After that time the custom of royal suicide disappeared.

The rulers of Napata and Meroe used traditional Pharaonic titles in their inscriptions. Nowhere in their titulature do we encounter a Meroitic word for king. The title *kwr* (read *qere*, *qer* or *qeren*) appears only in Psammetik II's account of his conquest of Kush when he mentions the king Aspelta. Though this title must have been the usual form of address of Kushite sovereigns, it was not allowed to intrude into the monuments of Kush.

The *candace*: the role of the queen-mother

The exact role played by royal ladies in the earlier periods is not quite clear, but there are many indications that they occupied prominent positions and important offices in the realm. During the Kushite rule over Egypt the office of the chief priestess (*Dewat Neter*) to the god Amun in Thebes was held by the daughter of the king and gave her great economic and political influence.

The queen-mother's important role at the election and coronation ceremonies of her son is mentioned by Taharqa and Anlamani in such a way as to leave no doubt about her decisive influence and specific status. She also exercised an influence through a complicated system of adoption, whereby the queen-mother, designated by the title Mistress of Kush, adopted the wife of her son. On the stele of Nastasen (−335 to −310) the upper scene shows his mother Pelekhs and his wife Sakhakh each holding a sistrum which seems to have been the sign of their office. The inscription of Anlamani says that he had dedicated each of his four sisters to one of the four temples of Amun to be sistrum players and to pray for him before this god.

In the later period these queens – either mothers or wives – started to assume political power and proclaim themselves sovereign, even adopting the royal title Son of Re, Lord of the Two Lands (*sa Re*, *neb Tawy*) or Son of Re and King (*sa Re*, *nswbit*). Many of them became famous, and in Graeco-Roman times Meroe was known to have been ruled by a line of *candaces*, *kandake* or queens-regnant.

The title is derived from the Meroitic *Ktke* or *Kdke* meaning queen-mother. Another title – *qere* – meaning ruler was not used until the Meroitic script appeared. As a matter of fact we have only four queens known to have used this title, namely

Amanirenas, Amanishekhete, Nawidemak and Maleqereabar, all by definition being *candaces*. It is noteworthy that in the royal tombs of Nuri, from Taharqa (died −664) to Nastasen (died about −310) there is no evidence of a queen having the full burial of a reigning monarch and during this period no reigning queen is known. The earliest attested reigning queen was Shanakdekhete, early in the second century before the Christian era and she was allowed a full royal burial in Begrawiya North. Most probably, in the beginning, the title and the office did not mean more than queen-mother. From Shanakdekhete onwards we have a series of reigning queens, but beginning with Amanirenas in the first century before the Christian era there seems to be another development. This was the close association of the first wife of the king and, perhaps, their eldest son on many of the important monuments. This suggests some degree of co-regency since the wife who survived her husband often became the reigning *candace*. However, this system did not last for more than three generations and seems to come to an end after Natakamani, Amenitere and Sherakarer in the first half of the first century of the Christian era. All this points to the internal development of a local institution which was not a copy of a foreign practice such as that of the Ptolemies in Egypt, for example Cleopatra. Indeed we can observe how these institutions grew in complexity over the centuries.

Central and provincial administration

At the centre of the administration stood the king, an absolute autocratic ruler, whose word was law. He did not delegate his power to any person, nor did he share it with anyone. In fact, there is a total absence of one administrator, such as a High Priest for all the temples, or a vizier in whose hands some degree of power was concentrated. The royal residence formed the centre of the administrative system. According to a recent survey of the evidence it seems that Meroe was the only town which can be regarded as the royal residence and centre of administration. Piankhi was rather vague as to his place of residence, while it is obvious that Memphis was the capital of his immediate successors of the Twenty-fifth Dynasty of Egypt. However, Taharqa clearly indicates that he was living among his royal brothers with his mother. From other inscriptions it is clear that these royal brothers lived at Meroe.

The central administration was run by a number of high officials whose Egyptian titles are preserved in two stelae of Asyelta. Among them we find – apart from army commanders – the chiefs of the treasury, seal bearers, heads of archives, the chief scribe of Kush and other scribes.

Military leaders appear several times on these inscriptions at critical points. They were charged with proclaiming the succession of a new king and carrying out the traditional ceremonies of coronation. In fact, they may have had some significant role in the choice of the successor. From this one can suppose that, most probably, the majority were members of the royal family, and perhaps even senior members. It was customary for the king not to go into battle but to stay in his palace, assigning the conduct of the war to one of the generals.

As for the administration of the provinces, there are traces of royal palaces to be found in many localities. Each palace formed a small administrative unit, headed perhaps by a chief seal bearer who kept the stores and accounts of the residence.

11.1 *Pyramid of King Natekamani at Meroe with ruins of chapel and pylon in foreground (Photo, Oriental Institute, University of Chicago)*

11.2 *Granite ram at Naqa (Photo, Oriental Institute, University of Chicago)*

However, in the later period starting perhaps towards the end of the first century before the Christian era we have enough records of provincial administrators to reconstruct at least the skeleton of the northern province of the kingdom which seems to have developed very fast in response to the unsettled conditions following the Roman conquest of Egypt and their unsuccessful attempt to advance farther south into Nubia. To meet this situation on the frontier a special administration for Lower Nubia was created. At its head was the *Paqar, qar* a prominent court personality, possibly a royal prince, if the first holder may be considered to have established the rule. The first was Akinidad, the son of Teritiqas and Amanirenas, who fought against the Roman invasion of Nubia. The same title was also borne by Arkankharor, Arikakhatani and Sherekarer (the king of the Djabal Ḳayli rock pictures) and the three sons of Natakamani and Amanitere (– 12 to + 12). Their names with the title *pqr* have been found on inscriptions from Napata, Meroe and Naqa.

Under the *Paqar*, the leading officer in charge of the administration was the *peshte*. Two other important posts under the *peshte* were the *pelmes-ate* (general of the water) and *pelmes-adab* (general of the land). These two officers seem to have been responsible for looking after the meagre, yet vital, communications of Nubia by land and by water, to ensure the flow of trade with Egypt, to control the frontiers and check the dangerous movements of the nomads both to the east and west of the Nile. These officials were helped by other minor officials, scribes, priests and local administrators.

Economic and social life

Ecology

The Kingdom of Kush depended on a broad basis of economic activity. It was as varied as the geographical diversity of the region which extended from Lower Nubia to the south of Sennār and to the Djabal Moya region in the southern Djazīra plain and included extensive areas between the Nile Valley and the Red Sea. Similarly large areas on the west of the Nile were probably under Meroitic influence, though their extent is still unknown. This wide area ranges from arid lands to those which receive appreciable summer rainfall. In Nubia economic activity was based on the type of agriculture usual in the Nile Valley where the river with its single course provides the only source of water. Recent archaeological work has indicated that the levels of the Nile were low and, since Nubia lies outside the rain-belt, the ecological conditions were not suitable for an agriculture designed to support an appreciable population. In fact it has been suggested that during the early part of the Napatan period Lower Nubia was for a considerable length of time entirely depopulated and that it was only from the third or second century before the Christian era, and as a result of the introduction of the *sāḳiya*, that it became repopulated.

In Upper Nubia flood plains, such as the Kerma Basin, the Letti Basin and Nuri, made cultivable thanks to the Nile flood or by the use of water-lifting devices, permitted the growth of large urban centres of considerable historical importance such as those at Barkal, Kawa, Tabo, Soleb or Amara. In this area agrarian economy played a greater role and plantations of dates and vines, in particular, are referred to several times in the inscriptions of Taharqa, Hersiotef and Nastasen.

From the junction of the River Atbara with the main Nile southward, the Nile is no longer that decisive single course which cuts through desert land. Instead, each of the Nile tributaries (the Atbara, Blue Nile, White Nile, Dinder, Rahad and so on) is equally important and offers the same agricultural and other economic possibilities, but with a wider area of cultivation.

Agriculture and animal husbandry

At the time of the rise of the Napata kingdom, animal husbandry had a millenary tradition and, together with agriculture, formed the main source of subsistence of the people. Apart from long-horned and short-horned cattle, the people bred sheep, goats and to a lesser extent horses and donkeys, as beasts of burden. Camels were introduced only comparatively late, at the end of the first century before the Christian era.

The primacy of cattle-breeding in the kingdom of Kush is attested in many ways: in iconography, in burial rites, in metaphors – an army without a leader is compared to a herd without a herdsman, and so on.

Offerings to the temples consisted mainly of livestock and it seems that the wealth of the kings, the aristocracy and the temple priests was measured in cattle. The accounts of classical authors, Strabo and Diodorus of Sicily, leave no doubt about the pastoralist character of Meroitic society, which in many respects was similar to later African cattle-breeding societies.

Throughout the whole history of Napata and Meroe, the development of agriculture in the northern parts was influenced by both climate and the scarcity of fertile land in the very narrow valley of the Nile. The chief irrigation machines at this time were the *shadūf*, to be superseded later by the *sāḳiya*. The latter, called in Nubian *kole*, appeared in Lower Nubia only in Meroitic times, but a more precise date is difficult to determine. The sites at Dakka and at Gammai, dating from the third century before the Christian era, seem to be the oldest to contain remains of *sāḳiya*. The introduction of this irrigation machine had a decisive influence on agriculture, especially in Dongola, as this wheel lifts water three to eight metres with much less expenditure of labour and time than the *shadūf*, which is driven by human energy; the *sāḳiya*, on the other hand, is driven by buffalo or other animals.

The main cereals cultivated were barley, wheat and, above all, sorghum or *durra* of local origin, and also lentils (*Lens esculenta*), cucumbers, melons and gourds.

Among technical crops, the first place belongs to cotton. It was unknown in Ancient Egypt but there are many indications that its cultivation in the Nile Valley started in the Kingdom of Kush before the beginning of the Christian era. Evidence from earlier times is scanty, but about the fourth century before the Christian era the cultivation of cotton and the knowledge of its spinning and weaving in Meroe reached a very high level. It is even maintained that the export of textiles was one of the sources of wealth of Meroe. The Axumite King Ezana boasted in his inscription that he destroyed large cotton plantations in Meroe.

An important branch of agriculture was the cultivation of fruit in orchards and grapes in vineyards. Many of these belonged to temples and were cultivated by slaves.

Generally speaking there existed in the Napata and Meroe periods the same branches of agriculture as in Ancient Egypt, but in another relationship. Animal husbandary dominated; agriculture and garden and orchard cultivation were less developed, though cotton started to be cultivated here much earlier than in Egypt. So far as is known the agricultural products were not exported, as they were hardly sufficient for local consumption.

Mineral resources

During antiquity the Kingdom of Kush, it is said, was one of the richest countries of the known world. This renown was due more to the mineral wealth of the border lands to the east of the Nile than to the core of the kingdom itself.

Kush was one of the main gold-producing areas in the ancient world. Gold was mined between the Nile and the Red Sea, mostly in the part to the north of the eighteenth parallel, where many traces of ancient mining are to be found. Excavations at Meroe and Mussawwarat es-Sufra have revealed temples with walls and statues covered by gold leaf. Gold and its export not only were one of the main sources of the wealth and greatness of the kingdom, but greatly influenced foreign relations with Egypt and Rome. It has been computed that during antiquity Kush produced about 1,600,000 kilograms of pure gold.

The eastern desert was rich in various precious and semi-precious stones such as amethyst, carbuncle, hyacinth, chrysolith, beryl and others. Even if these mines were not all controlled by the Meroitic kingdom, in the last resort all their products went through Meroitic trade channels, and so increased the fame of Meroe as one of the richest countries in the ancient world.

The problem of iron working

The large mounds of slag found near the ancient town of Meroe and elsewhere in the Butana have been the cause of much speculation on the importance of iron in Meroitic civilization. It has been maintained that the knowledge of iron smelting and iron working in many parts of sub-Saharan Africa was derived from Meroe. Already in 1911 A. H. Sayce declared that Meroe must have been the 'Birmingham of ancient Africa' and this view was current until quite recently among scholars, and became accepted theory in the majority of works dealing with African or Sudanese history.

In recent years this generally accepted view has been contested by some scholars who have raised a number of serious objections to it, pointing out that the iron objects found in graves are extremely few in number. In any case, one cannot deduce a knowledge of the smelting of iron from examples of its working-up into objects.

Towns, crafts and trade

It has been suggested that urban development in Lower Nubia followed political development and the growing interest of the Meroites in their northern borders with Egypt. They benefited from trade relations with Egypt and consequently large towns and thriving local communities located in strategic positions such as Ḳasr Ibrīm or

Djabal Adda grew up in Lower Nubia. Political and religious life centred round a local magnate or a family with hereditary administrative or military office. This aristocracy lived in castles like that at Karanog or in palaces like the Governor's Palace in Mussawwarat es-Sufra.

Pliny, quoting as his authorities Bion and Juba, has preserved the names of many Meroitic towns on both banks of the Nile, situated between the First Cataract and the town of Meroe.

The town of Faras, Pakhoras, was the main administrative centre of the province called *Akin*, which corresponded to Lower Nubia. Some official buildings have been excavated, among them the so-called Western Palace dating from the first century of the Christian era and built of sun-dried bricks, and a fortification situated on the river bank. South of Faras Meroitic settlements are rare. The region is inhospitable and the valley too narrow to meet the needs of a large population. Only at Kawa, opposite the modern city of Dongola, do we find wider lands and increased signs of ancient occupation.

Upstream from Kawa there are no sites of importance until Napata is reached. Its place in royal ceremonies and religious customs has already been stressed. The importance of this town derived from its location at the northern end of the caravan route which skirted the three scarcely navigable cataracts. All goods from the southern and central parts of the kingdom, as well as from the interior of Africa, had to go through Napata. Though the town site of Napata remains partly unexplored, the royal cemeteries at El-Kurru, Nuri and Djabal Barkal, as well as the temples of Djabal Barkal and Sanam, have all been investigated. We can thus assess the importance of Napata as a royal and religious centre in the earlier period of the history of Kush.

The next important urban centre in the Nile Valley was at Dangeil, five miles north of Berber, where the remains of brick buildings and walls have been discovered. The site itself seems to lie on an important route leading from Meroe to the north.

On the Island of Meroe, which corresponds roughly to the modern Butane plain lying between the Atbara and the Blue Nile, many traces of Meroitic settlement have been found.

Although the city of Meroe is mentioned for the first time in the last quarter of the fifth century before the Christian era, in the inscription of Amannateieriko in the Kawa temple under the name of *B.rw.t*, the lowest excavation strata show that a large settlement existed on this site already in the eighth century. The part hitherto excavated and examined is sufficient to show that Meroe at its height was an enormous city with all the attributes of urban life. As such Meroe must be numbered among the most important monuments of early civilization on the African continent. The main elements of the excavated parts of the city are the royal city with palaces, a royal bath and other buildings, and the Temple of Amun. In the vicinity were found the Temple of Isis, the Lion Temple, the Sun Temple, many pyramids and non-royal cemeteries.

Not far away from Meroe lies the site of Wad ben Naqa, consisting of ruins of at least two temples. Recent excavations have revealed a large building which was perhaps a palace, and a beehive structure which may have been an enormous silo. This and many scattered mounds in the vicinity indicate the importance of this town, the residence of the *candaces* and a Nile port.

Among other important sites, the following should be mentioned. Basa, lying in Wādī Hawad, has a temple and an enormous *hafir* surrounded by stone statues of lions. The most interesting feature is that this town did not grow haphazardly, but was strictly planned according to the terrain then covered by trees and shrubs. Of exceptional importance from many points of view is Mussawwarat es-Sufra in the Wādī al-Banat at some distance from the Nile. Its main feature, the Great Enclosure, consists of many buildings and walled enclosures surrounding a temple built in the first century before the Christian era, or a little earlier.

Apart from their administrative and religious functions, the Meroitic towns were also important centres of craft and trade. The existing evidence indicates a high technological and artistic level of crafts. Although in the earlier period Egyptian influence is unmistakable, from the third century before the Christian era, Meroitic craftsmen and artists created a highly original and independent artistic tradition.

Pottery is the best-known of all the products of the Meroitic civilization and owes its fame to its quality both of texture and of decoration. There are two distinct traditions: the hand-made pottery made by women which shows a remarkable continuity of form and style and reflects a deep-rooted African tradition, and the wheel-turned ware made by men which is more varied and responsive to stylistic changes.

Jewellery was another highly developed craft. It has been found in considerable quantities, mostly in royal tombs. As with other artefacts, the earlier jewellery was closely modelled on Egyptian styles and only later examples are characteristically Meroitic in style and ornamentation. The main materials were gold, silver and semi-precious stones, and the range of artefacts goes from plaques to necklaces, bracelets, ear-rings and finger-rings.

Cabinet-makers produced various kinds of furniture, especially beds, but also wooden caskets, strong-boxes and even musical instruments. Weavers made cotton and linen textiles. Tanners processed hides and leather.

All this indicates that in Meroe there existed a comparatively large class of craftsmen to which belonged also artists, architects and sculptors. How these crafts were organized is so far unknown, as the names of crafts in Meroitic inscriptions remain undeciphered. It is likely that workshops for the temple services existed as in Egypt and perhaps *ergasteries* were organized at the royal court.

The Kingdom of Kush formed an ideal entrepôt for the caravan routes between the Red Sea, the Upper Nile and the Nile–Chad savannah. It is therefore not surprising that foreign trade played an important role in the Meroitic economy as well as in its politics. Foreign trade was directed mainly to Egypt and the Mediterranean world and later perhaps to southern Arabia. The chief trade route went along the Nile, although in some parts it crossed the savannah, for instance, between Meroe and Napata, and Napata and Lower Nubia. The Island of Meroe must have been criss-crossed by many caravan routes and it was also the starting-point for caravans to the Red Sea region, northern Ethiopia, Kordofān and Dārfūr. The control of this large network of routes was a constant worry to the Meroitic kings, for the nomadic peoples very often raided the caravans. The rulers built fortresses at strategic points in the Bajude steppe –

between Meroe and Napata, for instance – to protect the trade routes and also dug wells along them.

Social structure

In the absence of any direct information, it is almost impossible to present a coherent picture of the social structure in Meroe. So far we know only about the existence of a higher or ruling class composed of the king and his relatives, of a court and provincial aristocracy that fulfilled various administrative and military functions, and of a very influential temple priesthood. At the opposite end of the social scale our sources often mention the existence of slaves recruited from prisoners of war. From indirect evidence we can surmise that, apart from cultivators and cattle-breeders who must have formed the majority of the Meroitic population, there existed a middle class of craftsmen, traders and various minor officials and servants, but nothing at all is known about their social status. Until more evidence becomes available, any attempt to characterize the type of social and production relationships would be premature.

Religion

General features

The Meroitic peoples derived most of their official religious ideas from Egypt. The majority of gods worshipped in Meroitic temples correspond to those of Egypt, and earlier Meroitic kings considered Amun the highest god, from whom they derived their rights to the throne. The priests of the temples of Amun exercised an enormous influence, at least to the time of King Ergamenes, who seems to have broken their former absolute control. But even later kings showed – at least in their inscriptions – a veneration for Amun and his priests, who were variously favoured by gifts of gold, slaves, cattle and landed property.

Along with Pharaonic divinities such as Isis, Horus, Thoth, Arensnuphis, Satis, with their original symbols, purely Meroitic gods were worshipped like the Lion-god Apedemak or the god Sebewyemeker (Sbomeker). The official cult of these gods began as late as the third century before the Christian era. It seems that they were formerly local gods of the southern parts of the empire and came to prominence only when the Egyptian influence began to fade and was replaced by more particularly Meroitic cultural traits.

Apedemak, a warrior god, was a divinity of great importance to the Meroites. He is depicted with a lion's head, and lions played some part in the ceremonies of the temple, especially in Musawwarat es-Sufra. At the same place we find another Meroitic god unknown to the Egyptians, Sebewyemeker, who was perhaps the chief local god, since he was considered as creator. Some goddesses are also depicted at Naqa, but their names and place in the Meroitic pantheon remain unknown.

The presence of two sets of divinities, one of Egyptian and the other of local origin, is reflected also in temple architecture.

Amun temples

Religious symbolism played an important role in the designing of temples in Ancient Egypt. The act of worship was expressed in elaborate and complex rituals and each part of the temple had a specific role in the progress of the ritual. These various parts, e.g. halls, courtyards, chambers, chapels, etc., were laid out axially producing a long processional corridor. Such temples were built in the Dongola region by Peye and Taharqa and their successors. The most important of these temples dedicated to Amun-Re in Napata was built at Djabal Barkal. Meroe does not figure in earlier coronation inscriptions as having a temple to Amun, but towards the end of the first century before the Christian era the city was honoured by the building of one of these temples and a long inscription in Meroitic script was set up in front. This temple became perhaps the leading temple of Amun-Re in the later period of the kingdom.

Lion temples

The name 'lion temple' is suggested by a marked preponderance of lion figures, whether sculptured in the round, guarding the approach and the entrance of temples, or in relief in a prominent position. The figure of the lion represents also the chief Meroitic god Apedemak. This does not mean that every temple of this kind was dedicated solely to Apedemak. The existence of this type has been observed by different authorities, but in the description of individual temples various names have been given to them. Thus, we hear of the Apis Temple, Isis Temple, Sun Temple, Augustus-head Temple, Fresco Chamber, and so on. The use of the term 'lion temple' would eliminate further misunderstanding, the figure of the lion being its most distinctive feature. Statues of rams are associated with Amun temples at Barkal, Kawa, Meroe, Naqa, where the lion statues are entirely absent, even when the lion-god Apedemak was probably one of the deities worshipped and when his figure appeared among those of the other deities. Although ram-headed deities, Amun-Re and Khnum, appear quite often on the reliefs of these lion temples there is no single instance of a ram statue being found associated with any of the lion temples.

Distribution and types of lion temples

Besides thirty-two recorded lion temples, there are fourteen other sites in which the presence of lion temples is almost certain. If we add to this the occurrence of priestly titles associated with temples in localities such as Nalete, Tiye, etc., the number of these temples must have been very great indeed. They seem to have been distributed throughout the whole realm of Meroe. From a study of this distribution it is apparent that there are four localities where several temples have been discovered: Naqa with eight temples, Musawwarat es-Sufra and Meroe with six temples at each site and Djabal Barkal with three temples.

All lion temples can be divided into two basic types. The first is a two-chamber temple, the earliest examples of this type being built of plain mud-brick without a pylon. The second type has a single chamber only and most of these temples have a pylon in front, although the earlier examples are without it.

Two local sources can be suggested for the appearance of the second type of lion temple. That it had developed from the first type seems evident from the fact that B 900 was reconstructed at a subsequent date with the plan of the second type. On the other hand, there are several small single-chamber structures at both Barkal and Kerma from which the second type might have derived its origin. The earliest examples of this type can be found perhaps below Meroe M 250, possibly dating from Aspelta, and below temple 100 of Musawwarat es-Sufra dating from before –500.

Although the two types of temple – Amun and lion temples – suggest at first glance two kinds of religion, a careful reconsideration shows that in fact there was only one religion in Meroe. For the coexistence of two religions would presuppose either a considerable degree of religious tolerance which can hardly be expected at that time, or fierce conflict and continuous religious wars and this does not appear on any form of record. On the contrary, the pantheon worshipped in the Amun temples seems also to have been worshipped in the lion temples, except that certain gods were given more prominence in one temple than in another. The gods are after all a mixture of Egyptian gods such as Amun-Re or the Osirian triad or indigenous local gods such as Apedemak, Mandulis and Sebewyemeker. The differences in the temple plans indicate differences rather in the rituals than in the religion. The rituals connected with coronation ceremonies needed an Amun-temple type to accommodate processions and festivities. This form of religious practice made it possible to incorporate various local gods and beliefs without conflict and hence helped to give coherence for a very long period to a kingdom composed of very diverse elements.

12

The spreading of Christianity in Nubia

The social structures and historical events of Nubia's early Christian period were shaped by two main factors. One of these was the decline of the Kingdom of Meroe. The other was the Romanization and then the Christianization of Egypt, its northern neighbour. After the fall of the Kingdom of Meroe, a Nobadian state was formed in northern Nubia between the First Cataract and the Dal, i.e. the area between the Second and the Third Cataracts. It emerged after a long series of struggles between the Blemmyes and the Nobades, who finally gained control of the Nile Valley and pushed the Blemmyes (Bega or Buga) out into the eastern desert.

The Polish excavations at Faras confirmed that ancient Pachoras was the capital of the Kingdom of the Nobades towards the end of its existence. It was the site of their sovereigns' palace, which was transformed later into the earliest cathedral.

The remains of their material culture show that the contrasts in their society's living standards were extreme. The masses were relatively poor. Their humble burial places made the British archaeologist, G. A. Reisner, use the term 'the X-Group Culture' – for lack of a more exact historical definition. In contrast to the common people's low level, the ruling classes, princes and court cultivated the traditions of Meroitic art and culture. The most representative remains of the material culture of the tenuous upper crust of society are the lavish tomb furniture of the well-known tumuli of Ballana, discovered in 1938 by W. B. Emery, and the sovereigns' palace of Nubia at Faras mentioned earlier.

The Polish excavations at Faras led to the discovery under the Nobadian sovereigns' palace of a Christian church built of unbaked bricks that must have antedated the end of the fifth century. This early dating has, it is true, recently been contested, but the facts are that among 'X-Group' tombs there have been found Christian graves and that Christian oil lamps and pottery, decorated with the sign of the cross, appear in X-Group settlements on Meinarti Island. This is strong evidence that very early, even before the official Christianization of Nubia by the mission headed by the priest Julianos which was sent out by Empress Theodora of Byzantium, the Christian faith had reached the Nobades and readily made converts among the poor. A further argument for an early penetration of Nubia by the Christian faith is the existence there of monasteries and hermitages since the end of the fifth century. It can, therefore, be confidently stated that the Christian religion had gradually infiltrated into Nubia before its official conversion which, according to John of Ephesus, took place in +543.

Many factors explain this early Christianization of the country of the Nobades. Both the Roman empire, still hostile to Christianity in the third century, and the Christian empire, in the fourth, fifth and sixth centuries, persecuted those who did not obey official injunctions with regard to religion. Hence many Egyptians perhaps, and also Nubians fleeing from Egypt, may have brought their faith to the Nobades dwelling south of Aswan. The traders' caravans passed through Aswan on their southward route, carrying beliefs along with the rest. Byzantine diplomacy, too, played anything but a small role in the fifth and sixth centuries, Byzantium being anxious to remain on good terms with Axum in the face of the Persian threat in the Red Sea. In +524 a formal treaty enabled Axum to send Blemmyes and Nobades to take part in the projected expedition in the Yemen. The priests were certainly not inactive in these transactions and relationships.

By order of Empress Theodora, the priest Julianos gave Monophysite baptism only to the sovereigns of the country. Under the influence of Christian Egypt most of its people had been strongly attracted to the new faith and had adopted it much earlier. A church on the banks of the Nile in an outlying district was serving a humble Christian community back in the sixth century. The conversion of the Nobadian rulers to Christianity was for them an important political act. They no longer had a well-defined religious ideology with which to hold the people's allegiance and Christianity now gave them access to Egypt, where since the fourth century the bishop had resided on the island of Philae. Through Egypt they could reach the Mediterranean and the centre of the civilization of that era – Byzantium.

The Kingdom of the Nobadae (Nūba in Arabic), known as Nobadia, extended from Philae to the Second Cataract. Its capital was Faras. In the south as far as ancient Meroe, another Nubian kingdom emerged in the sixth century with Old Dongola (Dūnkūla in Arabic) as its capital. This kingdom was later called Makuria (Muḳurra in Arabic). In contrast to northern Nubia, which had adopted the Monophysite doctrine, Makuria was converted to orthodox Melkite by a mission which Emperor Justinian sent out in +567 to +570.

As a result of the Polish excavations carried out at Old Dongola since +1964, four churches and the Christian royal palace have been identified. One of these buildings dates back to the end of the seventh or the beginning of the eighth century. Beneath it the remains of an earlier church built of unbaked bricks have been discovered. This religious building, which was not the cathedral, had five naves and was supported by sixteen granite columns 5.20 metres in height. In view of the magnitude of the remains discovered, there is reason to think that the enthusiastic descriptions given by an Arab traveller in the eleventh century were historically accurate: Dongola was an important capital, at least as regards its monuments.

Finally, between +660 and +700 the Makurites also adopted the Monophysite doctrine and the fact was not without important consequences. Towards +580, with the support of the Nobadae, a Byzantine mission came to Alodia and its leader, Bishop Longinos, noted that the country had already been partly converted by the Axumites. Towards the end of the sixth century Nubia was therefore a Christian country consisting of three kingdoms: Nobadia in the north, Makuria in the centre and Alodia in the south. Their mutual relations are not even yet entirely clear, at any rate in respect of the first period of their independence.

Since Monneret de Villard's research in 1938, many archaeological discoveries have been accumulated, particularly through the 'Nubian campaign' organized under the auspices of Unesco in 1960–5 to explore ground that was to be flooded by the Nile water above the Sadd al-'Āalī, the High Dam. In some parts of northern Nubia the slow rise of the water level in the storage basin allowed digging to continue until 1971, and at Ḳasr Ibrīm, which is not flooded, till the present day.

The results of the research of these years have often been exceptionally valuable and have brought the problems of Christian Nubia back into the foreground.

Although Nubia, unlike Egypt, was not part of the Byzantine empire, there undoubtedly existed between them definite links forged by the missions of the priests Julianos and Longinos. The organization of the Nubian government, as its nomenclature shows, was strictly modelled on the Byzantine bureaucracy. Though the Persian invasion of Egypt in +616 stopped at the northern frontier of Nubia, evidence exists that the northern kingdom was invaded by Sassanid detachments stationed south of the First Cataract. In any case the invasion by Chosroes II broke the direct links between Nubia and Egypt, by then Christian, and in particular the contacts between the Nubian clergy and the patriarchate of Alexandria, which officially supervised the church of Nubia. In +641 Egypt came under the rule of the Arabs. Christian Nubia was severed from the Mediterranean culture for centuries to come.

At first the Arabs did not consider the conquest of Nubia important, and only made raids into the north. Therefore, as soon as Egypt submitted, they signed with Nubia a treaty called a *baḳt*, which bound the Nubians to pay an annual tribute of slaves and certain goods and the Arabs to provide a suitable quantity of food and clothing. During the seven centuries of Christian Nubia's independence, both sides regarded the treaty as valid in principle, but more than one armed clash occurred. Thus, almost as soon as the *baḳt* was signed, the Amīr 'Abdallāh ibn Abū Ṣaḥr raided Dongola in +651–2; but that did not interrupt the constant trade between Nubia and Muslim Egypt.

Northern and central Nubia united to form one state, doubtless in consequence of the first skirmishes between the Arabs from Egypt and the Nubians. Maḳrīzī, quoting earlier Arab sources, states that in the middle of the seventh century the whole of central and northern Nubia as far as the Alodian border was ruled by the same king, Ḳalidurut. The Christian sources seem to prove that the union of Nubia was the work of King Merkurios, who came to the throne in +607 and is said to have introduced Monophysitism into Makuria. He set up the capital of the united kingdom in Dongola.

To this day the question of Monophysitism in Nubia is not entirely clear, especially as regards the kingdom's relations with the orthodox Melkite church. It is still possible that the Melkite doctrine persisted in some form in the interior of the kingdom. It is known that as late as the fourteenth century the province of Maris, the former kingdom of northern Nubia, was subject to a Melkite bishop who, as metropolitan resident in Tafa, ruled over a diocese which included the whole of

12.1 *Faras cathedral (Photo, Warsaw National Museum)*

Nubia. Moreover, except in the eighth century, Alexandria always had two patriarchs, a Monophysite and a Melkite.

When King Kyriakos learned that the Umayyad governor had imprisoned the Patriarch of Alexandria, he attacked Egypt on that pretext and penetrated as far as Fusṭāṭ. As soon as the Patriarch was released, the Nubians went home. Kyriakos' expedition to Fusṭāṭ proves that Nubia did not confine itself strictly to defence, but also took offensive action against Muslim Egypt.

Military expeditions, however, are not the sole evidence of the vigour of the Nubian state after the beginning of the eighth century. Archaeological discoveries have also proved the extraordinary development of culture, art and monumental architecture in Nubia during that period. In +707 Bishop Paulos rebuilt Faras Cathedral and decorated it with splendid murals.

Some important religious buildings in Old Dongola date from that period. Other Nubian churches, such as those of ʿAbdallāh Nirḳī and Al-Sabu'a, were splendidly decorated with murals, which became a constant feature of ceremonial decoration.

The Christian period was a time of rapid economic development in Nubia. The population of northern Nubia was about 50,000. The introduction of *sāḳiya* irrigation in the Ptolemaic and Roman periods had enlarged the area under cultivation by watering it between the abundant Nile floods of that time, and it produced wheat, barley, millet and grapes. The abundant date harvest from the palm plantations also raised the country's living standards.

Trade with neighbouring countries increased but extended far beyond them. The inhabitants of Makuria sold ivory to Byzantium and copper and gold to Ethiopia. Their merchants' caravans went to the heart of Africa, to the lands which are now Nigeria and Ghana. The well-to-do classes preferred Byzantine dress. The women wore long robes, often decorated with coloured embroidery.

As has already been said, the organization of power in Christian Nubia was modelled on Byzantium. The civil governor of the province was the eparch, whose authority was symbolized by the horned crown which he wore on a helmet decorated with a crescent. He usually wore a full robe held in by a scarf. The fringes of the bishops' stoles, which they wore over their rich and complex liturgical vestments, were adorned with small bells.

That the Nubians were famous archers is attested by many ancient and Arab authors. In addition to the bow they used the sword and the javelin.

Sacred buildings, with a few rare exceptions, were built of unbaked bricks. Only in the cathedrals of Ḳasr Ibrīm, Faras and Dongola were the walls made of stone or burnt bricks. Most churches were built in the basilical style, but cruciform or central-plan churches are sometimes found in Nubian architecture. The decoration of the first period, that is, until the end of the seventh century, can only be deduced from the monumental cathedrals mentioned above.

Except for parts of converted pagan buildings, for example at Faras, the decoration was of sandstone and repeated the traditional scroll-work pattern borrowed by Meroitic art from the Hellenistic art of the Roman east. Mention should be made of the beautiful sculptured volutes of the foliated capitals. Icons painted on wooden panels or carved were probably used at that time as ritual images.

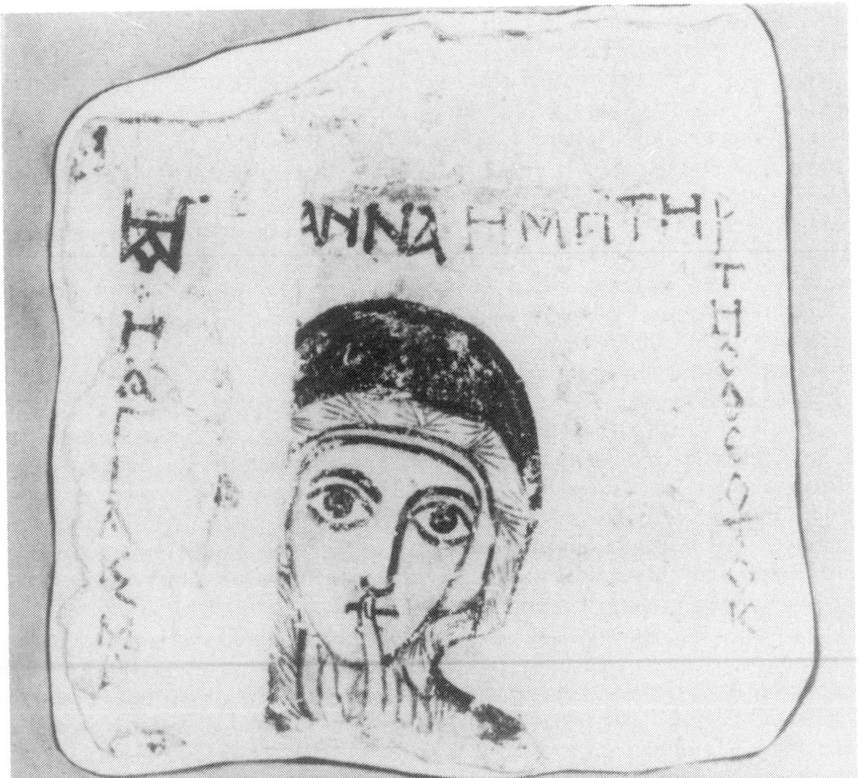

12.2 *Head of St Anne: a mural in North Aisle of Faras Cathedral (eighth century) (Photo, Warsaw National Museum)*

12.3 *Christian Nubian ceramic (G. Mokhtar)*

The oldest monuments of Christian art in Nubia are powerfully influenced by Coptic Egypt. This is chiefly shown by their subjects, e.g. the frieze of doves or eagles recalling their images on Coptic stelae.

From the eighth century onwards Nubian churches were decorated with *fresco secco* paintings. Thanks to the Faras discoveries of +1961–4, it is possible, from more than 120 mural paintings in perfect condition, including portraits of bishops whose dates of office can be found in the List of Bishops, to deduce a general evolution of style in Nubian paintings, which is confirmed by fragments of murals from other Nubian churches.

Faras was at that time undoubtedly the artistic centre at least of northern Nubia. The style of the paintings found north of Faras at ʿAbdallāh Nirḳī and Tamit, and south of it at Sonḳi Tino, is definitely provincial by comparison with the great works at Faras.

From the beginning of the eighth century to the middle of the ninth, Nubian painters preferred violet tones in their pictures. This period of Nubian painting was strongly influenced by Coptic art, the traditions of which were derived from the expressive style of the Fayyūm portraits. One of the most representative works of that period is the head of St Anne of Faras (now in the Warsaw Museum), but the influence of Byzantine art and its themes can also be seen.

Later that style developed, and until the middle of the tenth century white is clearly predominant. This may be due to the influence of Syro-Palestinan painting, which is distinguished by a characteristic way of rendering double folds of vestments and certain iconographic features. Perhaps the fact that Jerusalem was at that time a goal of pilgrimage for all the countries of the Christian East may account for this development in contemporary Nubian painting.

Very close ties between the Monophysite Kingdom of Nubia and the Monophysite sect of the Jacobites of Antioch are also known to have existed at that time. Deacon John and Abu Salih both mention that in the reign of King Kyriakos the Monophysite (Jacobite) Patriarch of Alexandria was the head of the Nubian church. A very strong realist trend then appeared for the first time in Nubian painting; its best example is the portrait of Bishop Kyros of Faras (now in Khartoum Museum).

Excavation has unearthed a vast quantity of artefacts, pottery being the most abundant. W. Y. Adams has made a systematic study of them. He finds that they yield evidence of interesting technical, stylistic and economico-social developments.

Even before +750, Aswan supplied the south with an appreciable proportion of the ceramics used there. This trade was not interrupted when the Muslims settled in Egypt.

To sum up, until the ninth century, Nubia enjoyed an initial period of prosperity which was not greatly disturbed by its usually peaceful Muslim neighbours. The cultural unity of early Christian Nubia is difficult to discern. In Faras, the aristocracy and the administrative officials spoke Greek, as did the dignitaries of the church. The clergy also understood Coptic, which was perhaps the language of many refugees. As for Nubian, while it was widely spoken by the population, the only traces remaining of a written form of the language date from a later period, probably not earlier than the middle of the ninth century.

Christian Nubia's golden age, around +800, was yet to come.

13 Pre-Axumite culture

The northern regions of Ethiopia, which were to emerge from prehistoric times about the fifth century before the Christian era, do not seem to have been very densely populated in an earlier age. The scant information we have, however, indicates that human groups developed there in much the same way as in the rest of the Horn of Africa.

During the last ten millennia before the Christian era pastoral peoples seemed to have lived here, who made drawings of their humpless, horned cattle on the rocky crags that stretched from the north of Eritrea to the land of the Hareri; their herds resembled those that were raised at the same period in the Sahara and in the Nile Basin. These peoples were in contact with the Egyptian world from a very early date.

Linguistically, the Kushite element is also of importance; it was of local origin and was beginning to be perceptible in other spheres. The recent discoveries made at Gobedra, near Axum, show that the practice of millet-growing and the use of pottery began in the third or fourth millenium. Thus there is reason to believe that, alongside pastoral activities, a recognizable Ethiopian type of agriculture began to develop from this time. The new techniques were probably associated with a more settled way of life, which created more favourable conditions for the development of higher civilization.

While the founding of the city of Axum and the appearance of a royal Axumite dynasty can be dated from the second century before the Christian era, from the evidence of the geographer Claudius Ptolemy, corroborated a hundred years or so later by the *Periplus Maris Erythraei* and by archaeological discoveries, ancient Greek and Latin writers tell us almost nothing about the centuries leading up to these events.

They merely tell us that, in the middle of the third century before the Christian era, Ptolemy II founded Philadelphus, the port of Adulis, which was enlarged by his successor Ptolemy III, and which Pliny, around the year +75, said he considered one of the most important ports of call on the Red Sea. He also mentions the numerous Asachae groups who lived by elephant-hunting in the mountains which were a five-day journey away from the sea. The association that is frequently suggested between this ethnic term and the name of Axum is highly conjectural.

Apart from legendary accounts, information must be sought in the series of archaeological discoveries that have been made since the beginning of the twentieth century. They enable us to reconstruct the pre-Axumite period, which, as we know from the studies of F. Anfray, consists of a south Arabian period and a transitional period.

The south Arabian period

This is the period when 'south Arabian influence was strong in northern Ethiopia'. The chief sign of this influence is the existence in Eritrea and Tigre of monuments and inscriptions which are akin to those current in south Arabia during the supremacy of the Kingdom of Saba. Thanks to the palaeographic and stylistic studies of J. Pirenne, the parallel examples found in south Arabia can be dated from the fifth and fourth centuries before the Christian era. It is generally agreed that the same dates apply to the finds made in Ethiopia, although the hypothesis put forward by C. Conti-Rossini of a time-lag between the two shores of the Red Sea cannot be definitely ruled out; according to F. Anfray, 'there is reason to think that in future it will be necessary to reduce the time-span, and perhaps to advance the dates of the south Arabian period'.

The only remaining architectural monument of this period is the temple of Yeha. It is built of large blocks, carefully fitted together, with bossage and corner-stones, and consists of a rectangular cella about 18.6 metres by 15 metres resting on an eight-tiered pyramidal base. As J. Pirenne points out, the façades, which are preserved up to a height of about 9 metres, are treated in a similar way to several buildings found in Mârib, the capital of the Kingdom of Saba, but the plan of Yeha is not like that of any of the south Arabian sanctuaries known to us. Another building in Yeha, badly ruined, comprises rectangular megalithic pillars standing on a high terrace; it is situated on Grat-Beal-Guebri and seems to date back to the same period. Similar pillars exist at two other sites. Some are to be seen at the top of the hill of Haoulti, south of Axum, where they are set up in no apparent order and may not be in their original position. At Kaskasé, on the road from Yeha to Adulis, there are six pillars whose arrangement is not yet understood, as the site has not yet been excavated. These pillars are reminiscent of the rows of gigantic four-cornered pillars that adorn the sanctuaries of Mârib (Awwam Bar'an) and Timna (the temple of Ashtar).

The sculptures found at Yeha also point to Mârib, as for example the frieze of ibexes and the fluted and denticulated plaques, which are also found in the Melazo region, at Haoulti and Enda Cerqos, and which may have served as wall coverings. The Melazo area has proved to be rich in sculptures dating back to the south Arabian period: as well as the stelae of Haoulti and the decorated plaques mentioned above, there are a number of works that were used again later in modified forms. The most outstanding examples are the *naos* and the statues discovered at Haoulti.

The monument that is called a *naos* on a proposal by J. Pirenne – a better term than the previously suggested 'throne' – is carved from a single block of fine local limestone about 140 centimetres high. It has four feet shaped like a bull's hooves which support a base decorated with two bars and surmounted by a niche covered with ornamentation except for the back, which is quite smooth. The niche is topped by a dais in the shape of a depressed arch 67 centimetres wide and 57 centimetres deep; along the edge, which is 7 centimetres high, there run two rows of reclining ibexes that converge towards a stylized tree standing on the tip of the *naos*; similar ibexes, pointing inwards towards the niche, cover the edges of both sides in superimposed metopes 13 centimetres wide.

The external surface of each side is decorated with the same scene in bas-relief: a small beardless figure holding a staff precedes a large bearded man holding a sort of fan. Their noses are slightly aquiline, giving them a Semitic appearance, and their hair is represented by small lozenges. The small figure wears a plain robe flaring right down to the ankles, and a mantle covering his shoulders; on the right-hand side of the *naos*, a masculine proper noun is written over his head in Sabaean script: 'RFS' (Rafash). The large figure wears a baggy loin-cloth with a flap falling down behind, held at the waist by a belt that appears to the knotted at the back with one end hanging free; a cloak thrown over his shoulders is held in place by two corners tied in a large, flat knot on his chest. On the left-hand bas-relief, he is holding an object described as a fan with both hands, but on the right-hand bas-relief he is wearing a quadruple bracelet on his left wrist and holding a sort of club in his right hand.

The same site at Haoulti yielded several statues of a similar type, only one of which is almost complete. It represents a seated woman with her hands on her knees, dressed in a long robe with narrow vertical pleats shown by grooves that follow the lines of her body. Over the robe she wears a wide necklace composed of three thick, ringed strands from which hangs a scutiform pectoral; this is counterbalanced between her shoulder-blades by an ornament in the shape of a trapeze with six vertical stems. The statue was meant to fit into a seat, for the backs of the legs are flattened and have a vertical lug, badly damaged, in the middle.

Apart from the fragments of at least two similar statues, there was a headless statue, less delicately executed than the one described above, but otherwise differing from it only in that its sole ornament was a three-stranded necklace and it was seated on a small stool decorated with a bar.

The posture of the Haoulti statues recalls that of a statuette discovered accidentally with miscellaneous other antiquities at Addi Galamo, on the western edge of the Tigre plateau. The statuette is only about 40 centimetres high. The hands rest on the knees, but hold two cylindrical cups that were probably intended to serve as receptacles for offerings. The hair is represented by lozenges, and there are grooves bearing the traces of a necklace with a counterweight and of bracelets that may have been made of some precious metal. The robe is not pleated, but is decorated with rosettes, probably inlaid, that may represent embroidery, and it ends in a fringe. The seat is decorated with a bar.

When F. Anfray excavated Matara, an important site in the neighbourhood of Kaskasé, a fragment of a head of the same type as the Haoulti head was unearthed in a pre-Axumite stratum of Mound B, but the workmanship is much more rudimentary and the details are in high relief.

Another statuette, on show at the National Museum of Rome (MNR 12113) has many points in common with the Haoulti statues. It represents a seated woman whose head and arms have been broken. Its height as it stands at present is 13.7 centimetres. The woman wears a long, fluted robe, a ringed, double-stranded necklace from which there hangs a row of beads, a pectoral and a counterweight. The lower part is in the shape of a base on which is inscribed a south Arabian name, Kanan. According to J. Pirenne, the script dates from the end of the fourth century before the Christian era.

South Arabia has so far only yielded objects presenting such general similarities as the seated position, some of which are feminine; representations of seated women on the funerary bas-reliefs of Mârib, Hâz and the Aden Museum, and the statue of 'Lady Bar'at at Timna', in which J. Pirenne sees the great south Arabian goddess.

As early as the ninth and eighth centuries before the Christian era the type of the seated woman or goddess, often holding a goblet, is very common in the area under Syro-Hittite control. There seems to be a real relationship between the Ethiopian statues and those of Asia Minor in the late seventh and early sixth centuries before the Christian era. J. Pirenne has pointed out certain affinities between the orientalized Greek art of the sixth century or the derived style of the fifth century and south Arabian art.

While analogies with the seated statues are found in the Semitic Near East and in the orientalized Hellenic world, there is evidence of an Egyptian, and more specifically Meroitic, influence in the counterweighted necklaces, inspired by the *mankhit*, and in the pleated robes which, as J. Pirenne has observed, recall the tunics of the queens of Meroe and the corpulence that they inherited from Ati of Punt, a contemporary of Hatshepsut.

Such comparisons highlight the diversity of the influences reflected in these seated women of Tigre, but they provide no definite answer to the question of what they represent. Neither can any conclusive argument be drawn from the inscribed base found at Addi Galamo, which seems to be associated with the statuette. One might even hesitate to regard them as queens or dignitaries or, as J. Pirenne maintains, as representations of the great goddess.

We would be inclined, then, to reject the hypothesis of an empty throne of the type found in Phoenicia, Adulis or Tacazzé, and to return to our first impression, considering, like J: Pirenne, that the object is 'a stone reproduction of a processional *naos*', in which a cult statue rested. Apart from a few fragments found at Haoulti which might come from a similar monument, this *naos* is unique of its kind. Although nothing analogous has come to light in south Arabia – which might be due to the present state of archaeological research in the Yemen – some of its features have been found there, treated in a rigorously identical fashion.

The same bull's hooves are seen on stone furniture identified by G. van Beek and on a marble statuette from Mârib. Reclining ibexes, often arranged in superimposed metopes and on the edge of a flat stele, an example of which was recently discovered at Matara, occur frequently in the Sabaean region (Mârib, Hâz).

We also find ibexes associated with a stylized tree, the fruits of which they seem to be eating, on an altar from Mârib. The religious significance of these ibexes, whether associated with a 'tree of life' or not, appears to be in no doubt: Grohmann seems to have proved that the ibex symbolized the god of the moon, Almaqah, to whom the bull was also dedicated.

While the technique of the lateral bas-relief is closer to the Persian Achemenidean

13.1 *Incense altar of Addi Galamo (Ethiopian Institute of Archaeology)*

style than to the south Arabian works known to us at present, which are apparently of later date, there are parallels between the figures represented and the bronze sculpture in the round from Mârib: hair, eyes, ears, loin-cloth and sandals.

The sculpture of the south Arabian period is also represented by sphinxes, although, apart from a small fragment discovered at Melazo, they have so far been found only in Erythrea. The best-preserved sphinx comes from Addi Gramaten, north-east of Kaskasé. Its hair is plaited, as it is in some Axumite pottery heads of a later period and as it is worn by the women of Tigre today, and round its neck is a three-stranded necklace. The necklace is also found on the forequarters of two sphinxes with hammer-wrought facets that stand out from a stone plaque found at Matara. Another sphinx, very badly damaged, has been found at Dibdib, south of Matara. J. Pirenne points out that these lions with human heads have nothing in common with the griffins and winged sphinxes of the Phoenician tradition which were produced in south Arabia at a later period. Perhaps we should look for Egyptian or Meroitic prototypes, origins already suggested for a south Arabian head with plaited hair and a necklace.

One category of objects carved in stone that is particularly well represented in northern Ethiopia is that of incense altars. Most of these belong to a type that is well known in south Arabia: a cubic altar with architectural decoration often standing on a pyramidal base. The most beautiful example, which, according to J. Pirenne, surpasses all the south Arabian examples, is the altar of Addi Galamo, but a series of altars in various states of preservation has been found at Gobochela in Melazo, several have been found at Yeha, and fragments have been found at Matara and also at unidentified places. A group of four altars found at Gobochela represents a hitherto unknown variety: the cylindrical incense altar on a base in the shape of a truncated cone. Here the decoration is confined to the south Arabian divine symbol of a crescent surmounted by a disc and to a frieze of triangles. As for the small cubic altar of south Arabia, we only have two objects which seem to belong to the south Arabian period. One, unearthed at Matara, is the first in Ethiopia to be referred to specifically as a perfume-burning altar, a *mqtr*. The second, found near the preceding site at a place called Zala Kesedmai, differs in the bas-reliefs that decorate its sides. On one side is the divine symbol of the disc and crescent, and on the opposite side a stylized 'tree of life' that recalls the 'tree of life' of Haoulti. The ibexes on the two remaining sides are turned towards this tree.

As in south Arabia, beside these incense-burning altars, we find libation altars, which can be recognized by the channel allowing the offered liquid to run out. At Yeha were found several platforms similar to those at Hureidha or the Mârib region, with a drainage channel in the shape of a bucranium. On others, there are fine inscriptions in relief and friezes of beam-ends like those of the perfume-burning altars. The first specimen mentioned, one of the second group, and a unique libation altar at Matara all bear the local name of this series of objects, *mtryn*, a term which is not corroborated in south Arabia. The Matara site also yielded thick sacrificial tables similar to the first one from Yeha. The libation altar of Addi Gramaten bears a much closer resemblance to the more elaborate type with a frieze of beam-ends and a tiered base. The altar at Fikya, near Kaskasé, which is in the shape of a bowl with protomes of sphinxes or lions, is rather more reminiscent, according to J. Pirenne, of shapes common in Meroitic art.

All that the archaeological excavations have given us in the way of material remains, apart from these sculptures, is a type of pottery which is as yet little known. F. Anfray attributes to this period tulip-shaped vases and large jars with handles and horizontal ridges that come from Matara and Yeha. He compares this material with what was found at Es-Soba, a few kilometres north of Aden, which seems to date from the sixth century before the Christian era.

The epigraphic documents that palaeography allows us to attribute to the most ancient period are all in south Arabian script but, according to A. J. Drewes, they fall into two groups. The first group consists of inscriptions on monuments written in the authentic Sabaean language with a few local peculiarities; the second includes inscriptions on rocks written in a script which imitates that of the first group but in fact transcribes a Semitic language thought to be only related to Sabaean.

The texts mention not only the terms used for cult objects such as perfume-burners or sacrificial tables, as we saw above, but also the names of a number of deities who constitute a pantheon almost identical with that of the Kingdom of Saba. The most comprehensive list known at present appears on a block that was re-utilized in the church of Enda Çerqos at Melazo: '. . . 'Astar and Hawbas and Almaqah and Dât-Himyam and Dât-Ba'dan . . .'

'Astar appears in two other inscriptions, one from Yeha and the other of unknown origin. It is simply the Ethiopian form of the name of the star-god Athtar, who is also associated with Almaqah in three votic texts, one at Yeha and two at Matara. At the latter site there is an altar dedicated to Shron, which is an epithet of this god, who is identified with the planet Venus.

The moon-god who seems to have been most venerated in Ethiopia, as well as in Saba, is Almaqah. In addition to the inscriptions of Matara, Yeha and Enda Çerqos we have already mentioned, all the texts at Gobochela in Melazo, as well as the altar at Addi Galamo and a libation altar at Yeha, are dedicated to him alone.

The solar cult is represented by a pair of goddesses, Dât-Himyam and Dât-Ba'dan, who seem to correspond to the summer sun and the winter sun.

Whereas dedicatory texts usually give only the filiation of the high-ranking persons concerned, the Gobochela texts reveal that the population was organized in clans. Four texts from this site and one from Yeha mention 'Lhy, of the Grb clan, of the family of (or son of) Yqdm'l Fqmm of Mârib'; this person is associated with his brother SBHHMW on some of the dedications; at Yeha, he consecrates his worldly goods and his son Hyrmh to 'Astar and Almaqah. It is probable that the terms YQDM'L and FQMM denote ethnic groups, but we are sure that GRB does. The expression 'of Mârib' and 'of Hadaqan' in the two Matara texts refer to toponyms rather than to ethnic groups; they may concern places founded in the north of Ethiopia by south Arabian colonists, but, according to L. Ricci, these terms would rather seem to indicate that these groups came originally from Arabia proper.

The political organization of northern Ethiopia during the south Arabian period seems to have been a hereditary monarchy, two of whose dynasts, Rbh and his son Lmm, bear the same title 'King Sr'n of the tribe of Yg'd *ḿukarrib* of D'iamat and of Saba' '; the first of these two sovereigns added on the altar of Addi Galamo: 'descendant of the tribe W'rn of Raydan'. The second is also mentioned on the altar of unknown origin dedicated to 'Astar; the same Lmm, or another sovereign bearing the same name, is mentioned in two texts at Matara, in one of which he is associated with a certain Sumu'alay, the name borne by a Sabaean *mukarrib*. The fact that the link with the Waren ethnic group of Raydan is explicitly mentioned shows the importance which these kings attached to their south Arabian descent.

Architecture, works of art, epigraphy and the data provided by the texts on religious beliefs and social organization in northern Ethiopia – all afford evidence of a strong south Arabian influence in the fifth and fourth centuries before the Christian era. As F. Anfray reminds us, the emergence of this predominantly Semitic culture was preceded by several centuries of silent penetration; 'small groups of immigrants peddled south Arabian culture', no doubt under the pressure of economic and demographic circumstances which we do not yet understand. It is not impossible, as the same investigator suggests, that these colonies introduced new agricultural techniques, in particular the use of the swing-plough, and built the first stone villages of Ethiopia.

The appearance of a cultural unit whose internal coherence is evident, however, throughout the northern part of the Ethiopian plateau must certainly have coincided with the rise to power and the survival as a dominant class of one group, but we shall probably never know whether this group consisted of descendants of south Arabian colonists or of indigeneous inhabitants who had assimilated this superior culture so well that they had made it their own.

The intermediary period

A much stronger impression of a local culture having assimilated foreign influence is conveyed by material dating from the second pre-Axumite period, which has been called the intermediary period.

Some characteristics of south Arabian origin are no doubt still perceptible but, as F. Anfray has made clear, it is no longer a case of direct influences but of internal developments growing from earlier contributions. Inscriptions in a much rougher script are used to transcribe a language less and less like the original south Arabian dialect. *Mukarribs* are no longer mentioned, but a text found at Kaskasé refers to a king bearing a south Arabian name, Waren Hayanat (W'RN HYNT), descendant of Salamat. The GRB clan, well vouched for at Gobochela in Melazo during the south Arabian phase, still exists, although its links with Mârib are no longer stated, for one of its members dedicates a cube-shaped incense altar with a pyramidal base to Almaqah; a crude statuette of a bull is also dedicated to the same deity. At Addi Gramaten, a later hand has added to the altar a second dedication to Dât-Himyam, and to the sphinx a name: Wahab-Wadd. The epigraphic documentation is completed by inscriptions composed of cursive south Arabian letters.

The architecture of the intermediary period is hardly represented except by the religious buildings unearthed in the region of Melazo. All the objects from Gobochela were found, either re-utilized for other purposes or else *in situ*, by J. Leclant in a rectangular structure oriented on an east–west axis; it consists of a surrounding wall 18.1 by 7.3 metres which encloses an esplanade leading to a cella 8.9 by 6.75 metres. The latter opens by a door in the middle of the western side, and the eastern part is occupied by a bench on which the sacred objects were placed.

A characteristic of this period is the great accumulation of objects in underground deposits such as the well tombs of Yeha and Matara or the pits of Sabea and Haoulti. Iron implements, the manufacture of which was probably introduced during this phase, are mainly represented at Yeha by rings, scissors, swords and daggers; a sword and some rings have also been found at Matara. Several fragments of iron objects have also been collected round the temples at Haoulti.

However, bronze is much more prevalent than iron, perhaps because of its greater resistance to corrosion. A large number of thick, open rings with a rectangular section was found at Sabea, and an object of the same type was lying on a bench in one of the sanctuaries at Haoulti. These rings were possibly worn as bracelets or anklets in the Meroitic fashion, but it may be asked whether they were not also used as money. Weapons are represented by a crescent-shaped axe or halberd and two riveted daggers from Haoulti, as well as two knives from Matara, one riveted and another with a crescent-shaped pommel. The Yeha tombs have further yielded cooking-pots, balance-pans and a small bell; fragments of receptacles were also collected on the hill-top at Haoulti. Needles and pins come from Haoulti, Yeha and Matara. Small bronze beads are reported from Sabea, Haoulti and Yeha.

There is one last category of bronze objects that reflect a south Arabian tradition, namely, the pierced plaques called identity badges. A. J. Drewes and R. Schneider distinguish between two classes. The first contains the plaques from Sabea and Haoulti and most of those from Yeha. The second class, which is only found at the Yeha site, is composed of larger, thicker plaques, fitted with a handle and shaped somewhat like a stylized animal, a bull, an ibex, a lion or a bird; the plaques in this class contain proper names written in cursive south Arabian.

When we consider the high technical level revealed by these objects, it seems plausible to attribute to the Ethiopian bronze-workers of this intermediary stage – as F. Anfray suggests – other works such as a miniature pair of bull's hooves near the Haoulti sanctuaries, and the powerful figurine of a bull from Mahabere Dyogwe, which would appear to afford further evidence of the cult of Almaqah.

Gold is used for ornaments such as finger-rings at Yeha and Haoulti, ear-rings, beads and coiled wire at Haoulti. Countless little pieces of necklaces of various colours, made of glass-paste or frit, are found on all the sites of this period, and pieces made of stone are also found at Sabea and Matara.

Other stone objects include small sandstone mortars or incense burners, disc-shaped or rectangular, found at Yeha, Matara and Haoulti, a seal found at Sabea, an alabaster vase and an incised ring made of serpentine found at Yeha.

Lastly, the deposit at Haoulti contained two earthenware amulets representing a Ptah-patec and a Hathoric head, while in the lower levels at Matara a cornelian amulet representing a Harpocrat was found. Among the finds at Addi Galamo were four bronze vessels, including a bowl decorated with finely engraved lotus flowers and frogs, and a fragment of a vase with an embossed line of cattle. This group of objects

13.2 *Bronze bull of Mahabere Dyogwere (Ethiopian Institute of Archaeology)*

is particularly interesting as they are of Meroitic origin and provide evidence of relations between Ethiopia and the Nile Valley. Some Meroitic influence can also be seen in the pottery of this period, which is highly characteristic.

While the ex-votos of Haoulti indicate that the basis of the economy was mainly agricultural and pastoral, the rapid progress made by metal-working in bronze, iron and gold, by the quantity production of stone or glass-paste objects, and by potters shows that a class of specialized craftsmen had now appeared. It certainly seems that the process of urbanization was under way in a number of centres founded during the south Arabian period, such as Melazo, Yeha and Matara, or in more recent settlements such as Adulis. While the memory of the south Arabian traditions had not yet died out, the new stimulus seems to have come from the Kingdom of Meroe, which played a primary role in the diffusion of metal-working techniques over Africa.

It is quite possible that the decline of Meroe, on the one hand, and the waning power of the south Arabian kingdoms, on the other, allowed the Ethiopians to control all trade in gold, incense, ivory and products imported from the Indian Ocean.

14

The civilization of Axum from the first to the seventh century

According to primary sources, the history of the Kingdom of Axum extends from the first century of the Christian era over almost a thousand years. It includes two armed incursions into south Arabia in the third, fourth and sixth centuries, an expedition to Meroe in the fourth century and, during the first half of that same century, the introduction of Christianity.

A score of kings, most of them known only from their coinage, succeeded one another on the Axum throne. The earliest king actually recorded is Zoscales, mentioned in a Greek text belonging to the end of the first century, but it is still an open question whether he is the same as the Za-Hakalé who occurs in the traditional lists of monarchs.

Our knowledge of Axumite civilization comes from various sources, from authors of antiquity, such as Pliny, who mentioned Adulis, to Arab chroniclers such as Ibn Hishām and Ibn Ḥawḳal. But these texts are mostly somewhat vague, and the greater part of our evidence comes from local epigraphy and the gradually increasing amount of archaeological material. Inscriptions, which are few, began to be collected in the nineteenth century. The discovery of the inscriptions by Ezana, by Kaleb, and by one of the latter's sons (Waazelia), in Greek, Ge'ez and pseudo-Sabaean, yielded all kinds of information, added to in the last twenty years by other evidence of a similar kind, including cave inscriptions and texts on sheets of schist found in Eritrea. These date from the second century, and are the earliest writings of the Axumite period.

Area

Archaeology shows the Axumite kingdom as a tall rectangle roughly 300 kilometres long by 160 kilometres wide, lying between 13° and 17° north and 30° and 40° east. It extended from the region north of Keren to Alagui in the south, and from Adulis on the coast to the environs of Ṭakkaze in the west. Addi-Dahno is practically the last-known site in this part, about 30 kilometres from Axum.

Proto-Axumite period

The name of Axum appears for the first time in the *Periplus Maris Erythraei* ('Circumnavigation of the Erythrean Sea'), a naval and commercial guide compiled by a merchant from Egypt. The work dates from the end of the first century. Ptolemy, the second-century geographer, also mentions the place.

The *Periplus* describes Adulis as 'a large village three days' journey from Koloè, a town of the interior and the chief market for ivory. From this place to the city of the people called the Axumites is another five days' journey. Here is brought all the ivory from the land beyond the Nile, across the region called Cyenum and thence to Adulis.' So this village served as an outlet for Axum, especially for ivory. The text says that rhinoceros horn, tortoise-shell and obsidian were also sold there. These things were among the exports from Adulis mentioned by Pliny before the *Periplus*; the name of Adulis is thus referred to before that of Axum. According to Pliny, Adulis was in the land of the Troglodytes. Since the first century the Romans and the Greeks knew of the existence of the Axumite people and of their 'towns' in the hinterland of Adulis.

Archaeology gives us little information about the material culture of the early centuries of the period. A few inscriptions of the second and third centuries are practically the only datable evidence. They offer the earliest forms of the Ethiopic alphabet, the use of which has survived to the present day. Even so they are not the oldest inscriptions found in the Axumite area: several others, of south Arabian type, belong to the second half of the last millennium before the Christian era. The south Arabian script was the model for the Ethiopic. The shape of the letters changed considerably in the second century of the Christian era, moving away from the south Arabian script.

Axumite sites

Adulis and Axum which, according to the *Periplus*, were at the two ends of the route used in antiquity, are the most important Axumite sites, and also the only ones where the ancient name, attested in texts and inscriptions, has been preserved locally down to the present. Adulis is a deserted site, but the people of the nearby villages still call the ruins Azuli. All, or nearly all, the other ancient sites have names which are certainly not those of Axumite antiquity.

Axum

The city of Axum enjoyed a great reputation in the third century of the Christian era, according to a text of the period attributed to Mani, which describes the kingdom as the 'third in the world'. And indeed in the town itself, great buildings and much other material evidence preserve the memory of a great historical epoch.

At the beginning of this century a German mission sketched and photographed all the visible monuments. In the western part of the town they uncovered the ruins of three architectural complexes which they rightly identified as the remains of the palace. Subsequent work, in particular that of the Institute of Archaeology, has brought new buildings to light and revealed a wealth of facts about the ancient royal city.

Of the three edifices known to tradition as Enda-Semon, Enda-Mikael and Taakha-

Maryam, all that remained were the basements, but today they can only be seen in the sketches and photographs of the German mission.

The ruins of another imposing building lie under the church of Maryam-Tsion, to the east of which, below the level of the terrace, the remains of a basement varying in width from 42 to 30 metres still survive.

To the west of the town, from 1966 to 1968, the Ethiopian Institute of Archaeology discovered and studied another architectural complex. These ruins, situated at Dongour, to the north of the Gondar road, are those of a castle belonging to about the seventh century. Four irregular groups of buildings, containing about forty rooms in all, are so arranged as to form a square enclosure around the main part of the castle. Three ovens of baked bricks have been uncovered in the western part of the site. In one room in the outbuildings, to the south, a brick structure bearing traces of flames seems to have been a heating device.

The Dongour site is the finest example of Axumite architecture that can be seen today. It does not seem to have been a royal residence; it was more probably inhabited by some leading citizen.

Another outstanding building, the remains of which are attributed by tradition to Kaleb and his son Guebra-Masqal, once stood on a hill to the north-east of Axum. A pair of what might be called chapels were raised over crypts consisting of several vaults built of and covered by stone slabs.

At Bazen, to the east of the town, some oven-type tombs are hollowed out of the rocky hillside. Some have a shaft, and vaults on each side at the bottom. The same sector contains a multiple tomb with a stairway of seventeen steps, also hollowed out of the rock, and dominated by a stele which in ancient times did not stand alone, since an English traveller at the beginning of the nineteenth century tells of having seen fourteen fallen 'obelisks' here.

The ancient city covered the area between the giant stelae and the Dongour site, and ruins lie everywhere under the surface. When excavations can be undertaken in the places traditionally called Addi-Kiltè and Tchaanadoug, they will bring to light a vast stretch of Axum's past.

Adulis

There are few remains on the surface of this site, which is not on the coast but about four kilometres inland. As far as can be judged from the evidence above ground, they lie within a rectangle roughly 500 metres long and 400 wide. In 1868 a British expeditionary force which landed near by dug up some remains of the buildings, but of the work undertaken since little remains apart from the walls uncovered by Paribeni's mission in 1906, and those found in 1961 to 1962 by the mission of the Ethiopian Institute of Archaeology.

At the beginning of 1906, Sundstrom, a Swede, discovered a large edifice in the northern sector, and shortly afterwards Paribeni uncovered two smaller ruins to the east and the west. All these ruins consist of the tiered and stepped basements of rectangular structures which are surrounded by outbuildings. Sundstrom called the one he uncovered a 'palace'.

The basement revealed to the west of this complex by Paribeni displays the same architectural features. It is about 18½ metres long. The upper part was covered by a pavement, and comprised the remains of the pillars of a nave. At the eastern end a semicircular apse between two rooms was a sufficient indication that the ruins were those of a basilica.

To the east of Sundstrom's discovery, Paribeni found the basement of another church. There were two striking features: a baptismal tank in the room south of the apse and, in the centre of the building, the remains of eight pillars arranged octagonally. A square plan and a rectangular plan are thus combined in the same building.

On the Erythrean plateau, 135 kilometres south of Asmara, near Sénafé, there is one of the oldest archaeological sites in Ethiopia: its lowest levels belong to a large building of the south Arabian period.

The Institute of Archaeology carried out systematic excavations of the Matara site between 1959 and 1970. These digs have revealed four large villas, three Christian churches, and an ordinary residential quarter consisting of some thirty houses. The four villas are of the now familiar type, with a main dwelling constructed over a tiered basement and surrounded by outhouses. As elsewhere, masonry piers buried under the rooms of the main building served as bases for the posts supporting the vestibules.

The ordinary houses consist of two or three rooms; the walls are of an average thickness of 70 centimetres. Remains of hearths, brick ovens and numerous receptacles have made it possible to locate the living quarters. There is another type of house intermediate in size between the villas and the ordinary dwellings.

To the south and east of the town there are religious edifices which are outwardly very much like the other structures: they have a central building surrounded by courtyards and outhouses; the method of construction was exactly the same.

Kohaito

On this site, which lies north of Matara at a height of 2,600 metres, many ruins of architectural interest can be seen. Ten or so mounds scattered over quite a large area contain the remains of large buildings belonging to the end of the Axumite period and, in all probability, fragments of still older structures. Several pillars are still standing on the mounds. It is thought that most of them belonged to churches of about same size as those at Matara. The walls on all the hillocks display the features of Axumite masonry work and are laid out on the same rectangular pattern as those visible on other sites of the period. As well as these ruined buildings, to the north-north-east there was a dam consisting of regular courses of perfectly fitted blocks of stone. Its function was to impound the waters on the south-eastern side of a natural basin commonly known as the Safra Basin.

To the east there is a rock-hewn shaft tomb which comprises two rooms or burial-vaults. A cross of the Axumite type cut into the rock adorns one of the sides of the tomb.

In a ravine near the site the rock is painted and carved with figures representing oxen, camels and other animals.

Towns and markets

The big settlements formed compact and crowded communities where dwellings stood close together and clustered round large buildings designed for various purposes. Excavations at Axum, Adulis and Matara have shown that these places were real urban centres. In the quarter of Matara inhabited by the common people there is a narrow winding alley between the houses. All this points to a comparatively large population whose activities were not wholly confined to agriculture.

The presence of coins sheds light on the development of the economy. Further evidence is afforded by the nature of the objects which have been unearthed: glassware and Mediterranean amphoras. Works of art (such as a bronze lamp and various articles made of gold) suggests that luxury was not unknown.

Axumite architecture–general characteristics

The chief characteristics of Axumite architecture are the use of stone, a square or rectangular layout, the regular alternation of projecting parts and recessed parts, tiered basements with large buildings erected over them, and a type of masonry which uses no other mortar but clay. In addition, there is the striking fact that these distinctive features are reproduced practically everywhere. All the major edifices, religious or otherwise, stand on the same type of tiered base and are reached by monumental stairways, often comprising seven steps. They are all surrounded by outbuildings from which they are separated by small courtyards.

It may be taken as certain that the castles and villas comprised at least one storey above the ground floor, which, given its height, ought rather to be called the first floor. Given the smallness of the rooms at this level, and the fact that they were cluttered with pillars or posts, it is probable that the real living quarters were on the floor above. It is an open question whether the big castles of Axum had several upper storeys.

The Axumites included timber among their building materials. The frames of doors and windows were of wood and at certain points in the walls, especially at the corners of rooms, joists were let into the masonry to strengthen it. The beams supporting the floors of rooms in upper storeys, or the roofs, which were probably flat, were of course wooden.

It was also the custom to make the basements of large buildings as solid as possible by laying large blocks of hewn stone at the corners or along the top in long rows. Many of these blocks are to be seen in buildings of the late Axumite period, some of them having been used before in a previous structure.

Monolithic monuments

The stelae of Axum are of several types. They are scattered about a field, and there is no doubt that in antiquity they marked the places of graves. Some are over 20 metres high. This type of stele is found in various places, though they are most plentiful near the group of giant stelae. There are seven stelae in this group. They are remarkable for their decorative carvings. Only one is still standing. Five lie broken on the ground. The seventh was taken to Rome and in 1937 it was erected near the Caracalla Theatre where it still stands.

The carvings imitate many-storeyed buildings. The tallest of the stelae, which was about 33 metres high, depicts nine superimposed storeys on one of its sides: a lofty dwelling, complete with door, windows, butt-ends of beams, is perfectly carved in hard stone. The meaning of this imaginary architecture is entirely unknown. There are practically no points of comparison between it and any other examples elsewhere. One of these stelae has lances carved on the pediment. Another, which is not one of those representing architecture, displays a sort of shield.

At Matara and Anza, on the eastern plateau, there are two round-topped stelae about five metres high. They display two distinctive features: a crescent which is the symbol of south Arabian religion and an inscription in Ge'ez. Such inscriptions have a commemorative significance; this has been definitely established, at least at Matara. Palaeographic factors indicate that they date from the third or the beginning of the fourth century. The workmanship of these monoliths is the same as that of the smooth stelae at Axum.

Thrones loomed large in Axumite culture. They are mentioned in two inscriptions of Ezana. In the sixth century, Cosmas noted the presence of a throne close to a stele at Adulis. 'The throne has a square base. It is made of excellent white marble' and 'entirely . . . hewn out of a single block of stone'. Both throne and stele were 'covered with Greek characters'. The inscription on the throne was composed by an Axumite sovereign who ruled in about the third century. The significance of these monuments is not clear. Are they thrones commemorating victories? Votive seats? Symbols of regal power? They are as much of an enigma as the great stelae.

The group near Maryam-Tsion is arranged so that all the thrones face east, in the same direction as the carved sides of the stelae. If this arrangement is the original one, it is possible that they were turned towards a temple which may have stood at that time on the site of the present church, where there are many ruins.

The inscriptions themselves are cut into the hard stone, a kind of granite. One of Ezana's texts, which is in three different scripts – Ethiopic, south Arabian and Greek – is engraved on both sides of a stone over two metres high.

This fondness for large-scale monuments appears to have prevailed in the case of statues too. At the beginning of the century a flat stone was discovered at Axum which displayed hollowed-out footprints 92 centimetres long. The stone had been used as the plinth for a statue, probably of metal. Ezana's inscriptions say that he erected statues in honour of the divinity. One such text reads: 'As a token of gratitude to Him who begot us, Ares the Unvanquished, we have raised statues, one of gold, another of silver and three of bronze, to His glory.' No Axumite statue has yet been recovered, but the archaeological investigations are far from complete. Few representations of animals have been discovered, either in stone or in metal. Cosmas tells us that he saw 'four bronze statues' of unicorns (no doubt rhinoceroses) 'in the royal palace'.

Pottery

Axumite sites yield large quantities of terracotta vessels, some broken and others intact. Such pottery, mainly utilitarian, has been found in both red and black terracotta, the former easily predominating. In many of the pots, the outer surface is finished in matt colour; some are coated with red slip. There is no evidence at all of the use of the wheel.

The vessels vary in size, and are not always decorated. When they are, the decoration usually consists of geometric designs, either carved, painted, moulded or stamped. The motifs are rarely taken from nature: just a few ears of corn, moulded birds and snakes. The Christian cross appears over and over again on the rims, sides or bottoms of vessels.

There is a difference between the pottery from the east of the plateau and that from the west. In the Axum area we find a kind of vessel with linear incisions on its sides, but this type is rare on the eastern plateau. There is a bowl from Matara, with a boss and ribs under the rim, of which no counterpart has so far been discovered in the Axum area, but here, on the other hand, we find a jar with a spout in the form of a human head which has not yet been paralleled elsewhere.

The information yielded by current investigations enables us to classify groups of pottery finds according to chronological series, but more excavation will have to be done before we have anything like accurate datings.

Imported pottery, mainly jars with handles and ribbed sides, is also found in the Axumite layer of all the sites. These amphoras, of which there are a large number at Adulis, are of Mediterranean origin. There is no trace of such amphoras in the pre-Axumite levels. In the Axumite layer are also found many fragments of glass phials, bottles and cups, and blue-glaze vessels dating from the end of the Axumite period and mostly imported from the Indian Ocean. There are also little cups which look like *terra sigillata*, probably imported from Egypt.

A few special objects

Archaeological research has led to the discovery of various objects, such as seals fashioned in stone or terracotta and engraved with geometric motifs or profiles of animals; little tools made of various metals; terracotta dice; fragments of blades; figurines of animals; female statuettes similar to the fertility figures of prehistory; and so on. Of special interest are a bronze lamp and a treasure hoard brought to light during excavations at Matara.

The first consists of an oblong bowl resting on a stem made to resemble a colonnade of stylized palm-trees. On top of the bowl is a round boss decorated with a pattern which represents a dog wearing a collar, in the act of catching an ibex. On the reverse of the bowl a bucrane is modelled in light relief. The lamp stands 41 centimetres high; the bowl is 31 centimetres long. To judge by its symbolism – which seems to be that of the ritual chase, especially in view of the presence of the bucrane – the lamp probably came from south Arabia, where similar objects have been discovered.

14.1 *Neck of a bottle (Ethiopian Institute of Archaeology)*

14.2 *Perfume pan, Alexandrian style (Ethiopian Institute of Archaeology)*

The treasure was found in a bronze vessel 18 centimetres high. It consists of two crosses, three chains, a brooch, 68 pendants, 64 necklace beads, 14 coins of Roman emperors of the second and third centuries (mainly the Antonines), and two bracteates. All the articles are of gold, and in a remarkably good state of preservation. Judging from where they were found, they must have been gathered together in about the seventh century.

Sometimes Axumite levels yield south Arabian inscriptions and fragments of perfume-braziers from the fifth century before the Christian era. The stones are usually broken and have been reused by Axumite builders. These levels also produce a few articles imported from Egypt or Nubia, or, as at Haoulti, terracotta figurines which, according to Henri de Contenson, the explorer of this site, 'seem related to those met with in India in the Mathura and Gupta periods'. He also points out, in this connection, that 'the first two centuries of the Christian era were precisely the heyday of the traders who established contacts between India and the Mediterranean via the Red Sea'.

Numismatics

Axumite coins are of special importance. It is through them alone that the names of eighteen kings of Axum are known.

Several thousand coins have been found. The ploughed fields around Axum throw up a good many, especially during the rainy season when the water washes away the soil. Most are of bronze, and they vary in size from 8 to 22 millimetres. The coins carry various symbols. Those of the early kings (Endybis Ousanas I, Wazeba, Ezana) bear the disc and crescent. All coins made after Ezana's conversion to Christianity depict the cross, either in the middle of one side or among the letters of the legend inscribed round the edge. In some cases the bust of the king is framed by two bent ears of corn or one straight ear is represented in the centre, as on the coins of Aphilas and Ezana. Perhaps the ears of corn were emblems of power to ensure the fertility of the land.

The legends are written in Greek or Ethiopic, never in south Arabian. Greek appears on the very earliest coins; Ethiopic begins only with Wazeba. The words of the legend vary: 'By the grace of God', 'Health and happiness to the people', 'Peace to the people', 'He will conquer through Christ'. And, of course, the name of the king is shown, with the title 'King of the Axumites', or 'King of Axum'.

Script and language

The earliest alphabet used in Ethiopia, which dates back to the fifth century before the Christian era, is of a south Arabian type. It transcribes a language that is akin to the Semitic dialects of south Arabia.

The first examples of Ethiopic script, properly so called, date from the second century of the Christian era. They are consonantal in form. The characters are still reminiscent of their south Arabian origin, but they gradually evolve their own distinctive shapes. The direction of the writing, which was initially variable, became fixed, and it then ran from left to right. The first inscriptions were engraved on tablets of schist. They are not numerous and comprise a few words. The oldest was discovered at Matara. An inscription engraved on a metal object has been found which dates from the third century. It mentions King Gadara and is the first Ethiopic inscription known to bear the name of Axum. Other texts were engraved on stone. The great inscriptions of King Ezana belong to the fourth century. It is with them that syllabism first appears, soon becoming the rule in Ethiopic script. Vocalic signs become integrated into the consonantal system, denoting the different tone qualities of the spoken language.

This language, as revealed in the inscriptions, is known as Ge'ez. It is a member of the southern group of the Semitic family. It is the language of the Axumites. About the fifth century the Bible was translated into Ge'ez.

The rise of Axumite civilization

Five centuries before the Christian era a special form of civilization marked by south Arabian influences was established on the northern Ethiopian plateau. It was essentially an agrarian civilization, and it prospered during the fifth and fourth centuries before the Christian era. In the course of the following centuries it declined, at least judging by the present lack of archaeological documentation. But the culture did not die out. Some of its characteristics were preserved in the Axumite civilization. It is also noteworthy that, especially on the eastern plateau, most Axumite buildings occupy the same sites as those of the pre-Axumite period. This betokens a kind of continuity.

However, the archaeological finds dating from the first centuries of the Christian era reveal many aspects that are new. Although the writing used in the inscriptions was derived from a south Arabian script, a considerable change is now apparent. Religion, too, has altered. The names of all the ancient gods have disappeared except for that of 'Astar. They are replaced in the Ezana texts by the names of the triad Mahrem, Beher and Meder. As regards architecture, while it continues to be characterized by the use of stone and wood and by the tiered basement of its buildings, it displays various new features. Pottery is very different in workmanship, shape and decoration, and imported ceramics are also found, while glassware occurs in all sites. The name of Axum appears (for the first time in the historical records of this period), and it is probably significant that the site seems to have had no appreciable past before the first century.

Economic factors

During the Axumite era, as in the preceding centuries, agriculture and animal husbandry formed the basis of economic life. But in Axumite times these developed along quite distinctive lines, no doubt because of two factors in particular.

All ancient sources indicate that maritime trade increased in the Red Sea in the course of the first two centuries. This is attributed to the Roman expansion in this area, which was facilitated by progress in navigation. We know that navigational methods improved at the beginning of the first century. The pilot Hippalus showed how sailors could make use of the winds to the best advantage, and this undoubtedly gave an impetus to sea traffic. Strabo records that 'every year, in the time of Augustus, a hundred and twenty ships set out from Myos Hormos'.

Commercial connections multiplied. Ships brought cargoes and made it possible to trade with India and the Mediterranean world. Adulis was the meeting-point for maritime trade, as it was – and this is the second factor – for inland trade. In the interior, a traffic was growing in a very valuable commodity – ivory. In fact, Pliny and the author of the *Periplus* place it first on the list of the exports from Adulis. Axum was the great collecting-centre for ivory from various regions. It was an article which was indispensable to the luxury-loving Romans. In the age of the Ptolemies the Ethiopian elephant was already highly prized. Armies used it as a sort of tank. Later it was hunted for its tusks. Whenever the authors of antiquity talked of Adulis, Axum or Ethiopia (East Africa), they always gave prominence to elephants and their ivory. They mentioned other goods – hippopotamus hides, rhinoceros horn, tortoise-shell, gold, slaves, spices – but they took a special interest in elephants. In 1962, the mission from the Ethiopian Institute of Archaeology found an elephant's tusk in the Axumite ruins at Adulis, and, in 1967, they discovered pieces of a terracotta figurine of an elephant in the walls of the castle at Dongour.

The African roots

The civilization of Axum developed in the first centuries of the Christian era, but its roots lie deep in prehistory. It was foreshadowed in the culture of the last five centuries before the Christian era. Archaeology is attempting to define its characteristic features, but only a few aspects of the subject have been investigated so far, and the cataloguing of the data of antiquity is by no means complete. The main task ahead is to determine what came from external influences and what was really indigenous: like other civilizations, that of Axum was the result of an evolutionary process aided by geographic condition and historical circumstances. The indigenous contribution is naturally of great importance, for there can be no doubt that Axumite civilization is, above all, the product of a people whose ethnic identity is progressively emerging from the study of its inscriptions, language and traditions. Archaeology is gradually revealing the unique character of Axum's material achievements. Much remains to be done, and future research will concentrate on interpreting the significance of the evidence dug out of the soil. But already we know that the civilization of Axum owes its particular quality to its African roots.

15 Axum: political system, economics and culture, first to fourth century

Historical sources of the second and third centuries record the rapid rise of a new African power: Axum. Claudius Ptolemy was the first to mention the Axumites as one of the peoples of Ethiopia. This situation in north-east Africa resembles that described in *Aethiopica*, the novel by Heliodoros, a Graeco-Phoenician author of the third century, who describes the arrival of the Axumite ambassadors as friends and allies of the Meroitic king. The *Periplus Maris Erythraei*, where one can find data on different periods from before +105 to the beginning of the third century of the Christian era mentions the 'metropolis of the so-called Axumites' as a little-known city and the kingdom of its ruler Zoscales as very young. Zoscales ruled all the Red Sea coast of Erythrea, but the hegemony in the Bēdja desert belonged to Meroe. The balance between these two powers – the old metropolis of the Meroites and the young metropolis of the Axumites – recalls the novel by Heliodoros. The earliest sources to mention the Axumites' expansion to south Arabia are the Sabaean inscriptions of the end of the second and the beginning of the third centuries which report on the 'Abyssinians' or Axumites who waged war in Yemen and occupied some of its territories. Between +183 and +213 the Axumite kings, Gadara and his son, seem to have been the most powerful rulers in southern Arabia and the real leaders of the anti-Sabaean coalition. At the end of the third and in the early years of the fourth centuries, 'Azbah, an Axumite king, also waged war in South Arabia'.

Subsequently, the Himarites united the country but the Axumite kings claimed to be their sovereign, as can be seen from their titles.

Wars in southern Arabia were also reported in two Greek inscriptions by Axumite kings whose names and dates of reign are unknown. The author of the longer inscription conquered the coastal parts of Yemen 'till the land of the Sabaeans' and vast territories in Africa 'from the frontiers of Egypt' to the land of incense of Somali.

By about +270 the fame of the new state had reached Persia. The 'Kephalaia' of the prophet Mani (+216 to +276) calls Axum one of the four greatest empires of the world.

What resources and organization did Axum have to achieve such successes?

Occupations

For the most part the Axumites were engaged in agriculture and stock-breeding, practically the same types of occupation as those of the present-day Tigre peasants. In the foothills and on the plains, cisterns and dams were constructed as reservoirs for rainwater and irrigation canals were dug. Inscriptions indicate that wheat and other cereals were sown; viticulture also existed. Large herds of cattle, sheep and goats were kept; other domestic animals were asses and mules. Like the Meroites, the Axumites had learned to capture and domesticate elephants, but these were reserved for the use of the royal court.

The crafts and trades of blacksmiths and other metal-workers, potters, builders, stonemasons and carvers, among others, attained a very high level of skill and artistry. The most important technical innovation was the use of iron tools. Another innovation was the introduction of a cohesive cementing solution in building, which led to the development of a form of stone and timber construction.

Political structure

Axum may have been initially a principality which in the course of time became the capital province of a feudal kingdom. History confronted its rulers with various tasks, the most urgent of which was the establishment of their power over the segmentary states of northern Ethiopia, and the assembling of these into one kingdom. It sometimes happened that a new ruler, on ascending the throne, was obliged to inaugurate his reign with a countrywide campaign to enforce at least formal submission on the principalities.

The founding of a kingdom served as the basis on which to build an empire. From the close of the second century up to the beginning of the fourth, Axum took part in the military and diplomatic struggle waged between the states of southern Arabia. Following this, the Axumites subjugated the regions situated between the Tigre plateau and the valley of the Nile.

The state was divided into Axum proper and its vassal kingdoms, the rulers of which were subjects of the Axum king of kings, to whom they paid tribute. The Greeks called the Axumite potentate the basileus (only Athanasius the Great and Philostorgius termed him tyrant); the vassal kings were known as archontes, tyrants and ethnarchs. Syrian writers, such as John of Ephesus, Simeon of Beth-Arsam and the author of the *Book of the Himyarites*, accorded the title of king (mlk') to the Axumite 'king of kings' and also to the kings of Himyar and 'Alwa, who were his subjects. But the Axumite term for all these was 'negus'. Mention is made of army neguses (nägästa särāwit). Apart from leading armies in time of war, these neguses assumed command of building operations. Among the neguses, the inscriptions name kings of four ethnic groups of Bega (Bēdja), each ruling over about 1,100 subjects, and the ruler of the Agabo principality whose subjects numbered scarcely more than between 200 and 275 grown men, or a total of 1,000–1,500 persons. Vassal kingdoms were situated on the Tigre plateau and in the region of Zula Bay (Agago, Metin, Agame, etc.), beyond the Taqqaze river (Walḳa'it, Samēn, Agaw), in the arid regions around the Ethiopian uplands (Agwezat) and likewise in the Arabian peninsula. After Ezana's victory, these kingdoms extended to Upper Nubia, between the Fourth Cataract and Sennar. A power hierarchy was thus created, from the Axum king of kings down to the chiefs of separate communities.

Two methods of collecting tribute existed: either the vassal rulers (such as Abraha, King of Himyar) sent a yearly tribute to Axum, or the King of Axum, accompanied by a numerous retinue, travelled round his domains gathering tribute and victuals for his attendants on the way. The vassal kings followed the same method. A compromise between these two methods was achieved by the vassals delivering tribute at appointed stages along the king's route.

The sources contain no information on the administrative system of Axum. Near relatives of the king assumed an important part in the direction of affairs. It is understandable, therefore, that the Roman emperor Constantine II addressed his letter not only to Ezana, but also to Se'azana, his brother. Military expeditions were led as a rule by the king, his brother, or other kinsmen. Armies of less importance, commanded by army kings, were made up of warriors from the communities or ethnic groups.

The rulers of Axum settled warlike groups along the borders of the state: Abyssinians in southern Arabia, four ethnic groups of Bega in the Matlia region, or in the Byrn land (which possibly lay in Begemdir).

Far too little is known about the history of this kingdom to enable us to trace the development of its political system. It may be assumed, however, that, at the time when the Axum monarchy flourished, something like a centralizing process took place in its structure.

The common norms of law that prevailed in the kingdom may be studied in the first juridical records of Axum: in the four laws from the Sāfrā.

Commerce and commercial policy

The position held by the Axum kingdom in world commerce was that of a first-rate trading power, as evidenced by the minting of its own gold, silver and copper coinage. It was the first state in tropical Africa to introduce a coinage. The minting of coin, especially gold, was not only an economic but also a political measure, proclaiming to the whole world the independence and prosperity of the Axum state. The first Axumite king to put his own coinage into circulation was Endybis (in the second half of the third century). The Axumite coins bore a basic resemblance to Byzantine coins of the same period.

The wares enumerated in the *Periplus*, with the exception of gold and emeralds, were only such as could be obtained by hunting, trapping and collecting. Agricultural and dairy produce, and goods produced by craftsmen or tradesmen, are not mentioned. If these were exported, it must have been in very limited quantities, and to places within the bounds of the Roman-Byzantine empire. The famous Ethiopian wheat may possibly have been exported to neighbouring countries, although the earliest, extremely vague, information about this dates from the tenth century. On the contrary, to judge from the accounts in the *Periplus*, Adulis imported certain foodstuffs such as small quantities of Laodicean (Syrian) and Italian wine and olive-oil; the ports of the Horn of Africa received cereals, wine and the juice of the young Diospolis grape from Egypt, wheat, rice, bosmor, sesame oil and sugar-cane from India. Apparently, some of these products, such as sugar-cane, must have been shipped to Adulis as well.

In general, archaeological data confirm and supplement the accounts left by the *Periplus*. Excavations in strata dating from the period under review at Axum, Adulis and Matara, and the finds at Hawila-Asseraw and Debre-Dāmo, yielded many objects of non-Ethiopian origin, some of which must have reached that country through trade. Most of the foreign wares came from the Roman-Byzantine empire, especially from Egypt; they included amphoras which evidently served as vessels for wine or oil; fragments of glassware, gold ornaments and necklaces of Roman silver coins (Matara), beautiful gem (Adulis), lamps of bronze and a bronze balance and weights (Adulis and Axum).

Objects of Indian origin have also been found: a seal in Adulis, terracotta figurines in Axum, 104 gold coins dating from the reigns of the Kushana kings before the year +200 in Debre-Dāmo. Pre-Islamic Arabia yielded silver and bronze coins found accidentally in Erythrea and during excavations at Axum and a lamp of bronze from Matara. Examples of Meroe workmanship are numerous: fragments of ceramic vessels have been found in many places, statuette-amulets in faience of Hathor and Ptah in Axum and in cornelian of Horus in Matara, sculptured stelae showing figures of Horus on crocodiles and bronze bowls found at Hawila-Asseraw. Some of these objects may have reached Ethiopia from Sudan in the course of trade, but probably most of them were spoils of war, or tribute.

The unification of a considerable part of north-east Africa by the Axumites soon enriched their nobility. Among these wealthy people, the Roman, Arabian and Indian merchants found customers for their luxury goods, which were the most profitable of all.

The profits accruing from the creation of the powerful Axum kingdom enriched not only the nobility but also the whole of the privileged ethno-social group of Axumites who were the citizens of the capital community. Many of the goods enumerated in the *Periplus* were imported for a wider stratum of the population. Bracelets of imported brass worked by local smiths, spears of imported iron and other metal articles in local use, as well as clothing made of foreign fabrics were transformed into saleable wares for local markets, by this means becoming available to both the urban and the rural populations. Finally, foreign merchants and other foreign groups settled in Adulis, Axum and different Ethiopian towns, and brought in quantities of imported goods. It was among these groups that wine and olive-oil found a ready sale. Excavated objects such as the balance and weights, the seal, Roman and Kushana coins were obviously traces left by Roman-Byzantine and Indian merchants who had lived in Adulis and Axum. Among those who traded with the Axum kingdom, Arab tradition recalls the Banū-Ḳuraysh from Mecca, Cosmas Indicopleustes speaks of islanders from Socotra, and 'Pseudo-Calisthenes' mentions Indians. The relative importance of overseas cities and countries for Ethiopian trade in the early sixth century may be judged by the number of ships that entered the Ethiopian harbour of Gabaza in the summer of +525. This list is to be found in the *Martyrdom of Aretha*, and a detailed analysis of it has been made by N. V. Pigulevskaya.

In Axum, as in other African kingdoms of antiquity, herds constituted wealth but it was extremely difficult to transform them into saleable merchandise. The systematic export of herds by sea was out of the question although the Axumites contrived to send some animals singly, even some elephants belonging to the army of Abraha. Cattle could, of course, be driven into the African interior for sale to the people there – Cosmas Indicopleustes mentions that caravans of Axumites drove cattle into Sasu – but a considerable proportion of these animals must inevitably have been needed for victualling the caravan itself.

One kind of merchandise for which the demand never slackened throughout the centuries was that of slaves. There are references in the Ezana inscriptions and sources connected with Axumite–Himyarite wars to prisoners taken in warfare who were regarded as desirable merchandise by foreign slave-traders. Gold and silver seized as spoils of war, or as tribute sent from Nubia, from the Bēdja, Agaw, Himyar and other countries were brought by caravans from Sasu and minted as coin which went to pay for the foreign goods required by the king and his nobles.

Although industry in Axum did not result in any important volume of saleable commodities, the abundance of agricultural and animal products permitted the Axumites to load trading vessels and caravans. Thus they provided their own food and commodities for home consumption and also for some trade with other countries.

Some idea of how they organized their commerce is given by Cosmas Indicopleustes in his account of how Sasu supplied gold to Axum from its many goldfields. 'From year to year the Axumite king sends, through the archon of Agaw, people to bring back gold. Many travel with these people for the same purpose, so that altogether there might be more than five hundred.' The gold conveyed from Sasu was in nuggets the size of the wolf-beans known as tankaras. It seems that the nucleus of a caravan consisted of the king's agents, accompanied by some other people, who might be nobleman's agents and rich Axumites, but not foreigners.

The political hegemony of the Axumite kingdom on the world's trade-routes proved no less profitable than direct participation in trade.

When he had subjugated Upper Nubia, southern Arabia, the Lake Tana region, and the peoples of the deserts surrounding Ethiopia, the King of Axum controlled the routes linking Egypt and Syria with the countries of the Indian Ocean, and also with the interior of north-east Africa. The Straits of Bab-al-Mandeb, which, like the Straits of Malacca and Gibraltar, constituted one of the three main sea highways of the ancient world, also came under Axumite control. In antiquity, Bab-al-Mandeb was a busy sea-route linking the Red Sea to the Persian Gulf, India, Ceylon, the Straits of Malacca, and the countries of south-east and eastern Asia. From the Gulf of Aden another route branched out along the coast of Somalia to East Africa. This route was explored and used by mariners from southern Arabia and in the earliest centuries of the Christian era – by those of India and the Roman empire as well.

During the period under review the Red Sea trade flourished, though stories of piracy were current at about the same time. Peoples from the African and the Arabian coasts of the southern Red Sea and the Gulf of Aden engaged in piracy. Roman authors characteristically attributed piratical attacks in this region to changes in the political attitude of Axum and other Red Sea states towards the Romans.

Roman merchants had a vital interest in the establishment of security along the trade-routes within the sphere of Axumite hegemony, and consequently in its unifying policy. For this reason they supported the union of the Roman-Byzantine empire with the Axumite kingdom. It would not, however, be correct to represent the Axum kings simply as promoters of Roman-Byzantine policy, including its religious and commercial aspects. They pursued an independent political course that corresponded with Byzantine policy, particularly when the predominantly economic interests of the two powers coincided. An instance of this may be drawn from the sixth century when, despite the frequent voyages of the Byzantines to India, they considered that the Ethiopians had more stable trade relations with that country.

In the fourth century and the beginning of the fifth, the harbours of Adulis and the Horn of Africa scarcely attracted the attention of Roman geographers. Between the fifth and sixth centuries, however, Adulis became the leading port between Clysme and the ports of India.

The fact that Adulis then reached a peak of prosperity which it never achieved before or after was due, not to successful resisting of any type of competition, but solely to the active patronage of the early feudal Axum state. It was understandable, then, that Adulis should be called 'the officially established market' in the *Periplus*.

Culture

The development of the early feudal empire was reflected in the ideology and culture of Axum over a period lasting from the second to the fourth century. The brief inscriptions devoted to the gods underwent a gradual transformation into detailed accounts of the victories won by the King of Kings. Particularly interesting in this respect are the Ethiopian and Greek inscriptions of Ezana, who attained the peak of epigraphic style in an inscription giving the fullest account of his Nubian campaign. The inscription reveals genuine eloquence, religious feeling and a free use of complex conceptions. King Ezana is represented as irreproachably fair-minded and magnanimous. This inscription may be justifiably termed a literary achievement. It has points in common with folk-poetry and Ethiopian literature of a later period.

A parallel evolution took place in the mottoes on Axumite coinage. Coins dating from the third to the mid-fourth century bear the ethnic sobriquet peculiar to each monarch, which consists of the word *be'esi* (man) and an ethronym relating to the name of one of the Axumite 'armies'. It was in some way associated with the ethnic and military structure of the Axum state and possibly stemmed from the military democracy of the Ethiopians of antiquity. Currency coined in the time of Ezana and his successors bore a Greek motto signifying 'May the country be satisfied!' It is evident that this demagogic device reflects an official doctrine, the first traces of which may be discovered in the inscriptions of Ezana. Clearly the king aimed at making himself popular with the nation. Later on, this motto gave place to pious Christian formulas.

In the recurrent change of mottoes on coins, and in the royal inscriptions of Axum, two warring tendencies can be seen in the ideology of officialdom: the monarchical idea bound up with Christian unity and the demagogic notion stemming from local traditions.

With the idea of empire came the development of the gigantesque in architecture and the figurative, such as the colossal monolithic stelae, 33.5 metres in height,

15.1 *Gold money from the reign of King Endybis. (Source unknown)*

15.2 *Greek inscription from Ezana (fourth century). (Source unknown)*

erected on a platform 114 metres in length; the monolithic basalt slab measuring 17.3 by 6.7 by 1.12 metres; the huge metal statues; the vast royal palaces of Axumite kings Enda-Mikael and Enda-Simeon; and particularly the palatial set of buildings, Taaka-Maryam, extending over an area of 120 metres by 80 metres – all these are unparalleled in tropical Africa. With the taste for the gigantesque, a tendency towards the decorative became noticeably stronger in architecture. The combination of stone and wood in building, with alternate stone blocks worked to a greater or lesser extent at various points in the edifice, with wooden beams and rubble filling cemented with a cohesive solution, greatly simplified the builders' task and made it possible to achieve a highly decorative effect. During this period architecture and sculpture in Ethiopia were of a striking originality which, however, did not exclude adaptation of different cultural influences from the Roman empire, southern Arabia, India and Meroe. Especially significant were the Syrian influences that stemmed from the spread of Christianity.

The four-towered palace of the Axumite kings is mentioned by Cosmas Indicopleustes. According to the reconstruction made by Dr Krenker, it was a castle, and the arrangement of the adjacent buildings – palaces, temples and other sanctuaries – made it the most inaccessible part of the city.

The pre-Christian religion of the Axumites closely resembled that of ancient southern Arabia. It was a complex polytheism with the characteristics of agricultural and stock-breeding cults. The deities worshipped were Astar, the embodiment of the planet Venus, and the chthonic deities Behēr and Meder, both symbolizing earth. Behēr and Meder (as a single deity) followed Astar in inscriptions. A relic of this form of worship was the Ethiopian Christian term Egziʾabhēr (God; or, literally, the god Behēr, or god of earth.)

The moon-deity Hawbas had been worshipped in southern Arabia and in pre-Axumite Ethiopia. Conti-Rossini produced evidence to show that the god Gad and his cult, against which medieval saints struggled, was none other than the god of the moon. Conti-Rossini connected this cult of the moon with the fact that the taurine antelope was held sacred in modern Eritrea.

Symbols of the sun and moon are found on stelae from Axum, Matara and Anza, and on the coinage of the Axumite kings of pre-Christian times. They refer probably to Mahrem, the dynastic and ethnic deity of the Axumites. In the 'pagan' bilingua of Ezana, the Mahrem of the Ethiopian text is given the Greek name, Ares. All the 'pagan' Greek inscriptions of the Axumite kings, with the exception of the Sembrythes' inscriptions in which the name of the god is absent, use the name Ares. As is well known, the Athenian Ares was worshipped as the god of war. It follows, then, that his double, Mahrem, was also worshipped as the god of war. In the Axumite inscriptions Ares-Mahrem, in his capacity of War-god, is termed 'invincible', 'unconquerable by his enemies' and ensuring victory. In his capacity as the ethnic progenitor, Ares is called the 'god of the Axumites' in the inscriptions from Abba-Pantalewon. As the dynastic deity, the kings called Mahrem-Ares their 'greatest god', ancestor of kings.

It is clear that Mahrem, god of war and monarchy, reigned supreme over the astral and chthonic deities in the same way that a consecrated monarch dominated a people;

at the same time, war, personified by Mahrem, predominated over peaceful labour and was looked upon as a more sacred task, more honourable than peasants' toil, sanctified though this might be by the precepts of their forefathers. Plainly discernible in the religion of Axum are the characteristic features of early class ideology, that of a feudal society in the process of formation.

The Axumites offered sacrifices to their gods. Domestic animals constituted the bulk of these offerings. One of Ezana's inscriptions records that a dozen oxen were offered up to Mahrem at a single sacrifice. According to ancient Semitic custom, some kinds of donation for sacrifice were brought in ritually immaculate clothing; for others this was not obligatory. But already in the pre-Axumite period the living sacrificial animal was supplanted by its consecrated image. Bronze and stone images of sacrificial bulls, rams and other animals, many bearing inscriptions, have been preserved.

Ancestor-cult, especially of dead kings, occupied an important place in the religion of the Axumites. It was customary to dedicate stelae to them: *häwelt*, a word stemming from the root *h-w-l*, means 'to go round', or 'to worship', and is comparable to the Islamic worship of the Kạʿba. Sacrifices were brought to the altars and to the pedestals of stelae carved in the form of altars, and the blood of the sacrifices flowed down into hollows hewn in the form of bowls. The graves of Axumite kings were regarded as the city's holy places. Vessels and other objects found in burial grounds indicate belief in a life beyond the grave. Some indirect references suggest the existence of a cult of 'lords of the mountains' reminiscent of corresponding cults in Arabia.

During the early Axumite period religious ideas from countries near and far penetrated into Ethiopia. In the *Monumentum Adulitanum* mention is made of Poseidon, a sea-god who was evidently worshipped by the inhabitants of Adulis and along the southern part of the Red Sea coast. The holy places of Almaqah, 'national' god of the Sabaeans, worshipped by King Gadara of Axum, were situated at Melazo and perhaps at Hawila-Asseraw. The recently discovered stele at Axum, with the Egyptian symbol of life, the ankh, and objects pertaining to the cult of Hathor, Ptah and Horus, as well as scarabs, suggests that adherents of the Egyptian-Meroe religion were residing at some time in Axum, Adulis and Matara. The small images of Buddha found at Axum were probably brought there by Buddhist merchants from India.

As a result of foreign cultural influences, the subculture of the Axumite monarchy was not only national, but also international in character. Side by side with Ge'ez, the Greek language was used as a state and international language. Apparently, kings like Za-Hekale and Ezana knew Greek (the *Periplus* reports that 'King Zoscales' was literate in Greek and Ezana's mentor was a Graeco-Phoenician, Frumentius, later the first bishop of Axum). The majority of Axumite kings of the third and fourth centuries minted coins with Greek mottoes. We know of six royal Greek inscriptions of Axum.

We have no reason to think that Sabaean was one of the official languages of the early Axumite kingdom. One of the three texts of Ezana pseudo-trilingual (in fact, Ge'ez–Greek bilingual) is written in later Himyaritic script and has some exaggerated peculiarities of Sabaeo-Himyaritic orthography. The same script is used in three other royal inscriptions of Axum by Ezana, Kaleb and Wa'azab. Thus together with an inscription of Tsehuf-Emni (Eritrea) we have five 'pseudo-Himyaritic' texts from Ethiopia. Their language is Ge'ez with very few Sabaean words.

It is not clear why Axumite kings used the 'pseudo-Himyaritic' scripts side by side with that of normal Ethiopic in their inscriptions of definitely official character. But in all cases it is evidence of south Arabian influence.

Perhaps the use of the Himyaritic script, as well as that of vocalized Ethiopic, and the introduced figures were innovations of Ezana's rule, and these innovations were interrelated.

The hypothetical Greek influence on the creation of the Ethiopic alphabet has not been proved, although the Greek origin of the system and the main signs of Ethiopic figures, as they first appeared in Ezana's inscriptions, is certain.

The vocalized Ethiopic alphabet so closely reproduces the phonematic system of Ge'ez that it is inconceivable that any but an Ethiopian could have been its creator. This alphabet, with the addition of some signs, has been in continuous use in Ethiopia till this day and is generally regarded as the outstanding achievement of the Axumite civilization.

Soon after its creation, the Ethiopic vocalized script began to influence the scripts of Transcaucasia. D. A. Olderogge suggested that Mesrop Mashtotz used the vocalized Ethiopic script when he invented the Armenian alphabet. Not long before this time (at the end of the fifth century) the Ethiopic script may have been introduced into Armenia by the Syrian bishop Daniel.

It was through the mediation of north Syria that Axum and Armenia had cultural relations at this time. We have some evidence about the Syrians in Axum and about Syrian influence on Axumite architecture, particularly in the grand monolithic stelae in the form of multi-storey buildings. Some analogy with south Arabian and Indian architecture of the time can also be seen. During the second and third centuries we may reasonably suggest that Meroitic influence predominated. All the articles of Meroitic handicraft found in Ethiopia belong to this period. Elephants may have been introduced into the Axumite royal ritual under the influence of India as well as that of Meroe.

The Axumite kingdom was not only an important trading power on the routes from the Roman world to India and from Arabia to north-east Africa, but also a great centre of culture which seeped down these routes. In their turn, many of the ancient civilized countries of north-east Africa and south Arabia determined many features of the Axumite culture under whose domination they lived.

16 Christian Axum

Traditional pre-Christian cults in Axum

Up to the eighteenth century, religion, whatever its form, played a major part in every human society. In general, polytheism preceded monotheism. Present-day Christian centres were once cradles of traditional religion. No nation has adopted Christianity without first passing through a period of traditional religion.

Ethiopia is no exception to that rule; it was not privileged to accept monotheism directly, without first practising the most diverse forms of worship. In a country like Ethiopia, it was natural for several cults to exist and to be transmitted from father to son.

Among the inhabitants of ancient Ethiopia the Kushitic groups, unlike the ruling classes, had escaped assimilation to Semitic culture, and worshipped different natural objects such as giant trees, rivers, lakes, high mountains or animals. All these were believed to shelter good or evil spirits, to whom various annual or seasonal offerings and sacrifices had to be made.

The peoples of Semitic origin who had not inherited the Kushitic cult, and the Semitized Kushites, fairly advanced as compared with the previous groups, worshipped nature in its celestial and terrestrial forms (the sun, moon and stars, the land and the earth) under the names of the triad Mahrem, Behēr and Meder. These were in rivalry with foreign or semi-national gods of south Arabia or Assyro-Babylonia such as Almuqah, Awbas, Astart, who in turn were assimilated to the Greek gods Zeus, Ares and Poseidon.

This somewhat arbitrary assimilation was allowed by certain kings of Axum whose culture was Greek. But it did not shake the foundations of the divinity of Mahrem, regarded as the national god. The Mahrem of the Axumites could be called Zeus by a Greek and Amon by a Nubian of Egyptian culture, since every man spoke in his own language. It will be remembered that when Alexander the Great made his triumphal entry into Egypt in −332, he was received by the priests as the son of Amon.

Old Ethiopian texts dating from the time of King Amde Tsion (+1313 to +1342) report the existence of a cult of the serpent 'arwe', side by side with the practice of the Law of Moses. This serpent was sometimes considered as a dragon-god and sometimes as the first reigning king, Arwe-Negus, father of the Queen of Sheba. The popular belief surely belongs to the legendary history of ancient Ethiopia, before the dawn of its authentic history. All nations have some such legend preceding their ancient and medieval histories.

The Semites who came from south Arabia and are the ancestors of the Tigre and the Amara, living on the high plateau, were said to have brought with them several south Arabian cults. The existence of these creeds, quoted confusedly by travellers, is confirmed by epigraphic and numismatic documents.

The practice of pre-Christian cults at the court of Axum before its conversion to Christianity is attested by the temple of Yeha (which is still standing), scattered stelae, castle sites and votive objects.

However, a point to be clarified is whether this comparatively developed religion was a royal and aristocratic preserve or was practised also by the people at large. As for the existence of Judaism in Ethiopia, several factors testify to the presence of a group which professed the Jewish religion; the history of the kings, *Tarike Neguest*, mentions it briefly. This was a group which perhaps even ruled for a certain time.

Even if we leave aside the fantastic story of *Kbre Neguest* (Glory of the Kings) which the Ethiopian clerics consider as a basic work of history and literature and in which all the kings of Axum are wrongly said to be linked with Solomon and Moses, certain traditions handed down through the centuries refer to the presence of believers in the Jewish faith.

But with the introduction of Christianity, which was either preceded or followed by a transfer of power into the hands of other groups (Sabaeans, Habesan and others), the Jews, as everywhere else, were victims of prejudice and violence and withdrew into less accessible areas.

The coming of Christianity to Axum

The new religion founded in Palestine by Christ and spread by his militants throughout all the empires of East and West arrived, in its turn, at the court of Axum, in the midst of a polytheistic cult followed by the Kushites and of a sub-Arabic religion practised by the Semites and the Semitized Kushites.

On the basis of the apocryphal texts of the Acts of the Apostles drawn up by a certain Abdia, part of the population mistakenly believes that Saint Matthew was the first to bring Christianity to Ethiopia. This view, however, is supported by no document worthy of belief.

The history of the kings, *Tarike Neguest*, attributes to the famous Frumentius the privilege of having introduced Christianity into the country. Frumentius is later called the Enlightener (Kessate Brhan) or Abba Selama, which means, Father of Peace. The arrival of Frumentius in Ethiopia, his departure for Alexandria and his return to Axum are described in detail by Eusebius and Rufinus.

According to Rufinus, a certain Meropius of Tyre wished to go to the Indies with two young relatives, Frumentius and Aedesius. On their return, his boat was attacked by the population of a port. Meropius died and the two young brothers were taken to the King of Axum. The younger one, Aedesius, became a cup-bearer, whilst Frumentius, owing to his Greek culture, became the king's counsellor and treasurer, as well as tutor to the royal children. This king seems to have been Ella Amida, father of King Ezana. After the death of Ella Amida, his wife became regent and asked the two young men to remain with her to administer the country until her son was old enough to reign.

So Frumentius brought up the young prince to love the new Christian religion. He then departed with his brother Aedesius. While Aedesius returned to Tyre to help his aged parents, Frumentius went to Alexandria to visit the Patriarch Athanasius, and told him of the favourable attitude of the royal family of Axum towards Christianity, urging Athanasius to send a bishop there. The patriarch, being unwilling to send a bishop who knew neither the language nor the customs of the country, therefore consecrated Frumentius himself as bishop of the church of Axum and sent him back to Ethiopia. Frumentius then baptized the king and all the royal family.

It is from this date, therefore, that Christianity spread in Axum. The first Christian king, educated and then baptized by Frumentius, appears to have been Ezana, the son of Ella Amida. And there is every reason to believe that the example of the king and the royal family was widely followed.

While recognizing the part played by Frumentius, we suggest that the change of religion should be attributed to another cause. Thanks to epigraphic and numismatic documents, and to travellers' reports, we know that the court of Axum was on friendly terms with Constantinople. There were considerable commercial and cultural exchanges between the two countries. Eusebius, in his *Vita Constantini*, mentions the presence of Ethiopians in Constantinople during the reign of Constantine. The use of the Greek script and the Greek language at the court of Axum is also very significant. King Zoskales in the first century of the Christian era spoke and wrote Greek, as did Ezana himself. All this clearly indicates the preponderance of Greek culture in the Axumite kingdom.

Now the Emperor of Constantinople, Constantine the Great, was the contemporary of King Ella Amida and of Ezana. The splendour of Constantine's court and his leaning towards Christianity were doubtless recounted and enlarged upon by other travellers, besides Frumentius, who are not mentioned in the annals. All this must have made a deep impression on the court of Axum and on Frumentius himself, who finally found the king and his family ready to embrace the new Christianity which was already widespread at the court of Constantinople.

The transfer from one religion to another is, of course, never easy, and it must have been even less so for the kings, who loved their god as their own father. A king's honour was always linked to his god. The interests of the court and of the religious leaders were almost everywhere identified with one another. When a king like Ezana called his god 'unconquerable', he was in fact thinking only of himself. Through the attribute he was seeking his own invincibility.

We can therefore imagine the difficulties that Ezana had to face, as did his contemporary, Constantine the Great. For indeed the Emperor of Constantinople, although he presided over Christian councils and arbitrated in the religious disputes of the patriarchs, was baptized only on his death-bed, since he feared betrayal by the believers in the old cults of Zeus and Ares.

Similarly, as Guidi and Conti-Rossini have pointed out, King Ezana and his family – through fear or pride – did not suddenly abandon their old god in favour of the Christian religion. The famous inscription registered by Deutsche Axum expedition (DAE) in Volume II, which begins with the words 'with the help of the Lord of Heaven and Earth' and which is considered by all Ethiopians as Ezana's first indication of his Christianity, clearly shows his desire to assimilate the new religion to the old belief in the gods Bēher and Meder, by avoiding any mention of the name of Christ, Christ's unity with God, and the Trinity which he forms with the Father and the Holy Spirit. The expression 'Lord of Heaven and Earth' – Igzia Semay Wem, first pronounced in the fourth century by the first Christian king – has remained in use down to the present day.

Neither foreign works nor local accounts so far published give any specific date for the introduction of Christianity to Axum. The history of the kings, *Tarike Neguest*, as well as the *Guedel Tekle Haymanot*, states that the brothers Frumentius and Aedesius arrived in +257 and that Frumentius returned to Axum as bishop in +315. Other sources of the same kind give the dates +333, +343, +350, and others. All these dates seem to be arbitrary. Certain foreign works state that King Ella Amida, father of Ezana, died about +320 to +335. Taking fifteen years as the age of majority, and allowing for the departure and return of Frumentius, the baptism of King Ezana must therefore have occurred between +350 and +360.

An inscription in Greek characters, discovered at Philae, mentions the visit in +360 of an Axumite viceroy, a Christian named Abratoeis, to the Roman emperor, who received him with all the honours due to his rank. The emperor must have been Constans II (+341 to +368), the son of Constantine the Great. Although a Christian, he had adopted the doctrine of Arius, who denied the unity and the consubstantiality of the three persons of the Holy Trinity and consequently the perfect equality of Jesus Christ with the Father. The Council of Nicaea, held in +325 and presided over by the father of Constantine II, had condemned the doctrine.

An implacable enemy of Arius was precisely Athanasius, who had consecrated Frumentius bishop of Axum. This patriarch was himself later ousted on the orders of the semi-apostate emperor, who nominated a certain George, very favourable to Arianism, to replace him.

The news of the arrival in Axum of Frumentius, a fervent supporter of the Patriarch Athanasius, who had consecrated him, was not likely to please the Emperor of Constantinople. He immediately dispatched a letter to King Aizanz (Ezana) and to his brother Saizana, generously calling them his 'greatly honoured brothers'. In a friendly manner, he requested them to send back Frumentius to the new patriarch, George, in Alexandria, so that his case could be examined by the latter and his colleagues, who alone had the power to decide whether or not Frumentius was worthy to head the bishopric of Axum.

Unfortunately, we do not possess the document that might have revealed the reaction of the two brothers on receipt of this letter. Although the national interest forced them to maintain friendly relations with the powerful Emperor of Constantinople, it would seem that they did not comply with his request. All the local sources affirm that Frumentius carried out his episcopal duties peacefully to the end of his life.

The spread of Christianity

The introduction and spread of Christianity by Bishop Frumentius and the two brother-kings (Abraha and Atsbaha) are widely recognized. All the local sources confirm this. A curious fact is that, in the many texts dating from this period and written before the end of the nineteenth century, there is no trace of the name Ezana, which appears to be the king's 'pagan' name. Nor, to my knowledge, does any epigraphic or numismatic inscription mention the name Abraha, which is presumably the king's baptismal name. So we have different names for the same man who, by good or bad fortune, was, like Constantine the Great, a semi-'pagan' and a semi-Christian during his reign.

The influence of the two brothers, and especially that of Abraha, was enormous in the country. He built the city of Axum and its first cathedral. Several churches and convents claim to have been founded by him, though we should not forget how much help was given in his work by his brother Atsbaha and by Bishop Frumentius, as well as by other religious leaders not mentioned in the sources.

The first proselytism in favour of the new religion seems to have been well received by a part of the population linked to the court by ethnic and cultural ties. These were Sabaean, Habesan, Himyard of Semitic stock, ancestors of the Tigre and the Amhara, who accepted their masters' religion without difficulty.

After the introduction of Christianity, and as those converted to the faith increased in numbers, journeys to the holy places became frequent. In a letter sent from Jerusalem in the year +386, a certain Paola wrote to her friend Marcella who lived in Rome: 'What should we say of the Armenians . . . of the Indian and Ethiopian people, who hasten to this place (Jerusalem); where they show exemplary virtue . . .?' Saint Jerome, doctor of the Latin church, also mentions the continual arrival of Ethiopians at the holy places.

The spread of Christianity in the Kingdom of Axum during the fifth and sixth centuries was the work of churchmen whom all the traditional texts describe as *Tsadkan* (Just) or *Tesseatou Kidoussan* (Nine Saints). But their arrival in the Kingdom of Axum involved the latter in the theological quarrels current at the time in the large cities of the Byzantine empire.

After the condemnation of Arius in +325, it was the turn of the Patriarch of Constantinople, Nestorius, to arouse a great polemic by publicly professing the humanity of Christ in opposition to the doctrine established at Nicaea on the divine nature of Christ. According to Nestorius, the two natures of Christ (human and divine) were quite distinct and separate. The Virgin Mary was the mother of Christ as a man, not as God, and therefore should not be called Theotokos, or Mother of God, but merely Christotokos, Mother of Christ.

This proposition met with strong opposition from Cyril, Patriarch of Alexandria, and from Pope Celestine of Rome. Nestorius was condemned in Ephesus (+431) as a heretic and thrown into prison.

His successor Flavian, Patriarch of Constantinople, put forward another idea on the two natures of Christ (human and divine), without, however, denying that Christ was true man and true God. In Flavian's view, each of Christ's two natures was perfect and distinct, and united only in the person of Christ. Dioscoros, Patriarch of Alexandria, at once opposed this viewpoint. Christ, he said, had but one nature, which was at once human and divine. This was the Monophysitism whose chief defender was the scholar Eutyches. Close argument degenerated into uproar during the Council held at Ephesus in +442. Dioscoros and Eutyches emerged victorious from this stormy debate; the loser, having been soundly flogged by his opponents, died very soon afterwards and Dioscoros returned triumphant to Alexandria.

A council composed of 636 prelates and doctors of the church was held in +451 in Chalcedon, under the presidency of the Emperor Marcian. The discussion became so confused that it was impossible to discern either victor or vanquished, and the question had to be put before the Pope of Rome, who was considered to be the supreme head of all the churches. Pope Leo the Great declared in a letter that he was in favour of the doctrine of the two separate natures of Christ. The Council therefore condemned Dioscoros. His opponents, armed on the one hand by the opinion of the supreme head of the universal church, and on the other by the support of the Emperor Marcian, went so far as to manhandle and beat Dioscoros in revenge for the ill-treatment of the Patriarch Flavian. Dioscoros was then banished to an island in Galatia.

Now, ever since the time of Frumentius, the Kingdom of Axum had, as we know, come under the jurisdiction of the patriarchate of Alexandria, whence it received its bishop and canon law. The kings and bishops of Axum were therefore naturally upholders of the Monophysite cause, which was later, in Ethiopia, to take the name of *Tewahdo*. The news of the ill-treatment inflicted on their patriarch filled them with great hatred of the supporters of the doctrine of the two natures of Christ. For the Monophysites life became unbearable throughout the whole Empire of Constantinople, since the conquerors of Chalcedon threatened and insulted them incessantly. To escape from this intolerable existence the Monophysites fled towards Egypt and Arabia. It was at this time that the famous Nine Saints arrived in the Kingdom of Axum, where they sought refuge with others who professed the same doctrine as themselves.

They carried out their apostolate in various places. Abba Aregawi went up to Debre-Dāmo, where the cult of the Python appeared to have taken root among the local population. Abba Guerima settled at Mettera (Madera) near Senafe, and Abba Aftse at Yeha, where one can still see the ancient temple dedicated to the god Almaqah (fifth century). Penteleon and Likanos remained in the city of Axum, while Alef and Tsihma went to Bhzan and to Tseden Tsedeniya; Ym'ata and Gouba settled in the region of Guerealta.

In the places where they lived, convents and churches dedicated to them are still to be seen today. Some are carved into giant rocks, and are accessible only by means of a rope. In the convent of Abba Ym'ata, also built on a rock, at Goh (Guerealta), there is a circular painting representing the Nine Saints.

Christianity, as introduced in the fourth century by Frumentius, was therefore consolidated by these saints. They were, of course, helped by the successors of King Ezana, such as Kaleb and Guebre Meskel, who were fervent Christians. In their

16.1 *Debre Damo (Tekle Tsadik Mekouria)*

teaching of the Gospel, the Nine Saints upheld the Monophysite doctrine for which so many Christians had suffered ill-treatment and exile.

However, the spreading of Christianity was not due solely to these nine monks who came from the Byzantine empire. Guided by bishops such as the famous Abba Metta'e, hundreds of native and foreign monks certainly helped to propagate the Christian faith, although they did not have the privilege, like the Nine Saints, of being mentioned by name in the annals. Starting from the northern regions, Christianity was implanted in other provinces such as Begemdir, Godjam and Shoa, among the Bēdja and the Amhara. The Christian religion benefited from the faithful support of kings, queens, princes, governors and dignitaries of the church, who had many convents and churches built in places where the traditional cults had flourished.

And now we come to the question of the language in which these monks, who came from all corners of the Byzantine empire, taught the Gospel. The people of the upper classes close to the court were more or less polyglot and spoke Greek, Syriac or Arabic; in their case there does not seem to have been any linguistic problem. But the foreign monks were obliged to study the language of the country before they could make themselves understood by the people in general. Possibly some of the pilgrims who went to the holy places in Jerusalem, Constantinople and Alexandria spoke Greek or Syriac and could act as interpreters, or could teach the people themselves directly.

The Kingdom of Axum and south Arabia

It has long been known that groups of peoples of Semitic origin crossed the Red Sea and settled in northern Ethiopia, probably seeking more fertile and richer lands than their own desert country. The newcomers possessed a higher form of civilization than that of indigenous peoples (most of whom were Bēdja, Aguew, and so on, of Kushitic origin) and ended by taking over the central power and founding the cities of Yeha, Matara, Axum and other places.

Other groups of the same origin (Sabaeans, Himyarites) remained in their native land, while those who had crossed the Red Sea became more and more powerful, to the point where the central government of Axum seemed strong enough to some to be considered the third world power. Royal castles, temples, circles and crescents, symbolizing the gods Mahrem and Almaqah all confirm the identity of the two peoples who lived on either side of the Red Sea.

Until the beginning of the fourth century the Semitic people on the opposite shores of the Red Sea practised the same traditional religion, that is, the worship of the moon, with the crescent as its symbol, which is still honoured today by the Muslim Arab states. Perhaps the Prophet Muḥammad did not require converts to abandon this symbol, whereas the bishops of Axum put pressure on the Christian kings to replace it by the Christian symbol of the cross.

Struggle between Christians and Jews in south Arabia

Other groups of Hebraic religion had been living in this same region of south Arabia for a long time, perhaps since the destruction of Jerusalem by Nebuchadnezzar in −587 and its occupation by the Lagidae. But their numbers increased greatly after the third destruction of Jerusalem by the Emperor Titus in +70, when Jews persecuted by the Romans received a welcome from their compatriots settled in south Arabia.

Furthermore, many Monophysites left the Byzantine empire and sought refuge in Arabia after the Council of Nicaea and even more after that of Chalcedon, when Arians were condemned and persecuted. There, with the help of the kings and the Christians of Axum, they founded a powerful community. Under the rule of the Emperor Justin I (+518 to +527), many Syrian Monophysites were expelled by order of the emperor, and left for Hira (Nadjaf, now in Iraq) and from there reached south Arabia and settled in Nadjrān. But the Christians, thanks to the unfailing help of the Axumites, increased in number and developed and organized their community. Many churches were built. Nadjrān and Zafar (Tafar), for instance, became great Christian cultural centres and major trading posts.

The Jews, too, with the talent they show in all fields, had formed a community in Saba and in Himyar and sought to control trade there. So a sharp rivalry developed between Christians and Jews.

Massacre of the Christians of Nadjrān by the Jews

While the Emperor Justin I reigned in Byzantium (+518 to +527), Kaleb was Emperor of Axum. It was at this time that the Jews, with the help of the Himyarites, massacred the Christians of Zafar and Nadjrān. This event is recorded mainly by the religious authors of the period, Procopius and Sergius.

Sergius, who claims to have gathered his information from eye-witnesses, gives the following version of the event which Conti-Rossini has translated into Italian in his *Storia di Ethiopia*. Dhū Nuwās or Nasruc, king of the Himyarites, persecuted the Christians, with the support of the Jews and the 'pagans'. Bishop Thomas therefore went to Abyssinia to seek aid, and found it. The Abyssinians, led by a certain Haywana, crossed the Red Sea and prepared to attack Dhū Nuwās. The latter, not being able to withstand so strong a force, signed a peace treaty with the Abyssinian leader Haywana who, after leaving part of his army behind him, returned home. With the bulk of the troops gone, Dhū Nuwās treacherously massacred the Christians of Zafar and burned all the churches, together with the 300 Christian soldiers left as a garrison. But the worst massacre described by the authors of this period took place in +523 at Nadjrān, the most highly developed of the Christian centres.

King Kaleb's maritime expedition

After the massacre of +523, a nobleman named Umayyah managed to get back to Axum and told King Kaleb and the bishop what had happened to the Christians. Other Christians escaped to Constantinople to inform the Emperor Justin. Through the Patriarch Timothy of Alexandria, Justin sent a letter to Kaleb urging him to avenge the bloodshed of Christians. So King Kaleb hastily assembled an army that would guarantee victory. He is said to have obtained 120,000 men and 60 warships from the Emperor Justin. However, other authors state that he left with his own ships which were anchored at Adulis, and that his army numbered no more than 30,000 soldiers.

Towards the end of May +525, Kaleb embarked and set sail with all his ships for south Arabia where the Himyarite king awaited them. In fact, when the king and his army arrived they found the enemy port blocked by chains and guarded by soldiers ready to defend themselves.

Without waiting for the end of the battle, King Kaleb looked for a more propitious place to land his troops. By chance, one of the family of Dhū Nuwās, who had been captured in battle, told them of such a place and the king, accompanied by some twenty boats, succeeded in disembarking. This enabled him to put the rest of the King of Himyar's soldiers to flight. It was while the main part of the contingent continued to fight that Dhu Nuwās fell into King Kaleb's hands, with seven of his companions. Kaleb, wishing to avenge the shedding of Christian blood, unhesitatingly killed him on the spot.

At Nadjrān, the king was present at a ceremony to commemorate the martyrdom of the Christians who had lost their lives in the massacre, and before he returned to Axum he had a monument built in Marib in memory of his victory. Kaleb also erected a monument in Marib, so that his name might be remembered by future generations. Before his return to Axum the king left a certain Summyapha Awsa at Zafar, under the orders of Abreha, who was the best-known Christian general at the court of Axum, as also in south Arabia.

A contingent of 10,000 men was left as a garrison. After his successful campaign, Kaleb received a triumphal welcome, as one can well imagine, on his return to Axum. Yet, instead of savouring the fruits of victory, this king, who was both religious and warlike, retired to the convent of Abba Penteleon to lead a monastic life and swore never to leave it. He sent his crown to Jerusalem, begging Bishop Yohannes to hang it before the door of the Holy Sepulchre in accordance with a vow he had made before the campaign.

The King's decision to abdicate after such a victory is admirable in itself, if the facts reported in the traditional texts are accurate. But another text states that Kaleb remained on his throne until +542. It is quite possible, if his war against Dhū Nuwās took place in Arabia in +525, that he reigned for another seventeen years, unless there is an error of dating, after his return to Axum.

Literature

Axum had several alphabets which were used by men of letters and by the court for its administration. Among the stelae of Axum, some carry inscriptions only in Sabaean, or in Ge'ez or sometimes in Greek, but seldom in all three languages together. Sabaean was the alphabet of the Sabaean peoples, which are thought to be among the ancestors of the Axumites, described in the traditional text as Neguede Yoktan (*ḳabīla* of Yoktan) and from whom the present-day Amhara, Tigre, Gouraghe, Argoba and Harrari (Aderes) are descended.

Greek, like English today, was the vehicular language of that period, a foreign tongue introduced into Axum because of the kingdom's cultural, economic and political relations with the Byzantine empire. In the end, it was Ge'ez, at first without vowel signs and later vocalized, that became from the sixth and seventh centuries onwards the official national language of the Axumites, the language of the Aga'izyan – another name given by the natives, which means liberators.

In general, the language provides research workers with useful pointers, but does not in itself enable the ethnic group to be identified. For a native might be of Semitic origin, of Axumite nationality and Greek culture and another might be of Bēdja or Blemmye stock, a Nubian by birth or nationality, and of Egyptian culture. Therefore a person who spoke or wrote Ge'ez was not necessarily an Axumite.

After the Arab conquest in the Middle East and North Africa during the seventh century, Greek and Sabaean gave way to Ge'ez, which began to be used in all circles – civil, military and religious. Greek maintained its influence only throught the translation of the Bible from Greek into Ge'ez, and through certain works of the fathers of the church such as Cyril of Alexandria or St John Chrysostom.

The first inscription which marks the beginning of Christian Axumite literature is the one which the DAE registered under No. II, in which King Ezana, newly converted, described his victory over the people of Noba (the Nubians), who had dared to dispute his power beyond the River Ṫakazi and had put his emissaries to death. One can believe in the moral sense of this conquering emperor when he accuses 'the Noba of ill-treating and oppressing the people of Mengourto, Hasa and Baria, the people of black and red colour (*Seb'a tselime, seb'a que'yh*), of having twice broken the oath they had taken.' Was this the result of his new religion?

The influence of Christianity appears also on the numerous coins of the kings of Axum, where the Christian symbol of the cross replaced the crescent, symbol of the ancient religion. Certain Axumite kings, wishing for publicity or to gain the sympathy of their people, had unusual legends inscribed on their coins. The coinage of King Wazed or Wazeba (son of King Kaleb – sixth century) had his effigy on one side and on the other the inscription: 'Let the people be joyful.' Most significant are the coins of King Lyouel, which bear his crowned head on one side (to the right of the crown there is a small cross) and a cross on the other, which would seem to indicate that he was a fervent Christian. On another coin of the same king the inscription 'Christ is with us' figures in Ge'ez, without a vowel sign. This is the first time the name of Christ is mentioned.

The Old Testament was gradually translated from Greek into Ge'ez during the fifth and sixth centuries. The Bible came into use in Ethiopia, and its teaching assumed vital importance in the court and in ecclesiastical circles, until it eventually became the sole basis of science and philosophy without, however, overshadowing certain works of the fathers of the church.

After the Council of Chalcedon in +451, the Nine Saints and their disciples arrived in Ethiopia and strengthened the influence of Monophysitism among the Ethiopian clergy. That is why the Ethiopian church systematically avoided all other works, of whatever value, that came from the West. One remembers the agreement between 'Amr ibn Alas, the companion of the Prophet Muḥammad, on one hand, and, on the other, the Patriarchs Benjamin and Chenouda, at the siege of Heliopolis in +640 during the conquest of Egypt. Their hatred of the Patriarch Mukaukis and of all those who professed the doctrine of the two natures of Christ led the Egyptian Monophysites to rally to the side of the Muslims.

For the Amhara dynasty, who were said to have descended from Solomon and were the legitimate heirs of the kings of Axum, the most revered kings were David and his son Solomon. Then followed Alexander the Great, Constantine the Great and Theodosius II, the two latter because of the help they had given to Christianity. The biblical persons of most renown for the monks were Joshua, Samson and Gideon. The Song of Songs, the Proverbs, the Book of the Wisdom of Solomon, the Wisdom of the Son of Sirach, etc., were considered works of true philosophy, more than the writings of Plato or Aristotle. Virgil, Seneca and Cicero and the medieval scholars of the West were totally unknown.

The Christian society of Ethiopia loves and admires David more than anyone else, considering him to be the ancestor of Mary and of the so-called Solomonian dynasty. The Ethiopian religious adore the Book of Psalms and believe that by reading the psalm for the day each morning they will be protected from all evil. Like David, they believe that Almighty God is their exclusive ally.

Whilst some religious use the psalms as prayers, others employ them for magico-religious purposes. The scholar knows by heart the appropriate psalm for each circumstance, to gain happiness or to avoid misfortune, to ward off a threatening plague or to be protected from gunfire. Generally they quote Psalms 6, 7, 10, 57 and others.

Part of the heritage that Ethiopia received from Christian Axum is the liturgical chants assembled in a work known as the *Degoua*. According to fourteenth-century local sources, the author was a native of Axum called Yared, a contemporary of King Guebre Meskel and of Abba Aregawi, one of the Nine Saints.

In reading this book of religious chants in detail, one sees that the texts are drawn from the Bible, from the works of the early patriarchs, from the famous theologians of the third to the eighth centuries, and from the apocryphal books. They are arranged poetically and concisely and form a great collection divided into several books, chapters and verses. Then all the verses are separated (the first line is usually written in red) and there is a verse for each annual and monthly feast. They are all written in praise of angels, saints, martyrs, the Virgin Mary and God, and are used for the morning and evening services.

Biblical literature and liturgical chants have a long traditional history, part authentic and part legend. They form part of the inheritance that Christian Axum has generously bequeathed to the Ethiopians over the centuries.

17

The proto-Berbers

The ethnic components of the Libyan population were more or less settled before the arrival of the Phoenicians on the African coasts at the beginning of the first millennium before the Christian era; they were not to alter at any time during the whole of antiquity, for it would not seem that the Phoenician and Roman demographic accretions were of any consequence. In fact the demographic contribution of the Phoenicians to Africa Minor cannot be assessed precisely. It is unlikely, however, that the Carthaginians would have had such constant recourse to mercenaries on the battlefield if those of Phoenician origin had been more numerous. The demographic contribution of the Romans is also difficult to evaluate.

At least thirteen millennia before the Christian era there existed a culture very improperly known as Ibero-Maurusian. Its bearers, the race of Mechta el-Arbi, were tall (1.72 metres on average) and dolichocephalic. They had low foreheads and long limbs and were addicted to the removal of the incisors. A trend towards mesobrachycephalism and signs of slenderness have been detected on certain sites, notably at Columnata in western Algeria towards −6000.

The Ibero-Maurusian culture, properly so called, disappeared at the end of the ninth millennium. This did not happen suddenly everywhere, however. It was supplanted by the Capsian culture in Cyrenaica, but yielded more indecisively to local cultures in western Algeria and Morocco. No evidence of its existence is to be found on the north-eastern coasts of Tunisia, and it left few traces in the Tangiers area. This culture could not have come from Europe, since it arose before the beginnings of navigation across the Straits and from and to Sicily. It is tempting to think that its origins were eastern, but it may have come rather from the north of the Nilotic Sudan, as J. Tixier claims. Subsequently, as they came under pressure from migrating peoples, the Ibero-Maurusians doubtless took refuge in the hills and may be regarded as constituting one of the anthropological components of the population of the djebels.

In about −7000 there appeared men of fairly tall stature, of Mediterranean race, but not devoid of negroid characteristics. They are known as Capsians, after the site of Capsa (now Cafsa). They flourished in an area which has not been exactly defined, but which certainly lay inland without, apparently, extending to the westernmost borders of North Africa or to the southern Sahara. They settled usually on a hillock or a slope near a source of water, but sometimes on plains featuring lakes or marshes, and their diet included snails. This culture also came from the east and it could not have spread by sea. It must be reckoned to have come to an end by about the year −4500. Although the Capsian crania are identical with many contemporary types, it is thought that true proto-Berbers were not in evidence until the Neolithic Age, since Capsian funeral rites do not appear to have survived in the Libyco-Berber world. It will be noted, however, that the custom of using and decorating ostrich eggs which characterized the Capsian way of life persisted throughout the Neolithic era up to the time of the Libyan peoples mentioned in historical records, such as the Garamantes. The latter, according to Lucian, used the eggs for countless purposes and this is confirmed by excavations at Abū Ndjem (inland Tripolitania). Nevertheless, Neolithic man in Africa Minor can doubtless be regarded as a cousin of the Capsian. At all events, the historical peopling of the Maghrib is certainly the result of a merger, in proportions not yet determined, of three elements: Ibero-Maurusian, Capsian and Neolithic.

It is generally agreed that the Neolithic Age began with the appearance of ceramics. Recent carbon-14 measurements indicate that the use of ceramics spread outwards from the central and eastern Sahara, within that area stretching from the Ennedi to the Hoggar. The ox had undoubtedly become domesticated by −4000 at the latest. It is not impossible that cattle were domesticated earlier in the Acacus. Evidence of a Neolithic culture in the Capsian tradition dates from a somewhat later period – in about −5350 at Fort Flatters, even a little earlier in the valley of the Sawura – and does not become established in the northern part of the Capsian area before −4500. In the region lying between these two currents which affect 'the Maghrib of the high lands and the Northern Sahara', Neolithic characteristics do not emerge until much later.

The humid period of the Neolithic Age came to an end towards the middle of the third millennium, as is attested by the dating of guano from the Taessa (Atakor in the Hoggar). Arkell's work on the fossil fauna and flora on Mesolithic and Neolithic sites in the Khartoum region gives some support to this finding as regards the valley of the upper Nile. From this time on North Africa, almost totally cut off from the whole continent by desert, found itself virtually an island, only able to communicate easily with the rest of Africa through the narrow corridor of Tripolitania.

As early as the close of the third millennium before the Christian era the painted potsherds of Gar Cahal, in the Ceuta area, bear a resemblance to the Chalcolithic ceramics of Los Millares. We must therefore assume sea-route contacts which may perhaps take us back to the fourth millennium.

From −2000, ivory and ostrich eggs were imported into Spain, while bell-shaped vessels of Iberian origin make their appearance in the Ceuta and Tetuan areas. Towards −1500, copper and bronze arrow-heads are to be found in the west of Africa Minor, no doubt first imported by Iberian hunters; but they do not appear to have spread westward beyond the region of Algiers. Because of the lack of tin, the use of bronze is hardly noticeable in North Africa. At the other end of Africa Minor, from Korba to Bizerta, the presence of flakes of obsidian originating from the Lipari Islands and worked in Sicily and Pantellaria provides evidence of the beginnings of navigation in the Messina Straits. G. Camps has drawn attention to the numerous borrowings made from then onwards by eastern Africa Minor from European neighbours:

rectangular tombs with short access passages and right-angled bays, cut into the cliffs and known as '*haounet*', existed in Sicily as early as −1300; the Algerian and Tunisian dolmens are of a type similar to those widely found in Sardinia and Italy; the Castellucio ceramics which were common throughout Sicily towards −1500, with geometrical designs painted in brown or black on a paler background, are the forerunners of Kabyle pottery; and so forth. More distant influences from Cyprus or Asia Minor came through Malta, Pantellaria and Sicily as soon as Aegean, and then Phoenician, sailors began to reach those islands.

The separateness of Africa Minor, lying on the borders of the continent, the result both of the drying-up of the Sahara and of the appearance of navigation, needs to be stressed. However, not all links with Africa south of the Sahara were broken. While the climate of North Africa in ancient times was very much the same as it is today, the marginal belt of the Sahara continued for a long time to be better watered and more wooded in its hilly expanses with aquifers lying much closer to the surface so that water was more accessible; the horse could therefore be used for Saharan travel. In the Fezzān in particular, surface overspills from aquifers persisted for a long time. We can regard as evidence of the original African unity the fact that, in ancient times, dark-skinned men whom the Greeks were later to call Ethiopians, that is, 'burnt faces', were in contact with the Libyco-Berber world, in most of the oases of the Sahara, in the Fezzān and on all the Saharan slopes of the Atlas range. They led a peaceful existence and engaged not only in food-gathering and hunting, but also in agriculture based on extremely ancient methods of irrigation.

It would certainly be a mistake to imagine a wholly Ethiopian Sahara in the Neolithic and proto-historical ages, even if we are careful to give the term 'Ethiopian' its broadest sense of 'man of colour' and refrain from interpreting it as 'Negro'. M. C. Chamla has recently thought it possible to establish that only one-quarter of the skeletons of this period could be identified with black men, while over 40 per cent show no negroid characteristics. On the other hand, the remains of a child discovered in a rock-sheltered deposit in the Acacus and dated approximately between −3446 and −180, are negroid. In the Punic burial grounds, negroid remains were not rare and there were black auxiliaries in the Carthaginian army who were certainly not Nilotics.

Libyco-Berbers (Maurii and Numidians on the coast, Getules on the plateaux), white or half-breed Saharans on the borders of the desert – such as Pharusians, Nigrites or Garamantes, 'Ethiopians' scattered from the Sūs to the Djarīd – these were the peoples of Africa Minor at the time of the first Phoenician sea voyages, and such they remained throughout antiquity.

The proto-Berbers in their relations with the Egyptians and the Peoples of the Sea

Libya's historical sources in the second millennium before the Christian era whether inscriptions or figured objects, are essentially Egyptian in character and concern Libyan populations in contact with Egypt who were able to settle in the north-west of the Delta before the unification of the Nile Valley.

As early as the pre-dynastic era, towards the middle of the fourth millennium, the ivory handle of the Djabal al-Arak knife may perhaps have portrayed long-haired Libyans, naked except for a belt holding up the phallic covering. This interpretation has, however, been contested and we cannot be certain of the Libyan identity in an iconography before the emergence of the first name given to the Libyans by the Egyptians, that of Tehenou. According to W. Holscher, this name appears on a fragment of a schist *palette* belonging to King Scorpio, and next on an ivory cylinder from Hierakopolis dating from the reign of Narmer (third millennium). This second object pictures the Pharaoh's booty and prisoners. But it is a bas-relief of the funeral temple of Sahure (First Dynasty, *c.* –2500) that enlightens us about the physical aspect and clothing of the Tehenou.

These men were tall, with sharp profiles, thick lips, full beards and a characteristic hair-style, with a heavy growth on the back of the neck, locks reaching to the shoulders and a small quiff upright above the forehead. They wore distinctive broad ribbons around their shoulders, crossing on the breast, and necklaces hung with pendants. They inhabited the Libyan desert and its oases during the third millennium.

Under the Sixth Dynasty, towards –2300, reference was made to the Temehou. These were not a branch of the Tehenou, as O. Bates surmised, but a new ethnic group with paler skins and blue eyes, including a considerable proportion of fair-haired individuals. It has been suggested that they are identical with the Group C people who settled in Nubia during the Middle Empire and the beginnings of the New Empire, and this hypothesis is strengthened by a resemblance between the pottery of that group and the pottery found in Wādī Howar, 400 kilometres south-west of the Third Cataract.

They often wore feathers in their hair and were sometimes tattooed. Their weapon is the bow, or sometimes a sword or boomerang. These features are also noted by Herodotus among the Syrtes Libyans of the fifth century.

The forays of the Temehou became more menacing during the Nineteenth Dynasty. After Seti I had driven them back *c.* –1317, Ramses II incorporated Libyan contingents into the Egyptian army and organized a defence line along the Mediterranean shore as far as el-Alamein. The stele at the latter spot confirms the occupation of the region by Ramses II and is the first object referring to the Libou. From the name of these people the Greeks derived the geographical term Libya, which then applied to their area of movement, and then, step by step, to the whole of Africa. Under Merneptah, in –1227, mention is made of the Meshwesh as western neighbours of the Libou. Both the Libou and the Meshwesh appear to have formed part of the broader group of the Temehou. Having occupied the oases of Baḥriyya and Farāfra, the combined ethnic groups were defeated north-west of Memphis by the Egyptians.

The two best-known Egypto-Libyan wars, however, are dated –1194 to –1188, in the reign of Ramses III. They are recorded in the Harris Grand Papyrus and in inscriptions and reliefs of the Pharaoh's funeral temple at Medinat-Habou. First the Libou, then the Meshwesh, tried in vain to overcome Egyptian resistance on the Nile, and were defeated one after the other.

The victories of Ramses III had one particularly important consequence: they enabled him to control the western oases through which the cult of the Theban

Amon was spreading, particularly the oasis of Siwa, gradually reaching Tripolitania along the 'thirst tracts' and, in the Punic period, exerting an undoubted influence on the cult of the god Ba'al Ammon, a near homonym.

Such are the first pieces of evidence which tell us something about the Libyans in the most easterly part of their wide area of settlement. It should be noted that the Peoples of the Sea are only mentioned once in an inscription at Karnak, as being in constant contact with the Libyans during the reign of Merneptah in −1227, and that this inscription itself may be the result of an amalgam of several campaigns. But, even if we grant that there were detachments of Peoples of the Sea among the Libyans, can we go on to assert that these were the peoples who taught the Libyans the use of chariots, first in the confines of Egypt and then throughout the Sahara?

This proposition has the support of some first-rate Sahara specialists, although there are few similarities between the Aegean and the Saharan portrayals of chariots, as is well demonstrated by an archaeologist of classical antiquity such as G. Charles-Picard and a specialist on the horse such as J. Spruytte. The Saharan chariots are seen in a horseman's perspective and not in profile; the platform is not raised and rests on the centre of the axle, well away from the wheels, thus limiting the passenger load in practice to one driver, whose hands hold a kind of short whip and not a weapon. The horses, mostly Barbaries, are harnessed by means of a collar-yoke, not a yoke resting on the withers. Although they are indeed shown in an extended position ('flying gallop'), neither their hocks nor their knees appear. In the Aegean documents, moreover, the 'flying gallop' is not the stance of harnessed horses. Thus the Saharan chariots would seem to be strongly characterized as somewhat fragile 'sporting' vehicles.

Therefore, we should probably distinguish the Saharan chariots from the war chariots of antiquity identified among the foes of Ramses III and later among the Garamantes (four-horse chariots), the Arbytes, the Zoeces, the Libyans in the service of Agathocles in the neighbourhood of Carthage, the Pharusians and the Nigretes. Rather than assume a borrowing from the Peoples of the Sea, we will be closer to the truth in allowing, with W. Holscher, that the Libyans borrowed the chariot from the Egyptians who had used it ever since the Hyksos invasion four or five centuries earlier. The origins of the Saharan chariots remain a mystery. They were made entirely of wood, the design was very simple, and they may have been constructed according to an original technique. Moreover, the Barbary (or Mongol) horse, of small size, having a convex face and forehead line, a prominent and hollow backbone with five lumbar vertebrae, and sloping hindquarters, cannot be derived from the Arab-Oriental breed with its square-cut profile, as ridden by both the Hyksos and the Aegeans. It may perhaps have spread from East Africa and the Sudan, but this is only a hypothesis. We may note that both in the Saharan rock carvings and in carvings of the Roman era within the *Limes*, portrayals of the Arab-Asiatic horse are exceedingly scarce, although they exist. However, even supposing that these cases do not confront us with a stylized image foreign to African realities, it remains true that until the arrival of the Arabs the Barbary horse was the dominant species in Africa Minor.

Life of the Berbers before the foundation of Carthage

As H. Basset and G. Camps have rightly underlined, agriculture was not introduced to the Libyco-Berbers by the Phoenicians, but had been practised by them since the close of Neolithic times. Engravings and paintings of the Metal Age represent a swing-plough in a more or less diagrammatic form at La Cheffia (eastern Constantine region), and in the High Atlas, west of Tebessa, in the region of the Douar Tazbent, a pattern of squares is what remains today of primitive hydraulic installations dating from much earlier than the epoch of native kingdoms. Users of these installations had equipment still partly made of stone.

They had already been familiar for a very long time with the harnessing of oxen, which is depicted both in Egyptian frescoes and in High Atlas engravings. On the other hand they do not appear to have known any mechanical method of threshing their crops before Punic times and were content to let the grain be trodden out by heavy cattle.

Botanists have shown that hard wheat (perhaps brought from Abyssinia) and barley were grown in North Africa long before the arrival of the Phoenicians, together with beans and chick-peas, although the latter derived their Berber name, *ikiker*, from the Latin *cicer*.

Archaeological research into funerary monuments confirms the existence in remote antiquity of large sedentary groups practising agriculture in Africa Minor. The tomb furniture testifies, as is well demonstrated by G. Camps, to the great antiquity of the Berber rural culture. We can agree with this scholar that a map of the distribution of the proto-historical burial grounds containing ceramics will give us a reasonably accurate notion of the geographical spread of agriculture. A study of ceramic shapes has enabled G. Camps to throw some light on the way of life of the Libyco-Berbers at this time. The typology is very close to that of contemporary ceramics: bowls, basins and goblets to contain liquids and broths, more or less shallow plates, large dishes somewhat similar to those used in our day for baking unleavened bread, griddlecakes and pancakes.

A kind of fruit-dish on a stem base is also found from the proto-historical age up to the present day. Perforations show that from the earliest times the Berbers hung their eating-vessels on the wall. On the other hand, there are no modern equivalents of the ancient filtering-pots, and G. Camps has wondered whether they were not used for separating honey or for preparing infusions.

Archaeologists have also established that the nomads of the southern sites carried ornamental weapons and wore bracelets, metallic pendants or porcelain beads more often than did the sedentary inhabitants. Some scraps of fabric indicate the use of striped cloth. Rock engravings found near Sigus attest to the existence in ancient times of the burnous, which is perhaps the origin of legends concerning headless men or men with their faces in their chests. Such cloaks were apparently also worn by the Blemmyes of the Arabian desert on the borders of Upper Egypt.

The chief source of wealth of the nomads was the raising of sheep, goats and cattle. An engraving showing a milking scene has been found at Djorf Torba, west of Colomb Béchar, in an area now completely barren. According to Elien (NA,

17.1 *Libyan stele from Abizar, south-east of Tigzirt (Photo, Museum of Antiquities, Algiers)*

VII, 10.1) these nomads did not have slaves, but used dogs instead; the same comments have been made regarding the Red Sea Troglodytes and the Ethiopians of the Nile swamps. Hunting was naturally a common activity, and Ptolemy mentions some Oreipaei hunters living in southern Tunisia near the Ethiopian border, who were neighbours of the Nybgenite Ethiopians roaming the lands south of the Djarīd.

Of the social organization of the Libyco-Berbers in times preceding those described in classical sources we know very little, at least if we ignore recurrent attempts at reconstitution based on later evidence. The imposing size of the mounds of the Rharb in Morocco, or of the mausoleum of the Medracen in the Constantine region, suggests that, in those parts of both the western and eastern Maghrib which were independent of Carthage, monarchies had sprung up at least as early as the fourth century. Nothing more can be asserted, for the brilliant picture of Libyan social organization painted by St Gsell is mainly based on Roman documents of the imperial age, and even on the evidence of the poet Corippus who was a contemporary of Justinian.

Religious beliefs of the Libyco-Berbers

It is difficult to gain an insight into the religious beliefs of the Libyco-Berbers before the impact of the Punic Phoenicians and, later, that of the Romans. Proto-historical archaeology never allows us to reconstitute more than rites, and even then, in the case of Africa Minor, the possibility is confined to funerary rites.

Among the Libyans, the sense of holiness appears to have crystallized around a great variety of objects. Supernatural power was often thought to be manifested in the surrounding countryside, hence the many fluvial or mountain genie worshipped in the inscriptions of Roman times. More precisely localized, divine power could reside in the commonest objects. Round or pointed stones, such as granite pebbles, symbolizing the human face or phallus, were objects of worship.

The animals which symbolize most obviously the power to procreate – the bull, the lion and the ram – are precisely those which the Libyans venerated. Athanasius (*Contra Gentes*, 24) informs us that the ram was considered as a divinity by the Libyans under the name of Amon. Mention should also be made of the fish-cult characteristic of the area which is now Tunisia: it partly explains the wealth of fish images found in Tunisian mosaics. The fish – a phallic symbol – warded off the evil eye. A fish-shaped phallus ejaculating between two female pudenda is shown in a mosaic from Susa. Alongside the fish, the shell was widespread as a symbol of the female sex throughout Africa Minor; it served the living as a charm and comforted the dead in their tombs.

Sacrifices in honour of the dead were performed in front of their tombs in a reserved area facing the rising sun. Sometimes the vital force of the dead man was symbolized by means of a monumental stone in the form of an obelisk or a stele. Herodotus (IV, 172) informs us that the Nasamonians consulted their ancestors about the future by sleeping on their tombs. G. Camps believes that this incubation ritual is the reason for the existence of the bazinas and tumuli of platform shape, but the Saharan monuments incorporating a chapel and chamber appear to be the best adapted to this custom. It was probably widespread throughout the Saharan populations, since

17.2 *Lions from Kbor Roumia (M. Christofle,* Le tombeau de la chrétienne, *1951)*

they expressed astonishment at the fact that the Atlantes (Herodotus, IV, 184) never had any visions in sleep.

The Libyans do not appear to have worshipped major god figures represented in a more or less human form. According to Herodotus (IV, 188) they only sacrificed to the sun and the moon. However, those of the Djarīd area were more inclined to offer sacrifices to Athena, Triton and Poseidon, while the Atarantians (IV, 184), the westerly neighbours of the Garamantes, cursed the sun. Cicero relates (*Rep.*, VI, 4) that Massinissa gave thanks to the sun and other divinities in the sky. The sun continued to be worshipped in several towns of Roman Africa such as Maktar, Althiburos, Thugga and Sufetula, but some Punic influence may have been at work here and there.

Apart from the two major heavenly bodies, both epigraphy and literary sources reveal a profusion of divinities, often mentioned only once, and sometimes even referred to collectively, e.g. the Dii Mauri. A carving found near Bēdja appears to picture a kind of pantheon of seven divinities. But this no doubt reflects a kind of polytheism introduced under Punic influence, which led the Libyans to personalize the divine powers. Left to themselves, the Libyans were always drawn more to the sacred than to the gods.

18

The Carthaginian period

The entry of the Maghrib into recorded history begins with the arrival on its coasts of sailors and settlers from Phoenicia. The reconstruction of the history of this period is complicated by the fact that the sources are almost all Greek and Roman, and for these two peoples the Phoenicians of the west, especially under the leadership of Carthage, were for most of it bitter enemies. Hence the picture in the sources is a hostile one. No Carthaginian literature has survived; the contribution made by archaeology is also limited because in most cases the Phoenician settlements are overlaid by much more substantial Roman towns, though in the last two decades some progress has been made. The development of the indigenous Libyan cultures before the third century is likewise to some degree obscure. The archaeological picture of the first millennium is one of continuing slow evolution, but with Phoenician influences operating with increasing effect from about the fourth century. The particular phenomenon of widespread, large, stone-built surface tombs appears to have no connection with the much earlier megalithic cultures of northern Europe. The largest, such as the tumulus of Mzora and the Medracen, are probably connected with the growth of larger ethnic units in the fourth or third centuries. Greek and Roman authors refer to a large number of different peoples by name, but for the period under review generally divide the non-Phoenician inhabitants of the Maghrib into three main groups. In the west, between the Atlantic and the Mulucca (Moulouya), were the Mauri, and the name Mauretania, earlier Maurousia, was given to their territory, but later the designation was extended much farther east beyond the Chelif. Between the Mauri and the maximum western extension of the Carthaginians inland territory (see below) were the Numidae with their territory Numidia. The third group were the Gaetuli, the name given to true nomads along the northern fringes of the Sahara. The classical names for these groups, and for individual peoples, are used throughout this chapter.

The earliest Phoenician settlements

Tyre and the other Phoenician cities (such as Sidon and Byblus) from about −1000 were the most active trading cities in the eastern Aegean and Near East, little interrupted by the growth of the Assyrian empire. The motive which sent Phoenician traders into the western Mediterranean was the search for sources of metal, in particular gold, silver, copper and tin. This led them at early date to Spain, which remained one of the chief sources of silver in the Mediterranean world even in the Roman period. Their power also increased through this commerce, carried on for a long time, and they were able to send out numerous colonists to Sicily and the neighbouring islands, to Africa, Sardinia and Spain itself. Traditionally the earliest Phoenician foundation in the west was on the site of the modern Cadiz, the name itself deriving from the Phoenician Gadir, meaning a fort, presumably representing its origin as a trading post. The Phoenicians used both a northern route, along the southern coasts of Sicily, Sardinia and the Balearic Islands, and a southern one, along the coast of North Africa. Along the latter route it has been estimated that there was probably an anchorage used by the Phoenicians every 30 miles or so, though the development of such anchorages into permanent settlements depended on various factors; the classic sites were offshore islands or promontories with landing-places on either side. In addition, general strategic factors led to the advancement of some sites as opposed to others; it is significant that three of the most important, Carthage and Utica (Utique) in North Africa, and Motya (Mozia) in Sicily, are all well placed on the narrows leading from the eastern into the western Mediterranean and dominate both the southern and northern routes.

Foundation of Carthage

The name Carthage (Latin: *Carthago*) represents the Phoenician name Kart Hadasht, meaning New City. This may imply that the place was destined from the start to be the chief settlement of the Phoenicians in the west, but we know too little of the archaeology of its earliest period to be certain of this. The traditional date for the foundation is −814, long after the traditional dates for Cadiz (−1110) and Utica (−1101). These latter dates have a legendary appearance. As for the date of Carthage, the earliest uncontested archaeological material is of the middle of the eighth century before the Christian era, that is, within a couple of generations of the traditional date. Nothing of historical value can be derived from the foundation legends transmitted to us in various versions by Greek and Roman authors. Material of about the same date comes from Utica, and of seventh- or sixth-century date from Leptis Magna (Lebda), Hadrumetum (Sousse), Tipasa, Siga (Rachgoun), Lixus (on the Oued Loukkos) and Mogador, the last being the most distant Phoenician settlement so far known. Finds of parallel date have been made at Motya in Sicily, Nora (Nuri), Sulcis and Tharros (Torre di S. Giovanni) in Sardinia and at Cadiz and Almunecar in Spain. It must be emphasized that, unlike the settlements which the Greeks were making in Sicily and Italy and elsewhere in the eighth and seventh centuries, all the Phoenician settlements, including Carthage itself, remained small places, with perhaps no more than a few hundred settlers at most, for generations. Furthermore, they long remained politically subordinate to Tyre, as was to be expected having regard to their prime function as anchorages and supply points.

Carthaginian leadership of the western Phoenicians

The emergence of Carthage as an independent city, followed by her leadership of the rest of the Phoenicians in the west and the creation of an empire based in North Africa, with profound historical consequences for the whole of the western Mediterranean area, began in the sixth century before the Christian era. During the seventh century there appears to have been no great conflict between Phoenicians and Greeks, and Greek imports are known from many Phoenician sites in the Maghrib; but in −580 the city of Selinus (Selinunte) and other Sicilian Greeks tried to drive the Phoenicians from their settlements at Motya and Palermo. Carthage appears to have taken the lead in repelling this attack, which if successful would have led the Greeks on to threaten the Phoenician settlements in Sardinia and opened the Spanish trade from which they had so far been excluded. Following this success, the Phoenician settlements on Sardinia were consolidated. A final success in this period was in Africa itself; a Spartan named Dorieus tried to found a settlement at the mouth of the Kinyps river (Wādī Oukirri) in Libya. Carthage regarded this as an intrusion and within three years was able to drive out the Greeks with help from the native Libyans.

The burden of leadership of the Phoenicians of the west seems to have been too heavy for the manpower available to Carthage. Up to the sixth century they relied on their own citizens. In the middle of the century, under the leadership of Mago, the policy of hiring mercenary troops on a large scale was initiated, a policy followed for the remainder of Carthaginian history. Of the non-Carthaginian elements which were hired, the Libyans provided the biggest share. They were particularly useful as light infantry. As mercenaries, or under treaties of alliance at a later date, Numidian and Mauretanian cavalry from the northern parts of modern Algeria and Morocco were a significant part of all large Carthaginian armies; Spanish, Gallic, Italian and finally Greek mercenaries are found in the service of Carthage at various dates.

The generation after the success against Dorieus saw profound changes among the Greek cities of Sicily, which reacted seriously on Carthage. Gelon, ruler of Gela and from −485 of Syracuse, initiated a war to avenge Dorieus and planned a campaign to conquer the area of Phoenician settlement around the Gulf of Gabes. As a result, Carthage sought friends in Sicily among those opposed to Gelon and in −480 put a large mercenary army into the island, perhaps taking advantage of the fact that the same year saw the invasion of Greece by Persia. A figure for the Carthaginian fleet at this date is given as 200 ships, which puts it on a par with that of Syracuse and not much less than that of Athens. However, the intervention ended in complete disaster with the destruction of the army and the fleet at a great battle at Himera. Gelon was unable or unwilling to follow up this success and allowed peace on a moderate war indemnity.

Expansion in North Africa

The defeat of Himera was followed by seventy years of peace in which Carthage avoided conflict with the Greeks, but was even so able to maintain her trading monopoly. More important, she turned towards the acquisition of territory in Africa itself. This change occurred as Carthage was increasingly isolated by Greek successes elsewhere, first against the Persians, in which the Phoenicians lost heavily, and then against the Etruscans in Italy. The new policy is associated with the Magonid family, led at this time by Hanno, son of Hamilcar who had been defeated at Himera, and who is loosely described by the late Greek writer Dio Chrysostom, as 'transforming the Carthaginians from Tyrians into Africans'.

While the amount of land conquered in the fifth century and the number of settlements now grown to towns, albeit small ones, is uncertain, it began to approach the maximum which Carthage ever controlled. Most important was the conquest of the Cap Bon peninsula and a considerable area of land to the south of Carthage, at least as far as Dougga. This included some of the most fertile land in Tunisia, an area where later Roman settlement was particularly dense. It provided the essential supply of food and the possibility of a much larger population in the city. Many Carthaginians had estates in Cap Bon at a later date. Land in Cap Bon counted as city land and the inhabitants were presumably reduced to servile or semi-servile status. Inhabitants of the rest of the conquered territory were obliged to pay tribute and provide troops. The number of Phoenician settlements on the coast was added to by those now established by Carthage herself, though we are ignorant of some of their names. Like the settlements, they were small places, of a few hundred inhabitants, established where native peoples came to trade their goods, as is indicated by the fact that the Greeks called them *emporia* – markets.

The boundary between the Carthaginian empire and the area of Greek colonization in Cyrenaica was on the Gulf of Sidra, but settlements on the coast of Libya were few. The most important was at Lepcis where it is probable that permanent settlement was made when the expedition of Dorieus to the vicinity showed that there was a danger of Greek intrusion. At Sabratha, there was a settlement by the early fourth century. Lepcis became the administrative centre of the settlements round the Gulf of Gabes and is known to have been a wealthy place at the end of the Carthaginian period, and its Phoenician culture even remained dominant for over a century under Roman rule. The source of its wealth is generally held to be trans-Saharan trade, since the area was the terminus of the shortest route by way of Cidamus (Ghadāmes) to the Niger. However, we do not know in what this trade consisted, except that semi-precious stones are mentioned. The agricultural wealth of the area in Roman times owed its origin to the Carthaginian settlers. Traditionally Lepcis Minor and Hadrumetum were founded from Phoenicia, not Carthage, and the latter became the largest town on the east coast of Tunisia. From Neapolis (Nabeul) a road ran across the base of Cap Bon to Carthage. West of Carthage lay Utica, second only to Carthage in importance; it was, like Carthage, a port though it is now ten kilometres inland.

The Empire of Carthage

Carthage was criticized by her enemies for the harsh treatment and exploitation of her subjects, and there were certainly several categories among these. The most privileged areas were doubtless the old Phoenician settlements and those established by Carthage herself, whose inhabitants were called Libyphoenicians by the Greeks. They appear to have had local officials and institutions similar to those of Carthage herself. They had to pay dues on imports and exports and sometimes troops were levied from them. After −348 they seem to have been forbidden to trade with anyone except Carthage. The position of Carthaginian subjects in Sicily was affected by their proximity to Greek cities; they were allowed their own institutions and issued their own coinage throughout the fifth century in a period when Carthage herself did not issue coins. Their trade does not seem to have been restricted; on the analogy of Roman practice when Sicily fell to Rome, a tribute of one-tenth of the produce was levied. The Libyans of the interior were the worst off, though ethnic structures appear to have been permitted to them. It seems that Carthaginian officials directly supervised the collection of tribute and the enrolment of soldiers. The normal exaction of tribute seems to have been one-quarter of the crops, and at a critical point in the first war with Rome half was taken.

Carthaginian trade and exploration

West Africa

There was general agreement among the Greeks and Romans that Carthage depended more on trade than any other city, and when they thought of a typical Carthaginian they thought of a merchant. Further, it was believed that Carthage was the wealthiest city in the Mediterranean world. However, it must be said that both the trade itself and the alleged wealth have left remarkably few traces for the archaeologist, much less, for example, than in the case of major Greek and Etruscan cities of the same era. Undoubtedly one major reason in the case of Carthage is that the bulk of her trade was in items which left no trace, primarily metals in unworked state – the primary object of Phoenician exploration in the first place – textiles, slaves and, increasingly as her fertile lands were worked, foodstuffs.

The profits from the trade with backward peoples, from whom gold, silver, tin and presumably iron were obtained in exchange for cheap manufacturers, are indicated by the vast mercenary armies she could raise in the fourth and third centuries and the minting of gold coinage far in excess of that of other advanced cities.

The active leadership of the state in major trading enterprises is indicated in our sources, particularly those concerned with West Africa. According to Herodotus (fifth century), the Egyptian King Necho (*c.* −610 to −594) sent Phoenician mariners to sail down the Red Sea and thence to circumnavigate Africa. They are said to have taken two years on the journey, having twice halted to sow and reap a crop of wheat. Herodotus believed that the voyage had been successful and it is not impossible, but it had no repercussions at the time; if it took place, the vast size of the continent thus revealed must have removed any ideas of a route from the Red Sea to the Mediterranean. The Carthaginians who, again according to Herodotus, believed that Africa could be circumnavigated, must have known of the venture, and of another of the early fifth century.

A Persian prince procured a ship in Egypt on orders to attempt the circumnavigation in the opposite direction; he appears to have sailed down the Moroccan coast a good distance beyond Cape Spartel but was forced to return. Herodotus also gives an account of Carthaginian trade on the Moroccan coast. This is the earliest description we have of the classic method of dumb barter. The gold trade is normally associated with a much-discussed Greek text which claims to be a translation of the report of a voyage down the Moroccan coast by one Hanno, identified as the leader of the Magonid family in the middle of the fifth century and the statesman responsible for Carthaginian expansion elsewhere in Africa.

The most southerly settlement mentioned in the report is called Cerne, generally identified with Hern Island at the mouth of the Rio de Oro:

> 'At Cerne, the Phoenicians [i.e. Carthaginians] anchor their *gauloi*, as their merchant ships are called, and pitch tents on the island. After unloading their goods they take them to the mainland in small boats; there live Ethiopians with whom they trade. In exchange for their goods they acquire the skins of deer, lions and leopards, elephant hides and tusks . . . the Phoenicians bring perfume, Egyptian stones [?faience] and Athenian pottery and jars.'

There is no mention of gold; Cerne appears as an anchorage rather than a settlement.

If gold was the objective, it is remarkable that all knowledge of the trade disappeared with the fall of Carthage even though some settlements on the Moroccan coast survived. The Greek historian Polybius sailed beyond Cerne after –146, but discovered nothing worth while, and in the first century of the Christian era the Roman writer Pliny wrote of the report of Hanno: 'many Greeks and Romans on the basis of it tell of many fabulous things and of many foundations of cities of which in fact neither memory nor trace remain'. Oddly enough, Mogador began to be visited again by sailors from the Roman client-state of Mauretania (see below), but it seems that fish rather than gold was the purpose.

The Atlantic

A report of another voyage led by Hanno's contemporary, Himilco, was known in antiquity, but only scattered references survive. Himilco explored the Atlantic coast of Spain and France, and certainly reached as far as Brittany. The object was probably to increase direct control of the trade in tin obtained from various sources close to the Atlantic coasts. A number of ancient writers were interested in the trade, no doubt because the Carthaginians allowed so little information to emerge. In fact the Carthaginian period was the last stage in the trade in tin along this coast which went back to prehistoric times, with south-west Britain as one of its most important sources. However, there is no evidence that any Phoenician ever reached Britain; no Phoenician object has ever been found there (nor, for that matter, in Brittany). If tin from Britain was obtained it was probably through the intermediary activity of peoples in Brittany. The likelihood is that most tin from British sources was transported across Gaul to the Rhône Valley and the Mediterranean, and that the Carthaginians got most of theirs from northern Spain. In any case, the most valuable mineral produced in Spain was silver; we know that in the third century the production reached impressive levels and it was undoubtedly of far greater importance than tin.

Mediterranean trade

As stated, Carthage exercised a monopoly of trade within her empire, either sinking any intruding vessel or arranging commercial treaties with possible competitors like the Etruscan cities and Rome. Normally foreign traders were not allowed to trade west of Carthage; this meant that goods they brought to that city were then moved and traded in Carthaginian vessels. It was by these ways that products from Etruria, Campania, Egypt and various Greek cities reached a large number of North African sites. The manufactures of Carthage are not easy to identify archaeologically because they lack individual style and merit. It was only in the fourth century that Carthage began to issue her own coins as her trade with advanced powers increased, and as the changed economic scene made it necessary also to pay mercenaries in coin.

Saharan trade

The question of Carthaginian contacts with Saharan peoples, and people living even farther south, is obscure. If communications or contacts existed, they must have been based on Leptis Magna and Sabratha, since it is in this region that there are the fewest natural obstacles. Carthaginian concern to keep Greeks from the area has been cited as evidence that trade of some substance with the interior existed, since suitable agricultural land for settlement is scarce. Unfortunately, up to the present such trade as existed has left no archaeological trace whatever, and in literature only carbuncles are mentioned as an article of desert commerce. Slaves were perhaps traded – the Garamantes are said to have pursued Ethiopians (i.e. negro peoples) in four-horse chariots; ivory and skins are suggested, though these were readily available in the Maghrib; and gold from the Sudan is still more problematical, though not impossible. Recent archaeological evidence from Djerma indicates that the earliest population growth is from the fifth or fourth century and that over succeeding centuries a considerable sedentary population based on agriculture grew up. This may be due to cultural influences extending from the Carthaginian sites on the coast. After the destruction of Carthage, the Romans penetrated both to Djerma and Ghadāmes and occasionally farther south, and there are some archaeological traces of imports from the Mediterranean world into the interior, but on a modest scale. The lack of camels in North Africa at this time explains the difficulty and irregularity of trans-Saharan travel.

The city of Carthage

Although Carthage had the reputation of possessing enormous wealth, there is no trace of this in the archaeology, even allowing for the complete destruction of the city by the Romans. This is not to say that there were no important buildings as in other ancient cities of similar size. Carthage had an elaborate double artificial harbour, the outer for the use of merchant ships – how many could see it at one time is not known – and the inner which had quays and sheds for 220 warships, together with a control building sufficiently high to give a view over intervening buildings out to sea. The city walls were of exceptional dimensions and held out against every attack till the final Roman assault. An inner citadel, with a circumference of about two miles, enclosed the hill known as the Byrsa, no doubt the oldest part of the city. Between the harbour and the Byrsa was an open public space equivalent to a Greek *agora*, but it does not seem that it ever had the regular planned or monumental aspect which came to characterize Greek cities. The city seems to have developed unplanned, with narrow winding streets, and we hear of buildings up to six storeys in height, as at Tyre itself and at Motya in Sicily. As for temples, although these are said to have been numerous, they are unlikely to have been substantial till the later stages of Carthaginian history when Greek cultural influence became pronounced, since most of the evidence goes to show that the Carthaginians were essentially conservative in religious matters and long remained faithful to the concept of simple enclosures without monumental buildings.

Carthaginian political institutions

The only aspect of Carthage to receive praise from the Greeks and Romans was its political constitution which seemed to ensure the stability so highly cherished in antiquity. Hereditary kingship prevailed in the Phoenician cities till Hellenistic times, and all our sources likewise refer to kingship at Carthage; for example, Hamilcar, defeated at Himera, and Hanno, the leader of the African expansion, are described as kings. It is probable that in calling them kings the classical authors were thinking as much of their sacral and judicial as of their political and military powers. The position was in principle elective, not hereditary, but several generations of the Magonid family held the position. During the sixth and fifth centuries they appear also to have been the military leaders of the state when occasion demanded. During the fifth century a process began whereby the power of the kings was diminished. This appears to be associated with the rise to power of the *sufets*, the only Carthaginian political term transcribed for us by Roman writers. The word combines the meaning of judge and governor and, since in the third century two (perhaps more) were elected annually, it was easy to compare them with Roman consuls; and the term *sufet* remained in use in North Africa in areas of Carthaginian culture for at least a century after the Roman conquest, to denote the chief magistrate of a town. The reduction in the power of the kings was similar to developments in Greek cities and in Rome. At the same time the power of a wealthy aristocracy increased. In addition to their exclusive membership of a council of state like the Roman senate, the aristocracy established a court of 100 members apparently with the specific function of controlling all organs of government. Although the citizen body had some say in the election of kings, *sufets* and other officials, it is certain that Carthaginian politics were always dominated by the rich – Aristotle considered the part played by wealth at Carthage to be a bad feature. Both birth and wealth were essential for election.

Carthaginian religion

While their political institutions were praised, Carthaginian religious life was severely criticized by classical authors, above all because of the persistence of human sacrifice. The intensity of religious beliefs was likewise commented on. Naturally the cults at Carthage have similarities with those of Phoenicia from which they were derived. The supreme male deity of the Phoenician world was known in Africa as Baal Hammon, the meaning of the epithet Hammon apparently being 'fiery' and expressive of his solar aspect. He was identified in Roman times with Saturn. In the fifth century he was outstripped, at any rate in popular worship, by a goddess named Tanit. The name is apparently Libyan and the growth of her cult is associated with the acquisition of territory in Africa, because it had pronounced fertility aspects, owing much to the Greek goddesses Hera and Demeter. Crude representations of a female figure with arms raised occur on hundreds of stelae from Carthage and elsewhere. These two deities overshadowed the rest, though we know also of Astarte, Eshmoun (identified with Aesculapius the divine healer) and Melkart, the particular protector of the mother city, Tyre. The institution of human sacrifice is proved archaeologically by discoveries not only at Carthage and Hadrumetum but also at Cirta, in Libyan territory but much influenced by Carthaginian culture, and at a number of settlements outside Africa. The discoveries are of sacred enclosures containing urns with the calcined bones of children, often marked by stelae referring to a sacrificial offering generally to Baal Hammon, but often to Tanit as well. According to our sources (which have doubtful features) the sacrifices were always of males, were annual, and an obligation on the leading families. The practice certainly declined, but an incident in −310 shows that it could be revived in moments of crisis when its neglect was held responsible for divine displeasure. There is no doubt that the emphasis of Carthaginian religious ideas was on the necessity of appeasing the capricious power of the gods. In spite of their contacts with Egypt, the Carthaginians appear to have attached little importance to the idea of life after death, in this respect being like the early Hebrews. Inhumation was the general rule and the grave-goods were moderate; many tombs contained small grotesque masks of terracotta which are assumed to have an apotropaic significance.

Conflicts with the Sicilian Greeks

The period of expansion in Africa and peace elsewhere which had lasted since the disaster at Himera ended in −410. The city of Segesta, a native Sicilian community but allied to Carthage, had been in part responsible for bringing the Athenians into Sicily and was now subject to a major punitive attack by the Greek city of Selinus. It appealed to Carthage. The appeal was accepted, presumably because, if Segesta were defeated, Greek control would reduce the Phoenician settlements to a mere toe-hold on the west of the island. In addition, the Carthaginian leader, Hannibal, turned the expedition into a war to avenge the defeat at Himera in which his grandfather had perished. In −409 a mercenary army of perhaps 50,000 laid siege to Selinus and took it by storm after nine days; shortly afterwards Himera was also taken and razed to the ground, with the massacre of all the inhabitants who had not previously fled. Hannibal then returned and disbanded the army, which indicated that there was no thought of extending the territory of Carthage, though it is clear that from this date the Phoenicians here, and in other territory in Sicily which they dominated, created in effect a Carthaginian province. However, in −406 Carthage was tempted to try for the first and only time to conquer the entire island, after attacks on her territory by some Syracusans. This left Carthage with a larger territory than she had had before, and more tribute. Furthermore it broke the isolation in which she had been living during most of the fifth century, and from this date we find that imports and trade in general with the Greek world revived, in spite of the frequent periods of war.

Africa itself was naturally secure from destruction, except that we hear of a revolt in −368 to −367 which was easily suppressed. Sometime in the −340s, a certain Hanno tried to stage a *coup d'état* by calling on the slave population, African subjects and Mauretanian peoples to join him, but it does not appear that this was a serious threat. Very different was the situation from −310 to −307 when Carthage was engaged in yet another war with Syracuse, now ruled by Agathocles. When his city was under siege, the Greek tried a desperate venture; eluding the Carthaginian fleet, he landed 14,000 men on Cap Bon, burned his ships and made for Carthage. Except at Carthage itself there were no strong points or garrisons, and a vast amount of damage was done within Carthaginian territory in the three years before Agathocles was forced to leave Africa.

The first war with Rome

These conflicts were, however, on a minor scale compared with the revolutionary changes in the east during the same period, when Alexander the Great created an empire stretching as far as India. But Carthage was soon herself to be engaged in a struggle of at least as great a world-historical importance, namely, with Rome. A treaty existed between them as early as −508 when Rome was just one of many Italian communities of moderate size. Another treaty was signed in −348, again regulating trade between the two powers, and, though Rome was by now much stronger, the treaty was very favourable to Carthage, simply because Rome's trading interests were negligible. In the next decades Rome broke through with dramatic rapidity to become the dominating power throughout Italy. The gap between the areas in which the two powers were interested closed even further when in −293 Carthage's old enemy Agathocles led a campaign in southern Italy. A few years later, King Pyrrhus of Epirus was invited into Italy to try to liberate the Greek cities of southern Italy, led by Tarentum, from Roman domination. Although he was unsuccessful, he was approached by the Sicilian Greeks to be their protector against Carthage. To try to prevent this, Carthage sent an impressive fleet to Rome to encourage Rome to continue the war with Pyrrhus. She was successful, but Pyrrhus came to Sicily in any case and had some modest but not decisive successes before he returned to Greece in −276.

Thus Carthage and Rome up to this date had no conflict of interests, yet a decade later were involved in a conflict which produced the heaviest losses on both sides of any known war up to that time. Though the result was of geopolitical significance, there is little doubt that the cause of the war was relatively trivial and that neither side had deep-seated aims. In −264 Rome accepted the submission of Messana (Messina) which had previously been an ally of Carthage against Syracuse. Roman politicians at the time were brimming with self-confidence; it appears to have been expected that Carthage would not react, and that there was booty to be obtained from the Greek cities of Sicily. Some also played on Roman fears that Carthage, if she held Messana, could dominate Italy, though in fact she had never had any interest whatever in doing so. Carthage determined to resist Roman intervention because it would mean a complete change in the balance of power which had existed in the island for a century and a half, and also no doubt because she felt that Roman policy was dangerously adventurist. The ensuing war (the first Punic war) lasted till −242 when the Carthaginian fleet was defeated off the Aegates Islands. This meant that Sicily could no longer be supplied, and a peace of exhaustion followed, in which Carthage gave up Sicily and agreed to a substantial indemnity.

Hannibal and the second war with Rome

The economic difficulties caused by the war made it difficult to pay the mercenaries, half of whom were Libyans. A revolt took place in Africa characterized by ferocious atrocities on both sides. Some 20,000 mercenaries were involved, one of the most effective leaders being a Libyan named Matho. Carthage itself was at risk and the rebels for a time controlled Utica, Hippo Acra and Tunis; they were well enough organized to issue their own coins with the legend 'Libyon' (meaning 'of the Libyans) in Greek. The intensity of the struggle, which ended in −237, testified to the harshness of Carthaginian treatment of the Libyans. At the same time the Romans high-handedly seized Sardinia while Carthage was in no position to resist. In −220 Rome became anxious about the Carthaginian recovery and engaged in a manoeuvre designed to prevent the consolidation or extension of Carthaginian control in Spain. Hannibal (and his government) rejected Rome's threats and decided, in the light of the adventurist Roman policies in −264 and −237, that war was inevitable. In −218 Hannibal crossed the Ebro on his way to the Alps and the road into Italy. The strategy was based on the assumption that Rome could only be finally defeated in Italy itself, and in any case it was necessary to forestall a Roman invasion of Africa, which could easily be mounted since Rome now controlled the sea. This war (the second Punic war) lasted till −202, again with tremendous losses on the Roman side. Hannibal's military genius welded together a superb fighting force, largely of Spaniards, but also with Gallic and African contingents. Notable victories were won at Lake Trasimene (−217) and Cannae (−216), Rome's greatest single defeat. While in Italy the defensive policy of Fabius Maximus was pursued, never allowing Hannibal again to exercise his genius in the field, Spain was won for Rome by the young Scipio Africanus in −206. Rome then prepared for an attack on Africa.

In this they were assisted by the situation in Numidia. The native peoples had now been exposed to Carthaginian civilization for several centuries. Much larger political units had evolved than before, and repeated service in Carthage's wars had increased their strength and sophistication. Syphax, chief of the largest Numidian ethnic group, the Masaesyli, whose territory extended from the Ampsaga (Oued el Kebir) in the east to the Mulucha (Moulouya) in the west, had defected from Carthage in −213, but had rejoined her in −208 when he married a daughter of a leading Carthaginian. Conversely Gaia, the chief of the Massyli, sandwiched between the Masaesyli and Carthaginian territory, had been loyal to Carthage during the period of Syphax's defection, and his son Masinissa rendered good service in Spain. When Rome was victorious, Masinissa decided to back what must have seemed to be the winning side and made his peace with Scipio. On returning to Africa he could not establish himself as head of his ethnic group, but gathered a private force and after two years of epic adventures was waiting to fight for Scipio when he landed. He played a major part in initial successes in −203 before Hannibal was finally recalled from Italy. The final battle took place at Zama (Sab Biar) in −202 when Hannibal suffered defeat. Masinissa, who had meanwhile driven Syphax out of his territory, provided 4,000 cavalry, contributing decisively to the Roman victory. Under the peace terms, Carthage gave up her fleet and had her territory in Africa limited by a line roughly from Thabraca to Thaenae; but she was also to return to Masinissa any land his ancestors ever held, a fruitful cause of disputes, and was forbidden to make war outside Africa, or even within it, without Rome's permission.

Masinissa and the Kingdom of Numidia

Carthage survived another fifty years, but this period of the history of the Maghrib is primarily that of a rapid advance in the economy and society of most of the peoples close to the Mediterranean. It was a historical paradox that the chief figure in this, which involved a more rapid spread of Carthaginian civilization than ever before, should have been Carthage's great enemy Masinissa. His personality was such that later, instead of merely being regarded as a useful deserter by the Romans after −206, he established close ties of friendship with a number of the most influential Roman politicians. He was rewarded after Zama with the eastern, more fertile, parts of Syphax's territory, and thus ruled from Cirta (Constantine) a territory which extended from somewhere west of that city to the new Carthaginian boundary. Trade in other products was limited and the only coins issued were of bronze and copper. Masinissa's capital, Cirta, would appear to have grown into a real city. The archaeology is not well known, but its urban aspect will have been almost entirely Carthaginian; more Punic stelae have been found there than in any other African site except Carthage itself, and there can be no doubt that the language of Carthage became increasingly used in Numidia and Mauretania.

The destruction of Carthage

Over a period of fifty years, Masinissa sought to exert increasing pressure on Carthaginian territory and probably hoped that in the end Carthage itself would fall to him with Roman assent. At first Rome had no interest in further weakening Carthage, which was also naturally a dependant, and down to −170 his gains in territory were small. From −167, however, Rome pursued increasingly ruthless policies, not only in Africa, and favoured Masinissa. Although it was true that Carthage had shown a remarkable recovery from the second Punic war, any idea that she could ever again be a threat to Rome was irrational. The Carthaginians were given the choice of abandoning their city and moving into the interior, or facing war and its consequences. When they chose the latter alternative, a Roman army was sent to Africa in −149. In spite of overwhelming superiority, Carthage held out till −146. Some Libyans still supported her, and Masinissa himself resented the Roman action which deprived him of his cherished hope, but had to acquiesce. Most of the old-established Phoenician and Carthaginian settlements, such as Utica, Hadrumetum, Thapsus and others, went over to the Romans and avoided inevitable destruction. Carthage itself was razed to the ground and the site ceremonially cursed, a symbolic action by Rome testifying to the fear and hatred which she had accumulated over a century for the power which most sternly resisted her domination over the Mediterranean world.

Post-Carthaginian successor states

Numidia

It was more than another century before Rome properly supplanted Carthage as the dominant political and cultural power in the Maghrib. For various reasons (see Chapter 20) Rome only took over a small part of north-eastern Tunisia after the destruction of Carthage and even this was largely neglected. In the rest of North Africa she recognized a series of client kingdoms which were generally left to their own devices. Within these kingdoms the cultural influence of Carthage continued and even increased as the older coastal settlements continued to flourish and many refugees from the last years of Carthage's struggle fled there. The Phoenician language in its later form known as Neo-Punic spread ever more widely. In Numidia, Masinissa died in −148 at the age of about 90 and was succeeded by Micipsa (−148 to −118). During his reign, trade between Numidia and Rome and Italy increased and we hear of numerous Italian traders at Cirta. On his death the kingdom was jointly ruled by two of his brothers together with Jugurtha, a grandson of Masinissa, who had the support of the Roman statesman Scipio Aemilianus, just as Masinissa had had that of an earlier Scipio. Jugurtha was a man of great vigour and sought to establish himself as sole ruler. The Romans attempted a formal division of the kingdom, but, when Jugurtha captured Cirta from one of his rivals and killed the Italian residents, Rome declared war. Jugurtha sustained a formidable resistance, causing some military humiliation to Rome until he was betrayed to the Romans by Bocchus, ruler of Mauretania. Rome then established as king another member of Masinissa's dynasty named Gauda, who was followed by his son, Hiempsal. Hiempsal is known to have written a book about Africa in the Punic language, and presumably continued the civilizing work of his dynasty. Hiempsal's son, Juba (−60 to −46), who had been publicly insulted as a young man by Julius Caesar, joined the Pompeian cause in −49 and rendered it a great deal of assistance in Africa, to the extent that he was said to have been promised the Roman province in Africa if the Pompeians won. He committed suicide after Caesar's victory at Thapsus, which was followed by the establishment of direct Roman rule over Numidia.

Mauretania

The Mauretanian kingdom is generally considered to have developed more slowly than Numidia, but this may be due to lack of information. Obviously the mountain massif of the Atlas remained as immune to Phoenician as it later did to Roman civilization, but there was some development of sedentary life in fertile regions such as the Moulouya Valley and along the Atlantic coast. It was in the mountainous regions that individual ethnic groups retained their identity into Roman times and even beyond. Mauri are referred to as early as the expedition to Sicily of −406, in Hanno's revolt in the −350s and the Roman invasion of Africa in −256. A king of the Mauri helped Masinissa at a critical point in his fortunes, but there were also Mauri in Hannibal's army at Zama. At a later date, Bocchus I at first helped Jugurtha against Rome, but later betrayed him, and was rewarded with substantial territory east of the Moulouya. In the next generation the area seems to have been divided. Bocchus II ruled the eastern part and in association with an Italian adventurer, P. Sittius, fought against Juba in the interest of Caesar, who was also supported by Bogud II, who ruled west of the Moulouya. Both were rewarded, Bocchus with further extension of his territory at the expense of Numidia. A few years later, Bogud II supported Mark Anthony against Octavian in the Roman civil war, and was driven out of his territory by Bocchus II in the interest of Octavian. As Bocchus died in −33 and Bogud was killed in −31, the whole vast area was now without a ruler. In −25 Augustus installed as king Juba, son of the last Numidian king, who had spent his boyhood since the age of four in Italy, and for whom the Numidian kingdom had been temporarily reconstituted from −30 to −25. Ruling for over 40 years as a completely loyal client king, Juba did to some degree in Mauretania what Masinissa had done in Numidia. He was fully Hellenized in culture, and the author of many books (now lost) written in Greek. There is no doubt that his capital Iol, renamed Caesarea (Cherchell), and probably also an alternative capital, Volubilis, became fully urbanized in his reign. He was succeeded by his son Ptolemaus who ruled till +40, when he was summoned to Rome by the emperor Gaius and executed, no reason being known. In +44 Mauretania was made into two provinces, thus completing the organization of the Maghrib under Roman rule.

The Phoenician heritage in the Maghrib

In general, the period of the independent Numidian and Mauretanian kingdoms saw the evolution and entrenchment of a culture. of mixed Libyan and Phoenician character, the latter element being culturally dominant, though naturally representing only a minority of the population as a whole. The strength of the mixed culture may be seen from the fact that the use of Neo-Punic on inscriptions lasted into the second century of the Christian era, and that over the same period the term *sufet* is known to have been used in at least thirty different towns as far apart as Volubilis in western Morocco and Leptis Magna in Libya. The strong persistence of Phoenician/Libyan religion in Roman times is also a fact with wide ramifications. In general historical terms, the establishment of the Phoenician settlements in the Maghrib constituted the only extension into the western Mediterranean area of the older civilizations of the ancient Near and Middle East, all of which Carthage outlived. This, along with the spread of the Greeks to the west, was part of the movement by which the entire western Mediterranean, and to a degree north-western Europe, till then inhabited by 'tribal peoples' of great variety, were brought within the range of influence of the civilizations of the Aegean and the East. In the history of Africa, the Phoenician period brought the Maghrib into the general history of the Mediterranean world, emphasizing its connections with the northern as well as the eastern shores. The geographical conditions which, till modern times at least, already associated the Maghrib with the Mediterranean world were emphasized. In view of the limitations of our historical sources, growth of more exact knowledge of the evolution of the native Libyan culture and its response to the introduction of Phoenician civilization must await the further work of the archaeologist.*

* *Note of the International Scientific Committee:* It is intended to give a more detailed account of the legacy and role of Libya during the period covered in this volume in the next edition. It is planned to hold a symposium which will deal with the contribution of Libya in classical antiquity, with particular reference to the role of Cyrenaica during the Greek era, Libya during the Phoenician period and the civilization of the Garamantes.

19 The Roman and post-Roman period in North Africa

PART I: The Roman period

The Roman occupation and the resistance of the indigenous population

After the destruction of Carthage in −146 and the reduction of her territory to the status of a Roman province, the fate of North Africa lay in the hands of Rome and the indigenous kingdoms. It would have been desirable to devote a special chapter to the study of the latter, from the advent of the Numidian kingdoms up to the end of the reign of the last King of Mauretania in +40. Thereafter, the whole of North Africa became Roman and remained so until the Vandal invasion.

The distinctive nature of the African wars emerges, more particularly, from the accounts of the phase of conquest. During the last quarter of the first century before the Christian era, a long series of triumphs celebrated by Roman generals over the Maurusiani, Musulamii, Gaetulians and Garamantes afford indisputable evidence that the indigenous populations were never completely subjugated, despite the Roman victories.

The best-known of these wars is that of the Numidian Tacfarinas, which lasted for eight years under the reign of Tiberius, and extended to all the southern confines of North Africa, from Tripolitania as far as Mauretania. The demands attributed by Tacitus to Tacfarinas give a clearer idea of the deep-seated causes of the resistance of the indigenous inhabitants. The Numidian leader took up arms to force the all-powerful emperor to recognize his people's right to land, for the Roman conquest had been immediately followed by the sequestration of all the fertile land. The fields of the sedentary Numidians were laid waste; the areas traditionally roamed by the nomads were steadily reduced and limited; veterans and other Roman and Italian colonists established themselves everywhere, starting with the richest parts of the country; tax-collecting companies and members of the Roman aristocracy, senators and knights, carved out huge estates for themselves. While their country was being exploited in this way, all the autochthonous nomads, and all the sedentary inhabitants who did not live in the few cities spared by the succession of wars and expropriation measures, were either reduced to abject poverty or driven into the steppes and the desert. Their only hope, therefore, lay in armed resistance, and their principal war aim was to recover their land.

Military operations continued throughout the first two centuries of the Christian era, and the Roman thrust towards the south-west stirred up the *ḳabīlas* which assembled and dispersed in the area stretching from the valley of the Moulouya to Djabal Amour and the Ouarsenis. Having easily established themselves in the coastal strip and in the north-east, the Romans advanced by stages in the southern part of what is modern Tunisia, as well as in the High Plateaux and the Saharan Atlas. Under the Julio-Claudian emperors, the frontier of the conquered territory stretched from Cirta in the west to Tacape in the south, and included Ammaedara, which was the headquarters of the Legio III Augusta, Thelepte and Capsa. Under the Flavian emperors, the legion established itself at Theveste and the boundary was pushed forward as far as Sitifis; the Nementcha region was incorporated under Trajan and the colony of Timgad was founded in +100. Finally, in +128, the legion set up a permanent garrison at Lambaesis and roads were driven through the Aures Mountains, which were defended against the *ḳabīlas* by a camp at Gemellae. Between the Roman provinces and the desert regions lying to the south into which the *ḳabīlas* had been driven, a frontier zone was created – the *limes*; this was gradually advanced in a south-westerly direction and consisted of a network, from 50 to 100 kilometres deep, of trenches and roads defended by a string of military posts and small forts. The aerial archaeological research work done by J. Baradez has revealed, among other things, the segments of a *fossatum*, bordered by an earth-bank or a wall and guarded at irregular intervals by square or rectangular towers.

However, Rome was powerless to root out the resistance of the Berbers, and never succeeded in keeping the nomads of the south and west permanently in check. Despite the efforts of Trajan and Hadrian, and notwithstanding the firm policy pursued by Septimius Severus on the borders of Tripolitania, the crisis of the third century put an untimely end to this enterprise. The desert, the mobility of the camel-mounted nomads and the ease with which communications could be kept open from west to east along the Saharan Atlas range, assured the indomitable Berbers of great freedom of movement. In this respect, the *ḳabīlas* which finally succeeded in wearing down the domination of Rome found their reservoir of manpower in Mauretania Tingitana and, later on, in the vast stretches of desert in the hinterland of Tripolitania. Up to the first quarter of the third century the centre and south of the country were defended from local raiders by the Legio III Augusta, whose theoretical strength of 5,000 to 6,000 men was reinforced as necessary by large numbers of auxiliaries. It has been calculated that the maximum number of soldiers may have amounted to between 25,000 and 30,000 in the second century. This is not by any means a high figure, although it is necessary to take account of the veterans still liable for service who settled on the land cleared for cultivation along the *limes*; in time of need, troops were also transferred from the legions stationed in the other provinces of the empire.

Administrative organisation and military problems

On 13 January −27, Octavian, on whom the title of Augustus was conferred three days later, divided the provinces of the empire, in accordance with the approved principle, between himself and the senate. Africa, which had long since been conquered and pacified and was bound to the senatorial class by many traditions of an economic as well as a political nature, fell among the provinces to be administered by the senate. The *provincia Africa*, to which the epithet *proconsularis* was applied, combined the two provinces successively established by Rome in North Africa: one had consisted of the Punic territory conquered in −146, and was known as Africa Vetus, and the other had been created by Caesar after his African campaign against the Pompeians and their ally, King Juba I of Numidia, and was called Africa Nova. In addition to these territories there were the four Cirtean colonies which Caesar had assigned to the Italian adventurer P. Sittius.

As in republican times, the Roman senate continued during the imperial period to delegate a governor in Africa. He was one of the two senior ex-consuls present in Rome at the time of drawing lots for the provinces; he therefore bore the title of proconsul and, unless his term of office was prolonged as an exceptional measure, he held his appointment in Carthage for only one year. In addition to his judicial prerogatives, by virtue of which he was the supreme judge of the province both in civil and in criminal cases, he was invested with administrative and financial powers; he directed the execution of major public works and sanctioned expenditure; he exercised supreme control over the department responsible for keeping Rome supplied with African corn, and over the operation of the fiscal system the proceeds of which were earmarked for the *aerarium Saturni*, the treasury of the senate. He was assisted by pro-praetor legates, one of whom resided in Carthage itself, and the other at Hippone, and by a quaestor, who was in charge of the financial administration. Furthermore, as already mentioned, he was provided with a small contingent of troops, about 1,600 strong, for the maintenance of law and order.

The emperor could intervene in the affairs of the senatorial province either directly or, as was most often the case, through a resident equestrian procurator, who was an imperial official responsible for the management of the vast imperial domains and for the collection of certain indirect taxes, sich as the *vicesima hereditatium*, which supplied the military treasury controlled by the emperor. The procurator also had a measure of judicial power, limited in principle to the settlement of tax disputes. From the year + 135 he was assisted by a *procurator Patrimonii*, for the administration of the domains, and *a procurator IIII Publicorum Africae*, for the administration of the fiscal revenues.

Meanwhile, proconsular Africa, unlike the majority of senatorial provinces, could not be deprived of troops. While the north-eastern part, which corresponded to the old province of Africa Vetus, was very quiet, this was not the case in the southern regions, where the Roman authorities needed a military garrison to guard and gradually to extend the supposedly pacified zone. These troops, consisting mainly of the Legio III Augusta, were commanded by an imperial legate subordinate to the proconsul, who was therefore in the position of being able to assert the military authority of the republican governors responsible to the senate. However, this situation could not last indefinitely without arousing the emperor's distrust. It was not long before Caligula decided, in pursuance of a general policy of restricting the powers of the civil governors and reducing the authority and autonomy of the senate, to make an important politico-military change in the organization of proconsular Africa: the military command was taken out of the hands of the civil government, and this resulted in the creation, *de facto* if not *de jure*, of a military territory of Numidia under the authority of the legate in command of the Legio III Augusta. As early as +39, the status of the official entrusted with this special command must have stood halfway between that of the legates who were governors of provinces and that of the legates who were deputies of the general of the legions.

Septimus Severus eventually regularized the position by raising the military territory to the dignity of a province: this was the province of Numidia, probably created in +198 to +199. It was administered by the legate of the legion, who was also called the *praeses* and was directly nominated and transferred by the emperor, and its western frontier still followed the left bank of the Ampsaga (Oued-el-Kébir), passed to the west of Cuicul and Zarai, cut across the Hodna plain and dipped southwards in the direction of Laghwāt.

Between the Ampsaga and the Atlantic there lay the Kingdom of Mauretania which had been bequeathed by King Bocchus the Younger to the Roman empire as far back as −33. Octavian, the future Augustus, accepted the legacy and availed himself of the opportunity to plant eleven colonies of veterans in the country, but in −25 he gave up the kingdom to Juba II, who was succeeded by his son Ptolemy in +23. In +40, Caligula, judging that the time for direct administration had arrived, caused Ptolemy to be assassinated. Finally, Claudius decided, at the end of +42, to organize the two provinces of Mauretania: Caesariensis to the east and Tingitana to the west, separated by the Mulucha (Moulouya). Like Numidia, both Mauretanian provinces came directly under the authority of the emperor.

The remodelling of the military system in North Africa became a necessity when the African legion, the III Augusta, was disbanded under Gordian III. The command was finally entrusted to the Count of Africa, who had the troops of all the African provinces under his authority. This army of the fourth century was very different from that of the earlier empire; the attacks by the Moorish *ḳabīlas* made it essential to build up a mobile army, a striking force always ready to take swift action in zones of insecurity. It was composed of legionary infantry units and cavalry detachments recruited mainly from the Romanized peasants living in the vicinity of the camps. However, military service gradually became a hereditary and fiscal obligation, and this inevitably impaired the value of the contingents. In addition to this mobile army, regarded as crack troops, there were the *limitanei*, peasant-soldiers who were allotted plots of land situated along the *limes*. They were exempted from the payment of taxes and were required, in return, to guard the frontier and repulse any raiding *ḳabīlas*. Like those in the east, the *limitanei* of Mauretania Tingitana were organized in traditional units – wings, cohorts – but all other African provinces were divided, instead, into geographical sectors, each taking its orders from a *Praepositus limitis*. Archaeological evidence of various kinds, found particularly in the eastern sector of the *limes*, shows that the *limitanei* were grouped around fortified farms and lived off the land, frequently introducing irrigation by canals. They thus contributed to the development of agriculture and human settlement on the confines of the Sahara and made the *limes* more a zone of trade and cultural contacts than a line of separation between the Roman provinces and the independent part of the country which had remained Berber.

Concurrently with the military reforms, there was a radical revision of the territorial organization of the provinces. It is now established, however, that the reorganization was carried out gradually, having regard to the needs and conditions prevailing in each province. In order to strengthen the imperial authority, while at the same time curtailing the authority of the proconsul whose power often played into the hands of usurpers, and to increase the revenue from taxes to finance defence measures against the threatened onslaughts on the frontiers, proconsular Africa was split into three autonomous provinces: in the north, Zeugitana, or the proconsular province in the proper sense of the term, extended southwards as far as a line running between Ammaedara and Pupput, near Hammamet; westwards, it included Calama, Thubursian Numidarum and Theveste. However, the proconsul in Carthage was still an important official. He was a *clarissimus* who, after his term of office, often reached the top of the consular hierarchy and ranked among the *illustres*. These proconsuls of the fourth century were not infrequently of African extraction. They were always assisted by two legates, who generally had family connections with them and resided one at Carthage and the other at Hippone.

The province of Byzacium was an offshoot of the proconsular province. It stretched from the Ammaedara–Pupput line as far as the gates of Tacape. Westwards, it included the regions of Mactar, Sufetula, Thelepte and Capsa. However, in the south, the guard posts of the *limes* did not come under the authority of the governor of the province of Byzacium, which, like the proconsular province, was without troops; the posts situated near the Shott al-Djarīd were therefore the responsibility of Numidia, while those in the south-west were under the authority of Tripolitania. The governor of Byzacium, who resided at Hadrumet, was at first of the rank of a knight and held the title of *praeses*; but possibly during the reign of Constantine and, in any case, after +340, he acceded to consular status.

In the south-east, the new province of Tripolitania comprised two different zones: a coastal strip stretching from Tacape to the Altars of the Philaeni, which came under the proconsul and very probably the legation at Carthage; in the interior, the *limes* region of Tripolitania was placed, until the third century, under the authority of the commander of the Legio III Augusta, governor of the province of Numidia. This region included the Djeffara and the Matmatas, and extended as far as the northern tip of the Shott al-Djarīd.

The province of Numidia had a narrow outlet to the sea between the Edough Mountains on the east and the mouth of the Ampsaga on the west, but towards the south its territory widened out and stretched from the eastern end of the Shott al-Hodna to the gates of Theveste. It was divided at first into two zones, one comprising the quiet region of the towns of the old Cirtean confederation around the capital city, Cirta, and the other consisting of the turbulent mountainous region in the south with Lambaesis as the principal settlement, but was reunified as early as +314. However, it continued to be ruled by a governor of the rank of knight exercising both the civil and the military powers, and holding the title of *praeses*, up to +316. In that year, the civil government was entrusted to senators bearing the new title of *consularis provinciae*, and then given the rank of *clarissimi*; the great majority belonged to the Roman aristocracy, on account of the landed interests which linked the latter to this rich province. Cirta became the only capital and took the name of Constantine, in honour of the emperor.

19.1 *Mosaic from Sousse: Virgil writing the Aeneid (Photo, Bardo Museum, Tunis)*

19.2 *Mosaic from Chebba: the triumph of Neptune (Photo, Bardo Museum, Tunis)*

The problem of the administrative reorganization of the provinces of Mauretania in the fourth century is dominated by a question of prime importance: were the interior of Tingitana and all the western part of Caesariensis evacuated by Diocletian just before his accession? In the light of recent research, it appears to be very doubtful whether the region lying to the west of Mauretania Caesariensis was relinquished. On the other hand, it is agreed that Diocletian evacuated all the territories south of the Oued Loukkos in Mauretania Tingitana in +285. Rome seems, however, to have maintained purely maritime relations with the coastal towns, which would explain how places like Sala could continue, under Constantine, to live within the Roman orbit. Furthermore, Diocletian detached the eastern part of Mauretania Caesariensis to make a new province: this was Mauretania Sitifensis, with Sitifis, the modern Sétif, as its capital. Lastly, Mauretania Tingitana was separated for administrative purposes from the rest of Africa and was attached to the diocese constituted by the Spanish provinces.

Colonization and municipal organization

Like Greek civilization, Roman civilization was essentially an urban phenomenon. The degree to which a province was civilized and Romanized was therefore determined by the closeness of the towns. In the African provinces, and particularly Africa Proconsularis, urban life was highly developed; at least 500 cities have been counted in North Africa as a whole.

In the republican period, no cities had yet been admitted to a share of Roman citizenship; there were only seven cities of Phoenician origin, enjoying a measure of autonomy which was not invulnerable to political vicissitudes: these were the cities which had sided with Rome during the last Punic war. Their traditional institutions were formally recognized and they were also exempted from the land tax, the *stipendium*. Meanwhile, Roman rule tolerated, but did not legally protect, the institutions of the other African cities, which continued to apply the Phoenician administrative system and to be headed by *suffetes* and councils of notables, while paying the *stipendium*. Colonists cannot, therefore, have lived only in Carthage; later on, at all events, they must have been scattered in a number of small towns. It was also necessary, no doubt, to expropriate the previous landowners and move them elsewhere. The fate of Rome's first attempt at colonization in Africa is well known: for political motives rooted in the hatred felt by the Roman aristocracy for G. Gracchus, the reformer and leader of the popular part, and also for economic reasons arising out of the fact that the settlers were humble and impecunious folk and rarely of peasant stock, the venture failed; so it was that this colonization project merely served, in the last analysis, as a pretext for overthrowing the popular party and permitting wealthy men, senators and knights, to carve vast estates out of the African territories conquered by the republic.

In reviving the plans of his adoptive father Julius Caesar, Augustus Octavius initiated a new epoch in the history of Africa, a new political pattern, and a far-reaching administrative, military and religious programme. According to the list supplied by Pliny, whose sources still give rise to much controversy, there were soon six Roman colonies, fifteen *oppida civium romanorum*, one *oppidum latinum*, one *oppidum immune* and thirty *oppida libera*.

The emperors who succeeded Augustus continued to apply his policy; under Marcus Aurelius there were more than thirty-five colonies distributed throughout the African provinces. As a general rule, the immigrants were veterans who had served in legions disbanded as a result of the reorganization of the army; there were also Italians who had been evicted or ruined by the agricultural crisis in the peninsula. The number of the latter was not so large, however, as to turn the African provinces into resettlement areas. But the rational implantation of these colonies took well into account defensive and economic considerations.

Economic life

The population

We have no contemporary estimate, however approximate, of the size of the population in Roman times. It was necessary, of course, to organize a census periodically for fiscal purposes, but the returns have not come down to us. In this field, therefore, we are reduced all too often to barely adequate methods of arriving at possible figures: the application of a mean density coefficient in computing the total number of inhabitants, and, especially, the use of the topographical argument, in combination with various considerations, in attempting to assess, in particular, the number of town-dwellers.

More recently, A. Lézine has presented a point of view regarding the urban population which is at variance with that of G. Charles-Picard; arguing, like the latter, that living conditions and density of population in the Tunisian Sahel were very similar during the Middle Ages to those existing in ancient times, he has attempted to calculate the size of the population of Sousse towards the end of the tenth century, and that of the population of Carthage between +150 and +238. He has finally arrived at the number of 1,300,000 town-dwellers. If we were to accept this conclusion, while retaining the figure of 4 million proposed by C. Courtois for the total population, the figure for country-dwellers would appear more reasonable. However, a fresh approach to these demographic problems has been suggested by recent research work; instead of relying only on the data yielded by the census of ancient times, the density of population, the relative numbers of *domus* and *insulae*, and the number of recipients of doles of corn, we now also take into account the number of tombs per generation and the *summae honorariae* paid by newly appointed magistrates at a rate varying according to their rank and the size of the town.

Agriculture

It is common knowledge that agriculture was the mainstay of the economy of ancient times; in Africa during the Roman period, the land was the principal and most highly prized source of wealth and social consideration. It is also a platitude to say that Africa was the granary of Rome. This expression has sometimes been used to imply that it once enjoyed proverbial abundance contrasting with the poverty of modern times, so as to bring in an ill-informed verdict relating to the degeneration of the population, totally disregarding the complex problems which have created the conditions of underdevelopment. Here we are really obliged to repeat a truth which cannot have been overlooked by historians: in point of fact, Africa was the granary of Rome because, being a vanquished country, it was forced to keep the conqueror supplied with corn by way of tribute. Under Augustus, for instance, 200,000 Romans received a free ration of 44 litres of corn per month, totalling about a million bushels. In any event the theory of Africa's remarkable prosperity and exceptionally high yields of corn in Roman times has been demolished by the geographer J. Despois.

At first, the Roman conquest brought in its wake a decline in agriculture, as in the African economy as a whole. The Carthaginian *chora* was laid waste and its arboriculture was abandoned, for Italy was then in control of the wine and oil market and saw to it that there was no competition in these lucrative branches of husbandry. Corn-growing was the only one to be carried on, and in the reign of Augustus it started to expand for a political reason which was to prevail up to the end of the Roman rule, namely, the need to ensure food supplies for the Roman plebs. After Rome had pushed the frontiers farther to the west and south and had embarked upon the policy of confining the *ḳabīlas* to circumscribed areas, while pursuing an active land development policy, particularly through the extension of the great hydraulic projects, there was a sharp rise in the figures for corn production. By the time that Nero was on the throne Africa, we know, was already keeping the capital of the empire supplied with corn for eight months of the year: it has thus been calculated that the African contribution was 18 million bushels, or 1,260,000 quintals. During the period of great prosperity in Africa, from the middle of the second century until +238, the position improved, owing, in particular, to the cultivation of the virgin lands of Numidia and also those of the Mauretanian provinces, but Africa had to meet new fiscal exactions, as when the military *annona* was converted, under Septimius Severus, into a regular pecuniary charge. From the second century onwards, however, large investments in public buildings are a sign of prosperity among the upper classes and, in particular, among the urban middle class. The truth is that, in this period, the imperial government allowed the provinces more freedom of action in developing their economy, whereas Italy was suffering from a crisis which had already become a problem under the Claudian emperors and was still unsolved.

From the very beginnings of the occupation, the mark of Roman colonization was a chequer-work of agrarian units – the centuriation; the soil of Africa was divided into squares measuring 710 metres across, which formed a perfectly symmetrical chess-board pattern. Having become the property of the Roman people by right of conquest, these lands were classified in several categories under complicated property laws which were constantly changing. Except in Mauretania, where no restrictions were placed on rights of way, ethnic property steadily lost ground to the ever-expanding area occupied by colonists. A huge operation designed to contain the *ḳabīlas* within certain areas was unremittingly pursued under the early empire, and was even stepped up in the Severan period when the *limes* was pushed forward in

19.3 *Cherchell aqueduct, Algeria (P. Salama)*

19.4 *Tripoli (the ancient town of Oea, Libya) triumphal arch of Marcus Aurelius (P. Salama)*

Tripolitania, Numidia and Mauretania, involving violent expropriation action against the *ḳabīlas*, who were driven into the desert. However, indigenous landowners living in the cities, whose property was not expropriated for the benefit of Roman or Latin settlers, generally kept their estates on condition that they paid the *stipendium* from which very few of the indigenous cities were exempt. Another real property category was composed of lands distributed to the Roman citizens – veterans, Roman or Italian immigrants of small means – who settled in the colonies, the *oppida civium romanorum*, the *pagi*. In course of time, however, the legal status of the lands of the indigenous cities and that of the properties of the Roman cities became indistinguishable as municipal constitutions developed a tendency to integrate the autochthonous communities.

The status and organization of the great imperial domains are known to us, thanks to four major inscriptions and other evidence yielded by the rich store of African epigraphs. They have handed down to us texts of prime importance, such as the *Lex Manciana* and the *Lex Hadriana* which are not 'laws' within the meaning of Roman public law, but working regulations. In the opinion of many writers, they applied to the whole of the *ager publicus* existing throughout the empire. In any event, we only have detailed knowledge of the management methods applying to the imperial domains. These were leased to contractors known as *conductores*, who employed managers *(villici)* to run them. The *villicus* developed the resources of part of the domain himself; he probably used slaves and farm labourers, as well as the compulsory services demanded of the colonists. These colonists were freemen who farmed the greater part of the domain as sub-tenants of the *conductores*. The main purpose of the *Lex Manciana* and the *Lex Hadriana* was to determine the rights and duties of the *conductores* and their *villici*, on the one hand, and those of the farmers (*coloni*), on the other hand; the principle was that, in return for the delivery of one-third of their annual crops and a specified number of days of labour on the land which was under the direct management of the *villicus*, the farmers enjoyed, on their respective plots of land, the right of use, which they could bequeath to their heirs and even sell, on condition that the new holder of the right left the farming cycle undisturbed for two consecutive years. The management of the domains was supervised by a strictly graded body of imperial officials.

Industry and trade

It has generally been noticed that epigraphs and figures carved on monuments yield much less information in Africa than in other western provinces about the life of craftsmen and hired workmen. However, while metal-working seems to have been less prevalent in the African provinces, we must not be tempted to indulge in generalizations; it could be pointed out, for example, that the epigraphical material contains very few references to builders and architects, although their works cover innumerable archaeological sites in Africa. In any event, the technological stagnation of the Roman period was not conducive to any large-scale development of the industries of antiquity. In these circumstances, the leading industries were concerned with the processing of agricultural products, and particularly the manufacturing of olive-oil; the ruins of olive-presses, which are found in such profusion in the area stretching from Sefetula to Thelepte and Tebessa, testify to the importance of oil in the economy of ancient times, not only as the staple fat for human consumption, but also as the sole fuel for lamps and an essential toilet requisite.

The pottery industry, which was associated to a variable degree with the olive-oil industry, met the demand for lamps and containers, in addition to producing domestic utensils. In Punic times, the local industry concentrated on turning out everyday articles, and the more delicate specimens of the potter's art were imported at first from Greece and Etruria and later from southern Italy.

Africa thus succeeded in breaking free from its economic dependence, and its foreign trade regained some of the importance of Punic times. Port facilities were extended to keep pace with the development of the exportable resources of the hinterland and to handle the quantities of grain and oil to be shipped to Italy; the main dealings were with Ostia, the harbour which was Rome's outlet to the sea. On the site of Ostia have been found, among the *scholae* (offices) of the shipping corporations, no fewer than nine buildings which belonged to the African corporations of Mauretania Caesariensis, Musluvium, Hippo Diarrhytus, Carthage, Curubis, Missus, Gummi, Sullectum and Sabratha. These *domini navium* or *navicularii*, who formed corporations, were collectively responsible for the transport of commodities to Italy; they were granted special privileges as early as the reign of Claudius, and they were organized, up to the time of Septimius Severus, according to the principle of free association.

Texts surviving from ancient times, as well as archaeological and epigraphical finds, have a great deal to tell us about Africa's internal trade. We know from such sources that *nundinae* (fairs) were held in rural centres on different days of the week, like the present-day *souks*. In villages, *macella* (provision-markets) were established on a site consisting of a square surrounded by porticoes on to which there opened the booths of the various merchants. A number of such sites have been excavated, notably at Leptis, where kiosks were equipped with standard instruments for measuring length and capacity which were inspected by the municipal *aediles*. Other deals and transactions were concluded on the forum or in the shops and covered markets of the towns (occupied by bankers and money-changers, tavern-keepers, cloth-merchants, and so on). The roads which were originally designed to serve the purposes of conquest and colonization soon had a stimulating effect on trade because, of course, they facilitated the transport of goods. Under Augustus and his successors, two roads of strategic importance linked Carthage with the south-west, via the valley of the Miliana, and with the south-east via the coast. The third side of the triangle was constituted by the Ammaedara–Tacape strategic highway, which was the first route attested by milestones. Under the Flavians and the first Antonines, the road system was greatly extended, in particular by the construction of the Carthage–Theveste highway; around the former military centres of Theveste and Lambaesis, a network of roads encircled the Aures and Nementcha Mountains and stretched northwards towards Hippo-Regius.

Much research has been done on the various technical questions relating to Roman roads: lay-out, structure, bridges and viaducts, auxiliary buildings for the use of travellers. The Roman rulers were very conscious of the strategic and colonizing importance of the highways, their administrative role, and also their economic role; in this connection, special attention has been devoted, for example, to the route of the marble trade between Simitthu and Thabraca, and a study has been made of the sites of the *horrea* and *mansiones* (barns and warehouses) situated at crossroads and at various points along the roads for the storage of the grain and oil delivered to the tax-collectors.

The relations between the African provinces and the peoples of the Sahara

It has long been known that the Romans had three great Saharan fortresses on the confines of the desert, in the south of Tripolitania: they were those of Bu Ndjem, Gheria al-Gherbia and Ghadāmes, which was called Cidamus in ancient times. They were situated on the borderline between the desert and a zone under Roman control inhabited by sedentary peasants who lived in fortified farms and were mainly engaged in the cultivation of olive-trees in the drainage basins of the wadis. In this region, an original type of civilization developed, bearing the mark of strong local traditions on to which Punic influences had been grafted. The indigenous traditions and the Punic imprint, illustrated, in particular, by the numerous inscriptions in local alphabets, and by the survival of the Punic language up to the eve of the Arab invasion, proved adaptable, however, to the new way of life introduced by the Romans. The fortresses commanded the main routes linking the coast with the Fezzān, the land of the Garamantes. As far back as –19, Cornelius Balbus had attacked these Garamantes and, according to Pliny, had subdued several of their towns and fortresses, including Garama and Cidamus. Later, possibly in the reign of Domitian, an expedition led by Julius Maternus set out from Leptis Magna and reached Garama. Accompanied by the King of the Garamantes and his army, the expedition then travelled as far as the country of the Ethiopians and the region of Agisymba where, we are told, rhinoceroses were to be seen. This shows that the Romans were primarily interested in the Fezzān in so far as this permanent caravan base enabled them to approach the fringe of trans-Saharan Africa. The caravan trade brought black slaves, ostrich feathers, wild beasts, emeralds and carbuncles from the Sahara. In exchange, the Roman provinces supplied wine, metal objects, pottery, textiles and glassware, as has been shown by the excavations carried out, in particular, at the necropolises of the Fezzān.

The rise of Romano-Berbers and problems of African society

Under Augustus and his successors, the population of the African provinces was composed of three groups distinguished from each other by the laws that governed them, as well as by their languages and customs: Roman or Italian immigrants; Carthaginians and settled Libyans who had incorporated Punic institutions and practices into their own traditions, the latter being in the majority; nomadic Libyans who were severely restricted to certain areas or were banished entirely from the regions containing the usable land they had been forced to surrender.

It has often been said, quite correctly, that the African provinces were not regarded

19.5 *Timgad, ancient city of Thamagudi, Algeria: avenue and arch of Trajan (P. Salama)*

19.6 *Lebda, ancient city of Leptis Magna, Libya: Roman amphitheatre (P. Salama)*

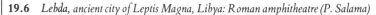

as resettlement areas: in the reign of Hadrian, colonies of veterans ceased to be founded in proconsular Africa, and those in Numidia were henceforth established for the benefit of soldiers recruited in African towns. As we have seen above, the status of the latter rose steadily until it had become completely Romanized: virtually all indigenous town-dwellers had been integrated, and particularly the most wealthy – who sought by this means to escape from the socio-economic and juridical inferiority imposed upon them as a result of the Roman conquest – by the time that the *constitutio Antonina* was promulgated in +212. This granted Roman citizenship to all the free inhabitants of the empire who had not yet acquired it, except for the *dediticii*. Septimius Severus had already followed the example of the Antonines in elevating an immense number of communities to the rank of *municipium* or even *colonia*; non-citizens came to be in the minority, so that the existence of inferior juridical rights became less and less defensible by comparison with the need to simplify the administrative and fiscal systems, and with the trends in favour of political, legal, ethical and religious universalism.

Thus, ethnic distinctions tended to disappear only in the cities, which, however, were very numerous, especially in proconsular Africa. Social distinctions took their place in urban communities. The two highest social classes, the senators and knights, enjoyed a status defined by the property qualification and reflected in insignia and titles. Although the property qualification was necessary, it was not sufficient in itself, whereas the principle of heredity was always applied; unless the emperor conferred the rank of senator or knight as a special favour, it was acquired solely by right of birth. The first senator of African stock came from Cirta; he lived in the reign of Vespasian. A century later, around the year +170, the number of African senators had risen to about a hundred, forming the second largest group, after the group composed of men of Italian stock. Similarly the first African knight known to history, who came from Musti, was given the gold ring by Tiberius, and by Hadrian's time there were several thousand knights in proconsular Africa and Numidia. We see that the rise of the Romano-Berbers was a prominent feature of the Antonine–Severan period, when Africans were playing an important role in Rome and the empire.

The main social force which had made it possible, under the early empire, and in the interests of the emperors themselves, to infuse fresh blood into the aristocratic orders, ensuring that the order of knighthood, in particular, maintained the high standard of professional competence and personal qualities required for the performance of its dual function, was undoubtedly the urban middle class, which might be called the municipal bourgeoisie.

The decurion middle class constituted the very backbone of Romanized communities in Africa. Under the early empire, it recruited its members almost entirely from a certain stratum of the land tenure structure: the decurion lived in town on the income derived from his property, but he did not own a *latifundium*, nor was he a peasant, and, even if he felt attached to his land, he preferred a bourgeois style of living. He might be very rich: to make a name for himself in the city and earn the gratitude of his fellow-townsmen, he had to be lavish with gifts, which he distributed on a scale dictated by his vanity as much as by his generosity. He organized municipal games, gave doles of food and money to the poor, or erected and maintained public buildings.

19.7 *Haidra, Tunisia: sixth century Byzantine fortress, general view (P. Salama)*

19.8 *Haidra, Tunisia: Byzantine fortress, detail (P. Salama)*

The cities were all determined to have their forum, complete with statues on their pedestals, their senate-house, their basilica for the courts of justice, baths, libraries, magnificent and costly edifices for the municipal games as well as a multitude of temples in honour of official or traditional gods.

Even though the theory of the decline of the towns in the fourth century now has to be revised, since there is epigraphical evidence of relatively intense building activity and archaeology has revealed sumptuously decorated dwellings even during the third century. The social pattern of urban life was very different under the late empire from that prevailing under the early empire. Agriculture was still the main source of the income of the best people in the towns, but the decurions, representing the middle class which had hitherto governed through the city councils, were supplanted by an oligarchy of great landowners, the municipal *primates* or *principales*, who had made their fortune by exporting the corn and oil of their estates and had thus gained admission to the imperial nobility. These men of substance, who enjoyed the support of the imperial government, acceded to the highest positions in municipal and provincial government; they reconstructed public buildings destroyed in the third century or restored those falling apart with age, and embellished their cities, knowing that such activities opened the way to a career. The emperors adapted their urban policy to these social changes; the essential aim was to encourage the growth of towns, not only because it was one of the principal factors on which the empire's taxation system was based, but primarily because towns formed a solid rampart against the menace of the alleged barbarians.

In rural areas, it was still unusual, during the fourth century, for great African landowners to live permanently on their estates in isolation from the rest of the world; they continued to take some interest in the embellishment of the cities and in municipal life. But at the end of the century the first signs appeared of a trend towards a seigneurial type of agriculture; the *dominus*, who had become progressively more independent on his lands, appropriated more and more of the prerogatives of the defaulting state, policing his own domain and even exercising the power of justice within its boundaries. With the introduction of the taxation system of the *iugatio-capitatio*, it was in the interests both of the imperial treasury and of the large landed proprietors that there should be no change, on a given property, in the productive units of labour and land. Lay and ecclesiastical landlords were thus able, with the aid on the imperial administration, to debar the *coloni* from attempting to improve their lot, and succeeded in trying them to the land.

Religious life and the advent of Christianity

Roman domination had practically no inhibiting effect upon the worship of the traditional deities venerated by the indigenous population. The old Berber cults often continued, in humble rural sanctuaries, to be observed in their ancestral forms, but in some cases they were absorbed into the cults of the Graeco-Roman deities. For instance, the cult of the god of fertility and health-giving waters was sometimes masked by that of Neptune, Aesculapius or Serapis. In the regions which had belonged to the Numidian kingdoms, where Punic influence was profound and durable, a pantheon of native gods was even adumbrated. But the majority of the population of the African provinces practised the cults of Saturn and the Graeco-Roman equivalents of the old gods of Carthage; the religion of this African Saturn was merely a continuation of that of Baal Hammon, just as Juno-Caelestis, the chief deity of Roman Carthage, was none other than Tanit, the great goddess of Punic Carthage.

As regards the empire's official cults, it was not long before they were honoured in the cities; loyalty to Rome had to be expressed, in particular, through the observance of religious practices, which was an integral part of Roman civilization. In each city the cult of the Capitoline triad, Jupiter, Juno and Minerva, that of Mars, father and protector of the Roman people, of Venus, Ceres, Apollo, Mercury, Hercules and Bacchus, were other official forms of the empire's religion and of Graeco-Roman spiritual life. Temples and statues, altars and sacrifices were everywhere to be found in honour of these deities.

The deities of the eastern regions of the empire, readily accepted in Rome, were also honoured in Africa where they were introduced by officials, soldiers and merchants, who spread the cult of Isis, Mithras or Cybele, these being sometimes identified with local gods, as, for example, Isis with Demeter or Cybele with Caelestis.

It is remarkable that Latin should have won recognition as the language of African Christianity from the outset, while the Roman church was still using Greek. According to Tertullian, who lived at the end of the second and the beginning of the third century, there were large numbers of Christians in Africa at that time, belonging to all classes and all occupations. It was possible to hold a synod of seventy-one bishops at Carthage around the year +220; ninety bishops attended another synod convened about +240. This shows that small Christian communities were scattered in many African cities, constituting what the empire no doubt regarded as a serious danger. It was true that by rejecting the imperial ideology and particularly by refusing to participate in the cult of the emperor, the Christians were resolutely adopting the stance of an opposition movement. In spite of its broad-minded outlook and its usually tolerant attitude towards new cults, Rome could not compromise with a sect which aimed to create an ever-widening network of groups pursuing a different ideal outside the framework of the official institutions. Harsh penalties were, therefore, inflicted upon the Christians.

There is no room in this brief account for a review of the history of African Christianity, which was at its zenith in the period between the peace won by the church in the fourth century and the establishment of the Arabs in North Africa. A special study might be devoted to this complex question, which involves more especially a survey of the Donatist schism and, of course, of Christian literature from Tertullian to Saint Augustine, whose personality and work were the last brilliant product of the Roman way of life in Africa.

African culture

After being long neglected by writers of Roman history, the art of the provinces and outlying cultures has now become the centre of attention. This is due to a clearer understanding of the limits of Romanization and the different forms it took in its contacts with indigenous societies. Furthermore, there is no denying the truth that the art of a given province cannot be dissociated from its economic, social and religious life.

In this connection, it became necessary, in order to study and appreciate the art developed in the African provinces under Roman rule, to take account of the enduring Libyco-Punic substratum which, moreover, continued to follow its own pattern of life and evolution for centuries.

Phoenician and Punic culture, mixed with Egyptian and Oriental elements, and impregnated with Hellenistic influences after the fourth century before the Christian era, was adopted and adapted by the native population before, but mainly after, the destruction of Carthage. Lastly, the Italo-Roman contributions, being more significant and more directly imposed, inevitably generated hybrid varieties which are often difficult to define. It has become customary, however, to distinguish between two cultures in Africa, one being official and Roman, and the other popular, indigenous and provincial. But there are monuments, of course, in which the two trends meet and contaminate each other, so that they lose their separate identities.

African architectural works generally reproduced types of public monuments which were prevalent throughout the Roman world, and accordingly derived their inspiration from an essentially Roman technique and ideal. Nor were ornamental sculptures and the great statues of gods, emperors and prominent men very different in style from their counterparts in Italy or in other provinces. However, architectural or sculptural creations linked with the religious or funeral traditions of the population, as well as certain special construction or decoration techniques, bear the stamp of local characteristics. This is evident in the temples raised to deities who retained their native individuality despite their apparent identification with Roman gods, in certain monumental sepulchres, in a special wall-building technique known as '*opus africum*', in domestic architecture and, lastly, in the votive stelae still imbued with pre-Roman influences.

The countless mosaics brought to light since the beginning of this century also display local tendencies and characteristics. Here we can only refer the reader to the specialized periodicals and to *La Civilization de l'Afrique Romaine* by G. Charles-Picard, who brings his chapter on the 'African baroque' to a close with the following words: 'To say the very least, therefore, Africa fully repaid her debt to Rome, and showed that she was capable of reaping benefits from her borrowings in a spirit which is neither that of Greece nor that of the Hellenized Levant.'

PART II: From Rome to Islam

When Roman domination ended in North Africa, after holding sway for four centuries in some regions, and for up to five in others, the internal situation presented a complex picture. Regional risings, religious conflicts, social unrest, all led to a worsening climate, but the soundness of administrative experience and the prestige of Latin culture gave this imported civilization a good many chances of survival.

Split into vanquished or independent zones according to the vicissitudes of foreign conquest or local resistance, post-Roman and pre-Islamic North Africa experienced one of the most distinctive periods in its history.

The regions under foreign occupation

Over a period of close on three centuries, two foreign invaders in turn took over the tutelage of Rome without ever succeeding in entirely reconstituting its frontiers.

The Vandal episode

Nothing could have been more unexpected in North Africa than these conquerors of Germanic origin. No domination was less in keeping with the actual circumstances of the country. Outstripping the other Germanic peoples who, like them, had swarmed over western Europe in +406, the Vandals settled first of all in the south of the Iberian peninsula which has seemingly perpetuated their name (Vandalusia = Andalusia).

They crossed the Straits of Gibraltar, 80,000 strong, under the leadership of their king Gaiseric (or Genseric) in +429. Their advance made lightning progress. In +430 they were already besieging the town of Hippone and the Romans acknowledged their possession of the Constantine region in +435. Three years later they took Carthage and, after a brief withdrawal in +442, commenced three large-scale operations in +455 – the final annexation of all the eastern zone of Roman Africa, the conquest of most of the major islands in the western Mediterranean and an audacious expedition to sack Rome itself. The eastern empire, hoping to oust these intruders, suffered a naval disaster in +468 and acknowledged the *fait accompli* – a treaty in +474 finally established good relations between Byzantium and the Vandals, who represented a major maritime power in the western Mediterranean.

The term 'vandalism', synonymous with the spirit of destruction, was coined only at the end of the eighteenth century, and today, in the light of much archaeological evidence, it seems clear that, in their poor management of the territory, the Vandals sinned more through omission than intention.

It seems that during this period neither agriculture nor trade experienced any obvious decline. External relations seem to have been prosperous and the whole group of Vandal possessions was termed the 'grain empire'. Symbolizing the wealth of the well-to-do classes, fine jewellery, Germanic in style, has been found at various times in Hippone, Carthage, Thuburbo Maius and Mactar.

On the political and religious sides the picture is darker. On the southern and western flanks of their North African domain, the Vandals experienced such assaults from the 'Moors', the general term for the North African rebels, that it is virtually impossible to fix a definite frontier to their zone of control. It was no doubt a fluctuating one and probably at no time extended westwards beyond the region of Djemila–Cuicul.

In religion there was a constant climate of crisis. The Vandals were Christian, but professed the Arian creed, a heresy that was intolerable to the traditional Catholic clergy. This led to the virtually systematic repression of the clergy by a central authority which was little inclined to put up with resistance on questions of dogma. Anti-Catholic fury reached its climax following a pseudo-council held in Carthage in +484.

This situation of moral and social crisis brought about a process of collapse, hastened, in fact, by the excesses or incompetence of Gaiseric's successors. In +530 the supplanting by Gelimer of King Hilderic, ally of Justinian, emperor of the eastern empire, sparked off the Byzantine conquest.

The Byzantine episode

The court at Constantinople, regarding itself as the legitimate successor of the Roman empire, resolved to expel the new Germanic states in the west from the territories they had usurped. It was in North Africa that this operation proved least ineffective.

In +533, on Justinian's orders, an expeditionary force commanded by Belisarius wiped out Vandal authority in three months and the Vandals as such disappeared from history. The first Byzantine measure, the famous edict of +534, which reorganized the country's administrative structures, set the pattern that was to be followed: a policy of both a military and legal kind, too closely based on that of the Romans. There was failure to realize that, after a hundred years and more of slackened discipline, the rural masses would no longer accept the rigidity of administrative conservatism; and what in fact the century and a half of Byzantine occupation in North Africa produced were some undeniable achievements in the field of building against a backcloth of perpetual insecurity.

One need only study a map showing the Byzantine strongholds in North Africa to understand that the strategy of fortresses barring the invasion routes, occupying all the crossing-points and defending the country to its very heart, was evidence of a perpetual state of alert, necessary because the enemy loomed everywhere. The old offensive spirit was accordingly replaced by defensive tactics, evincing an anxious state of mind.

The Roman towns continued to decline and their populations dwindled, in the shelter of the powerful fortresses which constituted their citadels, as at Tebessa, Haidra or Timgad. The old provinces, sometimes reconstituted artificially, received governors who were under the authority of a praetorian prefect established in Carthage; but this was quite separate from the military power. At the end of the sixth century a supreme head, the exarch or patrician, concentrated virtually all power in his hands.

Domestic policy, stemming from Roman methods, naturally sought to restore the tax revenue of old. The *annona*, the annual tax payable in wheat, was accordingly reintroduced. Following confiscation of the royal domains of the Vandals, private estates were given back to their former owners, the search extending, if necessary, to the third generation of their descendants. One can imagine the number of legal and material disputes this operation gave rise to. In every domain, taxation was regarded as a crushing burden. Economic life was, however, relatively prosperous. Maintenance of the monetary economy for all transactions, and the handing over of external trade to official agents, gave Carthage and its hinterland a reputation of great wealth in the

Mediterranean world, all the more so since the two sides of the straits of Sicily were under Byzantine authority. It is to be doubted whether the North African rural population benefited to any great extent from this general situation.

As regards religious affairs the new masters re-established the traditional cult, i.e. Orthodox Catholicism, and proscribed Arianism. A fresh revival of Donatism, which had formerly been rife in Roman Africa, was severely repressed; it was, quite rightly, regarded as a phenomenon of social strife. Byzantium even indulged in a dogmatic crisis, that of monotheletism, a futile discussion on the divine and human natures of Christ, and at the time of the Mohammedan conquest the North African clergy was torn apart by this question.

From this time on, the widespread administrative or military insubordination, abuse of power and corruption in high places, in the face of the constant Berber threat, portended sooner or later inevitable collapse. It took some fifty years, from +647 to +698, for a new and unexpected visitor, the Arab conqueror, to wipe out the Byzantine rule for ever.

The independent regions

If we bear in mind that Roman Africa of the later empire had already experienced a number of political and social transformations, we can realize the extent to which the arrival of the Vandals served as a liberating channel for these old tendencies. 'Eternal Africa' regained its rights and the foreign presence, near or far, was no longer regarded as a burden. It would be a delusion, then, to differentiate, in psychological terms, between the regions governed by Berber princes and nominally owing allegiance to Vandal or Byzantine sovereignty and those regions which were completely independent. The former, situated on the periphery of the zones under foreign occupation, were decentralized to such a point that they were constantly breaking away from the central authority. The Byzantine rulers in fact approved the grant of official investiture to Iavdas in the Aures, to Guenfan, Antalas and Coutzina in the high Tunisian steppes and to Carcazan in Tripolitania; all these 'vassals' freely administered the territories settled on them, and there was virtually no question of their ever being taken back from them.

As regards the zones which were quite free from external interference, some of them remote from Vandal or Byzantine strongholds, in the former Mauretania Caesariensis and Mauretania Tingitana, they enjoyed absolute independence from +429 onwards and their rulers did not interfere in their neighbours' affairs unless it was to gain some personal advantage.

Here we again come up against one of the main constants in the history of the Maghrib of classical times – the tendency towards territorial division and rivalry the moment a centralizing force has disappeared. Political division is then governed by geographical considerations.

Very little, unfortunately, is known of the structure of this post-Roman independent North Africa. Some kingdoms were formed there by large socio-political federations, only revealed to us by rare literary allusions or chance archaeological findings. There was, for instance, at the beginning of the sixth century, in the Altaya and

Tlemcen region, the government of Masuna, 'king of the Moors and the Romans'; a little later, in the Aures, the reign of a certain Masties, '*dux* for sixty-seven years, *imperator* for forty years', who never repudiated his faith 'either towards the Romans or the Moors'. Vartaia, another local ruler, pays his tribute; he is perhaps ruler of the zone of Hodna. There is no doubt that the town of Tiāret, a former citadel of the Roman *limes*, admirably situated at the junction of the nomad and settled worlds, was also, as far back as the fifth century, the capital of a dynasty whose power is still symbolized by the Djedars of Frenda, great tombs of impressive majesty. The powerful Garmul, King of Mauretania, who destroyed a Byzantine army in +571 ought also perhaps to be considered in this connection. Lastly, during the sixth and seventh centuries, an indigenous principality existed in distant Tingitana in the northern part of what is now Morocco, whose vitality is attested by the inscriptions at Volubilis and the Mausoleum of Souk el-Gour.

In most cases, the socio-political organization reveals a structure that is neither sketchy nor anarchical. Original institutions combined Berber traditions and the Roman administrative model. 'Moors' and 'Romans' were associated, a formula which certainly implies collaboration between the peasant element, non-Romanized, and the city-dwellers, with several centuries of Latin influence behind them. There was, then, no kind of challenge to an administrative and cultural heritage which was foreign in origin, and which at times was a source of some pride. The historical map for these regions shows the survival of small urban centres such as Tiāret, Altaya, Tlemcen and Volubilis, still Christian in character, where the use of Latin was still current practice until the seventh century.

Behind the tumultuous events of this time, which fanned violence over a long period until ultimately a balance was reached, we can imagine an economic and social background which led to the gradual impoverishment of the people in general. In statistics which we have, for example, for the number of dioceses in the year +484 in Mauretania Caesariensis we still find the names of most of the towns of classical Roman Africa. Even supposing that many of these had already been reduced to village status, they none the less existed. The fact that churches were still being built, often adorned with fine mosaics as at El Asnam, points to creative activity, necessarily based on remaining sources of wealth. No doubt benefit was still being reaped from the momentum of the previous epoch. Archeology, however, reveals virtually nothing comparable in the sixth and seventh centuries. The abandonment of the towns thus continued at the same time as the new society, of a basically rural type – one that was to be found everywhere in the Early Middle Ages – became consolidated.

What monumental remains did this final period bequeath to us? The districts close to the Mauretanian littoral, where the Byzantines were ensconced, were readily open to influences. For example, fine bronze candelabra dating from the sixth century were found in the ruins of Mouzaiaville to the south of Tipasa. The very site of Ténès was made famous by the discovery of one of the most remarkable treasures of gold and silverware in the ancient world, including more especially the official regalia of imperial dignitaries. Their existence in this remote place is still a mystery. It is the author's belief that all these jewels were stolen and are perhaps related to the sack of Rome which was perpetrated, the texts tell us, in +455 by

Vandal troops with Moorish contingents.

But once we move away from the coastal areas and the districts under foreign occupation, building activity ceases at the end of the fifth century. There are, however, two important exceptions to this rule, represented by the famous colossus-type tombs in which the art of building recovered its pristine excellence without necessarily being affected by any foreign influence. Thus in Morocco, the Mausoleum of Souk el-Gour, which can be dated to the seventh century, and, in Algeria, the Djedars of Frenda, extending chronologically from the fifth to the seventh(?) centuries, display an architectural vigour that would be inexplicable if the local context had been one of utter destitution. It is hardly surprising that the first Muslim kingdoms in the central and western Maghrib, that of Rustumids of Tiāret, and then of the Idrīsids of Walili (Volubilis), should have taken root precisely in these places.

And so the ancient period came to an end in these regions, a hybrid episode in which the action of social and political transformations gradually eroded Latin influence, revealing that unquenchable spirit of independence and immense steadfastness of purpose which is the constant hallmark of the history of North Africa.

20 The Sahara in classical antiquity

The traditional notion of 'classical antiquity' may appear a priori incompatible with the study of Saharan problems. These have a very particular classification. To take only one example: in Mediterranean archaeology, classical antiquity covers a period of roughly a thousand years, from the fifth century before the Christian era to the fifth century of the Christian era, but in the proto-history of the Sahara it would cover the end of the 'caballine' period and part of the 'Libyco-Berber', neither of these periods, moreover, being exactly datable. Any absolute chronology would therefore seem to be ruled out in this case.

Nevertheless, during that same millennium, the Saharan universe was the scene of highly important events which were connected in large part with the history of the Graeco-Roman world. So I have no hesitation in using classical chronological criteria, which are valid for the whole of the known world.

How is the question of the Sahara of antiquity approached by the historian? First, Graeco-Latin textual sources must be examined: while the information collected is not always reliable, and may induce error, it is in principle of value. The next step is to bring modern methods of scholarship to bear so as to correct the raw data little by little and shed light on the problem as a whole. That done, the Sahara of 'antiquity' will no longer be judged only from the outside. It will reveal its own personality.

Contemporary textual sources and their over-interpretation

We know the analytical methods of the ancient geographers and historians. Unable to visit inaccessible regions themselves, they gathered second-hand information which had a goodly share of error and fable. The Greeks, and later on the Romans, spoke only of Inner Libya, a very vague geographical expression signifying what lay beyond the North African territories, or Inner Ethiopia, a zone still farther south which derived its name from the dark skins of its inhabitants. Descriptions of these regions, which frightened contemporaries by their sheer mysteriousness, are therefore full of fabulous details in which men and animals often take on the aspect of ludicrous or terrifying monsters.

However, even if they could not always steer away from legends, serious authors did record valuable information and with time we find the quality of their work improves, in proportion, doubtless, as the progress of Graeco-Roman colonization in Africa made people aware of the realities.

As early as the middle of the fifth century before the Christian era, Herodotus obtained first-rate information as to the existence and the customs of Saharan populations. In his writings we find the Garamantes hunting Troglodytes in four-horse chariots (IV, 183). We find the Nasamonians (IV, 172–5) pushing beyond the wilderness of sand to discover, in a country of men with black skins, a great river full of crocodiles, like the Nile. We further learn (IV, 43) of the extraordinary exploit of Phoenician sailors who managed to circumnavigate the entire African continent, east to west, for Pharaoh in about −600, and then of the Persians' failure to do the same thing, but in the opposite direction, after venturing into the Atlantic (IV, 43). Finally, we see the Carthaginians exchanging their trade goods for precious gold dust on the West African coast (IV, 196).

At this point in our sources comes a celebrated document which can be dated from the first half of the fourth century before the Christian era, the *Periplus* of Hanno, a narrative of the voyage of a Carthaginian charged with exploring and colonizing that same coast (*Geographici Graeci Minores,* I). Full of picturesque scenery, savages, crocodiles and hippopotamuses, this short recital nevertheless gives two important landmarks: the island of Cerne, known from another source as a depot for ivory and skins of wild beasts (*Scylax Periplus*, fourth century before the Christian era, para. 112), and a great volcano called 'the Chariot of the Gods', the final stage of Hanno's voyage along the African coast. The existence of these two points was to be confirmed in the second century before the Christian era by the voyage of the Greek historian Polybius, though his narrative is only know at second hand, through another text (Pliny the Elder, *Natural History*, V, 9–10).

A most valuable text of Pliny the Elder's (*Natural History,* V, 5) tells of a raid in −19 by the proconsul of Africa, Cornelius Balbus, against the unruly Kingdom of the Garamantes of the Fezzān. Along with a few toponyms that are perfectly identifiable, like Rhapsa (Gafsa), Cidamus (G͟hadāmes) or Garama (D͟jerma), the list of Roman victories contains many others that are ambiguous and recall the sound of modern Saharan place names. This was taken as sufficient proof that the Romans reached the Niger.

The writer Marinus of Tyre (late first century of the Christian era) and his commentator, the celebrated geographer Claudius Ptolemy, whose African documentation goes back to the years +110 to +120, report that the Governor Septimius Flacchus, 'campaigning from a base in Libya, covered the distance from the country of the Garamantes to the Ethiopians in a three-months' journey southwards; while on the other hand Julius Maternus, coming from Leptis Magna and journeying from Garama on in the company of the King of the Garamantes, who was marching against the Ethiopians, reached Agisymba, an Ethiopian land where rhinoceros abound, after four months' unbroken travel southwards' (Ptolemy, *Geography*, I, 8, 4). This story took on the more importance in that Ptolemy backed up his seemingly vast knowledge of African geography with a mathematical system, longitudes and latitudes authenticating the places mentioned. His map of the interior was furbished out with the aid of phonetic similarities, and his work produced such an impression that once again people believed they had proof that the Romans were fully acquainted with the tropical regions of Africa, especially Niger and Chad.

Today this over-generous, exaggerated view no longer holds. Modern methods of analysis oblige us to rethink the history of the Sahara.

The approach of present-day scholarship

The new textual criticism

Modern historians have clearly seen that three major works were in question: the *Scylax Periplus* of Hanno, the episode of Cornelius Balbus and Ptolemy's *Geography*.

For several years the veracity of the *Scylax Periplus* has been under quasi-decisive attack. First, it has been established that ancient ships venturing beyond Cape Juby, but exposed on the return voyage to the full force of strong trade winds, would never have been able to get back to their base. This has therefore limited the geographical range of Hanno's voyage to the Atlantic coast of Morocco, where recent archaeological work has identified the ancient island of Cerne with the island of Essaouira-Mogador. What is more, a subtle method of philological comparisons goes to show that the tale of the *Scylax Periplus* is simply an unskilled plagiarism from a passage in Herodotus, hence an out-and-out forgery.

Second victim: Pliny's story of the raid by Cornelius Balbus. Analysis of manuscripts makes it possible to refute systematically any toponymic identification with regions of the central and southern Sahara. The Roman victory therefore covered only the south of the Maghrib and the Fezzān. Moreover, a proconsul, whose office only lasted for one year, could scarcely have gone any farther.

Finally, Ptolemy's *Geography*, an imposing work, turns out to be singularly restricted territorially. Its longitudes and latitudes, calculated according to the norms of antiquity, like its mountains, rivers, cities and peoples, bring us to the southern confines of the Maghrib; and its Niger, for example, is no longer anything but a waterway in southern Algeria. The Fezzān, then, would have been the most southerly zone known to the Romans, the problem of Agisymba, on the borders of *terrae incognitae,* remaining open.

Now that we are freed of textual constraints which were sometimes burdensome, we can try to see what the Sahara of antiquity itself has to show us.

What were its ecological, anthropological, sociological frameworks? What archaeological remains has it revealed to us?

The ecological problem

Palaeoclimatically, the Sahara is known to have reached the final phase of its desiccation in the era we are considering. But we have to qualify. Patches of resistance still preserved enough humidity for the life there to be far more intense than it is in our time. The Ahaggar, the Fezzān, the Tibesti and the northern Sahara still had a fairly high level of habitability. This may explain the survival of a wild fauna which has now disappeared: crocodiles in the wadis and *gueltas* (permanent water-holes), felines in hill country. But it is doubtful that large herbivores like the elephant or the rhinoceros could have gone on living this side of the Tibesti or even of the Kuar country, the northern fringe of the great tropical savannahs of Chad, where, naturally, they were plentiful.

Domestic animals held out along with men in the refuge-zones of habitation. There were modern bovine breeds and flocks of goats and sheep. But it is odd to find the donkey, beast of all work of the Saharan oases, virtually unrepresented in rock pictures.

The anthropological problem

For a long time it was supposed that the presence of a white population in the Sahara was a recent phenomenon only, a regular conquest, a result of the Romans' driving the steppe Berbers out of Maghrib territory.

Here too, the situation is becoming clearer in the light of recent work both in the Fezzān and in Saharan Algeria. It is now considered that during the proto-historical period – of which antiquity was merely the final stage – the central and northern Sahara was peopled mainly by white elements. Now, it seems that the origin of this physical type is no longer to be looked for towards the Maghrib but rather towards the north-east of the African continent. We may know more about this when definite conclusions are obtained by the technique for studying blood-groups. On the other hand, it is probable that the population of the southern Sahara, to the extent that it was inhabited on any considerable scale, consisted only of black-skinned people from the tropical savannah.

Civilization

In the absence of absolutely reliable chronology, it seems a priori difficult to assess the progress of Saharan civilization in antiquity, especially since it is not certain that the different zones of this vast territory developed along the same lines. A good means of studying the problem is to start from the cultural situation of the Sahara at the end of the Neolithic period and, on this basis, to follow the line of development in various fields.

Language and writing

The mother-language, which was pluridialectal and which for practical convenience is called 'Berber', belongs to the Hamitic-Semitic common trunk, but branched off from it long ago. Its ancient form, 'Libyan', is attested in all Mediterranean African territories and in the Canary Islands, through written examples. There is no doubt that this language was introduced into the Sahara from the north or the north-east with the immigration of white populations. No date can be put to the event, but Saharan writing, called 'Tifinagh', deriving from the Libyan alphabet of the Maghrib, is a fairly late phenomenon. In the northern territories there seems to be no unimpeachable evidence of Libyan writing before the third or second century before the Christian era and it is accepted that the Berbers came to write their language down under Carthaginian influence. The word 'Tifinagh' – 'Tifinar' in French transliteration – is itself based on the root FNR which in all Semitic languages designates the Phoenician people.

In the Sahara, Tifinagh writing gradually moved away from its Libyan ancestral form, 'Old Tifinagh' still being fairly close to it. We must therefore be particularly cautious in the dating of rock drawings called 'Libyco-Berber' with written characters on them. Very serious mistakes can be made. Moreover, the Berber language and alphabet may also have been used by negroid populations.

Socio-political organization

'Tribal' organization, inherent at that stage of evolution, was the basic political rule, but it gave rise to incessant wars – reported with exactitude in Herodotus and Ptolemy.

For two regions, however, we have more solid data: the Ahaggar and the Fezzān zone.

In the Ahaggar, in the second half of the fourth century of the Christian era, the socio-political pyramid culminated in a woman. When her tomb was discovered, intact, at Abalessa, the association was immediately made with the local legend of a Queen Tin Hinan who had come from Moroccan Tafilālet in distant times and was the ancestress of the Tuareg people. In the Berber world there were several examples of supreme authority being attributed to a holy woman; in any case the attitude towards women in Tuareg society is a liberal one. The funerary equipment of this 'princess' – seven gold bracelets, eight silver bracelets, several other precious jewels – can be approximately dated by the impression of a Roman coin of the emperor Constantine going back to between +313 and +324. As for the wooden bed on which the body was resting, when submitted to the radio-carbon test it revealed the date +470 (±130). As we shall see, this dignitary's wealth can only be explained by her privileged position both in the social hierarchy and in trans-Saharan trade. The great region called the Kingdom of the Garamantes – mentioned by Herodotus as early as the fifth century before the Christian era – opposed the Roman advance on the southern borders of the Maghrib. Defeated by Cornelius Balbus in −19 and then, finally, by the legate Valerius Festus in +69 the Garamantes seem to have become a sort of client-state of the empire. Archaeological research at and around Garama has revealed nearly ten centuries of a civilization which was partly founded on foreign relations, from the last Punic era to the coming of the Arabs.

Thus in the Ahaggar and the Fezzān, but also throughout the northern Sahara, in Tassili-n'-Ajjer during its last period and perhaps even in the Adrār des Ifoghas, supreme political power in antiquity was indisputably in the hands of an aristocracy of a white or near-white race.

In the absence of documents, it is impossible to say whether the position was the same on the edges of the Sahara bordering the Niger–Chad savannahs. It is very likely that white influence had not penetrated to those parts.

As regards religion, there is no doubt that the whole of the central and southern Sahara followed traditional religion. Only the people of the northern Sahara, in direct contact with the Mediterranean world, may have been converted to Christianity in late antiquity. One classical author asserts categorically that the Garamantes and the

Macuritae were converted at the end of the sixth century, but archaeological research has so far not confirmed this.

Saharan art of antiquity

In the great edifice of Abalessa which is preserved in the Ahaggar, we find disposed around the tomb of Tin Hinan an ambulatory which is peculiarly African in architecture. At Tin Alkoum, at the south-eastern opening of the Tassili-n'-Ajjer, a series of circular tombs of traditional Saharan workmanship can be dated through Roman funerary equipment of the fourth century, as can similar monuments at the nearby necropolis of Ghāt.

In the north-west Sahara, in the necropolis of Djorf Torba near Bechar – unfortunately ravaged by tourists – there were even to be found inside the edifices, curious figurative ex-votos: flat slabs, either carved or painted, some with Libyan inscriptions or drawings of horses or human figures, in a style similar to that of late antiquity in the Maghrib, and as yet devoid of Islamic elements.

But for the most impressive Saharan art we must above all look at the rock drawings. According to the traditional classification of the prehistorians, their antiquity corresponds to the penultimate stage of rock art, the Libyco-Berber period which follows the caballine era and precedes the Arabo-Berber. While this sequence is correct in itself, it lacks precise chronological bases, and dating of the Libyco-Berber as between −200 and +700 is still precarious. The presence of Old Tifinagh characters is perhaps the least uncertain criterion, though this type of writing carries over into the Muslim era. Since the horse and the wheeled vehicle were still coexisting, it is very hard to differentiate them chronologically. Are the war chariots at the flying gallop of the Fezzān and Tassili in an Egyptianized tradition which might go back to the fourteenth century before the Christian era or in a Graeco-Cyrenaican tradition acquired, at earliest, towards the sixth? Drawings of camels cover almost all Saharan regions, but their age, too, is hard to estimate. It is to be feared that very few of them fall within our historical frame of reference. Libyco-Berber works, residua of the admirable Neolithic works on whose traditions they drew, prove how vigorous pictorial art was in the Sahara at the moment when it was dying out in the lands to the north.

Economic life. Internal communications and foreign relations: a camel revolution?

From time immemorial economic life in the Sahara has been linked with the problem of communications. For classical antiquity, therefore, the enrichment of certain regions like the Fezzān is related to their sphere of influence, presupposing the existence of a fair amount of trading. Since internal trafficking, we know, was already limited, the cause of this prosperity must be sought in their relations with the outside world. This new situation was a fundamental contrast to that of the humid Sahara of prehistoric times.

In my opinion, the capture of wild animals was the principal source of profit for the territory. Of course at that time North Africa, too, still teemed with lions and

20.1 ◄ *The tomb of Queen Tin Hinan at Abalessa, main entrance (P. Salama, Bardo Museum, Algiers)*

20.2 ◄ *The tomb of Queen Tin Hinan at Abalessa: flagstones used for covering the ditch trench (P. Salama)*

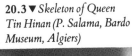

20.3 ▼ *Skeleton of Queen Tin Hinan (P. Salama, Bardo Museum, Algiers)*

tigers, antelopes and ostriches; but such was the scale of Roman demand that the hunt had to be extended to the interior of Africa. We have eloquent statistics on this subject. At the inauguration of the Flavian amphitheatre in Rome at the end of the first century, 9,000 wild animals were fought; for his triumph in +106 the Emperor Trajan exhibited 11,000. Most of these wild animals were 'Libycae' or 'Africanae' – that is, were exported from North Africa. In this inventory elephants and rhinoceroses came from the southernmost parts of the Sahara or even from Chad and Baḥr al-Ghazāl. In any event ivory must have had a place in trans-Saharan trade, the North African elephant having almost entirely disappeared by the second century of the Christian era. It will not be forgotten, however, that Nubia supplied Rome with a quota of wild animals.

I find it hard to believe that there was a trade with Europe in black slaves. The Western Roman world was not looking for black slaves. It has often been made out that convoys of gold dust from Mali and the Gulf of Guinea supplied the European market, prefiguring the trade situation of the Middle Ages. This opinion is mere hypothesis.

These few trade relations, which are not yet well understood, cast doubt on the use of Saharan itineraries. Here again one must be prudent. The only elements we have to go on in attempting to reconstruct the communications network are certain points like Ghadāmes or Phazania where natural arteries have their outlet, the territorial dispersal of Roman objects in the Sahara, and finally comparison with caravan routes before or after the period we are considering. Only the last two elements present a difficulty.

It seems that, generally speaking, Saharan lines of communication for foreign trade were mostly oriented towards the north and the north-east, with the Garamantes and their satellites siphoning traffic towards the Fezzān zone. From there well-attested itineraries led towards the great Syrtic ports (Sabratha, Oea and Leptis Magna), which were cities of great wealth as early as the Punic era. From Garama one could also join up with the valley of the Nile, either by a northern route through the oases of Zuila, Zella, Awdjīla and Sīwa, all of them points already known to writers of antiquity; or by a more southerly route where Kifra served as a crossroads. In these eastern regions of the Sahara, inevitably, we come back to the old problem of Neolithic and proto-historical communications for which Tibesti provided a staging-post. But it seems that relations declined first with Hellenistic, then with Roman Egypt, trade being increasingly diverted to the Mediterranean coast.

It is probably in the eastern Sahara, too, that we should seek the link which brought iron into the black world, in so far as this did not occur independently. The problem of the transition from the Stone Age to the Metal Age in the Saharan and Niger regions is of immense importance. Here again, geographical uniformity is lacking.

The question of the iron industry is different. The problem of how iron metallurgy made its appearance in the black world is extremely controversial, some maintaining that it was a specifically African invention, others that it was brought there by foreign intervention. The upholders of the second theory are themselves divided into two camps: some assume a Mediterranean influence, across the central Sahara; whilst others trace the origin of this technique to the land of Kush and assume that it followed the natural route linking the Niger to the Nile Valley via Kordofān and Dārfūr. Be this as it may, carbon-14 datings indicate that iron metallurgy existed in the area of Chad and northern Nigeria in the second and first century before the Christian era. The possibility of its having evolved locally is not to be rejected out of hand; but, if such was not the case, it was probably transmitted by the Meroitic civilization, so that the central Saharan routes were not involved.

Study of the means of transport can also help us better to locate the Saharan routes and check certain hypotheses. We know that the great desert was conquered by the horse before it was conquered by the camel. Here, as in other places, the 'caballine' period had as its first consequence the use of wheeled vehicles. We do not know when wagons and chariots disappeared, but, according to Herodotus, the Garamantes were still using them. Archaeology confirms his testimony. The most diversified drawings of wheeled vehicles abound in the Sahara. Systematic inventories have even made it possible to give a cartographic reconstruction of trans-Saharan wagon routes. It should be added that any Saharan itinerary used by horses, whether in harness or no, required either a system of watering-places, which we know the Garamantes had, or else the transport of a large store of provisions.

As for the camel – more exactly, the one-humped dromedary originating in the Near East – it appears in Saharan Africa only belatedly. This event has been discussed *ad infinitum*. On the continent itself, in fact, the camel was a late arrival. It is not found in Egypt until the Persian and Hellenistic periods (fifth and fourth centuries before the Christian era) and it is a likely supposition that it spread to the Sahara from the lower Nile Valley. The event seems very hard to date. All we have to go on are Libyco-Berber Saharan rock drawings which are of little use for accurate chronology and a large number of inscriptions and sculptures from Roman North Africa, all apparently subsequent to the second century of the Christian era.

Let me note in passing the symbolic presence of camels on the well-known Roman coins called 'spintrian', which were probably struck for the use of courtesans, the ancients believing that these ruminants had lascivious instincts which were quite exceptional!

I am inclined to agree with those historians who attach quite exceptional importance to the increasing use of camels in the Sahara. Camels meant increased mobility for individuals and for groups, an advantage which had been recognized for a long time in Arabia. It is even thought that changing the method of harnessing, especially by altering the position of the saddle, made it possible to train 'meharis', camels for racing and for use in battle.

Rome's 'Sahara policy'

Because of the lack of documents, we do not know whether Punic Carthage was much alarmed at the presence of powerful *ḳabīlas* on her southern frontiers. Excavations at Garama prove that, at least during the second and first centuries before the Christian era, the ports of the Syrtic coast, which then belonged to the Kingdom of Numidia, had trade relations with the Fezzān, relations on which their wealth was largely dependent.

Roman history is better known. The main lines of Latin policy can be briefly summarized as follows: occupation of the agricultural lands of the Maghrib required strategic cover to the south. In these regions the Saharan nomads were a nuisance. Their seasonal migrations into the colonized territory, unavoidable because essential to survival, had their uses in that they made the products of the steppe and the desert available to the settlers, but there was always the risk of their creating conflict with the settled *ḳabīlas*. Even the distant Garamantes seemed dangerous, inasmuch as they could at any moment reinforce the aggressive potential of the nomads. The mere fact of their power was a challenge.

So, as we have seen, we are not entirely without knowledge of the Sahara of antiquity, even though the information we have is incomplete. Several points are certain. The desiccation of the climate did not kill the desert. Human activity went on. Languages and writing were consolidated there. The increasing use of camels eased problems of transport and communication. The region played its own part in the history of the great Mediterranean states. Did the same perhaps hold true of tropical Africa? It is in this context of continued development that the medieval renaissance undoubtedly had its roots.

21 Introduction to the later prehistory of sub-Saharan Africa

Information obtained from archaeology

One of the main achievements of recent research in sub-Saharan African archaeology is the realization that peoples at different stages of technological development were living contemporaneously in different parts of Africa. There was no single end to the Stone Age, agricultural practices were adopted at different times and many of the communities with whom we will be concerned in the next few chapters were still living by hunting and food-gathering and using a Stone Age technology right up to the end of the first millennium of the Christian era. It is impossible to assign an exact closing date for the period under discussion in an area for which we have no fixed historical dates. Dates we have, but they are largely obtained from radio-carbon determination (carbon-14). Rather than fix a definite date for the close of the period, the chapters on sub-Saharan Africa deal largely with what is commonly known as the 'Neolithic' and Early Iron Age period. The period thus defined ends in most areas around −1000.

The 'Neolithic' in sub-Saharan Africa is a term which has been used in various inconsistent ways in the past either to denote an agricultural economy and/or to distinguish tool assemblages which include polished or ground stone cutting tools, pottery and, in many instances, querns or grindstones. Early farming communities were not necessarily characterized by the same tool assemblages. Recent research in many parts of Africa has demonstrated the time-trangressive nature of tools like the ground-stone axe which made its first appearance in parts of Africa amongst hunter and food-gatherer tool-kits of more than 7,000 to 8,000 years ago, whilst similar tools were probably still used in parts of the Zaire Basin (Uelian) less than a thousand years ago. Pottery seems similarly to have been used by hunter-gatherers in contact with their agricultural neighbours long before its users became farmers themselves. Grindstones first appeared regularly on the Late Stone Age sites in several parts of Africa and are an indication of the more intensive use of plant remains. By the Early Iron Age we mean the period during which there was a persistent use of an iron technology as opposed to the occasional use of iron tools. By and large the Early Iron Age in sub-Saharan Africa was characterized by the presence of small, relatively dispersed settlements and not by the development of states, which first arose in the Late Iron Age.

Unfortunately our knowledge of the physical nature of the inhabitants of sub-Saharan Africa is very limited. In West Africa there were certainly peoples who possessed some physical features similar to the present-day inhabitants of the area as early as the tenth millennium before the Christian era (Iwo-Eluru in Nigeria) and have been termed 'proto-Negroes'. In southern Africa the ancestors of the present-day Khoisan hunter-food-gatherers and herders of Namibia and Botswana (San and Khoi Khoi) were larger than their descendants and occupied areas as far north as Zambia for certain, and possibly even as far as the Semliki River in eastern Zaïre. Excellent evidence for this came from the Gwisho sites in Zambia at which the tool-kit and the inferred diet clearly indicate that the groups involved were ancestral San. Biogenetic studies by Singer and Weiner have indicated that the San and the Negro are closer to one another than they are to any outside group, which suggests that they are the lineal descendants of the original Stone Age inhabitants of Africa. They have also indicated the biological homogeneity of the African populations stretching from West Africa right through to South Africa. Only in the remote areas, e.g. the Zaïre forest home of the pygmies or the Kalahari environment of the San, were the populations significantly different and there the difference must be explained by genetic isolation. In areas like the Sahelian belt and on the fringes of north-east Africa and in Madagascar there is a mixture between largely Negro populations and populations which developed independently of those to the south such as the Malayo-Polynesians in the case of Madagascar, and peoples akin to those of the Mediterranean periphery and south-west Asia in north-eastern Africa and the Sahara.

The contribution of linguistics

Crucial to an understanding of the Early Iron Age in sub-Saharan Africa is an appreciation of the linguistic background. Two principal sets of events concern us in the period under review: first, the fragmentation of the Congo-Kordofanian language family, to use Greenberg's term, and secondly the dispersion of the Bantu-speaking peoples, who now comprise more than 90 per cent of the peoples south of a line drawn from the Bight of Biafra to the East African coast around Malindi. We know very little about the first set of events. All that can be said about them is that the Kordofanian languages are old, relatively numerous, often spoken by very small, in some cases minuscule, groups of people, with each language distinct from its neighbours and with the whole comprised within the modern province of Kordofan in the Republic of Sudan and principally concentrated around the Nuba Mountains. The Kordofanian languages have diverged widely from the Niger-Congo languages and are isolated from the linguistic groups around them. Nothing useful can be said about the time-scale involved in the separation of the Kordofanian from the Niger-Congo dialects of the proto-Congo-Kordofanian family except that it probably predates −10000 to −8000.

The fragmentation of the Niger-Congo languages may be related to the gradual expansion of peoples south from the Sahel with the growing desiccation of the Sahara. Painter has put a time-scale of around −6000 to −3000 on the fragmentation, but there are other views. Armstrong has suggested that the languages of southern Nigeria are as much as 10,000 years old which implies a much earlier movement to the south. Both views could of course be right, with some of the Niger-Congo language speakers having broken away from the main group and later having become isolated in a forest environment. These are perhaps the linguistic counterparts of the Iwo-Eluru proto-Negro inhabitants. Other Niger-Congo speakers spread later from the Sahel, once an agricultural way of life was established. A problem about this interpretation is that the earliest food-producers in the Sahel appear to have been pastoralists rather than arable agriculturalists. The suggestion made by Sutton in chapter 23 may be a solution to the problem since there is evidence of Sahelian pastoralists being associated with harpoons and other items identified as diagnostic of the aquatic culture. The linguistic divergence within the Niger-Congo family would, however, appear to be related to the geographical separation of different, largely agricultural groups, a separation far enough back in time for the individual components of the Niger-Congo family to have become linguistically very distinct.

When we turn to the Bantu languages, we are faced with a different situation. There are more than 2,000 Bantu languages in eastern, southern and central Africa which have vocabulary items and a structural framework in common and are thus related, a relationship which was recognized as early as 1862 by Bleek, who coined the name Bantu for them because of their common use of the word 'Bantu' for people. The divergence between the different Bantu languages is nowhere near as great as that between the different West African languages and most estimates put the divergence back to around 2,000 to 3,000 years. There are, however, various linguistic theories about how the Bantu separated from the West African languages, of which two have been the most often accepted. Joseph Greenberg approached the problem from the macro-level in his study of African languages as a whole and used grammatical as well as lexical evidence taken from some 800 languages. Using core words, he discovered that the Bantu languages are closer to the West African languages than is, for example, English to proto-German, which is a relationship which linguists have always regarded as close. He worked out that 42 per cent of the vocabulary of Bantu is present in the nearest West African languages, compared with only 34 per cent of the English words in proto-German. He thus placed the source area of the Bantu languages firmly in the Nigerian–Cameroon border area. The late Professor Guthrie worked on the micro-level after years of immersion in comparative Bantu studies and analysed some 350 Bantu languages and dialects. He isolated the roots of cognate words which had to have the same meaning in at least three separate languages. Using the general sets, he worked out a Common Bantu Index which indicated the percentage of the general words in any Bantu language. The isoglosses (or lines connecting equal Bantu indices) thus constructed indicated a nuclear area where the retention rate was over 50 per cent situated in the grasslands south of the Zaïre forest in the Zambezi–Zaïre watershed area. It was in this nuclear area that he assumed the proto-Bantu had developed. There is thus agreement on the ultimate ancestry of the Bantu languages in West Africa, but disagreement on the immediate centre of dispersion. Those authorities who are willing to propose a chronology would place the Bantu expansion somewhere between 2,000 and 3,000 years ago and accept that iron was in use by those who expanded, and all would agree to the rapid, some would say explosive, expansion of the Bantu.

The role of agriculture

Agriculture implies some control over one's food supply and a relatively settled existence, in contrast to the more constant movement of the hunter-gatherer. Group size increased and more complex social, and ultimately political, structures were able to develop. Agriculture, particularly arable agriculture and horticulture, also normally involved a higher population density and an increase in the total population figure. Archaeologists identify agricultural societies by both direct and indirect evidence. Direct evidence includes the discovery of seeds or grains in a carbonized state on archaeological sites or their retrieval using advanced archaeological recovery techniques. Indirect evidence, or circumstantial evidence, involves the discovery of implements and utensils assumed to have been used for cultivation, harvesting and the preparation of plant foods. Unfortunately the climatic conditions in much of sub-Saharan Africa militate against the discovery of very much in the way of direct evidence. Organic matter normally disintegrates within days of its disposal. The soils on most tropical sites are on the whole aerobic and do not allow for the preservation of pollen. Where pollen is found, as in the high-altitude swamps and lakes, the location is too far removed from land suited for arable cultivation to provide evidence for past agriculture. A further problem is that many of the tools and implements for agriculture are of an equivocal nature. A knife for peeling vegetable foods can be used for other purposes, grindstones can be used for pulverizing ochre for paint or for pounding and grinding non-cultivated foodstuffs, and are commonly found in many Late Stone Age contexts. Many of Africa's food crops like bananas, yams and other roots do not produce pollen and many are cultivated using wooden digging sticks to avoid damage to the tubers. Archaeologists thus have to rely on even more circumstantial evidence for inferring agriculture, such as the existence of large settlement sites, the presence of what appear to be permanent houses, the use of pottery or the existence of regular cemeteries. As will appear obvious from Chapter 26, the hunter-food-gatherers in Africa occasionally lived in large communities, often used pottery and, if their fishing or other specialized hunting or food-gathering occupation was successful, would indulge in the making of relatively permanent settlements such as those at early Khartoum or Ishango of Late Stone Age date. It is thus possible, regretfully, to conclude that as yet our evidence for untangling the story of early agriculture in sub-Saharan Africa is somewhat thin and that our conclusions can only be speculative.

Up to the end of the 1950s it was commonly assumed that agriculture was late in date in most of sub-Saharan Africa, in fact largely contemporaneous with the introduction of an iron technology in all but parts of West Africa, and that the idea had dispersed from the Nile Valley ultimately to the rest of Africa. New evidence from the Sahara and elsewhere is indicating, however, that the story is not so straightforward. The first question-marks against this orthodox view of the origins of

African agriculture were placed by Murdock, who postulated a source area for much of Africa's agriculture in the west of West Africa around the headwaters of the Niger and the Senegal in the Futa Jallon. Though much of Murdock's hypothesis cannot now be substantiated in detail, nevertheless it is apparent that yams, one form of rice (*Oryza glaberrima*), sorghum, the oil palm and many lesser staples were indigenous to West Africa.

Though the origins, date and mode of development of most African agriculture are somewhat controversial, it is generally agreed that, except for the possibility of some highly localized millet-growing communities in the Rift Valley of Kenya, the beginnings of arable agriculture, at least in most of Bantu-speaking Africa, are contemporaneous with the first appearance of an iron technology. It is also fairly widely agreed that many of the early staples of agriculture in Bantu Africa like the fruiting banana, the colocasias (coco yams), eleusine (finger millet) and sorghum were introduced ultimately either from West Africa, or in the case of the bananas indirectly from south-east Asia. The earliest cattle were pre-Iron Age in date and are found in East Africa as early as the beginning of the first millennium before the Christian era, and it would seem from the evidence referred to by Parkington in Chapter 26 that sheep had diffused as far south as the Cape in South Africa by the beginning of the first millennium of the Christian era. It may be that the spread of pastoralism had something to do with the dispersal of the aquatic culture described by Sutton in Chapter 23, as Ehret has convincingly indicated the evidence for the social influence of the Central Sudanic languages on the Bantu languages. He has described for instance, how words for 'cow' and terms used for milking activities were borrowed by the Bantu from their Central Sudanic neighbours, presumably along with the cattle and milking practices. On the basis of linguistic differentiation among the presumed proto-Central Sudanic speakers, Ehret infers that the cattle-keepers preceded the arable agriculturalists. He also sees this interaction as first taking place around the middle of the first millennium before the Christian era. He has indicated that the proto-Bantu words for 'hoe' and 'sorghum' were derived from the Central Sudanic languages, and we must therefore envisage a social interaction between Nilo-Saharan peoples and the ancestors of the Bantu, and a diffusion southwards of hoe agriculture and sorghum cultivation particularly into the Bantu world. Though some expansion of population may have taken place as a result of these developments by the first millennium before the Christian era, the archaeological evidence described in later chapters clearly indicates that the main expansion of agricultural peoples took place in the first millennium of the Christian era in most of Bantu Africa.

Iron

An important question in any discussion of the early expansion of agricultural people into the southern half of Africa is that of the origin of the diffusion of iron working. To clear scrub and bush, forest fringe and woodland, a slashing tool is the easiest implement to use. Stone Age man did not have such tools and in sub-Saharan Africa there was no Bronze Age. The earliest evidence for the use of copper comes from Mauretania, and the copper workings date from a period between the ninth and fifth centuries before the Christian era, which is only a little earlier that the earliest proven iron workings in West Africa at Taruga on the Jos plateau of Nigeria which date from the fifth or fourth century before the Christian era.

Considerable speculation has arisen over the question of the origins of early African iron working. There are several acceptable schools of thought, but none can as yet be proved correct. The older school opted for a spread of iron working from the Nile Valley, particularly Meroe, termed by Sayce the 'Birmingham of Africa'. There is, however, no firm evidence of a direct diffusion of iron working from the Nile Valley either westwards or southwards. Iron in Ethiopia, dating from the fifth century, probably came from south Arabia; alternatively it could have come from the Ptolemaic ports on the Red Sea, such as Adulis, with which these centres were in contact.

The discovery of the early dates for Nigerian iron working focused the attention of scholars on the possibilities of a North African source. The Phoenicians spread iron technology from the Levant to parts of the North African coast in the early part of the first millennium before the Christian era. Connah has postulated that as iron working is late, around +500, at Daima, near Lake Chad, which is situated on the likely corridor route from the Nile Valley, iron must have come from the north. Other relatively early dates for iron working come from Ghana, Hani (+80) and Senegal. It is just as possible, of course, to suggest that iron working could have come from North Africa via Mauretania in the trail of the copper workers and spread along the Sudanic belt westwards and southwards, though in that case the dates should be earlier in Senegal and Mauretania than in Nigeria. It is, of course, possible to suggest multiple lines of influence bringing iron working to tropical Africa with a line to Mauretania from the Maghrib, another across the Sahara to Nigeria and a third one across the Red Sea to Ethiopia, as well as others via the east coast from the Red Sea area, India or south-east Asia to East Africa.

The suggestion has recently been made that iron working may have developed indigenously in Africa. A strong proponent of this view is C. A. Diop, who is supported by Wai Andah in Chapter 24 of the main edition. It is further suggested that as many of the early sites for iron technology in West Africa, such as those associated with the Nok culture, or in Burkina Faso, are associated with stone tools, then the possibility must remain open that iron working took place in predominantly Late Stone Age contexts.

The apparently recent kilns which are now being investigated in the Congo have unfortunately added nothing new to our knowledge and will probably never yield any traces of the first period of their use. But, having been found and dated, they might give some indication of the route followed by the iron trade between Shaba and the sea and make it possible to establish some dates for this late development.

Far too few dates have so far been obtained for Early Iron Age sites as a whole to be certain even about the dates of the introduction of iron working into the various parts of tropical Africa. In the early 1960s, for instance, it was thought that iron working began in East Africa around 1000, and now the date has been pushed back by at least 750 years; the same is true of Ghana, where, until the discovery of the Hani furnace dating to the second century of the Christian era, the normally quoted date was around +900. Nevertheless, certain conclusions can be drawn. First, there is not

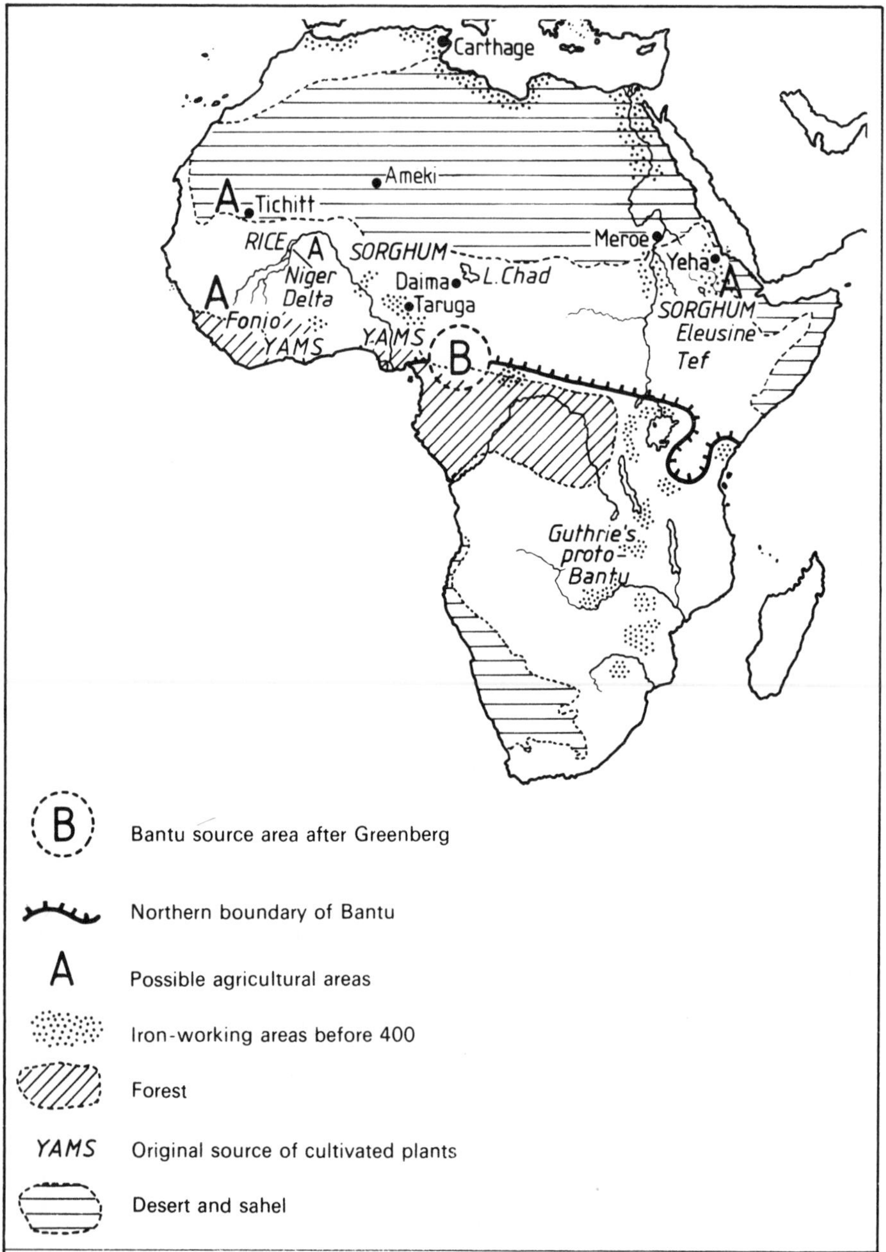

21.1 *Hypotheses concerning the origin of the Bantu and the beginning of iron working (from M. Posnansky)*

a great deal of evidence to suggest direct spread from the Nile Valley to West Africa, so that the idea of dispersion from Meroe had the least evidence to support it. Secondly, there is no positive evidence of kiln or pit-fired pottery in West Africa in the period before the Christian era and the ethnographic evidence for an indigenous development for iron working has not been extensively presented and refers at best to situations in the second millennium of the Christian era, so that we must reluctantly keep an open mind about the origins of iron working. The sparse evidence which does exist indicates earlier dates for West Africa than are available for East or Central Africa, which further suggests a spread from West Africa southwards and eastwards. Iron working spread remarkably rapidly, since the earliest dates in South Africa are around +400, i.e. a few centuries later than most of those for West Africa.

This rapid spread of iron working – some would call it explosive – thus matches the evidence from linguistics. The archaeological evidence from East or Central Africa, which further suggests a spread from West Africa of the first millennium of Christian era, shows definite similarities of shape and decoration over a wide area of tropical Africa, which can only be explained by postulating a common origin for the various wares (Soper, 1971, for East Africa, and Huffman, 1970, for southern Africa). After the initial similarities, strong regional diversity developed. This trend is well observed in Zambia where perhaps a more intensive study of Iron Age pottery has been made than elsewhere in tropical Africa. The conclusion of Ehret, who on the basis of linguistic evidence thinks in terms of 'loose collections of independent but mutually interacting communities' coexisting with unassimilated hunter-gatherers, is also very acceptable on archaeological grounds. As these Bantu communities became adapted to specific environments, so their interactions with more distant communities grew less and their languages and material cultures diverged.

Exchanges between the different regions of the continent

A further feature of the history of tropical Africa at this period which needs to be stressed is the continuing and intensifying influence of North Africa on the Sudanic belt.

The Sahara, as has been seen in the earlier chapters, was neither a barrier nor a no man's land, but an area with a detailed history of its own, much of which still needs to be unravelled. By its very nature as a desert, its population was sparse and nomadic, and in the period under review the majority of its population probably consisted of pastoralists who moved from the desert to the highlands, like the Hoggar, the Tassili, the Tibesti, and from the Sahelian belt northwards and southwards with the passage of the seasons. It is very difficult either to quantify the actual contact that existed or to describe its effects, though in recent years archaeological work in the Sudanic belt is clearly indicating that contact there was both indirect, such as that provided by the effects of nomadism, and direct, such as may have grown up through trade contacts and mineral exploitation. Our information at present consists of classical literary sources, rock paintings and engravings in the Sahara and archaeological evidence.

Before dealing with the literary evidence for contact across the Sahara, it is necessary to mention the two direct sea contacts reported to have been made from the

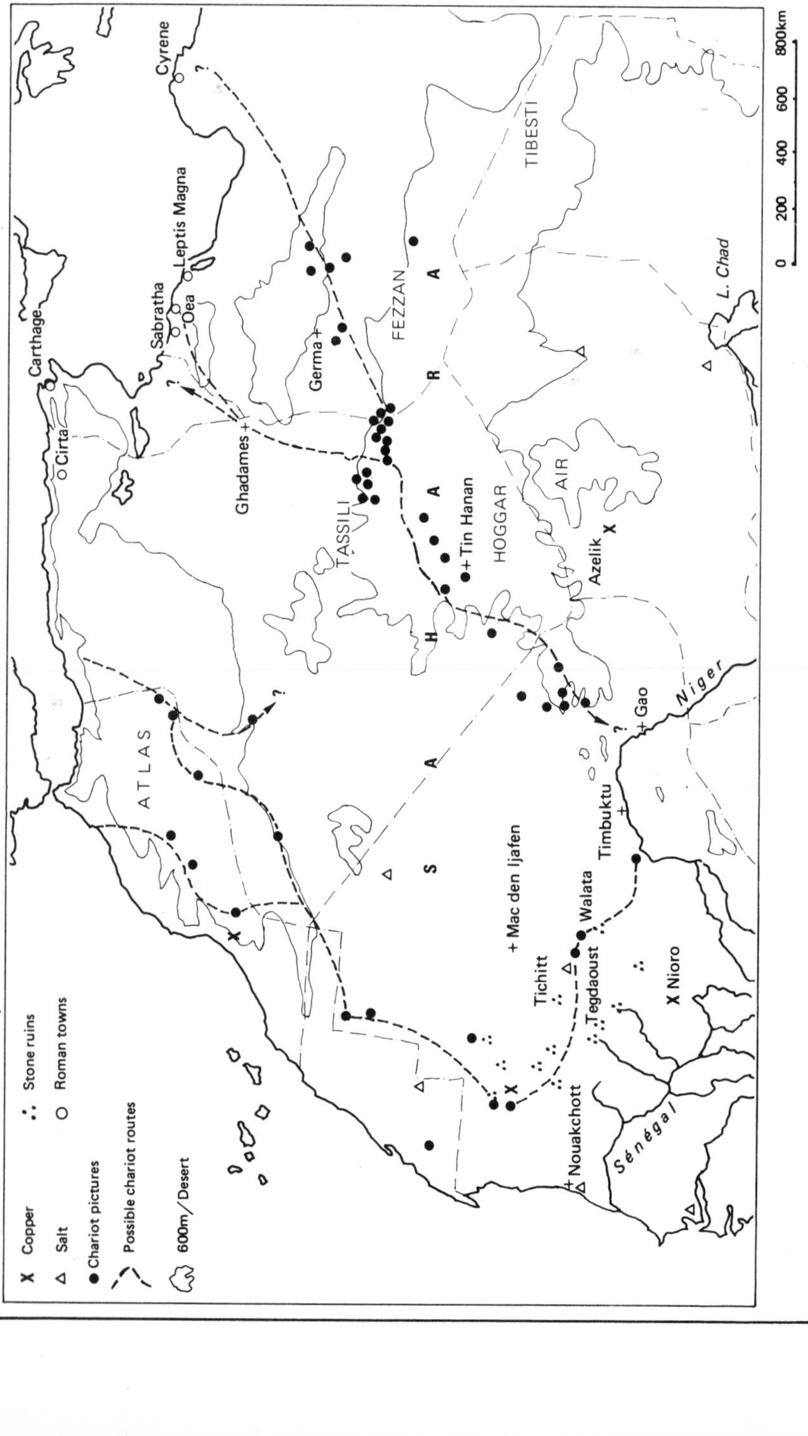

21.2 *Copper sources and caravan routes across the Sahara (after M. Posnansky, 1971)*

Mediterranean to West Africa. The first is the voyage of nearly three years said to have been made by Phoenician sailors in the service of Necho. Circumstantial evidence against the voyage is very strong. The second voyage is said to have been made by the Carthaginian, Hanno. Mauny (1960) has indicated that the same circumstantial evidence that adduced against Necho's reign would apply equally well to Hanno's voyage. If the voyages were made, they certainly had no impact on West Africa. No undoubted or well-authenticated and dated Carthaginian, Phoenician or Egyptian artefacts have been found along the West African coast. The Carthaginians certainly obtained gold along the Atlantic coast of Morocco as the account of the 'dumb barter' trading in Herodotus implies, but it is doubtful whether classical sailors reached further south than the Senegal River.

Much more evidence of contact in pre-Islamic times comes from the rock art and archaeological evidence. Rock art indicates that regular lines of communications were open to the Sudanic belt as early as −500. The drawings are mainly of chariots or carts, some horse-drawn and some bullock-drawn. Lhote (1953) has noted that there are no chariots in Aïr or the Tibesti except near the Fezzān. Most of the pictures of bullocks are found near the western route. We should perhaps not draw too many conclusions from the chariots. Daniels has suggested that they 'indicate the widely spread usage of a common type of vehicle rather that any complex system of Saharan roadways'. Where datable, as in the case of those associated with late Neolithic villages, they belong to the period −1100 to −400. We have to assume from the rock art that the routes across the Sahara were negotiable by horse, bullock and almost certainly by the versatile donkey. The eastern route has a strong concentration in the Tassili, and Lhote has indicated possible termini on the Tripolitanian coast in such centres as Leptis, Oea and Sabratha.

Earlier in this chapter we considered the evidence for copper working in Mauretania. The archaeological evidence would indicate that the western route was of greater direct importance than the eastern across the Tassili. The exploitation of the copper may have provided the incentive for a contemporaneous working of gold to the south. From the finds in the Senegal tumuli there is abundant evidence of Maghribian influence and one must infer that trade contacts slowly increased from their beginnings in the first or second millennium before the Christian era. It is even possible that camels were used in the trade on this western route before the arrival of the Arabs in the late eighth century of the Christian era: after all, camels were known in North Africa from at least the first century before the Christian era (Caesar mentioned their capture in −46) and they were quite common by the fourth century.

22 The East African coast and its role in maritime trade

One of the outstanding characteristics of the East African coast has been its relative accessibility, not only from the interior but also from the sea. Accessibility from the interior has been a vital factor in population movements into the coastal belt, and helps to explain its ethnic and cultural complexity. The sea, on the other hand, has been a means of contact with the outside world. One of the main features of the history of the East African coast over the last 2,000 years has therefore been not isolation but the interpenetration of two cultural streams to produce a new amalgam, the coastal Swahili civilization. The vehicle of that process has been trade, which facilitated the assimilation of the East African coast into the international economic system with its attendant consequences.

A dearth of historical sources, however, makes it difficult to reconstruct the history of the East African coast before the seventh century of the Christian era. All the available sources, both documentary and numismatic, are the products of international trade, and we have little material on the history of the coast before the establishment of international contacts. The earliest Graeco-Roman documentary sources make only indirect (though often valuable) references to the east coast of Africa. Strabo (− 29 to + 19), who witnessed the period of Roman expansion under Augustus, not only gives contemporary and sometimes eye-witness accounts of the Red Sea region and Indian Ocean trade, but also incorporates fragments of earlier geographies now lost. Pliny (+ 23 to + 79) describes the Roman empire at its height, and is most valuable for his descriptions of trade and navigation in the Indian Ocean, and of the luxurious and decadent style of imperial Rome. The most important source for the Indian Ocean during this period, and the first direct, though meagre, account of the East African coast, is the *Periplus Maris Erythraei*, written apparently by an unknown Greek commercial agent based in Egypt. The *Periplus* is basically an eye-witness account.

A considerable increase in knowledge of the Indian Ocean in general and of East Africa in particular is noticeable in Ptolemy's *Geography*, written about + 156. Ptolemy is fairly specific in acknowledging his indebtedness for the East African material to Marinus of Tyre, who was definitely his contemporary. The last documentary source for the period is the *Christian Topography* of Cosmas Indicopleustes, written during the first half of the sixth century of the Christian era. It is most useful for its information on Ethiopia and on the ascendancy of the Persians in the Indian Ocean, but it displays ignorance about the coast of East Africa south of Cape Guardafui.

Unfortunately we still lack firm archaeological evidence about the East African coast during this period to confirm and complement the available documentary sources. What we do have is a number of coin collections which have come to light on the coast over the last three-quarters of a century. It should be pointed out, however, that none of these collections was found at a known or excavated archaeological site, and that the circumstances under which they were found have unfortunately been poorly recorded. At best we can say that numismatic evidence does not conflict with the available documentary sources, and that it is valuable as a pointer to the rhythm of international trade along the East African coast.

The earliest find consisted of six coins discovered at Kimoni, north of Tanga, 'in a mound "under" trees about 200 years old', apparently buried for a long time. The find covered a span between the third and the twelfth centuries of the Christian era. Therefore it could not have been deposited as a hoard before the latter date, but whether the earlier coins were brought to East Africa in pre-Islamic times remains uncertain. The second find consisted of a single gold piece of Ptolemy Soter (– 116 to – 108) and may have come from somewhere along the coast.

A number of collections of unknown provenance came to light in the Zanzibar Museum in 1955. The first, in an envelope marked Otesiphon (capital of the Parthian and Sassanid empires near Baghdad), consisted of five Persian coins ranging from the first to the third centuries of the Christian era. According to Freeman-Grenville, when he examined them they still had the 'especial type of dirt' typical of Zanzibar sticking to them, and he was in no doubt that they had been found somewhere in Zanzibar. The other two groups of coins also had this dirt sticking to them and were probably found in Zanzibar or Pemba. They covered a wider range, from the second century before the Christian era to the fourteenth century of the Christian era, which suggests that they were not hoards but collections of chance finds.

The remaining two finds pose similar problems of interpretation. Haywood claimed to have found a large collection of coins and a vessel shaped like a Greek amphora at Bur Gao (Port Dunford) in 1913. The vessel got broken during a storm and he unfortunately threw away the pieces. The collection seems to fall into two distinct portions. The first, which seems to form the core of the collection, consists of seventy-five coins of Ptolemaic Egypt, Imperial Rome and Byzantium, covering the period from the third century before the Christian era to the first half of the fourth century of the Christian era. The second portion consists of thirteen coins of Mameluk and Ottoman Egypt, ranging from the thirteenth century of the Christian era onwards. Wheeler suggests that 'the significance of the discovery is not necessarily vitiated' by the addition of the later Egyptian coins. These could have been added to the collection in the long interval before they passed into the hands of the numismatist. The core of the collection could thus have been deposited some time after the first half of the fourth century.

The other collection is reputed to have been dug up at Dimbani in southern Zanzibar by an old farmer, Idi Usi, now dead; and it passed into the hands of an amateur collector. The coins have been only tentatively identified. The core appears to consist of twenty-nine Roman coins and one Parthian coin of the first to the fourth centuries of the Christian era. The collection also includes a late twelfth-century Chinese coin and some later Islamic, European and even colonial African coins of the period down to the late nineteenth century. It may be suggested that, as in the case of the Haywood collection, the later coins were perhaps added to the core at a later stage.

The continental factor

The earliest evidence about the population of the East African coast comes from the *Periplus*, which describes the inhabitants of the coast as 'very great in stature'. Oliver suggests that they were Kushites, comparable to the Late Stone Age agriculturists who inhabited the Kenya highlands from about −1000, who according to the available archaeological evidence were men of 'tall stature'. The fact that iron objects figure among the imports suggests that the coastal peoples did not yet know how to work iron. There are several Kushitic-speaking pockets close to the coast and within the above-mentioned corridors, such as the Sanye people near the Tana and the Mbugu in Usumbara, who may be remnants of this early coastal population.

Archaeological evidence indicates a rapid infiltration of iron-using, probably Bantu-speaking people, into the coastal hinterland during the early centuries of the Christian era. They may well have moved up the coastal belt from the south and occupied the south Pare and Kwale areas behind Mombasa. Sunsequently they appear to have moved up the coast as far as Barawa, and up the Pangani corridor to the north Pare and Kilimanjaro region by the middle of the first millennium of the Christian era. In their expansion they probably assimilated the pre-existing population of the coastal belt.

From the available evidence it is difficult to obtain an adequate picture of the coastal economy and society before international commercial links were established. The people may have been agriculturalists, like the Late Stone Age Kushites of the interior. From the *Periplus* it is clear that fishing played an important role in the economy, and the document gives a very accurate description of fish-trapping using 'wicker baskets', a method still common along the coast. But the population appears to have been essentially coast-bound. They had dug-out canoes and small 'sewed boats', but not apparently deep-sea dhows. Unfortunately we have no evidence about socio-political organization in this period, for, though the *Periplus* mentions chiefs at each of the market-towns, international trade may have been a crucial factor in the rise of the chiefs and also of the market-towns. It thus appears that the population of the East African coast before the establishment of international commercial links was at a rather low level of technological, and probably also of socio-political, development. Hence, when international trading links were established, the initiative lay with the mariners from the northern rim of the Indian Ocean, with all the consequences that followed from that situation.

The oceanic factor

If accessibility from the land has made the East African coast historically an integral part of Africa, accessibility from the sea has subjected it to a long history of commercial contact, cultural influence and population movements from the lands across the Indian Ocean. The history of the western Indian Ocean until the seventh century is therefore to a considerable extent the history of interaction along two distinct lines, between East Africa and the Middle East, and between the latter and India; and also of the intermediary role played by the Middle East between the Indian Ocean and the Mediterranean.

Such interaction was made possible by the development of a suitable marine technology and the harnessing of the winds and currents of the Indian Ocean. The most important geographical characteristic of the Indian Ocean is the seasonal reversal of the monsoon winds. It is clear that by the beginning of the Christian era Indian Ocean mariners were already acquainted with the use of these winds. They had also overcome the technical problem of building a large enough vessel in an area without iron by resorting to 'sewing' planks together with vegetable fibres.

The spatial extent of reliable monsoons and the level of commercial organization in East Africa help to define the normal radius of action of the monsoon dhows. With a rather simple commercial organization involving a more direct exchange between foreign vessels and the market-towns, which appears to have been the case before the seventh century, the northern dhows are unlikely to have gone much farther south than Zanzibar.

Development of trade in the western Indian Ocean

The earliest historical evidence about the western Indian Ocean suggests that, contrary to common assertion in textbooks, there was no commercial intercourse, direct or otherwise, between East Africa and India before the seventh century of the Christian era. Even trade between India and the Middle East until the time of the *Periplus* appears to have been confined to a few luxuries. It seems likely that apart from gold and some other precious goods India was largely self-sufficient, especially in the staple 'forest' products that East Africa could have supplied. Indeed, India appears to have been an active exporter of ivory at this time, which probably delayed the exploitation of African ivory resources.

That exploitation appears to have been stimulated by the intense rivalry among Greek successor states after the death of Alexander. The firm control exercised by the Seleucids over the land-routes to India induced the Ptolemies of Egypt to seek ivory from elsewhere. The immediate need was to secure elephants. They therefore turned to the African coast of the Red Sea, establishing a series of elephant-hunting posts as far as the mouth of the Red Sea. The effect of the Ptolemies' policy was thus a tremendous expansion of the ivory trade.

The loss of Syria under Ptolemy V (−204 to −181), and the growing demand in Italy for Arabian and Indian commodities at a time when the immediate hinterland of the Red Sea coast was apparently being depleted of ivory, forced Egypt to turn to the southern sea-route in order to maintain some commercial contact with India. By the end of the second century before the Christian era, Eudoxus took advantage of a shipwrecked Indian pilot to make the first direct voyage to India. Indian trade continued to grow sufficiently in importance for officers to be appointed 'in charge of the Red and Indian Seas' between −110 and −51. Egyptian trade with India at that time was therefore largely indirect, through the south-west Arabian entrepôts. South-west Arabia thus occupied a crucial middleman's position and appropriated its share of commercial profit which became proverbial.

The south-west Arabians also appear to have controlled the other branch of trade which led down the East African coast. It has already been suggested that one of the driving forces for Ptolemaic commercial expansion down the Red Sea was the increasing demand for Oriental luxuries, including ivory. It is therefore possible that the Arabs extended their commercial activities to the East African coast at this time to supply that demand for ivory. Exactly how early and how far down the coast these trading connections extended in the pre-Roman period is difficult to determine in the absence of archaeological evidence. To date, only one Ptolemaic gold coin of the late second century before the Christian era has allegedly been found in the vicinity of Dar es-Salaam, while the twenty-two Ptolemaic coins in the Haywood collection could not have been deposited before the fourth century of the Christian era at the earliest.

Expansion of trade under the Romans

The establishment of the Roman empire under Augustus resulted in a tremendous increase in the demand for Oriental commodities in the Mediterranean. As Pliny complained: 'By the lowest reckoning India, China and the [Arabian] peninsula take from our empire 100 million sesterces every year – that is the sum which our luxuries and our women cost us.' The expansion of the market under Augustus brought about a more aggressive policy in the Red Sea designed to break the Arab monopoly over the Oriental trade. The Romans sought to establish a direct sea-route to India, and to control the southern end of the 'incense route' with an expedition in −24 under Gallus.

Despite the Roman entry into the Indian Ocean trade, however, the *Periplus* itself gives a picture of a very lively trade still in the hands of the Indians and Arabs. The Indians traded actively in the Persian Gulf and the Red Sea, but apparently not south of Cape Guardafui. While the Arabs shared the Indian trade with the Indians and increasingly the Romans, they seem to have enjoyed a virtual monopoly over the trade with the East African coast, a fact which is corroborated by Roman ignorance of the African coast south of Cape Guardafui before the *Periplus*. Moreover, though the latter document is undoubtedly an eye-witness account of the East African coast, the fact that only four paragraphs are devoted to it suggests that the region still lay beyond the normal range of Graeco-Roman activities.

Assimilation of the East African coast into the Roman economic system

Whatever the level of Arab commercial activity along the East African coast in the pre-Roman period, it is almost certain that it received a fresh stimulus as a result of the economic unification and increased opulence of the Roman empire. The demand for ivory grew enormously as the Romans began to use it not only for statues and combs but also for chairs, tables, bird-cages and carriages; there was even an ivory stable for the imperial horse. By the first century of the Christian era, ivory could be obtained only from far into the interior in the Upper Nile region, coming down to Adulis. Consequently the supply of ivory from the East African coast, though it was considered to be of a lower quality than that of Adulis, assumed a greater importance. It served to integrate the region even further into the international system of trade centred on the Mediterranean through the south-west Arabian state of Himyar. The assimilation of the East African coast into the international system was therefore not only at the level of commerce, but also involved political domination and social penetration. The latter may thus have begun the process of creating a class of coastal sea-going and trading people of mixed parentage, who acted as local agents for the international system of trade.

Azania, as the Romans called the east coast of Africa south of Ras Hafun, was probably not economically unified. It consisted rather of a series of market-towns each with its own chief, each dependent on its own narrow hinterland for export commodities and each visited directly by the monsoon dhows. The *Periplus* mentions a number of places such as Sarapion, probably a few miles north of Merca, Nikon, probably Bur Gao (Port Dunford), and the Pyralean Islands, which have been identified with the Lamu archipelago. South of the Lamu archipelago there is indeed a change in the character of the coastline, as the *Periplus* so accurately described. Two days' sail beyond lay the island of Menouthias, 'about 300 stadia [about 55 kilometres] from the mainland, low and wooded'. Pemba is the first major island that the northern mariners would encounter, and probably the only one that could have been reached in two days from Lamu. Moreover Pemba is in fact 50 kilometres from the mainland, as against 36 kilometres in the case of Zanzibar.

The only market-town along the coast south of Ras Hafun mentioned in the *Periplus* was Rhapta, which was probably located between Pangani and Dar es-Salaam. Rhapta was apparently governed by a local chief but under the overall suzerainty of the south-west Arabian state.

The *Periplus*, however, gives the impression that that suzerainty consisted of little more than a monopoly of external trade exercised by Arab captains and agents of Muza. The most important economic function of the port was the export of 'a great quantity of ivory', rhinoceros horns, high-quality tortoiseshell and a little coconut-oil. These were exchanged primarily for iron goods, particularly 'lances made at Muza especially for this trade', hatchets, daggers and awls, various kinds of glass and 'a little wine and wheat, not for trade, but to serve for getting the goodwill of the savages'.

That trade was growing rapidly in the early centuries of the Christian era is indicated by Ptolemy during the first half of the second century. Along the Somali coast a new emporium had arisen called Essina, and Sarapion and Nikon (Toniki) are now described as 'port' and 'emporium' respectively. But the most spectacular development had occurred at Rhapta, which is now described as a 'metropolis' (in Ptolemaic usage implying the capital of a state), and there is no longer any reference to Arab suzerainty.

Thus by the middle of the second century a large part of the East African coast and at least part of the Pangani corridor had been drawn into the international system of trade. The momentum which had pushed the commercial frontier into East African waters began to weaken as the Roman empire entered its long period of decline in the third century. A shift occurred in international trade from spices, precious stones and ivory to cotton and industrial products. Direct trade may have ceased altogether, as the marked gap in numismatic evidence suggests, but there was a brief revival at the end of the third and the beginning of the fourth centuries with the political reconsolidation of the empire. Existing numismatic evidence for East Africa is unsatisfactory, though it seems to show a similar fluctuation. The Haywood collection included six Imperial Roman coins dated to the mid-second century of the Christian era, followed by a gap until the end of the third and the fourth centuries which is represented by seventy-nine coins. In the Dimbani collection there seems to be only one coin of the first century, while the rest of the identified Roman coins seem to belong to the third and fourth centuries of the Christian era.

The realignment of East Africa's external relations

The disintegration of the system of international trade probably had a similarly catastrophic effect on another state which had become dependent on it: Himyar in south-west Arabia. The decline in the Roman demand for the frankincense it produced, and for other Oriental luxuries for which it was the middleman, undoubtedly affected its well-being, and laid it open to invasions from Ethiopia and later Persia. On the sea it may have lost much of its middleman's role partly to the Ethiopians, whose port of Adulis emerged as a centre for the export of upper Nile ivory to the Mediterranean.

The Ethiopians, however, do not appear to have been able to step fully into the shoes of the Arabs as carriers of trade in the western Indian Ocean. Farther east, Persia was emerging as a significant maritime power. The command of the western Indian Ocean by the Persians in the sixth and seventh centuries, especially in view of the decline of the Arabs and the inability of the Ethiopians to replace them, strongly suggests that they had a dominant commercial influence over the East African coast. No archaeological evidence from the pre-Islamic period has so far been unearthed along the coast, except for the five Parthian and Sassanid coins of the first three centuries of the Christian era which may have been dug up somewhere in Zanzibar.

The Persians may also have begun to play an important role as an intermediary between East Africa and India. The collapse of the Roman empire had deprived East Africa of its major ivory market at a time when India was still largely self-sufficient. But already by the beginning of the sixth century Indian demand for ivory for the manufacture of bridal ornaments seems to have begun to outstrip local supply. That demand was securely based on the regular ritual destruction of these ornaments upon the termination of the Hindu marriage by the death of either of the partners. By the tenth century India and China were the most important markets for East African ivory.

23 East Africa before the seventh century

It is easier to acquire knowledge of the situation of the peoples and societies in East Africa after +100 than during the earlier periods. A great deal of research is now being done on these latter periods and the findings are leading to a constant revision of all or parts of the previous conclusions.

Study of the 2,000 years from −1000 to +1000 is difficult. It calls for sophisticated methods and a vast amount of information which archaeology has so far been largely unable to furnish.

The study which follows is therfore conjectural, hypothetical and even provocative on more than one point, in order to stimulate reflection and research.

The approach to the early history of East Africa is therefore a cultural one essentially, an attempt to reconstruct the way or ways of life, as far as the combined archaeological, anthropological and linguistic evidence will allow. Reference is frequently made to language groups. Linguistic definitions and classifications of peoples are commonly the most clear and convenient for anthropologists and historians. Those used in this chapter are clarified in the accompanying chart. They follow in general the scheme originally laid down in *Zamani* (edited by Ogot and Keiran, 1968), which was based on Greenberg's classification of African languages.

The southern savannah hunting tradition

Throughout the savannahs and light woodlands which cover most of Africa to the east and south of the great equatorial forest belt, the main population for many thousands of years before the Iron Age consisted of hunter-gatherers using bows and arrows and advanced stone-working techniques. These peoples were generally of a physical type which is represented now by the so-called San and Khoi Khoi inhabiting the Kalahari and its margins. Their language would have been of the Khoisan family. Nowadays these languages are confined to the Khoi and San of southern and south-western Africa, and in East Africa to two small separate groups living in north-central Tanzania – the Sandawe and Hadza.

The Hadza remain hunters and gatherers, few in number, fairly mobile and expert in finding and winning the wild food resources of their territory. The Sandawe, on the other hand, have for some time been growing crops and keeping goats and cattle.

Interesting, again, is the observation that this very territory of the Hadza and

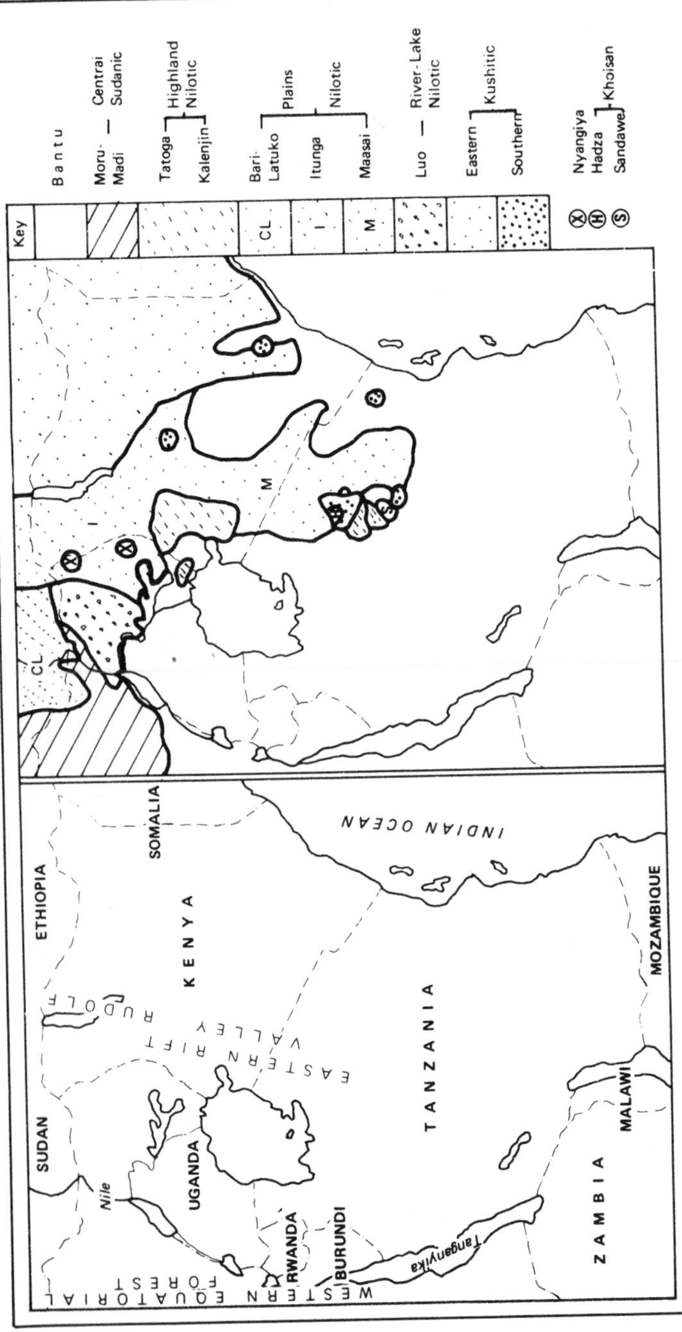

23.1 *East Africa: political map and map showing the distribution of languages and peoples (from J. E. G. Sutton)*

Sandawe and that which lies between them contains, unlike the rest of eastern Africa, numerous examples of hunter rock art, painted on the inner walls of natural shelters which were used from time to time during the Late Stone Age as temporary camps and family bases. These paintings have a social and often religious significance which is as yet poorly understood; but they also provide valuable indications of hunting methods, diet and daily life.

This extensive savannah hunter-gatherer way of life had a cultural sophistication and economic viability of its own. If it was the gathering side which produced the bulk of the food consumed, the more difficult and respected task of winning meat was essential for a balanced diet and for satisfying the appetite. All this depended on a degree of mobility, with seasonal camps but no permanent settlements, as the groups followed the game or exploited the vegetable resources of a territory, and this would have restrained population growth and perhaps inhibited change.

The greater part of the vast region once occupied by the hunter-gatherers became afterwards the domain of Bantu cultivators. In a number of these Bantu regions stories are told of chance encounters with small, strange folk who once lived and hunted in the bush and forest. These stories are not historically precise, yet they very likely reflect a core of vague memory handed down from the period a thousand years ago and more when the Bantu were colonizing this expanse of south-central Africa and gradually confining and assimilating the sparser Sandawe population with its very different way of life. A contrasting way in which this old hunting tradition may be reflected in later agricultural times is the prominence accorded to hunting feats and skills in Bantu legend.

But not the whole of East Africa became part of the Bantu world. As will be explained below, northern Uganda, much of Kenya and parts of north-central Tanzania have long been occupied by a range of distinct populations, with Kushitic, Nilotic and other languages, some of whom became established there during the Iron Age, others earlier. Here, as further south, there is clear ethnographic and archaeological evidence of the existence in both recent and ancient times of numerous hunter-gatherer communities.

These northerly regions of East Africa may well have constituted during much of the Late Stone Age a fluctuating frontier zone, partly determined by climatic changes, between the cultures of San-type populations of the southern savannahs and others of north-eastern and middle Africa. Of these regions much remains to be learned. However, at least two other distinct cultural traditions and broad ethnic entities, also lacking either agriculture or livestock, are identifiable within or bordering East Africa in recent millennia. They are the subjects of the following two sections.

The collecting and trapping tradition of the equatorial forest

In the rain-forest of the Congo Basin, and especially its easterly edges bordering on Rwanda and south-western Uganda, there live pygmy Negroes. Their range and numbers are smaller than in earlier times because of the gradual expansion of settled agricultural peoples, Bantu mainly, who have cleared much of the forest and reduced the natural food resources on which the pygmies used to live. Many of the latter have been assimilated, but others survive as independent bands, though maintaining relations with the neighbouring Bantu and speaking the latter's languages.

Although this forest life of the pygmies was, like that of the San, based economically on the hunting and collecting of wild animals and vegetables, it demanded a very different type of ecological adjustment and technological specialization. To include both pygmies and San under the same 'hunter-gatherer' label is to overlook their distinct ways of living and thinking, as alien to each other as either is to that of Bantu cultivators. The pygmy way of life, like that of the San, must represent an ancient cultural and economic tradition attached to a special environment, in this case the dense forest whose nature helps explain the distinctive physical features and short stature of these people.

However, historical evidence of any sort bearing on the pygmies and their former geographical extent is extremely scant, although in the Congo Basin some very tentative attempts have been made at correlating certain Late and Middle Stone Age remains (the Lupembo-Tshitolian complex). The distribution and dating of this complex does at least indicate an important forest and woodland tradition, ancient in origin and persisting into quite recent times. Its later phases are not well represented eastward of Rwanda; so, should it be the work of pygmies, it would not support a view of their extension into East Africa during the Late Stone Age, even at times when rainfall was higher and forests greater. There are, it is true, allusions to the former presence of pygmies in scattered parts of East Africa in random historical and anthropological writings. Some of these appear to be based on ethnographic misconceptions, others on folklore or vague oral-traditional evidence mentioning small hunter-gatherer peoples in the past. In so far as these accounts relate to specific peoples and relatively precise periods of time, they probably refer in most cases to San-type hunters of the savannah tradition or in the northerly portion of East Africa to separate groups, so-called Dorobo and other backwoodsmen.

The aquatic tradition of middle Africa

The question of the aquatic tradition, which has been neglected for so long, is taken up in the previous volume of this history. It will suffice here, therefore, to consider the final development of this interesting way of life.

By −5000 the climate of East Africa had turned markedly drier and the lakes had fallen far below their previous high levels, being fed by fewer and smaller rivers. Thus the geographical continuity and, in places, the economic basis of the aquatic way of life was undermined. The days of its cultural dominance were over. However, around −3000, conditions turned more humid again for a while and lake levels correspondingly rose (but not as high as in the seventh millennium). In the eastern Rift Valley in Kenya a modified aquatic culture was resuscitated at this time, perhaps through new migrations or contacts with the middle and upper Nile. Remains of this late aquatic phase, with unusual pottery styles and shallow stone bowls, have been found above Lakes Rudolf and Nakuru, dating generally, it seems, around −3000. Despite the apparent absence of harpoons from sites of this period, these people certainly fished. But very likely the diet was less predominantly aquatic than in the main phase of between three thousand and five thousand years earlier. By −2000, with the dry trend re-established, the viability of an aquatic culture was finally undermined in much of the eastern Rift Valley.

It appears that the population of this later aquatic phase was also basically negroid. Direct clues as to its language are lacking. But the most reasonable argument is that it belonged to one branch or other of the Chari-Nile family (the eastern division of Nilo-Saharan).

One would expect the great aquatic civilization, both its main phase between −8000 and −5000 and its later revival around −3000, to be represented along the rivers and swamps of the upper Nile Basin and in particular along the old shorelines of East Africa's biggest lake, Victoria Nyanza. Oddly, signs of this seem to be lacking for the millennia in question. However, by the first millennium before the Christian era, there were people who camped on islands and in rock-shelters and open stations, by the lake itself and by rivers in the region, whose diet included fish and molluscs, but also the flesh of bush game and perhaps of cattle and sheep. Whether some of these people cultivated at all is very uncertain; but there is some interesting evidence of forest clearance around Lake Victoria at this time, which is indicative at least of some new and relatively intensive form of land use. The pottery of these people, known as Kansyore ware, bears some striking affinities to the much older dotted wavy-line ware of the early aquatic tradition. As far as is known, these wares had been superseded long before in the Nile Valley; and it is unlikely therefore that the Kansyore types were simply introduced to Lake Victoria as late as the first or second millennium before the Christian era. More likely, the aquatic tradition stretches back several millennia here as elsewhere, but all that has been recognized of it so far is its most recent and run-down phase immediately before the Iron Age.

While there are no direct clues to the language-group to which these Lake Victoria people of the first millennium before the Christian era belonged, it is possible that it was Central Sudanic (a division of Chari-Nile). This region and that to the south was from the beginning of the Iron Age populated by Bantu; and, according to one linguistic school of thought, these Bantu in their process of settlement assimilated an older and smaller population of Central Sudanic speakers from whom they learned about sheep and cattle and how to keep them. Having no words of their own for these things, the Bantu borrowed them from the earlier inhabitants of these regions whose own languages have become extinct. South of Lake Victoria no reasonable archaeological support for this hypothesis has yet been found; but around the lake itself a case can be made for identifying the sites with Kansyore ware with the Central Sudanic language-group, especially if the association in some places with the remains of sheep and cattle in the first millennium be correct. Maybe an isolated and very declined aquatic tradition was at this time reinvigorated by contact on its eastern side with a new pastoral tradition which established itself in the Kenya highlands.

The Kushitic pastoral tradition

As the drier climatic regime became firmly established by the second millennium, not only did the lakes retreat to approximately their present levels (and the fish become extinct in some cases), but the forests receded also, leaving in their place, most notably in the eastern Rift and across the adjacent plateaux, fine upland pastures. And, though around Lake Victoria and by several other lakes and rivers one could still fish and maintain some of the elements of the old aquatic life, this tradition had now lost its great geographical continuity and the cultural assurance which formerly went with it. The new prestige in much of the middle African belt, and especially its eastern end, was cattle-keeping, and to continue to live by and off the water was commonly seen as backward and intellectually stagnant. It was not only an archaic way of life: it was, in the view of the more successful pastoral groups, uncouth and unclean. The first pastoralists in East Africa identified themselves not only by their Kushitic speech and their insistence on circumcision, but also by a taboo against fish.

For a long time now cattle, in those parts of East Africa with grass of sufficient quality and quantity and free from tsetse and endemic diseases, have been an object of prestige and an indication of wealth. But it is important to understand that this cattle ideology is based on hard economic sense. Cattle provide meat and, more important, milk; and, even among people who rely on their fields for most of their food, livestock are an important source of protein and also a safeguard against famines periodically caused by drought or pests. Moreover, one should not overlook the important role of goats and sheep, which commonly provide the main sources of meat to communities concentrating on cattle-keeping and on agriculture alike.

The economy was not exclusively pastoral. Antelopes and other game were hunted, especially perhaps by some of the poorer communities. It is not yet known for certain whether types of sorghum or millet or other foods were cultivated by these people, but the likelihood is strong. To begin with, the amount of pottery at some of the sites suggests that part at least of the population was more settled than would have been the case in a purely pastoral community, while the grinding equipment also hints at the cultivation, preparation and consumption of grain. However, these big, flat grindstones and the accompanying pestles could have been used for crushing wild vegetables or even non-food items. For instance, some of those left in graves are stained with red ochre with which the corpses had been adorned. But this observation need not rule out a utilitarian purpose in everyday life. A more persuasive argument for assuming some cultivation is that, without the ability to turn to alternative sources of food in times of severe crisis following prolonged droughts or cattle epidemics, it is unlikely that such societies could have survived long; and hunting and gathering would have sufficed as a temporary stopgap and main source of food for only very small and dispersed groups. Nevertheless, a cultural accent on cattle-keeping and a predominant economic reliance on livestock is illustrated by the geographical distribution of these people, virtually confining themselves to those regions with fine extensive grasslands. The crater highlands in northern Tanzania, containing the green bowl of Ngorongoro with its cemeteries of this period, were the essential southern limit of this long pastoral zone. A people more committed to combining their stock-raising with agriculture would have spread out farther into fertile districts on their eastern and western sides and could have continued farther southwards.

The pottery styles and certain other features of the material culture of these early pastoralists of the highlands and Rift Valley of Kenya and northern Tanzania betray influences from the middle Nile region. But the reflection is a pale one, the influences probably indirect. They do not necessarily mean that the cattle and their herders originated in that region. Rather, they may result from contact with and assimilation of the late aquatic population with its own more ancient Nile connections which was previously established by the Rift Valley lakes. An illustration of this is the continuity of the strange stone bowls in this region through some two thousand years, from late aquatic times to early pastoral ones.

Difficult though it is to generalize on physical types, one gets the clear impression that the populations to the west of this line are very typically negroid and that those in the highlands and plains to the east are rather less so. Language studies point to influences from Ethiopia to the East African highlands, keeping all the time a little to the east of the cultural divide. Ethiopia is the ancient home of the Kushitic language-family; and most of the present Bantu and Nilotic languages of Kenya and of north-eastern and north-central Tanzania reveal evidence of borrowing from Kushitic tongues. In a few places, notably at the southern end of this zone, such southern Kushitic languages actually persist, though of course highly diverged from the old Kushitic forms. Among the important cultural-historical messages which the word-borrowings provide is the contribution to cattle-keeping made by the early Kushitic populations in East Africa.

The Kushitic cultural element in East African history is reflected in other ways, and up to a point in the non-chiefly social and political institutions, based on age-organization, of the peoples of the plains and highlands of Kenya and parts of northern Tanzania. But this observation is a very general one, and not all aspects of these systems need be traceable to the original Kushitic settlement. Of more specifically Kushitic origin must be the custom of circumcision in initiation, whose distribution coincides remarkably closely with that of substantial word-borrowings from Kushitic and the aversion to fish in the same broad region.

We gain then a picture of a pastoral Kushitic-speaking people, tall and relatively light-skinned, expanding southwards and making themselves masters of the rich grasslands, the plains and more especially the plateaux, of Kenya and northern Tanzania about three thousand years ago. All this may sound just like a restatement of the now rejected Hamitic myth. The point is that, while the more illogical and romantic aspects of the various and vaguely stated Hamitic hypotheses do derive from prejudiced European scholarship and grostesque attitudes towards Africa and black peoples, the factual bases of these views were not entirely fictitious. Some of the observations were acute and certain of the historical interpretations very judicious. The error of the Hamitic school lay in its presuppositions and its obsession with origins of peoples and ideas. Failing to appreciate the local scene, it emphasized a particular set of external influences, that is, the Kushitic element and the pastoral prestige, rather than seeing this as but one of many parts of the East African historical and cultural experience – an experience in which the old savannah hunting tradition, the aquatic one established during the wet millennia, and more recently the Bantu with their attachment to iron and agriculture have been equally important elements.

The Bantu agricultural and iron-using tradition

While pastoralism and the associated fish taboo provided the cultural and ethnic hallmark of the Kushites in one zone of East Africa during the first millennium, that of the early Bantu during the following millennium was the working and use of iron. Much more important than this question of origin is the evident fact that the early Bantu depended on iron and were identified as the people who possessed its secrets. Probably the earlier peoples of East Africa were unfamiliar with it. For tools and weapons they had taken suitable stones and worked them by ancient techniques. For instance, the eastern Rift Valley in the Kushitic zone is blessed with sources of an unusually fine stone called obsidian (opaque volcanic glass), from which excellent blades of different sizes were readily producible for all sorts of purposes, including spearheads and probably circumcision-knives. The contemporaneous but distinct communities living around Lake Victoria, among whom the aquatic tradition persisted in part, were less fortunate than those in the Rift Valley in the stones available to them, but succeeded none the less in manufacturing complex tool-kits from quartz, chert and other stones with good flaking properties, as also did the savannah hunters in the regions southward. To all such varied peoples, the first contact with strangers practising an iron technology must have been a shattering intellectual experience.

The main expansion of the Bantu was vast and fast, not a series of gradual stages as some have argued. But it was a matter neither of purposeless nomadic wandering, nor of organized military conquest. It was a remarkable process of *colonization* – in the true sense of the word – the opening up of essentially empty lands. This Bantu expansion did not engulf the whole of the area considered here. About one-third of East Africa has remained non-Bantu on account of the resilience and adaptability of some of the earlier populations, especially in the long zone of the eastern Rift with its old Kushitic populations, augmented during the Iron Age by the arrival of certain Nilotic divisions. (See the linguistic map and the preceding and succeeding sections.)

This interpretation of Bantu expansion and settlement in East Africa (and in countries to the south and west) at the beginning of the Iron Age is based on a combination of linguistic and archaeological evidence, as well as general ethnographic considerations. The obvious point about the numerous Bantu languages, especially those outside the Congo forest, is their close common relationship which points to a quite recent separation and differentiation, of the order of some one or two thousand years. Another thing which emerges from a comparative study of Bantu languages is an acquaintance with iron and the skills of working it from early times. This is one reason for associating the early Iron Age archaeological sites, dating from the early and middle parts of the first millennium of the Christian era, in many districts of eastern and south-central Africa with the Bantu colonization. But a more compelling reason for confidently identifying these sites as those of the early Bantu is simply that their distribution agrees so nicely with that of present Bantu peoples. There are no sensible grounds for theorizing that a quite different population covered this same broad region, only to disappear completely no more than a thousand years ago.

The most frequent and diagnostic objects found on these early Bantu sites are not iron tools and weapons (for these were usually too valuable to be discarded and, even

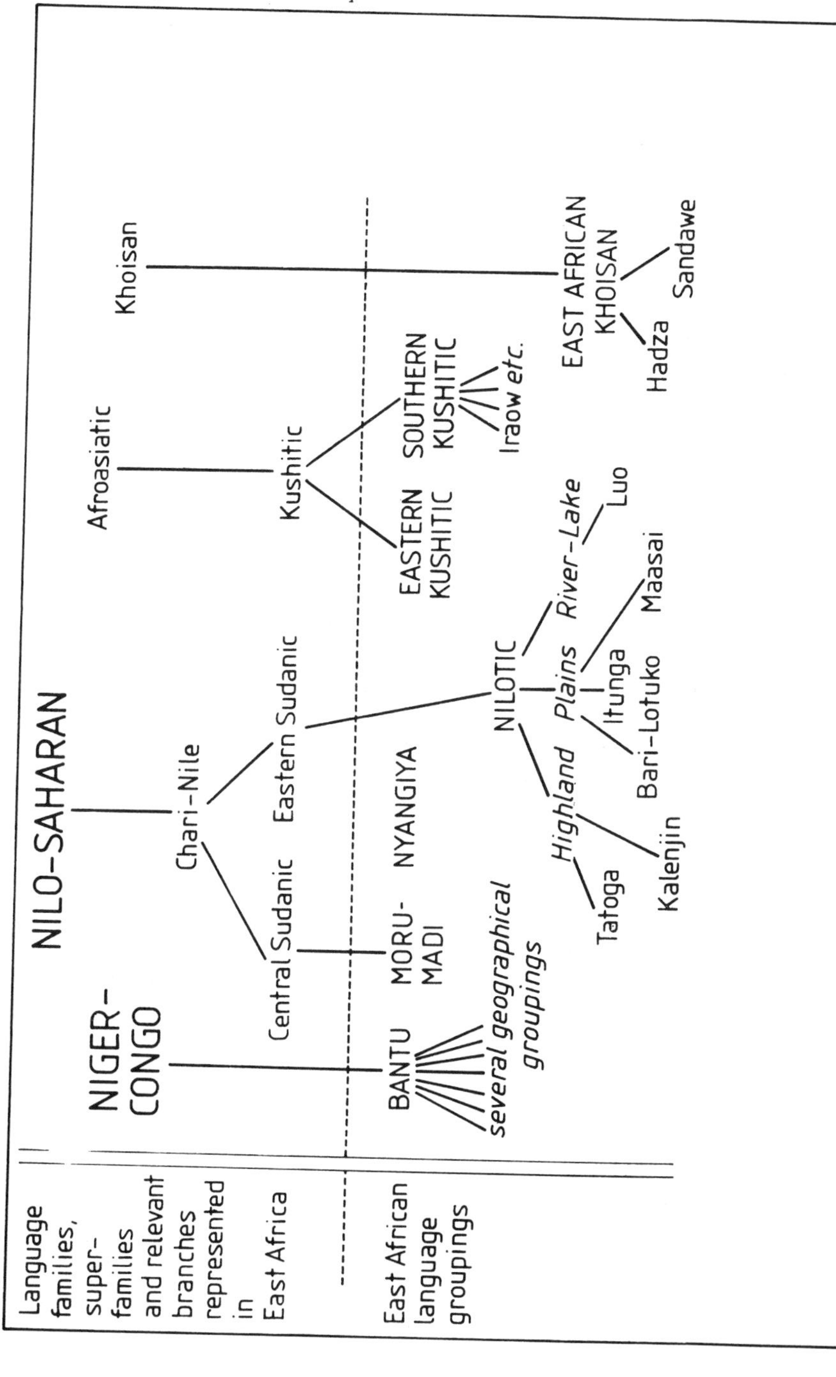

23.2 *East African language groupings and relationships (from J. E. G. Sutton)*

if they had been, would normally have corroded completely), but the broken pieces of earthenware pots. From the very beginning these pottery wares were by no means identical region by region throughout the enormous span of Bantu settlement. New types are being recognized continually by archaeologists. Perhaps the best known are the dimple-based (or Urewa) wares found around Lake Victoria and further west, extending to the northern end of Lake Tanganyika and the woodlands south of the forest in Zaïre. Besides the dimples on the bases of some of these vessels, many have elaborately shaped rims and remarkable decoration in scrolls and other patterns. To the south and east of the dimple-based zone, the early Iron Age wares fall into two main groupings. In north-eastern Tanzania and south-eastern Kenya, that is beyond the great Kushitic bulge, Kwale ware, as it is called, occurs from the highland edges down to the coastal plain. At the southern end of Lake Tanganyika, and in the countries farther south, a whole plethora of regional wares has been identified. (These include those in Zambia previously known as 'channelled').

The Nilotes: adaptation and variation

Beside the Bantu, another language group – or rather series of distantly related language groups – occupied much of East Africa during the Iron Age. These were the Nilotes. While their physical features differ in certain general respects from those of the Bantu, the Nilotes are very pronouncedly negroid. It is true, nevertheless, that those Nilotic-speakers who have moved furthest eastward and southward into the old Kushitic zone of Kenya and northern Tanzania have assimilated some of the previous Ethiopoid population. This helps to account for the original negroid features of the present Itunga, Maasai, Kalenjin and Tatoga groupings. These are the people who were in the past classified as 'Nilo-Hamites'. Their partly Kushitic ancestry is further shown – but in a variety of ways among these different groups – in their cultural heritage. This has involved considerable word-borrowing from Kushitic tongues. But basically their languages remain Nilotic.

The divisions within the Nilotic languages – between the Highland, River-Lake and Plains Nilotes – are deep and ancient (considerably more so than those in Bantu, for instance). And, while a date for the break-up of 'parent Nilotic' cannot be accurately estimated, it could not have been less than two thousand years ago. This would have occurred somewhere in the southern Sudan, possibly towards the Ethiopian border. From this general region representatives of each of the three divisions have moved into northerly, and even central parts of East Africa during the last two thousand years. However, the extensions of Plains Nilotes (notably the Itunga group in eastern Uganda and north-western Kenya, and the Masai in Kenya and northern Tanzania) and the River-Lake Nilotes (the Lwoo of Uganda and the Kenya lake-shore) belong to the present millennium and are therefore the concern of later volumes of this *History*. In this volume our main concern is limited to the Highland division of Nilotic, represented nowadays by the Kalenjin of the western Kenya highlands and the Tatoga scattered over various grasslands in northern Tanzania.

The early Highland Nilotes are not yet known archaeologically; but their present distribution and internal linguistic comparison show that they must have established themselves in Kenya quite a thousand years ago. It is possible that their emergence as a group with an identity, culture and language of their own had begun with the coming of iron to the upper Nile Basin and the Ethiopian borderlands. In these regions and in the Kushitic zone, it is likely that the knowledge of iron and the skills of working it derived from a northerly source. This would have been independent of its adoption by the early Bantu, who were probably responsible for the expansion of iron-working in western and southern parts of East Africa.

The majority of the Nilotes remained in the Nile Basin, mainly in the southern Sudan. Here they were not directly influenced by Kushitic ways, and they usefully combined stock-keeping, grain cultivation and fishing. However, the Plains division eventually split into three principal branches, and it is instructive to observe their range of cultural and environmental adaptations from north-west to south-east. Among the Bari-Lotuko cluster in the southern Sudan and the borders of northern Uganda, a fairly typical Nilotic life has been maintained. In the rather dry hills and plains which cross from northern Uganda into Kenya, herded by the Itunga grouping (Karamojong, Turkana, Teso, etc.), fishing is infrequent, though this may be attributable to the scarcity of opportunities as much as to a cultural prohibition. Beyond the Itunga, the third branch of the Plains Nilotes, the Maasai, has extended across a very large part of the highlands and plateau grasslands of Kenya and northern Tanzania. Here in recent centuries they have assimilated and been strongly influenced by the earlier settled Highland Nilotes and, directly or indirectly, by the southern Kushitic. They have adopted not only the fish taboo, but also circumcision. In these fine pastures, in fact, the central Masai sections succeeded recently in pursuing the pastoral ethic to its ultimate extreme.

These are by no means all the examples that could be cited of Nilotic expansion and assimilation often of a seemingly haphazard sort – assimilation of other Nilotic divisions and sudivisions as well as of non-Nilotes, and processes of expansion frequently demanding both ecological and cultural adaptations. In the southern Sudan and in northern and eastern Uganda the interactions which have taken place during the present millennium, and probably the preceding one too, between certain branches of the Plains and River-Lake Nilotes have been quite as complex as those just noted between Nilotes and Kushites and between older Nilotes and newer Nilotes in the Kenya and northern Tanzania highlands.

The East African 'megalithic' problem

In older literature on eastern Africa and its history there was considerable discussion of advanced civilizations in antiquity. These were posited in the interlacustrine region and more particularly in the highlands of Kenya and northern Tanzania (the old Kushitic zone, interestingly), among others. Such historical views were based on a mixture of ethnographic traits, unscientifically collected 'oral traditions' and archaeological observations, the last consisting of the remains of supposed 'engineering' works and the ruins of buildings and terraces of dry stone (that is 'megalithic'). Unfortunately, much of the primary evidence was inaccurately recorded or, even where accurate, was illogically interpreted or correlated with quite irrelevant materials to please fanciful historical outlooks which were fashionable at the time, notably the notorious Hamitic ideas. This tendency was all too eagerly taken up by secondary writers who uncritically accepted, and in some cases irresponsibly exaggerated, the supposed primary evidence. Equally illogical was the presumption so often made that various types of archaeological features, whether genuine or bogus, whether with or without stonework, distributed over a wide region, should be attributable to a single people or culture at a particular period of the past. Such a presumption underlay Huntingford's theory of an Azanian civilization in Kenya and northern Tanzania, which he attributed to Hamites, and equally Murdock's hypothesis of megalithic Kushites having once inhabited the same general region. (Murdock, by the way, was specifically opposed to the Hamitic prejudices of earlier writers.)

The word megalithic is thus a loaded one which serves no cultural or historical purpose in East Africa. It is worth, nevertheless, briefly noting and commenting on those features which have been cited as evidence of ancient megalithic cultures. Not all are in fact stone constructions. Many, if not most, of the cairns (or stone mounds), which represent graves, frequently encountered in the pastures of Kenya and northern Tanzania date from the end of the Late Stone Age between two and three thousand years ago and are probably the work of Kushitic-speaking peoples. But some may be more recent. It is possible, but by no means certain, that some of the rock-cut wells which occur in the drier pastures of southern Masailand in Tanzania, and also of eastern and northern Kenya, may date back to the same period when cattle were introduced. So, perhaps, may some of the so-called ancient roads in the highlands, which are in fact nothing more than cattle-tracks accidentally eroded by the continual passing of herds across ridges and down slopes to water over periods of time. Many of these are still being enlarged, and new ones started. Less likely to extend back so far are the practices of irrigated agriculture pursued on and below several of the Rift escarpments and mountain passes of northern Tanzania and Kenya. On the other hand, it can be demonstrated that these are at least a few centuries old in places. Much more rare and much less important for historical argument, despite what has been written, are hillside agricultural terraces. Only in very peculiar or marginal situations were these constructed. Some accounts even speak of monoliths and stone phalli in the East African interior: it is highly doubtful whether any such things ever stood there!

There is, however, a little more to the East African megalithic issue than this. One also reads of stone houses and enclosures and pit-dwellings. Though here again there have been some inaccurate description and misinterpretation, there are some bases of archaeological fact to be faced. The features in question consist of types of dry-stone walling and revetting and lie in two separate areas. Culturally, too, these two complexes were quite separate from each other, interesting though it is that they were roughly contemporary, each dating essentially to the middle centuries of the present millennium (incidentally, well outside the period properly covered in this volume). The first of these complexes comprises the so-called Sirikwa Holes, which are extremely numerous over the whole of the western highlands of Kenya. The second complex lies similarly on the western side of the great Rift Valley, but some distance to the south beyond the Tanzania border.

24 West Africa before the seventh century

Critical appraisal of the available archaeological and other relevant data does not support the popular belief that outside cultural influence was mainly responsible for the origins, development and overall character of the Neolithic and 'Iron Age' societies of West Africa. In particular, it is wrong to claim that ideas and peoples from outside, usually from the north across the Sahara, stimulated or generated most major developments pertaining to early food production or the earliest working of iron and copper. The data suggest rather that complex regional, sub-regional and local factors were variably important and that West African Neolithic and Iron Age sites, explicable to a greater or lesser extent within systems of sites, integrated as much as possible with the major ecological constraints at work.

The origins of agriculture and animal husbandry

Plant succession and soil studies of prehistoric sites (hitherto grossly neglected) have a major role to play in understanding how and when the change from hunting and gathering occurred in West Africa – especially as 'direct' evidence is often lacking.

Domestication in this context means the process of withdrawing animals from natural selection processes; directing their reproduction; making them serve man (by their work and/or their products); and modifying their characteristics by selective breeding, while losing some old character traits. Plant cultivation here refers to the deliberate planting of tubers or seeds and the protection of fruit trees, vines, etc., with a view to obtaining for human use an appreciable quantity of these tubers, seeds and fruits.

Ecological studies indicate, first, that animal domestication is feasible in the semi-arid tropical and subtropical savannah areas because the soil pH is fairly high (± 7.0), and consequently the macro-elements (nitrogen and phosphorus) are relatively readily assimilable and pastures have a relatively high protein content. Secondly, and in contrast, such studies indicate that domesticated animals are not an important feature of food production in the humid tropical regions partly because the soil pH and the assimilability of the macro-elements nitrogen, phosphorus and calcium are generally low; hence the pasturage is high in cellulose and crude fibre, and has a high heat increment value. Heat production and dissipation by the animals are thus real problems for livestock in the humid tropics. To maintain thermal equilibrium in such regions, cattle are usually small, giving them a large surface area per unit weight and facilitating heat dissipation. Where some domesticated animals were in fact kept, the problem of high temperatures appears to have been overcome by the selection of small livestock which could adapt to tropical conditions.

Thirdly, ecological studies show that the annual plants cultivated in most of West Africa, in complete contrast to those of the Middle East, were and still are adapted to growth in a season of high temperature and high humidity. Except in the cool and relatively dry highlands, Middle Eastern cereals fail completely because of their inability to withstand pathogens that flourish at high temperatures.

Palaeontological, botanical, ecological, ethnographic and archaeological data, all combined, suggest that at the general level the food-producing complexes first adopted were farming (crop cultivation), pastoralism, and mixed farming (i.e. a combination of animal rearing and plant cultivation). At the specific level, these food-producing complexes varied according to the kinds of crops cultivated, the animals kept and the ways in which these were harvested or reared and the settlement and social systems adopted.

Indeed, archaeological and ethnographic data suggest the existence in West Africa of (i) early cattle herding in the northern and eastern Sahara; (ii) early seed-crop complexes, possibly practising permanent field systems, on the slopes and scraps of the central Saharan highlands; (iii) seed-cropping complexes in parts of the Sahel and northern savannah regions, with influences impinging on these from both north and south (in this connection, it appears that the inland delta of the Niger, the edge of the Futa Jallon hills in the upper basin of the Senegal, Niger and Gambia rivers, and the Sudanic environments in general, may have been nuclear areas for crops like rice (*Oryza glaberrima*), millets (*Digitaria*), guinea corn and bulrush millets); (iv) mixed farming and cattle herding in the central and eastern Sahel regions and parts of the northern savannah regions, where the desiccation of the Sahara may have played an important role; and (v) root and tree complexes in the forest fringe regions to the far south.

These early 'Neolithic' complexes were characterized by distinctly different artefact complexes, as well as (largely inferred) different settlement and social patterns and land-use methods. In some areas, however (e.g. Tiemassas, Senegal and Paratoumbian, Mauretania), two or more traditions met and overlapped.

Early cattle-herding Neolithic complexes of the north

Remains of domestic shorthorn cattle have been found at Uan Muhuggiag, south-west Libya, and Adrār Bous, Aïr, and the dates obtained suggest domestication of cattle from −5590 (±200) in the former area and −3830 to −3790 in the latter. At Uan Muhuggiag the remains of sheep were also found. The short-horned type of cattle does not, however, appear to have existed in the Nile Valley before the Eleventh Dynasty (−2600), although there is evidence for the long-horned type at Kom Ombo in Egypt during the Pleistocene.

Cultural evidence suggests that in Libya there may have been an early instance of transition from hunting and gathering to pastoralism, which extended as far to the south-east as Adrār Bous (Tenereen, −4000 to −2500) and as far to the south-west as

Tishīt (Khimiya phase, post –1500). In these areas the pastoralists appear to have been direct descendants of earlier inhabitants and the new way of life probably replaced or was combined with a seed-cropping Neolithic. If so, it means either that the concept of cattle domestication was transferred to these areas, or that they were on the outskirts of a large nuclear zone of cattle domestication. Radio-carbon dates from sites reporting domesticated *Bos* indicate possible expansion of cattle from the Saharan heartlands into the southern Sahara and Sahel zones of West Africa, and some form of relationship with the desiccation of the desert region.

Early seed-cropping Neolithic complexes

The central Saharan highlands

Such evidence as exists suggests that seed-cropping, but *not any other form of cultivation*, probably occurred much earlier here than anywhere to the south. The earliest evidence for this early form of Neolithic comes mainly from rock-shelter sites at Amekni and Meniet in the Hoggar. At Amekni in contexts dated to –6100 and –4850, Camps recovered two pollen grains which are considered, because of their size and shape, to represent a domesticated variety of *Pennisetum*. From Meniet, Pons and Quezel identified two pollen grains belonging to a level dated to about –3600 which may be a cultivated cereal.

Other less conclusive evidence for seed-crop cultivation in this area comes from the rock shelter at Sefar in the Tassili, radio-carbon dated to about –3100. Paintings in this shelter appear to depict cultivation, while linguistic evidence suggests a considerable antiquity for sorghum cultivation in the central Sahara. Apart from occupying rock shelters, the prehistoric people of this region also occupied relatively large permanent villages or settlements on hillsides and the edges of escarpments overlooking lakes or wadis. They made polished and flaked axes, grinders and querns, dimple stones, rubbers, pottery and many kinds of flake tools.

The southern Sahara, the Sahel and parts of the savannah regions of West Africa

The Neolithic in these parts of West Africa has often been regarded as the result of northern influences; and there may well be some justification for this view, since some of the Late Stone Age products in this area show affinities with the post-Palaeolithic complexes of the Hoggar or of the eastern Sahara and the Maghrib. But the main archaeological traditions characteristic of the Early Neolithic (Late Stone Age) in this area show distinctive traits, especially in pottery, tools and settlement size and pattern. Most settlements at that time were located on escarpments or on flat land near lakes or wadis. Three main traditions may be discerned, probably reflecting differences in economic and social patterns:

(i) At the northern fringe of this region are industries, such as those of the Tenereen and Bel-air (Senegal), which are based on blades, and include a variety of geometrical microliths and/or projectiles, few or no polished or ground stone items; settlement areas are relatively small.

(ii) In the central areas, such as Borku, Ennedi, Tilemsi, Ntereso and Daima, industries are found which lack geometrical microliths, but have a variety of

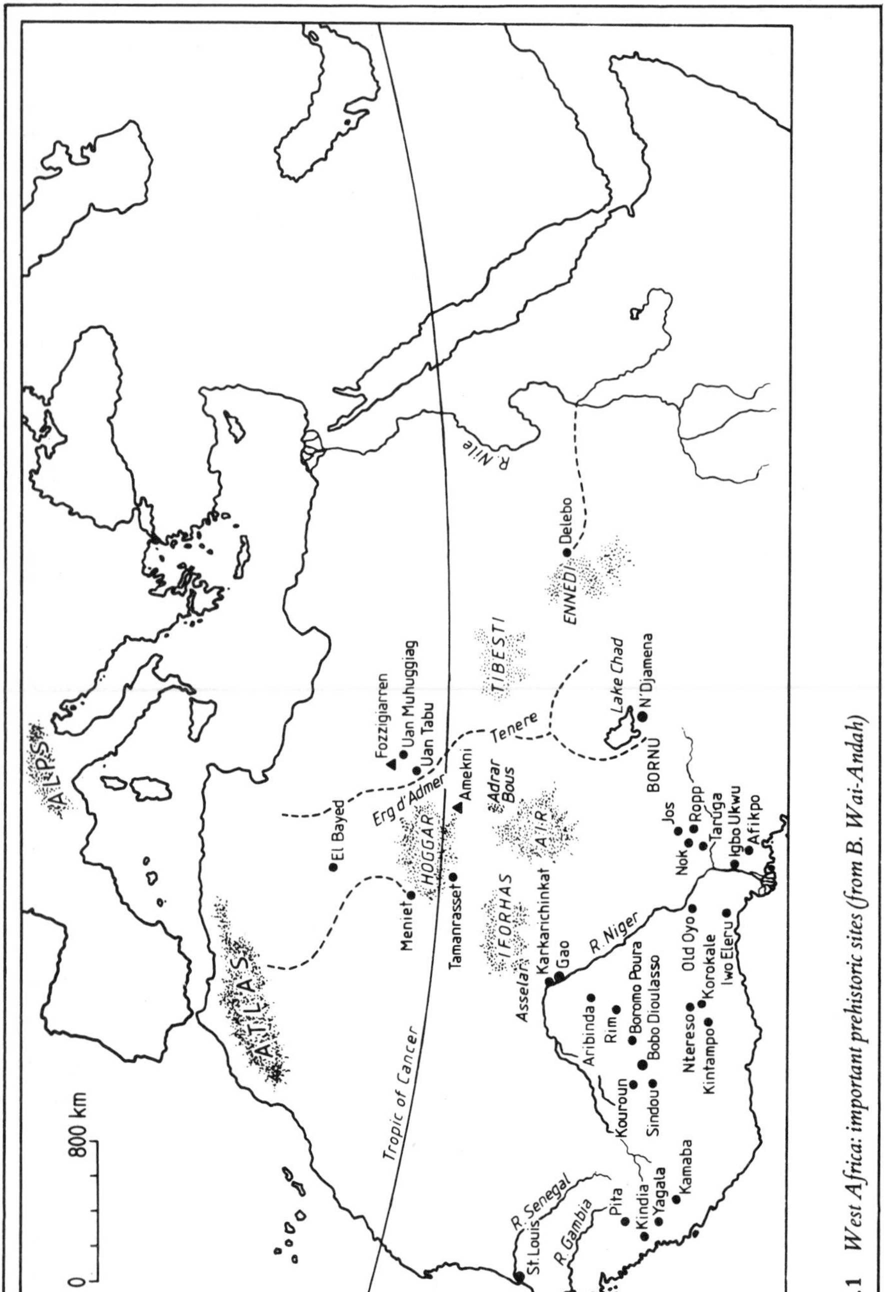

24.1 *West Africa: important prehistoric sites (from B. Wai-Andah)*

projectiles, fish-hooks and harpoons, and some polished and ground stone items. Settlement areas here are relatively large.

(iii) The third group of industries to the south, represented principally by Nok and Kintampo, is virtually devoid of blades, geometrical microliths and projectiles, but is rich in polished and ground stone tools. This group is characterized by relatively larger and apparently more permanent settlements.

The Tilemsi Valley complexes

Evidence from the Karkarichinkat sites shows that, during at least the later part of the most recent wet phase of the Sahara (– 2000 to – 1300), this area was inhabited by pastoral peoples with a way of life not very dissimilar from that of some present-day semi-nomadic pastoralists such as the Nuer of the Sudan and the Fulbe of West Africa. The Karkarichinkat South sites resemble fishing and herding camps, as witness the abundance of bivalve shells, fishbones and *Bos* remains with few or no stone artefacts except fish-hooks. In contrast the abundance of pottery, clay figurines of animals and stone artefacts (especially a great variety of projectiles) at Karkarichinkat North all suggests a shift away from standing water and a greater involvement in herding, hunting and possibly some plant cultivation.

The cultural groups who lived in northern Tilemsi, around Asselar, had an industry similar to the Tenereen of the Sahara region (Tixier, + 1962) and at least as old (skeletal material has been dated to – 4400). Both groups contain grindstones, polished axes and scrapers; geometrical microliths are rarer in the lower Tilemsi, and their projectiles and pottery are different. At Asselar and Karkarichinkat it would seem that besides herding cattle the people also hunted wild animals. Studies by Camps in the Admer Erg south of Tassili-n-Ajjer suggest that pastoralists with industries similar to the Tenereen existed as far north as this as well as occupying the Tassili-n-Ajjer and bordering plains from at least the fourth millennium before the Christian era.

The D͟hār Tis͟hīt region

Research in this part of southern Mauretania has revealed an eight-phase, well-dated, Late Stone Age sequence containing subsistence data which shed some light on the problem of early food production in this area in particular and in the region of the Senegal/Niger headwaters generally.

A plausible explanation for the development trend reported at Tis͟hīt, because it fits the archaeological data much better, would be as follows – special rearing and propagation of *Cenchrus biflorus* in the Khimiya phase (– 1500), then the intensification and expansion of this practice of incipient production and propagation of plants to include several other plants during the dry Naghez phase (– 1100).

The region south of Lake Chad

This region known as the *Firki*, comprises black clay plains which stretch away from the southern margins of Lake Chad and are thought to have been formed from lagoon deposits on the edge of a formerly larger lake. The zone is comparatively fertile and well watered. The soil is very retentive of moisture once it has absorbed it; and this retentiveness is now artificially increased by the construction of low banks round the fields. Seasonal inundation rendered this area attractive for settlement by both farmers and herders, while seasonal extremes considerably restricted habitable sites and the constant use of such areas in the past resulted in the accretion of occupation mounds and tells.

Excavation of some of these mounds in northern Nigeria, Cameroon and Chad has so far revealed successive occupations over periods of time known in some cases to approach and exceed 2,000 years. Lebeuf, working principally in Chad, is convinced that the mounds are connected with the Sao of oral traditions. Even if this term has much cultural or ethnic value, this writer shares Connah's reluctance to use oral tradition to identify peoples some of whom lived 2,500 years ago.

The Daima evidence suggests that by the early sixth century before the Christian era there were Late Stone Age herdsmen living in this area, keeping cattle and sheep or goats, using polished stone axes, the material for which had to be carried many kilometres into this completely stoneless region, and making tools and weapons of polished bone. These earliest occupants of the site probably built only in grass and wood, and lacked metals of any kind.

Findings from sites like Rop and Dutsen Kongba strongly suggest that a fully stone-using Neolithic level also immediately preceded the famous Nok Iron Age culture (i.e. before −2500) of the Jos Plateau. The Nok people may well have traded polished and ground stone tools to peoples occupying the stoneless regions to the north, and perhaps also the pottery, which at Daima is best represented by a fine ware with burnished red surfaces often decorated with toothed comb or roulette patterns.

The Kintampo–Ntereso complexes, Central Ghana

Archaeological evidence indicating the existence of a negroid group practising food production at least as early as −1300 to −1400 has so far been found in four main areas of Ghana: east of the Banda hills, the high ground around Kintampo, riverine sites scattered among the open woodlands of the inner Volta Basin, and the Accra plains to the far south.

These groups of sites can now be distinguished from one another more by environmental setting than by evidence of material culture. Burnt daub is fairly common at the Kintampo site and points to more or less fixed abodes. The widespread distribution of polished axes and 'rasps' (also called 'terracotta cigars') into areas where suitable rocks are absent points to the practice of some kind of inter-regional trade. Evidence at three of the Kintampo sites also shows that the Kintampo complex was preceded by another with a distinctly different pottery tradition, stone tools and animal remains, reflecting intensive hunting and gathering and/or incipient cultivation.

The forest fringe areas

A distinctly local industrial complex, different in character from the Late Stone Age industries, directly succeeded the latter in the forest fringe areas of West Africa, as well as in the open grassland regions of north-central Burkina Faso. The same industry overlaps with a more northern Neolithic complex in parts of Senegal, Mali and Mauretania (Vaufrey's Paratoumbien).

The early food-producing peoples of the forest region (the so-called Guinea Neolithic) occupied rock shelters and caves as well as open-air sites. Examples of shelters are Yengema, Kamabai and Yagala all in Sierra Leone; Kakimbon, Blande and Monkey Caves in Guinea; Bosumpra in Ghana; and Iwo Eleru and Ukpa in Nigeria. From Iwo Eleru also comes evidence suggesting that the predecessors as well as the Neolithic peoples were negroid. The best-known open sites include the valley and hill-slope sites of Rim in north-central Burkina Faso, and the Senegal coastal sites of Rarenno, Tiemassas and Cap Manuel.

Significantly, the archaeological evidence from the Mali–Mauretania–Senegal nexus seems to lend support to Portères's thesis that the red-skinned African rices (*Oryza glaberrima* and *Oryza stapfili*) could have been first domesticated by an indigenous wet cultivation method at least 3,500 years old in the extensive flood plains of the upper Niger between Segu and Timbuktu in Mali, an area where the Niger divides into several streams and lakes (the inland Niger Delta); and from there such cultivation may have spread down the Gambia and Casamance rivers to the coastal peoples of Senegambia. It is worth noting also that the botanical evidence clearly rules out the idea of rice cultivation having resulted from the introduction of knowledge of cereal cultivation. Portères has pointed out that, whereas the ancestral form of wheat (emmer) gave edible seeds so that cultivation could have developed from grain collection, this was not possible for African rice, since its ancestral forms did not yield a collectable crop.

All in all, then, the data suggest that the central Saharan and adjoining Sahel highland areas were the centre for the earliest and an independent cultivation of some grain crops, especially *Pennisetum* and sorghum, whilst the forest fringe areas of Nigeria saw the earliest indigenous cultivation of certain root (yams, coco-yams) and tree (oil palm) crops. On the other hand the forest fringe area to the extreme west was the nuclear area for rice cultivation. Dealing specifically with sorghum, Portères noted that, of the three regions which possessed basic wild stocks of sorghum (West Africa, Ethiopia and East Africa), West Africa was of special significance because unlike East Africa (and Asia) its current types are unique instead of being crosses between the three primary forms.

While radio-carbon data indicate that the 'Neolithic' of the central Saharan area (*c.* −7000) was the earliest of all the primary farming Neolithics, it also shows that the transition to food production in the forest fringe areas was much earlier than the same event in the Sudanic and Sahel zones to the north. At Iwo Eleru this change dates to just after −4000 (−3620) and continued until −1500. At Ukpa rock shelter near Afikpo (5° 54′N, 7° 56′E; Shaw, +1969) the Neolithic pottery and hoe-containing level dates to −2935 (±140) continuing to −95.

The Guinea Neolithic occurs slightly later in Sierra Leone to the east and in Burkina Faso to the north. At Yengema cave, thermoluminescent dating of pottery representing 'more or less the beginning and the end of the ceramic Neolithic' indicates a period from −2500 to −1500. At Kamabai the Neolithic levels span a period from −2500 to +340 (±100). In the north central region of Burkina Faso (Rim), the same type of industry has been dated to between −1650 and +1000.

But the distinctive character of the Guinea Neolithic of the forest fringe areas, and its dating in relation to the early food-producing cultural complexes in the savannah and Sahel zones, suggest not only that the change to food production occurred earlier in the forest areas but that it was independent of northern influences.

To say that the West African 'early Neolithic' complexes had distinctly local features, many of which reflect independently evolved economic and social adaptation measures for uniquely local ecologies, is not to say that each was an isolated enclave. The scanty skeletal evidence available suggests that the populations of most of these areas were negroid.

In the Sahara, Neolithic man seems to have been a mixture of the Mediterranean and Negro races who settled in the Tassili area in Neolithic times. In moving southward, these people probably gave rise to several of the dark-skinned groups who inhabit what is now savannah.

That the early Neolithic negroid peoples of West Africa were not living in isolated cultural enclaves is also illustrated by similarities in pottery features (e.g. rockering technique and comb-shaped decoration). If the dating is correct, then it is likely that these pottery features probably spread from the central Sahara to parts of the Sahel and savannah. On the other hand, roulette decoration was a more specifically southern feature, while the dotted wavy-line and wavy-line decorations typical of the Nilotic regions were completely absent in the south, but were just present in some eastern and central Saharan complexes.

It now appears that there were at least four primary areas of Neolithic development, two of which were in the far north of West Africa. Particularly in the open plains of the northern region, the pastoral form of transhumance was established very early. In lacustrine areas and the valleys and surrounding hill slopes, seed-cropping and in some cases mixed farming were prominent. On the other hand, the lowlands and forest fringe areas of the south were primary centres for root and tree crop cultivation.

Two main nuclear areas have been identified in West Africa, one to the north in the Sahel/Sudanic transitional zone, the other to the south on the fringes of the forest area. Both were thus located in regions with contrasting seasons, one season being unfavourable to growth (heat, drought or cold). Plants in such habitats store up reserves to enable them to resume vigorous new life when the 'favourable' weather returns. These reserves were in the form of roots and tubers in the south and seeds in the northern Sudanic zone.

In the forest and savannah areas with little or no seasonal climatic variation on the other hand, plants grew at a slow and regular pace. They did not need to struggle for survival, or to accumulate reserves – a feature which by example probably encouraged domestication ventures in both nuclear areas. The central savannah zone, sandwiched between the two nuclear areas, appears to have been a meeting-point for influences from both of them.

In all three main cultural regions, however, the transition from food gathering to food growing modified man's attitude towards his natural environment and his human group in several ways. From being a gatherer, he became a producer and 'storer', and subsequently (through long-distance trade) exchanged some of the resources which his neighbours lacked for commodities which his own group needed. The economic change also encouraged the development of handicraft activities and new technologies (ceramics, metal working, etc.) as well as active and complex trading networks, in addition to more profound social changes. But these social changes varied in kind and degree according to the type of agricultural base that was established.

The early Iron Age

Iron Age developments do not seem to have differed markedly from Neolithic trends, except that the earliest instances of transition to the Metal/Iron Age in West Africa occurred at both ends of the Sahel/savannah zone rather than in the forest regions to the south. In this respect, as with early food production, all the cultural and chronological evidence strongly suggests that there was much that was indigenous in this venture into metal working.

As set out in detail elsewhere, the evidence about the Early Iron Age in West Africa may be typologically and to some extent chronologically and stratigraphically divided into assemblages containing: (i) pottery, iron and ground stone tools; (ii) pottery, iron and/or other metals, sometimes in conjunction with special (pot) burial practices; and (iii) pottery alone.

Sites where traces of iron working are mixed with a more or less flourishing stone industry are usually the oldest types of Iron Age assemblage, and probably reflect the transition from the Stone to the Iron Age. Sites belonging to such transitional industries have been identified in several parts of West Africa, as well as elsewhere (e.g. in the Great Lakes region of East Africa). Such industries generally contain iron slag, knife blades, fragments of arrow and spearheads, hooks and bracelets, hammer-stones, a variety of axe/adze forms, stone discs (rings), querns and rubbing stones. There are distinct regional trends: for example, terracotta figurines seem to be particularly characteristic of northern Nigeria.

Regional variation is also evident in pottery from the Early Iron Age. For example, Bailloud's sequence from Ennedi of two related styles, Telimorou and Chigeou, which span the Late Neolithic/Early Iron Age transition, appear to be related to Coppens' *céramique cannelée* from Chad and Courtin's Taimanga style from Borku. Telimorou is associated with the earliest open village sites, and has been tentatively dated to the first millennium before the Christian era. Both Bailloud and Courtain point out the resemblance of these pottery styles to that of the C-group in Nubia, though the dating of the latter seems likely to be considerably earlier (starting about −2000) in Nubia. Examples of stone tools still in use included grinders and dimple stones as well as polished and flaked axes. Even within the same period, and when circumscribed by the same artistic tradition, some Nok sites contained unique features suggesting regional variation. For instance, polished axes were entirely absent from Taruga and there are differences in domestic pottery between Samun Dukiya, Taruga and Katsina Ala.

Not only was Nok culture firmly established well over 2,500 years ago, but its influence appears to have been far-reaching. For instance, some of the stylistic features of Nok culture are paralleled in the clay figurines at Daima, where iron working started about the fifth or sixth century of the Christian era.

Connah suggests that around the eighth century the original people at Daima were replaced by others who were fully iron-using and predominantly cereal-cultivating people with rather wider contacts than their predecessors. But the tradition of burial by crouched inhumation was continued, as was the making of clay figurines. At no stage did they bury their dead inside the enormous pottery jars usually referred to as So pots, although this type of pottery is present in the upper part of the mound.

Many important ancient village mound sites, some up to half a kilometre long, were found on artificial or natural hillocks on the banks of rivers in the lower Chari Valley in the Chad Republic, within a radius of 100 kilometres from Fort Lamy. These yielded some of the same finds as at Nok and Daima, including fine terracotta figurines, both human and animal, stone ornaments, copper and bronze weapons, and many thousands of potsherds. Huge funerary pots were also used here and the villages were surrounded by defensive walls.

Southern Nigeria

Willet observes that 'so many features of the Nok culture, particularly of its art, are found in later cultures elsewhere in West Africa, that it is difficult not to believe that the Nok culture as we know it represents the ancestral stock from which much of the sculptural tradition of West Africa derives'. True or not, there are certainly many similarities between Nok and Ife art which are unlikely to be coincidental. As at Nok, a naturalistic sculpture tradition dates back to at least +960 (±130), and an elaborate bead-work was present at Ife and Benin and to a lesser extent at other ancient Yoruba towns.

The Igbo-Ukwu excavations clearly indicate that iron working in south-eastern Nigeria is at least as early as the ninth century of the Christian era, but there is nothing to suggest that it could not have been earlier. Because iron smithing was a highly skilled occupation, it remained exclusive to certain communities and lineages. The most famous of the Igbo smiths are those from Awka, east of Onitsha, who apparently first obtained iron (ore?) from the Igbo smelters of Udi, east of Awka, and only much later received supplies of European iron. Other foci of metal working among the Igbo were the Abiriba iron smelters, among the Cross River (eastern) Igbo; the iron and brass smiths located near the Okigwe–Arochuku ridge, and the Nkwerre smiths in the southern part of this region.

One excavation in the Awka area yielded fifteen iron gongs and an iron sword similar to those still made by the Awka smiths, as well as a large number of cast bronze bells and other objects dated to +1495 (±95) which cannot be so readily attributed to Awka smiths.

It is not clear what the time/cultural relationship is between Ife and Igbo-Ukwu, although Willett thinks it possible that Ife may be much earlier than is at present supposed and may even be much nearer Nok than present evidence (*c.* thirteenth to fourteenth centuries of the Christian era) suggests. If the Ife beads are indeed the same as the 'akori' beads of the Guinea coast, as both Frobenius and ethnographic evidence from southern Nigeria suggest, then it is conceivable that the Igbo-Ukwu glass beads were manufactured at Ife. If so, it would mean that Ife culture dates at least as far back as the Igbo-Ukwu finds (ninth century of the Christian era). In this connection it may also be significant that a discontinuity of tradition at Ife in the stone sculpture, glass industry and clay figurines is largely paralleled at Daima, and that the cultural discontinuity at Daima dates from between the sixth and ninth centuries of the Christian era.

The Iron Age in the extreme west

The Iron Age in the extreme western section is even less well known than that of Nok and neighbouring areas. For instance, such information as exists for Mauretania relates not to an Iron Age but to a 'copper age'. In the middle Niger region, and particularly in Senegambia, only a partial chronological sequence has so far been obtained.

Excavations by N. Lambert at Akdjudjt indicate that copper smelting in the western Sahara dates as far back as –570 to –400; this may also have been the date of the trans-Saharan trade in copper. Estimates at one of the sites suggest that 40 tons of copper were extracted from it, and it is possible that some of this output was exported from the western Sahara to the Sudan.

The vast number of copper objects from sites and museum collections and also those mentioned in written sources suggest that the use of this metal, scarce though it was, was widespread in West Africa for a very long time – although it was not as important as wood, iron or clay. Copper and its alloys, when imported, came in a number of forms which changed little over the centuries, such as bars, manillas, rings, wires, bells and basins.

African peoples made a distinction between red copper, that is, copper in its pure form, bronze and yellow copper or brass. Unfortunately such precision is lacking in much of the literature. Spectrographic analysis needs to be carried out to establish the actual metal content of an object and the preferences of the earliest users of copper and its alloy (bronze).

The middle Niger region

Artificial earth mounds, either settlement sites or graves (tumuli), are known from three main areas in this region. They are:

(i) the Niger–Bani confluence in the Bani Valley;
(ii) north and north-east of Macina and Segu; and
(iii) far to the east of the bend, in Burkina Faso.

A large, thick-walled ware decorated chiefly with a twisted-string roulette was consistently present in all three areas, and often served as a burial pot. In places burial pots occur in twos and threes, with accompanying domestic equipment. In Burkina Faso (Rim), the main associated tools were iron, polished and ground stone tools and domestic pottery. Bronze and copper objects were also present in the Niger bend area. Also present in the Macina and Segu areas, but not at Bani or Rim (Burkina Faso) far to the east, is a distinctive slipware having polymorphic forms; fine, thin-walled dishes and bowls, some of which were carinated, pedestalled or flat-based; footed cups; and jugs and conical jars.

In Segu and Timbuktu some of these 'Iron Age' people were mainly farmers cultivating millet and rice, while others were mainly fishermen using nets with terracotta weights instead of bone harpoons. There were impressive pre-Islamic monuments, with artistically dressed stones, and some of the finds cover several acres, indicating major settlements. But very few, if any, of these sites have been investigated and then only superficially, although many were extensively looted by the French.

At Kouga excavations of a tumulus yielded a date of −950 (± 120) at a relatively late level containing a traditional white-on-red painted ware. Surface sherds bore impressions of millet, wheat and perhaps maize. Both at this site and at several others in this part of West Africa the indications are that there was an earlier Iron Age level mostly characterized by impressed or undecorated sherds, bone and stone tools, and bracelets. A related cultural tradition in Burkina Faso yielded even earlier dates in the fifth/sixth century of the Christian era.

The Senegambia region

Burial tumuli have been discovered in parts of this region, especially at Rao at the mouth of the River Senegal and in northern Senegal along the river. Again, although most of these are yet to be investigated closely, superficial study indicates that burials were made in wooden chambers covered by mounds at least four metres high, and that they contained iron tools, copper bracelets, beads, gold, jewellery and several simply shaped pots, bowls, beakers and jars, unpainted but closely decorated with elaborate designs, executed by scoring and pricking, and without comb impressions. Recent excavations date these burials to +750, which is later than the period which concerns us in this chapter.

A study of several shell middens on the coast in Lower Casamance in an area 22 by 6 kilometres has revealed a cultural sequence extending from −200 to +1600 overlapping with early modern Dyula material culture. Sapir believes that the earliest phase so far known (−1200 to +200), found only in the Loudia and Quolof sites, represents a late rather than an early Neolithic phase. Cultural contacts and/or influences are indicated by he pottery of this period, which shares decorative techniques such as wavy-line incision with Neolithic pottery widely distributed from Cap Vert to southern Algeria and even Central Africa.

Inland archaeological data of this period reflect sparse settlements in small encampments on low sandy ridges, probably covered by grass and shrubs and surrounded by forest. Shellfish gathering was not practised, and, as the only animal bones reported are a few unidentifiable mammal remains, the means of subsistence is not clear.

The complete absence of mollusc remains or fish-bones and the presence of sherd rather than shell-tempered pottery are considered by the original investigator as indications that these 'early inhabitants' of the coast were not in fact adapted to coastal life. Aubreville considers that thick forest once covered the whole area surrounding the Cussouye Plateau until it was ravaged by fire and converted into open paddy fields. If correct, this may mean that these Period I inhabitants were already farmers, perhaps of mountain or dry rice.

During the subsequent occupations (Periods II to IV, i.e. after +300), the rich fauna of the mangrove channels and creeks was exploited, and agriculture may also have been practised, although a systematic search for the remains of rice or other plants has yet to be carried out.

On our present view, this sequence seems too recent to shed much light on the origins of wet rice agriculture in the area. It may be useful, however, to note here that, according to Portères, Senegambia was a secondary centre of *Oryza glaberrima* propagation, the primary centre being somewhere near the middle Niger.

The lower Casamance sites appear to represent an advanced stage of wet rice cultivation. At this time the use of iron tools makes it possible to reclaim mangrove swamps and to ridge heavy alluvial clay soils for paddy fields. We may in fact do well to look for the first centres of *Oryza glaberrima* cultivation in the looser soils of drained inland valleys where it would have been possible to cultivate dry land or mountain rice by broadcasting or punch-hole planting after clearing the trees by girdling with stone implements.

It has been suggested by scholars such as Arkell that the West African iron-working traditions were derived from Egypt or Nubia, whilst others, such as Mauny, favour Carthage. In fact copper and bronze were later worked in much the same way as iron, whereas in Egypt and Nubia copper and iron were worked by very different methods. Available dating evidence gives no more support to either variant of the diffusion theory of iron working than does directly retrieved cultural evidence. It appears, for instance, that the Garamantes of Libya and the Meroitic people began using chariots, and probably iron tools, at about the same time (– 500) as iron working started in the Nok region of northern Nigeria. Indeed, dates from some sites suggest that iron working may even have occurred in the Nok region as early as – 1000.

The diffusion theory for iron working in West Africa does not give proper consideration to the many problems connected with the process: how, when and in what places (not necessarily in one place) steps were taken to change rock or earthy material into new, tough, durable metals which would be more effective than stone for weapons and also have a wide variety of other uses. In this respect Diop and Trigger have correctly noted that 'the early dates for Iron Age sites in West Africa and in Southern Africa should serve to remind us that the possibility should be kept open that iron working may have developed independently at one or more points south of the Sahara'.

Prehistoric trade and the earliest states of West Africa

Goods recovered from Fezzān tombs indicate that Roman items were being imported between the first and fourth centuries of the Christian era. It seems that, after replacing the Carthaginians on the Tripolitanian coast in the late second century before the Christian era, the Romans in their turn imported ivory and slaves from the

Sudan, with the Garamantes acting as intermediaries. After the decline of Roman rule trade declined, but later revived with the Byzantine reconquest after +533 and before the Arabs overran the Fezzān. Recent archaeological research thus clearly shows that an important element of long-distance trade in prehistoric times was carried on with the peoples of the Sahara and North Africa. But this by no means justifies claims such as those made by Posnansky that 'to discover the origins of long-distance trade in West Africa our search has to begin in the sands of the Sahara'. However well-intentioned such a claim may be, the emphasis is wrong and the far-reaching implications false. For one thing, it ignores the fact that an internal system of long-distance trade existed in West Africa which much preceded (and indeed made possible) the development of trans-Saharan trade.

In the view of this author, existing evidence points to the existence from Early Iron Age times of a complex and extensive network of long-distance trade, thriving on local complementary craft industries, especially (e.g. in fish and salt) between coastal peoples and inland farming peoples on the one hand, and also between the latter peoples to the south and more pastoralist societies to the north on the other. Important local products traded included iron and stone (for tools and weapons), leather, salt, grain, dried fish, cloth, pottery, woodwork, kola nuts and stone and iron personal ornaments.

The patterns of internal trade and crafts (industry) developed within West Africa shaped and sustained trade routes between the West African and the Saharan worlds. Such internal trade also fostered the growth of larger villages and towns in the Late Neolithic and Iron Age times. Archaeological information which is now accumulating, even for the forest areas of West Africa, continues to indicate that the subsequent emergence of the Asante, Benin and Yoruba states, as well as the Igbo-Ukwu culture, depended essentially on a highly successful exploitation of their environment by earlier iron-using (and in some cases non-iron-using) peoples.

25 Central Africa

Two problems fundamental to the history of Africa are the diffusion of metallurgy and the amazing spread of the Bantu languages.

For a long time there has been a distinct tendency to link the two questions and explain them in terms of one another. The diffusion of metallurgy is seen as a consequence of the spread of the Bantu-speaking peoples, and, conversely, this expansion is supposed to have been facilitated by the possession of iron tools which made it possible to tackle the equatorial forest.

Language specialists were the first to put forward the theory that the Bantu languages originated on the plateaux of Nigeria and Cameroon. Archaeologists followed suit and tried to make the findings in their respective fields fit in with that hypothesis. But the areas covered by these sciences do not exactly coincide, and it is a pity that the word 'Bantu', a linguistic term, should have come to be used for the ethnological concept of the Bantu peoples and their societies, and thence for the archaeological concept of a Bantu Iron Age.

Geographical background

The region dealt with in this chapter is Central Africa, i.e. the republic of Zaïre and the neighbouring countries of Gabon, Congo, the Central African Republic, Rwanda, Burundi and northern Zambia.

It forms a huge basin with an average altitude of 400 metres. Around this vast inner plain the ground rises in steps to become mountains or high plateaux. The regions near the Equator have abundant rainfall all the year round. To both north and south are belts with two rainy seasons that merge into one; from about latitudes 5° or 6° there is one rainy season. Mean annual temperatures are fairly high, the range widening with distance from the Equator.

The central basin is covered by dense equatorial forest bordered with savannah. In areas with a defined dry season, grass predominates, but there are often strips of forest along the rivers.

Late Stone Age

Late Stone Age societies of hunter-gatherers used increasingly specialized tools. A distinction is generally made between two opposing traditions, that of the Tshitolian

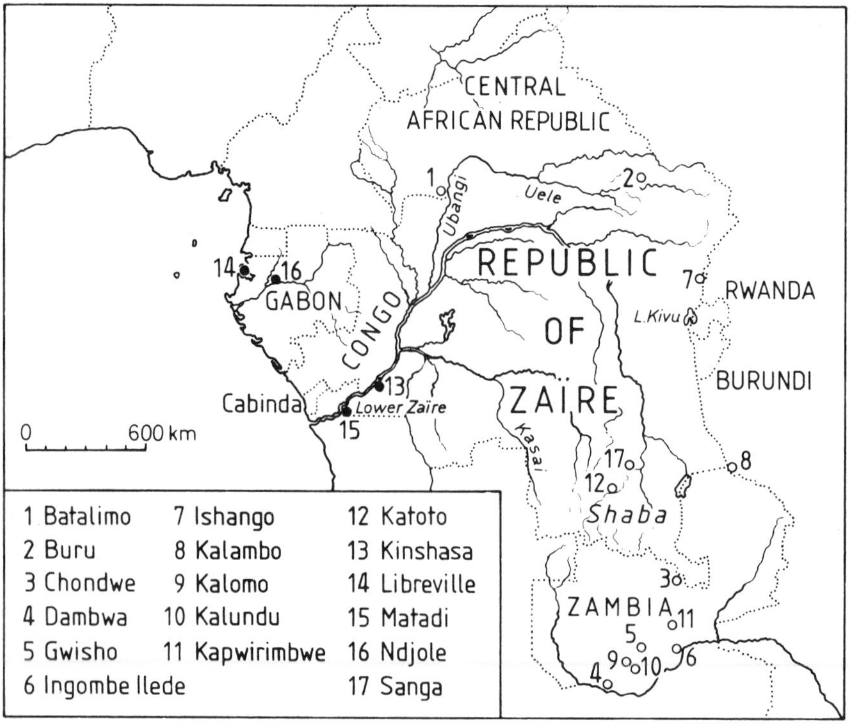

25.1 *Central Africa showing places mentioned in the text (from F. Van Noten)*

industrial complex and that of the complex of microlithic industries, of which the Nachikufan and the Wilton are the best-known examples.

The Tshitolian stands out fairly clearly from the other Late Stone Age industries of Central Africa. Geographically it belongs to the southern and, above all, the south-east areas of the Zaire Basin. The Tshitolian seems to continue the tradition of the Lupembian complex, from which it is separated mainly by a tendency to reduce the size of instruments and by the appearance of new forms: leaf-shaped and tanged flaked arrowheads, geometric microliths (segments, trapeziums). Some polished tools are also found towards the end of the Tshitolian. Chronologically, the Tshitolian appears to have stretched roughly from −12000 to −4000, perhaps to −2000 or even, locally, to the beginning of the Christian era.

The Nachikufan is an essentially microlithic industry which seems to have been established in the north of Zambia over 16,000 years ago. It had three successive stages. The oldest produced microlithic tools in association with a large number of pierced stones and grinding equipment. The second stage, which began about −8000, is characterized by the presence of polished tools. The last stage of this industry, beginning about −2000, is marked by a great abundance of small segments, pottery and a few articles made of iron – these last probably the result of trade. The Nachikufan tradition appears to have lasted down to the nineteenth century.

There is evidence of the Wilton, a purely microlithic industry, in southern Zambia and a large part of South Africa. Polished tools also appeared towards the end of its development.

Houses seem to have consisted of huts of branches and grass similar to those of the San of the Kalahari Desert. The dead were buried on the spot, with no goods in their graves. The bodies lay in various positions.

Neither agriculture nor animal husbandry was practised. Excavations have shown that the food was comparable to that of present-day peoples and consisted basically of a large variety of vegetable products, gathered from wild plants, supplemented by hunting and fishing. The inhabitants of Gwisho lived off quite a large area, and hunted animals both of the plain and of the forest.

There are a large number of microlithic industries in Central Africa which have been inadequately described and cannot be classed with those listed above. Probably some of them are merely local variants, adapted to special materials or activities.

There is little evidence to justify a distinction between the Late Stone Age and the Neolithic. However, the technological features traditionally attributed to the Neolithic do predominate in certain regions, for example Uele, Ubangi, and, to a lesser extent, Lower Zaïre. This led the early archaeologists of Central Africa to distinguish a Uelian, a Ubangian and a Leopoldian Neolithic. But these so-called industries are practically unknown except for their polished tools collected on the surface of the ground or acquired by purchase.

As regards Ubangian, there is now an excavated site at Batalimo, south of Bangui, in the Central African Republic. This site has produced hewn hatchets or adzes, an axe with a partly polished cutting edge, an abundant non-microlithic industry, and richly decorated pottery: tall wide-necked jars and flat-bottomed pots, and bowls. Thermoluminescent dating places the pottery around +380 (±220). This date may

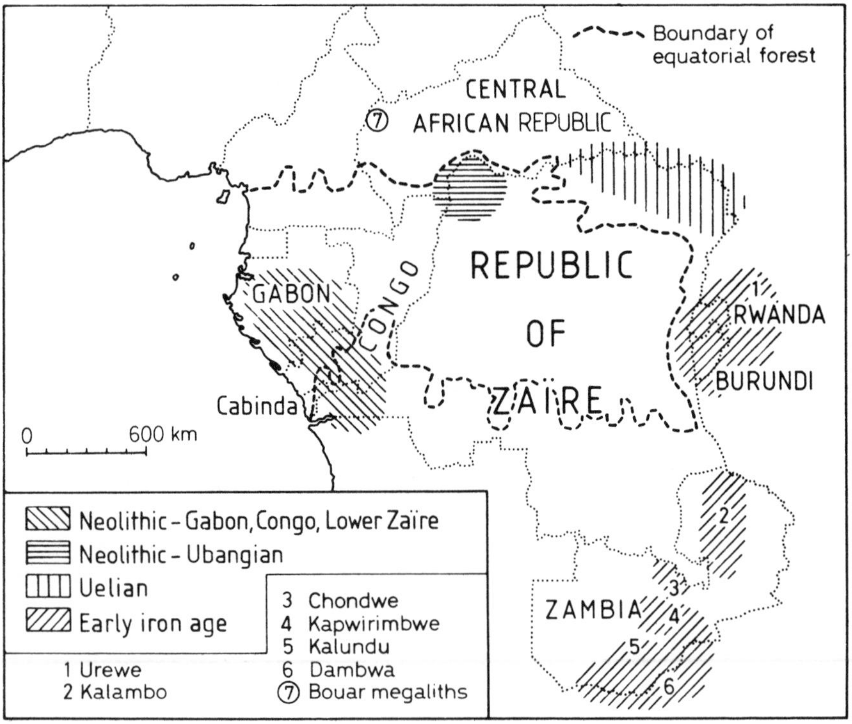

25.2 *Central Africa showing areas of 'Neolithic' and 'Early Iron Age' occupation (from F. Van Noten)*

seem too recent to some, but in the absence of other evidence it cannot be rejected.

In Lower Zaïre, from Matadi to Kinshasa, axes with more or less polished edges are found, sometimes in association with flat-bottomed pottery. During a recent trial excavation in a cave of this region a polished axe was found in association with this pottery and with wood ash, and a sampling of it, radio-carbon dated, gave a calibrated age of −390 to −160. Trial excavation of another cave about six miles away also yielded a polished axe in association with this same pottery.

In Gabon the stratigraphy of various sites, such as that of Njole, 120 miles east of Libreville, has revealed a Neolithic level containing axes with polished edges, pottery and fragments of quartz.

Early Iron Age

There were contacts between the peoples of the Stone Age that was drawing to an end and the first workers in metals. That fact is generally established. But we do not know if this technological change brought about far-reaching changes in the societies concerned.

The Early Iron Age is customarily associated with dimple-based pottery. This pottery, described for the first time in +1948, is now known as Urewe. It is attested in parts of Kenya, in Uganda and in the lake region. Some examples found at Kasai also seem to belong to this vast area of distribution. Most dates for these ceramic types fall between +250 and +400. But in at least one site at Katuruka, in Buhaya, Tanzania, considerably earlier dates have been obtained. Unfortunately it is still hard to assess the implications of this discovery.

Urewe ware presents a very homogeneous appearance, and it has often been suggested that the various examples had a common origin and that the differences they present are local variants rather than different chronological stages. It is true that they are never found stratigraphically superimposed on one another.

From the very beginning, iron working seems to have been associated with certain cultural traits such as pottery making and the building of daub villages. It is also generally agreed that agriculture and animal husbandry were practised at the same period.

The presence of Urewe pottery is well attested in the lake region (Kenya, Uganda, Rwanda, Burundi, Tanzania) and also in Zaïre, in the region of Kivu. For a long time Zambian pottery of the Early Iron Age (channel-decorated ware) was grouped with dimple-based pottery. But in fact it seems it can be broken down into several regional types.

Some vestiges of structures for habitation or storage have been preserved. A series of eight pits with straight parallel edges, something over a metre in diameter and nearly two metres in average depth, contained pots and potsherds, fragments of moulds, objects made of iron, and iron slag. Four of the pits were surrounded by a circular trench, possibly the remains of a superstructure.

There is only indirect evidence that there were agricultural activities. Nor is there any sure trace of animal husbandry.

Many pieces of iron slag, especially one great block of dross from the base of a furnace, and several fragments of pipes show that iron-smelting was practised, if not in the living sites, at least in their neighbourhood.

Among the iron objects unearthed from the pits may be mentioned many spear- and knife-tips, arrow-tips, bracelets or anklets, rings for fingers or toes. Bracelets or anklets and other ornaments were also made of copper.

The use of stone continued, as is evidenced by many mill-stones and pestles, stampers, hammers (including a smith's hammer), an anvil, and many crude artefacts which were used for scratching, cutting or rubbing. White clay and red ochre were used as pigments.

The lip of pottery in most cases is rounded and flaring, thickened at the rim. All the bases are rounded, except on two pots which have a dimple pressed in by the fingers. Decoration, which was applied before firing, is most often seen on or above the shoulder. The patterns consist of bands of parallel horizontal grooves broken by herring-bones and spirals. A network of slanting and criss-cross incisions of rows of triangular impressions and punctuations occasionally form the pattern of false relief covering the neck and shoulder.

Examples of pottery similar to that at Kalambo Falls have been found in eleven sites in the northern province of Zambia, distributed over an area of more than 97,000 square kilometres.

In the absence of extensive excavations and absolute datings, the few data we have are very conjectural. Four pots, two of them dimple-based, found near Tshikapa, seem to belong to the Urewe type; on the other hand many jars and shards found in a cave near Mbuji-Mayi rather closely recall the pottery of the Kalambo Falls industry.

Further study of the Kalambo pottery reveals the existence of many groups, some of them quite widely diffused. None of these groups is related to Urewe ware. Since excavation has not been extensive, we cannot attempt a chronology of this pottery or of the objects in metal.

In the Bouar region of the Central African Republic there are several barrows of various sizes with squared stones on top sometimes three metres high. Sometimes there are rows of vaults, and it seems that these cairns were intended for burial places. No bones have been found, however, though articles made of iron have been discovered. Six radio-carbon datings are available. Two belong to the sixth and fifth millennia before the Christian era and the other four range from the seventh century before the Christian era to the first century of the Christian era. The first date seems to be that of the building of the barrows, the second that at which they came into use again in the Iron Age.

The cemeteries of Sanga and Katoto are in the Upper Zaïre valley, in the Upemba tombs, and are the best-known Early Iron Age sites in the republic of Zaïre.

Situated on the edge of Lake Kisale, near Kinkondja, the Sanga burial ground, discovered some time ago, was systematically excavated in 1957 and 1958. New excavations were undertaken in 1974. A total of 175 graves have been opened, but it is clear that a large part of the cemetery has still to be explored.

After the excavations of 1958 three groups of pottery were distinguished and it looked as if a chronology could be worked out for them. The Kisalian group (the most abundant) seemed the oldest, followed by the Mulongo group (from the name of a place north-east of Sanga), and finally by red slipware.

The 1958 excavations revealed that these three groups were at least in part contemporary with one another. In the absence of internal chronology, two radiocarbon datings enable us to estimate the age of the cemetery: +710 ($\pm$120) and +880 ($\pm$200).

The older date was obtained from a grave in which the position of the body was quite unusual and the single pot, though Kisalian, untypical. The other date comes from a grave without goods characteristic of any of the three cultures. Therefore we do not know exactly what is dated.

Moreover, the vagueness of these dates detracts considerably from their value. All we can safely say is that, to within a couple of hundred years, some of the graves at Sanga go back to between the seventh and ninth centuries of the Christian era.

The excavations give us an idea of the burial ground itself, and, through that, a glimpse of ancient Sanga society. Burial rites seem to have been rather complex. Most of the graves are pointed towards the north or north-east – the ones containing Mulongo or red slipware towards the south. The dead person usually lay *decubitus dorsal* and was accompanied with objects presumably intended to make things easier for him in the other world. The pottery shows no signs of wear and the strong resemblance among certain vessels in a given tomb seem to indicate that it was made for exclusively funerary purposes. The jars were probably filled with food and drink. The corpse was adorned with jewellery of copper, iron and ivory. It seems as if premature infants, too, were buried. In some cases the dead person has a bundle of little crosses in his hand. There is a clear tendency for the size of the jars to be in proportion to the age of the dead person.

The general picture one gets of Sanga is of a civilization where the people attach more importance to hunting and fishing than to agriculture. However, hoes and bedstones have been found in the graves, as have remains of goats and fowls.

As the bones have not been analysed, the only anthropological datum we possess is an odontological study of some of the human remains. This study shows in particular the frequency of mutilated teeth. We do not know the whole extent of the burial ground, which would have given some idea of the size of the population.

The Sanga civilization, then, seems to have been a brilliant phenomenon, but, so far as our present knowledge goes, an isolated one. Probably the discoveries as a whole cover a longer period than that suggested by the two radio-carbon datings.

New excavations were undertaken in 1974. The main purpose was to learn just how long the burial ground had been in use and establish its internal chronology, to delimit its area, and to try to find the habitat site. Thirty new graves were explored; they will probably enable us to complete the chronology and form some idea of the size of the burial ground. But because of the expansion of the modern village the habitat site could not be found.

However, at Katongo, six miles from Sanga, excavations seem to have revealed a habitat level at the foot of a hill less than half a mile from a cemetery; excavations also revealed the existence of pottery groups recognized at Sanga.

The grave-goods are just as rich as at Sanga, and here too suggest a prosperous society with a high level of technical development. The presence of numerous hoes and millstones indicates that agriculture was important, but hunting and fishing must have been practised too.

The presence of glass beads and ornaments made of shells from both the Atlantic and the Indian Ocean indicates fairly far-flung trading activities.

Katoto pottery is original, like that at Sanga, and seems somewhat less stereotyped. Some decorative motifs are reminiscent of Urewe ware, but as none of the latter has been found in the Shaba area it cannot be said that Katoto pottery is a development of the Urewe type, rather than a simple case of convergence. As a matter of fact most of these common motifs, such as the spiral, strapwork, herring-bone and concentric circles, are very widespread. The pits are later than the graves, and sometimes disturb them. One of them has been given a radio-carbon dating: +1190 (±60).

The burial ground at Katoto completes the picture suggested by the excavations at Sanga. But it seems astonishing that two such large settlements, quite close to each other and apparently contemporary, should have had so little to do with each other.

Despite the abundance of grave-goods, we do not know very much about the people buried in these necropolises. We do not know who they were, where they came from or what they died of, and we have but scant means of imagining how they lived. The size of the two burial grounds suggests that towards the end of the first millennium of the Christian era, the banks of the upper Lualaba were the site of large concentrations of people, which gave rise to brilliant civilizations. The excavations now under way at several new sites should teach us more about those civilizations.

Origin of the Bantu

As we have said, the word 'Bantu' designates in the first place a group of languages. But it has gradually acquired an ethnographical, and even an anthropological, connotation. In fact it was linguistic classification that served as a basis for researchers in other disciplines.

In the absence of written evidence, archaeology does not enable us to establish direct correlations between existing evidence of the Iron Age and the linguistic notion of Bantu.

Many attempts have been made to link the success of 'Bantu' groups to the knowledge of working in iron. But one observes, comparing metallurgical terms in the Bantu languages, that there is great diversity in the basic vocabulary of forging. However, certain reconstructions suggest the use of iron at proto-Bantu level, for instance the expressions for forging, hammer and bellows. Were these words in the language before the division, or did they enter it as borrowings at some unknown stage in the ramification process? It is not impossible that those words which are widely attested result from a shift in meaning from proto-Bantu to the present-day languages. Thus the word for 'forge' would be only a special application of the word for 'beat'. Finally, other metallurgical terms seem to have the same origin in both Bantu and non-Bantu languages, which seems to indicate that in both instances it is a matter of borrowings.

When one thinks of how important the ability to work metals was in traditional

African societies, it is difficult to see why, if the 'Bantu' worked in iron before their expansion, we find no obvious linguistic traces of it.

Finally, very little research in physical anthropology has been done on the 'Bantu'. An article by J. Hiernaux (+ 1968) is alone in supplying a few facts. Hiernaux shows the biological resemblances between Bantu-speaking peoples. So little work has been done in this area of human palaeontology that it is very difficult to distinguish a complete present-day 'Bantu' skeleton from one belonging to some other African, or even European, group. What can be said, then, of the damaged or fragmentary skeletons which are often all that archaeology affords?

The only human fossil remains that have been properly studied come from Ishango, in Virunga Park in Zaïre. Unfortunately the age of these remains cannot be accurately determined, and it has not been possible to ascribe them to a definite physical type.

Nature of societies in the Early Iron Age

Little is known about the kind of life people lived at the beginning of the Iron Age. Such evidence as there is varies with the extent of the research that has been carried out: the sites in Zambia and the burial grounds at Sanga and Katoto, in Shaba, provide the most concrete data.

Remains of habitats are rare in Central Africa. The only ones known are at Gombe, Kalambo Falls and perhaps Katongo. The only proof of agricultural activity at the beginning of the Iron Age consists of iron hoes practically identical in form with modern ones. Holes dug in the ground have been regarded as store pits, and small daub constructions as granaries. The fact that there are numerous remains of mill-stones is less convincing, as societies which lived by hunting and food-gathering also had grinding implements.

Excavations have yielded arrowheads and spearheads, and the remains of what must have been hunting dogs. Snares and nets were probably also used. The importance of fishing is shown by the hooks found in the graves at Sanga and Katoto. The trefoil braziers of Sanga are very much like those used in their canoes by boatmen in the equatorial part of Zaïre.

A distinction needs to be made between two kinds of trade, regional trade, mostly in metals, pottery, basketwork, dried fish and salt, and long-distance trade, the latter dealing in shells – cowries and conuses (cone-shells) – glass beads, and metals like copper. In Zaire, at Sanga and at Katoto, all the shells and beads came from the east coast, with the exception of a conus at Katoto from the Atlantic, a distance of some 1400 kilometres as the crow flies. Little copper crosses, used as a sort of coin, have been found quite a long way from copper-producing areas.

Brick furnaces for iron smelting have been found in association with dimple-based ware in Kivu, Rwanda, Burundi and Buhaya in north-west Tanzania. It should be noted that in the only description of iron smelting in Rwanda, given by Bourgeois (1957), a circle of baked bricks is used in the building of a furnace rather similar to the remains found by Hiernaux and Maquet.

Pottery remains are not decisive evidence of the Iron Age since, as we have seen, pottery is also found in the context of the Late Stone Age and the Neolithic. It is generally impossible to distinguish Iron Age pottery as such from that of the earlier periods.

Jars were made by patting and pulling the clay into strips or cords which were often arranged in a coil. The variety of shapes and decoration is so great that we show here only a few of the most characteristic.

As far as archaeology enables us to judge, societies of the Early Iron Age were not essentially different from those of today and must have presented the same sort of diversity. The agricultural techniques then practised were not favourable to the establishment of large settlements, and involved a certain mobility.

The burial grounds at Sanga and Katoto are exceptional in that they are the result either of very long occupation, or of a large concentration of people on the banks of the Lualaba. The richness of the goods in some graves, especially at Katoto, may be a sign of social inequalities.

The abundance and workmanship of objects of iron, copper, stone, wood, bone and clay reflect not only the skill of the craftsmen but also, probably, some degree of specialization.

All the graves discovered give evidence of elaborate burial practices. The dead wore many ornaments – bracelets, rings, necklaces, pendants, strings of beads and shells. Cowries, conuses and beads of glass or stone may have served, among other things, as coin in the same manner as the small crosses. Lastly, the most ancient dated wood sculpture of Central Africa comes from Angola and has been dated +750.

Conclusion

I have several times stressed the danger of using the provisional findings of one science to back the conclusions of another. Hasty correlation too often leads to general theories which within the rigorous framework of their proper discipline would be difficult to maintain. Nevertheless, any attempt at describing the nature of Early Iron Age societies, or the origin of the Bantu-speaking peoples, involves collating archaeological and non-archaeological data.

The anthropological-archaeological-linguistic explanation which linked the spread of the Bantu languages to the diffusion of working in iron chimed very well with the idea of evolution from beginnings in the Fertile Crescent, while denying that Africa could have arrived at discoveries independently.

Recent developments have caused these theories to be reconsidered. Linguisticians call in question the methods and results of glottochronology. New datings throw fresh light on the origin of metallurgy in Central Africa. Vestiges of iron workings at the Katuruka site have been dated as belonging to about −500 or −400.

In the present state of our ignorance, and taking the new evidence into account, it is clear that the problems connected with the diffusion of iron and the origin of the Bantu languages are more complex than was thought, and cannot be reduced to an over-simple explanation beset by contradictions.

It therefore seems pointless to go on constructing new hypotheses for migrations and for the origin of metallurgy each time that an excavation results in new datings. We can nevertheless attempt to relate certain relevant facts. In regard to the origin of

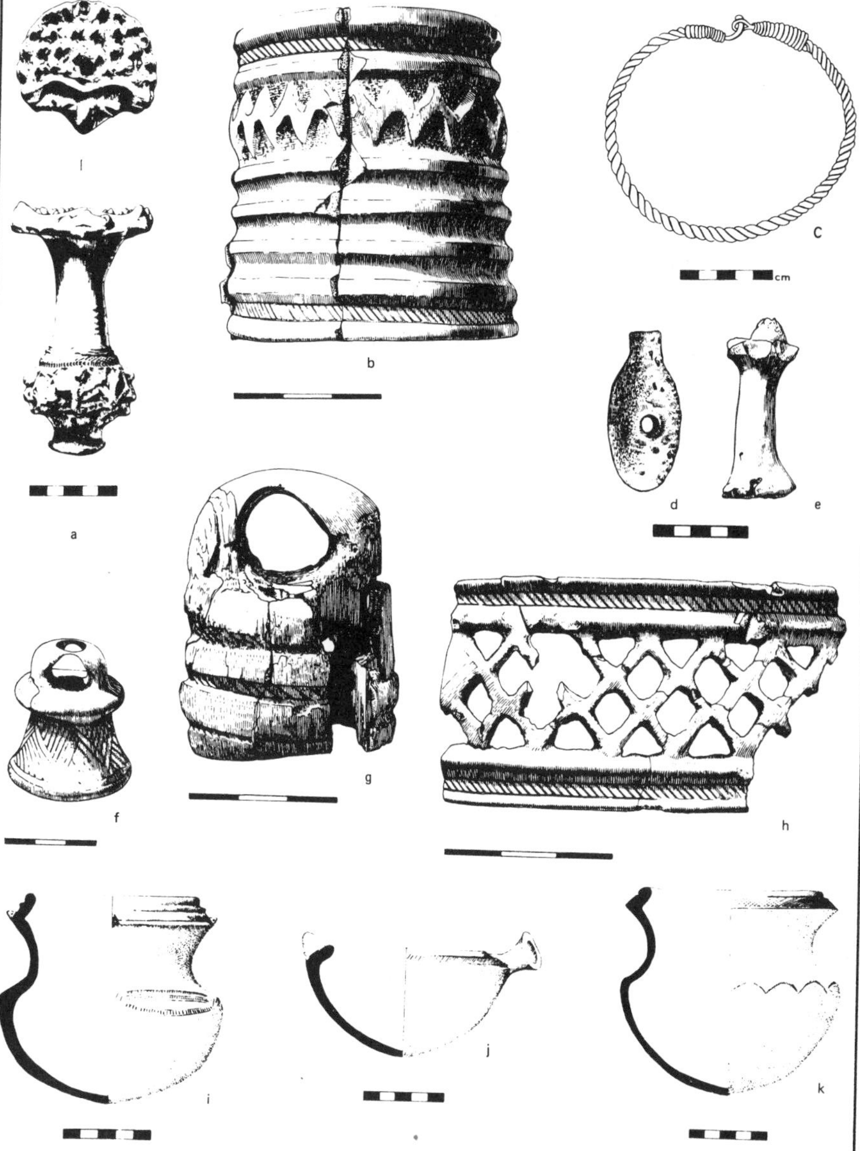

25.3 *Objects found at Sanga: a) Vessel with anthropomorphic decoration; view from above and from side: b) Ivory bracelet; c) Copper necklace; d) Iron whistle; e) Terracotta counter; f) Stone pendant; g) Ivory pendant; h) Fragment of ivory half necklace; i), j), k), Types of pottery (Tervuren Museum: J. Hiernaux, E. De Longrée and J. De Buyst, 1971)*

iron working, the new dates proposed for Katuruka seem to imply a connection with the almost contemporaneous dates put forward for Meroe. It is therefore possible to conceive of metal working having spread southwards from Meroe, but the spread would appear to have taken place very quickly. One cannot consequently at present rule out another origin which could even be local.

As the reader will have observed, our information about the Early Iron Age in Central Africa is of unequal value and very fragmentary; early research led to the construction of theories that now totter beneath the accumulated weight of new data. Much work – more extensive, more systematic and better co-ordinated – must be done before we can arrive at a convincing explanation of the events of this crucial period in the history of Central Africa.

26 *Southern Africa: hunters and food-gatherers*

Recent research has shown that iron-using peoples had moved south of the Limpopo by at latest the fourth or fifth century of the Christian era. Although much detail remains unpublished, it seems clear that the Iron Age inhabitants of the Transvaal and Swaziland were agriculturalists and herdsmen, and manufactured pottery similar to that known from Zimbabwe, Zambia and Malawi at about the same time. It is not known whether the apparently rapid diffusion of Iron Age peoples continued farther south at the same pace, but the earliest dates for iron-working in Natal are somewhat later, around −1050. Nor is it yet possible to say at what time the iron-using groups reached the most southerly extent of their distribution, around the Fish River in the eastern district of the Cape. Despite these uncertainties, which will no doubt be the focus of much further work, it is known that the Iron Age populations disrupted and displaced indigenous groups of hunter-gatherers who were largely ignorant of metal-working, stock-breeding and plant domestication. Only in areas unsuitable for occupation by mixed farmers, such as the rugged Drakensberg escarpment, were hunters able to survive the expansion of the Early Iron Age. Even these retreats were ineffective against the deprivations of today.

A second, and in many ways more destructive, population expansion began from the Cape in the middle of the sixteenth century. The indigenous people either migrated, drifted into the growing colony as servants or succumbed to diseases introduced by the colonists. Indigenous peoples were initially lumped together under the term 'Ottentoo' or 'Hottentot', but gradually the distinction between herdsmen (Khoi Khoi, many of whose ethnic names were known) and hunters (San, or *bosjesmen*, also known as Sonqua Khoi Khoi) was recognized and used. These groups were obviously closely related since they spoke similar languages, shared a good deal of subsistence technology and material culture, and were physically not unlike one

Note by the International Scientific Committee:

The International Scientific Committee would have preferred this chapter, like all the others, to have been presented within the chronological framework strictly laid down for Volume II. It therefore requested the volume editor to put this point to the author. The latter did not consider it possible to make any radical alteration to his text. The Committee is therefore publishing it in the form agreed after discussion with the author. It nevertheless maintains serious reservations regarding the method used, particularly in paragraph one, and regarding the resulting confusion for the reader, who is presented at one and the same time with information on the Palaeolithic and the contemporary periods.

another. Since in these respects they were clearly distinct from the other indigenous population group, the iron-using farmers farther to the north and east, they were generally identified as a separate element and would now be known as Khoi Khoi herdsmen and San hunters, often fused to produce the term 'Khoisan'.

It seems impossible in this case to keep within the chronological limits strictly laid down for this volume, but the author has attempted to describe the lasting and relatively stable aspects of a way of life, leaving it to the authors of the other volumes concerned with these regions to draw attention to the changes which have occurred over the centuries in the life of these groups as a result of contact with the outside world, and to the part they themselves have played in the general history of southern Africa. In this way the risk of overlapping will be minimized.

The Khoisan

This chapter will describe what is known of the way of life of hunters and herdsmen trapped between Iron Age farmers and European colonists in the southern parts of southern Africa. Since the colonists were literate and the Iron Age farmers were not, the documentation on traditional San and Khoi Khoi life and Khoisan relations with other groups is heavily biased towards the western Cape. In some ways this bias has been compounded by the rich archaeology of the Cape mountain belt as compared with many other parts of southern Africa. But the descriptions offered, though often relating to the south and west, should illuminate Khoi Khoi and San life-styles throughout the region, though much detail of local conditions will, of course, be missing.

For various reasons there is a good deal of evidence as to how the Khoisan groups lived. Because they survived until fairly recently, there is much archaeological evidence in the form of artefactual remains and plant and animal food residues. Because they came into contact with literate societies, there is a body of historical documentation on their indigenous ways of life. In addition, at least some of the indigenous groups left their own documents in the form of rock paintings and engravings, which are a valuable source of social, economic, technological and probably religious information. An important fact is that the environment in many parts of southern Africa has not changed radically since the time when it was first occupied by hunters and herdsmen. After 250 years of agricultural activity, it is still possible to document and monitor the spatial and seasonal factors in the environment which must have, to some extent, determined the nature of prehistoric settlement.

Since neither the Khoi Khoi herdsmen nor the San hunters used metals for their cutting, scraping or chopping tools, they fall within the scope of Stone Age studies, and have been viewed in the past very largely in terms of the stone artefacts they produced.

San hunter-gatherers

Recent ethnographic studies of hunter-gatherers have shown the very considerable importance of the gathered or collected component of the diet of groups in this economic category. It is clear from the accounts of the Kung and the G/wi of the Kalahari that the foods collected by the women tide the group over from day to day, though men and children also gather such *veldkos*. The importance of gathered foods, much but not all of which may be vegetable, is that they are predictable in their location and may be relied upon on a daily basis. High-protein meat, hunted or snared by men, is also of importance but being less predictable is not part of the daily staple food. The implication is not that hunters should be renamed gatherers, but that the balance between the food resources available to hunting and gathering groups needs to be recognized. Such groups keep themselves alive on collected foods, but benefit periodically from successes in the hunt.

Most of the historic accounts of the animal part of the prehistoric diet mention 'game' generally and the implication is that a wide range of species was taken. This is confirmed by the faunal lists from large excavations such as those at Die Kelders and Nelson Bay Cave, where the range extends from shrews to elephants and even whales. But the fauna from these sites show a strong bias towards smaller animals such as tortoises, dassies, dune mole rats and small territorial herbivores such as the steenbok, the grysbok and the duiker. The bones of carnivores are rare, perhaps reflecting occasional kills to obtain pelts; the larger herbivores such as hartebeest, eland and buffalo are much rarer than the smaller animals, and only occasional traces of elephant, hippo or rhino have been recovered. Whilst the proportions in part reflect a tendency for the prehistoric groups to bring back smaller animals to their home base and to butcher larger game where hunted, there is no doubt that ground game and the smaller herbivores were the prime targets or most frequent victims in the hunt.

The diet of San groups is well documented, both historically and archaeologically, although the distribution of excavations is very uneven and some areas are virtually unexplored or lacking in well-preserved deposits. In general terms, the day-to-day staples were collectable items, including roots, other plant foods, honey, and insects such as locusts, grasshoppers, termites and caterpillars. These were supplemented by small animals such as tortoises, dassies and dune mole rats, by the smaller herbivores, and less frequently by larger animals. The groups along the coast caught fish, rock lobsters, seals and sea-birds, and gathered quantities of shellfish, notably limpets and mussels.

The technology by which these resources were exploited is reflected in the assemblages of stone, bone, wood and fibre from caves and shelters throughout southern Africa, and in the descriptions of early travellers in the region. There are many rock paintings depicting women with weighted digging-sticks (see Fig. 26.1) who often seem to be carrying leather bags, no doubt to transport the foodstuffs home. Leatherwork is fairly commonly found in the dry environments of the rock shelters and caves of the Cape.

Almost all commentators on San hunting refer to the bow and poisoned arrows as being the principal weapon. Though complete implements are rarely met in excavations, there are examples of all components of this equipment from caves in the western and eastern Cape. Possible bow fragments, reed mainshafts, notched reed lengths, polished bone points and linkshafts, knotted sinew and painted aloe fragments, represent the discarded or lost remnants of San hunting equipment. Many animals,

26.1 *Rock painting: women with digging sticks weighted with perforated stones (J.E. Parkington)*

26.2 *Rock painting: a large group of figures, most of them recognizable as male, depicted in what might be a dancing scene (J.E. Parkington)*

however, were not shot with the bow but caught in snares made of vegetable twine and set out in the veld. Other hunting techniques have been mentioned in historical accounts, but have not yet been supported by archaeological evidence. For example, a number of travellers in the eighteenth century described large pits dug close to river-banks with pointed stakes set upright within them. These were usually interpreted as designed to trap larger game such as elephant, rhino, hippo and buffalo, and have a wide geographical distribution extending south from the Orange River and east as far as the Gamtoos.

Obviously a number of fishing techniques were used by hunter-gatherers and most of them are documented archaeologically. Perhaps the most spectacular are the funnel-shaped reed-basket traps of the lower Orange River described by both Lichtenstein and Barrow and ascribed by them to *bosjesmen*, almost certainly San. These traps were placed in the streams and were described as having been made from 'osiers, twigs of trees, and reeds' in a pointed or funnel-shaped design, no doubt similar to that still used in the Kafue and Limpopo rivers. Though no traces of these have been excavated, a number of rock paintings from Lesotho and east Griqualand undoubtedly depict sets of these traps connected by reed or wooden fences and catching large numbers of freshwater fish.

All in all, San technology seems to have included a wide range of hunting and gathering techniques, using implements made from materials such as stone, bone, wood, fibre, reed, leather, shell, ivory, sinew and leaf and often including composite tools in which raw materials were combined. Stone seems to have formed only the tip or cutting or scraping edge of more complex tools, and stone artefacts were clearly as often as not mounted in mastic on wooden or bone handles. For these artefacts, fine-grained homogeneous rocks such as chalcedony, agate, silcrete or indurated shale were preferred, whilst the more brittle quartz was also used and quartzite pebbles and boulders were turned into upper and lower grindstones for grinding pigments or foodstuffs. It is interesting that few of the seventeenth- and eighteenth-century travellers specifically mention or describe the manufacture of stone artefacts, perhaps indicating the gradual replacement of at least some stone artefacts by bone, wooden or metal versions. The implications of this picture of wide raw material usage are obvious to those who wish to classify and distinguish between groups on the basis of stone assemblage comparisons alone.

Archaeological research is increasingly directed at the conditions which governed the settlement of San groups. The result is that it is becoming possible to describe the patterns of need of hunter-gatherers in ecological terms which were not familiar to early travellers. Nevertheless, historical records and information from rock paintings can obviously add to the evidence now emerging from large-scale excavation and detailed analyses of animal bones and plant remains.

Compared with the hunter-gatherers of the Kalahari and farther afield, it is likely that San groups would have been small and highly mobile units. The only exceptions to this are, for example, the groups of 150 and 500 people described by Barrow and a camp of fifty huts reported by Thunberg, both in the late eighteenth century, when hunters were gathering in unusually large numbers to defend themselves against European raids. The size of groups represented in rock paintings seems to confirm that the most frequent social unit was under twenty people, though larger groupings are found. There is good evidence, in the form of a high correlation between women and digging-sticks and between men and bows in rock art, that there was a fairly strict division of labour amongst the San groups.

It has been shown repeatedly that hunter-gatherer groups tend to move in units of variable size in order to increase the efficiency of their use of resources: fission into small family groups when resources are spread thinly, and fusion into larger gatherings when the type of subsistence requires the use of considerable manpower, or when resources are highly concentrated and thus capable of supporting large gatherings. This pattern also serves to maintain the kinship web between neighbouring groups who use the occasional large gathering to pass on news, exchange items, technological innovations and perhaps women, through whom the web of kinship obligations is traced. In times of catastrophe, these obligations are a lifeline allowing one group to survive by temporarily using another's resources. Moreover, personal difficulties can be solved by one or other party leaving a group and either temporarily or permanently joining another in which there are relatives. Though the recognition of these features remains a goal of archaeological research, the most explicit information about them, at present, comes from historical records and, perhaps questionably, from rock art.

One study of the size of groups depicted in the rock art of the western Cape resulted in a mean group size of about fourteen persons, a figure very similar to that recorded in the diaries of the late eighteenth-century commandos. However, there are examples of rock paintings which illustrate up to thirty or forty men in a single scene, which must mean a gathering of around a hundred persons or more (see 26.2).

The storage of foodstuffs from times of plenty to times of scarcity is not characteristic of recent Kalahari groups, who seem to have regarded the environment as a natural larder which always provided some combination of foods and which required little supplementing. It seems that, by carefully planning an annual beat around the available resources and conserving the more common foods for difficult times, the need to store food was minimized. Food was usually collected and consumed the same day, or over a few days in the case of unusual bounties such as large game. The situation farther south seems to have been similar, since evidence of storage pits is rare in the archaeological record and the early travellers never described storage as an important aspect of San subsistence. Kolb, who had access to the information of many observers of Khoi Khoi and San life at the end of the seventeenth century, noted that 'though the fields abound with wholesome and very nourishing fruits and roots which they might lay up in plenty against a rainy day, yet it is the custom of the women to . . . gather only such a quantity . . . as will serve their families for the day'. Other early authorities mention the storing of dried grasshoppers, the pounded roots of the canna plant and dried apricots, items which were probably not as economically important as the roots, tubers and corms. In the southern Cape there is evidence, as yet unpublished, of large numbers of storage pits associated with San cave sites. As yet unconfirmed reports suggest that the seeds recovered from these pits may have been collected for their oil content rather than as food.

From the evidence that has been presented, it seems clear that San groups were highly organized, small, mobile groups with an intimate knowledge of the resources available to them and of how these resources varied through time and space. The subsistence base, the range of hunting, fishing and gathering techniques and the settlement patterns employed are becoming increasingly better documented, using data from a variety of sources.

Khoi Khoi pastoralists

The picture of hunting and gathering within defined environmental contexts is, of course, seriously incomplete when dealing with the immediate precolonial period, say, since −2000. At every site marked on 26.3, with the exception of Bonteberg and Gordons Bay (where they have not been actively sought), there are the remains of domestic stock in a Late Stone Age context. Since there are no indigenous sheep, goats or cattle, and since these assemblages predate contact with European or negro herdsmen, it must be assumed that this records the appearance of herded stock from another source. The earliest radio-carbon dates associated with domestic animals and the potsherds at sites from Angola to the eastern Cape are summarized in 26.4. Also included is the rather sparse information on these items from inland areas and, for reference, the earliest dates presently available for the penetration of iron-using, Bantu-speaking mixed farmers into southern Africa. Although the apparent pattern may change with further research, it seems worth while risking some interpretations in terms of the origin and speech of Khoi Khoi herdsmen.

The most obvious point is that potsherds appear for the first time in sites from Angola to the southern Cape during the period −2000 to −1600. As more shards are found, dating will become more accurate, and it may be that radio-carbon dating will ultimately point to the same dates for the appearance of patterns throughout the whole region. Only four dates before −2000 have been reported, and there are reasons for supposing that all of these are either seriously contaminated or pre-pottery.

A second and no less important observation is that, wherever a search for traces of domestic animals has been specifically made, they appear as early in the archaeological record as do potsherds. This may not be true in *every site*, but, when dates from neighbouring sites are combined to form local sequences, then they appear concurrently. Although this approach may seem unjustified, it can be defended as ironing out problems raised simply by sampling phenomena. The implication is that potsherds and domestic stock diffused quickly, at the same time and through the same area. The word 'diffused' seems inescapable since, whereas pottery could be independently invented, domestic animals obviously could not. Moreover the pottery shows no signs of being crude or early inefficient attempts at a technological innovation.

Although research continues into the spread of iron and domestic animals into southern Africa along an easterly route, present evidence suggests the fourth or fifth century of the Christian era for their introduction south of the Limpopo. Thus the set of Late Stone Age dates associated with both pottery and domestic stock predates that of the Iron Age farther north and east by fully two to three hundred years, an interval surely not accountable to radio-carbon dating.

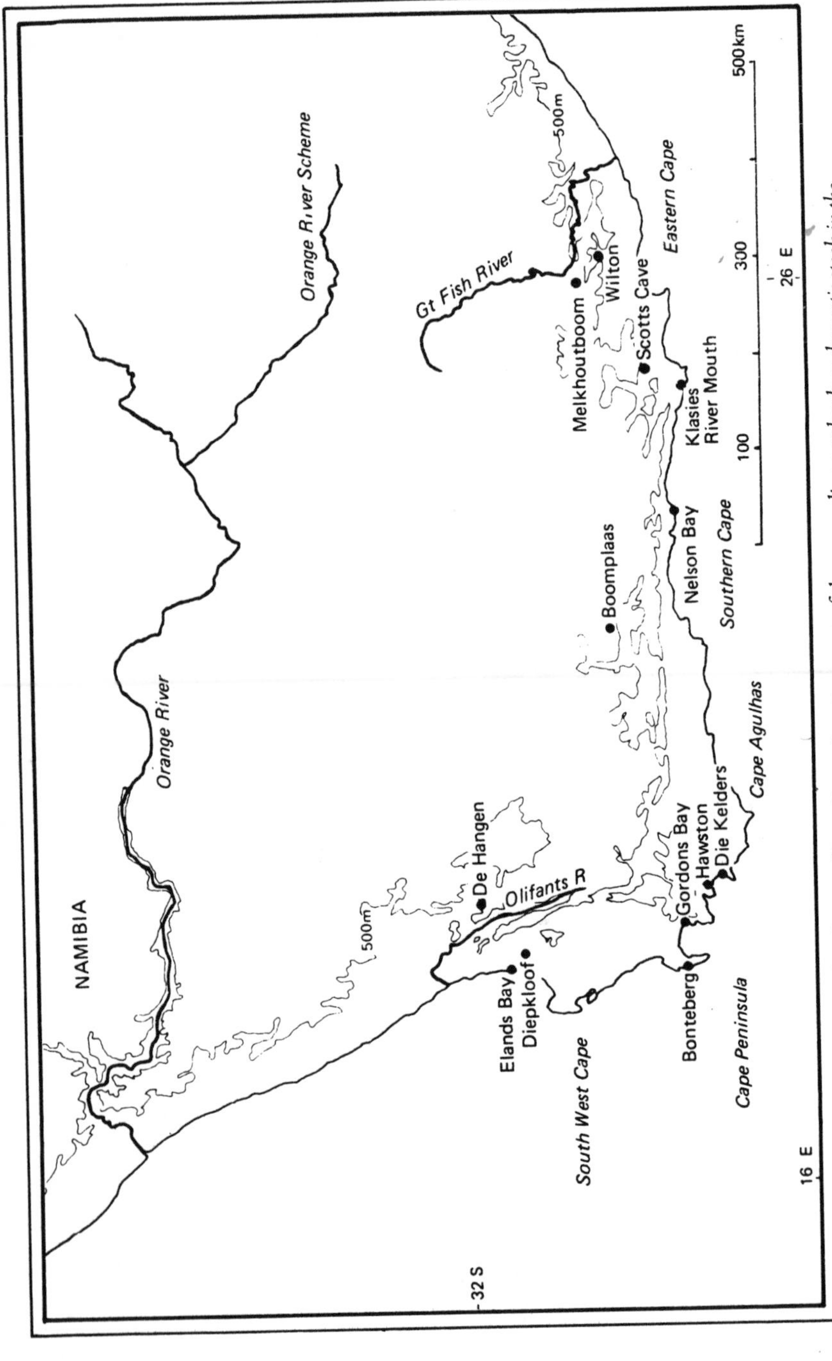

26.3 *Southern Africa, showing the distribution of Late Stone Age sites, most of them revealing potsherds or domestic stock in the first centuries of the Christian era (J. E. Parkington)*

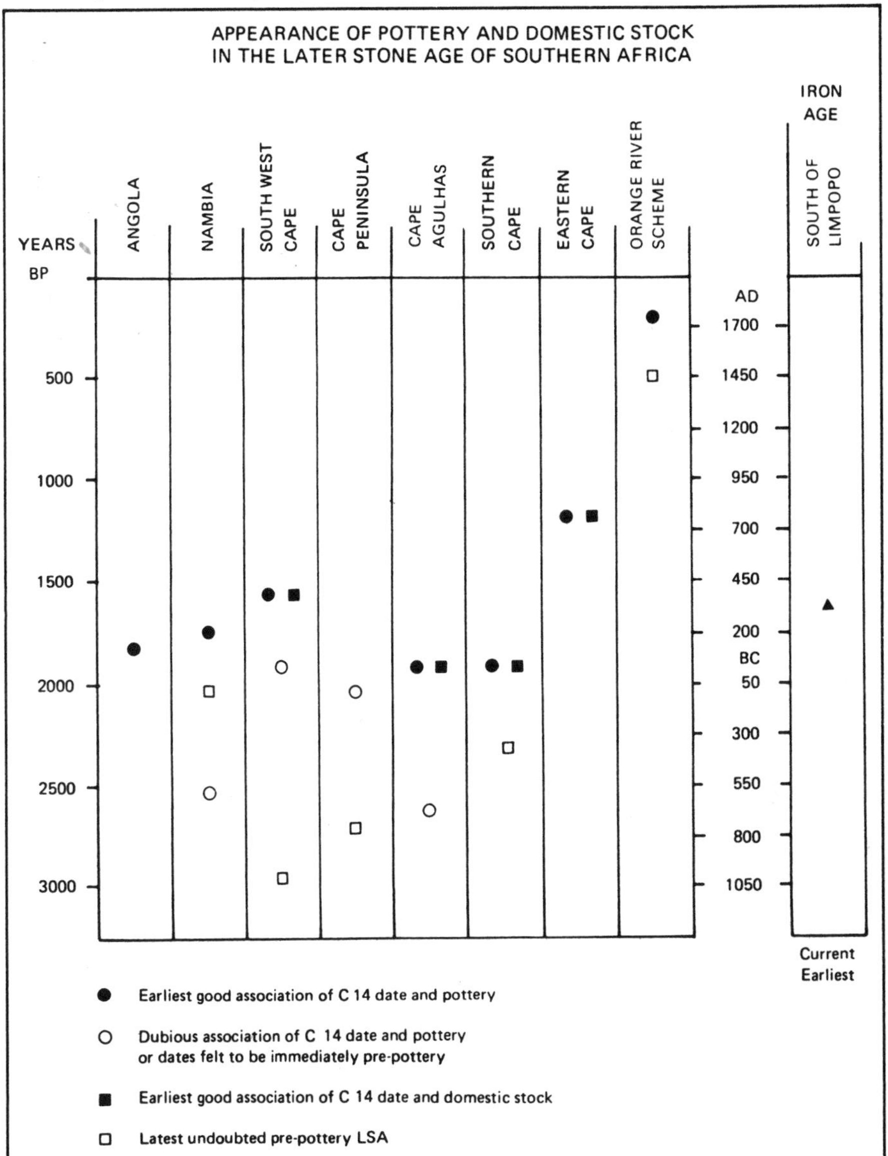

26.4 *The earliest dates available for the appearance of pottery and domestic stock in later Stone Age contexts in Southern Africa (J. E. Parkington)*

The implication of this contextual, distributional and chronological pattern seems to be that herding peoples with pottery spread rapidly into the southern Cape along a westerly coastal route around −2000. No doubt groups of hunters were integrated into the pastoralist societies and there must have been some important readjustments in demographic and economic patterns, though these remain largely undocumented. It seems inescapable that these intruders were the Khoi Khoi pastoralists.

It is, of course, of considerable interest to speculate on the origins, causes and circumstances of this intrusion, but with so few data such speculation must be very imprecise. Research in Zambia and Zimbabwe has tended to be rigidly divided into Iron Age and Stone Age, with the result that surface levels in cave, shelter or open sites containing pottery have often been written off as Stone Age with Iron Age contamination. The fact is that in these areas there may well have been populations of a technically Stone Age character, but whose economy included the herding of some domestic stock, and who manufactured pottery recognizably different from local iron-using agriculturists. In Zimbabwe the so-called Bambata pottery is fairly generally recognized as distinct from Iron Age pottery and was often recovered with 'Wilton', that is Late Stone Age, artefacts. Whether this reflects a pre-Iron Age spread of pastoralists or not remains contentious, but corroboration for the idea may be sought in the distribution of paintings of fat-tailed sheep from Zimbabwe, generally believed to be of Stone Age associations. These were the sheep herded by Khoi Khoi pastoralists at the Cape in the fifteenth, sixteenth and seventeenth centuries of the Christian era.

Should the distribution of Stone Age sheep-herding peoples be extended through Zimbabwe and Zambia, the possibility arises of some origin in East Africa where cultural, linguistic and even biological antecedents have been postulated. The existence of herding peoples who make pottery with lugs, the survival of 'click languages' in the Hatsa and Sandawe, and the claimed 'Hamitic' features of 'Hottentot' populations have all at one time or another been quoted as evidence of a north-eastern origin for the herding, non-iron-using populations of southern Africa. Whilst these connections may be dubious or in some cases rejected, the continuity of traits such as ceramics, sheep-herding, sheep and cattle types, non-iron technology, ground stone artefacts and possibly language, if proven, would argue strongly for an ultimate East African origin for Khoi Khoi pastoralists. This in turn would suggest that the disruptions which caused the movements of Bantu-speakers in a predominantly eastern wave southwards may also have prompted a western move, perhaps towards the Cape. The absence of 'Hottentot' or 'Cape Coastal' pottery from the Transvaal, Swaziland, Natal, the Orange Free State or the Transkei may merely reflect the facts that agriculture is a more feasible pursuit in these better-watered, summer-rainfall areas and that highly mobile herding peoples without crops were more capable of spreading through the dry landscapes of Namibia and the northern Cape and thence to the pastures of the western and southern Cape.

It is conceivable that sheep were brought along the western route but that cattle were obtained by Khoi Khoi pastoralists from the east, from Bantu-speaking populations by then resident in the Transkei region. Support for this may come from the abundance of presumed Late Stone Age paintings of fat-tailed sheep in the western

Cape and the absence of similar paintings of cattle, although cattle were painted in the areas now settled by Bantu-speakers. Furthermore the presence of cattle-bones as early as sheep-bones in Late Stone Age excavations in the southern Cape is not yet firmly documented.

Thus there are grounds for speculating that sheep-herding peoples, related to stone-using hunters and distinct physically from Bantu-speakers, having received stock and pottery from neighbours in East Africa, migrated west and then south in search of pasture, to arrive finally at the Cape soon after −2000. Such populations may have incorporated, fought with or simply learned to live with locally existing hunters and subsequently met with and interacted with Bantu-speakers in what is today the Transkei. The sparse distribution of pottery, ground stone artefacts and animal bones along the route just described may mean nothing more than that they were highly mobile, leaving debris so thinly dispersed as to be archaeologically practically invisible.

There is no evidence that the Cape Khoi Khoi were habitual metalworkers before the arrival of European settlers, but the Namaqua were quite obviously able to work copper into beads and discs in the seventeenth century.

Relations between San, Khoi Khoi and other groups such as immigrant colonists or iron-using agriculturalists were probably as varied as those between San and Khoi Khoi. In the west both San and Khoi Khoi were driven from their lands and exterminated or assimilated into colonial society. A number of rock paintings from the western Cape depict the covered wagons, mounted horsemen and weapons of the trekking farmers. In the east the conflict between Iron Age farmers and hunters is largely undocumented, but again rock paintings depict cattle thefts in which small bowmen steal from larger figures with spears and shields. The later stages of this interaction are recorded when literate colonists moved into Natal and on the slopes of the Drakensberg Mountains. Khoi Khoi herdsmen, perhaps having more in common with Bantu-speaking mixed farmers than did the San, seem to have established more harmonious relations with, for example, Xhosa and Tswana groups. The description of the Gonaqua by Le Vaillant suggests a history of close ties between them and near-by Xhosa, including considerable intermarriage. It is probably quite wrong to imagine clear economic, linguistic, physical or cultural distinctions between the various prehistoric peoples of southern Africa. Even more unlikely, perhaps, is the possibility that any such distinctions would have coincided exactly.

27

The beginnings of the Iron Age in southern Africa

The cultural episode in southern Africa known to historians as the Early Iron Age saw the introduction into the area of a way of life which contrasted sharply with those which had gone before, and one which established the character of subsequent historical developments throughout the region. Early in the first millennium of the Christian era a substantial population movement brought to southern Africa a negroid farming people whose economy, settlement-type, perhaps even their physical appearance and their language, were in marked contrast with those of the earlier inhabitants, and who introduced the knowledge of the arts of metallurgy and pottery which were, in this area, previously unknown. It is with the nature, origin and development of these Early Iron Age societies that this chapter is concerned.

Archaeologists now recognize a broad cultural similarity among the communities who introduced Iron Age material culture into southern Africa. The remains of these communities are attributed to a common southern African Early Iron Age industrial complex which is distinguished from other, later, Iron Age industries, both by its chronological integrity and by the clear designation of its associated pottery to a common tradition. The distribution of this Early Iron Age industrial complex extends far beyond the southern African region here discussed. Numerous regional subdivisions within the complex may be recognized primarily on the basis of ceramic stylistic variation, and in many areas these groupings may be confirmed by further unrelated cultural traits.

The Early Iron Age ceramic tradition appears to have been introduced throughout its area of distribution during the first few centuries of the Christian era and to have survived in most areas until its displacement by distinct and more heterogeneous Late Iron Age traditions, most frequently around the beginning of the present millennium. This terminal date varies in some areas, the Early Iron Age being displaced by the eighth century in certain regions, while in others there may be demonstrated a considerable degree of typological continuity between the Early Iron Age and the modern traditional ceramic industries. For convenience, in the context of the present multi-volume work, I have taken it upon myself to discuss the Early Iron Age cultures up to the time of their displacement or until the eleventh century of the Christian era, whichever is the earlier in each region. I have thus left the later survivals of the Early Iron Age cultures for discussion elsewhere in the context of their Late Iron Age contemporaries.

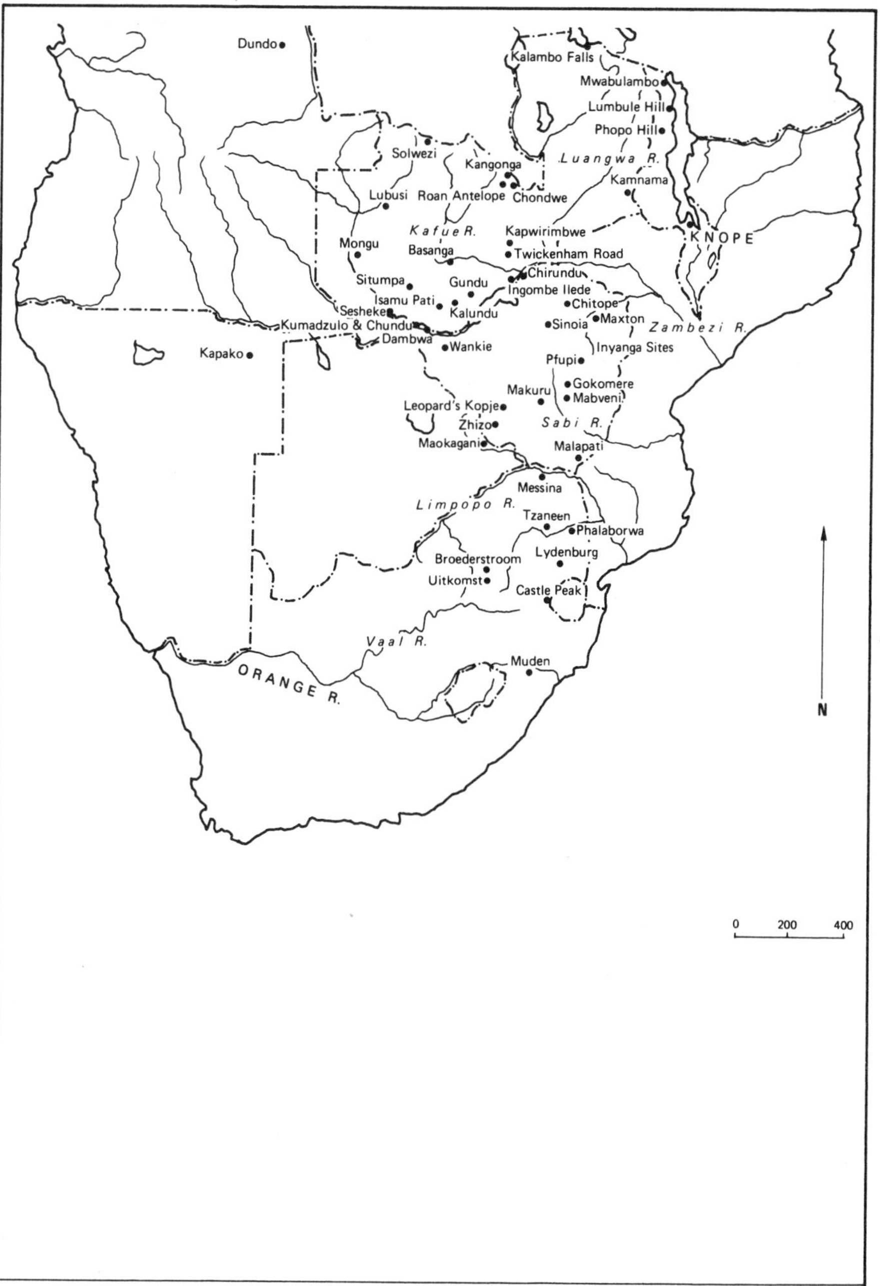

27.1 *Southern Africa: sites (from D. W. Phillipson)*

It is clear that the Early Iron Age represents but one sector of human activity in southern Africa during the first millennium of the Christian era. In many areas 'Late Stone Age' folk continued to practise their traditional way of life throughout this period; while some of their counterparts farther to the south, beyond the southernmost penetration of the Early Iron Age, appear to have adopted certain new cultural traits which are best seen as derived from contact, both direct and indirect, with Early Iron Age settlers. These 'Late Stone Age' and related populations are discussed by J. E. Parkington in Chapter 26 of the present volume.

Reconstruction of the Early Iron Age in southern Africa must be based first and foremost on archaeological evidence. Unlike events of the later periods of the Iron Age, those of this time – which corresponds broadly with the first millennium of the Christian era – lie effectively beyond the range of oral tradition. As has been shown in an earlier chapter, attempts have been made to base historical reconstructions of the pre-literate Early Iron Age societies of this region on purely linguistic evidence. In the present state of our knowledge, however, it seems preferable generally to admit the conclusions of historical linguistics as secondary evidence for comparison with a sequence which has first been established on the basis of archaeology.

Regional survey of archaeological evidence

Southern Zambia, Angola, Malawi

A regional survey of the Zambian Early Iron Age has recently been undertaken by the present writer; and a number of distinct groups have been recognized primarily on the basis of the typology of the associated pottery. Here, we are only concerned with the evidence from the southern part of the country. Two closely related groups may be discerned in the Copperbelt region and on the Lusaka plateau. The Chondwe group of the Copperbelt is characterized by pottery vessels with thickened or undifferential rims, the most frequent decorative motifs being lines of alternately facing triangular impressions forming a chevron design in false relief and also chardate areas of comb-stamping delineated by broad grooves. The score of village sites which have so far yielded pottery of this type are distributed alongside rivers and streams, generally close to the tree-lines of the dambos which fringe the upper reaches of the Kafue head-water tributaries. Radio-carbon dates for the Chondwe group sites of Kangonga and Chondwe cover the sixth to the eleventh centuries of the Christian era, but study of pottery typology suggests that certain other sites may be earlier. Iron and copper working is evident throughout the time range of the known sites. However, exploitation of the area's copper deposits appears to have been on a small scale in Early Iron Age times, although it attracted widespread trade contacts.

To the south, centred on the Lusaka plateau, are the Early Iron Age sites attributed to the Kapwirimbwe group, the pottery of which is distinguished from that of the Chondwe group by the greater degree and frequency of rim-thickening and by the extreme rarity of all comb-stamped decoration, the place of which is taken by a variety of incised designs. At the village of Kapwirimbwe, 13 kilometres east of Lusaka, the apparently brief occupation has been securely dated from around the fifth century of the Christian era. There were extensive remains of collapsed *daga* structures, many of which appear to have been iron-smelting furnaces.

In western Zambia few Early Iron Age sites have so far been discovered. At Sioma Mission on the upper Zambezi, a settlement is dated from the middle centuries of the first millennium; another, beside the Lubusi river west of Kamoa, belongs to the last quarter of that millennium. These sites have yielded pottery which, although undoubtedly belonging to the Early Iron Age, is markedly distinct from that of the groups recognized farther to the east.

At this point it is convenient to note that Iron Age sites dating from the first millennium of the Christian era are now known from more southerly areas of Angola, as at Feti la Choya where the earliest Iron Age occupation is dated from the seventh or eighth century. The relationship of this site to the Early Iron Age industrial complex cannot be determined since no details of the associated artefacts, beyond the bare fact that iron and pottery were present, have so far been made available. In the extreme north of Namibia, the site of Kapako has yielded pottery, described in a preliminary and provisional account as akin to that from Kapwirimbwe, associated with a radio-carbon date in the late first millennium.

South of the Kafue, in the fertile plateau regions of the Southern Province of Zambia, several sites of large Early Iron Age villages have now been discovered. Individual sites were apparently settled for a much longer time than was general elsewhere; the earliest such occupations apparently took place around the fourth century. This Early Iron Age settlement seems to have been denser than in most other populations whose counterparts elsewhere long survived the arrival of agriculture and metallurgy.

The Zambezi Valley area around Livingstone is probably the best-explored region of southern Africa from the point of view of Iron Age archaeology. The Early Iron Age Dambwa group of this area shares features both with the Kalundu group and with the Gokomere sites in Zimbabwe. It has been suggested that, after an initial and little-known phase best illustrated by the small assemblage of shards from the Situmpa site near Machili, the main florescence of the Dambwa group may have been derived from a secondary centre of dispersal of Iron Age culture situated south of the Zambezi. Copper does not occur in the region and must have been brought in by trade, the two nearest known sources being in the Kafue Hook region of Zambia and around Wankie in Zimbabwe. Copper artefacts found on Dambwa group sites include bangles and trade-bars.

In the Eastern Province of Zambia the Early Iron Age population appears to have been established by the third century of the Christian era, but to have been sparse; the majority of the Christian inhabitants of this area probably retained their 'Late Stone Age' way of life well into the present millennium, until long after the inception of the Late Iron Age. The pottery of these Kamnama group sites of eastern Zambia is clearly closely related to that from contemporary settlements in adjacent regions of Malawi, where an outline Iron Age archaeological sequence is now available for the greater part of the country lying to the west of the lake.

In northern Malawi, a site on the South Rukuru river beside Phopo Hill has yielded evidence for prolonged Early Iron Age occupation dated to between the

27.2 *Southern Africa: location of Early Iron Age and related sites mentioned in the text (from D. W. Phillipson)*

second and fifth centuries of the Christian era. Potsherds, wild-animal bones and evidence of iron-smelting were recovered, together with shell disc beads. No glass beads were found. The pottery is clearly akin to that from Kamnama; and the general affinities of this material to the Early Iron Age wares of East Africa, especially that from Kwale inland from Mombasa, are clear. Comparable material from Lumbule Hill near Livingstonia is dated to about the middle of the first millennium. In northern Malawi the Mwavarambo site appears to represent the local form of the Early Iron Age, showing some affinities with the Malambo group of northern Zambia. Mwavarambo is dated from the eleventh to the thirteenth centuries. In southern Malawi, the finds from the numerous sites attributed to the Nkope group indicate comparable settlements of the period from the fourth to the eleventh centuries.

The Early Iron Age ceramics from Malawi and adjacent regions of Zambia form a clear typological link between the contemporary wares of East Africa and those of Zimbabwe, but they are markedly distinct from those of the Chondwe, Kapwirimbwe and Kalundu groups in the trans-Luangwan regions to the west. Unfortunately, no data are available on Early Iron Age sites, if any do indeed occur, in the country to the east of Lake Malawi.

Africa south of the Zambezi

In Zimbabwe the same general picture of regionally differentiated Early Iron Age industries belonging to a common industrial complex is continued. We have already referred to the industries of two northern regions of the country, which are closely related to Zambian groups. Over most of the rest of Zimbabwe the Early Iron Age cultures show considerable basic similarity. There is general acceptance for a tripartite division of the associated pottery. Ziwa ware appears centered on the eastern highlands around Inyanga and extending both westwards towards Salisbury and southwards along the Mozambique border areas towards the Low Veld: Zhizo ware (formerly known as Leopard's Kopje I) is found in the south-west around Bulawayo. Gokomere ware is widely distributed in the south-central area. The typology shows that the three groups are intimately related; indeed recent work has shown that in several areas there is considerable typological overlap between the groups and suggests that they may not always be so sharply defined as are some of the Zambian Early Iron Age groups.

A clear picture of Zimbabwean Early Iron Age settlement is obtained at Mabveni in the Chibi district, where remains of three pole-and-*daga* structures have been investigated; one of these was interpreted as a storage bin which was originally raised above the ground on stones. Traces of dry-stone walling could not be linked unequivocally with the Early Iron Age settlement, but are architecturally distinct from structures of more recent date. The pottery was characterized by necked vessels with diagonal comb-stamped decoration on the thickened rim-band, and a variety of open bowls. Clay figurines of sheep and humans were also recovered, as were beads made of iron, copper and shell. Contact with coastal trade is demonstrated by the presence of marine shells and glass beads. Sheep were the only domestic animals represented. The site is dated from some period within the first two-thirds of the first millennium.

Confirmatory evidence for much of the above comes from a rock shelter at Gokomere Mission north of Fort Victoria, where the animal bones included a horn-core of the domestic goat. The Early Iron Age settlement at Gokomere is dated from between the fifth and seventh centuries. The earliest Iron Age occupation of the 'Acropolis' at Great Zimbabwe is a further example of the Gokomere Early Iron Age industry, the end of which is dated between the third and fifth centuries.

Significant economic development is indicated in this area during the later centuries of the Early Iron Age. It is only in its later forms that Ziwa ware is found associated with imported glass beads. Comparable pottery is also found on sites with simple terraces and stone walling, as well as in gold and copper mines, indicating that its makers were involved in the more comprehensive exploitation of their territory's natural resources than had been their predecessors, and also that they were in contact with the trade network of the Indian Ocean.

It is at this time, too, that domestic cattle are first attested in the archaeological record of Zimbabwe. Remains of these animals are markedly absent from sites of the earliest phase of Iron Age settlement south of the Zambezi, where the only domestic species represented are sheep and goats. Cattle are first recorded on sites dated to the eighth century. They do not, however, become frequent before the inception of the Late Iron Age.

Centred on Bulawayo, the sites yielding Zhizo-type pottery have much in common with the Early Iron Age industries farther east. It now appears that this pottery does not represent the initial Early Iron Age occupation of the area; this is probably seen in such sites as Mandau and Mandiliyangwa in the Matopo Hills, where the sherds have close typological connections both with the early Gokomere wares and with the earliest Iron Age pottery of the Dambwa group in the Victoria Falls region. It seems probable that in much of south-western Zimbabwe the Early Iron Age population remained sparse until the development of the Zhizo industry late in the first millennium. Rock-art studies indicate the substantial survival of Late Stone Age peoples throughout this time, especially in the Matopo Hills.

Excavations at Zhizo Hill in the Matopos have yielded fragments of pole-and-*daga* structures and collections of stones which are interpreted as the supports for grain storage bins, together with pottery decorated primarily with comb-stamped motifs; this material is dated between the ninth and twelfth centuries.

The spread of the Early Iron Age industrial complex south of the Limpopo during the first millennium is now indicated, but the evidence is sparse and incomplete. Pottery similar to that from Malapati has been discovered at Matakoma in the Soutspansberg of the northern Transvaal; no absolute dates for the site are available, but the similarity with the dated Malapati assemblage makes a date in the second half of the first millennium appear probable. Near Tzaneen in the north-eastern Transvaal, pottery of Early Iron Age type has been dated from the third or fourth century, indicating that the spread of this complex south of the Limpopo did not long postdate its introduction into Zimbabwe.

Even farther to the south, several occurrences of Iron Age artefacts have been dated from the first millennium, but their attribution to the Early Iron Age industrial complex remains uncertain. At Castle Peak, Ngwenya, in western Swaziland, an Iron

Age presence is securely dated from the fourth or fifth century. The excavators' preliminary note indicates that the pottery, which was found associated with stone mining tools, occasional iron objects and artefacts of 'Late Stone Age' type, may be attributable to the Early Iron Age.

Archaeological synthesis

Despite the uneven distribution and quality of archaeological research into the Early Iron Age, which will have become apparent from the foregoing summary, several broad overall trends may be discerned. Within the area under review, study of the pottery typology permits the recognition of two major divisions within the Early Iron Age. One, best known in central and southern Zambia where it is represented by the Chondwe, Kapwirimbwe and Kalundu groups, extends for a considerable but unknown distance to the west. The other occupies Malawi, eastern Zambia and the area of known Early Iron Age settlement south of the Zambezi. The Dambwa group in the Victoria Falls area of the Zambezi valley shares features in common with both divisions. This classification is confirmed to a certain extent by the study of selected economic aspects of the Early Iron Age, as attempted below.

Food-producing economy

Detailed evidence for the food-producing economy of the Early Iron Age societies has only rarely been recovered. The presence of relatively large, semi-permanent villages is, of course, suggestive of an economy based to a substantial extent on food production, while the discovery of occasional iron hoes and large numbers of grindstones is indicative of some form of agriculture. More specific evidence for the identity of the cultigens and domesticates involved has, however, only been forthcoming from comparatively few sites.

Bones of domestic cattle, however, come from early contexts only at the southern Zambian sites of Kapwirimbwe, Kalundu and Kumadzulo. South of the Zambezi cattle do not appear to occur before the eighth century, as at Coronation Park, Makuru and Malapati. That sheep were introduced into Zimbabwe before cattle may also be inferred from the study of the rock paintings of that country, where fat-tailed sheep are frequently represented, but cattle never. Recent evidence from Broederstroom, however, suggests that cattle may have occurred earlier in the Transvaal, where they probably came from the west.

Mining and metallurgy

Only three metals were worked on any substantial scale during the southern African Iron Age: these, in decreasing order of importance, were iron, copper and gold.

Iron ore in one form or another is extremely widespread throughout the region; where richer ores were not available, ferricrete or bog iron appears to have been smelted, despite their low yield. Iron-working seems to have been introduced throughout the region contemporaneously with the arrival of the other diagnostic traits which constitute Iron Age culture as here defined. There is no evidence that iron was generally mined other than by the excavation of shallow pits; often the ore was simply collected from the surface. Details of the iron-smelting furnaces of the southern African Early Iron Age are not known, but it is interesting to note that smelting appears frequently to have been conducted within the confines of the villages, as if the taboos, which in later periods ensured that smelting operations were carried out away from all contact with women, did not at that time apply. The objects made of iron were generally of domestic utilitarian purpose: knives, arrows and spearheads and the like. There was probably little long-distance trade in iron or iron objects.

Copper deposits have a far more restricted distribution than do those of iron. Copper artefacts are, however, widely distributed on Early Iron Age sites, although they are not so common as they are on those of later periods. It cannot be demonstrated that copper-working technology was practised in all areas at such an early date in the Early Iron Age as were the corresponding techniques for iron; in the Lusaka region, for example, copper appears not to have been known until a late phase of the Early Iron Age. Copper was clearly regarded as a relative luxury and its use was largely restricted to the manufacture of small items of personal adornment such as beads and bangles of thin, twisted strip. The metal was traded in the form of bars, of which the best example from an Early Iron Age context is that from Kumadzulo. No copper-smelting furnaces of the Early Iron Age have been investigated.

Iron Age gold-mining in southern Africa appears to have been restricted largely to Zimbabwe and immediately adjacent regions. Small-scale prehistoric workings in Zambia, South Africa and elsewhere have been reported, but no detailed investigations have been conducted. In contrast, well over a thousand prehistoric gold-mines have been recorded in Zimbabwe and closely bordering regions of Botswana and the Transvaal. Most of the ancient workings have been destroyed by further mining within the past eighty years and only in very few cases are detailed descriptions available. Dating the prehistoric exploitation of the Zimbabwean gold deposits is correspondingly difficult. The earliest radio-carbon dates for ancient mines in this region are from the Aboyne and Geelong mines, both around the twelfth century.

Although substantial quantities of gold objects have been recovered from Zimbabwean Iron Age sites, the great majority of these were removed by treasure-seekers during the early years of the European occupation; in hardly any cases, therefore, are data available concerning the provenance and archaeological associations of such discoveries. The few finds of gold which have been made in controlled archaeological excavations have all come from Late Iron Age contexts.

Architecture

Only a few sites have yielded information permitting the reconstruction of architectural plans and structural details attributable to the Early Iron Age in this region; and there must remain some doubt as to the extent to which these sites are characteristic of the architecture of southern Africa as a whole during this period. Kumandzulo produced evidence of the plans of eleven houses of pole-and-*daga* construction. These were sub-rectangular in outline with substantial corner posts; the maximum wall-length was only 2.3 metres. No comparable evidence has been recovered from other Early Iron Age sites in southern Africa, but fragmentary traces from a number of other sites such as Dambwa and Chitope suggest that the general method of construction illustrated at Kumandzulo was frequently used, although the sub-rectangular shape of the Kumadzulo houses cannot be paralleled elsewhere.

Building in stone was widespread in the Iron Age in regions south of the Zambezi, but the practice seems not to have spread into Zambia except on a very small scale during the closing centuries of the Late Iron Age.

Conclusion

Such, in outline, is the present state of our knowledge concerning the Early Iron Age in southern Africa. Elucidation of the events of this cultural episode is here regarded as primarily an archaeological exercise. Historical linguistic investigations can clearly also make a major contribution to Early Iron Age studies; these have been discussed in an earlier chapter.

Within the southern African region here discussed, two major divisions of the Early Iron Age may be recognized in the archaeological record. They may best be regarded as primary divisions of the common Early Iron Age industrial complex, but they may be readily distinguished from each other by the typology of the associated pottery. One division displays a distribution extending southwards between the Luangwa Valley and Lake Malawi to Zimbabwe and the northern Transvaal; its people were herders of sheep and goats, but appear initially to have lacked cattle. The second division is best known from central and southern Zambia, but there are indications that it also extended over an enormous area farther to the west. In this region cattle were known in Early Iron Age times and it was probably from these folk that cattle were passed to the early Khoisan pastoralists of the most southerly regions of the continent, to which the Early Iron Age industrial complex itself did not penetrate.

The very uneven distribution of archaeological research prevents a more detailed view of the broader subdivisions of the Early Iron Age. In particular, the whole of Mozambique is a complete blank on the distribution maps, so events throughout the area between the Indian Ocean and Lake Malawi remain entirely unknown. Most of Angola and much of South Africa have so far been very inadequately investigated. When these deficiencies have been remedied, it is probable that very major revisions will be required to the synthesis here proposed.

It has been shown that the culture introduced to southern Africa by the Early Iron Age people was responsible for establishing many of the main trends in the subsequent culture-history of the region until quite recent times. Of particular interest to the historian in this context is the extent to which the regionally differentiated characteristics of later times may be traced back to the Early Iron Age. The stone-building tradition of Zimbabwe and the Transvaal, the gold-mining of Zimbabwe and the copper-working of the Copperbelt area, for example, are all seen to have their inception in the context of the Early Iron Age in their respective regions, although they did not reach their full florescence until later times. Continuity between the Early and Late Iron Ages in many areas was thus presumably more marked than has often been assumed; but it is only when more intensive research has been conducted, particularly in those areas which remain virtually unexplored by archaeologists, that the full contribution of the Early Iron Age to southern African history may be evaluated.

28 Madagascar

Cultural investigations

The population of Madagascar has been the subject of many studies, yet, despite several often valid hypotheses, its origins are still veiled in mystery. Most authors agree that, while the neighbouring African continent has made ethnic contributions to Madagascar, the Malayo-Polynesian elements, which are just as obvious, especially in the central highlands, should also be stressed. The double ethnic origin of the Malagasy would explain the physical differences among the inhabitants of the island, who all speak an Indonesian language. Although this language is divided into three dialects, its linguistic unity is unquestionable.

Linguistics

The Dutchman de Houtman was the first scholar to suggest that Malagasy belongs to the Malayo-Polynesian linguistic group.

Van der Tuuk later established scientifically the relationship between Malagasy and the Indonesian languages. Dahl pointed out that Malagasy had been influenced by Bantu, not only in its vocabulary, but also in its phonology. This fact is of prime importance for the discussion of African–Indonesian interactions, which will be described later. Hébert has shown in several of his works that there is often a bipartition among the Indonesian terms in Malagasy that demonstrates the heterogeneity of its south-east Asian origins. Dez has made an analysis of the vocabulary of Indonesian origin that allows us to infer what type of civilization was brought to Madagascar by the emigrants. And lastly glottochronology has confirmed the deeply Indonesian nature of the basic vocabulary (94 per cent) and provides an idea of the length of time that separates Malagasy from the proto-language. But, although the main elements of the basic Malagasy linguistic corpus belong to the Indonesian subgroup, we should not forget that other elements, Indian, Arabic and African, have also been incorporated into the language. The contacts implied by these elements help us to understand the contacts and admixtures of the Indonesian diaspora westwards.

Physical anthropology

Research in this field has confirmed that the Malagasy belong both to the mongoloid and to the negroid stock. Rakoto-Ratsimamanga has come to important conclusions

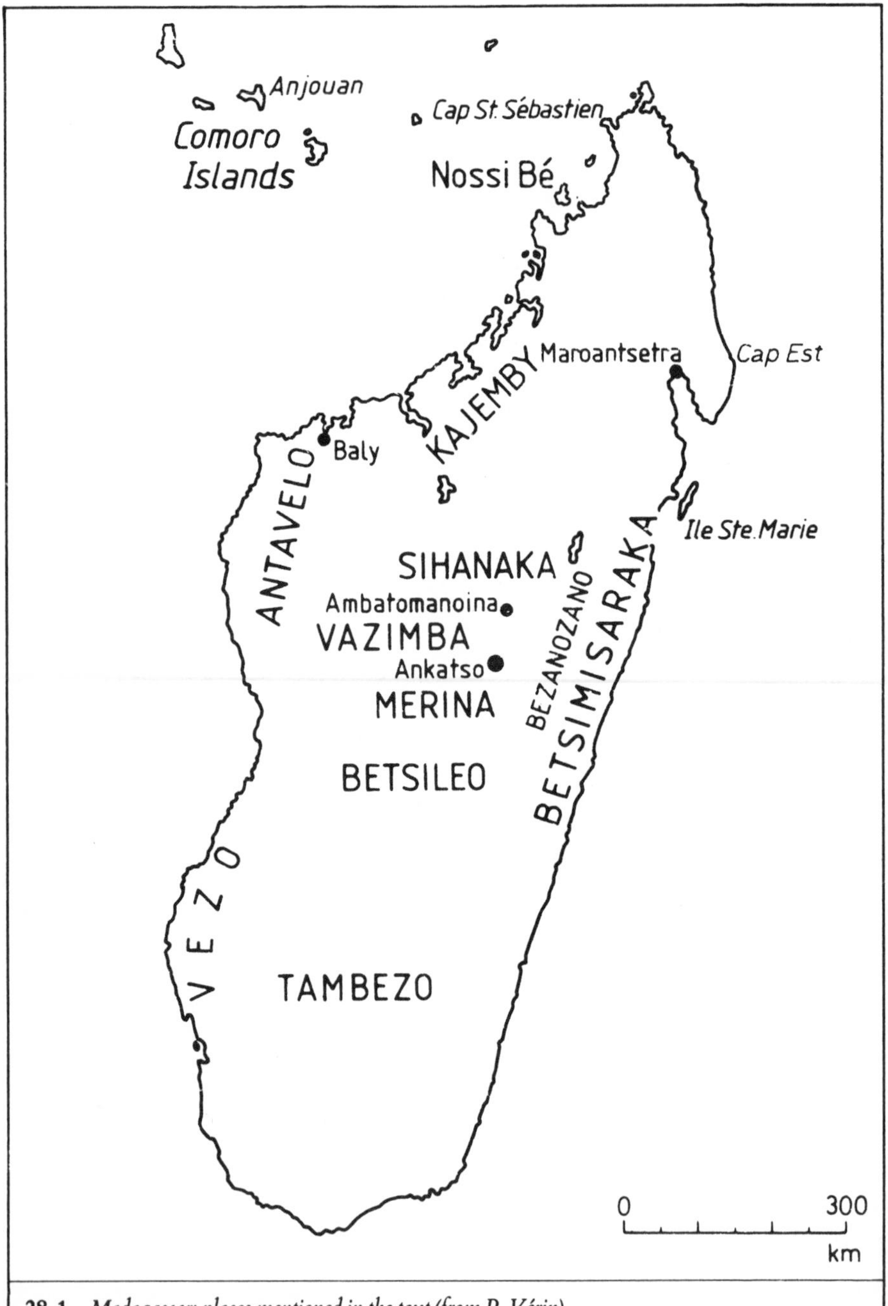

28.1 *Madagascar: places mentioned in the text (from P. Vérin)*

on the distribution and nature of the pigmentation most frequently found among the inhabitants of the central highlands. He distinguishes four morphological types among which the population is divided in the following proportions:

Indonesian-mongoloid type	37%
Negro-Oceanic type	52%
Negro-African type	2%
European type	9%

One might question whether such a large proportion of the negroid element is really of Oceanic origin.

Haematological research carried out by Pigache shows very clearly that the Malagasy negroids are of African and not Melanesian origin.

Ethnology

It was H. Deschamps who first attempted to distinguish between the Indonesian and the African contributions to Malagasy civilization. Certain African cultural features are found, such as elements of the cattle complex, the snake-cult addressed to dead kings in the west and in Betsileo, and some features of the socio-political organization found in the coastal regions.

Malagasy civilization owes much to the east, including most house forms, rice culture on irrigated terraces, some aspects of ancestor-worship and a whole technological complex, including the double-valved bellows, the outrigger canoe, the underground oven containing porous volcanic rock, and less well known objects, such as the rotating bow drill and the mounted file for opening coconuts that have been studied on the west coast of Madagascar and that are found as far away as Western Polynesia, identical in form.

One can conclude that the ancestors of the Malagasy are both Indonesian and African in origin, and that the predominantly Indonesian nature of the language need not minimize the role played by Africa in the settlement of Madagascar. That great neighbouring continent contributed physically to the majority of the population and also gave Madagascar many features of its culture and its socio-political organization. Such a hybrid situation is not to be found in the Comoro Islands or on the coast of Africa where Indonesian influxes are also supposed to have occurred.

The different theories as to the origins of the Malagasy in fact hover between two extremes, Africa and Indonesia, though it is true that some authors such as Razafintsalama (who maintained, on the basis of several thousand suspect etymological derivations, that the great island had been colonized by Buddhist monks) hold completely deviant points of view. A. Grandidier attributed an exaggerated importance to Asia, believing that apart from the recent Makua arrivals all the ancestors of the Malagasy came from south-east Asia, including the negroids that he calls – for this purpose – Melanesians. G. Ferrand accepted this view which is in defiance of the geographical evidence, though less unreasonably, and stressed the more African aspects of the origins of the Malagasy. He distinguished the following historical phases:

a possible pre-Bantu-speaking period;
a Bantu-speaking period dating to before the Christian era;
a pre-Merina Indonesian period from the second to the fourth century with emigration from Sumatra during which the newcomers established their supremacy over the Bantu-speaking peoples;
arrival of the Arabs from the seventh to the eleventh centuries;
a new wave of Sumatrans in the tenth century, among whom we find Ramini, the ancestor of the Zafindraminia, and Rakuba, the ancestor of the Hova;
lastly, the Persians and, in about 1500, the Zafikasinambo.

The first settlements in Madagascar

Before going more deeply into the Indonesian and African origins of the Malagasy people, we should evaluate the theories that attempt to credit Madagascar with very ancient migrations from the Mediterranean region.

Phoenicians, Hebrews or people of the *Periplus?*

In dealing with countries beyond the fringes of the ancient world the Phoenicians, Egyptians, Sabaeans, Greeks and Hebrews are often credited with clearly exaggerated contributions to the history of those countries. For instance Bent (1893) attributed the founding of Zimbabwe to the Phoenicians, and C. Poirier identified the region of Sofala with the countries of Punt and Ophir.

According to some authors ancient voyagers even reached Madagascar. F. de Mahy thought he had found Phoenician remains at Majunga, but Ferrand and I are unable to confirm his hypothesis. A. Grandidier in his account states that the Greeks, and of course the Arabs, visited Madagascar. According to him, 'ever since ancient times this island was known to the Greeks and the Arabs, by the names of Menuthias, Djafouna and Chezbezar which they gave it, and the accurate but very short description which they have left us of it, did not catch the attention of European geographers, who only learned of its existence through the Portuguese in 1500'.

In fact the only Greek name, 'Menuthias', which occurs in Ptolemy and the *Periplus*, is more likely to denote the island of Pemba, or perhaps Zanzibar or Mafia. A certain F. Du Mesgnil took it into his head to write a work with the title, *Madagascar, Homer and the Mycenaean civilization*, which gives a clear picture of the speculations that the work contains.

The legends of Jewish migrations are more difficult to dismiss. Father Joseph Briant, in his slim volume *The Hebrew in Madagascar*, is convinced that there were, not one, but two Jewish migrations to Madagascar. He supports his arguments with several hundred comparisons between Malagasy and Hebrew words.

Such researches into the Jewish origins of certain of the Malagasy go back to Flacourt, who believed that the first foreigners to come to the east coast of Madagascar were 'the Zaffe-Hibrahim, or those of the lineage of Abraham, the inhabitants of the Isle of the Blessed Mary and the neighbouring lands', and in his foreword to the *History of the Great Isle of Madagascar* Flacourt justifies his hypothesis by the existence of biblical names, the practice of circumcision and the fact that working on Saturday is forbidden.

G. Ferrand denies the possibility of these Jewish migrations. He believes that the few Semitic names on the island can be attributed to the Malagasy who were converted to Islam, and as for the fact that working on Saturday is forbidden, Saturday is simply a *fady* (taboo) day, a common occurrence in Malagasy custom; on the east coast *fady* still occurs on Tuesdays, Thursdays or Saturdays according to the region. Moreover it seems that in the seventeenth century the existence of circumcision among several exotic peoples led Christian French authors to try to find a Jewish origin for them.

A different theory as to the origins of the pre-Islamic Malagasy has recently been put forward by Poirier, who sees a duality in the Muslim contributions to Madagascar. While his predecessors felt that the attenuated Muslim practices that survive in Madagascar suggested a Jewish origin, Poirier considers that they are a primitive form of religion that came to Madagascar from Arabia. However, archaeological data from East Africa and Madagascar give no support to this theory. The massive Arab infiltrations that fertilized Swahili culture commenced in the eighth century.

The first Indonesian immigrants

Although it would be rash to attempt to put a definite date to the migration of the first Indonesians, for reasons that we shall go into later, we can conjecture that their departure took place from the fifth century of the Christian era. They may have continued moving until the twelfth century, as Deschamps thinks. The name Palaeo-Indonesians is given to the first migrants who made contact with the Africans and who probably also made alliances with them. The later arrivals, known as Neo-Indonesians, were the ancestors of the Merina. This last wave has preserved its original biological identity better, possibly because it followed a more direct route, but it is probable that because of its smaller numbers it adopted the language of Palaeo-Indonesians who arrived earlier in Madagascar.

If some stone artefacts were found, they would enable us to know more about the earliest phase of Malagasy history, but up to now none has been found, and I am of the view that the first Malagasy to live on the island were acquainted with metal. We know that on the African coast the Stone Age was superseded by the Iron Age between the first and fourth centuries of the Christian era. The Bronze Age in Indonesia was far earlier, and, what is more important, very different civilizations coexisted there; there were even a few isolated groups in Indonesia that continued to use stone tools after the tenth century. Whether or not stone objects exist in Madagascar is a matter of controversy.

As far as means of transport are concerned, it has often been asked whether the Indonesians of the first millennium of the Christian era had ships capable of covering such long distances. In the east Indian Ocean, as Deschamps has shown, there were ships that could be taken on the high seas; the earliest picture of such a ship appears in the sculpture of the Borobudur temple (Java, eighth century) depicting a ship with an outrigger, two masts and sails.

Having recognized the Indonesian contribution to the settlement of Madagascar, it remains to discover the routes that they may have taken. Many authors have pointed out the existence firstly of the great south equatorial route which, in theory, might lead from Java to Madagascar; this south equatorial current is strong between the southern coasts of Java and the neighbouring region of the Amber Cape from August to September. Sibrée has pointed out that the pumice stones which came from the Krakatoa explosion travelled along such a route that brought them eventually to the coast of Madagascar.

Although not absolutely untenable, the idea of a direct route from the Indian Archipelago to Madagascar remains unlikely for reasons Donque explains perfectly: although a priori a direct route between Java and Madagascar meets with no insurmountable obstacles during the southern winter, when tropical cyclones are absent from the region, yet we should note the existence of factors that might invalidate such a hypothesis, for the direct journey covers a distance of nearly 4,000 miles over a marine desert without a single port of call. We should, therefore, rather envisage a route that called in at southern India and Sri Lanka (Ceylon). Deschamps alludes to references made to pirate incursions in these regions in the first half of the first millennium of the Christian era.

The journey from southern India to Madagascar does not pose any great problem. The route along the southern coasts of West Africa had been known since the period of the *Periplus*, and the abundance of Chinese coinage found later at Sīrāf testifies to the importance of trade between the Far East and the Middle East by sea. From the Middle East travellers went down the African coast, as they had done in the days of Rhapta's prosperity, and it is probable that the discovery of the Comoro Islands was an intermediary step to that of Madagascar.

The Indonesians who stayed on the African coast may, as Deschamps believed (as also did Kent, in a different but quite as hypothetical a form), have formed a nucleus for the settlement of Madagascar. The impact of the Indonesians on the African coast has been exaggerated, for the 'Malaysian complex' of plants imported into Africa from south-east Asia is not necessarily linked to Indonesia: according to the *Periplus* sugar-cane, and probably the coconut-palm, arrived independently.

The fact that the outrigger canoe is found throughout the Indian Ocean is certainly an indication of the extent of Indonesian influence, as Hornell realized. Deschamps believes that it shows the route taken by the migrants to Madagascar, a plausible idea which is, however, still under discussion, for the close links between Swahili and Malagasy culture may have encouraged such loans.

The end of Indonesian migration to the west

It is possible that it was the increased influence of Islam from the beginning of the second millennium that put a stop to the voyages of the Indonesians.

The Indonesian voyages to the coast of Africa ceased quite early, but this does not mean that relations were broken off between the Far East and the western Indian Ocean. On the contrary, there are indications of the expansion of Indian Ocean trade that was probably largely in the hands of the Muslims who became more and more familiar with the trade-routes. Ibn Majid's chart gives precise latitudes for the towns on the African coast and for the Indonesian territories and entrepôts across the ocean, which could, in those times, be crossed in thirty to forty days.

28.2 *Chinese pottery, Vohemar civilisation (Art and Archaeology Museum, Madagascar)*

28.3 *Antalaotse tomb of Antsoheribory (P. Vérin)*

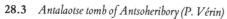

It is not inconceivable that, though the Indonesians had stopped frequenting the coast of Africa, they continued to sail straight to Madagascar, perhaps from the southern regions of India. The Neo-Indonesians may also have followed this route.

The African and Swahili immigration

This discussion of the various hypotheses as to the Indonesian origins of the Malagasy should not allow us to forget that an important – and possibly major – contribution to the settlement of Madagascar was from Africa. Deschamps has put forward two hypotheses to explain this Afro-Asian symbiosis, firstly that there was ethnic and cultural mixing on the east coast of Africa itself, and secondly that the Indonesians may have raided the neighbouring coast from Madagascar. Kent also sees the symbiosis in terms of strong Indonesian influence in Africa and a subsequent colonization of Madagascar. However, at present we have no archaeological information whatsoever from the southern coastal sites of Africa (Tanzania–Mozambique), and I personally refuse to consider such theories except as mere hypotheses. It is quite possible that the Afro-Indonesian symbiosis may have begun in the Comoro Islands or in north Madagascar.

The often-repeated idea, that Madagascar was originally inhabited by pygmies, defies all geological and navigational evidence since Madagascar has been an isolated island since the Tertiary era and the pygmies are no sailors and did not share in the expansion of the Swahili maritime civilization. Moreover, such ethnic groups as the Mikea, who were once thought to have been the last of the pygmy inhabitants, are not particularly small.

In my opinion the Malagasy of African origin are Bantu-speaking people; it is probable that they started arriving in the island at the latest from the ninth century on, as did the Indonesians, but it is unlikely that the African migration continued until the dawn of recent historical times (sixteenth century). It would appear that most of the Africans arrived at the same time and in the same way as the Muslims or the non-Muslim Swahili.

Though the Malagasy vocabulary is predominantly Indonesian, we should not forget the Bantu contribution. Similarly the Creole spoken in the Antilles consisting of 95 per cent French with some African elements should be noted. The Bantu contribution to Malagasy is on two levels, principally that of vocabulary, but also that of word structure. The fact that Bantu words occur in all the dialects of Madagascar shows that the African settlement of the country was not particularly belated; their influence is found in the very roots of Malagasy civilization. The Malagasy language bears traces of a very pronounced Bantu influence. This influence is so great, and of such a character, that it is inexplicable unless a Bantu substratum is assumed. Moreover, although it is at present impossible to unravel the succession of cultural contributions, many authors have been conscious of the heterogeneous character of the settlement of north and west Madagascar. Mellis, throughout his book on the north-west, stresses the contrast between the people of the sea-coast (*antandrano*) and the people of the interior (*olo boka antety*); this contrast is reflected in some of their funerary rites.

The movements of the coast-dwelling Bantu-speakers from the ninth century

28.4 *Statue of Antsary: Antanosy art near Fort-Dauphin (P. Vérin)*

account for the African contribution to the settlement of Madagascar, but we still have to explain why the Indonesian language became the *lingua franca*. Some of the Bantu-speakers must have come into contact with the Indonesians, and it is possible that between different Africans speaking different languages or dialects Indonesian may have been a language of convenience. However, Madagascar must have continued to be a linguistic and ethnic chequerboard for quite a while, at least on the coast around Baly and Maintirano (Mariano's Bambala), on the Tsiribihina (according to Drury), and among certain Vazimba groups in the interior (according to Birkeli and Hébert). The ancient Vazimba led a rather primitive life economically. They lived as fishermen on the coasts, but in the interior they probably depended to a great extent on a crude use of the natural resources at their disposal. Gathering berries, hunting and collecting honey were probably sufficient for their needs. According to Drury, the Vazimba of the Tsiribihina were river fishermen, and excavations have shown great heaps of shells from shellfish eaten by these berry-gathering peoples near Ankazoaka and Ankatso.

The symbiosis between the Indonesians and Africans started at the very beginning of the settlement of Madagascar. By the tenth century a few of the coastal Bantu-speakers must have converted to Islam. I find striking the fact that the Muslims of Madagascar share with all the peoples of the west and north-west coasts the same myth as to their origins, the myth of Mojomby, or 'the lost island'. Elsewhere I have recounted the myth in literary form as it was told to me by the Antalaotse of Boina Bay. According to my informants, Selimany Sebany and Tonga, the ancestors of the Kajemby and the Antalaotse once lived together on an island between the African coast and the Comoros. They lived by trade and practised the Muslim religion. But when impiety and discord appeared on the island, Allah decided to punish them: the island sank beneath a raging sea and only a few righteous men escaped. Some say that they were miraculously saved, others say that God sent a whale to carry them away. Kajemby and Antalaotse were descended from these righteous men. It seems likely, therefore, that the Muslims did not superimpose their culture on Madagascar, but rather played a catalytic role among the Africans who had migrated there.

29 The societies of Africa south of the Sahara in the Early Iron Age

In the last few chapters we have looked at the archaeology of different regions of sub-Saharan Africa in the closing millenium before the Christian era and during the first millenium of the Christian era. The purpose of this chapter is to try to assess some of the major trends which seem to have been developing in the history of Africa during the period under review. The changes which took place in all areas were of a fundamental nature. The economy was transformed from one which was largely parasitic on the landscape to one which was in control of its means of food production from both plants and animals. The technology was equally transformed from a simple one based largely on stone and wood to a far more complex one based on various metals as well as stone. During the period the foundations had been laid for the African societies we know today – the boundaries between different linguistic groups were to alter slightly, the population was to expand radically, and social and political groupings were to become more complex as states emerged, but by and large many of the fundamental demographic and economic aspects of sub-Saharan Africa had been established by the last quarter of the first millennium of the Christian era.

One of the problems in trying to delineate the emergent trends lies in the unevenness of the archaeological coverage. Vast areas still remain archaeologically unexplored, particularly in some of the largest countries such as Angola, Mozambique, Zaire, the Central African Republic, Cameroon, Benin, the Ivory Coast, Mali, Burkina Faso, Niger, Sierra Leone and Madagascar. Even where significant research has been undertaken it is highly localized, as in Senegal or Chad. It is important to note that, whereas organizations concerned with antiquities date from the nineteenth century for parts of North Africa (e.g. Egypt, 1858), many sub-Saharan countries have only initiated research with independence and the establishment of national museums and universities. Nevertheless, the establishment of radio-carbon chronology has revolutionized our knowledge of the Early Iron Age and allows some broad generalizations to be made about the time-scale involved in the various economic developments.

Mineral exploration

Copper

Copper was first mined in Mauretania probably by the first quarter of the first millennium before the Christian era. The form of the copper artefacts found in the area suggests that the stimulus for the mining came from contact with Morocco. Very little is known of the form that the original mines took, though it is believed that they were relatively shallow undertakings. The Mauretanian mines were the only ones that we know for certain were operational before +1000. Other sources of copper occur in Mali and Niger in the Nioro and Takedda areas, and were certainly being exploited by the second millennium of the Christian era, but when they were first discovered or worked is unknown.

There is evidence from Arab writers and also classical sources to suggest that copper was an element in trans-Saharan trade as early as the first millennium of the Christian era, coming south, perhaps, in return for the gold going to the north. The finding of ingots at Macden Idjafen in the western Sahara is evidence of the importance of the trade at a slightly later period (eleventh or twelfth century of the Christian era). Of vital importance for an appreciation of the scale of the trade is the material from Igbo-Ukwu in eastern Nigeria. If it is really of the ninth century, as claimed by the excavator Thurstan Shaw, and also by Wai-Andah in Chapter 24 of the main edition, it clearly indicates that the trade must have been on a large scale by the eighth or ninth centuries of the Christian era in order to account for the large number of cuprous objects and for the implied even larger numbers which still await discovery in similar sites.

An important copper source worked at this time was that in the Shaba region of Zaïre, where the excavations at Sanga and Katoto have revealed an abundance of copper objects. Nevertheless, it is worth noting that in the tripartite cultural division suggested by the excavator, Nenquin, the earliest phase, the Kisalian, is represented by twenty-seven graves, of which only two contained copper ingots. This suggests that during the Kisalian period, dating from the seventh to the ninth centuries of the Christian era, copper, though being exploited and made into ornaments, was not really abundant. The copper belt in northern Zambia was also exploited at this time with a date for copper-mining of +400 ± 90 being reported from Kansanshi. Copper items, however, were more numerous in southern than in northern Zambia at this time. The first and far from numerous copper items in southern Zambia were probably obtained from the Sinoia area of Zimbabwe and sources in eastern Zambia. So far we know nothing about the exploitation methods in either of these areas. Elsewhere in Africa copper was a very scarce resource: it has not been found on sites in eastern Africa until a much later date.

Salt

Salt is a mineral that was in great demand particularly with the beginning of an agricultural mode of life. Hunters and food-gatherers probably obtained a large amount of their salt intake from the animals they hunted and from fresh plant food.

Salt only becomes an essential additive where fresh foods are unobtainable in very dry areas, where body perspiration is also normally excessive. It becomes extremely desirable, however, amongst societies with relatively restricted diets, as was the case with arable agriculturalists. We have no idea when the salt resources of the Sahara at Taghāzā and Awlīl were first extracted. That they were an element in the trade of the Sahara by the first millennium of the Christian era is evident from Arabic texts of the last quarter of the millennium. It is probable that some of the salt extraction is as old as the copper-mining and the development of the Tishīt settlements in Mauretania, both areas where a sedentary life would have imposed the need for salt supplies. We know quite a lot about mining activities in the medieval period, which will be discussed in later volumes, but nothing about them at this time. It is probable that at this period the mining operations were of a fairly simple kind. Salt would have been available as a surface deposit in various parts of the Sahara as a result of the desiccation process after −2500. Perhaps man noted which dried-up lakes, swamp or pond beds attracted wild animals. Surface salts are often quite obvious from their colour.

Iron

Iron ores were worked as early as Middle Stone Age times in Swaziland for use as pigments. It is clear that body pigments and iron oxide ochres for body pigments, and later for decorating rock surfaces, were eagerly sought after from Early Stone Age times. A piece of haematitic colouring matter was even brought into the Olduvai Basin by very early Stone Age tool-users. By Late Stone Age times, manganese, specularite, and haematite were being regularly mined at localities in Zambia, Swaziland and the northern Cape. An excavation in some of the workings at Doornfontein indicated regular mining operations involving galleries and chambers from which up to 45,000 metric tons of specularite may have been obtained, probably by Khoisan-speaking groups from the ninth century of the Christian era onwards. It is likely that the existence of such mines, and the implied knowledge of metallic ores and their properties, helped the rapid growth of an iron technology in the first half of the first millennium of the Christian era.

Elsewhere in sub-Saharan Africa we do not have such clear indications of mining for iron and it seems that the lateritic crust of the tropical areas was the most likely source of iron ores. Bog iron, however, was used in the lower Casamance Valley in Senegal and at Machili in Zambia.

Gold

Gold was almost certainly mined in West Africa during the period under review, as well as being collected by alluvial panning. Though implied by the Arabic sources, no actual gold-mines have been located, excavated or dated, nor has evidence for the refining processes been recovered. These were probably similar to those well documented for later periods. The main areas for which there is evidence of gold exploitation – largely from non-contemporaneous sources – were located near the headwaters of the Niger and Senegal rivers in present-day Guinea and Mali and are known as Bambuk and Bure. There is rather better evidence (discussed by

Phillipson in Chapter 27 of the main edition) for gold-mining by means of shallow adits or stopes in north-eastern Zimbabwe, but there is no undisputed evidence that the activity is older than the eighth or ninth century of the Christian era. The ores seem to have been crushed, using pounding stones.

Stone

Stone was almost certainly quarried for various purposes, the most important of which was to provide the raw material for ground and polished stone tools and for the manufacture of querns. Many societies used fixed querns, taking their grains to a rocky outcrop where they could also lay out foods to dry and where they could grind grains or pound vegetable foods. But such outcrops are not available everywhere and it is evident that rock for grindstones, both the upper and lower varieties, had to be searched for and often moved over considerable distances. All over sub-Saharan Africa grooves, normally 10–12 centimetres wide and up to 50 centimetres long, mark the spots where suitable flaked stone rough-outs were ground to make axes, adzes and chisels. It is probable that the process of quarrying, albeit on a small scale, grinding, polishing and trading of either the rough-outs or the finished products went on throughout the period in diminishing intensity as iron replaced stone. In some areas ground-stone tools were, however, still in use in the second millennium of the Christian era. Surprisingly few ground-stone tools have been found in East and southern Africa, though they are extremely common in West Africa.

Another relatively unexplored activity which certainly took place was the search for suitable semi-precious stones to make into beads: cornelian and various forms of chalcedony, such as agates and jaspers, as well as crystalline quartzes or rock crystal, were the most common. Beads of these materials are found all over sub-Saharan Africa – often in graves such as those at the Njoro river cave site in Kenya, dated to the tenth century before the Christian era, and also on habitation sites. At Lantana in Niger a mine for red stone (jasper) which is still traded to Nigeria for bead-making is believed to be very old, but it is impossible to date its origin. Rarely abundant, stone beads nevertheless indicate a deliberate search for well-known rock types. Such beads were, of course, made as long ago as Stone Age times, and were to continue being made right throughout the Iron Age until gradually replaced by the cheaper, more easily made and eventually more accessible glass trade-beads.

Trade

Some form of exchange has gone on between communities probably from relatively early Stone Age times. The exchange of bright or useful stones and honey for meat, and occasionally even womenfolk, probably marked the gatherings of foraging peoples, if models based on the study of modern hunters and food-gatherers are any guide. Such exchanges, which were of both a ritual and economic significance, would have become regular as societies entered into an agricultural existence, though even in Late Stone Age times specialized fishermen, seafood collectors or hunters must have led relatively settled lives and thus required for their tools stones and other materials which were not locally available. It is possible that certain bone implements, such as harpoons, which required more than average expertise, may have been traded. But it is fair to conclude that agriculture, implying a sedentary or a seasonal or periodically shifting existence, would have involved an increase in trade. Much of this trade was probably on a relatively restricted scale and local in scope, but would have included such commodities as salt, certain types of stone and later iron tools, beads, shells, possibly plants for medicinal or ritual use, meat for arable communities and grains and root crops for pastoral groups, specialized utensils or substances like poisons for fishing or hunting, dried fish and all sorts of objects with a scarcity value such as strange seeds, animal claws, teeth, curious stones, bones, etc., which might have had a magical significance and which even today are the stock-in-trade of certain stalls in West African markets. Except for the polished stone tools, quern stones and salt which have been referred to in the previous section, nothing is known about this trade.

With the advent of metals, however, trade took on a different character. Copper and gold are more localized than stones and were in demand by communities both to the north of the Sahara and to the east around the Indian Ocean. There is no reason to suppose that the trade was on a very big scale at this date even across the Sahara, but the networks had been established. We also have little evidence of markets or distribution centres in sub-Saharan Africa, though Arabic references to the old Ghana capital suggest that they probably existed before the acceleration of the trade brought about by the Arab conquest of North Africa.

Glass beads have come from several sites in Zambia, Shaba (Zaïre) and Zimbabwe from contexts in the last half of the first millennium and they were certainly imports.

Emerging themes in sub-Saharan African history

In the last quarter of the first millennium of the Christian era

It is now necessary to see whether, from the mass of descriptive data presented in the last eight chapters, any conclusions can be drawn about the state of African society at the end of the Early Iron Age. The period witnessed the transformation of the economy of sub-Saharan Africa from one of hunting and gathering to one mainly dependent on agriculture. Population certainly grew and settled life, villages and larger social units were the outcome. It is difficult to ascertain the social structures involved, but it is likely that over most of Africa we are dealing with relatively small villages consisting of one or more lineage groups with wider affinities based on clan relationships. Population densities must have been small in most areas: probably only a handful to the square kilometre. Following the initial rapid movement consequent upon the advent of iron, allowing clearance of the more wooded areas of Africa, communities had settled down. We have evidence of their isolation in the divergence of different members of the same language families and in the increasingly varied pottery forms and decorations which were developing in most areas around +600 to +1000. Demographic estimates, based both on the historical evidence available in North Africa and on extrapolation from ethnographic data and colonial census figures, indicate a population of well under 10 million for the whole of sub-Saharan Africa before +1000. If indications from oral traditions of change from matrilineal to patrilineal societies in the past five hundred years, particularly in East Africa, are any guide, we are dealing very much with matrilineal societies over most of the areas of tropical Africa.

Curiously it is more difficult to discover details about the religious beliefs of this time than about those of the preceding hunter-gatherers of the Late Stone Age. The latter provided many clues in their rock art. The earliest agriculturists possibly painted the rocks and may have been responsible for the stylized art of much of East and Central Africa, particularly of the area around Lake Victoria and of Zambia. Though we have some idea when this art tradition was finishing, we have no idea when it originated. The practice of burial is in itself often an expression of religious belief and the goods that were buried with the dead would in many cases indicate a sense of the need for such items in the after-life. This is not, of course, the only possible explanation. The size of the grave, the splendour of the grave-goods and the munificence of the accompanying ceremony can also serve to demonstrate the status, whether political, ritual, economic or social, of the family of the bereaved. The scale of the funeral activities would also help to establish the genealogy of the chief mourners. It should be remembered, however, and we have excellent twentieth-century parallels for the practice, that non-religious societies often build very striking mausoleums. The existence of impressive burial mounds or funerary monuments need not necessarily imply a belief in a given god or group of gods; but it certainly indicates confidence in the future on the part of society, and represents a political gesture of continuity by a ruling or elite group.

It is apparent that in the period under review states of some kind were emerging. The two key areas were the Sudanic belt and the area of Central Africa around the headwaters of the Lualaba. In the Sudanic belt there were possibly three nuclear areas, around Ghana in southern Mauretania and Senegal, in the inland Niger Delta above Segu and around Lake Chad. All were areas where long-distance trade was beginning to be important and where agriculture probably developed earlier than in areas farther to the south. The oral traditions and rituals of the ruling group would provide the state religions, which would thus help to ensure and rationalize the mystique of its authority. The head of the elite group, if he were not so in reality, would become the supposed unilineal descendant or reincarnation of the original conqueror, with definite divine characteristics. The divinity of the ruler in such a model is not original, but is acquired, often slowly, mostly deliberately but often probably incidentally, as a defence mechanism to preserve the distinctive integrity of the chief.

Turning from hypothesis to fact, the only area in which we can convincingly assert that a kingdom existed in the period under review was at the western edge of the Sudan, where the Kingdom of Ghana was certainly in existence by +700 and could have been emerging for up to a thousand years. The reasons for its growth must have been its control of valuable mineral resources (copper, iron and gold, in the probable order of their exploitation); its control of the salt trade; and possibly its location in an area of primary development of an agricultural mode of life, as represented by the Tis̲hīt sequence. A detailed account of the state will be found in the next volume; but it is probably no coincidence that the growth of Ancient Ghana, the building of the Senegambian megaliths and the rich burial mounds of Senegal were contemporaneous developments. They were probably related parts of the same pattern of economic growth.

As we have seen in the preceding chapters, there is no uniform ending to the period under review as there is for North Africa; nevertheless the arrival of the Arabs in North Africa was ultimately to affect either directly or indirectly much of West and East Africa. We have seen that by +800 most of Africa was firmly in the Iron Age. The forest margin was being slowly eroded by the advance of agriculture, both in West Africa and in southern Central Africa. Population was increasing. The first phase of the agricultural revolution had involved the rapid expansion of small groups of arable cultivators, who probably obtained a great deal of their protein by using the age-old, well-tried methods of their Stone Age hunting and gathering ancestors. Much of their hunting equipment was the same as their predecessors': nets, bone and horn fish-hooks and wooden spears and arrows, perhaps still barbed at times with microliths or the sharpened ends of antelope horns or similar natural substances. In a few cases it was supplemented by more efficient, though costly, iron arrowheads and more quickly made fish-hooks. Much of their mythology and religion must also have been derived from their foraging forebears, but as life became more settled they developed new beliefs based on the mysteries of agriculture and metal-working. Some of these beliefs had probably been passed on by the people who transmitted the new mysteries. The Iron Age farmers were more creative, moulding pots, carving drums, making baskets, smelting iron, forging tools. Their religion was becoming centred on creative deities, and their systems of belief were aimed at ensuring salvation from the vicissitudes of a Nature to which the agriculturalist is more vulnerable. Their ritual and music were probably more elaborate, their material culture was more varied and their sense of tradition and social continuity was more firmly established. Fundamental changes had taken place in society which ultimately affected all the succeeding periods of African history.

Conclusion

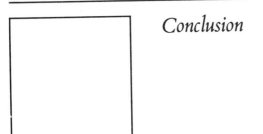

In this volume an attempt has been made to show, as far as possible, the main trends in the early history of Africa: the major changes that occurred, the fundamental contacts between its various regions, and the state of African societies and groups during the period under review.

The volume outlines a general framework for research, and the main lines along which studies should be directed. However, it already seems possible to reach some conclusions and to recognize some hypotheses, although it should be clearly and strongly emphasized that a great deal remains to be done and that long, in-depth studies are needed.

The chapters on Ancient Egypt demonstrate that before the third millennium before the Christian era, Egypt had achieved a high intellectual, social and material standard, compared with most other parts of the world. The Ancient Egyptian civilization, besides being old, original and rich in initiative, lasted for almost three thousand years. It resulted not only from favourable environmental factors, but also from the efforts to control those factors and put them to beneficial use. There is no doubt that the natural elements played an important and remarkable role in the development of the Ancient Egyptian civilization. But, on the other hand, this role was supplemented and became effective only through the Egyptians' struggle to tame their environment, to overcome the difficulties and problems it posed, and so to render it beneficial for their own prosperity.

Although Egypt was open to cultural currents coming especially from the East, this volume shows how the Egyptian civilization rested to a great extent on an African foundation and also that Egypt, which is a part of Africa, was one of the main centres of universal civilization in ancient times and that a great deal of scientific knowledge, art and literature emanated from that region, and influenced Greece in particular. In the fields of mathematics (geometry, arithmetic, etc.) astronomy and the measurement of time (the calendar), medicine, architecture, music and literature (narrative, poetry, tragedy, etc.), Greece received, developed and transmitted to the West a great part of the Egyptian legacy – from Pharaonic and Ptolemaic Egypt. Through Greece and Phoenicia, the Ancient Egyptian civilization entered into contact not only with Europe, but also with North Africa and even the Indian sub-continent. Wide differences of opinion exist about the peopling of Egypt, which is still a subject of serious and deep study. It is hoped that the great progress in the methodology of physical anthropology will enable definitive conclusions on this subject to be reached in the near future.

According to records mentioned in this volume, Nubia has been closely connected with Egypt since the earliest times as a result of various factors: physical factors, particularly similar geographical features, especially between Nubia and the extreme southern part of Upper Egypt; historical and political factors, which are important in themselves and were greatly strengthened by the physical aspect; social factors, which are reflected in culture and religion. Thus, since the beginning of the First Egyptian Dynasty, and through the Old Kingdom, the Egyptians paid a great deal of attention to the northern area of Nubia, which they considered as a complementary part of their own country. They organized a flow of trade with the Nubians, exploited Nubian natural resources, and when any Nubian resistance was shown they sent military missions to end it.

However, since prehistoric days Nubia had constituted a distinct geographical and social unit. Since the dawn of history, it had been inhabited by people whose culture was identical with that of the northern valley of the Nile. But, starting from about −3200, the Egyptians began to outstrip their southern neighbours in the cultural domain, and made vast strides towards civilization, while Nubia remained stationary at the prehistoric level for a considerable time. In the first half of the second millennium before the Christian era, the so-called Kerma culture, a rich and prosperous civilization, flourished in Nubia. Although greatly influenced by Egyptian culture, it possessed its own local characteristics. But, after the beginning of the first millennium before the Christian era, when the power of Egypt waned, a native monarchy began to be established, with Napata as its capital, which later ruled Egypt itself. The fifty-year Nubian domination in Egypt during the seventh period (the first part of the Twenty-fifth Dynasty) effected a union of Egypt and Nubia. The glory of this great African power was outstanding, as shown by classical writers.

After the transfer of the capital to Meroe, Nubia experienced a period of progress and prosperity and resumed contacts with its neighbours, until nearly the ninth century. The expansion of the Meroitic monarchy to the west and south, its role in diffusing its ideas and techniques and its transmission of Eastern and Western influences are still under study and discussion. Also, even after the publication of this volume, further stimulus should be given to the efforts to decipher the Meroitic script. The 900 documents which exist would reveal information of many kinds. It would also make available, side by side with the Pharaonic language, a new classical language that was strictly African.

From the fourth century of the Christian era, Christianity began to spread to Nubia, where the temples were converted into churches. The role of Christian Nubia was also great, its achievements were numerous, and its influence on its neighbours was remarkable.

Nubia, because of its geographical location, played a special and sometimes involuntary role as an intermediary between Central Africa and the Mediterranean. The Kingdom of Napata, the Empire of Meroe and the Christian kingdom showed Nubia as a link between north and south. Through it, culture, techniques and materials found their way through surrounding regions. It is by the stubborn pursuit of research that we may discover that the Egypto-Nubian civilization played a role in Africa similar to that of the Graeco-Roman civilization in Europe.

Although Ethiopia was influenced at the beginning by various motives, it established a cultural unit whose central coherence could be identified as coming from southern Arabia. Material sources dating back to the second pre-Axumite period indicate that a local culture existed which had assimilated foreign influences.

The Kingdom of Axum, which lasted from the first century of the Christian era for about one thousand years, adopted a quite distinct form, different from that of the pre-Axumite period. The civilization of Axum, like that of Ancient Egypt, was the result of a cultural development, whose roots went back to prehistory. It was an African civilization, which was produced by its people, although some Meroitic influence can be traced in the pottery of the second pre-Axumite period.

During the second and third centuries, the Meroitic influence predominated in Ethiopia. The newly discovered stele of Axum with the Egyptian symbol of life (Ankh), and objects connected with Hathor, Ptah and Horus, as well as scarabs, show the influence of the Egyptian Meroitic religion on Axumite beliefs.

The Axumite kingdom was an important trade power on the routes from the Roman world to India and from Arabia to North Africa, and also a great centre of cultural dissemination. So far, only a few aspects of Axumite culture and its African roots have been investigated and much still remains to be done.

The arrival of Christianity in Ethiopia – as in Egypt and Meroe – brought great changes in the culture and life of the people. The role of Christianity and its continuity in Ethiopia, its influence inside and outside that country, are interesting subjects which deserve in-depth study in the near future.

In view of the limitations of our historical sources, increased knowledge about the evolution of the native Libyan culture and its reaction to the introduction of the Phoenician civilization must wait until the archaeologists and historians have carried out further studies.

In the present state of our knowledge we must therefore consider that the entry of the Maghrib into recorded history begins with the arrival of the Phoenicians on the coast of North Africa, although Carthaginian contacts with the peoples of the Sahara and even with people living farther south remains obscure. At the same time, it should be pointed out that the culture of North Africa is not indebted solely to the Phoenicians for its early inspiration, which was mainly African.

The Phoenician period brought the Maghrib into the general history of the Mediterranean world, since the Phoenician culture was mixed with Egyptian and oriental elements and depended on trade relations with other Mediterranean countries. Nevertheless, the later period of the Numidian and Mauretanian kingdoms saw the evolution of a culture of mixed Libyan and Phoenician character.

Although we have very scarce and incomplete knowledge about the Sahara and its culture in antiquity, several points can be made. It is certain that the desiccation of the climate did not kill the desert and that human activity continued there; that languages and writing were consolidated; that with the increased use of camels, means of transport were developed which allowed the Sahara to play an important role in cultural exchanges between the Maghrib and tropical Africa.

We can therefore conclude that the Sahara was neither a barrier nor a dead zone, but an area with its own culture and history which still needs to be studied to discover the continuing influence of the Maghrib on the Sudanic belt. There were always active cultural contacts across the Sahara with sub-Saharan Africa which greatly affected African history.[1]

Hitherto, it has often been customary to situate the beginning of the history of Africa south of the Sahara at approximately the fifteenth century of the Christian era[2] for two main reasons, namely, the dearth of written documents and the dogmatic cleavage which historians have made mentally between that part of the continent on the one hand and Ancient Egypt and North Africa on the other.

This volume, despite the gaps and incompleteness of the research so far undertaken, has helped to demonstrate the possibility of a cultural unity of the entire continent in the most widely varying fields.

The theory of the genetic kinship between Ancient Egyptian and the African languages has been discussed. If research confirms this theory, it will prove the deep-rooted linguistic unity of the continent. The similarity of royal structures, the relationship of rites and cosmogonies (circumcision, totemism, vitalism, metempsychosis, etc.), the affinity of material cultures (tilling equipment is one example), are all matters to be deeply studied in the future.

The cultural heritage left to us by the societies which lived in Egypt, Nubia, Ethiopia and the Maghrib is of great importance. The monotheism imposed by the Christians, and before them by the Jews, in these regions was strong and expressive and no doubt facilitated the entry of Islam into Africa. These well-known facts stand on the credit side of the Africans; on the debit side are unclear areas where a vast amount of work remains to be done, and many uncertain points to be clarified.

Likewise, completion of the third condition for the writing of Volumes I and II, i.e. the reconstruction of the ancient African road network since proto-historical times, and a determination of the extent of cultivated areas during the same period from the analysis of photographs taken from satellites for that purpose, would singularly broaden and deepen our knowledge of both the intra-continental cultural and trade relations of the time and the degree to which the land was occupied.

More extensive work on ethnonyms and toponyms should make it possible to determine migratory currents and unsuspected ethnic relationships from one end of the continent to the other.

I hope this volume will persuade the African countries to show more interest in, and give more help to, the archaeology of ancient Africa.

1 See Chapter 29, 'The societies of Africa south of the Sahara in the Early Iron Age'. It deals with the results obtained in the last ten chapters of this volume concerning sub-Saharan Africa.

2 Some writers in both Anglophone and Francophone Africa paid a good deal of attention to sub-Saharan Africa before the fifteenth century.

Bibliography

The publishers wish to point out that although every effort has been made to ensure that the details in this Bibliography are correct, some errors may occur as a result of the complexity and the international nature of this work.

Abbreviations and List of Periodicals

AA *American Anthropologist*, Washington D.C.
AB *Africana Bulletin*, Warsaw University, Warsaw
Actas VIII Congr. Intern. Archeo. Crist. *Actas del VIII Congresso Internazionale di Archeologia Cristiana*, Barcelona, 1972
Actes Coll. Bamako I *Actes du ler Colloque International de Bamako organisé par la Fondation SCOA pour la Recherche Scientifique en Afrique Noire* (Project Boucle du Niger), Bamako, 27 January–1 February 1975
Actes Coll. Intern. Biolog. Pop. Sahar. *Actes du Colloque International de Biologie des Populations Sahariennes*, Algiers, 1969
Actes Coll. Intern. Fer. *Actes du Colloque International. Le Fer à travers les âges*, Nancy, 3–6 October 1956, Annales de l'Est, Mém, no. 16, Nancy, 1956
Actes 1er Coll. Intern. Archéol. Afr. *Actes du 1er Colloque International d'Archéologie Africaine*, Fort Lamy, 11–16 December 1966, Etudes et documents tchadiens, Mém. No. 1, Fort Lamy, 1969
Actes 7e Coll. Intern. Hist. Marit. *Actes du 7e Colloque International d'Histoire Maritime* (Lourenço Marques, 1962), published 1964, SEVPEN, Paris
Actes Coll. Nubiol. Intern. *Actes du Colloque Nubiologique International au Musée National de Varsovie*, Warsaw, 1972
Actes Conf. Ann. Soc. Phil. Soudan *Actes de la Conférence Annuelle de la Société Philosophique du Soudan*
Actes 2e Conf. Intern. Afr. Ouest *Comptes Rendus, 2nd International West African Conference*, Bissau, 1947
Actes 2e Congr. Intern. Et. N. Afr. *Actes du 2e Congrès International d'Etudes Nord Africaines (Congresso Internazionale de Studi Nord Africani), Revue de l'Occident Musulman et de la Méditerranée* (Aix-en-Provence, 1968), published Gap, Ophrys, 1970
Actes XIV Congr. Intern. Et. Byz. *Actes du XIVe Congrès International d'Etudes Byzantines*, Bucharest, 1971
Acts III Cong. PPQS *Acts of the Third Pan-African Congress of Prehistory and Quaternary Study*, Lusaka, 1955
Acts IV Congr. PPQS *Acts of the Fourth Pan-Africa Congress of Prehistory and Quaternary Study*, Leopoldville, 1959, AMRAC 40
Acts VI Congr. PPQS *Acts of the Sixth Pan-African Congress of Prehistory and Quaternary Study*, Dakar, 1967, Chambéry, Impr. réunies
Acts VII Congr. PPQS *Acts of the Seventh Pan-African Congress of Prehistory and Quaternary Study*, Addis Ababa, 1971
AE *Annales d'Ethiopie*, Paris, Institut Ethiopien d'Etudes et de Recherches, Section d'Archéologie
AEPHE *Annuaire de l'Ecole Pratique des Hautes Etudes*, IVe section (Section des Sciences Historiques et Philologiques), Paris
ÄFU *Ägyptologische Forschungen* (ed. A. Scharff), Glückstadt, Hamburg, New York
AHS *African Historical Studies*, Boston University African Studies Centre (became *IJAHS* in 1972)
AI *Africana Italiana*, Rome

AJA *American Journal of Archaeology*, journal of the Archaeological Institute of America, Boston, Mass.
ALS *African Language Studies*, School of Oriental and African Studies, London University
AMRAC *Annales du Musée Royal de l'Afrique Centrale*, séries in 8°, Sciences humaines, Tervuren, Belgium
Ant. Afr. *Antiquités Africaines*, Editions du Centre National de la Recherche Scientifique, Paris
Antiquity *Antiquity*, Gloucester
AQ *African Quarterly*, New Delhi
Archaeology *Archaeology*, Archaeological Institute of America, Boston, Mass.
ARSC *Académie Royale des Sciences Coloniales; Classe des Sciences Morales et Politiques*, N.S., Brussels
AS *African Studies*
ASAM *Annals of the South African Museum*
ASR *African Social Research*
Atti IV. Congr. Intern. Stud. Et. *Atti del IV Congresso Internazionale de Studi Etiopici*, Rome, 10–15 April 1972, Academia nazionale dei Lincei, Rome
AUEI *Avhandlinger Utgitt av. Egede Instituttet*, Oslo, Egede Instituttet
Azania *Azania*, journal of the British Institute of History and Archaeology in East Africa, Nairobi
BAA *Bulletin d'Archéologie Algérienne*, Algiers
BAM *Bulletin de l'Académie Malgache*, Tananarive
BHM *Bulletin of Historical Metallurgy*
BIFAN *Bulletin de l'Institut Français* (later re-named *Fondamental*) *d'Afrique Noire*, Dakar
BM *Bulletin de Madagascar*, Tananarive
BO *Bibliotheca Orientalis*, Netherlands instituut voor Het Nabije Oosten, Leyden
BS *Bulletin Scientifique*, Ministère de la France d'Outre-Mer, Direction de l'Agriculture
BSAC *Bulletin de la Société d'Archéologie Classique*
BSFE *Bulletin de la Société Française d'Egyptologie*, Paris
BSPPG *Bulletin de la Société Préhistorique et Protohistorique Gabonaise*, Libreville
BWS 56 *Burg Wartenstein Symposium no. 56 on the origin of African domesticated plants*, 19–27 August 1972
CA *Current Anthropology*, Chicago
CEA *Cahiers d'Etudes Africaines*, Mouton, Paris
CM *Civilisation Malgache*, Tananarive, Faculté des Lettres et Sciences Humaines, Université de Madagascar
CQ *Classical Quarterly*, London
C-RAI *Compte Rendu des Séances de l'Académie des Inscription et Belles Lettres*, Klincksieck, Paris
C-RGLCS *Compte Rendu des Séances du Groupe Linguistique d'Etudes Chamito-Sémitiques*, Ecole Pratique des Hautes Etudes, Sorbonne, Paris
CSSH *Comparative Studies in Society and History*, The Hague
CTL *Current Trends in Linguistics*, The Hague
EAGR *East African Geographical Review*, Kampala
EHR *Economic History Review*, Economic History Society, Cambridge
GJ *Geographical Journal*, London
GNQ *Ghana Notes and Queries*, Legon
HAS *Harvard African Studies*, Harvard University Press, Cambridge, Mass.
Hesperis *Hesperis*, Institut des Hautes Etudes Marocaines, Rabat
IJAHS *International Journal of African Historical Studies*, New York (formerly *AHS*)
JA *Journal Asiatique*, Paris
JAH *Journal of African History*, Cambridge University Press, London, New York
JAOS *Journal of the American Oriental Society*, New Haven, Conn.
JARCE *Journal of the American Research Center in Egypt*, Boston, Mass.
JCH *Journal of Classical History*, London
JEA *Journal of Egyptian Archaeology*, London
JGS *Journal of Glass Studies*, Corning, New York
JRAI *Journal of the Royal Anthropological Institute of Great Britain and Ireland*, London
JRAS *Journal of the Royal Asiatic Society of Great Britain and Ireland*, London
JRS *Journal of Roman Studies*, Society for the Promotion of Roman Studies, London
JS *Le Journal des Savants*, Paris
JSA *Journal de la Société des Africanistes*, Paris

JSAIMM *Journal of the South African Institute of Mining and Metallurgy*, Johannesburg
Kush *Kush*, Journal of the Sudan Antiquities Services, Khartoum
LAAA *Liverpool Annals of Archaeology and Anthropology*, Liverpool
Lammergeyer *Lammergeyer*, Journal of the National Parks Game and Fish Preservation Board, Pietermaritzburg
Libyca *Libyca*, Bulletin du Service d'Antiquités of Algeria, Direction de l'Intérieur et des Beaux Arts, Algiers
MADP *Malawi Antiquities Department Publications*, Zomba
MAGW *Mitteilungen der Anthropologischen Gesellschaft in Wien*
MAI *Mitteilungen des deutsches Archaologischen Instituts*, Harvasowitz, Wiesbaden
Man *Man*, New York
MEJ *Middle East Journal*, Washington, DC
Mém. CRAPE *Mémoires du Centre de Recherches Anthropologiques, Préhistoriques et Ethnographiques*, Institut Français des Sciences Humaines en Algérie
NA *Notes Africaines*, Bulletin d'Information de l'IFAN, Dakar (see BIFAN above)
OPNM *Occasional Papers of the National Museums of Southern Rhodesia*, Bulawayo
Optima *Optima*, Johannesburg
Paideuma *Paideuma, Mitteilungen zur Kulturkunde*, Frankfurt am Main
Proc. PS *Proceedings of the Prehistoric Society*, Cambridge
RA *Revue Africaine, Journal des Travaux de la Société Historique Algérienne*, Algiers
R. Arch. *Revue Archéologique*, Paris
REA *Revue des Etudes Anciennes*, Bordeaux
RFHOM *Revue Française d'Histoire d'Outre-Mer*, Paris
RH *Revue Historique*, Paris
ROMM *Revue de l'Occident Musulman et de la Méditerranée*, Aix-en-Provence
RSE *Rassengna di Studi Etiopici*, Rome
RUB *Revue de l'Université de Bruxelles*, Brussels
SAAB *South African Archaeological Bulletin*, Cape Town
SAJS *South African Journal of Science*, Johannesburg
SASAE *Supplément aux Annales du Service des Antiquités d'Egypte*, Cairo
SLS *Society for Libyan Studies*
SM *Studi magrebini*, Naples, Istituto Universitario Orientale
SNR *Sudan Notes and Records*, Khartoum
TJH *Transafrican Journal of History*
TNR *Tanganyika (Tanzania) Notes and Records*, Dar es Salaam
Trav. IRS *Travaux de l'Institut de Recherches Sahariennes*, University of Algiers, Algiers
Ufahamu *Ufahamu*, Journal of the African Activist Association, Los Angeles
WA *World Archaeology*, London
WAAN *West African Archaeological Newsletter*, Ibadan
WAJA *West African Journal of Archaeology*, Ibadan
ZAS *Zeitschrift fur Agyptische Sprache und Altertumskunde*, Osnabruck, Zeller
ZMJ *Zambia Museum Journal*, Lusaka

Bibliography

Abel, A. (1972) 'L'Ethiopie et ses rapports avec l'Arabie préislamique jusqu'à l'émigration de ca. 615', *IVth CISE*

Abraham, D. P. (1962) 'The early political history of the Kingdom of Mwene Mutapa, 850–1589', *Historians in Tropical Africa* (Salisbury: University College of Rhodesia and Nyasaland)

Abraham, D. P. (1964) 'The ethnohistory of the empire of Mutapa, problems and methods', in J. Vansina, R. Mauny and L. V. Thomas (eds.), *The Historian in Tropical Africa* (London/Accra/Ibadan: Oxford University Press for the International African Institute), pp. 104–26

Adams, W. Y. (1962a) 'Pottery kiln excavations', *Kush*, 10, pp. 62–75

Adams, W. Y. (1962b) 'An introductory classification of Christian Nubian pottery', *Kush*, 10, pp. 245–88

Adams, W. Y. (1964a) 'Post-pharaonic Nubia in the light of archaeology', *JEA*, 50, pp. 102–20

Adams, W. Y. (1965b) 'Architectural evolution of the Nubian church 500–1400 AD', *JARCE*, 4, pp. 87–139

Adams, W. Y. (1965c) 'Post-pharaonic Nubia in the light of archaeology II', *JEA*, 51, pp. 160–78

Adams, W. Y. (1966a) 'The Nubian campaign: retrospect', *Mélanges offerts à K. Michalowski* (Warsaw), pp. 13–20

Adams, W. Y. (1966b) 'Post-pharaonic Nubia in the light of archaeology III', *JEA*, 52, pp. 147–62

Adams, W. Y. (1967) 'Continuity and change in Nubian cultural history', *SNR*, XLVIII, pp. 11–19

Adams, W. Y. and Nordström, H. A. (1963) 'The archaeological survey on the west bank of the Nile, third season 1961–2', *Kush*, 11, pp. 10–46

Adams, W. Y. and Verwers, C. J. (1961) 'Archaeological survey of Sudanese Nubia', *Kush*, 9, pp. 7–43

Addison, F. S. A. (1949) *Jebel Moya (The Wellcome Excavation in the Sudan)*; 2 vols. (London: Oxford University Press)

Aldred, C. (1980) *Egyptian Art in the Days of the Pharaohs* (London: Thames and Hudson)

Alexander, J. (1980) 'The spread and development of iron using in Europe and Africa', in R. E. F. Leakey and B. A. Ogot (eds.), *Proceedings of the 8th Panafrican Congress of Prehistory and Quaternary Studies*, pp. 327–30

Alexander, J. and Coursey, D. G. (1969) 'The origins of yam cultivation', in P. H. Ucko and G. W. Dimbleby (eds.), *The Domestication and Exploitation of Plants and Animals* (London: Duckworth), pp. 123–9

Ali Hakem, A. M. (1972) 'Meroitic settlement of the Butana central Sudan', in P. H. Ucko, R. Tringham and G. W. Dimbleby (eds.), *Man, Settlement and Urbanism* (London: Duckworth), pp. 639–46

Allen, J. W. T. (1949) 'Rhapta', *TNR*, 27, pp. 52–9

Amblard, S. (1984) *Tichitt Walata – Civilisation et Industrie Lithique*, Editions Recherche sur les civilisations, Mémoire no. 35, (Paris: ADPF)

Andah, B. W. (1973) 'Archaeological reconnaissance of Upper-Volta', thesis (Berkeley, University of California)

Andah, B. W. (1979) 'Iron Age beginnings in West Africa: reflections and suggestions', *WAJA*, 9, pp. 125–41

Anfray, F. (1963) 'Une campagne de fouilles à Yeha', *AE*, 5 (February–March 1960), pp. 171–92

Anfray, F. (1967) 'Matara', *AE*, 7, pp. 33–97

Anfray, F. (1968) 'Aspects de l'archéologie éthiopienne', *JAH*, 9, pp. 345–66

Anfray, F. (1972) 'L'archéologie d'Axoum en 1972', *Paideuma*, XVIII, p. 71, plate VI

Anfray, F. (1974) 'Deux villes axoumites: Adoulis et Matara', *Atti IV Congr. Intern. Stud. Et.*, pp. 752–65

Anfray, F. and Annequin, G. (1965) 'Matara. Deuxième, troisième et quatrième campagnes de fouilles', *AE*, 6, pp. 49–86

Anfray, F., Caquot, A. and Nautin, P. (1970) 'Une nouvelle inscription grecque d'Ezana, roi d'Axoum', *JS*, pp. 260–73

Anquandah, J. (1982) *Rediscovering Ghana's Past* (London: Longman)

Applegate, J. R. (1970) 'The Berber languages', *CTL*, VI, pp. 586–661

Arkell, A. J. (1949) *Early Khartoum. An Account of the Excavations of an Early Occupation Site carried out by the Sudan Government Antiquities Service* 1944–1945 (Oxford: Oxford University Press)

Arkell, A. J. (1961) *A History of the Sudan from the Earliest Times to 1821* (London: University of London, Athlone Press), 2nd edn revised

Arkell, A. J. (1966) 'The iron age in the Sudan' *CA*, 7, 4, pp. 451–78

Armstrong, R. G. (1964), *The Study of West African Languages* (Ibadan: Ibadan University Press)

Atherton, J. H. (1972) 'Excavations at Kambamai and Yagala rock shelters, Sierra Leone', *WAJA*, 2, pp. 39 ff

Aubreville, A. (1948) 'Etude sur les forêts de l'Afrique équatoriale française et du Cameroun', *BS*, 2, p. 131

Aumassip, G. (1986) *Le Bas-Sahara dans la Préhistoire* (Paris: Editions du Centre National de la Recherche Scientifique)

Aurigemma, S. (1940) 'L'elefante di Leptis Magna', *A1*, pp. 67–86

Badawy, A. (1968) *A History of Egyptian Architecture (The New Kingdom): From the Eighteenth Dynasty to the End of the Twentieth Dynasty 1580–1085 BC* (Berkeley, Calif. Los Angeles: University of California Press)

Bailloud, G. (1969) 'L'évolution des styles céramiques en Ennedi (République du Tchad)', *Actes ler Coll. Intern. Archéol. Afr.*, Fort Lamy, 1966, pp. 31–45

Balout, L. (1967) 'l'Homme préhistorique et la Méditerranée occidentale', *ROMM*, Aix-en-Provence, 3

Baradez, J. (1949) *Vue aérienne de l'organisation romaine dans le Sud-Algérien. Fossatum Africae* (Paris: AMG)

Barraux, M. (1959) 'L'auge de Sima', *BAM*, n.s., XXXVII, pp. 93–9

Barrow, J. (1801–4) *An Account of Travels into the Interior of Southern Africa in the Years 1797 and 1798*, 2 vols (London: T. Cadell and W. Davies)

Basset, H. (1921) 'Les influences puniques chez les berbères', *RA*, 62, p. 340

Bates, O. (1914) *The Eastern Libyans* (London: Macmillan)
Bates, O. and Dunham, D. (1927) 'Excavations at Gammai', *HAS*, 8, pp. 1–122
Bayle des Hermans, R. de (1972a) 'Aspects de la recherche préhistorique en République Centrafricaine', *Africa-Tervuren* XVIII, 3/4, pp. 90–103
Bayle des Hermens, R. de (1972b) 'La civilisation mégalithique de Bouar. Prospection et fouille 1962–6 par P. Vidal, Recension', *Africa-Tervuren*, XLII, 1, pp. 78–9
Beauchêne, M. C. de (1963) 'La préhistoire du Gabon', *Objets et Mondes*, III, 1, p. 16
Beauchêne, M. C. de (1970) 'The Lantana mine near the Rapoa/Niger confluence of Niger', *WAAN*, 12, p. 63
Beck, P. and Huard, P. (1969) *Tibesti, carrefour de la préhistoire saharienne* (Paris: Arthaud)
Bedaux, R. and Bollamd, R. (1980) 'Tellem, reconnaissance archaéologique d'une culture de l'Ouest africain au Moyen Age: Les textiles', *Journal des Africanistes*, 50, 1, pp. 9–24
Beek, G. W. Van (1967) 'Monuments of Axum in the light of south Arabian archaeology', *JAOS*, 87, pp. 113–22
Bénabou, M. (1976) *La résistance africaine à la romanisation* (Paris: Maspero)
Bermus, S. (1983) 'Découvertes, hypothèses, reconstitution et preuves: Le cuivre médieval d'Azelik-Takedda (Niger)', in M. Echard (ed.), *Métallurgies africaines: nouvelles contributions*, Mem. Soc. Afr., pp. 153–71
Bermus, S. and Echard, M. (1985) 'Metal-working in the Agadez region (Niger): An ethno-archaeological approach', in P. T. Craddock and M. J. Hughes (eds.), *Furnaces and Smelting Technology in Antiquity* (London: British Museum, Occasional Paper, 48) pp. 71–80
Bisson, M. S. (1975) 'Copper currency in central Africa: the archaeological evidence', *WA*, 6, pp. 276–92
Blankoff, B. (1965) 'La préhistoire au Gabon', *BSPPG*, pp. 4–5
Bloch, M. and Verin, P. (1966) 'Discovery of an apparently neolithic artefact in Madagascar', *Man*, I, pp. 240–1
Boshier, A. and Beaumont, P. (1972) 'Mining in southern Africa and the emergence of modern man', *Optima*, 22, pp. 2–12
Boubbe, J. (1959–60) 'Découvertes récentes à Sala Colonia (Chellah)' *BSAC*, pp. 141–5
Bourgeois, R. (1957) 'Banyarwanda et Barundi, Tombe I – ethnographie', *ARSC*, XV, pp. 536–49
Bovill, E. W. (1968) *The Golden Trade of the Moors* 2nd edn (London: Oxford University Press)
Brabant, H. (1965) 'Contribution odontologique à l'étude des ossements trouvés dans la nécropole protohistorique de Sanga, République du Congo', *AMRAC*, 54
Breasted, J. H. (1951) *A History of Egypt from the Earliest Times to the Persian Conquest* 2nd edn (London: Hodder and Stoughton)
Briggs, L. C. (1957) 'Living tribes of the Sahara and the problem of their prehistoric origin', *Third Pan-African Congress on Prehistory*, Livingstone, 1955 (London: Chatto), pp. 195–9
Budge, E. A. T. Wallis (1928) *A History of Ethiopia, Nubia and Abyssinia, according to the Hieroglyphic Inscription of Egypt and Nubia and the Ethiopian Chronicle*, 2 vols (London: Methuen)
Budge, E. A. T. Wallis (1966) *A History of Ethiopia*, vol. I (Netherlands: Cosferhout NB, Anthropological Publications)
Bynon, J. (1970) 'The contribution of linguistics to history in the field of Berber studies', in D. Dalby (ed.), *Language and History in Africa* (London: Cass), pp. 64–77
Cabannes, R. (1964) *Les Types hémoglobiniques des populations de la partie occidentale du continent africain (Maghrib, Sahara, Afrique noire occidentale)* (Paris: CNRS)
Callet, F. (1974) *Histoire des rois de Tantaran'ny Andriana*, vols. 1–3, translated by G. S. Chaput and E. Ratsimba (Tananarive: Librairie de Madagascar)
Caminos, R. A. (1975) *New Kingdom Temples of Buhen*, 2 vols (London: Egypt Exploration Society)
Camps, G. (1954) 'L'inscription de Béja et le problème des Dii Mauri' *RA*, 98, pp. 233–60
Camps, G. (1960a) 'Les traces d'un âge du bronze en Afrique du Nord', *RA*, 104, pp. 31–55
Camps, G. (1960b) 'Aux origines de la Berbérie: Massinissa ou les débuts de l'histoire', *Libyca*, 8, 1
Camps, G. (1961) *Monuments et rites funéraires protohistoriques: aux origines de la Berbérie* (Paris: AMG)
Camps, G. (1970) 'Recherches sur les origines des cultivateurs noirs du Sahara', *ROMM*, 7, pp. 39–41
Camps, G., (1974) 'Le Gour, mausolée berbère du VIIe siècle', *American Anthropologist*, VIII, pp. 191–208
Camps, G. (1982) 'Beginning of pastoralism and cultivation in Northwest Africa and the Sahara', *The Cambridge History of Africa* (Cambridge: Cambridge University Press), pp. 584–623
Camps, G. Delibrias, G. and Thommeret, J. (1968) 'Chronologie absolue et succession des civilisations préhistoriques dans le Nord de l'Afrique', *Libyca*, XVI, p. 16
Camps-Fabrer, H. (1953) *L'Olivier et l'huile dans l'Afrique romaine* (Algiers: Imprimerie officielle)

Caquot, A. and Leclant, J. (1959) 'Ethiopie et Cyrénaique? A propos d'un texte de Synesius', *AE*, III, pp. 173–7

Carter, P. L. (1970) 'Late stone age exploitation patterns in southern Natal', *SAAB*, 25, 98, pp. 55–8

Carter, P. L. and Flight, C. (1972) 'A report on the fauna from two neolithic sites in northern Ghana with evidence for the practice of animal husbandry during the 2nd millennium BC' *Man*, 7, 2, pp. 277–82

Carter, P. L. and Vogel. J. C. (1971) 'The dating of industrial assemblages from stratified sites in eastern Lesotho', *Man*, 9, pp. 557–70

Castiglione, L. (1970) 'Diocletianus und die Blemmyes', *ZAS*, 96, 2, pp. 90–103

Caton-Thompson, G. (1929) 'The Southern Rhodesian ruins: recent archaeological investigations', *Nature*, 124, pp. 619–21

Caton-Thompson, G. (1929–30) 'Recent excavations at Zimbabwe and other ruins in Rhodesia', *JRAS*, 29, pp. 132–8

Chaker, S. (1973) 'Libyque: épigraphie et linguistique', *Encyclopédie berbère*, 9

Chamla, M. C. (1970) 'Les hommes épipaléolithiques de Columnata (Algérie occidentale)', *Mém. CRAPE*, XV, pp. 113–14

Chamoux, F. (1953) *Cyrène sous la monarchie des Battiades* (Paris: de Boccard)

Chaplin, J. H. (1974) 'The prehistoric rock art of the Lake Victoria region', *Azania*, IX, pp. 1–50

Charles-Picard, G. (1954), *Les Religions de l'Afrique antique* (Paris: Plon)

Charles-Picard, G. and C. (1958) *La Vie quotidienne à Carthage au temps d'Hannibal, IIIe siècle avant Jésus-Christ* (Paris: Hachette)

Charles-Picard, G. (1959) *La Civilisation de l'Afrique romaine* (Paris: Plon)

Charles-Picard, G. (1968) *Les Cahiers de Tunisie. Mélanges Saumagne*, pp. 27–31

Chastagnol, A. and Duval, N. (1974) 'Les survivances du culte impérial dans l'Afrique du Nord à l'époque vandale. Mélanges d'histoire ancienne offerts à W. Seston', *Publications de la Sorbonne*, Etude IX, pp. 87–118

Chittick, N. (1966) 'Six early coins from new Tanga', *Azania*, 1, pp. 156–7

Chittick, N. (1969) 'An archaeological reconnaissance of the southern Somali coast', *Azania*, IV, pp. 115–30

Clark, J. D. (1970) *The Prehistory of Africa* (London: Thames and Hudson)

Clark, J. D. (1974) 'Iron age occupation at the Kalambo Falls', in J. D. Clark (ed.), *Kalambo Falls Prehistoric Site*, vol. II (Cambridge: Cambridge University Press), pp. 57–70

Clark, J. D. and Fagan, B. M. (1965) 'Charcoal, sands and channel-decorated pottery from northern Rhodesia', *American Anthropologist*, LXVII, pp. 354–71

Clark, J. D. and Walton, J. (1962) 'A late stone age site in the Erongo mountains, south west Africa', *Proc. PS*, 28, pp. 1–16

Cohen, D. and Maret, P. de (1974) 'Recherches archéologiques récentes en République du Zaïre', *Forum-Université Libre de Bruxelles*, 39, pp. 33–7

Connah, G. (1967) 'Excavations at Daima, N.E. Nigeria', *Actes VI Congr. PPEQ*, pp. 146–7

Connah, G. (1981) *Three Thousand Years in Africa* (Cambridge: Cambridge University Press)

Connah, G. (1987) *African Civilizations: Precolonial Cities and States in Tropical Africa: An Archaeological Perspective* (Cambridge: Cambridge University Press)

Contenson, H. de (1960) 'Les premiers rois d'Axoum d'après les découvertes récentes', *JA*, 248, pp. 78–96

Contenson, H. de (1961) 'Les principales étapes de l'Ethiopie antique', *CEA*, 2, 5, pp. 12–23

Contenson, H. de (1963a) 'Les subdivisions de l'archéologie éthiopienne. Etat de la question', *R. Arch.*, pp. 189–91

Contenson, H. de (1963b) 'Les fouilles de Haoulti en 1959. Rapport préliminaire', *AE*, 5, pp. 41–86

Contenson, H. de (1963c) 'les fouilles à Axoum en 1958. Rapport préliminaire', *AE*, 5, pp. 3–39

Contenson, H. de (1965) 'Les fouilles à Haoulti en 1959; rapport préliminaire', *AE*, 5, pp. 45–6

Cooke, C. K. (1971) 'The rock art of Rhodesia', *SAJS*, special issue 2, pp. 7–10

Coon, C. S. (1968) *Yengema Cave Report* (Philadelphia, Pa.: University of Pennsylvania)

Coppens, Y. (1969) 'Les cultures protohistoriques et historiques du Djourab', *Actes ler Coll. Intern. Archéol. Afr.*, pp. 129–46

Cornevin, R. (1967) *Histoire de l'Afrique. Vol. I: Des origines au XVIe siècle*, 2nd edn (Paris: Payot)

Cosmas Indicopleustes (1909) *The Christian Topography of Cosmas Indicopleustes*, translated by E. O. Winstedt (Cambridge: Cambridge University Press). *Topographie chrétienne*, translated by W. Walsca (Paris: Cerf)

Coulbeaux, J. B. (1928) *Histoire politique et religieuse d'Abyssinie depuis les temps les plus reculés jusqu'à l'avènement de Menelik II*, Vol. I (Paris: Geuthner)

Crowfoot, J. W. (1911) 'The island of Meroe', *Archaeological Survey of Egypt, Memoire 19* (London) p. 37

Crowfoot, J. W. (1927) 'Christian Nubia', *JEA*, XIII, pp. 141–50

Culwick, A. L. and G. M. (1936) 'Indonesian echoes in central Tanganyika', *TNR*, 2, pp. 60–6

Dahl, O. Ch. (1951) 'Malgache et Maanjan, une comparaison linguistique', *AUEI*, 3

Dahle, L. (1889) 'The Swahili element in the new Malagasy English dictionary', *Antananarivo*, III, pp. 99–115

Dalby, D. (1970) 'Reflections on the classification of African languages', *ALS*, II, pp. 147–71

Dalby, D. (1967) 'The prehistorical implication of Guthrie's comparative Bantu. II. Interpretation of cultural vocabulary', *JAH*, XVII, pp. 1–27

Daniels, C. M. (1968a) *Garamantian Excavations: Zinchecra 1965–1967* (Tripoli: Department of Antiquities)

Daniels, C. M. (1968b) 'The Garamantes of Fezzan', in *Libya in History* (Beirut, Lebanon)

Daniels, C. M. (1970) *The Garamantes of Southern Libya* (Wisconsin: Cleander Press)

Daniels, C. M. (1972–3) 'The Garamantes of Fezzan. An interim report of research, 1965–73', *SLS*, IV, pp. 35–40

Daniels, S. G. H. and Phillipson, D. W. (1969) 'The early iron age site at Dambwa near Livingstone', in B. M. Fagan, D.W. Phillipson and S. G. H. Daniels (eds.), *Iron Age cultures in Zambia* (London: Chatto and Windus), vol. II, pp. 1–54

Dart R. A. and Beaumont, P. (1969a) 'Evidence of ore mining in southern Africa in the middle stone age', *CA*, 10, pp. 127–8

Dart, R. A. and Beaumont, P. (1969b) 'Rhodesian engravers, painters and pigment miners of the fifth millennium BC', *SAAB*, 8, pp. 91–6

Datoo, B. A. (1970a) 'Misconception about the use of monsoons by dhows in East African waters', *EAGR*, 8, pp. 1–10

Datoo, B. A. (1970b) 'Rhapta: the location and importance of East Africa's first port', *Azania*, V, pp. 65–75

Datoo, B. A. and Sheriff, A. M. H. (1971) 'Pattern of ports and trade routes in different periods', in L. Berry (ed.), *Tanzania in Maps* (London: University of London Press), pp. 102–5

Davies, N. M. (1958) *Picture Writing in Ancient Egypt* (London: Oxford University Press for Griffith Institute)

Davies, O. (1962) 'Neolithic Culture in Ghana', *Proceedings of the Fourth Panafrican Congress of Prehistory*, vol. 2 (Brussels) pp. 291–302

Davies, O. (1964) *The Quaternary in the Coast Lands of Guinea* (Glasgow: Jackson)

Davies, O. (1967a) *West Africa before the Europeans: Archaeology and Prehistory* (London: Methuen)

Davies, O. (1967b) 'Timber construction and wood carving in West Africa in the 2nd millennium BC', *Man*, 2, 1, pp. 115–18

Davies, O. (1971) 'Excavations at Blackburn', *SAAB*, 26, pp. 165–78

Deacon, H. J. and J. (1972) 'Archaeological evidence for demographic changes in eastern Cape during the last 2000 years', *Report at AGM of the Archaeological Association, University of Witwatersrand*, Johannesburg

Derricourt, R. M. (1973) 'Archaeological survey of the Transkei and Ciskei: interim report for 1972', *Fort Hare Papers*, 5, pp. 449–55

Desanjes, J. (1963) 'Un témoignage peu connu de Procope sur la Numidie vandale et byzantine', *Byzantion*, XXXIII, pp. 41–69

Desanges, J. (1975) 'L'Afrique noire et le monde méditerranéen dans l'antiquité. Ethiopiens et gréco-romains', *RFHOM*, 228, pp. 391–414

Desanges, J. (1976) 'L'Iconographie du noir dans l'Afrique du nord antique', in J. Vercoutter, J. Leclant and F. Snowden (eds.), *L'Image du noir dans l'art occidental. Vol. I: Des pharaons à la chute de l'empire romain* (Fribourg: Menil Foundation), pp. 246–68

Desanges, J. and Lancel, S. (1962–74) 'Bibliographie analytique de l'Afrique antique', *BAA*, pp. 1–5

Descamps, C., Demoulin, D. and Abdallah, A. (1967) 'Donnėes nouvelles sur la préhistoirė du cap Manuel (Dakar)', *Acts VI Congr. PPEQ*, pp. 130–2

Descamps, C. and Thilmans, G. (1972) *Excavations at DeNdalane (Sine Saloum) 27 November–16 January 1972*

Deschamps, H. (1960) *Histoire de Madagascar* (Paris: Berger-Levrault) (3rd edn, 1965)

Deschamps, H. (ed.) (1970) *Histoire générale de l'Afrique noire, de Madagascar et des Archipels, Vol. I: Des origines à 1800* (Paris: PUF), pp. 203–10

Devic, L. M. (1883) *Le pays des Zendj d'après les écrivains arabes* (Paris)

Diop, C. A. (1955) *Nations Nègres et Cultures. De l'Antiquité Négro-Egyptienne aux problèmes culturels d'Afrique Noire d'Aujourd'hui* (Paris: Présence Africaine)

Diop, C. A. (1967) *Antériorité des civilisations nègres: mythe ou vérité historique* (Paris: Présence Africaine)
Diop, C. A. (1968') 'Métallurgie traditionnelle et l'âge du fer en Afrique', *BIFAN*, B, XXX, I, pp. 10–38
Diop, C. A. (1973) 'La métallurgie du fer sous l'ancien empire égyptien', *BIFAN*, B, XXXV, pp. 532–47
Diop, C. A. (1977) 'Parenté génétique de l'égyptien pharaonique et des langues africaines: processus de sémitisation' and 'La pigmentation des anciens Egyptiens, test par la mélanine', *BIFAN*
Dixon, D. M. M. (1964) 'The origin of the kingdom of Kush (Napata-Meroe)', *JEA*, 50, pp. 121–32
Donadoni, S. (1970) 'Les fouilles à l'église de Sonqi Tino', in E. Dinkler (ed.), *Kunst und Geschichte Nubiens in christlicher Zeit: Ergebnisse und Probleme auf Grund der jüngsten Ausgrabungen* (Recklinghausen: Verlag, Aurel Bongers), pp. 209–18
Donadoni, S. and Curto, S. (1965) 'Le pitture murali della chiesa di sonki nel Sudan', *La Nubia Cristiana, Quaderno N° 2 del Museo eglizio di Torino* (Turin: Fratelli Pozzo-Salvati), pp. 123 ff
Doresse, J. (1957) 'Découvertes en Ethiopie et découverte de l'Ethiopie', *BO*, 14, pp. 64–5
Doresse, J. (1960) 'La découverte d'Asbi-Déra', *Atti del Convegno. Intern. Stud. Et.*, Rome, 2–4 April 1959, pp. 229–48
Dornan, S. S. (1915) 'Rhodesian ruins and native tradition', *SAJS*, 12, pp. 501–16
Drewes, A. J. (1954) 'The inscription from Dibbid in Eritrea', *BO*, 11, pp. 185–6
Drewes, A. J. (1956) 'Nouvelles inscriptions de l'Ethiqpie', *BO*, 13, pp. 179–82
Drewes, A. J. (1962) *Inscription de l'Ethiopie Antique* (Leiden: Brill)
Drewes, A. J. and Schneider, R. (1967, 1970, 1972) 'Documents épigraphiques de l'Ethiopie I, II, III', *AE*, VII, pp. 89–106; VIII, pp. 57–72; IX, pp. 87–102
Drouin, E. A. (1882) 'Les listes royales éthiopiennes et leur autorité historique', *RA*, August–October
Drury, R. (1731) *Madagascar or, Robert Drury's Journal during Fifteen Years of Captivity on that Island* (London: J. Brotherton)
Du Mesgnil, F. (1897) *Madagascar, Homère et la civilisation mycènienne* (Saint-Denis, Réunion: Dubourg)
Dunham, D. and Bates, O. (1950–7) *Royal Cemeteries of Kush, I: El-Kurru; II: Nuri; III: Royal Tombs at Meroe and Barkal* (Cambridge: Mass.: Harvard University Press)
Duval, N. (1971–) *Recherches archéologiques à Sbeitla* (Paris: de Boccard)
Duyvendak, J. J. L. (1949) *China's Discovery of Africa* (London: Probsthain)
Ehret, C. (1967) 'Cattle-keeping and milking in eastern and southern African history: the linguistic evidence', *JAH*, VIII, pp. 1–17
Ehret, C. (1971) *Southern Nilotic History: Linguistic Approaches to the Study of the Past* (Evanston: Northwestern University Press)
Ehret, C. (1972) 'Bantu origins and history: critique and interpretation', *TJH*, II, pp. 1–19
Ehret, C. (1973) 'Patterns of Bantu and central Sudanic settlement in central and southern Africa (*c*.1000 BC–500 AD)', *TJH*, III, pp. 1–71
Ehret, C. (1974) *Ethiopians and East Africans: the Problems of Contacts* (Nairobi: East African Publishing House)
Ehret, C. et al. (1972) 'Outlining southern African history: a re-evaluation AD 100–1500', *Ufahamu*, III, pp. 9–27
Elphick, R. H. (1972) 'The Cape Khoi and the first phase of South African race relations', thesis (Yale University)
Emery, W. B. (1965) *Egypt in Nubia* (London: Hutchinson)
Erman, A. (1927) *The Literature of the Ancient Egyptians*, translated by A. M. Blackman (London: Methuen)
Erroux, J. (1957) 'Essai d'une classification dichotomique des blés durs cultivés en Algérie', *Bulletin de la Société d'Histoire Naturelle de l'Afrique du Nord*, 48, pp. 239–53
Esperandieu, G. (1957) *De l'art animalier dans l'Afrique antique* (Algiers: Imprimerie Officielle)
Evans-Pritchard, E. E. (1968) *The Nuer: Description of Modes of Livelihood and Political Institutions of a Nilotic People* (London: Oxford University Press)
Fagan, B. M. (1969) 'Early trade and raw materials in south central Africa', *JAH*, X, I, pp. 1–13
Fagan, B. M. and Noten, F. L. Van (1971) 'The hunter–gatherers of Gwisho', *AMRAC*, 74, XXII
Fagan, B. M., Phillipson, D. W. and Daniels, S. G. H. (eds.) (1969) *Iron Age Cultures in Zambia* (London: Chatto and Windus)
Fagg, A. (1972) 'Excavations of an occupation site in the Nok valley, Nigeria', *WAJA*, 2, pp. 75–9
Fairman, H. W. (1938) 'Preliminary report on the excavations at Sesebi and Amarah West, Anglo-Egyptian Sudan, 1937–8', *JEA*, XXIV, pp. 151–6

Fairman, H. W. (1939) 'Preliminary report on the excavations at Amarah West, Anglo-Egyptian Sudan, 1938–9', *JEA*, XXV, pp. 139–44
Fairman, H. W. (1948) 'Preliminary report on the excavations at Amarah West, Anglo-Egyptian Sudan, 1947–8', *JEA*, XXXIV, pp. 1–11
Fattovich, R. (1972) 'Sondaggi stratigrafici. Yeha', *AE*, 9, pp. 65–86
Faublée, J. and M. (1964) 'Madagascar vu par les auteurs arabes avant le XIXe siècle', communication at the 8e Congrès. Inter. Hist. Marit. and Studia, 11
Ferrand, G. (1891–1902) *Les Musulmans à Madagascar et aux îles Comores*, 2 vols. (Paris: Leroux)
Ferrand, G. (1904) 'Madagascar et les îles Uaq-Uaq', *JA*, pp. 489–509
Ferrand, G. (1908) 'L'origine africaine des Malgaches', *JA*, pp. 353–500
Firth, C. M. (1910–27) *The Archaeological Survey of Nubia, Report for 1907, 1908, 1910, 1911* (Cairo: National Print Department)
Flacourt, E. (1661) *Histoire de la grande île de Madagascar* (Paris: Clougier)
Flight, C. (1972) 'Kintampo and West African Neolithic civilizations', *BWS*, 56
Forbes, R. J. (1954) 'Extracting, smelting and alloying', in C. Singer, E. J. Holmyard and A. R. Hall (eds.) *History of Technology*, 4 vols (Oxford: Clarendon Press), pp. 572–99
Franchini, V. (1954) 'Ritrovamenti archeologici in Eritrea', *RSE*, 12, pp. 5–28
Fraser, P. M. (1972) *Ptolemaic Alexandria*, 3 vols. (Oxford: Clarendon Press)
Freeman-Grenville, G. S. P. (1960) 'East African coin finds and their historical significance', *JAH*, 1, pp. 31–43
Frend, W. H. C. (1968) 'Nubia as an outpost of Byzantine cultural influence', *Byzantinoslavica*, 2, pp. 319–26
Frend, W. H. C. (1972) 'Coptic, Greek and Nubian at Qasr Ibrim', *Byzantinoslavica*, XXXIII, pp. 224–9
Gabel, C. (1965), *Stone Age Hunters of the Kafue. The Gwisho A site*, (Boston, Mass.: Boston University Press)
Gadallah, F. F. (1971) 'Problems of pre-Herodotan sources in Libyan history', *Libya in History* (Benghazi), pt 2, pp. 43–75 (Arabic edition, résumé in English, pp. 78–81)
Galand, L. (1969) 'Les Berbères, la langue et les parlers', *Encyclopedia Universalis* (Paris), pp. 171–3
Galand, L. (1974) 'Libyque et berbère', *AEPHE*, pp. 131–53
Garlake, P. S. (1969) 'Chiltope: an early iron age village in northern Mashonaland', *Arnoldia* (Rhodesia), IV, 19
Garlake, P. S. (1970a) 'Iron age sites in the Urungwe district of Rhodesia', *SAAB*, XXV, pp. 25–44
Garlake, P. S. (1970b) 'Rhodesian ruins. A preliminary assessment of their styles and chronology', *JAH*, XI, 4, pp. 495–513
Garlake, P. S. (1973) *Great Zimbabwe* (London: Thames and Hudson)
Garstang, J., Sayce, A. H. and Griffith, F. L. (1911) *Meroë, the City of the Ethiopians: an Account of a First Season's Excavations on the Site 1909–10* (Liverpool: University at Liverpool Institute of Archaeology)
Germain, G. (1948) 'Le culte du bélier en Afrique du Nord', *Hesperis*, XXXV, pp. 93–124
Goodchild, R. G. (1962) *Cyrene and Apollonia: an Historical Guide* (Libya: Antiquities Department of Cyrenaica)
Goodwin, A. J. H. (1946) 'Prehistoric fishing methods in South Africa', *Antiquity*, 20, pp. 134–9
Gostynski, T. (1975) 'La Libye antique et ses relations avec l'Egypte', *BIFAN*, 37, 3, pp. 473–588
Grandidier, A. (1885) *Histoire de la Géographie de Madagascar* (Paris: Imprimèrie Nationale)
Gratien, B. (1978) *Les cultures Kerma; essai de classification*, (Lille)
Greenberg, J. H. (1955) *Studies in African Linguistic Classification* (New Haven, Conn.: Compass)
Greenberg, J. H. (1972) 'Linguistic evidence regarding Bantu origins', *JAH*, XIII, 2, pp. 189–216
Griffith, F. L. *Karanog. The Meroitic Inscriptions of Shablul and Karamog* (Philadelphia)
Griffith, F. L. (1911–12) *Meroitic Inscriptions*, 2 vols (London: Archaeological Survey of Egypt)
Griffith, F. L. (1913) *The Nubian Texts of the Christian Period* (Berlin: Akedemie der Wissenchaften)
Griffith, F. L. (1921–8) 'Oxford excavations in Nubia', *LAAA*, VIII, 1; IX, 3–4; X, 3–4; XI, 3–4; XII, 3–4; XIII, 1–4; XIV, 3–4; XV, 3–4
Griffith, F. L. (1925) 'Pakhoras-Bakharas-Faras in geography and history', *JEA*, XI, pp. 259–68
Grobbelaar, C. S. and Goodwin, A. J. H. (1952) 'Report on the skeletons and implements in association with them from a cave near Bredasdorp, Cape Province', *SAAB*, 7, pp. 95–101
Grunderbeek, Van, M. C., Roche, E. and Doutrelepont, H. (1983) *Le premier âge du fer au Rwanda et au Burundi: Archéologie et environnement* (Brussels: IFAQ/CQS)
Gsell, S. (1913–28) *Histoire ancienne de l'Afrique du Nord*, 8 vols (Paris: Hachette)
Gsell, S. (1926) 'La Tripolitaine et le Sahara au IIIe siècle de notre ère', *MAI*, XLIII, pp. 149–66
Guidi, I. (1906) *The Life and Miracles of Tekle Haymanot* (London) vol. II

Guthrie, M. (1962) 'Some developments in the pre-history of the Bantu languages', *JAH*, III(2), pp. 273–82

Guthrie, M. (1967–71) *Comparative Bantu: an Introduction to the Comparative Linguistics and Pre-history of the Bantu Languages*, 4 vols (Farnborough: Greeg International)

Guthrie, M. (1970) 'Contributions from comparative Bantu studies to the prehistory of Africa', in D. Dalby (ed.), *Language and History in Africa* (London: Frank Cass), pp. 20–49

Hailemarian, G. (1955) 'Objects found in the neighbourhood of Axum', *AE*, I, pp. 50–1

Halff, G. (1963) 'L'onomastique punique de Carthage', *Karthago*, XIII

Hall, M. (1981) *Settlement Patterns in the Iron Age of Zululand: an Ecological Interpretation* (Oxford: British Archaeological Reports)

Hallo, W. W. and Simpson, W. K. (1971) *The Ancient Near East: A History*, (New York)

Hamy, E. T. (1969) in G. Parrinder (ed.), *African Mythology*, 2nd edn (London: Hamlyn)

Harden, D. B. (1963) *The Phoenicians*, rev. edn (London: Thames and Hudson)

Hartle, D. (1966) 'Bronze objects from the Ifeka gardens site, Ezira', *WAAN*, 4, p. 26

Harlan, J. R., Wet, J. M. J. de and Stemler, A. (eds.) (1976) *Origins of African Plant Domestication* (The Hague: Mouton; Paris: World Anthropology Series)

Harris, J. R. (1966) *Egyptian Art* (London: Spring Books)

Havinden, M. A. (1970) 'The history of crop cultivation in West Africa: a bibliographical guide', *EHR*, 2nd ser., XXIII, 3, pp. 532–55

Haycock, B. G. (1954) 'The kingship of Kush in the Sudan', *CSSH*, VII, 4, pp. 461–80

Hayes, W. C. (1953–9) *The Scepter of Egypt: A Background for the Study of Egyptian Antiquities in the Metropolitan Museum of Art*, 2 vols. (Cambridge, Mass.: Harvard University Press)

Hébert, J. C. (1968a) 'Calendriers provinciaux malgaches', *BM*, 172, pp. 809–20

Hébert, J. C. (1968b) 'La rose des vents malgaches et les points cardinaux', *CM*, 2, pp. 159–205

Hébert, J. C. (1971) 'Madagascar et Malagasy, histoire d'un double nom de baptème', *BM*, 302–3, pp. 583–613

Hellstrom, P. and Langballe, H. (1970). *The Rock Drawings, Scandinavian joint expedition to Sudanese Nubia* (Stockholm/New York)

Herzog, R. (1968) in *Punt*, Proceedings of the German Archaeological Institute of Cairo, 5 (Glückstadt)

Hiernaux, J. (1968a) *La Diversité humaine en Afrique subsaharienne* (Brussels: Université Libre de Bruxelles, L'Institut de sociologie)

Hiernaux, J. (1968b) 'Bantu expansion: the evidence from physical anthropology confronted with linguistic and archaeological evidence', *JAH*, IX, 4, pp. 505–15

Hiernaux, J. and Maquet, E. (1957) 'Cultures préhistoriques de l'âge des métaux au Rwanda-Urundi et au Kivu (Congo Belge)', lère partie, *ARSC*, pp. 1126–49

Hiernaux, J. and Maquet, E. (1960) 'Cultures préhistoriques de l'âge des métaux au Rwanda-Urundi et au Kivu (Congo Belge)', 2e partie, *ARSC*, X(2), pp. 5–88

Hiernaux, J., Maquet, E. and Buyst, J. De (1973) 'Le cimetière protohistorique de Katoto (vallée de Lualaba, Congo-Kinshasa)', *Actes IV Congr. PPQS*, pp. 148–58

Hintze, F. (1968) *Civilizations of the Old Sudan* (Leipzig)

Histoire et Tradition Orale (1975) 'L'Empire du Mali', *Actes Coll. Bamako I*, Fondation SCOA pour la recherche fondamentale en Afrique noire

Hobler, P. M. and Hester, J. J. (1969) 'Prehistory and environment in the Libyan desert', *South African Archaeological Journal*, 23, 92, pp. 120–30

Holl, A. (1986) 'Transition from Late Stone Age to Iron Age in the Soudano-Sahelian Zone: A case study from the perichadian plain', presented at the World Archaeological Congress, Southampton, England

Hölscher, W. (1955) 'Libyer und Ägypter, Beitrâge zur Ethnologie und Geschichte Libyscher Völkerschaften', *AFU*, 5

Hornell, (1934) 'Indonesian influences on East African culture', *JRAI*

Huard, P. (1966) 'Introduction et diffusion du fer au Tchad', *JAH*, VII, pp. 377–404

Huard, P. and Leclant, J. (1972) *Problèmes archéologiques entre le Nil et la Sahara* (Cairo)

Huard, P. and Massip, J. M. (1967) 'Monuments du Sahara nigéro-tchadien', *BIFAN*, B, pp. 1–27

Huffmann, T. N. (1970) 'The early iron age and the spread of the Bantu', *SAAB*, XXV, pp. 3–21

Huffmann, T. N. (1971a) 'A guide to the iron age of Mashonaland', *OPNM*, pp. 20–44

Huffmann, T. N. (1971b) 'Excavations at Leopard's Kopje main Kraal: a preliminary report', *SAAB*, XXVI, pp. 85–9

Huffmann, T. N. (1973) 'Test excavations at Makuru, Rhodesia', *Arnoldia*, (Rhodesia) V, p. 39
Huffmann, T. N. (1974) 'Ancient mining and Zimbabwe', *JSAIMM*, LXXXIV, pp. 238–42
Huffmann, T. N. (1982) 'Archaeology and ethnohistory of the African Iron Age', *Ann. Rev. Anthrop.*, II, pp. 133–50
Jakobielski, S. 'Polish excavations at Old Dongola', *Nubische Kunst*, pp. 167 ff
Jakobielski, S. (1975a) 'Polish excavations at Old Dongola 1970–72', *Actes Coll. Nubiol Intern.*, pp. 70–5
Jakobielski, S. (1975b) 'Old Dongola 1972–3' *Etudes et Travaux*, VIII, pp. 349–60
Jakobielski, S. and Krzysaniak, L. (1967–8) 'Polish excavations at Old Dongola, third season, December 1966–February 1967', *Kush*, XV, pp. 143–64
Jakobielski, S. and Ostrazs, A. (1967) 'Polish excavations at Old Dongola, second season, December 1965–February 1966', *Kush*, XV, pp. 125–42
Jamme, A. (1957) 'Ethiopia. Annales d'Ethiopie', *BO*, 14, pp. 76–80
Jenkins, G. K. and Lewis, R. B. (1963) *Carthaginian Gold and Electrum Coins* (London: Royal Numismatic Society)
Jones, A. H. M. (1968) 'Frontier defence in Byzantine Libya', *Libya in History* (Benghazi: University of Benghazi), pp. 289–97
Jones, A. H. M. (1969) 'The influence of Indonesia: the musicological evidence reconsidered', *Azania*, IV, pp. 131–90
Jones, N. (1933) 'Excavations at Nswatugi and Madiliyangwa', *OPNM*, I, 2, pp. 1–44
Julien, C. A. (1966) *Histoire de l'Afrique du Nord. Tunisie, Algérie, Maroc, de la conquête arabe à 1830* 2nd edn (Paris: Payot)
Julien, C. A. (1975) *Histoire de l'Afrique du Nord: des origines à la conquête arabe* (Paris: Payot)
Julien, G. (1908–9) *Institutions Politiques et Sociales de Madagascar d'après des documents authentiques et inédits*, 2 vols. (Paris)
Kadra, F. (1978) *Les Djedars, monuments funéraires berbères de la région de Farenda* (Algierş)
Kanawati, N. (1977) *The Egyptian Administration in the Old Kingdom: Evidence on its Economic Decline* (Warminster: Aris Phillips)
Katznelson, I. S. (1966) 'La Candace et les survivances matrilinéaires au pays de Kush', *Palestinskij Sbornik*, XV, 78, pp. 35–40
Kemse, F. (1985) 'The initial diffusion of iron to Africa', in R. Haaland and P. Shinnie (eds.), *African Iron Working* (Oslo: Norwegian University Press), pp. 11–27
Kent, R. (1970) *Early Kingdoms in Madagascar, 1500–1700* (New York: Holt, Reinhardt and Winston)
Klapwijk, M. (1973) 'An Early Iron Age site near Tzaneen, North-Eastern Transvaal', *SAJS*, LXIX
Klapwijk, M. (1974) 'A preliminary report on pottery from the North-Eastern Transvaal, South Africa', *SAAB*, 29
Kieran, J. A. and Ogot, B. A. (1968) *Zamani: a Survey of East African History* (Nairobi/London) (rev. edn 1974)
Kirk, W. (1962) 'The North-East Monsoon and some aspects of African history', *JAH*, III
Kolb, P. (1719) *The Present State of the Cape of Good Hope: or a particular account of the several nations of the Hottentots . . . with a short account of the Dutch settlements at the Cape*, translated by Mr Medley (1731), 2 vols. (London: Innys)
Kolendo, J. (1970) 'Epigraphie et archéologie: le praepositus camellorum dans une inscription d'Ostie', *Klio*, pp. 287–98
Kolendo, J. (1970) 'L'influence de Carthage sur la civilisation matérielle de Rome', *Archeologia*, XXI (Warsaw)
Lambert, N. (1981) 'L'apparition du cuivre dans les civilisations préhistoriques', in C. H. Perrot, Y. Person, J. P. Chrétien and J. Devisse (eds.), *Le Sol, la Parole et l'Ecrit, Mélanges en hommage à Raymond Mauny*, Société Française d'Histoire d'Outre-Mer, pp. 214–26
Lancel, S. and Pouthier, L. (1957) 'Première campagne de fouilles à Tigisis', *Mélanges de l'école française de Rome* (Rome: Institut Français), pp. 247–53
Lapeyre, G. G. and Pellegrin, A. (1942) *Carthage punique (814–146 avant J. C.)* (Paris: Payot)
Lassus, J. (1956) 'Fouilles à Mila. Une tour de l'ancienne Byzantine', *Libyca*, IV, 2, pp. 232–9
Lassus, J. (1975) 'La forteresse byzantine de Thamugadi', *Actes XIV Congr. Intern. Et. Byz*, pp. 463–76
Lauer, J. P. (1974) *Le mystère des pyramides* (Paris)
Law, R. C. (1967) 'The Garamantes and trans-Saharan enterprise in classical times', *JCH*, pp. 181–200
Leclant, J. (1956a) 'Egypte-Afrique, quelques remarques sur la diffusion des monuments égyptiens en Afrique', *BSFE*, 21, pp. 29–41
Leclant, J. (1956b) 'Le fer dans l'Egypte ancienne, le Soudan et l'Afrique', *Actes Coll. Intern. Fer.*, pp. 83–91

Leclant, J. (1961) 'Découverte de monuments égyptiens ou égyptisants hors de la vallée du Nil, 1955–60', *Orientalia*, 30, pp. 391–406

Leclant, J. (1964–7), 'Au sujet des objets égyptiens découverts en Ethiopie', *Orientalia*, 33, pp. 388–9; 34, p. 220; 35, p. 165; 36, p. 216

Leclant, J. (1965) 'Le musée des antiquités à Addis-Ababa', *BSAC*, 16, pp. 86–7

Leclant, J. (1970a) 'L'art chrétien d'Ethiopie. Découvertes récentes et points de vue nouveaux', in E. Dinkler (ed.), *Kunst und Geschichte Nubiens in christlicher Zeit. Ergebnisse und Probleme auf Grund der jüngsten Ausgrabungen* (Recklinghausen: Verlag Aurel Bongers), pp. 291–302

Leclant, J. (1970b) 'La religion méroïtique', *Histoire des Religions*, published under the direction of M. Brillant and R. Aigrain (Paris: Blond et Guy)

Leclant, J. (1973) 'Glass from the meroitic necropolis of Sedeinga (Sudanese Nubia)', *JGS*, XV, pp. 52–68

Leclant, J. (1976a) 'Koushites et Méroïtes. L'iconographie des souverains africains du Haut Nil antique', in J. Vercoutter, J. Leclant and F. Snowden (eds.), *L'image du noir dans l'art occidental. Vol. I: Des Pharaons à la chute de l'empire romain* (Fribourg: Menil Foundation), pp. 89–132

Leclant, J. (1976b) 'L'Egypte, terre d'Afrique dans le monde gréco-romain', *L'image du noir dans l'art occidental*, Vol. I (see J. Vercoutter), pp. 269–85

Leclant, J. and Miquel, A. (1959) 'Reconnaissance dans l'Agamé: Goulo-Makeda et Sabéa (Octobre 1955 et Avril 1956)', *AE*, III, pp. 107–30

Lee, R. B. (1968) 'What hunters do for a living, or how to make out on scarce resources', in R. B. Lee and I. De Vore, *Man the Hunter* (Chicago: Aldine Press), pp. 30–48

Lee, R. B. (1972) 'The Kung bushmen of Botswana', in M. G. Bicchieri (ed.), *Hunters and Gatherers Today* (New York: Holt, Rinehart and Winston)

Leglay, M. (1966) *Saturne africain, histoire* (Paris: de Boccard)

Leglay, M. (1967) *Saturne africain, monuments*, 2 vols. (Paris: Arts et Métiers Graphiques)

Lepelley, C. (1967) 'L'Agriculture africaine au Bas-Empire', *Ant. Afr.*, I, pp. 135–44

Lepelley, C. (1968) 'Saint Léon le Grand et l'église mauritanienne. Primauté romaine et autonomie africaine au Ve siècle', *Mélanges Ch. Saumagne* (Tunis), pp. 189–204

Leschi, L. (1945) 'Mission au Fezzan', *Trav. IRS*, pp. 183–6

Levaillant, F. (1970) *Voyage de Monsieur le Vaillant dans l'intérieur de l'Afrique par le Cap de Bonne Espérance, dans les années 1780, 81, 82, 83, 84 et 85*, 2 vols (New York/London: Johnson Reprint) (English translation)

Lewis-Williams, J. D. (1983) *The Rock Art of Southern Africa* (Cambridge: Cambridge University Press)

Levtzion, N. (1973) *Ancient Ghana and Mali* (London: Methuen)

Lézine, A. (1960) 'Sur la population des villes africaines', *Ant. Afr.*, 3, pp. 69–82

Lhote, H. (1954) 'L'Expédition de C. Balbus au Sahara en 19 av. J.C. d'après le texte de Pline', *RA*, pp. 41–83

Lhote, H. (1955) *Les Touareg du Hoggar* (Ahaggar) 2nd edn (Paris: Payot)

Lhote, H. (1958) *The Search for the Tassili Frescoes*, translated by A. H. Broderick (1959) (London: Hutchinson)

Lhote, J. (1963) 'Chars rupestres du Sahara', *C-RAI*, pp. 225–38

Lhote, H. (1967) 'Problèmes sahariens: l'outre, la marmite, le chameau, le délou, l'agriculture, le nēgre, le palmier', *BAM*, VII, pp. 57–89

Lhote, H. (1970) 'Découverte de chars de guerre en Air', *NA*, pp. 83–5

Lichtheim, M. *Ancient Egyptian Literature: A Book of Readings*: (1973) *Vol. I: The Old and Middle Kingdoms*; (1976) *Vol. II: The New Kingdom*; (1980) *Vol. III: The Late Period* (Berkeley, Calif.: University of California Press)

Macadam, M. F. L. (1949, 1955) *The Temples of Kawa*. Vol. I: *The Inscriptions*; Vol. II: *History and Archaeology of the Site* (London: Oxford University Press)

MacIver, D. R. (1906) 'The Rhodesian ruins, their probable origins and significance', *GJ*, 4, pp. 325–47

McIver, D. R. (1906) *Mediaeval Rhodesia* (London: Frank Cass)

MacIver, D. R. and Woolley, C. L. (1911) *Buhen* (Philadelphia, Pa.: University Museum), 2 vols

McIntosh, R. J. and S. K. (1984) 'Early Iron Age economy in the Inland Niger Delta (Mali)', in J. D. Clark and S. A. Brandt (eds.), *From Hunters to Farmers: The Causes and Consequences of Food Production in Africa* (Berkeley, Calif.: University of California Press)

McMaster, D. N. (1966) 'The ocean-going dhow trade to East Africa', *EAGR*, 4, pp. 13–24

Maingnard, L. F. (1931) 'The lost tribes of the Cape', *SAJS*, 28, pp. 487–504

Maître, J. P. (1966) 'Etat des recherches sur le Néolithique de l'Ahaggar', *Trav. IRS*, pp. 95–104

Maître, J. P. (1971) *Contribution à la préhistoire de l'Ahaggar* (Paris: AMG)

Maître, J. P. (1976) 'Contribution à la préhistoire récente de l'Ahaggar dans son contexte saharien', *BIFAN*, 38, pp. 759–83
Mahjoubi, A. (n.d.) *Les Cités romaines de la Tunisie* (Tunis)
Mahjoubi, A., Ennabi, A. and Salomonson, J. W. (1970) *La Nécropole de Raqqada* (Tunis)
Marliac, A. (1973) 'Etat des connaissances sur le Paléolithique et le Néolithique du Cameroun-Yaoundé', *ORSTOM* (Office de la Recherche Scientifique et Technique Outre-Mer), roneo
Mason, R. J. (1973) 'First early iron age settlement in South Africa: Broederstroom 24–73, Brits District, Transvaal', *SAJS*, LXIX, pp. 324–5
Mason, R. J. (1974) 'Background to the Transvaal iron age discoveries at Olifantspoort and Broederstroom', *JSAIMM*, LXXXXIV, 6, pp. 211–16
Mathew, G. (1963) 'The East African coast until the coming of the Portuguese', in R. A. Oliver and G. Mathew (eds.), *History of East Africa* (Oxford: Clarendon Press), vol. I
Mathew, G. (1975) 'The dating and significance of the Periplus of the Erythraean Sea', in R. I. Rotberg and H. N. Chittick (eds.), *East Africa and the Orient* (New York/London: Africana Publishing)
Mauny, R. (1952) 'Essai sur l'histoire des métaux en Afrique occidentale', *BIFAN*, XIV, pp. 545–95
Mauny, R. (1954) 'Gravures, peintures et inscriptions de l'ouest Africain', *BIFAN*, XI
Mauny, R. (1956) 'Monnaies antiques trouvées en Afrique au sud du Limes romain', *Libyca*, pp. 249–61
Mauny, R. (1960) *Les Navigations médiévales sur les côtes sahariennes antérieures à la découverte portugaises* (Lisbon)
Mauny, R. (1970) *Les Siècles obscurs de l'Afrique Noire* (Paris: Fayard)
Meillassoux, C. (1960) 'Essai d'interprétation du phénomène économique dans les sociétés traditionnelles d'auto-subsistance', *CEA*, 4, pp. 38–67
Mekouria, T. T. (1967) *L'Eglise d'Ethiopie* (Paris)
Mellaart, J. (1979) 'Egyptian and Near-Eastern chronology: a dilemma?' *Antiquity*, 53, pp. 6–18
Mellis, J. V. (1938) *Nord et nord-ouest de Madagascar. 'Volamena et Volafotsy' suivi d'un vocabulaire du nord-ouest expliqué, commenté et comparé au Merina* (Tananarive: Pitot de la Beaujardière)
Mendelessohn, K. (1974) *The Riddle of the Pyramids* (London)
Meyerowitz, E. L. R. (1960) *The Divine Kingship in Ghana and Ancient Egypt* (London: Faber and Faber)
Michalowski, K. (1962) *Faras: Fouilles Polonaises* (Warsaw: Polish Academy of Science)
Michalowski, K. (1965a) 'La Nubie chrétienne', *AB*, 3, pp. 9–25
Michalowski, K. (1965b) 'Polish excavations at Faras, fourth season, 1963–64', *Kush*, XIII, pp. 177–89
Michalowski, K. (1966a) 'Polish excavations at Old Dongola: first season (November–December 1964)', *Kush*, XIV, pp. 289–99
Michalowski, K. (1966b) *Faras, centre artistique de la Nubie chrétienne* (Leiden: Nederlands Instituut voor her Nabije Oosten)
Michalowski, K. (1967) *Faras, die Kathedrale aus den Wüstensand* (Einsiedeln/Zurich/Cologne: Benziger Verlag)
Michalowski, K. (1970) 'Open problems of Nubian art and culture in the light of the discoveries at Faras', in E. Dinkler (ed.), *Kunst und Geschichte Nubiens in Chrislicher Zeit. Ergebnisse und Probleme auf Grund der jüngsten Ausgrabungen* (Recklinghausen: Verlag Aurel Bongers)
Michalowski, K. (ed.) (1975) 'Nubia, récentes recherches', *Actes Coll. Nubiol. Intern.*
Miller, S. F. (1969) 'Contacts between the later stone age and the early iron age in southern central Africa', *Azania*, 4, pp. 81–90
Miller, S. F. (1971) 'The age of Nachikufan industry in Zambia', *SAAB*, 26, pp. 143–6
Mills, E. A. C. and Filmer, N. T. (1972) 'Chondwe iron age site, Ndola, Zambia', *Azania*, VII, pp. 129–47
Moorsel, P. Van (1972) 'Gli scavi olanolesi in Nubia', *Actas VIII Congr. Intern. Argueo. Crist'*, pp. 349–95
Morel, J. P. (1968) 'Céramique à vernis noir du Maroc', *Ant. Afr*, 2, and 'Céramique d'Hippone', *BAA*, I, 1962–5
Mori, F. (1964) 'Some aspects of the rock art of the Acacus (Fezzan, Sahara) and dating regarding it', in L. Pericot Garcia and E. Ripoll Parello (eds.), *Wartenstein Symposium on Rock Art of the Western Mediterranean and the Sahara: Prehistoric Art of the Western Mediterranean and the Sahara*. (New York: subscribers edn distributed through *Current Anthropology* for the Wenner-Gren Foundation for Anthropological Research), pp. 247–59
Mori, F. (1972) *Rock Art of the Tadrart Acacus* (Graz)
Mortelmans, G. (1957) 'La préhistoire du Congo Belge', *RUB*, 2–3
Munson, P. J. (1967) 'A survey of the Neolithic villages of Dhar Tichitt (Mauretania) and some comments on the grain impressions found on the Tichitt pottery', *Actes VI Congr, PPQS*

Munson, P. J. (1968) 'Recent archaeological research in the Dhar Tichitt of south central Mauretania', *WAAN*, 10, pp. 6–13

Munson, P. J. (1969) 'Engravings of ox-drawn chariots', *NA*, 122, pp. 62–3

Munson, P. J. (1970) 'Corrections and additional comments concerning the Tichitt Tradition', *WAAN*, 12, pp. 47–8

Munson, P. J. (1972) 'Archaeological data on the origin of cultivation in the south-western Sahara and its implications for west Africa', *BWS*, 56

Murdock, G. P. (1959) *Africa: Its Peoples and Their Culture History* (New York: McGraw Hill)

Murnane, W. J. (1977) *Ancient Egyptian Coregencies* (Chicago)

Muzzolini, A. (1986) *L'art rupestre préhistorique des massifs centraux sahariens* (Oxford: BAR)

Nenquin, J. (1959) 'Dimple-based pots from Kasai, Belgian Congo', *Man*, 59, 242, pp. 153–5

Nenquin, J. (1961) 'Protohistorische Metaaltechniek in Katanga', *Africa-Tervuren*, VII, 4, pp. 97–101

Nenquin, J. (1963) 'Excavations at Sanga, 1957. The protohistoric necropolis', *AMRAC*, 45

Noten, F. Van (1968) 'The Uelian. A culture with a Neolithic aspect, Uele Basin (NE Congo Republic)', *AMRAC*, 64

Noten, F. Van (1972a) 'Les tombes du roi Cyirima Rujugira et de la reine-mère Nyirayuhi Kanjogera', *AMRAC*, 77

Noten, F. Van (1972b) 'La plus ancienne sculpture sur bois de l'Afrique centrale', *Africa-Tervuren*, XVIII, 3–4, pp. 133–5

Noten, Van, F. (1982) *The Archaeology of Central Africa* (Graz: Akademische Druck-V Verlagsanstaft)

Obenga, T. (1973) *L'Afrique dans l'antiquité – Egypte pharaonique – Afrique noire* (Paris: Présence Africaine)

O'Connor, D. B. (1971) 'Ancient Egypt and Black Africa – early contacts', *Expedition*, 14, pp. 15–38

Odner, K. (1971) 'A preliminary report of an archaeological survey on the slopes of Kilimanjaro', *Azania*, VI, pp. 131–50

Ogot, B. A. and Kieran, J. A. (eds.) (1974) *Zamani: A Survey of the East African History* (Nairobi/London: East African Publishing House/Longmans)

Oliver, R. A. and Fagan, B. M. (1975) *Africa in the Iron Age, c.500 BC to AD 1400* (Cambridge: Cambridge University Press)

Oliver, R. A. and Mathew, G. (eds.) (1963) *Oxford History of East Africa* (London: Oxford University Press)

Painter, C. (1966) 'The Guang and West African historical reconstruction', *GNQ*, 9, pp. 58–66

Palmer, J. A. B. (1947) 'Periplus Mari Erythraei; the Indian evidence as to its date', *CQ*, XLI, pp. 136–41

Pankhurst, R. K. P. (1961) *An Introduction to the Economic History of Ethiopia from early times to 1800* (London: Lalibela House)

Parkington, J. E. and Pöggenpoel, C. (1971) 'Excavations at De Hangen 1968', *SAAB*, 26, pp. 3–36

Paterson, W. (1789) *A Narrative of Four Journeys into the Country of the Hottentots and Caffraria, in the Years 1777, 1778, 1779* (London)

Perret, R. (1936) 'Recherches archéologiques et ethnographiques au Tassili des Ajjers', *JSA*, 6, pp. 50–1

Pflaum, H. G. (1957) 'A propos de la date de la création de la province de Numidie', *Libyca*, pp. 61–75

Phillipson, D. W. (1968a) 'The early iron age in Zambia – regional variants and some tentative conclusions', *JAH*, IX, 2, pp. 191–214

Phillipson, D. W. (1968b) 'The early iron age at Kapwirimbwe, Lusaka', *Azania*, III, pp. 87–105

Phillipson, D. W. (1969) 'Early iron-using peoples of southern Africa', in L. Thompson (ed.), *African Societies in Southern Africa* (London: Heinemann), pp. 24–49

Phillipson, D. W. (1970) 'Excavations at Twickenham Road, Lusaka', *Azania*, V, pp. 77–118

Phillipson, D. W. (1971) 'An early iron age site on the Lubusi river, Kaoma district, Zambia', *ZMJ*, II, pp. 51–7

Phillipson, D. W. (1972a) *Prehistoric Rock Paintings and Engravings of Zambia* (Livingstone, Zambia: Exhibition catalogue of Livingstone Museum)

Phillipson, D. W. (1972b) 'Early iron age sites on the Zambian copperbelt', *Azania*, VII, pp. 93–128

Phillipson, D. W. (1973) 'The prehistoric succession in eastern Zambia: a preliminary report', *Azania*, VIII, pp. 3–24

Phillipson, D. W. (1974) 'Iron Age history and archaeology in Zambia', *JAH*, XV, pp. 1–25

Phillipson, D. W. (1975) 'The chronology of the iron age in Bantu Africa', *JAH*, XVI, pp. 321–42

Phillipson, D. W. (1977) *The Later Prehistory of Eastern and Southern Africa* (London: Heinemann)

Phillipson, D. W. (1985) *African Archaeology* (Cambridge: Cambridge University Press)

Pirenne, J. (1965) 'Arte Sabeo d'Etiopia', *Encyclopedia dell'arte antica* (Rome), vol. VI, pp. 1044–8

Pirenne, J. (1967) 'Haoulti et ses monuments. Nouvelle interprétation', *AE*, 7, pp. 125–33
Poirier, C. (1954) 'Terre d'Islam en mer malgache', *BAM*, cinquantenaire, pp. 71–115
Poirier, C. (1965) 'Données écologiques et démographiques de la mise en place des proto-malgaches', *Taloha* (Tananarive), pp. 61–2
Pommeret, Y. (1965) *Civilisations préhistoriques au Gabon. Vallée du Moyen Ogooné*, 2 vols (Libreville: Centre culturel français St. Exupéry), vol. II 'Notes préliminaires à propos du gisement lupembien et néolithique de Ndjole'
Pons, A. and Quézel, P. (1957) 'Première étude palynologique de quelques paléosols sahariens', *Trav. IRS*, 16, 2, pp. 27–35
Portères, A. (1962) 'Berceaux agricoles primaires sur le continent africain', *JAH*, 3, 2, pp. 195–210
Posnansky, M. (1966) 'The origin of agriculture and iron-working in southern Africa', in M. Posnansky (ed.), *Prelude to East African History* (London: Oxford University Press), pp. 82–94
Posnansky, M. (1967) 'The iron age in east Africa', in W. W. Bishop and J. D. Clark (eds.), *Background to Evolution in Africa* (London/Chicago: University of Chicago Press), pp. 629–49
Posnansky, M. (1969) 'Yams and the origins of west African agriculture', *Odū*, I, pp. 101–7
Posnansky, M. (1969–70) 'Discovering Ghana's past', *Annual Museum Lectures*, p. 20
Posnansky, M. (1971) 'Ghana and the origins of west African Trade', *AQ*, XI, pp. 110–25
Posnansky, M. (1972a) 'Archaeology, ritual and religion', in T. O. Ranger and I. Kimambo (eds.), *The Historical Study of African Religion: with special reference to East and Central Africa* (London: Heinemann), pp. 29–44
Posnansky, M. (1972b) 'Terminology in the early iron age of east Africa with particular reference to the dimple-based wares of Lolui island, Uganda', *Actes VI Congr. PPQS*, pp. 577–9
Posnansky, M. (1973a) 'Aspects of early west African trade', *WA*, 5, pp. 149–62
Posnansky, M. (1973b) 'Review of T. Shaw, "Igbo Ukwu"', *Archaeology*, 25, 4, pp. 309–11
Préaux, C. (1943) 'Les Egyptiens dans la civilisation hellénistique d'Egypte', *Chronique d'Egypte*, XVIII, pp. 148–60
Préaux, C. (1950) 'La singularité de l'Egypte dans le monde gréco-romain', *Chronique d'Egypte*, XXV, pp. 110–23
Préaux, C. (1952) 'Sur la communication de l'Ethiopie avec l'Egypte hellénistique', *Chronique d'Egypte*, XXVII, pp. 257–81
Rahtz, P. A. and Flight, C. (1974) 'A quern factory near Kintampo, Ghana', *WAJA*, 4, pp. 1–31
Rebuffat, R. (1969–70) 'Zella et les routes d'Egypte', *Libya Antiqua* (Tripoli), VI–VII, pp. 181–7
Rebuffat, R. (1970) 'Route d'Egypte et de la Libye intérieure', *SM*, 3, pp. 1–20
Rebuffat, R. (1972) 'Nouvelles recherches dans le sud de la Tripolitaine', *C-RAI*, pp. 319–39
Rebuffat, R. (1974) 'Vestiges antiques sur la côte occidentale de l'Egypte au sud de Rabat', *American Anthropologist*, VIII, pp. 25–49
Rebuffat, R. (1975) 'Trois nouvelles campagnes dans le sud de la Tripolitaine', *C-RAI*, pp. 495–505
Reisner, G. A. (1910) *The Archaeological Survey of Nubia. Report for 1907, 1908* (Cairo: National Printing Department), vol. I
Reisner, G. A. (1918) 'The Barkal temples on 1916', *JEA*, V
Reisner, G. A. (1918–19) 'Outline of the ancient history of the Sudan', *SNR*, 1, pp. 3–15, 57–79, 217–37; II, pp. 35–67
Reisner, G. A. (1923a) *Excavations at Kerma* (Cambridge, Mass.: HAS), vols. V and VI
Reisner, G. A. (1923b) 'The meroitic Kingdom of Ethiopia: a chronological outline', *JEA*, 9, pp. 33–77
Reisner, G. A. (1929) 'Excavations at Simna and Uronarti by the Harvard Boston expedition', *SNR*, XII, pp. 143–61
Reisner, G. A. (1931) 'Inscribed monuments from Gebel Barkal', *ZÄS*, 66, p. 100
Reusch, R. (1961) *History of East Africa* (New York: Ungar)
Reygasse, M. (1950) *Monuments funéraires préislamiques de l'Afrique du Nord* (Paris: Arts et métiers graphiques)
Reynolds, V. (1967) *The Apes: the Gorilla, Chimpanzee, Orangutan and Gibbon, their History and their World* (New York: Dutton)
Riavi, S. A. (1967) 'Zanj: its first known use in Arabic literature', *Azania*, II, pp. 200–1
Ricci, L. (1955–8) 'Retrovamenti archeologici in Eritrea', *RSE*, 14, pp. 51–63
Roberts, A. D. (1974) 'Precolonial trade in Zambia', *ASR*, 10, p. 720
Robertshaw, P. (1984) 'The archaeology in Eastern Africa: recent development and more dates', *JAH*, 25, pp. 369–93

Robineau, C. (1966) 'Une étude d'histoire culturelle de l'île d'Anjouan', *RH*, 35, pp. 17–34

Robinson, E. S. G. (1956) 'The Libyan hoard', *Numismatic Chronicle*, LVI, p. 94

Robinson, K. R. (1961a) *Archaeological Report in Rhodesian Schoolboys' Exploration Society Expedition to Buffalo Bend* (Salisbury)

Robinson, K. R. (1961b) 'An early iron age site from the Chibi district, Southern Rhodesia', *SAAB*, XVI, pp. 75–102

Robinson, K. R. (1963) 'Further excavations in the iron age deposits at the tunnel site, Gokomere Hill, Southern Rhodesia', *SAAB*, XVIII, pp. 155–71

Robinson, K. R. (1966a) 'The Sinoia caves, Lomagundi district, Rhodesia', *Proceedings of the Rhodesian Science Association*, LI, pp. 131–55

Robinson, K. R. (1966b) 'The Leopard's Kopje culture: its position in the iron age in Southern Rhodesia', *SAAB*, 21, pp. 81–5

Robinson, K. R. (1966c) 'A preliminary report on the recent archaeology of Ngonde, northern Malawi', *JAH*, VII, pp. 169–88

Robinson, K. R. (1966d) 'The iron age in Southern Rhodesia', *SAAB*, XXI, pp. 5–51

Robinson, K. R. (1970) 'The iron age in the southern lake area of Malawi', *MADP*, 8

Robinson, K. R. (1973) 'The iron age of the upper and lower Shire Malawi', *MADP*, 13

Robinson, K. R. and Sandelowsky, B. (1968) 'The iron age in northern Malawi: recent work', *Azania*, III, pp. 107–46

Rosenbaum, E. (1960) *A Catalogue of Cyrenaican Portrait Sculpture* (London: Oxford University Press)

Rotberg, R. T. and Chittick, H. N. (eds.) (1975) *East Africa and the Orient* (New York/London: Africana Publishing)

Rowe, A. (1948) 'A history of ancient Cyrenaica. New light on Aegypto-Cyrenaean relations. Two Ptolemaic statues found in Tolmeita', *SASAE*, Cah. no. 12. Report by J. Leclant in *REA*, 52, 1–2, pp. 337–9

Rudner, J. (1968) 'Strandloper pottery from south and south-west Africa', *ASAM*, 49, pp. 441–663

Salama, P. (1954) 'L'occupation de la Maurétanie césarienne sous le Bas-Empire', *Mélanges Piganiol*, pp. 1292–311

Salama, P. (1973) *Un point d'eau du limes maurétanien (Maghreb et Sahara), Etudes géographiques offertes à J. Despois* (Paris: Société de Géographie)

Salama, P. (1976) 'Les déplacements successifs du Limes en Maurétanie césarienne. Essai de synthèse', *Akten XI Intern. Limeskong*, pp. 577–95

Sampson, C. G. (1974) *The Stone Age Archaeology of Southern Africa* (New York: Academic Press)

Säve-Söderbergh, T. (1963) 'Preliminary report of the Scandinavian joint expedition: archaeological investigations between Faras and Gemai, November 1962–March 1963', *Kush*, 12, pp. 19–39

Säve-Söderbergh, T. (1965) *The C-Group, Nubia Abu Simbel* (Stockholm: Kungl. Boktreycheriet, P. A. Norstedt Soner)

Säve-Söderbergh, T. (1970) 'Christian Nubia, the excavations carried out by the Scandinavian joint expedition to Sudanese Nubia', in E. Dinkler (ed.), *Kunst und Geschichte Nubiens in christlicher Zeit. Ergebnisse und Probleme auf Grund der jüngsten Ausgrabungen* (Recklinghausen: Verlag Aurel Bongers), pp. 219–44

Sayce, A. H. (1909) 'A Greek inscription of a king of Axum found at Mercoe', *Proceedings of the Society of Biblical Archaeology*, XXXI, London

Sayce, A. H. (1911) 'Second interim report on the excavations at Meroe in Ethiopia II. The historical results', *LAAA*, IV, pp. 53–65

Schapera, I. (1930) *The Khoisan Peoples of South Africa: Bushmen and Hottentots* (London: Routledge and Kegan Paul) (2nd edn, 1951)

Schapera, I. (1933) *The Early Cape Hottentots described in the Writings of Olfert Dappe, 1668, Willem Ten Rhyne (1686) and Johannes Guliemus de Grevenbroek (1695)* (Cape Town: Van Riebeeck Society) (2nd edn, 1951)

Schneider, R. (1965a) 'Notes épigraphiques sur les découvertes de Matara', *AE*, 6, pp. 89–142

Schneider, R. (1965b) 'Remarques sur les inscriptions d'Enda Čerqos', *AE*, 6, pp. 221–2

Schneider, R. (1974) 'Trois nouvelles inscriptions royales d'Axoum', *Atti IV Congr. Intern. Stud. Et.*, I. pp. 87–102

Schonback, B. (1965) *The Late Stone Age and the A-Group, Nubia Abu Simbel* (Stockholm: Kungl.; Boktryekeriet, P. A. Norstedt Stoner)

Schweitzer, F. R. (1970) 'A preliminary report of excavation of a cave at Die Kelders', *SAAB*, 25, pp. 136–8

Schweitzer, F. R. and Scott, K. (1973) 'Early appearance of domestic sheep in subSaharan Africa', *Nature*, 241, pp. 547–8

Sergew Hable Selassie (1972) *Ancient and Medieval Ethiopian History to 1270* (Addis Ababa: United Printers)
Shackleton, N. J. (1973) 'Oxygen isotope analysis as a means of determining season of occupation of prehistoric midden sites', *Archaeometry*, 15, 1, pp. 133–41
Shahid, I. (1971) 'The martyrs of Nağran, new documents', *Société des Bollandistes* (Brussels), pp. 242–76
Shaw, T. (1969) 'The late stone age in the Nigerian forest', *Actes ler Coll. Intern. Archéol. Afr.*, pp. 364–73
Shaw, T. (1970) *Igbo-Ukwu: an Account of Archaeological Discoveries in Eastern Nigeria*, 2 vols. (London: Faber, for the Institute of African Studies, University of Ibadan)
Shaw, T. (1971) 'Africa in prehistory; leader or laggard?', *JAH*, XII, I, pp. 143–53
Shaw, T. (1972) 'Early crops in Africa: a review of evidence', *BWS*, 56
Shinnie, P. L. (1971) 'The legacy to Africa', in J. R. Harris (ed.) *The Legacy of Egypt* (Oxford: Clarendon Press), pp. 434–55
Slim, H., Mahjoubi A. and Belkodja, Kh (n.d.) *Histoire de la Tunisie*, vol. I: *L'Antiquité* (Tunis)
Smith, A. B. (1974) 'Preliminary report on excavations at Karkarichinkat north and south, Tilemsi valley, 1972', *WAJA*, 4, pp. 33–55
Smith, H. S. (1966) 'The Nubian B-group', *Kush*, 14, pp. 69–124
Smith, H. S. (1976) *The Fortress of Buhen: the Inscriptions* (London: Egypt Exploration Society)
Smith, W. S. (1965) *The Art and Architecture of Ancient Egypt* (Harmondsworth: Penguin Books)
Smith, W. S. C. (1981) *The Art and Architecture of Ancient Egypt*, revised with additions by W. K. Simpson (Harmondsworth: Penguin Books)
Smits, L. (1967) 'Fishing scenes from Botsabelo, Lesotho', *SAAB*, 22, pp. 60–7
Snowden, F. M. Jnr (1970) *Blacks in Antiquity: Ethiopians in the Greco-Roman Experience* (Cambridge, Mass.: Harvard University Press)
Solheim, W. (1965) 'Indonesian culture and Malagasy origins', *Taloha* (Tananarive), I, pp. 33–42
Soper, R. C. (1967a) 'Kwale: an early iron age site in south eastern Kenya', *Azania*, II, pp. 1–17
Soper, R. C. (1967b) 'Iron age sites in north eastern Tanzania', *Azania*, II, pp. 19–36
Soper, R. C. (1971) 'A general review of the early iron age in the southern half of Africa', *Azania*, VI, pp. 5–37
Souville, G. (1958–9) 'La pêche et la vie maritime au Néolithique en Afrique du Nord', *BAM*, II, pp. 315–44
Spencer, J. E. (1968) 'Comments on the origins of agriculture in Africa', *CA*, 9, 5, 501–2
Spruytte, J. (1968) 'Le cheval de l'Afrique ancienne', *Le Saharien*, 48, pp. 32–42
Spruytte, J. (1977) *Etudes expérimentales sur l'attelage* (Paris: Crepin-Leblond)
Stahl, A. B. (1985) 'Re-investigation of Kintampo, a rock shelter. Ghana: implications for the nature of culture change', *African Archaeology Review*, 3, pp. 117–50
Summers, R. F. H. (1958) *Inyanga. Prehistoric Settlements in Southern Rhodesia* (Cambridge: Cambridge University Press)
Summers, R. F. H. (1969) 'Ancient mining in Rhodesia', *Mining Magazine*, 3 (Salisbury)
Summers, R. F. H., Robinson, K. R. and Whitty, A. (1961) 'Zimbabwe-excavations', *OPNM*, III, 23a
Sutton, J. E. G. (1966) 'The archaeology and early peoples of the highlands of Kenya and northern Tanzania', *Azania*, I, pp. 37–57
Sutton, J. E. G. (1971) 'The interior of east Africa', in P. L. Shinnie (ed.), *The African Iron Age* (Oxford: Clarendon Press)
Sutton, J. E. G. (1973) *The Archaeology of the Western Highlands of Kenya* (Nairobi/London: British Institute of Eastern Africa)
Sutton, J. E. G. (1974) 'The aquatic civilisation of middle Africa', *JAH*, XV, pp. 527–46
Sutton, J. E. G. (1985) 'Temporal and spatial variability in African iron furnaces', in R. Haaland and P. Shinnie (eds.), *African Iron Working (Ancient and Traditional* (Oslo: Norwegian University Press), pp. 164–96
Tamrat, T. (1972) *Church and State in Ethiopia 1270–1527* (Oxford: Clarendon Press)
Trigger, B. G. (1965) *History and Settlements in Lower Nubia* (New Haven, Conn.: Yale University Publications in Anthropology no. 69)
Trigger, B. G. (1969) 'The myth of Meroe and the African iron age', *IJAHS*, II, 1, pp. 23–50
Trigger, B. G., Kemp, B. J., O'Connor, D. B. and Lloyd, A. B. (1983) *Ancient Egypt: A Social History* (Cambridge: Cambridge University Press)
Turcan, R. (1961) 'Trésors monétaires trouvés à Tipasa. La circulation du bronze en Afrique romaine et vandale aux Ve et VIe siècles ap. J.C.', *Libyca*, pp. 201–57
Twisselmann, F. (1958) 'Les ossements humains du site mésolithique d'Ishango', *Exploration du Parc national*

Albert, Mission J. de Herzelin de Braucourt (1950), facsimile 5 (Brussels)

Tylecotte, R. F. (1970) 'Iron working at Meroe, Sudan', *BHM*, 4, pp. 67–72

Unesco (1963–7) *Fouilles de Nubie* (Cairo)

Vaal, J. B. (1943) 'In Soutpansbergse Zimbabwe', *SAJS*, XL, pp. 303–18

Vandersleyen, C. (ed.) (1975) *Das Alte Agypten* (Berlin)

Vansina, J. (1962) 'Long-distance trade routes in central Africa', *JAH*, III, 3, pp. 375–90

Vansina, J. (1966) *Kingdoms of the Savanna* (Madison, Wis.: University of Wisconsin Press)

Vansina, J. (1984) 'Western Bantu expansion', *JAH*, 25, pp. 129–45

Vantini, J. (1970) *The Excavations at Faras: a contribution to the History of Christian Nubia* (Bologna: Nigriza)

Vercoutter, J. (1958) 'Excavations at Sai 1955–57', *Kush*, VI, pp. 144–69

Vercoutter, J. (1959) 'The gold of Kush. Two gold-washing stations at Faras East', *Kush*, VII, pp. 120–53

Vercoutter, J. (1964) 'Excavations at Mirgissa I (October–December 1962)', *Kush*, XII, pp. 57–62

Vercoutter, J. (1976) *L'Egypte ancienne*, no. 247 (Paris: PUF)

Villiers, A. (1949) 'Some aspects of the Dhow trade', *MEJ*, pp. 399–416

Vinnicombe, P. (1965) 'Bushmen fishing as depicted in rock paintings', *Science South Africa*, 212, pp. 578–81

Vita, A. di (1964) 'Il limes romano de Tripolitania nella sua concretezza archeologica e nella sua realta storica', *Libya antiqua* (Tripoli), pp. 65–98

Vogel, J. O. (1969) 'On early evidence of agriculture in southern Zambia', *CA*, X, p. 524

Vogel, J. O. (1970) 'The Kalomo culture of southern Zambia: some notes towards a reassessment', *ZMJ*, I, pp. 77–88

Vogel, J. O. (1972) 'On early iron age funerary practice in southern Zambia', *CA*, XIII, pp. 583–8

Vogel, J. O. (1973) 'The early iron age at Sioma mission western Zambia', *ZMJ*, IV

Vychichl, W. (1961) 'Berber words in Nubian', *Kush*, 9, pp. 289–90

Wainwright, G. A. (1947) 'Early foreign trade in East Africa', *Man*, XLVII, pp. 143–8

Wainwright, G. A. (1951) 'The Egyptian origin of a ram-headed breastplate from Lagos', *Man*, LI, pp. 133–5

Wainwright, G. A. (1962) 'The Meshwesh', *JEA*, 48, pp. 89–99

Walsh, P. (1965) 'Masinissa', *JRS*, LV

Warmington, B. H. (1954) *The North African Provinces from Diocletian to the Vandal Conquest* (Cambridge: Cambridge University Press)

Warmington, E. H. (1963) 'Africa in ancient and medieval times', in E. A. Walker (ed.), *Cambridge History of the British Empire* (Cambridge: Cambridge University Press), vol. VIII

Warmington, B. H. (1964) *Carthage* (rev. edn, 1969) (London: Robert Hale)

Weeks, K. (ed.) (1979) *Egyptology and the Social Sciences: Five Studies* (Cairo)

Weitzmann, K. (1970) 'Some remarks on the sources of the fresco paintings of the cathedral of Faras', in E. Dinkler (ed.), *Kunst und Geschichte Nubiens in christlicher Zeit, Ergebnisse und Probleme auf Grund der jüngsten Ausgrabungen* (Recklinghausen: Verlag Aurel Bongers), pp. 325–46

Wendt, W. E. (1972) 'Preliminary report on an archaeological research programme in south-west Africa', *Cimbebasia B*, 2, 1, pp. 1–45

Wenig, S. (1978) *Africa in Antiquity: Vol. II, The Arts of Ancient Nubia and the Sudan* (The Catalogue, The Brooklyn Museum), New York

Willett, F. (1967) *Ife in the History of West African Sculpture* (London: Thames and Hudson)

Williams, B. (1980) 'The lost pharaohs of Nubia', *Archaeology*, 33, pp. 12–21

Williams, D. (1969) 'African iron and the classical world', in L. A. Thompson and J. Ferguson (eds.), *Africa in Classical Antiquity* (Ibadan: Ibadan University Press), pp. 62–80

Wilson, J. A. (1951) *The Burden of Egypt. An Interpretation of Ancient Egyptian Culture* (Chicago: University of Chicago Press)

Woldering, I. (1963) *Egypt, the Art of Pharaohs*, translated by A. E. Keep (London: Methuen)

Yoyotte, J. (1958) 'Anthroponymes d'origine libyenne dans les documents égyptiens', *C-RGLCS*, 8, 4

Zabkar, L. V. (1975) *Apedemak, Lion God of Meroe: A Study in Egyptian Meroitic Syncretism* (Warminster: Aris and Phillips)

Index

Abalessa, 290, 291, *292*
Abba Ym'ata, 229
'Abdallāh Nirki, 189, 191
Abizar, *242*
Abū Hāmād, 147, 156
Abu Simbel, 76, 158, 170
Abusir, 64
Abydos, 4, 63; temples, 47, 76
Achilles Tatius, 26, 38
Addi-Dahno, 203
Addi Galamo, 194, 195, *196*, 197, 198, 199, 200
Addi Gramaten, 197, 199
Adulis, 192, 195, 202, 203, 204, 205–6, 207, 209, 213, 216, 217, 219, 311, 312
Aeschylus, 26, 38
Africa: impact of environment, 2–3, 9; language similarities, 28–31, 32, 40–1, 54–5, 57–61; population, 2
Africa, Central, *340*, 342; iron age, 343–50; stone age, 339–43
Africa, East, *321*; aquatic culture, 316–17; coins, 307–8, 310, 312; hunter-gatherers, 313, 315; Kushitic pastoral tradition, 317–19; languages, 313, *314*, 315, 317; maritime trade, 306–12; megalithic cultures, 323–4
Africa, North: Byzantine period, 282–3; contact with Sudanic belt, 303–5; independent regions, 283–5; Roman period, 261–80; Vandal conquest, 281–2
Africa, southern: iron age, 362–72, *363*, *366*, metal-working, 369–70; prehistoric settlement, 297, 351–2, 360–1; rock art, *354*, 355, 356, 361
Africa, sub-Saharan: agriculture, 299–300; archaeology, 296–7; contact with North Africa, 303–5; early iron age, 383–9; emergence of states, 388; iron-working, 296, 300–3; languages, 297–9, 300; population, 387; relations with Egypt, 12–14, 90–102, 142–7; religion, 388, 389
Africa, West, 297, 300, 301, 303, 305; crops, 325–7, 331; early iron age, 333–7; languages, 298; Neolithic period, 325–33, *328*; prehistoric trade, 337–8
Africa Minor, 237, 238, 240, 241, 243
Agatharchides, 125
Agaw, 218
Agisymba, 274, 287, 288
agriculture, 79–80, 178–9, 269–70, 278, 296–7, 325–7, 331
Ahaggar, 288, 290, 291
Ahhotep, 84
Ahmose I (Amosis), 73, 98, 156
Ahmose, Admiral, 156
Ahmosis Nefertari (Ahmes-Nefertari, Ahmose-Nofretari), 17, 84
Akan, 90, 102
Akhenaton (form. Amenhotep IV), 73, *74*, 75, 87, 157
Akhot Aton, 75
Al-Kab, 141
Alexander the Great, 8, 63, 78, 119, 121, 127, 224, 235, 255
Alexandria, 107, 119, 120–4, 126, 128, 189, 191, 226, 229, 232; Library of, 4, 123; Lighthouse, 121, *122*, 123; Roman, 131, 132, 133–4, *135*, 138, 139
Algeria, 236, 238, 288, 289
Alodia, 186, 187
Altaya, 284
Amanishakheto, 167, 168, *169*
Amani-nete-yerike, 172–3
Amanitere, 168, 177
Amannoteyerike, 165
Amara, 168, 177; West, 157
Amasis, 84
Amde Tsion, 224
Amenemhet I, 69, 71, 152
Amenemhet II, 71
Amenemhet III, 71
Amenhophis I, 17
Amenhotep I, 73, 84
Amenhotep II, 73, 157
Amenhotep III, 73, 84, 115, 157, *159*
Amenhotep IV, 114, 157
Amenophis, *see* Amenhotep
Ameny, 152
Amhara, 228, 231, 234–5
Ammaedra, 262, 273
Ammianus Marcellinus, 26, 38
Ammonium (Siwa), 44, 91, 121, 127, 240, 293
Amon, 45, 75, 77, 83, 84, 87, 98, 102, 157, 161, 162, 163, 164
Amosis, *see* Ahmose I
Ampsaga river, 264, 265
Amratian period (Nagada I), 10–11
Amun temples, 183
Amyrtaios, 78
anchorites, 139
Angola, 348, 357, 365, 371
Aniba, 95
animals: domestication, 325, 326–7; wild, 291, 293
Anlamani, 164, 173, 174
Anne of Faras, St., *190*, 191

Antalaotse, 382
Antef, 152
anthropology, 34, 37, 38, 50–2, 56
Antinopolis, 134
Antiochus III, 131
Antoninus Pius, 134, 137
Antsary, *381*
Antsoheribory, *379*
Anu, 17, 47
Anza, 208
Apedemak, 168, 182, 183
Apollodorus, 21, 38
Apollonia (Susa), *see* Cyrene
Apollonius of Perga, 124
Arabia, South, 140, 193–202, 209, 214, 215, 217, 218, 223, 225, 231–5
Arabia Felix, 98
Arabs, 103, 140, 187, 189, 191, 234, 283, 285, 290, 305, 310, 312, 376, 377, 378, 389
archaeology, 154–5, 193–202, 203–13, 294, 296–7, 305, 326, 329; Alexandria, *135*; lack of evidence, 1–2, 13–14, 141–2; radio-carbon dating, 47, 237, 327; Sudan, 36
Archimedes, 124
Argo, isle of, 168
Arianism, 139, 227, 228, 232, 281, 283
Aristippus, 128
Aristo, 125
Aristotle, 21, 38, 253
Arsinoe (Tokra), *see* Tauchira
art, 117, 126, 128; Axumite, 209–11; Byzantine, *190*, 191; North African, 280; Saharan, 291; South Arabian, 195–9; *see also* rock art
Artaxerxes III, 78
Arwe-Negus, 224
Asachae, 192
Asante, 338
Asia, 13, 71, 119, 162
Aspelta, 164, *166*, 174, 184
Asselar, 329
Assyria, 77, 95, 162
astronomy, 113, 124
Aswan, 2, 115, 124, 125, 144, 150, 154, 167, 186, 191
Asyelta, 175
Asyut, 160
Aterians, 44
Athanasius, 226, 227, 243
Atlanarsa, 164
Aton, 73, 75, 157
Augustine, Saint, 279
Augustus, 131, 141, 167, 259, 262, 264, 268, 270, 273, 274
Aurelian, 136
Avaris (Hat-Wret), 71
Awka, 334
Axum, 170, 186, 192, 193, 203–13, 392; architecture, 207–8, 212, 219, 221, 223; art, *210*, 211; city of, 204–5, 207, 213; language, 211–12, 231, 233–4; literature, 234–5, political system, 215–16, pottery, 209, 212; religion, 221–2, 224–35, trade, 213, 216–19
Ay, 75

Bab-āl-Mandeb, strait of, 98, 218
baboon, 46, 57
Baḥr el G̲hazāl, 91
Ballana, 147, 170
Bani Valley, 335
Bantu, 102, *302*, 303, 308, 315, 317, 319, 320, 322, 323, 346–7, 360, 380, 382; language, 41, 297, 298, 300, 320, 348, 376
Baouit art, *135*
Barka (Al-Merg), 127, 128, 133
Barkal, 177, 183, 184
Basa, 181
Baṭn al-Had̲jar, 144, 145, 148, 165
Battiad dynasty, 127
Bēdja, 36, 214, 215, 216, 218, 231
Bedōuins, 68, 86, 94
Bel-air, 327
Benī Ḥasan, 116, 152
Benin, 90, 334, 338
Berbers (Libyco-Berbers), 48, 236–45, 262, 264, 274, 276, 283, 289, 290, 291
Berenice (Benghazi), 119, 127
Berlin Papyrus, 111
Bible, 27, 38, 42, 43, 95, 137, 212, 225, 234, 235
Bizerta, 237
Blemmyes, 136, 164, 170, 171, 185, 186, 241
blood-groups, 20, 37
Bocchoris, 77
Botswana, 297, 370
Brittany, 251
bronze, 62, 200, *201*
Bu-Nd̲jem, 274
Buddhism, 222, 375
Buhen, 94, 95, 142, 149, 152, *153*, 154, 156; temple, 156, 157
Bulawayo, 368
burial practices, 88–9, 148, 154–5, 344–6, 348, 388
Burkina Faso, 34, 301, 330, 331, 335, 336
Burundi, 339, 343, 347
Bushmen, 39, 351
Butana, 163, 179
Byblos, 60, 82, 246
Byzacium, 265
Byzantium, 42–3, 140, 186–91, 219, 232, 281, 282–3

Caesar, Julius, 258, 268
Caesarea (Cherchell), 259, *271*
Calama, 265
Caligula, 263, 264
Callimachus, 123, 128
Cambyses, 78, 111, 165
camels, 294, 305
Cameroon, 330
candace (queen-mother), 174–5
Cap Bon, 249, 255
Cape province, 351, 352, 360, 361, 385; rock art, 353, 356
Cape Guardafui, 98
Capsa (Cafsa), 236–7
captives, *22*, 39, 86, 91, *92–3*
Caracalla, 134
Carthage, 243, 246–60, 263, 265, 269, 273, 278, 279, 281, 282, 305; city, 252–3; destruction, 257–8; foundation, 247; religion, 253–4; trade, 250–3
Casamance, 336, 337, 385
cattle-breeding, 9, 178, 318, 324, 326–7, 329
Central African Republic, 339, 341, 344
ceramics, Neolithic, 237–8; *see also* pottery
Cerne island, 251, 287, 288
Chad, 3, 36, 91, 94, 99, 147, 288, 289, 293, 294, 330, 333, 334, 383
Chalcedon, Council of, 139, 229, 234
Chalcolithic (Cuprolithic) period, 62, 148, 150
Champollion, Jean-Francois, 4
Chebba, *271*
Cheops (Kheops, Khufu), 17, *23*,

45, 64; boat, *106*, 108–9
Cherchell, *see* Caesarea
China, 378, *379*
Chitope, 371
Christianity, 137–40, 169–71, 185–91, 225–35, 279, 281, 283, 290, 391, 392, 393
Cidamus (Ghadāmes), 249, 252, 274, 287, 293
circumcision, 21, 28, 31, 45
Cirta (Constantine), 254, 257, 258, 262, 263, 276
Claudius, 264, 273
Claudius II, 136
Cleopatra VII, *129*, 131, 175
Colchians (Colchidians, Colchoi), 21, 26, 45
Comoro Islands, 375, 378, 380
Congo, 301, 315, 316, 339
Constantine, *see* Cirta
Constantine the Great, 138, 226, 235, 290
Constantinople, 138, 139–40, 226, 282
copper, 62, 80, 105, 142, 149, 300, *304*, 305, 335, 364, 365, 370, 371, 384, 387
Coptos, 119
Copts, 26; language, 4, 28, 41, 137, 191
Cornelius Balbus, 274, 287, 288, 290
Coronation Text, 164
Cosmas Indicopleustes, 217, 218, 221, 306
Cyrenaica, 127–30, 236, 249, 260
Cyrene, 127, 128
Cyril, 139, 228, 234

Dahshur, 64, 108
Daima, 301, 327, 330, 334, 335
Dakar, 53, 56
Dakhila oasis, 91
Dambwa, 365, 368, 369, 371
Dangeil, 180
Dara, 44
Dar-es-Salaam, 310, 311
Dārfūr, 34, 36, 55, 57, 58, 91, 94, 147, 170, 181, 294
Darius I, 119, 165
Darius II, 78
David, King, 235
Debro-Dāmo, 217, 229, *230*
Deir al-Medina, 95
Deir el-Bahri, 69, 95, 98
Demetrius of Phaleron, 123
Denderah, 17
Dhar Tishīt, 329
Dhū-Nuwās, 232, 233
Dinkas, 55
Diocletian, 137–8, 170, 171, 268
Diodorus of Sicily, 26, 38, 124, 125, 165, 172, 174, 178
Diogenes Laertius, 38
Djabal Adda, 180
Djabal Ahmar, 44
Djabal Barkal, 157, 162, 163, 164, 173
Djedars, 284, 285
Djer, 149
Djerma, 253
Djeser, *19*
Djorf Torba, 291
Djoser, *see* Zoser
Dongola, 48, 155, 161, 178, 180, 186, 187, 189
Dongour, 205, 213
Dorieus, 248, 249
Doroba people, 316
Drakensberg mountains, 351, 361
Dufufa, 154–5

Ebers Papyrus, 111
Egypt: Arabs, 189, 191; division of, 136; geography, 3–4, 9; importance of Nile, 9; Lower, 63, 77; Middle, 69, 75, 94, 132, 134; racial types, 9–10; toponomy, 42; Upper, 63, 68, 69, 77, 91, 132, 133
Egypt, Pharaonic, 2, 11–12, 63–78, 82–4, 390, 391, 392, 393; animals, 80, 82; architecture, 114–16; burial practices, 88–9, 148, 154–5; chronology, 47–8, *66–7*; contacts with Africa, 12–14, 31, 35–6, 90–102, 142, 144, 147; cultural legacy, 116–17; fishing, 80, *81*; industry, 80, 104–5, 107–9; irrigation, 9; language, 28–31, 32, 39–41; law, 88; military organization, 84, 86; prehistory, 62–3, 103–4, 326; and proto-Berbers, 239–40; racial origins, 15–27, 34–57; relations with Nubia, 142, 144, 145, 147, 149–60; religion, 86–8, 117; science, 109–14; transport, 82; Twenty-Fifth dynasty (Ethiopian), 77, 161–3; writing, 10–12, 79, 116
Egypt, Ptolemaic: Alexandria, 107, 119, 120–4, 126, 128; Hellenistic culture, 123–7; trade, 119–20, 309–10
Egypt, Roman, 131–40
El Asnam, 284
El-Derr, 76
El-Kurru, 161, 173, 180
El Omari, 49
elephants, 213, 223, 293, 309
Ella Amida, 225–6, 227
Endybis, 216, *220*
Ennedi, 3, 237, 327, 333
Enthronement Text, 164
Erasistratus, 124–5
Eratosthenes, 123–4, 128, 170
Ergamenos, 165, 174, 182
Eritrea, 192, 193, 203
Esna, 44
Esneh, 17
Essina, 311
Ethiopia, 44, 45, 94, 95, 125, 301, 312, 319, 392; alphabet, 204, 211, 223; early history, 192–202, 224–5; languages, 58, 61; migrations to, 26; *see also* Axum
Euhesperides, 127
Eusebius, 225, 226
Ezana (Abraha, Aizanz), 170, 215, 216, 227, 228; coins, 211, 219; inscriptions, 178, 203, 208, 212, 218, *220*, 223, 226–7, 234

Farafira, 91
Faras, 149, 157, 180, 185, 186, 189, 191; cathedral, *188*
Fayyūm, 44, 71, 77, 87
Fezzān (Phazania), 91, 238, 274, 287, 288, 289, 290, 291, 293, 294, 305
Firki, 329–30
Fon, 102
Frenda, 284, 285
Frumentius, 225–6, 227, 228
Fundj, 36

Gabaza, 217
Gabes, Gulf of, 248, 249
Gabon, 339, 343
Gadara, 212, 214, 222
Gaetuli, 246

Garama (Jerma), 274, 287, 293, 294
Garamantes, 237, 238, 240, 252, 260, 261, 274, 287, 290, 293, 294, 295, 337
Garmul, 284
Gematon, *see* Kawa
geography, 123–4, 125
Gezira, 144
Ghadāmes, *see* Cidamus
Ghana, 90, 102, 301, 330, 331, 387, 388
Ghat, 291
Gheria el-Gherbia, 274
Ghudamis, 91
Giza, 64, 106; pyramid, 115
glass-making, 80, 107, 120
Gloger's Law, 15, 37
Gnostics, 137
Gobedra, 192
Gobochela, 197, 198, 199
Goh (Guerealta), 229
Gokomere, 365, 367, 368
gold, 62, 80, 94, 104, 179, 370, 371, 385–6, 387
Gombe, 347
Gonaqua, 361
Great Lakes, 47, 147
Greeks, 4, 21, 26, 38, 45, 63, 77, 286–7, 376, 390; in Alexandria, 133; and Axum, 204, 215, 224, 226–7, 233–4; Egyptian influences, 103, 107, 111, 116, 119–30; and Phoenicia, 246, 248–55
Guinea, 331, 332, 385
Gwisho, 341

Hadrian, 133–4, 262, 274, 276
Hadrumetum, 249, 254, 258
Hadza people, 313, 315
Haidra, *277*, 282
Halwan, 44
Ham, 38, 42
Hamilcar, 253
Hamitic theory, 319, 324
Hani, 301
Hannibal, 131, 254, 256–7
Hanno, 249, 251, 253, 255, 287, 288, 305
Haoulti, 194, 197, 200, 202
Hapidjefa, 154
Hareri, 192
Harkuf, 99, 150
Harsiotef, 165, 172
Hatsa, 360
Hatshepsut, *72*, 73, 84, 98, 156, 157
Hâz, 195
Hecataeus of Miletus, 125
Heka-Nefer, 95
Heliodorus, 214
Heliopolis, 17, 64, 87, 234
Heptanomis, 136
Heptastadion, 121
Heracleopolis, 69
Heraclius, 140
Heri-Hor, 77, 160
Herkhuf, 68
Hermonthis, 17
Herodotus, 4, 8, 21, 28, 38, 45, 99, 112, 125, 172, 239, 243, 245, 250, 251, 287, 288, 290, 294, 305
Herophilus, 124
Hersiotef, 165, 172, 178
Hiempsal, 258
Hiera Sycaminos (Muharraqa), 167
Hierakonpolis, 17, 149, 239
hieroglyphic writing, 10–12, 118, 167
Himarites, 214
Himilco, 251
Himyar, 218, 232, 233, 311, 312
Hippocrates, 111
Hippone, 263, 265, 281
Hittites, 48, 75–6
Hka-Hasut, 71
Hoggar, 237, 303, 327
Homo sapiens, 9–10, 15–16, 37, 39, 43, 44–5, 47, 52
Hor-aha, 149
Horemheb, 75, 157
Hottentots, 351
human sacrifice, 253–4
Huny, 64
Hyksos, 46, 71, 95, 144, 147, 154, 155, 156, 240

Ibero-Maurusian culture, 236–7
iconography, 35, 37–8, 46, 52–4
Ife, 334–5
Igbo, Igbo-Ukwu, 334–5, 338, 384
Imhotep (I-em-htp, Imeuthes, Imouthes), 63, 111
India, 119, 211, 213, 216, 218, 219, 223, 309, 312, 378, 380
Indian Ocean, 125, 306, 377, 378; trade, 308, 309–10, 312
Indonesia, 373, 375–80, 382
Intermediate periods, 68–9, 71
Iol, *see* Caesarea
Ipu-wer, 69
Irhtet, 94, 150
iron, 62, 104, 179, 200, 300–3, 320, 385
Iron Age, 320, 322, 333–7, 343–50; southern Africa, 351, 362–72, *363*, *366*; sub-Saharan Africa, 383–9
irrigation, 62, 71, 79, 115, 189
Ishango, 347
Isis, 27, 86, 117, 120, 128, 130, 170, 171
Islam, 378, 380, 382, 393
Israel, 76, 77, 95
Issessi, 68
Ithet-Tawi, 71
Itunga people, 322, 323
ivory, 13, 94, 213, 293, 309, 310, 311
Iwo-Eluru, 297, 298, 331

Java, 377, 378
Jerusalem, 231, 232, 233
Jews, 27–8, 95, 127, 133, 134, 139, 140, 225, 231–2, 376–7
Jos plateau, 330
Juba, 258, 259, 263
Juba II, 264
Jugurtha, 258, 259
Julianos, 185, 186, 187
Justin I, Emperor, 232
Justinian I, 4

Kadesh, 76, 84
Kafue, 364, 365
Kajemby, 382
Kalahari, 297, 313, 353, 355, 356
Kalambo, 344, 347
Kaleb, 232–3
Kalenjin people, 322
Kamabai, 331
Kamose, 95
Kangonga, 364
Kansyore ware, 317
Karanog, 168, 180
Karkarichinkat, 329
Karnak, 173; temples, 4, 73, 75, 76, 156, 162
Kasekhem, 149
Kaskasé, 197, 199
Kasr Ibrīm, 167, 171, 179, 187, 189; *see also* Primis
Katongo, 344, 345, 347
Katoto, 346, 347, 348, 384
Katuruka, 348, 350

Kau, 94
Kaw-Kaw, 55, 57; language, 57
Kawa (Gematon), 157, 162, 163, 164, 167, 173, 177, 180, 183
Kbor Roumia, *244*
Kenya, 44, 47, 300, 308, 315, 316, 317, 318, 319, 322, 323–4, 343, 386
Kephren, *70*
Kerma, Kingdom of, 144–5, 154–6, 161, 391
Khababash, 165
Khafre (Chefren, Chephren), 64
Khaliut, 164
Khamois, 84
Khargah (Khariyah), 44, 91
Khartoum, 36, 60, 61, 142, 237, 299
Kheops, *see* Cheops
Khoi Khoi, 297, 313, 352, 356, 357, 360–1
Khoisan, 297, 313, 352, 371, 385
Khor Abu Anga (Sai Island), 44
Khufu, *see* Cheops
Kifra, 293
Kilimanjaro, 308
Kintampo, 329, 330
Kisalian, 385
Kohaito, 206
Konosso island, 157
Korba, 237
Kordofān (El Obeid), 58, 147, 170, 181, 294, 297
Korti, 147
Kouga, 336
Kuban, 158
Kumadzulo, 370, 371
Kurgus, 156
Kush, 82, 95, 102, 144, 145, 152, 155, 156, 158, 160, 161–71, 174, 175, 177, 181; *see also* Meroe; Napata
Kushites, 48, 145, 164, 224, 225, 308, 318–19, 323, 324
Ḳustul (X-group), 147, 170–1
Ḳwale, 308
Kyriakos, 189, 191

Lahun, 115
Lambaesis, 262, 265, 273
languages: Axum, 211–12, 231, 233–4; Chari-Nile, 317; Egyptian-Wolof, 28–31, 32, 39–41, 54; Khoisan, 313; Malagasy, 373; Meroitic, 57–61; Nilotic, 322; sub-Saharan Africa, 297–9
Lebanon, 13, 68, 73
Lebda, *see* Leptis Magna
leopard (panther), 46, 57
Lepcis, 249
Leptis Magna (Lebda), 130, 247, 252, 259, 273, 274, *275*, 287, 293, 305
Lesotho, 355
Levallois, 44
Libou, 239
Libya, 13, 86, 127–30, 236–45, 286, 287, 326; and Phoenician culture, 259–60
Libyans, *22*, 39, 64, 68, 71, 75, 76, 86, 91, *92–3*, 274
Libyco-Berbers, *see* Berbers
linguistics, 28–31, 32, 39–42, 54–5, 57–61; *see also* languages
lion temples, 183–4
Lipari islands, 237
Lucian, 21, 38
Lupembo-Tshitolian complex, 316
Luxor, 152; temple, 73, 76
Lyouel, King, 234

Maasai, 322, 323
Mabveni, 367
Madagascar, 297, 373–82; immigration from Africa, 380, 382; languages, 373, 380, 382; settlement, 376–82
Madja, 94, 145
Magh̄rib, 134, 237, 243, 246, 258–60, 283, 288, 289, 295, 392, 393
Makuria (Muḳurra), 186, 187, 189
Malagasy, *see* Madagascar
Malapati, 368, 369
Malawi, 364, 365, 367, 369
Mali, 331, 384, 385
Manetho, 4, 63, 125
Manicheans, 137
Mankaure (Mycerinus), 64
Marcus Aurelius, 134, 269, *271*
Mârib (Awwam Bar'an), 193, 195, 197, 233
Mariette, 37
Marinus of Tyre, 287, 306
Maris, 187
Mark Anthony, 131, 259
Masaesyli, 256
Masinissa, 257–8, 259
Masties, 283
Masuna, 283
Matara, 194, 197, 198, 200, 202, 206, 207, 208, 209, 212, 217, 231
mathematics, 112–13, 124
Matopo Hills, 368
Matuar, 142
Mauretania (form. Marousia), 246, 251, 257, 258–9, 283, 284, 326, 329, 331, 335, 384, 385, 388; copper, 300, 301, 305; Roman rule, 261, 262, 264, 268, 270
Mbugu, 308
Meadi-Heliopolis, 49
Mechta el-Arbi, 236
medicine, 111–12
Mediterranean, 3, 120; race, 16, 37
Medracen, 243, 246
Meidum, 64
Meinarti Island, 185
Melanesians, 375
melanin, 15, 20, 37
Melazo, 193, 197, 198, 199, 202, 222
Melchite doctrine, 186, 187, 189
Memphis, 47, 63, 87, 111, 121, 158, 162, 175
Menes, *see* Narmer
Menouthias, island of, 311
Menthuhotep I, 17, *24*, 69
Menthuhotep II, 69, 152
Menthuhotep III, 152
Merenre, 68, 150
Merimda Beni Salama, 104
Merimde, 45, 49
Merina, 377
Merneptah, 76, 239, 240
Merneptah-Siptah, 158, 160
Meroe, 57, 95, 107, 125, 133, 141, 147, 163, 164–5, 167–70, 202, 214, 391; economic and social life, 177–82; language, 40, 57–61, 167; political organization, 172–7; pottery, 181; religion, 182–4; towns and trade, 179–81
Meshwesh, 239
Mesolithic, 36, 39, 47
Mesopotamia, 12, 103
metal-working, 62, 104–5, 120, 200–2; *see also* mining
Mettera (Madera), 229
Middle Kingdom, 62, 69–71, 84, 94, 152–4, 155
migrations, 2–3, 46–9, 55, 56–7
Mikea, 380
mining, 80, 105, 179, 300–3, 333,

335, 337, 384–5
Mirgissa, 155
Mittani, 73
Moeris, Lake, 80
Mogador, 251
Mojomby, 382
monasticism, 139
Monophysitism, 139, 186, 187, 189, 229, 231, 232, 234
Monumentum Adulitanum, 222
Moors, 264, 281, 283, 284
Morocco, 236, 243, 251, 259, 284, 285, 288, 305, 384
Mozambique, 371
Mulucha (Moulouya), 256, 262, 264
mummies, 20, 28, 37, 109, 111
Muslims, *see* Arabs; Islam
Mussawwarat es-Sufra, 168, 179, 180, 181, 182, 183, 184

Nachikufan complex, 341
Nadjrān, 232, 233
Nagā, 167, 168
Nagada, 36
Nahas, 27
Namaqua, 361
Namibia, 297, 360, 365
Napata, 39, 40, 57, 91, 147, 161, 162, 163–4, 167, 168, 172–84, 391
Naqa, *176*, 177, 182, 183
Narmer (Menes), 11, 17, 48, 53, 63, 239; palette, 11
Nasalsa, 164
Nasamonians, 243, 287
Nastasen, 165, 172, 173, 174, 175, 178
Natakamani, 168, *176*, 177
Natal, 351, 360, 361
Natoufians, 44
Naucratis, 133
Neapolis (Nabeul), 249
Necho, 250, 305
Necho II, 99
Nefertari, 84
Negadah people, 16
negroids, 147, 297, 315, 317, 331; in Egypt, 10, 15–21, 26–7, 35, 37–8, 39, 40, 42, 43, 45, 48, 50–4
Nehesi (Nubians), 94
Nementcha, 262
Neolithic, 45, 46, 47, 49, 62, 103–4, 237–8, 296–7; climate in North Africa, 3, 9, 12; West Africa, 325–33
Nero, 133, 168, 270
Nestorius, 228
New Kingdom, 69, 73–7, 80, 82, 83, 84, 86, 147
Ngorongoro, 318
Nicopolis, 133, 134
Niger (country), 384, 386
Niger (region), 335–6, 337
Niger (river), 91, 288, 294, 326, 331
Niger-Congo languages, 297–8
Nigeria, 294, 297, 301, 330, 331, 334–5, 384, 386
Nikon, 311
Nile Delta, 13, 48–9, 55, 56, 62–3, 69, 71, 76, 77, 79–80, 91, 104, 119, 132, 136, 140, 162
Nile river, *65*, 125, 178; floods, 8, 9, 11, 79
Nile valley (Nile Corridor), 134, 139, 141, 177; Egypt and Nubia, 12; historical sources for, 4–7; importance of, 3–4; irrigation, 79; relations with Africa, 12–14; settlement of, 9–10, 15, 34–57, 62, 103–4
Nilotes, 322–3
Nine Saints, 229, 234, 235
Nitokris, 84
Nobades, 136, 171, 185, 186
Nobadia, 186, 187
Nok culture, 301, 329, 330, 333–4, 337
Nubia, 13, 34, 36, 38, 42, 47, 57, 64, 68, 71, 73, 76, 80, 82, 84, 86, 94, 95, 105, 116, 136, 161, 162, 163, 167, 172, 177, 180, 391; A-group, 148–9; B-group, 149; C-group, 150–2, 239; Christianity, 185–91; early history, 142–7, *143*, *146*; geography of, 141; lack of evidence about, 141–2; link between Africa and ancient world, 144–7; Middle Kingdom, 152–5; New Kingdom, 156–8; racial types, 10, 17, 27, 45, 48, 51; relations with Egypt, 142–7, 149–60, 187, 191; settlement of, 48, 49; Unesco campaign, 187; writing, 12, 142; X-group, 170–1, 185; *see also* Kush
Nubian Corridor, 142–7
Nuer, 55
Numidia, 238, 246, 256, 258; Roman period, 263, 264, 265, 270, 274, 294

Octavian, *see* Augustus
Oea, 293, 305
Old Kingdom, 9, 10, 53, 63–8, 69, 80, 83, 94, 108, 142, 144
On, 17
Orange Free State, 360
Osiris, 13, 26, 27, 46, 55, 63, 84, 86, 87, 90, 99, 128, 162
Ostia, 273
Ouad ben Naga, 167–8
Ouadji, 149

Pa-Ramesses, 75
Pachomius, 139
Pachoras (Pakhoras), 180, 185
Palaeolithic, 39, 44, 47
Palermo Stone, 4, *5*, 7, 64, 149
Palestine, 13, 21, 44, 68, 71, 73, 75, 76, 77, 118, 162
Palmyra, 136, 168
Pangani corridor, 308, 312
papyrus, 80, 107, 116, 120
Pare, 308
Pedibast, 77
Pemba, 307, 311, 376
Pepi I, 68
Pepi II, 68, 99, 144, 150
Periplus Maris Erythraei, 192, 203–4, 213, 214, 216, 217, 219, 222, 287, 306, 308, 309, 310, 311, 376, 378
Persia, 47, 55, 78, 140, 165, 187, 214, 248, 287, 312, 376
Petrie, Sir Flinders, 17, 63
Peye, *see* Piankhi
Pharos island, 121
Phazania, *see* Fezzān
Philadelphus, 192
Philae, 167, 170, 171, 186, 227
Phoenicia, 21, 117–18, 236, 238, 241, 246–9, 259–60, 287, 301, 376; *see also* Carthage
Piankhi (Peye), 77, 175; stele of, 161–2
plants: cultivation, 325, 326, 327
Pliny, 180, 192, 203, 204, 213, 251, 268, 274, 287, 288, 306, 310
Pnubs (Tabo), 163
Polynesia, 373, 375
pottery: A-group, 148; Axumite,

209, 212; Bambatu, 360; C-group, 150–2, *151*; Chondwe, 364, 367, 369; Kalambo, 344; Kalundu, 369; Kansyore, 317; Kapwirimbwe, 364–5, 367, 369; Katoto, 346; Kwale, 322; Urewa, 322, 343–4; West African iron age, 333–4; Wilton, 360; X-group, 171; Zhiso, 367, 368; Ziwa, 367, 368
Primis (Ḳasr Ibrīm), 167
Probus, 136
Protests of the Eloquent Peasant, 69
Psammetik, 77
Psammetik II, 164, 174
Ptolemais (Tolmeta), *see* Barca
Ptolemy I Soter, 121, 123, 124, 127
Ptolemy II Philadelphus, 119, 121, 123, 131, 137, 192
Ptolemy III Eurgetes, 119, 123, 127, 192
Ptolemy V, 167
Ptolemy VI, 167
Ptolemy Apion, 127
Ptolemy Philopator, 131
Ptolemy, Claudius, 192, 204, 214, 287, 288, 290, 306
Punic culture, 274, 280
Punic wars, 256
Punt, 68, 73, 82, 95, 98, *100–1*, 376
pygmies, 99, 144, 297, 315–16
pyramids, 17, 63, 64, 108, 113, 114–16, 168

race classification, 20, 50–2
Ramses I, 157
Ramses II, 20, *25*, 76, 84, 91, 157–8, 239
Ramses III, 76, 91, 160, 239–40
Ramses IV, 77, 98
Ramses XI, 77, 160
Ramses-Siptah, 158
Ras Hafun, 311
Red Sea, 12, 36, 39, 58, 94, 98, 109, 119, 133, 134, 140, 163, 192, 193, 212, 218, 231, 243, 250, 306, 309, 310
Rekh-mi-Re, *96–7*
religion: Axum, 221–2, 224–35; Carthaginian, 253–4; Egyptian, 62–3, 99, 102, 117, 120, 128, 137–40; Ethiopian, 198, 212; Libyco-Berbers, 243, 245; Roman North Africa, 278–9
Rhapsa (Gafsa), 287
Rhapta, 311
Rift valley, 316–17, 318–19, 320, 324
rock art, 36, 38, 305, 353, *354*, 355, 356, 361, 388
Romans, 103, 107, 116, 127, 171, 177, 236, 306; and Axum, 204, 212–13; and Carthage, 246, 249–60; in East Africa, 310–12; in Egypt, 131–40; and Meroe, 167, 168; in North Africa, 261–80; and the Sahara, 286–7, 293, 294–5; in West Africa, 337–8
Rwanda, 315, 316, 339, 343, 347

Saba, 193, 195, 232, 233; language, 198
Sabratha, 130, 249, 252, 293, 305
Sahara, 15, 34, 36, 37, 44, 45, 47, 49, 57, 90–1, 102, 238, 252, 274, 326, 327, 329, 331, 332, 335, 338, 392, 393; Graeco-Roman period, 286–95; salt, 385; trade, 384; use of chariots, 240, 294
Sahel, 297, 298, 326, 327, 331, 332
Sahure, 64, 68, 239
Sai Island, 44, 156
Saitic Kingdom, 77
Sakkara (Saqqara), 39, 63, 64, 114, 116
salt, 384–5
San people, 44, 297, 313, 316, 352–3, 355, 356–7, 361
Sandawe people, 313, 315, 360
Sanga, 344–5, 347, 348, *349*, 384
Sangoan period, 44
Sanye people, 308
Sao people, 330
Sarapion, 311
Sassanid, 140
Sasu, 218
Satyrus, 125
Scipio Africanus, 256, 257
sculpture: Axumite, 207–8; South Arabian, 193–9
Sea Peoples, 76, 86, 240
Sebek-Hotep, 55, 152
Sebeknefru, 84
Sedeinga, 157
seed-cropping, 326, 327
Sefar, 327
Segu, 325, 336
Sekhem-Khet, 64
Seleucids, 119, 309
Semenekh-Ka-Re, 75
Semites, *22*, 27–8, 45, 52, 68, 225, 231; language, 32, 54, 211, 212, 290
Semna, 145, 152, 154, 157
Senegal, 28, 55, 301, 305, 326, 331, 336, 383, 385, 388, 389
Senegambia, 331, 335, 336–7
Senkamanisken, 164
Sennār, 36, 170
Senusret I, 71, 152
Senusret II, 71
Senusret III, 71, 154, 156, 157
Septimus Severus, 134, 262, 264, 270, 273, 276
Serapis, cult of, 120, 128, 130
Sesebi, 157
Sesostris I, 17
Sesostris III, 108, 115, 145
Sethnakhr, 76
Seti I (Sethos), 20, 75, 91, 157, 158, 239
Seven Wonders of the World, 64, 115, 121
Shaba, 55, 301, 346, 347, 384
Shabaka, 162
Shanakdakhete, 167, 175
Sheba, Queen of, 224
sheep-herding, 360–1, 369
Shellal, 152
Shenout of Atripa, 139
Sherekarer, 177
Sheshonq, 77
Shilluk, 55
ship-building, 108–9
Sicily, 248, 250, 254–6
Sidon, 246
Sierra Leone, 331
silver, 80, 104
Sirikwa Holes, 324
Sitifis, 268
Sīwa, *see* Ammonium
slavery, 83, 218, 252, 293
Smendes, 77
Smith Papyrus, 109, 111
Snefru, 64, 115, 142, 149
Socotra, 217
Sofala, 376
Soleb, 73, 157, *159*, 177
Solomon, 77
Somalia, 98, 119
Souk-el-Gour, 284, 285
Sousse, *266*

South Africa, 300, 303, 341, 370, 371
Spain, 247, 251
Sphinx, *25*
stelae: of the Appanaging of the Princesses, 164; of the Dream, 162; of Excommunication, 164; of Victory, 161–2
stone, 104, 108, 114, 386
Stone Age, 296, 316, 324, 327–33, 339–43, *358*, *359*, 385, 386; hunter-gatherers, 352–6; *see also* Neolithic; Palaeolithic
Strabo, 26, 38, 112, 123, 124, 125, 174, 178, 213, 306
Sudan, 36, 44, 77, 125, 148, 156, 172, 297, 300, 323, 335, 388; languages, 59, 60, 61; relations with Egypt, 94, 95, 161–3
Sudds, 144
Suez, 3, 13
Sumatra, 376
surgery, 109, 111
Susa, 165
Swahili culture, 306, 377, 378, 380
Swaziland, 351, 360, 368, 385
Syene, *see* Aswan
Syria, 13, 21, 55, 68, 73, 75, 76, 118, 133, 139, 140, 162, 223
Syrtes Libyans, 239

Ta-Seti, 141, 142
Tabo, 177
Tacape, 262, 265, 273
Tacfarinas, 261
Taharqa, 162, 173, 174, 175, 178
Tangayika, Lake, 322
Tanis, 77
Taniydamani, 167
Tanoutamon, 162
Tanwetamani, 173
Tanzania, 313, 315, 318, 319, 322, 323–4, 343, 347
Tarike Neguest, 225, 227
Tassili n'Ajjer, 290, 291, 303, 305, 327, 329
Tatoga people, 322
Tauchira, 127
Tauosre, 84
Tebessa, 272, 282
Teda, 17
Tehenou, 239
Tell-al-Amarna, 73, 75, 114, 115
Temehou, 239
Tenereen, 326, 327, 329
Ténès, 284
Teqorideamani, 170
Tera-Neter, 17, *18*
Tertullian, 279
Teye, 73, 84, 157
Thebaid, 136
Thebes, 44, 55, 69, 75, 77, 83, 87, 95, 98, 114, 131, 144, 145, 147, 160
Theodora, Empress, 185, 186
Theodosius II, 235
Theophrastus, 124
Theveste, 262, 265, 273
Thinis, 63
Thinite kings, 79
Thutmose I, 73, 147, 156
Thutmose II, 73, 156
Thutmose III, 20, 90, 95, 147, 156
Thutmose IV, 73, 157
Tiāret, 284, 285
Tiberius, 133, 261, 276
Tibesti, 3, 91, 288, 289, 293, 303, 305
Tishīt, 327, 385, 388
Tifinagh writing, 289–90
Tigre, 193, 194, 195, 197, 215
Tilemsi valley, 329
Timgad, 262, *275*, 282
Timna, 193
Timosthenes, 125
Tin Hinan, Queen, 290, 291, *292*
Tingitana, 262, 264, 268, 283, 284
Tinis, 17
Tore (Sanam), 163
totemism, 28, 31
trade: East Africa coast, 306–12; between Egypt and Africa, 13, 14, 68; Ptolemaic Egypt, 119–20; sub-Saharan Africa, 386–7
Trajan, 133, 262, *275*, 293
Transkei, 360, 361
Transvaal, 351, 360, 368, 369, 370, 371
Triacontaschone, 167
Tripoli, *271*
Tripolitania, 128, 130, 237, 240, 261, 262, 265, 270, 274, 283
Troglodytes, 287
Tshitolian complex, 341
Tsiribihina, 382
Tswana, 361
Tuareg, 290
Tubu, 17
Tumbus, 156
Tunisia, 236, 238, 243, 249, 258, 262, 283
Turin Papyrus, *6*, 7
Tutankhamun (form. Tut-Ankh-Aton), 75, 107, 157
Tyre, 246, 247, 253, 254

Uganda, 44, 315, 322, 323, 343
Ukpa, 331
Ule, 102
Utica (Utique), 247, 249, 256, 258

Vandals, 281–2, 283
Vazimba, 382
Vespasian, 133
Victoria, Lake, 317, 318, 320, 322, 388
Volney, 26, 38
Volubilis, 259, 284

Wad ben Naqa, 180–1
Wādī Abū Dom, 147
Wādī Halfa, 36, 44, 150, 152
Wādī Hamamat, 44
Wādī Hawad, 181
Wādī Muḳaddam, 147
Wādī Oukirri, 248
Wādī Tumilat, 44
Walili, 285
Waren tribe, 199
Wawat, 94, 150, 152, 156
Wazed (Wazeba), 234
Wilton complex, 341
Wolof language, 28–31, 32, 40, 41, 54–5
writing: development of, 2, 103, 118; in Egypt, 10–12, 79, 116, 142; Ethiopian, 211–12, 222–3; in Meroe, 167; Tifinagh, 289–90

Xerxes, 107, 165
Xhosa, 361

Yam, 68, 94, 99, 150
Yeha, 193, 197, 198, 200, 202, 225, 229, 231
Yemen, 195, 214
Yengema cave, 331
Yoruba, 102, 334, 338

Zafar (Tafar), 232, 233
Zahi, 71

Zaire, 90, 297, 298, 322, 341, 343, 344, 347, 384, 387
Zaire Basin (Uelian), 296, 341
Zambesi valley, 365
Zambia, 297, 303, 339, 341, 344, 351, 360, 364–5, 367, 370, 371, 384, 385, 387, 388
Zanzibar, 307, 309, 311, 312, 376
Zeugitana, 265
Zimbabwe, 351, 360, 365, 367–8, 370, 371, 376, 384, 386
Zoscales, 203, 214
Zoser (Djosar, Zozer), 17, 63, 64, 111, 114
Zula Bay, 215